Handbook of Research-Based Practices for Educating Students with Intellectual Disability

The *Handbook of Research-Based Practices for Educating Students with Intellectual Disability* provides an integrated, transdisciplinary overview of research-based practices for teaching students with intellectual disability. This comprehensive volume emphasizes education across life stages, from early intervention in schools through the transition to adulthood, and highlights major educational and support needs of children and youth with intellectual disability. The implications of history, recent research, and existing information are positioned to systematically advance new practices and explore promising possibilities in the field. Driven by the collaboration of accomplished, nationally recognized professionals of varied approaches and philosophies, the book emphasizes practices that have been shown to be effective through multiple methodologies, so as to help readers select interventions based on the evidence of their effectiveness.

Michael L. Wehmeyer is the Ross and Mariana Beach Distinguished Professor of Special Education and Director and Senior Scientist at the Beach Center on Disability, University of Kansas, USA. He is a past president of the American Association on Intellectual and Developmental Disabilities and founding co-editor of the AAIDD journal *Inclusion*.

Karrie A. Shogren is Professor of Special Education and Senior Scientist and Director of the Kansas University Center on Developmental Disabilities, University of Kansas, USA. She is founding co-editor of the AAIDD journal, *Inclusion,* and co-editor of the journal, *Remedial and Special Education.*

Handbook of Research-Based Practices for Educating Students with Intellectual Disability

Edited by Michael L. Wehmeyer
and Karrie A. Shogren

Routledge
Taylor & Francis Group

NEW YORK AND LONDON

First published 2017
by Routledge
711 Third Avenue, New York, NY 10017

and by Routledge
2 Park Square, Milton Park, Abingdon, Oxon OX14 4RN

Routledge is an imprint of the Taylor & Francis Group, an informa business

Library of Congress Cataloging in Publication Data
A catalog record has been requested for this book

ISBN: 978-1-138-83209-1 (hbk)
ISBN: 978-1-138-83210-7 (pbk)
ISBN: 978-1-315-73619-8 (ebk)

Typeset in Bembo
by Apex CoVantage, LLC
Printed at CPI on sustainably sourced paper

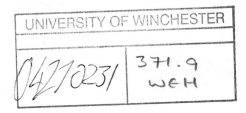

Contents

Contents

Part I

Understanding Intellectual Disability

Historical Understandings of Intellectual Disability and the Emergence of Special Education

Michael L. Wehmeyer, J. David Smith

This text is intended to serve as a resource for researchers, graduate students, educators, and others involved in the enterprise of educating learners with intellectual disability. In Chapter 2, you will learn about contemporary ways of understanding what is meant by what we now call "intellectual disability" and how the field of special education developed from civil rights legislation ensuring a free, appropriate public education for all children to today's context of evidence-and research-based practices—the focus of this text.

The editors of this text believe, however, that to understand the current context and the challenges for the future with regard to the education of students with intellectual disability, one must understand the past. In far too many situations, the practices established in the mid-1970s by the newly emerging field of special education reflected only the limited knowledge available at that time with regard to educating this population—knowledge derived from a history of segregation (Jackson, Ryndak, & Wehmeyer, 2010). The history of special education in America did not begin with the passage of Public Law (P.L.) 94–142 in 1975. It began in a small village in the north of the Languedoc-Roussillon-Midi-Pyrenees region of southern France in the late 1700s; in a private school established in 1840 in Paris; at a physician's residence in Barre, Massachusetts in 1848; in a wing of the Perkins School for the Blind in 1848; on the grounds of an institution in Vineland, New Jersey; and in the halls of early 20th-century New York City public schools. And, at every stage of the development of this field, practices were shaped by how intellectual disability was understood. This chapter provides a necessarily abbreviated introduction to that history and those meanings through to the passage of federal special education legislation in the mid-1970s.[1]

Educating the "Idiot:" Itard, Seguin, and the Infancy of Special Education

We begin this exploration in the 17th century. Even that early, the term *idiot* was the predominant term to describe people who had difficulty performing daily life activities. Idiot or idiocy referred, in general, to the observable "differentness" of people with intellectual disability. The term itself was derived from the Greek words *idatas* and *idios*. *Idatas* refers to a private person, and *idios* means "peculiar." Together, they refer to a person who is peculiar, set aside, different. That differentness has always been associated with how what we refer to as intelligence has been understood. Of course, the intelligence construct is a fairly modern invention, but even back to antiquity, societies praised and valued what we might now call "intelligence." The Greeks saw "intelligence" (*sophos*, or a wise person, someone who has attained the wisdom a philosopher seeks) as associated with the divine, and individuals manifesting clear intellectual and physical impairments were not highly valued (Privateer, 2006).

Appeals for the decent treatment and education of people considered to be inferior because of race, ability, social class, or gender were rare during the 17th century. Calls for more equal treatment and humane care of stigmatized people are not readily evident in historical records. Individual acts of compassion, concern, and advocacy were likely numerous but these are not documented because such actions were performed by people who were not in a social position to express their concerns in a broader way, and in a manner that would become part of the historical record. Surviving documents rarely provide arguments for more equal treatment and humane regard for people with disabilities in particular. It is important that before exploring the efforts of Jean Marc Gaspard Itard and other early pioneers in educating people with intellectual disability, to consider those unusual instances in which a person of some prominence and visibility stepped forward as an advocate for these people.

The Enlightened Voices of Jonathan Swift and Daniel Defoe

One example of an influential person in the 17th and 18th centuries who did demonstrate advocacy and action on behalf of people with intellectual disability is the life of Jonathan Swift. As a social critic and satirist, Swift is best known for *Gulliver's Travels* and *A Modest Proposal*. Swift saw charity as a moral obligation, and he practiced what he preached. His account books show expenditures for "charity," "poor woman," "gave old woman," and "poor boy." He was also supportive of numerous hospitals and schools for poor children, and an active director of several charities (Damrosch, 2013).

Swift left his entire fortune to establish a hospital in Dublin for *idiots and lunatics*. At the end of his own satiric obituary, *Verses on the Death of Dr. Swift*, he sarcastically penned:

He gave the little wealth he had
To build a house for fools and mad,
And showed by one satiric touch
No nation wanted [needed] it so much.
(Damrosch, 2013, p. 416)

Daniel Defoe, the English author, journalist, and social critic who lived during the years 1659 to 1731, provides an even more compelling example of disability advocacy in the 17th and 18th centuries. After business failures and bankruptcy earlier in his life, he changed both his name (from Foe to Defoe), and his values (Frank, 2011). Defoe was an early proponent of the novel as a literary form and is best known for his book *Robinson Crusoe*. It is within several of his other works, however, that his sensitivity to the needs, treatment, and education for people considered to have intellectual disability becomes apparent.

Defoe's first publication was entitled *An Essay Upon Projects*. The 1697 book consisted of a series of proposals for social and economic improvements in English society. In this publication, Defoe spoke of people who were at the time referred to as "fools." Defoe (1697) stated that, of all of the "persons who are the object of our charity, none move my compassion like those whom it has pleased God to leave in a full state of health and strength, but deprived of reason to act for themselves" (p. 63). He went on to say that the lack of care for these people was a cultural oversight and that the time had come in this "wise age" to care for these people as one would do for younger siblings.

Defoe (1697) therefore proposed that a "fool-house" be erected by governments "into which all that are natural or born fools, without respect or distinction, should be admitted and maintained" (p. 63). The most interesting aspect of Defoe's proposal is his idea for funding the "fool-houses." He asked that the houses be supported by those who profited from their extraordinarily high intellectual abilities. That is, he thought that the best way of doing so was by making the care of people with lesser intellectual ability a contribution by those of higher ability. To do so, he proposed that "without damage to the persons paying the same, [funds] might be very easily raised by a tax upon learning, to be paid by the authors of books" (p. 2). To supplement the tax support for these houses, Defoe (1697) further asked that additional funds be raised voluntarily by the means of a lottery.

> I propose to maintain fools out of our folly. And whereas a great deal of money has been thrown about in lotteries, the following proposal would very easily perfect our work . . . for a hundred thousand tickets at twenty shillings each . . . an immediate sum of one hundred thousand pounds shall be raised.
>
> *(p. 3)*

Of greater relevance to his earlier writings with relation to the history of the education of people with intellectual disability, however, is his pamphlet titled *Mere Nature Delineated,* published in 1726. His observations concern a boy who was found in a forest in northern Germany, a scenario we will see play out at the end of the 17th century as well. He was described as being discovered naked, and as living on grass, mosses, and the leaves of trees. He was uncommunicative and walked on his hands and knees. He was thought to be about 12 years old and came to be known as Peter the Wild Boy. Speculations concerning Peter's condition ranged from having been raised by wild animals to being an incurable idiot (Moorhouse, 2010). Peter was soon brought to London and attracted the attention of the leading intellectuals of the time including both Jonathan Swift and Defoe. He was adopted into the household of King George I and lived to be approximately 65 years old (Historic Royal Places, 2013).

Defoe's (1726) assessment of Peter differed radically from the speculations of others:

> . . . however, he gives us a view of mere nature, perhaps, the clearer for that . . . his soul is capable of improvement, [and] differs from us only in the loss it has sustained under so long a denied education. If that be the case, he is then only to be considered as an infant, and that he is just now in the mere state of infancy and childhood.
>
> *(Defoe, 1726, p. 60)*

Defoe (1726) went on to express his faith in education as the only answer to the mysteries of human diversity. He showed significant confidence in the malleability of the human condition, becoming consequently an early proponent of universal educability. He stated:

> Education seems to me to be the only specific remedy for all the imperfections of nature; that all the difference in souls, or the greatest part at least, that is to say, between the dull and the bright, the sensible and insensible, the active and the indolent, the capable and the incapable, are owing to, and derive from this.
>
> *(Defoe, 1726, p. 61)*

Jean Marc Gaspard Itard and Victor

Defoe's (1726) observations on the case of Peter presages an event that is often referred to as the initiation of the much later concept of special education, that of Jean Marc Gaspard Itard and another young boy found in a forest, this one named Victor. The perspectives of Swift and Defoe to the contrary, most people—and particularly most professionals in medicine—held pessimistic views of the malleability of intelligence (as we would now think of it).

Take, for example, Philippe Pinel (1745–1826), who is regarded as the founder of psychiatry. Pinel was a distinguished physician spurred to study mental illness as a result of the suicide of a close friend who had developed a mental disorder. As a physician at the Bicetre, a French asylum for people who were considered insane, he studied mental illness up close. Later, he became chief physician for the Salpetriere (a Paris hospital for the mentally ill). To Pinel are attributed many advances in the treatment of people with mental illness and intellectual disability, including the removal of restraints (chains, straightjackets) and the abandonment of techniques like bleeding and leaches in favor of a more humane, observational treatment method called the *Traitement Moral*, or moral treatment method. In spite of Pinel's accomplishments and improvements in care, like most physicians at the time, he regarded people with intellectual disability—who were often institutionalized along with people with mental illnesses—to be incurable and uneducable.

One of Pinel's students at the Salpetriere, Jean Etienne Esquirol (1772–1840), provided the first systematic differentiation between mental illness (dementia) and intellectual disability (amentia). Writing in *Mental Maladies*, the first modern text on mental disorders, Esquirol proposed that:

> . . . idiocy is not a disease but a condition in which the intellectual facilities are never manifested or have never been developed sufficiently to enable the idiot to acquire such amount of knowledge as persons of his own age reared in similar circumstances are capable of receiving.
>
> *(Esquirol, 1838, p. 26)*

Although Esquirol's distinction between mental illness and intellectual disability is an important road mark in the history of intellectual disability, it is perhaps his adherence to Pinel's view of the ineducability of people with intellectual disability that had the most direct effect on the field of special education: "Idiots are what they must remain for the rest of their lives" (Esquirol, 1838, p. 26).

Pinel, Esquirol, and, indeed, almost all physicians and psychiatrists, believed the ineducability of people with intellectual disability to be an immutable and unchangeable fact. Into this milieu walked Jean Marc Gaspard Itard (1775–1838)—who was Chief Physician at The National Institution for Deaf-Mutes in Paris and who had been a student under Pinel—and a young boy who was discovered by hunters on January 8, 1800 in the woods near Aveyron, a small village in south-central France (Lane, 1976). At the time it was thought that the boy, later named Victor, had lived in the wild for most, if not all, of his 11 or 12 years, thus earning him the epithet, "The Wild Boy of Aveyron." Victor was examined by Philippe Pinel and declared, not surprisingly, an "incurable idiot."

Eventually, though, Victor came under the care of Itard, who did not share his teacher's conviction of Victor's ineducability, and so he began a series of interventions to teach Victor to speak, recognize words and letters, and care for himself. Among other firsts, Itard's efforts were the first to emphasize the importance of an enriched environment in remediating deficits. Ironically, Itard considered his work with Victor a failure because of his pupil's inability to acquire speech, but in reality Victor gained a number of social, academic, and independent living skills (Lane, 1976).

Edouard Seguin and the Physiological Method

In 1837, Itard was approached by the director of a children's hospital about the possibility of taking on another pupil like Victor. Itard, whose health was failing and who was experiencing considerable pain, declined, but suggested that a young doctor who had previously studied under him, Edouard Seguin (1812–1880), might be willing to work with the boy. Seguin was persuaded to take up the cause, though he was not entirely persuaded Itard was correct in his optimism regarding educability and intellectual disability (and despite the fact that Esquirol told him he would be wasting his time). He was, however, sympathetic to Itard's devotion to people like Victor, who were so poorly treated. Consequently, he took up the challenge and began working with the child, adapting, adopting, and refining his mentor's methods and continuing the work even after Itard's death one year later. Unlike Itard's experience with Victor, 18 months after he began, Seguin's pupil was much improved, having acquired the ability to speak, write, and count. Seguin took on a few more children and, in 1839, established the first school to educate students we would now refer to as having intellectual disability (Smith & Wehmeyer, 2012).

Seguin had come to believe that idiocy was not the result of deficiency or malformation of the brain or nervous system, but was simply an arrest of mental development that occurred either before, at, or after birth due to variety of causes. Moreover, in Seguin's view, the disability could be overcome by appropriate treatment. That treatment was called the *Physiological Method* and was propagated in Seguin's important 1844 text, *Traitement Moral, Hygiene, et Education des Idiots*.

This notion of intellectual disability resulting from arrested mental development that could be overcome by training of the senses did, apparently, resonate with Esquirol, who assisted Seguin to further his experimental work at the *Hospice des Incurables Bicetre*. Although Seguin's Physiological Method was not fully formulated in *Traitement Moral, Hygiene, et Education des Idiots*, the theoretical considerations underpinning the treatment were. Seguin's interventions drew on several beliefs he held as foundational for intervention. Seguin based his intervention on the rudimentary knowledge of the neural system that was available at that time, emphasizing the importance of sensory stimulation via auditory and visual input, and on his understanding of typical child development, particularly motor and cognitive development.

The pedagogy Seguin derived from these theoretical foundations included physical training to stimulate sensory and motor development. Seguin developed exercises, and built the apparatus to implement these exercises, that emphasized learning through movement, manipulation, and sensory input. The "idiot" children under his care climbed onto swingboards, suspended by a rope from the ceiling, and were pushed so that their feet touched a wall near the swing, thus giving them the sensation of the pressure to their soles; they walked aided by parallel bars adjusted to be armpit high; they climbed stairs and rope ladders and hung from rings; felt texture boards with differing surfaces, from a metal rasp to a velvet cloth; arranged manipulative objects by size and shape; performed pegboards and figureboards; and learned to grasp, hold, release, and manipulate toys (Smith & Wehmeyer, 2012).

Coming to America

The first public school for feebleminded children in America was established by social reformer Samuel Gridley Howe in Boston in 1848. In 1843, Howe was honeymooning in Europe with his new bride, Julia Ward Howe, accompanied by Horace Mann, secretary of the board of education for the state of Massachusetts and leader of the common school movement, and his new wife, Mary Tyler Peabody. Howe and Mann mixed business with pleasure and toured institutions for the blind and deaf across Europe trolling for new ideas to take back with them to the United States. A year earlier, Mann had visited Europe and had met with Edouard Seguin. Upon his return, he wrote several articles that appeared in Boston area newspapers and magazines. During Mann and Howe's 1843 excursion, Howe came to see the education of idiots as yet another cause for civil libertarians such as himself and, thus, a personal challenge, and was introduced to and became impressed with Seguin's efforts.

When he returned to the United States, Howe pressured the Massachusetts legislature to establish a school for idiots. In early 1846, Howe was appointed chairman of a committee to explore what, if anything, might be done for the "idiots" of Massachusetts. Howe's committee issued its first report in March of 1847, with a full version published in 1848 titled *On the Causes of Idiocy*. In October 1848, Howe converted a wing of the Perkins Institute for the Blind, where he was superintendent, as an experimental school for four boys classified as idiots.

While Howe's school was the first public school for so-called idiots, it was not the first such American school. That distinction belonged to a private school opened in Barre, Massachusetts in the home of Hervey B. Wilbur, a young physician who had read about Mann's earlier visit and acted upon

Mann's challenge, opening a school (eventually called the Elm Hill School) for idiots in his small, white frame home in Barre, about 45 miles from Boston (Smith & Wehmeyer, 2012).

Howe was already a pioneer in the education of children with disabilities based upon his work with Laura Bridgman. Laura Bridgman was born in 1829. At two years of age she was rendered deaf and blind by scarlet fever. Her senses of smell and taste were also damaged by the illness. She became unable to communicate with the world around her except by touch. In 1837 she came to live at the Perkins Institute for the Blind, where she was tutored by Howe. He devised a method for teaching her based on her ability to feel the differences in shapes. Through drill and practice Howe taught her the names of objects using raised print. Subsequently she learned to form words with movable letters. Eventually he shifted his communication with her to fingerspelling. He spelled words into her hand and associated them with objects and actions. This was the method that Anne Sullivan, another student at Perkins, acquired through communicating with Laura, and that she used later in her teaching with Helen Keller. The miracle of Anne and Helen began with Dr. Howe and Laura. But Laura's fame and Howe's success with her were later eclipsed by the extraordinary accomplishments of Helen and Anne (Howe, 1893; Smith, 2003).

The Perkins Institute provides a lesson in both inclusion and exclusion. Due to Howe's actions, new methods for educating children who were deaf and blind would lead to greater opportunities for many people, beginning with Laura Bridgman. For children who were deemed to be idiots, the door opened a crack for public education. Both the Barre institution and Howe's Perkins Institute shared a common feature: They implemented Edouard Seguin's systematic approach for instruction. Descriptions of the educative activities employed on behalf of the children in Barre and at Perkins often emphasized motor movements and motor-related issues. And yet, the historical emphasis on segregating people with intellectual disability that prevails today also inserted itself into the Howe story. The school was initially housed at Perkins Institute, but, according to two of his daughters, Howe soon discovered that his students who were blind deeply resented the presence of students with intellectual disability in "their" school. His daughters interpreted this resentment to be an expression of the fear that they might come to be associated with the perceived inferiority of these "weaker brethren" (Smith, 2003, p. 122).

The same year that the Perkins and Barre schools opened, 1848, Edouard Seguin moved to the United States. In 1866, he published an updated and revised version of his original text in English, titled *Idiocy and Its Treatment by the Physiological Method*. The text soon became the standard for use in the institutions that states were establishing in the late 1800s. Although they would become very different in their missions, these institutions were originally founded to provide educational experiences for youth and young adults who, only a century before, had been deemed as uneducable and incurable idiots.

Appearance of Ungraded Classes

The 1870s were a mixed bag for public education for children who were not able to perform at typical levels. In 1874, the California Supreme Court held, in *Ward v. Flood*, that a principal of a public school could refuse to admit a child who had not had sufficient education to perform at the lowest grade of the school. Mary Ward, the plaintiff, was an African-American child who, in 1872, was denied entrance to a California public school by that school's principal (Flood) on the grounds that there were separate schools for colored children and that Mary could not master the curriculum for the lowest grade at San Francisco's Broadway Grammar School.

Though primarily a test of the legality of separate schooling for African-American children, the right of Flood to refuse Mary's admittance to his San Francisco elementary school was also based on the right of principals to refuse admittance to students who, essentially, would not be able to master the content in the school. And yet, despite this climate, the first "ungraded" classes—established for students who for one reason or another could not succeed in general education classes—were established during the 1870s, including an ungraded class for disobedient youth in New Haven Connecticut in 1871, a class for truant boys in New York City in 1874, and a similar class for incorrigible and truant boys in 1876 in Cleveland. These classes shared the characteristic of being exclusively for boys who were perhaps able to master the curriculum, but whose behavior or attendance limited their performance.

In 1896, the first public classes for "feebleminded" children opened in Boston and Providence, Rhode Island and, in 1899, the Chicago public schools opened classes for "crippled" children. That same year the National Education Association established a Department of Special Education, though the impetus for this pertained to education efforts for children who were deaf as spearheaded by Alexander Graham Bell. Significantly, in an 1893 decision, *Watson v. City of Cambridge* (Massachusetts), a feebleminded child was expelled from public school and denied reinstatement because the child was so limited, mentally, that he would not benefit, made "uncouth" noises, and was not able to take of himself, physically (Smith & Wehmeyer, 2012).

Educating the "Feebleminded:" Elizabeth Ferrell and the Emergence of Special Education

The trends established in the 1890s expanded dramatically in the early 1900s, with ungraded classes for some children being established, including classes for epileptic children in Cleveland in 1906, public classes for students with heart disease in New York City in 1906, and for children with defective speech in that city in 1908. At the same time, children who were feebleminded who were served in ungraded classes were, by and large, the most capable of these children, and other, less-capable children were sent to institutions.

For a variety of reasons, the terms used to describe people with cognitive impairments began to change. In the context of the early 20th century, with the explosion of interest in biology brought about by the rediscovery of Mendel's laws of heredity, the burgeoning efforts of psychologists to measure intelligence, and the applications of Darwinian principles of natural selection to social issues such as immigration and human welfare, how intellectual disability was understood began to change. From emphasizing an unspecific sense of "differentness," medical and educational language began to reflect misunderstandings of intellectual disability with terms such as *weak mindedness* and *mental defectiveness,* referring to a general "weak-mindedness." The primary terms used during this era, however were *feeblemindedness, idiocy,* and *imbecility. Imbecile* derives from the Latin term *imbecillus,* referring to weak mindedness. *Feeblemindedness,* which soon became the term of choice in the US, referred as well to weak-mindedness.

Goddard, Wallin, and Farrell, and the Expansion of Intelligence Testing and Ungraded Classes

The emergence of special education, the adoption of compulsory education laws, and the expansion of IQ testing occurred at roughly the same time. As evidenced by the continued prevalence of IQ testing to determine eligibility for special education, the use of intelligence testing influenced the growth of special education. The introduction of intelligence testing in America was also very much aligned with the growth of the eugenics movement in the US. This was particularly evident in the career of Henry Herbert Goddard. In 1906, Goddard, with a freshly minted Ph.D. in psychology, was hired as the director of the psychological laboratory at the New Jersey Training School for Feeble-Minded Boys and Girls (Vineland Training School), the first such laboratory in the United States to be housed outside of a university. Goddard's tenure at The Vineland Training School was marked by a series of historically important events in the field of intellectual disability, including coining the term *moron* to define certain segments of the population of people labeled as "feebleminded," and introducing the Binet-Simon Intelligence Scale to an American audience of psychologists.

In 1905, French psychologist Alfred Binet and his doctoral student, Theodore Simon, were commissioned by La Societe' Libre pour l'Etude Psychologique de l'Enfant (Free Society for the Psychological Study of the Child) to develop a measure of intelligence that would differentiate between students who were succeeding in school and those who were not. The intent of the measure was to identify students who were not succeeding so that they could receive the support they needed to do so. Binet did not believe in ranking children by scores on his tests. They were to used to identify students in need of academic assistance and to identify individual differences among children. Binet was convinced that intelligence, whatever it was, could be measured and demonstrated only in the context of a person's interaction with his or her environment, not simply through a quickly administered test (Smith & Wehmeyer, 2012).

In 1908, Goddard traveled to Europe, during which time he learned of the Binet-Simon scale. Upon his return to the United States, Goddard had the measure translated into English and began using it with the inmates of the Vineland Training School. Goddard translated two subsequent revisions and conducted a large standardization trial of the 1911 version. This version became widely adopted at the institutions that housed people with intellectual disability and quickly became linked to the diagnosis of intellectual disability, first using age-related norms and, later, using the calculated mental age.

Based upon his work with the Binet-Simon scale, Goddard was asked by the New York City school board to participate in the New York City School Survey of 1911–1912. The survey was in response to efforts of William Maxwell, the New York City Schools Superintendent, and Elizabeth Farrell, the Inspector of Ungraded Classes for the New York Public Schools.

Perhaps the first large-scale effort to educate students (including students who were feebleminded) occurred in the New York City Public Schools under Farrell's direction. Inspired by social welfare movements, Farrell established the first ungraded class in the New York City Public Schools in the late 1800s. Ungraded classes expanded through the New York system rapidly, with 10 in place by 1903, 14 by 1906, 61 by 1908, and 131 by 1912. The growth of these ungraded classes elicited concern from school board members who challenged both the need for such classes as well as the cost. The New York City School Survey of 1911–1912 was a means to gather information by the board that was quickly realized by Superintendent Maxwell for what it was: an attempt to curtail spending and restrict his power. This brought Goddard and his intelligence test in direct contention with Farrell and her ungraded classes. Unfortunately for Farrell, the identification of children for these ungraded classes was haphazard, mainly by teacher and principal referral. Goddard's report, titled *School Training of Defective Children*, was released in 1913 and emphasized the importance of using the Binet-Simon to identify children who were feebleminded and, particularly, using the test to determine the subclassifications in use at that time: idiot, imbecile, and moron. According to Goddard, only those children in the higher subclassification (moron) would benefit at all from school. Based loosely upon the sample of children he'd tested in the schools using the Binet-Simon, Goddard estimated the prevalence of feebleminded children at 2% of the population, a number much higher than the total number of students being served at that time. And, consistent with the viewpoint of someone who worked at an institution and held eugenic perspectives, Goddard's final recommendation was that the schools should establish a separate school system for defective children.

Elizabeth Farrell's response to Goddard's report was swift. In a report prepared for the board of education, Farrell provided a point-by-point rebuttal of Goddard's report. Goddard had, Farrell intimated, made the data fit his world view. Further, she argued that the test items—some of which referred to butterflies, grass, and trees—might be foreign to children who had grown up in the streets of New York City.

In the end, Goddard and Farrell's skirmish ended in a draw: The board of education implemented actions suggested from both reports. Goddard's recommendations to exclude children testing in the idiot and imbecile ranges were largely irrelevant because these children were not among the children in these early ungraded classes anyway, and were, instead, placed in the expanding system of institutions. Goddard's suggestion for a separate school district was not implemented, the board choosing to stick with Farrell's model of self-contained classrooms in regular schools.

Goddard's criticism of Farrell's methods for identifying students for ungraded classes stung enough, though, that she established a diagnostic clinic that included psychologists, social workers, health care professionals, and educators. In time, like nearly everyone else, Farrell became a proponent of using intelligence tests, though by this time Stanford Professor Lewis Terman had significantly revised the instrument, now referred to as the Stanford-Binet scale. Farrell went on to teach in Columbia University's Teachers College, and in 1922, while teaching a summer course at Teachers College, Farrell and her students formed the International Council for the Education of Exceptional Children, now known just as the Council for Exceptional Children (CEC), and she became that organization's first president (Kode, 2002).

Another early pioneer in special education who also had links to the CEC was John Edward Wallace Wallin, after whom the CEC lifetime achievements award is named. Wallin was a psychologist who worked for a brief time with Goddard at Vineland, but was an early critic of the Stanford-Binet. Primarily, however, Wallin's criticisms focused on who should administer such a measure: teachers or trained psychologists. During his career, Wallin established clinics for diagnostics, called at the time, psycho-educational clinics, in schools in St. Louis, Baltimore, and throughout Delaware.

Ferguson (2014) analyzed the records from the St. Louis schools and the papers of Wallin, and described how "the growing class of specialists in clinical psychology and psychometrics gained a foothold in the schools as educational gatekeepers for student placements along an increasingly elaborate 'continuum of care'" (p. 86). Farrell's early ungraded classes included a smorgasbord of children who had one characteristic in common: They weren't doing very well in school. But, as intelligence testing advanced and was widely adopted, "what had been a jumble of labels with only one or two placement options became, at least in theory, a growing continuum of both diagnostic categories and specialized educational settings" (Ferguson, p. 91). Ferguson concluded his review by noting that:

> It is also important to see this creation of the continuum in special education as part of an understandable effort by clinical psychologists inside and outside the schools and institutions to legitimize their professional and bureaucratic control of the mentally subnormal population.
>
> (p. 92)

As we consider what are evidence- and research-based practices in the field of intellectual disability, it is important to keep in mind that practices that remain, such as the continuum of placements, were not based upon anything other than political and professional factors.

Educating the "Mentally Retarded:" Special Education up to P.L. 94–142

The pathway from ungraded classes provided at the discretion of a school district to the passage of legislation ensuring free, appropriate public education for all was laid out by the parent movement in the area of intellectual disability. It emerged in the early 1950s and was then enhanced by the Kennedy administration and its personal experience with intellectual disability. By then, the term that was predominantly used was *mental retardation,* referring to slow mental processes. The term had changed, but not the meaning.

Growth of the Parent Movement

Efforts to organize groups of parents of children with intellectual disability had begun in the 1930s and expanded dramatically in the post-WWII years. Parents became increasingly dissatisfied with the options available for their children for a variety of reasons. For one, the conditions in the institutions that increasingly housed more and more people deteriorated to the extent that they were clearly not places parents would want to send their children. In 1950, 124,304 people lived in state-run, large institutions for "the mentally retarded." The institution census peaked in 1967 at 194,650 people. The prosperity and optimism of post-WWII America led parents to desire that their children with intellectual disability have the opportunity to live at home and attend schools, like their other children. These parents found other parents in the same situation, formed groups that began to advocate for the right to education, and established classes for children with intellectual disability in their religious communities and charitable organizations.

By 1950, there were enough of these groups to form a national organization, and in September 1950, representatives from 23 of those parent groups met in Minneapolis, Minnesota to form the National Association of Parents and Friends of Mentally Retarded Children (Abeson & Davis, 2000, p. 19). By 1975, when P.L. 94–142 was passed, approximately 218,000 members were organized in 1,700 state and local chapters in what was by then called the National Association for Retarded Citizens (and now is, simply, The Arc of the United States).

Among the early priorities of this newly established national organization was to change the public's perceptions of children with mental retardation, and to work to establish services for children and adults who, to that point, were denied access to education, work, day care, and preschool programs. Their progress was impressive. By 1959, 49 states provided classes for children considered educable and 37 states provided classes for children considered "trainable" (IQs of 25 to 50). This still left children with the most severe disabilities unserved in many states, and no state served children classified as "dependent" retarded (IQs under 20). They were considered to be totally unable to learn, needing only custodial care (*President's Committee on Mental Retardation*, 1977).

Part of the problem of states providing adequate education for children with mental retardation was the lack of qualified teachers. New educational methods and approaches were necessary in order to individualize instruction for children who exhibited diverse learning styles, functional levels, and needs. In response, The Arc advocated for legislation and funding, and in 1958, Public Law (P.L.) 85–926, an *Act to Encourage Expansion of Teaching in the Education of Mentally Retarded Children Through Grants to Institutions of Higher Learning and to State Education Agencies*, was enacted (Weintraub, Abeson, Ballard, & LaVor, 1976). It was the first federal legislation passed that provided support for university training programs for leaders and teachers in special education for children with mental retardation. Most important, this law also established a federal role in supporting people with mental retardation and their families in the United States.

The federal role in the area of intellectual disability took a significant step forward when John F. Kennedy, the brother of a sibling with intellectual disability, was elected president. In 1960 President Kennedy, with the urging of his sister, Eunice Kennedy Shriver, established the President's Panel on Mental Retardation. In October of 1962, the panel issued a report to the president titled "A Proposed Program for National Action to Combat Mental Retardation," which included 97 recommendations, many of which formed the basis for legislation and funding streams that benefit people with intellectual disability and their families to this day. Only weeks before his assassination, President Kennedy signed legislation taking this nation's first steps toward a community-based system of supports, and then spoke with members of the National Association for Retarded Children at their annual meeting in Washington, DC, about that historic legislation (Wehmeyer, 2013).

The opening paragraph of the President's Panel report illustrates the tone of the time, both progressive and, still, bound by parameters of intellectual disability as a defect and disease:

> Modern science and action by our social institutions have demonstrated that many even badly handicapped individuals need not be relegated to uselessness and to unemployment—to being heavy burdens upon their families or upon the public. We now have the means for giving a great number of such people hope and opportunity to be self-reliant and useful. Through educational

services, vocational rehabilitation, and training and retraining, supplemented by effective coun-seling and guidance, they can be given the incentive and the skills to become productive and self-supporting.

(President's Panel on Mental Retardation, 1962, p. 143)

The panel's report estimated that only about one-fifth of more than 1,250,000 school-age children with intellectual disability were receiving any type of special education in public schools. The report called for an additional 55,000 teachers trained to work with children with intellectual disability and for a federal extension and improvement program to support states and local districts to fund special education services.

Through the efforts of parents, family members, and the federal government, legislation leading up to the 1975 Education for All Handicapped Children Act (EHA, P.L. 94–142) was passed, beginning with the aforementioned P.L. 85–926 (*Act to Encourage Expansion of Teaching in the Education of Mentally Retarded Children Through Grants to Institutions of Higher Learning and to State Education Agencies*); to the *Training of Professional Personnel Act* of 1959 (P.L. 86–158), which expanded P.L. 85–926 to further efforts to train teachers to work with children with intellectual disability; to the *Mental Retardation Facilities and Community Mental Health Centers Construction Act* (P.L. 88–164), passed in 1963, which expanded training programs across disability categories.

Importantly, the *Elementary and Secondary Education Act* of 1965 (P.L. 89–10), part of President Lyn-don Johnson's "great society" legislation intended to combat poverty and racial inequality, included resources to states to educate disadvantaged children, and was amended in the 1966 *Education of the Handicapped Act* (P.L 91–230) to include children with disabilities.

Along with progress in legislation, the cause of equal access to education was taken up in courts; two landmark decisions, *Pennsylvania Association for Retarded Citizens v. Commonwealth* (1971) and *Mills v. Board of Education of the District of Columbia* (1972), established the rights of children with intellectual disability to receive a public education under the 14th amendment to the Constitution.

Conclusions

When, in 1975, P.L. 94–142 (EHA) was passed, assuring all children with disabilities access to a free appropriate public education, it did not appear fully formed and ready to implement at that time. Indeed, the law and how it came to be interpreted was one step in a process that began with the earliest historical efforts to educate people deemed, in the vernacular of the time, to be idiots, to the establish-ment of ungraded classes for the feebleminded, and in the efforts of the parent movement to ensure that children with mental retardation had access to education. What went into the law and how it was interpreted was a function of what had happened in the decades before 1975. From the prevalent role of intelligence testing and its influence on the continuum to the notion of a least-restrictive alterna-tive embodied in EHA, what is now the *Individuals with Disabilities Education Act* of 2004 (IDEA) was shaped within the context of a history of segregation and isolation.

IDEA requires, to this day, that children with disabilities be educated with their nondisabled peers unless the "nature or severity of the disability of a child is such that education in regular classes with the use of supplementary aids and services cannot be achieved satisfactorily" [IDEA 2004, Title 1(B) Sec. 612(a)(5)(A)]. The original language in P.L. 94–142 (EHA) requires that:

The State has established . . . (B) procedures to assure that, to the maximum extent appropriate, handicapped children, including children in public or private institutions or other care facilities, are educated with children who are not handicapped, and that special classes, separate schooling, or other removal of handicapped children from the regular educational environment occurs only when the nature or severity of the handicap is such that education in regular classes with the use of supplementary aids and services cannot be achieved satisfactorily.

[P.L. 94–142 20 USC 1412, Sec. 612(5)(B)]

This so-called least-restrictive environment language was included in P.L. 94–142 because state statutes enacted before the federal law included such language:

Many recently passed state statutes that require due process also mandate the use of placement schemes that emphasize the least restrictive alternative. That policy is based on the assumption that there are various types of settings that differ in terms of programs offered and their distance from the regular education program. As the distance from the regular education setting increases, the amount of the restrictiveness on the child's functioning as well as the possibility of stigma increases.

(Weintraub, Abeson, Ballard, & LaVor, 1976, p. 88)

So, there was a clear preference for educating students with disabilities with their nondisabled peers. Yet, P.L. 94–142 also allowed for alternative placements. Again, Weintraub, Abeson, Ballard, and LaVor (1976) commented on this:

While clearly and forthrightly invoking the right of handicapped children to instruction in the "least restrictive" educational environment, the federal government at the same time is concerned that each child's individual educational needs will be fully met. P.L. 94–142 requires that all handicapped children "to the maximum extent appropriate" shall be educated "with children who are not handicapped." P.L. 94–142 acknowledges that "special classes, separate schooling or other removal from the regular educational environment will be required to meet the appropriate instructional needs of many children when 'the nature or severity of the handicap is such that education in regular classes with the use of supplementary aids and services cannot be achieved satisfactorily.'"

(p. 88)

Given the discussion in this and subsequent chapters about how disability has been understood, and what was expected of people with intellectual disability over time, and given the history of segregation and exclusion, the presumption of P.L. 94–142 that "special classes, separate schooling or other removal from the regular educational environment will be required to meet the appropriate instructional needs of many children" (and, we would note, that probably means many children with intellectual disability, primarily) is understandable. But was it right? As a result of such presumptions, the inclination toward educating children with disabilities with their nondisabled peers has never been interpreted as a right or, even, as a requirement before an alternative placement. In a letter to Chief State School Officers from the Office of Special Education and Rehabilitation Services (OSERS) in 1994, this was stated quite clearly: "IDEA does not require that every student with a disability be placed in the regular classroom regardless of individual abilities and needs."

In this text, readers will learn about innovations in supports planning; alternate assessment; multitiered systems of supports; universal design for learning; positive behavior interventions; promoting access to the general education curriculum; promoting inclusive classrooms; teaching reading, literacy, math, and science; and more. And yet, even as these chapters are being written, students with intellectual disability are being excluded from involvement in multitiered systems, excluded from regular education classrooms, and not being provided opportunities to learn core content knowledge and skills in the general education curriculum. As per the latest report to Congress on IDEA's implementation, only 17% of students served under the category of intellectual disability spend 80% or more of their day in regular education and almost half (49%) of students with intellectual disability are educated in the regular class less than 40% of the day. Overall, about 57% of students with intellectual disability are educated in substantially segregated settings more than 60% of their school day.

Morningstar, Kurth, and Johnson (2015) calculated an "inclusion index" based upon placement rates reported through the IDEA reports to Congress from 2000 to 2010. This index took the log of the ratio of the number of students in general education at least 80% of the day to students in general education settings 40% or less of the school day. In this index, a zero indicates that students have an equal probability of being in general education 80% or more of the day or 40% or less of the school day. Students with high-incidence disabilities were more than four times as likely to be educated in the general education classroom 80% of the day than less than 40% of the day (index = 1.27) in 2000, a proportion that increased to nine times more likely by 2011 (index = 2.09). Students with low-incidence disabilities were four times more likely to spend 40% or less of their day in general education in 2000 (index = −1.27). In the intervening decade, things improved, but students with low-incidence disabilities were still 1.5 times more likely to be in general education 40% of the day or less than to be in the general education setting 80% of the day or more (index = −0.49).

Soukup, Wehmeyer, Bashinski, and Bovaird (2007) observed 19 elementary students with intellectual disability for a total of 1,140 minutes and recorded intervals in which students were working on grade-level content standards or content linked to any general education standard (below grade-level). Students in general education contexts were observed working on an activity linked to any general education content standard in 98% of intervals, and on an activity linked to their specific grade-level content standard in 83% of these intervals. Students not included in general education contexts were observed working on an activity linked to any general education content standard in only 46% of intervals, and there was not a single interval (0%) in which these students were observed working on a grade-level content standard.

"What is past is prologue," Antonio says in Act II of Shakespeare's The Tempest. As we look at evidence-and research-based practices to educate students with intellectual disability, it is wise to bear in mind that our present is very much built upon our past. The findings from Congress for the IDEA reauthorization of 2004 state that "improving educational results for children with disabilities is an essential element of our national policy of ensuring equality of opportunity, full participation, independent living, and economic self-sufficiency for individuals with disabilities." The methods, practices, and strategies discussed in the rest of this text are intended to achieve these outcomes, but they likely will not succeed if we do not heed the lessons from the past and change how we understand disability and how we design supports based upon those understandings. That is the topic of the next several chapters.

Note

1. The terms used medically, clinically, or educationally describe people with intellectual disability up until the 21st century have, over time, become stigmatizing, pejorative, and insulting. And yet, these terms also reflected how the condition we now call intellectual disability was understood at the time. We have opted to use these now-offensive terms in their historical context.

References

Abeson, A., & Davis, S. (2000). The parent movement in mental retardation. In M. L. Wehmeyer & J. R. Patton (Eds.), *Mental retardation in the 21st century* (pp. 19–34). Austin, TX: ProEd.

Damrosch, L. (2013). *Jonathan Swift: His life and his world.* New Haven: Yale University Press.

Defoe, D. (1697). *An essay upon projects.* London: Kessinger. Retrieved from https://books.google.com/books?id=-5oxAQAAMAAJ.

Defoe, D. (1726). *Mere nature delineated or a body without a soul: Being observations upon the young forester lately brought to town from Germany: With suitable applications: Also, a brief dissertation upon the usefulness and necessity of fools, whether political or natural.* London: T. Watson.

Esquirol, J.E. (1838). *Mental maladies: A treatise on insanity* (E. Hunt, Trans.). New York: Hafner.

Ferguson, P.M. (2014). Creating the continuum: J.E. Wallace Wallin and the role of clinical psychology in the emergence of public school special education in America. *International Journal of Inclusive Education, 18*, 86–100.

Frank, K. (2011). *Crusoe: Daniel Defoe, Robert Knox and the creation of a myth*. London: The Bodley Head.

Historic Royal Places (2013). Retrieved from http://www.hrp.org.uk.

Howe, S. (1893). *The education of Laura Bridgman*. Boston: Perkins Institute.

Jackson, L., Ryndak, D., & Wehmeyer, M. (2010). The dynamic relationship between context, curriculum, and student learning: A case for inclusive education as a research-based practice. *Research and Practice in Severe Disabilities, 33–34*(1), 175–195.

Kode, K. (2002). *Elizabeth Farrell and the history of special education*. Arlington, VA: Council for Exceptional Children.

Lane, H. (1976). *The wild boy of Aveyron*. Cambridge, MA: Harvard University Press.

Moorhouse, R. (2010). Peter the wild boy. *History Today 60*(4), 17–27.

Morningstar, M.E., Kurth, J.A., & Johnson, P.E. (2015). *Examining the past decade of education settings for students with significant disabilities*. Manuscript submitted for publication.

President's Committee on Mental Retardation (1977). *MR 76: Mental retardation past and present*. Washington, DC: Author.

President's Panel on Mental Retardation (1962). *A proposed program for national action to combat mental retardation*. Washington, DC: Author.

Privateer, P.M. (2006). *Inventing intelligence: A social history of smart*. Malden, MA: Blackwell Publishing.

Smith, J. (2003). *In search of better angels: Stories of disability in the human family*. Thousand Oaks, CA: Corwin Press.

Smith, J.D., & Wehmeyer, M.L. (2012). *Good blood, bad blood: Science, nature, and the myth of the Kallikaks*. Washington, DC: American Association on Intellectual and Developmental Disabilities.

Soukup, J.H., Wehmeyer, M.L., Bashinski, S.M., & Bovaird, J.A. (2007). Classroom variables and access to the general curriculum for students with disabilities. Exceptional Children, 74, 101–120.

Wehmeyer, M.L. (2013). *The story of intellectual disability: An evolution of meaning, understanding, and public perception*. Baltimore: Paul H. Brookes.

Weintraub, F.J., Abeson, A., Ballard, J., & LaVor, M. (1976). *Public policy and the education of exceptional children*. Reston, VA: The Council for Exceptional Children.

2

Reframing Educational Supports for Students with Intellectual Disability through Strengths-Based Approaches

Karrie A. Shogren, Michael L. Wehmeyer,
Robert L. Schalock, James R. Thompson

Introduction and Overview

As described in Chapter 1, throughout history and continuing into modern times, deficit-based models have dominated the intellectual disability field and shaped the organization of services and supports. Such models, when applied to the education of students with intellectual disability, have contributed to the widespread use of segregated educational programs and restricted curricular content for students with intellectual disability. Students with intellectual disability continue to be educated in segregated classrooms and schools, with progress toward more integrated placements stalling in recent years (Kurth, Morningstar, & Kozleski, 2014).

This ongoing separation of students with intellectual disability has been influenced by assumptions inherent in deficit-based approaches to disability, namely that such students are best served in homogeneous groups to allow for remedial education (Jackson, Ryndak, & Wehmeyer, 2008–2009). This separate, remedial model is driven by assumptions about the importance of quantifying deficits and implementing strategies to remediate deficits. This assumption leads to a focus on structuring educational services to address deficits, rather than building on and supporting student's strengths (Snell et al., 2009; Wehmeyer et al., 2008). The general result of these practices has been detrimental socially (e.g., lack of opportunity to interact with and learn from peers) and academically (e.g., lack of access to a challenging academic curriculum) (Ryndak, Jackson, & White, 2013).

Strengths-based approaches provide an alternative view, suggesting that rather than focusing on deficits in functioning, it is important to understand the demands of age-appropriate, inclusive environments where people with and without disabilities live, learn, work, and play. Based on an understanding of the demands of these environments, the supports that are needed to build on the student's strengths and maximize personal growth and participation can be identified and implemented to improve human functioning and personal outcomes. These supports do not necessitate segregation, and, in fact, are based on the assumption that the reference environment should be inclusive environments that are age-appropriate and accessible to all, including people with intellectual disability.

Shifting educational practices to align with strengths-based approaches has significant implications for restructuring the organization and delivery of educational services and supports for students with intellectual disability. In that regard, this chapter has three purposes. First, we identify those factors that have precipitated the movement toward strengths-based approaches; second, we describe the components of a strengths-based approach; and third, we briefly discuss the implications of employing a strengths-based approach to reframe educational supports and services for students with intellectual disability. This approach will be elaborated on in Chapter 4. Throughout this chapter, a strengths-based approach is defined as one that: (a) focuses on personal development; (b) uses individualized support strategies to enhance functioning in major life activity areas, personal well-being domains, and the dimensions of human functioning; and (c) evaluates the impact of support strategies on personal outcomes.

Factors Contributing to the Shift to Strengths-Based Approaches

Multiple, interrelated movements in the disability and related fields have contributed to the shift to strength-based approaches. These movements include normalization, the disability rights movement, the right to education in the least restrictive environment, the emphasis on self-determination, the social-ecological model of disability, the focus on human capabilities, and positive psychology. Each is described in this section of the chapter.

Normalization

The normalization movement emerged from the work of Bengt Nirje (1969, 1972) and has been identified as one of the most influential movements in the intellectual disability field (Scheerenberger, 1987). The basic principle of the normalization movement is that people with intellectual disability should be supported to live their lives and have experiences similar to their age-peers without disabilities in community environments that are valued by the vast majority of others in society, rather than in segregated environments. The normalization movement described the right and the importance of enabling people with intellectual disability to obtain an existence as close to normal as possible (Nirje, 1969), making available the patterns and conditions of everyday life that all people experience.

The normalization principle and associated movement significantly challenged existing models for organizing services for people with intellectual disability, leading to significant changes in the frameworks used to design and deliver supports and services. Chief among these changes was a greater focus on the rights of people with intellectual disability to fully access all of the resources in their community and to engage in age-appropriate activities and experiences that all people value.

Disability Rights Movement

Building on the emergence of the normalization principle and civil rights movements led by women and African Americans, the disability rights movements emerged, beginning with the independent living movement led by people with physical disabilities followed by the self-advocacy movement led by people with intellectual disability. Critical to these movements was the emergence of organizations organized and led by people with disabilities. In the 1980s groups for people with intellectual disability began to emerge that emulated the structure and intent of existing self-help groups and that also provided a vehicle for personal advocacy. These groups became known as "self-advocacy groups," and were organized and run by people with intellectual disability (Dybwad & Bersani, 1996). In 1990, leaders in the self-advocacy movement founded Self-Advocates Becoming Empowered (SABE), which provided a national presence for self-advocacy groups.

The importance of these consumer-organized and controlled organizations on strengths-based approaches cannot be underestimated. Not only did such organizations provide opportunities for leadership by people with disabilities, they provided opportunities for the recognition of the capacities of people with intellectual disability, and the critical influence that environments have in terms of creating (and limiting) opportunities.

Right to Education in the Least Restrictive Environment

As discussed in Chapter 1, the disability rights and parent advocacy movement (Turnbull, Shogren, & Turnbull, 2011) contributed to the passage of laws establishing the right to education for all students. In 1975, the *Education for All Handicapped Children Act* (P.L. 94–142), now known as the *Individuals with Disabilities Education Improvement Act* (IDEA, 2004), was signed into law. This public law ensured the right of all children with disabilities to a free appropriate public education (FAPE). IDEA defined special education as *specially designed instruction* to promote an equal opportunity for educational benefit for students with disabilities that prepares youth for "future education, employment, and independent living."

The 1997 and 2004 amendments to IDEA made clear that each student's educational program, and resultant specially designed instruction, should be based upon two sources: (a) the general education curriculum, defined as the same curriculum as that provided to all other students; and (b) the student's unique learning needs. The "access to the general education curriculum" mandates require that all students receiving special education services have the supports necessary for them to be involved with and progress in the general education curriculum, as well as goals and modifications to address their unique learning needs. This emphasis represented a major shift in curricular focus, particularly for students with intellectual disability, as historically the educational emphasis for these students had been on remediating deficits in adaptive skills and the application of a "functional curriculum" (Browder, Spooner, & Meier, 2011), or a curriculum focused only on specialized instruction to meet their unique, functional learning needs (e.g., daily living skill instruction).

In addition to the right to a free appropriate public education, IDEA presumes that specially designed instruction should be provided in the *least restrictive environment* (LRE). As discussed in Chapter 1, the law states that "to the maximum extent appropriate, children with disabilities . . . are educated with children who are not disabled, and special classes, separate schooling, or other removal of children with disabilities from the regular education environment occurs only when the nature or severity of the disability of a child is such that education in regular classes with the use of supplementary aids and services cannot be achieved satisfactorily." The LRE presumption emphasizes that special education should not be linked to a specific setting, but instead should be delivered in environments best suited to access the general education curriculum and meet the student's unique learning needs, with the presumption being placement in the general education classroom with appropriate supplementary aids and services. Research has also established that students with intellectual disability who are educated in the general education classroom are more likely to be working on academic tasks that are aligned with grade-level or near-grade-level curricular content than are their peers in self-contained classrooms (Matzen, Ryndak, & Nakao, 2010; Soukup, Wehmeyer, Bashinski, & Bovaird, 2007) and that if provided instruction to do so, students with intellectual disability can make progress on core content instruction in the general education setting (Lee, Wehmeyer, Soukup, & Palmer, 2010; Roach & Elliott, 2006; Shogren, Palmer, Wehmeyer, Williams-Diehm, & Little, 2012). These findings suggest that receiving education in general education classrooms has a profound influence on the extent to which students have access to challenging, grade-level curriculum (Lee et al., 2010; Wehmeyer, Lattin, Lapp Rincker, & Agran, 2003). Despite this presumption, many schools still operate a placement continuum and continue to make decisions on where to educate students with intellectual disability based on severity of disability and ingrained school processes, procedures, and programs (Jackson, Ryndak, & Wehmeyer, 2008–2009). Although there has been a slight increase in inclusive placements since the passage of the IDEA, the majority of students with intellectual disability are still served primarily in segregated classrooms and schools (Kleinert et al., 2015; Morningstar, Kurth, & Johnson, 2015). The passage of IDEA, with its the emphasis on access to the general education curriculum, has promoted a greater understanding of the capacities of students with intellectual disability, their right to general education curricular content as well as instruction linked to unique learning needs, and the role of the environment in shaping opportunities for the expression and development of student strengths.

Emphasis on Self-Determination

In the early 1990s, a growing emphasis in the field of special education concerned promoting the personal self-determination of students with intellectual disability. This was directly linked to the principles of the normalization and disability rights movements and highlighted the importance of assuring that all people, including people with intellectual disability, have the right and should be supported to govern their own lives (Ward, 1996). The movement toward promoting self-determination also pushed the field to focus on understanding and supporting the development of positive, strengths-based characteristics associated with human capacities and positive psychology (described subsequently). The emphasis on self-determination emerged in the intellectual disability field as increased attention was directed toward the poor outcomes that students with disabilities were experiencing as they transitioned from school to adult life in the late 1980s and early 1990s (Blackorby & Wagner, 1996), despite the passage of IDEA in 1975.

Despite policy changes, data continued to suggest that students with intellectual disability were experiencing poor outcomes. Promoting self-determination, or supporting students to develop skills and attitudes that would enable them to be causal agents over their lives, emerged as one way to promote better outcomes. Under deficit-based conceptualizations of disability, limited attention was directed to how students with intellectual disability could play an active role in making choices and decisions and setting goals for their lives. In fact, many people questioned whether this was possible for people with significant intellectual disability. However, researchers began to document the negative effects of a lack of choice and control on people with disabilities (Shogren, Bovaird, Palmer, & Wehmeyer, 2010; Wehmeyer & Palmer, 1997), and increased attention was directed toward innovative strategies to support students with intellectual disability to be self-determining (Ward, 2005).

Self-determination has received significant attention in disability and special education fields, and it contributed to the shift toward recognizing the importance of building on positive dispositions and enabling students with intellectual disability to become casual agents over their lives. This shift has been linked to the attainment of positive academic (Konrad, Fowler, Walker, Test, & Wood, 2007; Lee, Wehmeyer, Palmer, Soukup, & Little, 2008; Shogren et al., 2012) and adult outcomes (e.g., employment, independent living) (Shogren, Wehmeyer, Palmer, Rifenbark, & Little, 2015; Wehmeyer & Palmer, 2003; Wehmeyer & Schwartz, 1997). Research has also linked enhanced self-determination with enhanced quality of life and life satisfaction (Lachapelle et al., 2005; Nota, Ferrari, Soresi, & Wehmeyer, 2007; Shogren, Lopez, Wehmeyer, Little, & Pressgrove, 2006; Wehmeyer & Schwartz, 1998). As such, the emphasis on self-determination shaped the growing adoption of strengths-based approaches and the social-ecological model of disability in education contexts.

Social-Ecological Model of Disability

The social-ecological model of disability exemplifies the interaction between the person and his/her environment. The model encompasses a multidimensional understanding of human functioning, and focuses on the role that individualized supports play in enhancing human functioning. The social-ecological model defines disability as a function of the fit between a person's competencies and environmental demands and has been adopted by the World Health Organization in its International Classification of Functioning, Disability, and Health (World Health Organization, 2001, 2007) and the

American Association on Intellectual and Developmental Disabilities (AAIDD) in its Terminology and Classification system (Luckasson et al., 2002; Luckasson et al., 1992; Schalock et al., 2010).

When mismatches between personal competency and environmental demands are present, it is necessary to identify and arrange supports that effectively address the mismatches and enhance human functioning. As discussed by Buntinx and Schalock (2010), Schalock et al. (2010) and the World Health Organization (2001), *human functioning* is an umbrella term for all life activities and includes five dimensions: intellectual abilities, adaptive behavior, health, participation, and context. As a contributing factor in shifting to strengths-based approaches, a social-ecological model of intellectual disability (a) recognizes the vast biological and environmental complexities associated with intellectual disability, (b) captures the essential characteristics of a person with this disability, (c) establishes an ecological (i.e., person x environment) framework for the provision of a system of supports across ecologies (i.e., micro, meso, and macrosystems), and (d) recognizes that the manifestation of intellectual disability involves the dynamic, reciprocal engagement among multiple factors that involve intellectual ability, adaptive skills, health, participation, and context.

The social-ecological model of disability also facilitates a functionality approach to intellectual disability that provides a framework for going beyond classical theory, dogma, or vague notions of a phenomenon to a recognition of the ecological factors effecting the person. This change facilitates a more holistic approach to understanding and enhancing human functioning and personal well-being. As defined and discussed by Luckasson and Schalock (2013), a functionality approach to intellectual disability encompasses a systems perspective that includes human functioning dimensions, interactive systems of supports, and human functioning outcomes.

The "functionality approach" should not be confused with a "functional curriculum," although at first glance it may seem as if the two terms are related. A functionality approach to intellectual disability within educational systems involves an integrative understanding of human functioning; a unified language; the alignment of assessment, intervention, and outcomes; and the adoption of evidence-based practices. A functional curriculum is one where the focus is teaching and learning daily living, vocational, and community living skills (Bouck & Satsangi, 2014).

From a social-ecological perspective, the ultimate goal of identifying disability is to build systems of supports that promote optimal human functioning. The purpose of diagnosis and classification is to identify needed supports to enhance human functioning (Thompson et al., 2009). In the education context, these supports may be instruction to promote new skill development, environmental modifications through universal design, natural supports, technology supports, or any other resources and strategies to "promote the development, education, interests, and personal well-being of an individual and that enhance human functioning" (Schalock et al., 2010, p. 175). Further, the person should be the causal agent over these supports, playing a primary role in setting goals and creating visions for the future. Schalock et al. (2012) emphasized the importance of identifying supports for participation and for learning in inclusive contexts, and the role of structuring the environment through collaborative teaming and planning to promote access to inclusive environments for students with intellectual disability.

Focus on Human Capabilities

Another factor that has influenced the movement toward strengths-based approaches is the capabilities framework. As discussed by Brown, Hatton, and Emerson (2013), Burchardt (2008), Nussbaum (2009, 2011), and Reinders and Schalock (2014), the capabilities framework provides an understanding of what societies need to do to achieve social justice and inclusive environments. The capabilities emphasized by the authors are not synonymous with skills or abilities; rather, they *are substantial freedoms or combined capabilities*. Exercising these capabilities requires both internal capabilities (i.e., states of the person amenable to change, including learned skills, but also states such as self-confidence) and the social, political, and economic conditions in which people can develop and apply their internal capabilities (Nussbaum, 2011). From this perspective, functioning refers to how capabilities are realized in peoples' lives.

The capability framework has contributed to a shift to a strengths-based approach in three ways. First, because the framework focuses on "what each person is able to do and to be," it removes any threshold for capabilities needed for inclusion and emphasizes the combined capacities of all people in any environment (Nussbaum, 2009; Wolff, 2009). Second, Burchardt (2008) has developed on the basis of empirical investigation what he refers to as "valuable capabilities" that include life, health, and bodily integrity; individual, social, and family life; legal security; adequate standard of living; participation, influence, and voice; identity, self-expression, and self-respect; education and learning; and productive and valued activities. Third, the focus on human capacities is consistent with the principles inherent within the disability rights movement, including self-worth, self-determination, subjective well-being, pride, and engagement; it augments core themes of positive psychology, including abilities, talents, resilience, developmental processes, and fulfillment; and it facilitates quality-of-life enhancement strategies associated with empowerment, self-determination, valued roles, active participation, personal control, choices, and inclusive environments (Pazey, Schalock, Schaller, & Burkett, in press; Schalock & Verdugo, 2013).

Positive Psychology

In parallel to efforts occurring within the disability field to change ways in which disability has been understood, and supports and services have been organized to enhance functioning, psychologists have also began challenging the deficit-focused history and traditions in the discipline of psychology. Specifically, there has been an increasing call to reframe the science of psychology to emphasize the positive aspects of human functioning. Seligman (1999), as president of the American Psychological Association, called for a "reoriented science that emphasizes the understanding and building of the most positive qualities of an individual," which he called "positive psychology" (p. 559).

Seligman's call for positive psychology has had a substantial impact on psychology and related disciplines, including special education. It has emphasized a framework for understanding and researching strengths. Although research on constructs associated with positive attributes and values had existed throughout the history of psychology, positive psychology provides a strengths-based model of understanding human functioning rather than a deficit-based model. Seligman and Csikszentmihalyi (2000) characterized positive psychology as focusing on three "pillars": (a) valued subjective experience, (b) positive individual traits, and (c) civic values and the institutions that support them.

Since the introduction of positive psychology, there has been an "explosion" of research on positive psychology (Yen, 2010) in the general population. *Character Strengths and Virtues: A Handbook and Classification* (Peterson & Seligman, 2004) was published as a definition and classification system for strengths and virtues, much like the *Diagnostic and Statistical Manual* defines and classifies mental disorders. Tools have been developed to measure character strengths and virtues in youth (Park & Peterson, 2006), and these tools have been validated with youth with intellectual and developmental disabilities (Shogren, Wehmeyer, Forber-Pratt, & Palmer, 2015; Shogren, Wehmeyer, Lang, & Niemiec, 2014). Further, there has been alignment of work within the fields of positive psychology and disability, integrating a focus on human capacities and person-environment fit models. In the disability field, research focused on building on strengths and positive psychology constructs and processes has increased (Shogren, Wehmeyer, Pressgrove, & Lopez, 2006). The application of positive psychology has been explored for people with intellectual disability (Dykens, 2006; Niemiec, Shogren, & Wehmeyer, in press; Shogren, 2013; Wehmeyer, 2013), and constructs like self-determination and character strengths have been explored in adolescents with intellectual disability, providing access to strengths-based interventions that can be used in educational contexts to promote valued outcomes.

In summary, the normalization principle, disability rights movement, education rights movement, emphasis on self-determination, social-ecological model of disability, focus on human capabilities, and positive psychology have each contributed to the emergence of strengths-based approaches in education and disability, and a shift in the way in which people with disabilities are understood. These movements have also shaped the characteristics of current strengths-based approaches. We describe these characteristics next.

Characteristics of Strengths-Based Approaches

Strengths-based approaches need to be differentiated from those associated with a deficit-based approach to provide direction for the application of strengths-based supports that enhance human functioning and the attainment of educational goals. The following sections will discuss the key areas of emphasis within strengths-based approaches, followed by a brief introduction to the applications of a strengths-based approach to educational supports for students with intellectual disability.

Focuses on Personal Development

This first characteristic of a strengths-based approach is consistent with the notion of promoting human flourishing, derived from positive psychology (Seligman, 2011) and the capabilities approach (Nussbaum, 2011). Flourishing emerges as people develop capabilities through self-determined actions. The capabilities approach (described previously) and the tenants of self-determination and positive psychology all emphasize the need to focus on the process of developing strengths leading to valued personal outcomes. The focus is not on what the person is unable to do or will not achieve, but instead is on what the person can do and become. Further, with the introduction of a social-ecological approach and supports, it is possible to provide supports that enable participation in inclusive and age-appropriate environments. This approach emphasizes the process that leads to positive outcomes and the role of self-determined motivation in allowing people to realize their capabilities.

As a strengths-based characteristic, personal development occurs whenever students enlarge their world of experience and have the opportunity to engage in self-determined action and normal activities. Seen in this way, personal development is best understood as embarking on a journey, rather than planning a state of affairs to be realized at a given time. As a journey, personal development is a continuous process throughout a student's education that emphasizes building on strengths and capabilities to bring the student's capabilities to fruition. It entails the discovery of new opportunities that enable people to grow, develop, and flourish (Reinders & Schalock, 2014).

Uses Individualized Support Strategies

Since the mid-1980s, the social-ecological model supports paradigm has brought together the practices of person-centered planning, personal development and growth opportunities, community inclusion, self-determination, empowerment, and outcomes evaluation. These supports (which comprise the second characteristic of a strengths-based approach) are defined as resources or strategies that are designed for the person to support him/her in everyday life and that aim to promote the development, education, interests, functioning, and individual's personal well-being (Thompson et al., 2009). Services are an organized means for delivering supports, instruction, therapies, or other assistance.

Support strategies are the actual techniques one uses to help bridge the gap between "what is" and "what can be." Individualized support strategies contribute to a strengths-based approach in educational services in at least three important ways. First, they organize potential support strategies into a system through which individualized supports can be planned and implemented according to the student's personal goals and assessed support needs. Second, they provide a framework for coordinating the procurement and application of individualized supports across the sources of support. Third, they provide a framework for evaluating the impact of individualized supports on the individual's functioning level and personal outcomes.

Support strategies can be used to enhance a student's functioning in major life activity areas, the domains of personal well-being, and/or the dimensions of human functioning. Table 2.1 provides an overview of the components of these three support areas. Moreover, it is important to stress that supports should be arranged not only to compensate for any relative limitations or vulnerabilities a person may experience, but also to take advantage of and build upon areas of personal strengths and accomplishments.

Although it is beyond the scope of this chapter to describe specific support strategies for each of these targeted areas, in Table 2.2 we list a number of exemplary support strategies and their anticipated effects that will be elaborated on in other chapters in this volume. It is important to note, however, the importance of supports for both learning and participation in inclusive education environments.

Table 2.1 Targeted areas for supports provision

Major Life Activity Areas (Student)	Domains of Personal Well-Being	Dimensions of Human Functioning
Exceptional medical support needs	Personal development	Intellectual functioning
Exceptional behavioral support needs	Self-determination	Adaptive skills
Home life activities	Interpersonal relations	Health
Community and neighborhood activities	Social inclusion	Participation
School participation activities	Rights	Context
School learning activities	Emotional well-being	
Health and safety activities	Physical well-being	
Social activities	Material well-being	
Advocacy activities		

Table 2.2 Exemplary support strategies and their anticipated effects

Focus Area	Exemplary Support Strategies	Anticipated Effect
Personal development and self-determination	- Facilitate personal goal setting	- Facilitates motivation
	- Teach self-regulation and implement self-management, self-evaluation, self-instruction programs	- Enhances successful performance and internal locus of control
		- Increases sense of self-efficacy
	- Build on character strengths and virtues	- Increases motivation
		- Facilitates learning and independence
	- Promote choice making and preference assessment	- Facilitates communication and increases access
	- Maximize self-determined motivation	- Facilitates self-esteem and sense of empowerment
	- Implement skill development programs	- Facilitates internal locus of control
	- Provide technical assistance	- Facilitates independence, productivity, and community integration
Interpersonal Relations	- Use social media	- Increases communication and social engagement
	- Involve peer groups	- Increases social support, mentorship, and perceived societal contribution
	- Maximize family involvement	- Facilitates ongoing support and nurturance

Evaluates Personal Outcomes

The third characteristic of a strengths-based approach is to evaluate personal outcomes, which are the benefits derived from educational and supports services. At the individual level, evaluation focuses on short-term outcomes related to character strengths, major curricular domains, life activity areas, progress in general education curricular content, individualized learning goals, personal well-being domains, and/or the dimensions of human functioning. Further progress in these areas should be linked to supports provided, including supports for learning and participation. The evaluation of long-term outcomes at the personal level focuses on postsecondary living, employment, and education status (Pazey et al., in press).

Evaluating personal outcomes extends beyond the traditional approach to monitoring and assessing instructional objectives related to a student's Individualized Education Program (IEP). As the trend towards using evidence-based practices continues, with the corresponding focus on outcomes evaluation, this characteristic of a strengths-based approach will increasingly encompass collecting and using evidence strategically, employing outcome enhancement practices, assessing character strengths and virtues as well as personal outcomes, and analyzing all of the information to inform and improve support implementation practices (Schalock & Verdugo, 2013).

Application of Strengths-Based Approaches to the Education of Students with Intellectual Disability

Turnbull, Turnbull, Wehmeyer, and Shogren (2013) suggested that as strengths-based approaches have been adopted, there has been a greater focus on inclusive education, and that the movement towards inclusion and strengths-based practices can best be described as three generations of related, though distinct, activities. The first generation focused on addressing the question of "where" to provide educational services and supports. This generation of practice focused primarily on getting students into inclusive environments, ensuring that students had opportunities to access the general education classroom and curriculum, and that options beyond segregated schools and classrooms were available. Principles guiding the first generation focus were that: (a) all students receive education in the school they would attend if they had no disability, (b) school and general education placements are age- and grade-appropriate, and (c) special education supports exist within the general education class.

The second generation focus shifted to the "how" of inclusion, and more specifically, how educators could identify and implement supports for participation and learning that facilitated the student's success in general education classrooms. Various supports for learning and participation were identified through research and practice, including co-teaching, differentiation, universal design, collaborative planning and teaming, and family/professional partnerships. In both first- and second-generation inclusive practices, the primary focus was on where students were receiving their education and how to support success in that environment.

Since the 1990s there has emerged a convincing database with regard to the impact of inclusive practices on educational outcomes (Ryndak et al., 2013). Researchers have documented the impact of inclusive education on academic, social/communication, and behavioral skills, suggesting that students with intellectual disability (a) exhibit growth in academic achievement and use of academic skills when participating in inclusive settings (Dessemontet, Bless, & Morin, 2012; Kurth & Mastergeorge, 2012); and (b) show increased communication (Foreman, Arthur-Kelly, Pascoe, & King, 2004), social (Carter, Cushing, Clark, & Kennedy, 2005; Fisher & Meyer, 2002), and employment skills, in addition to skills leading to self-determination (Hughes, Cosgriff, Agran, & Washington, 2013), when educated in general education settings.

Researchers have also suggested that students with intellectual disability have greater growth in social skills, largely as a result of access to social networks and peer models (McDonnell, Johnson,

25

Polychronis, & Riesen, 2002). Placement in general education settings has also been found to increase teachers' learning expectations for students (Kurth & Mastergeorge, 2010). There is sufficient evidence that students with disabilities who receive their education in inclusive settings attain positive outcomes, including enhanced opportunities to interact socially with peers, enhanced task engagement, improved skills acquisition, enhanced social competence, and enhanced access to the general education curriculum. This is achieved without cost to students without disabilities, who realize socially valued outcomes as well as have access to resources and supports in inclusive classrooms that promote success for all students (Carter & Kennedy, 2006; Shogren et al., 2015).

The third generation of inclusive practices has emerged over the past decade as school reform efforts have begun to emphasize "what" the student is learning. Third-generation practices shifted the focus from individual classrooms to schoolwide provision of high-quality instruction for all students, with more intensive instruction as necessary for students who have exceptional support needs. The notion is that all students—including students with intellectual disability—benefit when the focus is on the provision of high-quality instruction based on an analysis of the mismatches between the personal characteristics (e.g., learning progress) of students and environmental demands (e.g., achievement expectations embedded in the curriculum).

The need for the reference environment to be the general education classroom and curriculum, with high-quality instruction in place, is central to third-generation inclusive practices and is consistent with the tenants of strengths-based approaches that create opportunities for embedding strengths-based supports related to self-determination, personal capabilities, and strengths and character development. Researchers have established that students with intellectual disability who are educated in the general education classroom are more likely to be working on academic tasks that are aligned with grade-level or near-grade-level content compared to peers in self-contained classrooms (Matzen et al., 2010; Soukup et al., 2007). Furthermore, when provided instruction to do so, students with intellectual disability can make progress on core content instruction in the general education setting (Lee et al., 2010; Roach & Elliott, 2006; Shogren et al., 2012). This finding suggests that access to challenging expectations and content can lead to valued outcomes.

Conclusion

This chapter identified current movements that are shifting the focus of education supports to strengths-based approaches and discussed the characteristics of a strengths-based approach. This approach emphasizes that all students with intellectual disability have strengths, virtues, and capacities that, if built on, create opportunities for flourishing in education and other valued life areas.

As mentioned, however, even today too many students with intellectual disability continue to be educated in segregated classrooms and schools. Thus, efforts to reframe educational services and supports must persist. Namely, not only emphasizing those factors that have contributed to the shift towards strengths-based approaches and practices, but also applying those practices through focusing on strengths development, using systems of supports, and evaluating outcomes to determine the effectiveness of educational efforts. Such information is critical to assure that educational improvement and the attainment of valued outcomes is not an episodic effort, but rather an ongoing process. These necessary activities and efforts are elaborated on in subsequent chapters.

References

Blackorby, J., & Wagner, M. (1996). Longitudinal postschool outcomes of youth with disabilities: Findings from the National Longitudinal Transition Study. *Exceptional Children, 62*, 399–413.

Bouck, E. C., & Satsangi, R. (2014). Evidence-base of a functional curriculum for secondary students with mild intellectual disability: A historical perspective. *Education and Training in Autism and Developmental Disabilities, 49*, 478–486.

Browder, D., Spooner, F., & Meier, I. (2011). Introduction. In D. Browder & F. Spooner (Eds.), *Teaching students with moderate and severe disabilities* (pp. 3–22). New York: Guilford Press.

Brown, I., Hatton, C., & Emerson, E. (2013). Quality of life indicators for individuals with intellectual disabilities: Extending current practice. *Intellectual and Developmental Disabilities, 51*, 316–332. doi: 10.1352/1934–9556–51.5.316

Buntinx, W. H. E., & Schalock, R. L. (2010). Models of disability, quality of life, and individualized supports: Implications for professional practice in intellectual disability. *Journal of Policy and Practice in Intellectual Disabilities, 7*, 283–294.

Burchardt, T. (2008). Monitoring inequality: Putting the capability approach to work. In G. Craig, T. Burchardt, & D. Gordon (Eds.), *Social justice and public policy* (pp. 205–220). Briston, UK: Policy Press.

Carter, E. W., Cushing, L. S., Clark, N. M., & Kennedy, C. H. (2005). Effects of peer support interventions on students' access to the general curriculum and social interactions. *Research and Practice for Persons with Severe Disabilities, 30*, 15–25.

Carter, E. W., & Kennedy, C. H. (2006). Promoting access to the general curriculum using peer support strategies. *Research and Practice for Persons with Severe Disabilities, 31*, 284–292.

Dessemontet, R. S., Bless, G., & Morin, D. (2012). Effects of inclusion on the academic achievement and adaptive behaviour of children with intellectual disabilities. *Journal of Intellectual Disability Research, 56*, 579–587. doi: 10.1111/j.1365–2788.2011.01497.x

Dwbwad, G. & Bersani, H. J. (1996). *New voices: Self-advocacy by people with disabilities.* Cambridge, MA: Brookline.

Dykens, E. M. (2006). Toward a positive psychology of mental retardation. *American Journal of Orthopsychiatry, 76*(2), 185–193.

Fisher, M., & Meyer, L. H. (2002). Development and social competence after two years for students enrolled in inclusive and self-contained educational programs. *Research and Practice for Persons with Severe Disabilities, 27*, 165–174. doi: 10.2511/rpsd.27.3.165

Foreman, P., Arthur-Kelly, M., Pascoe, S., & King, B. (2004). Evaluating the educational experiences of students with profound and multiple disabilities in inclusive and segregated classroom settings: An Australian perspective. *Research and Practice for Persons with Severe Disabilities, 29*, 183–193. doi: 10.2511/rpsd.29.3.183

Hughes, C., Cosgriff, J., Agran, M., & Washington, B. (2013). Student self-determination: A preliminary investigation of the role of participation in inclusive settings. *Education and Training in Autism and Developmental Disabilities, 48*, 3–17.

Jackson, L. B., Ryndak, D. L., & Wehmeyer, M. L. (2008–2009). The dynamic relationship between context, curriculum, and student learning: A case for inclusive education as a research-based practice. *Research and Practice for Persons with Severe Disabilities, 33–34*, 175–195.

Kleinert, H., Towles-Reeves, E., Quenemoen, R., Thurlow, M., Fluegge, L., Weseman, L., & Kerbel, A. (2015). Where students with the most significant cognitive disabilities are taught: Implications for general curriculum access. *Exceptional Children, 81*, 312–328.

Konrad, M., Fowler, C. H., Walker, A. R., Test, D. W., & Wood, W. M. (2007). Effects of self-determination interventions on the academic skills of students with learning disabilities. *Learning Disability Quarterly, 30*, 89–113. doi: 10.2307/30035545

Kurth, J. A., & Mastergeorge, A. M. (2010). Individual education plan goals and services for adolescents with autism: Impact of grade and educational setting. *Journal of Special Education, 44*, 146–160. doi: 10.1177/0022466908329825

Kurth, J. A., & Mastergeorge, A. M. (2012). Impact of setting and instructional context for adolescents with autism. *The Journal of Special Education, 46*(1), 36–48. doi: 10.1177/0022466910366480

Kurth, J. A., Morningstar, M. E., & Kozleski, E. B. (2014). The persistence of highly restrictive special education placements for students with low-incidence disabilities. *Research and Practice for Persons with Severe Disabilities, 39*(3), 227–239. doi: 10.1177/1540796914555580

Lachapelle, Y., Wehmeyer, M. L., Haelewyck, M. C., Courbois, Y., Keith, K. D., Schalock, R., . . . Walsh, P. N. (2005). The relationship between quality of life and self-determination: An international study. *Journal of Intellectual Disability Research, 49*, 740–744. doi: 10.1111/j.1365-2788.2005.00743.x

Lee, S. H., Wehmeyer, M. L., Palmer, S. B., Soukup, J. H., & Little, T. D. (2008). Self-determination and access to the general education curriculum. *The Journal of Special Education, 42*, 91–107.

Lee, S. H., Wehmeyer, M. L., Soukup, J., & Palmer, S. B. (2010). Impact of curriculum modifications on access to the general education curriculum for students with disabilities. *Exceptional Children, 76*, 213–233.

Luckasson, R., Borthwick-Duffy, S., Buntinx, W. H. E., Coulter, D. L., Craig, E. P.M., Reeve, A., . . . Tasse, M. J. (2002). *Mental retardation: Definition, classification, and systems of support* (10th ed.). Washington, DC: American Association on Mental Retardation.

Luckasson, R., Coulter, D. L., Polloway, E. A., Reiss, S., Schalock, R. L., Snell, M. E., . . . Stark, J. A. (1992). *Mental retardation: Definition, classification, and systems of supports* (9th ed.). Washington, DC: American Association on Mental Retardation.

Luckasson, R., & Schalock, R. L. (2013). Defining and applying a functionality approach to intellectual disability. *Journal of Intellectual Disability Research, 57*, 657–668.

Matzen, K., Ryndak, D., & Nakao, T. (2010). Middle school teams increasing access to general education for students with significant disabilities: Issues encountered and observations across contexts. *Remedial and Special Education, 31*, 287–304.

McDonnell, J., Johnson, J. W., Polychronis, S. C., & Riesen, T. (2002). The effects of embedded instruction on students with moderate disabilities enrolled in general education classes. *Education and Training in Autism and Developmental Disabilities, 37*, 363–277.

Morningstar, M. M., Kurth, J. A., & Johnson, A. (2015). *Examining the past decade of education settings for students with significant disabilities.* Manuscript submitted for publication.

Niemiec, R. M., Shogren, K. A., & Wehmeyer, M. L. (in press). Character strengths and intellectual and developmental disability: A strengths-based approach from positive psychology. *Education and Training in Autism and Developmental Disabilities.*

Nirje, B. (1969). The normalization principle and its human management implications. In R. B. Kugel & W. Wolfensberger (Eds.), *Changing residential patterns for the mentally retarded* (pp. 179–195). Washington, DC: President's Committee on Mental Retardation.

Nirje, B. (1972). The right to self-determination. In W. Wolfensberger (Ed.), *Normalization: The principle of normalization in human services* (pp. 176–193). Toronto: National Institute on Mental Retardation.

Nota, L., Ferrari, L., Soresi, S., & Wehmeyer, M. (2007). Self-determination, social abilities and the quality of life of people with intellectual disability. *Journal of Intellectual Disability Research, 51*, 850–865. doi: 10.1111/j.1365-2788.2006.00939.x

Nussbaum, M. C. (2009). The capabilities of people with cognitive disabilities. *Metaphilosophy, 40*, 331–351.

Nussbaum, M. C. (2011). *Creating capabilities: The human development approach.* Cambridge, MA: Belknap Press of Harvard University Press.

Park, N., & Peterson, C. (2006). Values in action (VIA) inventory of character strengths for youth. *Adolescent & Family Health, 4*, 35–40.

Pazey, B. L., Schalock, R. L., Schaller, J., & Burkett, J. (in press). Incorporating quality of life concepts into education reform: Creating real opportunities for students with disabilities in the 21st century. *Journal of Disability Policy Studies.*

Peterson, C., & Seligman, M. E. P. (2004). *Character strengths and virtues: A classification and handbook.* New York: Oxford University Press/Washington, DC: American Psychological Association.

Reinders, H., & Schalock, R. L. (2014). How organizations can enhance the quality of life of their clients and assess results: The concept of QOL enhancement. *American Journal of Intellectual and Developmental Disabilities, 119*, 291–302.

Roach, A. T., & Elliott, S. N. (2006). The influence of access to general education curriculum on alternate assessment performance of students with significant cognitive disabilities. *Educational Evaluation and Policy Analysis, 28*, 181–194. doi: 10.3102/01623737028002181

Ryndak, D., Jackson, L. B., & White, J. M. (2013). Involvement and progress in the general curriculum for students with extensive support needs: K–12 inclusive education research and implications for the future. *Inclusion, 1*, 28–49. doi: 10.1352/2326–6988–1.1.028

Schalock, R. L., Borthwick-Duffy, S., Bradley, V., Buntix, W. H. E., Coulter, D. L., Craig, E. P. M., . . . Yeager, M. H. (2010). *Intellectual disability: Definition, classification, and systems of support* (11th ed.). Washington, DC: American Association on Intellectual and Developmental Disabilities.

Schalock, R. L., Luckasson, R., Bradley, V., Buntinx, W., Lachapelle, Y., Shogren, K. A., . . . Wehmeyer, M. L. (2012). *User's guide for the 11th edition of intellectual disability: Diagnosis, classification and systems of support.* Washington, DC: American Association on Intellectual and Developmental Disabilities.

Schalock, R. L., & Verdugo, M. A. (2013). The transformation of disability organizations. *Intellectual and Developmental Disabilities, 51*, 273–286.

Scheerenberger, R. C. (1987). *A history of mental retardation: A quarter century of promise.* Baltimore: Paul H. Brookes.

Seligman, M. E. P. (1999). The president's address. *American Psychologist, 54*, 559–562.

Seligman, M. E. P. (2011). *Flourish: A visionary new understanding of happiness and well-being.* New York: Free Press.

Seligman, M. E. P., & Csikszentmihalyi, M. (2000). Positive psychology: An introduction. *American Psychologist, 55*, 5–14.

Shogren, K. A. (2013). Positive psychology and disability: A historical analysis. In M. L. Wehmeyer (Ed.), *The Oxford handbook of positive psychology and disability* (pp. 19–33). New York: Oxford University Press.

Shogren, K. A., Bovaird, J. A., Palmer, S. B., & Wehmeyer, M. L. (2010). Examining the development of locus of control orientations in students with intellectual disability, learning disabilities, and no disabilities: A latent growth curve analysis. *Research and Practice for Persons with Severe Disabilities, 35*, 80–92.

Shogren, K. A., Gross, J. M. S., Forber-Pratt, A. J., Francis, G. L., Satter, A. L., Blue-Banning, M., & Hill, C. (2015). The perspectives of students with and without disabilities on inclusive schools. *Research and Practice for Persons with Severe Disabilities, 40*, 243–260. doi: 10.1177/1540796915583493

Shogren, K. A., Lopez, S. J., Wehmeyer, M. L., Little, T. D., & Pressgrove, C. L. (2006). The role of positive psychology constructs in predicting life satisfaction in adolescents with and without cognitive disabilities: An exploratory study. *The Journal of Positive Psychology, 1*, 37–52.

Shogren, K. A., Palmer, S. B., Wehmeyer, M. L., Williams-Diehm, K., & Little, T. D. (2012). Effect of intervention with the self-determined learning model of instruction on access and goal attainment. *Remedial and Special Education, 33*, 320–330. doi: 10.1177/0741932511410072

Shogren, K. A., Wehmeyer, M. L., Forber-Pratt, A. J., & Palmer, S. B. (2015). *VIA inventory of strengths for youth (VIA-Youth): Supplement for use when supporting youth with intellectual and developmental disabilities to complete the VIA-Youth.* Lawrence, KS: Kansas University Center on Developmental Disabilities.

Shogren, K. A., Wehmeyer, M. L., Lang, K., & Niemiec, R. M. (2014). *The application of the VIA Classification of Strengths to youth with and without disabilities.* Manuscript submitted for publication.

Shogren, K. A., Wehmeyer, M. L., Palmer, S. B., Rifenbark, G. G., & Little, T. D. (2015). Relationships between self-determination and postschool outcomes for youth with disabilities. *Journal of Special Education, 53*, 30–41. doi: 10.1177/0022466913489733

Shogren, K. A., Wehmeyer, M. L., Pressgrove, C. L., & Lopez, S. J. (2006). The application of positive psychology and self-determination to research in intellectual disability: A content analysis of 30 years of literature. *Research and Practice for Persons with Severe Disabilities, 31*, 338–345.

Snell, M. E., Luckasson, R. A., Borthwick-Duffy, S., Bradley, V., Buntix, W. H. E., Coulter, D. L., . . . Yeager, M. H. (2009). The characteristics and needs of people with intellectual disability who have higher IQs. *Intellectual and Developmental Disabilities, 47*, 220–233.

Soukup, J. H., Wehmeyer, M. L., Bashinski, S. M., & Bovaird, J. A. (2007). Classroom variables and access to the general curriculum for students with disabilities. *Exceptional Children, 74*, 101–120.

Thompson, J. R., Bradley, V., Buntinx, W. H. E., Schalock, R. L., Shogren, K. A., Snell, M. E., . . . Yeager, M. H. (2009). Conceptualizing supports and the support needs of people with intellectual disability. *Intellectual and Developmental Disabilities, 47*, 135–146.

Turnbull, A. P., Turnbull, H. R., Wehmeyer, M. L., & Shogren, K. A. (2013). *Exceptional lives* (7th ed.). Columbus, OH: Merrill/Prentice Hall.

Turnbull, H. R., Shogren, K. A., & Turnbull, A. P. (2011). Evolution of the parent movement: Past, present, and future. In J. M. Kauffman & D. P. Hallahan (Eds.), *Handbook of special education* (pp. 639–653). New York: Routledge.

Ward, M. J. (1996). Coming of age in the age of self-determination: A historical and personal perspective. In D. J. Sands & M. L. Wehmeyer (Eds.), *Self-determination across the life span: Independence and choice for people with disabilities* (pp. 1–14). Baltimore, MD: Paul H. Brookes.

Ward, M. J. (2005). An historical perspective of self-determination in special education: Accomplishments and challenges. *Research and Practice for Persons with Severe Disabilities, 30*, 108–112.

Wehmeyer, M. L. (Ed.) (2013). *The Oxford handbook of positive psychology and disability.* Oxford: Oxford University Press.

Wehmeyer, M. L., Buntix, W. H. E., Lachapelle, Y., Luckasson, R. A., Schalock, R. L., Verdugo, M. A., . . . Yeager, M. H. (2008). The intellectual disability construct and its relation to human functioning. *Intellectual and Developmental Disabilities, 46*, 311–318. doi: 10.1352/1934–9556(2008)46

Wehmeyer, M. L., Lattin, D. L., Lapp Rincker, G., & Agran, M. (2003). Access to the general curriculum of middle school students with mental retardation: An observational study. *Remedial and Special Education, 24*(5), 262–272.

Wehmeyer, M. L., & Palmer, S. B. (1997). Perceptions of control of students with and without cognitive disabilities. *Psychological Reports, 81*, 195–206.

Wehmeyer, M. L., & Palmer, S. B. (2003). Adult outcomes for students with cognitive disabilities three-years after high school: The impact of self-determination. *Education and Training in Developmental Disabilities, 38*, 131–144.

Wehmeyer, M. L., & Schwartz, M. (1997). Self-determination and positive adult outcomes: A follow-up study of youth with mental retardation or learning disabilities. *Exceptional Children, 63*, 245–255.

Wehmeyer, M. L., & Schwartz, M. (1998). The relationship between self-determination and quality of life for adults with mental retardation. *Education and Training in Mental Retardation and Developmental Disabilities, 33*, 3–12.

Wolff, J. (2009). Cognitive disability in a society of equals. *Metaphilosophy, 40*(3–4), 402–415. doi:10.1111/j.1467-9973.2009.01598.x

World Health Organization. (2001). *International classification of functioning, disability, and health.* Geneva, Switzerland: Author.

World Health Organization. (2007). *International classification of functioning, disability and health: Children and youth version.* Geneva: Author.

Yen, J. (2010). Authorizing happiness: Rhetorical demarcation of science and society in historical narratives of positive psychology. *Journal of Theoretical and Philosophical Psychology, 30*, 67–78.

3

Supports and Support Needs in Strengths-Based Models of Intellectual Disability

James R. Thompson, Karrie A. Shogren,
Michael L. Wehmeyer

Chapter 2 provided an overview of how normalization, the disability rights movement, the right to education in the least restrictive environment, the emphasis on self-determination, the social-ecological model of disability, the focus on human capabilities, and positive psychology have led to the emergence and evolution of strengths-based models of intellectual disability. In this chapter, the focus will be on the supports model, which adopts a strengths-based approach to understanding and building systems of supports for people with intellectual disability based on the social-ecological model of disability. The fundamental premise of the chapter is that understanding children, youth, and adults with intellectual disability by their support needs and arranging supports to address those needs is the key to high-quality education and supports, as well as a high quality of life for children, youth, and adults with intellectual disability.

Social-Ecological Model of Disability

As described in Chapter 1, intellectual disability has traditionally been understood from a deficit-based perspective—and this perspective has led to limited expectations and opportunities for students with intellectual disability to access settings and activities that most others in society value. For example, service models were developed that created separate schools, curricula, and experiences for students with intellectual disability. These schools were established on the erroneous assumption that students with intellectual disability could not learn academic skills or otherwise benefit from access to the general education curriculum. Historically, the rationale for relegating many children and adults with intellectual disability to separate settings was that their deficits posed insurmountable barriers to meaningful participation in school and society.

The social-ecological model of disability (Schalock et al., 2010; World Health Organization, 2001) provides an alternative conceptual model for understanding people with disabilities that focuses on building on strengths and capacities. In the social-ecological model, disability is understood as a state of functioning characterized by a significant and chronic mismatch between a person's competencies and the demands of settings and activities associated with participating in an inclusive society. Understanding people with disabilities through a social-ecological lens draws attention to people's unique strengths and support needs instead of their deficits.

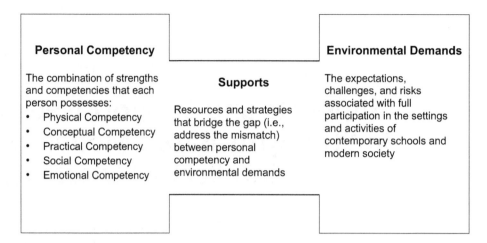

Personal Competency

The combination of strengths and competencies that each person possesses:
- Physical Competency
- Conceptual Competency
- Practical Competency
- Social Competency
- Emotional Competency

Supports

Resources and strategies that bridge the gap (i.e., address the mismatch) between personal competency and environmental demands

Environmental Demands

The expectations, challenges, and risks associated with full participation in the settings and activities of contemporary schools and modern society

Figure 3.1   The supports model: Supports as a bridge between personal competency and environmental demands

In the social-ecological model, information about deficits in personal competence is not the most salient information (as it was in the deficit-based model). While people with intellectual disability do have differences in personal competencies when compared to the general population, particularly in the domains on intellectual functioning and adaptive behavior (Schalock et al., 2010), and there is an association between intellectual functioning, adaptive behavior, and support needs (Thompson et al., 2009), these are not the same constructs and support needs are influenced by a much broader range of personal strengths, competencies, and environmental demands.

Overall, the critical implication of a social-ecological conceptualization of disability is to focus attention on the supports model and on the importance of identifying and arranging the supports people need to negotiate the demands of the settings and activities in which they wish to participate. Figure 3.1 depicts the supports model and the role of supports in bridging the gap between personal competencies and environmental demands. In considering the application of the supports model to students with intellectual disability, it is understood that students with intellectual disability will generally need more supports (i.e., extraordinary support) in order to fully participate in culturally valued activities than people without intellectual disability. From a social-ecological perspective, the chronic mismatch is the disability; the unique profile of strengths and competencies and environment demands demonstrated by each student with intellectual disability influences the pattern and intensity of support needs. Each component of the supports model described in Figure 3.1 is discussed in the following sections.

Personal Competency

Personal competence refers to the combination of strengths, skills, and abilities that each person possesses. Each person, including each person with intellectual disability, has a unique profile of strengths and limitations. Individual differences in personal competence are self-evident; no two people are exactly the same. Some people have talents in music; others struggle to carry a tune. Some people are able to do complex calculations quickly; others need longer periods of time and supports such as a calculator. Thompson, McGrew, and Bruininks (1999) provided a "big picture" framework of personal competence, discussing (a) the concepts of maximal and typical performance, and (b) five dimensions of adaptive behavior drawn from their review of factor analytic studies of adaptive behavior scales.

The five dimensions include physical competence, conceptual competence, practical competence, social competence, and emotional competence. As shown in Figure 3.2, the model describes personal competence as an amalgam (i.e., mixture) of the influence of these five dimensions. Although the five dimensions are distinct from one another, they most certainly influence each other. For example, as anyone who has been physically ill and needed to take an exam can attest, physical health (which is part of physical competence) affects conceptual proficiency. In the following sections, we first define

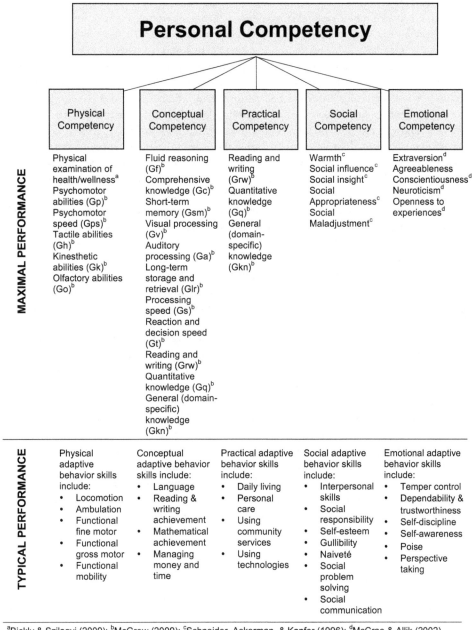

[a]Bickly & Szilagyi (2009); [b]McGrew (2009); [c]Schneider, Ackerman, & Kanfer (1996); [d]McCrae & Allik (2002)

Figure 3.2 Multidimensional and hierarchical model of personal competency

maximal and typical performance; then we describe the five dimensions of personal competence and maximal and typical performance within each of them.

Maximal and Typical Performance

The model of personal competency in Figure 3.2 describes the five dimensions of personal competency in terms of maximal performance (i.e., what people are able to do under the very best conditions) and typical performance (i.e., how people normally perform). In the field of intellectual disability, the distinction between typical and maximal performance has traditionally been made in relation to assessing intelligence and adaptive behavior. Because tests of intellectual functioning (i.e., IQ tests) were intended to measure general aptitude, it was essential to assure that assessment data were gathered under maximal performance conditions because a person's best performance was needed for the results of an IQ test to be valid. For example, an IQ test would not be considered valid if the assessor felt that the person was not displaying his or her best performance, whether it be due to testing conditions (e.g., a person who became fatigued because the testing session was too lengthy or distracted because the testing setting was too noisy) or motivation (e.g., a child who lost focus because he or she was missing out on a preferred classroom activity during the time of the assessment). In contrast, measures of typical performance, such as adaptive behavior scales, focus on identifying a person's performance in everyday "real life" tasks (e.g., assessors want to know if a person can cross a busy street safely on a regular basis, not just on their best day; Salvia, Ysseldyke, & Bolt, 2013).

The distinction between maximal and typical performance is conceptually important when attempting to understand personal competency because personal competency must be considered in terms of what a person is *capable of doing at the current time* as well as how a person *actually functions in daily life*. In the framework of personal competency shown in Figure 3.2, no ceiling on what someone might be able to accomplish in the future is implied. Not only is it impossible to make definitive claims on what any human being will or will not be able to do in the future, but history is replete with examples of deleterious effects stemming from making judgments about people's long-term abilities or potentials (see Gould, 1996).

Listed under each dimension of personal competency (Physical, Conceptual, Practical, Social, and Emotional) are examples of what measures could be used to understand maximal and typical performance. It is important to note that these are examples; we make no pretense that there was any attempt to validate any of the measures in relation to the various factors, nor are we claiming that our examples fully capture the universe of potential measures related to any factor. The purpose of Figure 3.2 is to illustrate that personal competency is a comprehensive, multidimensional construct, and attempts to understand a person holistically in regard to personal competency requiring multiple measures and considerations. It is also important to note that while examples are provided of intelligence tests and adaptive behavior scales, and their alignment with maximal and typical performance, as shown in Figure 3.2, these are not sufficient nor necessarily the only or most useful measures for understanding personal competency. Personal competencies cut across multiple domains, and they reflect strengths and abilities often not typically measured on traditional tests of intelligence and adaptive behavior.

Maximal Performance

The maximal performance indicator examples provided in Figure 3.2 draw heavily on broad ability domains associated with the Cattell-Horn-Carroll Theory of Cognitive Abilities, or CHC Theory as it has come to be known. CHC Theory is recognized by many contemporary intelligence theorists as the most comprehensive and empirically supported theory regarding the structure of human intelligence (McGrew, 2009; Schneider & McGrew, 2012), and thus provides important (but not comprehensive) information on a range of personal competencies. It is a multiple intelligence psychometric-based theory, with the multiple intelligences arranged in a hierarchical structure. At the top is a single general factor (the "g factor"), although there is debate among CHC theorists on whether a general factor (that influences all of the multiple intelligences below) actually exists. Depending on one's perspective, either below the "g factor" or at the top of the pyramid are 10 broad ability domains, and at the most specific level are more than 80 narrow ability domains (Flanagan & Dixon, 2014; McGrew, 2005, 2009; Schneider & McGrew, 2012; Taub & McGrew, 2014).

McGrew (2009) and Schneider and McGrew (2012) pointed out that CHC Theory has been, and continues to be, dynamic in the sense that structure of intelligence posited by CHC theorists evolves over time in response to new data and analyses. For example, recent research findings from Taub and McGrew (2014) suggested "intermediate factors" that may operate between the broad ability domains and narrow ability domains. If these findings are replicated, additional layers may be added to the theory. In an effort to encourage future researchers to continue to refine CHC Theory, McGrew (2009) described six additional broad ability domains (16 total), emphasizing that only 10 of the 16 have extensive empirical support, but that the additional six factors had some empirical support and should be further investigated. McGrew suggested the additional domains as a means of encouraging researchers to identify new assessment items that may align with the new domains (but not align with existing domains), as well to encourage a broader perspective regarding the nature of personal competency and intelligence. Because we wanted to be as comprehensive as possible in the personal competency model shown in Figure 3.2, we included all 16 of McGrew's (2009) broad ability domains as potential measures of maximal performance in the competency dimension with which they were most aligned. Because these domains are associated with aspects of intelligence, they would be assessed under the umbrella of maximal performance. Additional measures are also included and are noted in Figure 3.2 and will be further discussed with regard to each domain of personal competency.

Typical Performance

In regard to indicators of typical performance in Figure 3.2, we provided a truncated list of sample indicators that are commonly associated with developmental motor scales (e.g., BOT-2; Bruininks & Bruininks, 2005), adaptive behavior scales (e.g., VABS; Sparrow, Cicchetti, & Balla, 2005), and behavioral checklists (e.g., CTP 3; Conners, 2015). It is worth repeating that the purpose of typical performance indicators is to assess how people function in their daily life, which may or may not correspond with how they function in maximal performance situations. For example, two people may have a combination of competencies across the five dimensions of personal competency that would suggest their skills are aligned with a specific job in the community; thus, they would have similar competency profiles in terms of maximal performance. Under typical performance conditions, however, there could be vast differences. For a variety of reasons, to be successful in the job environment one person might need limited supports while another might need multiple supports. In the following sections, we discuss each personal competency dimension in regard to maximal and typical performance measures.

Personal Competency Dimensions

Physical Competency

The first dimension, Physical Competency, is one that has not traditionally been considered in association with the construct of intellectual disability, but it most certainly has a significant impact on personal competency and support needs. Protocols used by physicians (see Bickley & Szilagyi, 2009) to conduct annual physical examinations in regard to general physical health and well-being, and several broad CHC domains (e.g., psychomotor, tactile, kinesthetic, olfactory) capture the essence of the Physical Competency domain. In terms of everyday, typical performance, tasks associated with locomotion, ambulation, mobility, and activities involving fine and gross motor skills would be critical to consider (e.g., getting up off the floor by oneself; walking short, intermediate, and long distances; coordinating the fine motor muscles to operate household technologies).

Conceptual Competency

This factor, along with Practical Competency and Social Competency, are the three domains that have traditionally been most closely associated with intellectual disability. Maximal performance indicators of Conceptual Competency are focused on the power of the "mental machine" (i.e., the brain), and measuring them involves assessing mental processes such as those which have been of interest to human information processing researchers (see Chubb, Dosher, Lu, & Shiffrin, 2013). These include how effectively and efficiently people use their brains to process sensory information (e.g., visual and auditory processing) as well the power of their short- and long-term memory. Other influences on Conceptual Competency include fluid reasoning ability, reaction and decision speed, and mental processing speed. Proficiency in core academic areas (i.e., Grw and Gq in Figure 3.2), as well as domain-specific knowledge (i.e., Gkn in Figure 3.2), have also been considered essential to measures of Conceptual Competency, especially in terms of ease of learning and speed of acquisition. In regard to typical performance, the acquisition and use of language and communication skills, the extent of achievement in areas of literacy and mathematics, and reasoning/problem-solving skills (e.g., perceiving cause-and-effect relationships) are plausible indicators of the Conceptual Competency factor.

Practical Competency

In contrast to Conceptual Competency, Practical Competency is not concerned with mental processes, but rather the focus is on knowledge that has been acquired and that can be applied. Although three of the same CHC competencies under the Conceptual Competency factor are listed under the Practical Competency factor (i.e., Grw, Gq, and Gkn), the critical distinction is that in Practical Competency the focus is on how competent one is in *applying* what has been learned. Maximal performance indicators would examine proficiency in using literacy skills (i.e., reading, writing, and speaking) as well as numerical/quantitative reasoning and application. Demonstration of advanced knowledge and the ability to use the knowledge in any field (mathematics, history, cosmetology, plumbing, etc.) would also be reasonable maximal performance indicators. Typical performance indicators of the Practical Competency factor would include the multitude of practical adaptive skills that can be found on adaptive behavior scales. These include daily living skills (e.g., cooking), personal care skills (e.g., getting dressed), and community living skills (e.g., riding a bus), as well as functional academic skills (e.g., reading instructions for a recipe, making correct change).

Social Competency

Social Competency is the third factor that has been historically linked to intellectual disability, although many have argued that it has not been given the emphasis it deserves (see Greenspan & Grandfield, 1992; Greenspan, Loughlin, & Black, 2001; Greenspan, Switzky, & Woods, 2011). Social Competency refers to proficiency in socially interacting with others, maintaining positive relationships with others, and successfully negotiating a variety of social contexts (including recognizing when one is being manipulated or exploited). Because people live in an interdependent world (i.e., everyone depends on others in order to meet basic needs such as food, safety, and shelter, as well as higher-order needs such as love/belonging and esteem), Social Competency is critical to success in modern society. For maximum performance indicators of Social Competency, we elected to use the factor structure proposed by Schneider, Ackerman, and Kanfer (1996) that forms the basis of the Social Competency Questionnaire. We did, however, leave out two of their factors (Extraversion and Social Openness) as these were redundant with dimensions of the Emotional Competency factor in Figure 3.2 (discussed next).

In regard to intellectual disability, Greenspan (1999) pointed out that intellectual disability "is not a global disorder of social competency per se, but rather involves significant deficits in one aspect of social competency, namely social intelligence" (p. 14). Greenspan's discussion of social intelligence most closely corresponds to the "social insight" factor provided by Schneider et al. (1996). It can be true that limitations in social insight create additional needs for support. All aspects of Social Competency are important to consider, however, because relative strengths and limitations in any aspect can have important implications in regard to people's functioning. In terms of typical performance, indicators of Social Competency include gullibility (e.g., naiveté), interpersonal skills (e.g., manners, conversational skills), social responsibility (e.g., personal boundaries, respect for others' property), and social problem solving (e.g., how to resolve a conflict).

Emotional Competency

Emotional Competency refers to the ability to understand and regulate one's emotions, as well as to express or release emotions in a constructive manner. There is certainly an overlap between the Emotional and Social Competency factors, but we believe there is enough distinction between the two to justify considering them separately (versus a combined Social-Emotional factor). In terms of indicators of maximal performance, we chose to draw from McCrea and Costa's (2003) "Big Five" Personality Theory, which was developed through extensive factor analytic studies. The Big Five dimensions of personality are understood as traits on which people can be high, low, or anywhere in between. Extraversion refers to how active, assertive, energetic, and outgoing people are. Agreeableness is related to people's gratefulness, kindness, trustworthiness, and cooperativeness. Conscientiousness refers to the extent to which people are dependable, organized, capable planners, and responsible. Neuroticism is concerned with how anxious, insecure, and distressed people are. Openness to Experiences refers to people's ranges of interests, level of curiosity, originality, and extent of imagination.

Unlike the other dimensions of personal competency in Figure 3.2, being relatively "high" or "low" in any of the Big 5 personality traits is not necessarily advantageous nor detrimental. For instance, the qualities associated with Agreeableness are generally considered to be positive human characteristics, but people who are too agreeable may lack the healthy dose of skepticism and cynicism that is necessary to reject bad ideas or question the status quo. Likewise, although being extremely high in Neuroticism would seem to have few advantages, being extremely low on the trait could also be a concern. For instance, a person especially low in terms of Neuroticism could be extremely calm, but calmness taken to the extreme might translate into a lack of passion/excitement about anything. In contrast to the maximal performance indicators, the sample typical performance measures within the Emotional Competency factor are all stated positively. These include control of temper (i.e., managing anger), dependability and trustworthiness, poise, self-discipline and self-awareness, understanding the perspectives of others, and carefulness (i.e., regulating impulsivity).

The Big Picture of Personal Competency

Taking a "big picture" view of personal competency has several advantages over a narrow perspective (e.g., just focusing on Conceptual Competency) or a simplistic indicator (e.g., an IQ score). The advantages of understanding differences between maximum and typical performance were alluded to earlier. Understanding whether discrepancies exist (as well as the extent of the discrepancies), and examining potential reasons for discrepancies has critical implications when planning supports and services. For example, on one hand if a discrepancy between maximal and typical performance is due mostly to low motivation, then addressing issues of motivation is a reasonable course of action. On the other hand, if there are no meaningful discrepancies between typical and maximal performance, attempts to further motivate a person to perform better may do more harm than good. In such cases, using strategies to accommodate an area of relative weakness/difficulty would be a more productive course of action.

A "big picture" perspective on personal competency is useful to counteract the potentially negative effects that disability labels have on understanding people, because it provides a far more complete understanding of a person's *strengths and competencies* compared to a diagnostic term. Disability labels tend to draw attention away from individual differences. As was discussed earlier, intellectual disability has been traditionally understood in relation to Conceptual, Practical, and Social Competency. People with intellectual disability, however, not only have relative strengths and limitations in these three areas of personal competency, but they also have relative strengths and limitations in the other areas—including those not traditionally connected to the diagnosis (i.e., Physical Competency and Social Competency). Knowing that a person has a diagnosis of intellectual disability actually provides very little information about a person, and the "information void" gets filled by oversimplified images and/or preconceived notions about people with intellectual disability.

A "big picture" approach to understanding people's competencies can encourage a better description and appreciation of people's unique abilities and needs, and can counteract the "myth of homogeneity" that seems to inevitably accompany disability labels. Theoretically, if there was a comprehensive accounting for all of the elements of personal competency (and the more than 80 indicators identified in CHC Theory provide a good start), there would be no need for disability categories or labels. People could be described in terms of their profile of relative strengths and weaknesses.

The final point to be made about the "big picture" approach to personal competency is that if it were to be fully embraced, it would shift assessment activities from what is largely a search for deficits (in order to meet diagnostic criteria) to a search for relative strengths and limitations in order to capture an accurate understanding of a person's competency profile. Limitations in personal competency have important implications for planning teams working to address a person's needs. With that said, limitations and deficits are only part of the profile. Identifying strengths, whether the strengths are relative to the rest of the population's competencies or are relative only to the person's profile of competencies, is just as important for purposes of planning supports and informing decision making.

For example, a person with strengths in both maximal and typical performance in the Social Competency factor (e.g., the person is likable, trustworthy, conscientious, and has an even temperament and charming disposition) is likely to be a person who can acquire considerable social capital if the correct supports are in place. Gotto, Calkins, Jackson, Walker, and Beckman (2010) explain that "social capital refers to a set of relationships and social ties, with organizations and to individuals, that can expand one's choice-making opportunities, increase one's options, and lead to a more enriched quality of life" (p. 1). If a person with a disability has strengths in certain areas of Social Competency and Emotional Competency, developing extensive connections/social ties with others and arranging a network of informal supports (i.e., accumulating social capital) is readily achievable. If these are not areas of strength, then supports can be built around the person that enable the development of social networks. Considering personal competency in a holistic, "big picture" manner will logically lead to planning processes where a person's unique array of relative strengths are capitalized upon, relative weaknesses are accounted for, and personal nuances are thoughtfully considered.

Environmental Demands

Returning to Figure 3.1, a social-ecological understanding of disability calls for personal competency to be considered in the context of environmental demands. The environment refers to the settings and activities in which people are engaged during the course of their daily lives. Every child and adult must function in a variety of environments, and when combining all of the environments in which a person participates over the course of a day, month, or year, it is clear that no two people operate in *exactly* the same environments. That is, each person has his or her own unique environment, and therefore, each person experiences unique environmental demands that create specific needs for support.

Despite this uniqueness, there is much commonality in the environmental demands that people encounter. For example, consider transportation by school bus. Although some school systems may have quite idiosyncratic bus transportation practices, these would be outliers. The vast majority of communities providing bus transportation to school have the same environmental demands. Namely, children must be able to make it to their bus stop in the morning, successfully interact with other children who are waiting at the bus stop, wait for the bus to arrive, board the bus, find an empty seat, behave in a manner during transport that does not pose any safety concerns or other difficulties for fellow riders on the bus (e.g., remain in the seat throughout the trip), know when and how to interact with the bus driver or bus monitor if experiencing a problem, successfully exit the bus when it arrives at school, and finally, locate and travel to the classroom they are supposed to attend at the start of the school day. Whether a school bus is operating in upstate New York, southern Alabama, or western Arizona, the environmental demands involved in "riding the school bus" are very similar.

In this chapter we focus on environmental demands that are common to many children and adults with intellectual disability (Chapter 6 provides guidance about assessing and addressing environmental demands that are unique to an individual). Although there are countless ways to categorize various environments for consideration, we have organized our discussion around school and nonschool environments.

School Environments

Curricular Demands

The word *curriculum* refers to the content that is taught in a school or in a specific course or program of study. Curricular content (and thus curricular demands) have changed in important ways over the past 60 years since children with intellectual disability first entered public schools in the United States on a widespread basis during the 1950 and 1960s. Historically (as described in Chapter 1) IQ-based approaches to classifying students with intellectual disability drove educators' expectations for achievement ceilings, which in turn drove the curriculum. This led to limitations in the expectations held for students: The focus was on learning basic skills associated with early-childhood learning milestones (e.g., communicating essential wants and needs, naming colors and body parts, and learning self-care skills such as dressing and toileting; see Scheerenberger, 1983 for an historical overview, as well as classic special education textbooks by Gearheart & Litton, 1975 and MacMillan, 1977 that describe curricular approaches for different populations). Regardless of the classification designation, prior to the "mainstreaming" movement of the late 1960s and early 1970s (see Dunn, 1968), efforts to provide children with intellectual disability access to general education classrooms were not a priority because it was assumed that the curricular content taught to typically developing children was beyond the capacity of children with intellectual disability to understand.

Throughout the 1970s and 1980s a new consensus regarding best practice emerged in regard to the curricular emphasis for children with intellectual disability. Based on a concern that time was not being well spent on teaching children prerequisite skills that had little relationship to their future lives, educators were called upon to make curricular decisions based on the "criterion of ultimate functioning" (Brown, Nietupski, & Hamre-Nietupski, 1976). The crux of the argument was that (a) it took students with intellectual disability a longer time to learn new skills compared to their peers; (b) instructional time in school was limited, and there were a multitude of useful skills that needed to be taught and learned; and therefore (c) it made little sense to squander instructional time by teaching things to children with intellectual disability that they were not going to use in their later lives, because doing so displaced instruction time in areas that were relevant to future life experiences. The curricular emphasis for children with intellectual disability shifted to teaching functional skills in authentic environments (e.g., grocery shopping taught in grocery stores).

In regard to academics, although efforts to develop basic literacy skills were sometimes targeted in the curriculum, the focus was on functional academic skills (e.g., teaching writing in regard to skills needed to complete a job application) instead of core content skills (e.g., decoding text). Further, a focus on content skills was limited to students with fewer support needs. A review of the professional literature of that time period reveals that functional curricula were more likely to be emphasized for students with moderate/severe levels of intellectual impairment, and developing core academic skills was perceived to be a more suitable goal for students with mild levels of intellectual impairment (Bouck & Satsangi, 2014).

Despite differences in the curricular focus for students with intellectual disability and students from the general population, calls for increased integration in general education classrooms became more forceful during the 1980s and 1990s. Two important educational reform movements were focused on increasing the amount of time children with intellectual disability were educated alongside same-aged peers without disabilities. The *Regular Education Initiative (REI)* was targeted to children with high-incidence disabilities, which included children with intellectual disability in the "mild" IQ range. For example, Wang and Birch (1984) proposed the *Adaptive Learning Environment Model* (ALEM) as a means to eliminate special education pull-out programs such as resource rooms in general educational schools through adapting instruction in the general education classroom. The *Inclusive Education Movement* was initially focused on students with low-incidence disabilities, specifically the inclusion of children with moderate to severe levels of intellectual impairment and children described as having multiple or severe disabilities in general education classrooms (e.g., see Lipsky & Gartner, 1991). *REI* and *Inclusive Education* proponents eventually came together, unified by a shared vision of general education classrooms with far greater capacity to educate children with special education needs than what was common in the public schools. There were diverse views, however, among those calling for inclusive education. For example, some argued for the complete elimination of a continuum of special education placements outside of the general education classroom. Others saw the value of preserving a continuum of options despite the fact that such options had been traditionally overused (see Stainback, Stainback, and Moravec's 1992 critique of Brown et al.'s 1991 proposal for a system of inclusive education).

Central to the argument of *REI* and *Inclusive Education* was that general education classrooms offered a richer learning environment (e.g., higher expectations for student achievement, and access to more incidental learning opportunities to develop communication and social skills) than did segregated settings (see Brown et al., 1991; Wang & Birch, 1984). The importance of accessing grade-level content in the general education curriculum, however, was simply not emphasized until the amendments to the Individuals with Disabilities Education Act (IDEA) of 1997. This law required that curricula for children receiving special education services be grounded in the same curriculum taught to typically developing children.

IDEA 1997, the No Child Left Behind Act of 2001, and IDEA 2004 significantly challenged expectations for what students with intellectual disability were expected to be taught and to learn while attending school. The regulatory language of these laws was explicit in requiring that all children who receive special education services be entitled to access to the general education curriculum, which was defined by the same academic standards and the same expectations that applied to all other students. Moreover, large-scale standardized testing that was aligned with general education curriculum needed to be completed in order to gauge educational success (i.e., to determine if students were making adequate yearly progress, or AYP), and students with intellectual disability needed to be included in standardized testing. Finally, the performance of these students on the tests (along with the performance of other students with Individualized Education Programs, or IEPs) constituted a subgroup of students that had to, as a whole, meet criteria for AYP in order for a school and school district to be rated by the government as "successful." Thus, unlike any other time in the history of educating children with intellectual disability, the achievement of these children had substantial ramifications for all educators, schools, and school districts. Although nothing in public policy prevented schools from teaching functional skills or any other type of content outside of the general education curriculum, progress on grade-level, general education content standards became fundamental driver of what was taught in US schools to students with intellectual disability.

Curricular decisions in the United States were traditionally the responsibility of local school districts (which were required to select textbooks and other materials, as well as offer courses, that were aligned with their state's learning standards). Partly due to concerns with inconsistency in the scope and quality of learning standards between states, the National Governor's Association launched the *Common Core State Standards Initiative* (CCSSI) in 2009. According to the National Governors Association (2011), the CCSSI is an "effort to establish a single set of clear educational standards for English-language arts and mathematics that states can share and voluntarily adopt. . . . Governors and state commissioners of education from 48 states, 2 territories and the District of Columbia committed to developing these standards. They are informed by the best available evidence and the highest state standards across the country and globe and developed in collaboration with teachers, parents, school administrators and experts" (para 1).

The CCSSI is intended to assure that students graduating from a high school are prepared to enter credit-earning (i.e., not remedial) courses at the college/university level or enter the workforce. Although learning standards are not the same as the curriculum, learning standards most certainly set the parameters (i.e., scope and breath) for what is going to be taught in schools. Therefore, the school environment for today's students with intellectual disability includes the expectation that they will learn grade-level content that is aligned with the general education curriculum.

Children with intellectual disability often experience a gap (or mismatch) between the learning demands of general education content and the teaching approaches and achievement expectations associated with general education classrooms. To bridge the gap, students with intellectual disability need supports that modify the curriculum (while still maintaining the essence of the content that is being taught) and modify the teaching strategies and options for demonstrating learning and achievement.

Informal Curricular Demands

Not everything a child needs to know and/or learn in school is taught through the general education or formal curriculum. Participation in school entails participating in a complex and diverse community outside of structured course lessons. This community has a multitude of informal rules and processes, social expectations and norms, and social taboos (some of which are applicable across different people and environments, and some of which are not). It is not unusual for children with intellectual and related developmental disabilities to have support needs in the informal curriculum, as well as in the formal or academic curriculum (Carter, Hughes, Guth, & Copeland, 2005; Hughes et al., 1999; Scheard, Clegg, Standen, & Cromby, 2001).

The informal curriculum includes understanding social and behavioral expectations (e.g., knowing what to do during lunchtime, including how to secure food, where and with whom to sit, and transitioning to the activity following lunch), problems that are encountered (e.g., how to handle oneself when targeted by a bully), as well as situations involving expressing preferences and choices (e.g., how to express interest and become involved in a sports team or musical group). It is important to acknowledge that many of the best opportunities for establishing friendships arise during the "unstructured" times before, during, and after school. Students must be able to navigate the challenges associated with the informal curriculum in order to take advantage of such opportunities.

It is important that students have the opportunity to fully participate in the less formal portions of the school day in order to fully benefit from their schooling. Higher levels of Social Competency have been found among students with intellectual disability who were provided more opportunities to spend time with peers in unstructured, social activities compared to those who had fewer opportunities (Brooks, Floyd, Robins, & Cahn, 2015). In addition, participation in structured co-curricular activities has been shown to help students form positive social relationships and become socially accepted (Siperstein, Glick, & Parker, 2009). As is the case with students from the general population, students with intellectual disability who have an array of positive social relationships with others at school are less likely to be lonely and less likely to display challenging behavior (Wiener & Tardif, 2004).

Unfortunately, the unstated rules and customs that many students learn incidentally may not be readily apparent to some students with intellectual disability. Limitations in experience, knowledge, Social Competency, and executive functioning skills all contribute to creating needs for support in social situations. A student's success and the supports that he or she is provided in navigating the informal curriculum will have a profound impact on his or her happiness and satisfaction with schooling (Wiener & Tardif, 2004), and therefore any mismatch between personal competency and the demands of the informal curriculum need to be identified and addressed.

Outside-of-School Environments

Environments outside of schools can be classified in many ways. Adaptive behavior scales have often been organized around environmental domains. The Checklist of Adaptive Living Skills (Morreau & Bruininks, 1991), for example, is organized around the domains of Personal Living, Home Living, Community Living, and Employment. Dever (1988) embarked on an ambitious project to identify a taxonomy of skills needed for participation in community life, and he classified skill indicators within five broad domains: Personal Maintenance and Development, Travel, Leisure, Vocational, and Home-making and Community Life. Thompson, McGrew, Johnson, and Bruininks (2000) took an empirical approach to identifying domains of community adjustment by analyzing postschool follow-up data from nearly 400 former students who had been out of school for one to five years. Using confirmatory factor analytic procedures they identified five domains: Employment-Economic Integration, Recreation/Leisure Integration, Community Assimilation and Acceptance, Social Network Integration, and Residential Integration. Two other factors that were not related to community adjustment also emerged from their analyses of postschool outcome data. One pertained to a psychological construct (i.e., need for support) and the other to a quality-of-life factor (i.e., personal satisfaction). Because the five dimensions of community adjustment presented by Thompson et al. (2000) have empirical support, we choose their structure to guide our discussion of environmental demands encountered outside of school settings.

Table 3.1 shows the five domains of community adjustment (employment-economic integration, recreation-leisure integration, community assimilation and acceptance, social network integration, and residential integration) and provides descriptions of each dimension. The descriptions were drawn from the work of Thompson et al. (1999) as well as earlier work from McGrew and Bruininks (1994) Corresponding to each dimension are examples of environmental demands that people must navigate in order to fully participate in the settings and activities associated with the dimension. No pretense is made that these examples are comprehensive; listing all potential environmental demands for any of the domains would be exhaustive, if not impossible, to create. Rather, the examples are merely intended to highlight the complexity inherent in navigating community environments.

As Table 3.1 makes clear, any attempt to delineate all of the competencies needed to successfully adjust to community life would be an enormous, if not impossible, undertaking. The vast majority of people from the general population require some mentoring and/or guidance, as well as a fair amount of time, before they are fully competent in each domain. Further, the specific demands that

Table 3.1 Domains of community adjustment and corresponding environmental demands

Community Adjustment Domains and Descriptions	Examples of Environmental Demands Inherent to the Domain
Employment-Economic Integration—the extent to which people are involved in stable and integrated daily work or related activities and are economically self-sufficient	Employment requires that one embark on a job search and obtain gainful employment. To keep a job one must perform duties acceptably (e.g., display proper work speed and quality), maintain good relationships with supervisors and coworkers (e.g., regular attendance and punctuality at work; working in a manner that does not jeopardize the safety of oneself or others). Economic self-sufficiency requires using money to purchase good and services, and managing money effectively
Recreation/Leisure Integration—the extent to which people are actively involved in formal and informal recreation-leisure activities	Participating in recreation activities in the community requires that one understands how to participate in an activity (e.g., knows rules and etiquette of the sport/game) and can get to and from activities. Participating in informal leisure activities in the community (e.g., walking in the park) or at home (e.g., hobby, such as knitting) demands that one has developed preferences to spend free time and understands how to occupy oneself during that time.
Community Assimilation and Acceptance—the extent of engagement with neighbors and others in the community	Engaging with others in the neighborhood or community requires that one understands and is able to maintain boundaries (e.g., respect for others' privacy, culturally accepted physical proximity including touching) as well as recognize potentially dangerous situations (e.g., interactions with strangers who may attempt to exploit).
Social Network Integration—the extent to which individuals have a social support network	Establishing and maintaining a social network requires expressing oneself respectfully and maintaining meaningful communication/conversation with others. Additionally, understanding the reciprocity involved in maintaining close relationships is essential.
Residential Integration—the extent of independent living and integration into the community	Residential integration demands that one know how to safely operate technology and equipment in the home. Additionally, taking care of oneself (personal hygiene, grooming, dressing) and preparing food are critical requirements.

each person encounters in each domain will vary based on the specific environments that the person encounters. Thus, while students with intellectual disability will likely have support needs based on the environmental demands they encounter in each of these domains, the specific supports needed will vary based on their environment.

It is important to note that the domains in Table 3.1 originated from data on the life experiences of young adults with disabilities; however, it is not difficult to envision how each domain aligns with the life experiences of children. While children are not expected to work on paid jobs, age-appropriate expectations for completing chores at home as well as managing small amounts of money point to the applicability of the Employment-Economic Integration domain for all age groups. In terms of

Recreation/Leisure Integration, children (many more so than adults) participate in many organizations outside of school. Examples are scouting organizations, religious groups (e.g., Sunday school, worship-affiliated youth groups), or a nonschool related sports club. Community Assimilation and Acceptance is aligned with integration in local neighborhoods and could also include local children's activities such as day camps and swim lessons. Moreover, children have considerable unstructured free time, and as they get older they are expected to keep themselves occupied and entertained during times of the day when adults are not supervising or directing their activities. Social Network Integration is certainly as applicable to childhood as adulthood, and friendships (or lack of friendships) become increasingly important to children as they age. Also, it can be argued that children with intellectual disability are even more vulnerable than adults in terms of being potential targets for exploitation or harm. Finally, Residential Integration is centered around life in the family home for most children. The need for services to support families with children with intellectual disability has been well documented (see Turnbull, Turnbull, Erwin, Soodak, & Shogren, 2015) and the formal service system has been involved in efforts to support families for many years.

This brief overview of outside-of-school environmental demands only scratches the surface of the complexity of issues faced by children and adults with intellectual disability in modern society. Participating in the real world presents major challenges for all people, and therefore highlights the need to adopt a supports model for identifying, creating, and evaluating systems of support for students with intellectual disability to enable them to meaningfully access community settings and participate across environmental domains. Understanding people by means of their support needs and identifying and arranging supports to address their needs is the hallmark of a social-ecological conceptualization of intellectual disability, and is the focus of the supports model that is described in the next section. Systems of support that address the demands of the official school curricula, the informal curriculum, and non-school school settings will be discussed.

The Supports Model: Bridging the Gap between Personal Competency and Environmental Demands

Fundamental to a social-ecological understanding of people with intellectual disability is that intellectual disability is a state of functioning, not a deficit trait. People with intellectual disability are distinct from others in the general population in that they experience a chronic mismatch between their personal competency and what is expected of them in school and community activities and settings (i.e., environments). A contextual understanding of disability as a "state of being" instead of a "personal trait" is applicable to any disability population, not just people with intellectual disability.

Figure 3.1 provides an overview of the supports model. The chronic mismatch that people with intellectual disability experience between their personal competency and the demands of the environments they encounter in their daily lives creates extraordinary support needs. Support needs are addressed by providing a person with supports. Therefore, the purpose of supports is to bridge the gap between personal competency and environmental demands. Supports should compensate for skill limitations, build on personal strengths, and account for environmental expectations and conditions.

Schalock et al. (2010) provide formal definitions of supports and support needs. According to these authors, supports are "resources and strategies that aim to promote the development education, interests and personal well-being of a person and that enhance individual functioning" (p. 224) and support needs are "a psychological construct referring to the pattern and intensity of support necessary for a person to participate in activities linked with normative human functioning" (p. 224). It is most certainly true that each person has unique support needs because each person has unique strengths and limitations in personal competency and no two environments are exactly the same. There are, however, many commonalities between the support needs of different people. Therefore, resources and strategies that have proven to be useful in addressing the support needs of many people in the past will likely have application for many people in the future. Of course, it is the application of strategies and resources that need to be tailored to meet individual needs. The classes of support resources and strategies described next have been used to promote success in the general education curriculum, the informal curriculum, and the community.

People as Supports

In one sense, it is difficult to think of a support that does not involve people to some extent. In order for a support to be put into place somebody must envision the support, implement the support, and evaluate the support to see how useful it is. But the focus of this section is on using people to provide hands-on support to a child or adult with intellectual disability.

One approach is to use people who are already in the environment as supports: such individuals are referred to as *natural supports* (Cimera, 2007). In a general education classroom, this would include peers (peer supports) who provide assistance to a student with a disability that is qualitatively and/or quantitatively different than support that would be provided to most other peers. The most researched form of peer support is peer tutoring. Utley and Mortweet (1997) defined peer tutoring as "a class of practices and strategies that employ peers as one-on-one teachers to provide individualized instruction, practice, repetition, and clarification of concepts" (p. 9). Peer tutoring has shown positive outcomes across a wide range of instructional settings, ages, and content areas (Okilwa & Shelby, 2010), and the model is certainly as applicable in the informal curriculum as it is for structured courses where academic content is taught. In employment settings, coworkers have often been sought out as sources of natural supports with positive results. Cimera (2001) reported that supported employees who were trained by coworkers had longer tenures at their jobs than those trained by a job coach employed by a service provider agency.

People supports also include those who are part of the educational environment and provide support, including teachers, paraprofessionals, and related service personnel. There has been an ongoing concern that paraprofessionals are overused in today's schools. A paraprofessional who oversupports a child can unwittingly interfere with meaningful inclusion (e.g., in situations where the paraprofessional closely supervises a child throughout the day, the paraprofessional and child become their own classroom within a classroom). Concerns that paraprofessionals are overused is supported by data pertaining to hiring trends in special education. For example, Suter and Giangreco (2009) found that between 1990 and 2005 there was a 300% increase in paraprofessionals in one state. The use of paraprofessionals versus special education teachers or related service professionals to implement teaching and support strategies has been questionable in terms of the lack of use of expert and highly trained personnel in supporting students.

Technology Supports

Distinguishing between instructional technology and assistive technology is useful when considering the use of technology to support people with intellectual disability. Instructional technology is focused on facilitating student progress in a content area. An example would be a mathematics software program that is intended to develop a child's basic computational skills (i.e., addition, subtraction, multiplication, division). In contrast, assistive technology is not intended to expand the user's skills. Rather, it is intended to enable users to participate in settings and activities in ways that they otherwise could not. An example would be an augmentative communication device that enables a child to participate in conversations and class discussions more efficiently than if he or she had to rely on spoken communication. Increasingly, technology can serve both purposes, particularly if technology is universally designed and as apps and other technology advances create more universal access to devices and technologies that support all people.

Technologies can be high tech (e.g., an electric wheelchair for people who have difficulty getting from place to place in their environments), mid tech (a mobile word processor for students who have difficulty writing their notes in class), and low tech (a timer to remind an employee to complete a task by a certain time). For the purpose of our discussion, the critical consideration is that technology that is used as a support should enhance a person's participation and achievement in an important way.

An ongoing challenge in identifying and using technologies to support people with intellectual disability has been the tendency for planning team members to focus too much on device features and too little on how technology might be actually be used by a person or how to teach a person to use a technology effectively. With any new technology there is typically a learning curve, and users must anticipate a learning process. The issue of technological abandonment (i.e., buying a device for a person that he or she never uses) continues to be a major concern among educators and other professionals (Lauer, Longenecker-Rust, & Smith, 2006), and reflects the need to consider and promote the use of universal design and cognitive accessibility in all technologies that are developed.

Several processes for assessing technology needs, selecting technology, and implementing technological solutions have been proposed. One such process that aligns very well with a social-ecological understanding of a person with intellectual disability is Zabala's (2016) SETT (Student-Environment-Task-Tools) Framework. The SETT process calls for a planning team to explore the student's relative strengths and limitations, analyze the environments in which the student needs to use the technology, identify the tasks (i.e., what the student needs to do in the environments), and as a final step make decisions on choosing which tools might provide the best technological support.

Adaptations, Modifications, and Accommodations as Supports

Adaptations, accommodations, and modifications refer to changes in the environment to make it more accessible, meaningful, or engaging to students with intellectual disability. Examples include changes to instructional delivery, learning materials, classroom processes, or performance expectations that provide an opportunity for a student with a disability to more fully participate and/or find success in the school or community (e.g., work). Technically, the three terms have different meanings.

Adaptations is most often used as an umbrella term that includes both accommodations and modifications. Janney and Snell (2006) drew distinctions between curricular adaptations (where instructional content is changed by adding supplementary goals, simplifying goals, or introducing alternative goals), instructional adaptations (where different content is taught and/or learning is demonstrated differently), and alternative adaptations (where alternative/parallel learning activities are used). The term *adaptations* is also used to refer to adapted equipment (e.g., a special seat that a child with a physical disability may use to sit upright) or adapted materials (e.g., books on tape used by a child who has difficulty reading; Pisha & Stahl, 2005).

Modifications typically refers to *changes in what is being taught to or expected from a student*. For example, changing an assignment so the student with intellectual disability is not doing work that is as difficult/advanced as most other students is an example of a modification. *Accommodations* refers to changes that provide students with access to content taught in the curriculum, but do not change the difficulty level or the performance expectations. Allowing a student who has difficulty writing to orally give his answers to essay questions on a history test is an example of an accommodation.

For the purpose of this chapter, the distinctions between terminology (i.e., adaptations, modifications, accommodations) is not nearly as important as the concept that the school environment includes what and how students are taught, and what is expected of students in terms of performance. When there is a mismatch between a student's competency and the demands of a school environment, changes in the environment through adaptations, modifications, and accommodations are critical supports to offer. These supports can allow a student access to their school and the general education curriculum, and provide opportunities for success that otherwise would not be possible. The same principles apply to life in the community. A public bus driver (e.g., natural support) who is willing to remind a student with intellectual disability that this is the stop where he or she needs to exit the bus has made an important modification to the environment. Instead of being required to recognize one's bus stop by reading street signs or noting a landmark, the rider now is required only to pay attention when the bus driver informs him or her of the bus stop. Further, GPS technologies remove the need for relying on people supports and create more opportunities for navigation around the community. Just like in school, an accommodation or modification in the community may not always be required. When people's support needs change (in time, the person may be able to recognize his or her bus stop) they no longer need the extraordinary support.

Conclusion

Strength-based models of intellectual disability shift the focus from what students cannot do because of their deficits to what they can do with the right supports. This chapter focused on understanding people holistically in terms of their relative strengths and limitations, understanding the demands of environments in which people need to function, and understanding the array of support strategies that can be helpful to bridge any person–environment gaps that exist.

References

Bickley, L. S., & Szilagyi, P. G. (2009). *Bates' guide to physical examination and history taking* (10th ed.). Philadelphia, PA: Wolters Kluwer Health, Lippincott Williams & Wilkins.

Bouck, E. C., & Satsangi, R. (2014). Evidence-base of a functional curriculum for secondary students with mild intellectual disability: A historical perspective. *Education and Training in Autism and Developmental Disabilities, 49*, 478–486.

Brooks, B. A., Floyd, F., Robins, D. L., & Chan, W. Y. (2015). Extracurricular activities and the development of social skills in children with intellectual and specific learning disabilities. *Journal of Intellectual and Disability Research, 59*, 678–687. doi: 10.1111/jir.12171

Brown, L., Nietupski, J., & Hamre-Nietupski, S. (1976). The criterion of ultimate functioning and public school services for severely handicapped students. In M. A. Thomas (Ed.), *Hey, don't forget about me: Education's investment in the severely, profoundly and multiply handicapped* (pp. 2–15). Reston, VA: Council for Exceptional Children.

Brown, L., Schwarz, P., Udvari-Solner, A., Kampschroer, E., Johnson, F., Jorgensen, L., & Gruenewald, L. (1991). How much time should students with severe intellectual disabilities spend in regular classrooms and elsewhere? *Journal of the Association for Persons with Severe Handicaps, 16*, 39–47.

Bruininks, R. H., & Bruininks, B. D. (2005). *Bruininks–Oseretsky test of motor proficiency* (BOT-2) (2nd ed.). Minneapolis, MN: Pearson Assessment.

Carter, E. W., Hughes, C., Guth, C. B., & Copeland, S. R. (2005). Factors influencing social interaction among high school students with intellectual disabilities and their general education peers. *American Journal on Mental Retardation, 110*, 366–377.

Chubb, C., Dosher, B. A., Lu, Z., & Shiffrin, R. M. (Eds.). (2013). *Human information processing: Vision, memory, and attention.* Washington, DC: American Psychological Association.

Cimera R. E. (2001). Utilizing coworkers as "natural supports": Evidence on cost-efficiency, job retention, and other employment outcomes. *Journal of Disability Policy Studies, 11*, 194–201.

Cimera, R. E. (2007). Utilizing natural supports to lower the cost of supported employment. *Research and Practice for Persons with Severe Disabilities, 32*, 184–189.

Conners, K. C. (2015). *Conners continuous performance test (CPT 3)* (3rd ed.). Toronto, Canada: Multi Health Systems.

Dever, R. B. (1988). *Community living skills: A taxonomy.* Washington, DC: American Association on Mental Retardation.

Dunn, L. (1968). Special education for the mildly retarded—is much of it justifiable? *Exceptional Children, 35*, 5–22.

Flanagan, D. P., & Dixon, S. G. (2014). The Cattell-Horn-Carroll theory of cognitive abilities. In C. R. Reynolds, K. J. Vannest, & E. Fletcher-Janzen (Eds.), *Encyclopedia of special education.* Retrieved from http://onlinelibrary.wiley.com/doi/10.1002/9781118660584.ese0431/full

Gearheart, B. R., & Litton, F. W. (1975). *The trainable retarded: A foundations approach.* St. Louis, MO: C. V. Mosby Company.

Gotto, G. S., Calkins, C. F., Jackson, L., Walker, H., & Beckman, C. (2010). *Accessing social capital: Implications for persons with disabilities.* Kansas City, MO: National Gateway to Self Determination.

Gould, S. J. (1996). *The mismeasure of man.* New York: W. W. Norton.

Greenspan, S. (1999). What is meant by mental retardation? *International Review of Psychiatry, 11,* 6–18.

Greenspan, S., & Grandfield, J. M. (1992). Reconsidering the construct of mental retardation: Implications of a model social competence. *American Journal of Mental Retardation, 96,* 442–453.

Greenspan, S., Loughlin, G., & Black, R. (2001). Credulity and gullibility in persons with mental retardation. In L. M. Glidden (Ed.), *International review of research in mental retardation* (Vol. 24, pp. 101–135). New York: Academic Press.

Greenspan, S., Switzky, H. N., & Woods, G. W. (2011). Intelligence involves risk-awareness and intellectual disability involves risk-unawareness: Implications of a theory of common sense. *Journal of Intellectual and Developmental Disability, 36,* 242–253.

Hughes, C., Rodi, M. S., Lorden, S. W., Pitkin, S. E., Derer, K. R., Hwang, B., & Cai, X. (1999). Social interactions of high school students with mental retardation and their general education peers. *American Journal on Mental Retardation, 104,* 533–544.

Janney, R. E., & Snell, M. E. (2006). Modifying schoolwork in inclusive classrooms. *Theory Into Practice, 45,* 215–223.

Lauer, A., Longenecker-Rust, K., & Smith, R. O. (2006). Factors in Assistive Technology Device Abandonment: Replacing "Abandonment" with "Discontinuance". ATOMS Project technical Report, Retrieved from http://www.r2d2.uwm.edu/atoms/archive/technicalreports/tr-discontinuance.html

Lipsky, D. K., & Gartner, A. (1991). Restructuring for quality. In J. W. Lloyd, A. C. Repp, & N. N. Singh (Eds.), *The regular education initiative: Alternative perspectives on concepts, issues, and models* (pp. 43–56). Sycamore, IL: Sycamore.

MacMillan, D. L. (1977). *Mental retardation in school and society.* Boston, MA: Little, Brown and Company.

McCrea, R. R., & Costa, P. T. (2003). *Personality in adulthood: A five-factor theory perspective.* New York: Guilford.

McGrew, K. S. (2005). The Cattell-Horn–Carroll theory of cognitive abilities. In D. P. Flannagan & P. L. Harrison (Eds.), *Contemporary intellectual assessment: Theories, tests, and issues* (2nd ed., pp. 136–181). New York: Guilford Press.

McGrew, K. S. (2009). CHC Theory and the human cognitive abilities project: Standing on the shoulders of the giants of psychometric intelligence research. *Intelligence, 37,* 1–10.

McGrew, K. S., & Bruininks, R. H. (1994). A multidimensional approach to the measurement of community adjustment. In M. Hayden & B. Abery (Eds.), *Community living for persons with mental retardation and related conditions* (pp. 65–79). Baltimore: Paul H. Brookes.

Morreau, L. E., & Bruininks, R. H. (1991). *Checklist of adaptive living skills (CALS) manual.* Allen, TX: DLM.

National Governors Association. (2011). Common Core Standards Initiative. Retrieved from http://www.nga.org/cms/home/special/col2-content/common-core-state-standards-init.html

Okilwa, N. A., & Shelby, L. (2010). The effects of peer tutoring on academic performance of students with disabilities in grades 6 through 12: A synthesis of the literature. *Remedial and Special Education, 31,* 450–463. doi: 10.1177/0741932509355

Pisha, B., & Stahl, S. (2005). The promise of new learning environments for students with disabilities. *Intervention in School and Clinic, 41*(2), 67–75.

Salvia, J., Ysseldyke, J. E., & Bolt, S. (2013). *Assessment in special and inclusive education* (12th ed.). Boston, MA: Houghton Mifflin Company.

Schalock, R. L., Borthwick-Duffy, S., Bradley, V. J., Buntinx, W. H. E., Coulter, D. L., Craig, E. M., . . . Yeager, M. H. (2010). *Intellectual disability: Definition, classification, and systems of supports* (11th ed.). Washington, DC: American Association on Intellectual and Developmental Disabilities.

Scheard, C., Clegg, J., Standen, P., & Cromby, J. (2001). Bullying and people with severe intellectual disability. *Journal of Intellectual Disability Research, 45,* 407–415.

Scheerenberger, R. C. (1983). *A history of mental retardation.* Baltimore, MD: Paul H. Brookes.

Schneider, R. J., Ackerman, P. L., & Kanfer, R. (1996). To "act wisely in human relations": Exploring the dimensions of social competence. *Personality and Individual Differences, 21,* 469–481.

Schneider, W. J., & McGrew, K. S. (2012). The Cattell-Horn-Carroll model of intelligence. In D. Flanagan & P. Harrison (Eds.), *Contemporary intellectual assessment: Theories, tests, and issues* (3rd ed., pp. 99–144). New York: Guilford.

Siperstein, G. N., Glick, G. C., & Parker, R. C. (2009). Social inclusion of children with intellectual disabilities in a recreational setting. *Intellectual and Developmental Disabilities, 47,* 97–107. doi: 10.1352/1934-9556-47.2.97

Sparrow, S. S., Cicchetti, D. V., & Balla, D. A. (2005). *Vinland adaptive behavior scales* (2nd ed.). Circle Pines, MN: American Guidance Services.

Stainback, W., Stainback, S., & Moravec, J. (1992). Using curriculum to build inclusive classrooms. In S. Stainback & W. Stainback (Eds.), *Curriculum considerations in inclusive classrooms: Facilitating learning for all students* (pp. 65–84). Baltimore: Paul H. Brookes.

Suter, J., & Giangreco, M. F. (2009). Numbers that count: Exploring special education and paraprofessional service delivery in inclusion-oriented schools. *The Journal of Special Education, 43*, 81–93. doi: 10.1177/0022466907313353

Taub, G. E., & McGrew, K. S. (2014). The Woodcock-Johnson tests of cognitive abilities III's cognitive performance model: Empirical support for intermediate factors within CHC theory. *Journal of Psychoeducational Assessment, 32*, 187–201. doi: 10.1177/0734282913504808

Thompson, J. R., Bradley, V., Buntinx, W., Schalock, R. L., Shogren, K. A., Wehmeyer, M. L., . . . & Yeager, M. H. (2009). Conceptualizing supports and the support needs of people with intellectual disability. *Intellectual and Developmental Disabilities, 47*, 135–146.

Thompson, J. R., McGrew, K. S., & Bruininks, R. H. (1999). Adaptive and maladaptive behavior: Functional and structural characteristics. In R. L. Schalock (Ed.), *Adaptive behavior and its measurement: Implications for the field of mental retardation* (pp. 15–42). Washington, DC: American Association on Mental Retardation.

Thompson, J. R., McGrew, K. S., Johnson, D. R., & Bruininks, R. H. (2000). Refining a multidimensional model of community adjustment through an analysis of postschool follow-up data. *Exceptionality, 8*, 73–99. doi: 10.1207/S15327035EX0802_1

Turnbull, A. A., Turnbull, H. R., Erwin, E. J., Soodak, L. C., & Shogren, K. A. (2015). *Families, professionals, and exceptionality: Positive outcomes through partnerships and trust* (7th ed.). Upper Saddle River, NJ: Pearson.

Utley, C. A., & Mortweet, S. L. (1997). Peer-mediated instruction and interventions. *Focus on Exceptional Children, 29*(5), 1–23.

Wang, M. C., & Birch, J. W. (1984). Comparison of a full-time mainstreaming program and a resource room approach. *Exceptional Children, 51*, 33–40.

Wiener, J., & Tardif, C. Y. (2004). Social and emotional functioning of children with learning disabilities: Does special education placement make a difference? *Learning Disabilities Research and Practice, 19*, 20–32. doi: 10.1111/j.1540-5826.2004.00086.x

World Health Organization. (2001). *International classification of functioning, disability, and health (ICF)*. Geneva: Author.

Zabala, J. (2016). Sharing the SETT Framework. Retrieved from http://www.joyzabala.com/

4

Implications of Strengths-Based Models of Disability for the Education of Students with Intellectual Disability

Michael L. Wehmeyer, Karrie A. Shogren

The first three chapters have built a case for the importance of strengths-based approaches emphasizing social–ecological models of disability and a supports paradigm for the education of students with intellectual disability. In this chapter, we examine how practice in special education is shaped by these strengths-based approaches and what methods and strategies become important in such contexts. This chapter, in essence, serves as an advance organizer for content in the remaining chapters.

As has been discussed, by defining disability as a function of the reciprocal interaction between the environment and the capacities of a person, the focus of the 'problem' to be solved for students to learn shifts from being a deficit within the student to being the relationship between the student's functioning and the environment and, subsequently, to the identification and design of supports to address the student's functioning within that context. Historic models of special education services determined eligibility for special education and created the 'programs' in which to deliver those services based on student labels, with a label serving as a proxy, essentially, for a presumed set of common deficits. Students were grouped by label, in homogenous and often segregated settings, and provided an educational program based upon presumptive need as a function of the category or level of impairment. Social–ecological models of disability, in contrast, focus on the design of personalized supports instead of programs.

Personalized Supports in General Education Instead of Label-Specific Programs

Because of presumptions about the learning of students with intellectual disability predicated on historical understandings of disability that resulted in segregated services, the education system for students with disabilities has largely been segmented by a student's diagnosis/label and the severity of his or her cognitive impairment. As was argued in Chapter 2, despite the strong preference in federal law for children with disabilities to be educated with their nondisabled peers in regular classroom settings, students with intellectual disability are routinely placed in alternate, substantially segregated settings without any consideration of being educated in the general education classroom (Kurth, Morningstar, & Kozleski, 2014).

Subsequent chapters discuss issues pertaining to promoting access to the general education curriculum (Chapter 8), multitiered systems of supports (Chapter 12), and inclusive practices (Chapter 17). Probably the first implication of changing understandings of disability is that special education moves from a model of label- or category-specific programs to a model in which students who need additional or extraordinary support (in the form of instructional methods, materials, and strategies) get that in the context of the general education classroom.

As discussed in Chapter 3 (and again, in Chapter 6 when discussing measurement of supports), supports are "resources and strategies that aim to promote the development, education, interests, and personal well-being of a person and that enhance individual functioning" (Luckasson et al., 2002, p. 151). Supports, then, are resources and strategies to enhance human functioning. Education itself is a category or type of support, enhancing human functioning by increasing a person's capacity to function in a wide array of environments. Students, of course, vary in the level, type, and intensity of supports they will need to succeed, even within the same disability categories; they vary, essentially, in their need for supports or support needs. *Support needs* is a psychological construct referring to the pattern and intensity of supports necessary for a person to participate in activities linked with normative human functioning (Thompson et al., 2009).

Importantly, supports are individually designed and determined with the active involvement of key stakeholders in the process. This approach contrasts with traditional educational service delivery models designed in a top-down manner and delivered in the form of programs, as discussed previously. Supports added to a student's school day can take many forms but must be designed to alter the elements of the curriculum, a classroom, a lesson, or an activity only if necessary to enable students to be educated with his or her nondisabled peers. Many supports will be faded once the student participates in an activity with success and masters new competencies; however, if supports are more intrusive than needed, they will be more difficult to eliminate or reduce. When supports call unnecessary attention to the student, participation is accompanied by stigma. Sometimes the involvement of peers can help professionals design less intrusive classroom adaptations and accommodations (Janney & Snell, 2013); in other cases, supports provided by current electronic and information technologies (iPads, tablets, smartphones, etc.) replace stand-alone devices that might be more stigmatizing.

Additionally, a supports model requires an active and ongoing evaluation of the ecological aspects of the disability, since the disability can be defined only within the context of the functional limitations and the social context. Thus, efforts to design supports focus heavily on changing aspects of the environment or social context and providing students with additional skills or strategies to overcome barriers in those environments. In education's case, this contextual focus involves modifications to the classroom and the curriculum. Obviously, issues of Universal Design for Learning (UDL) come into play here, as discussed subsequently and in Chapter 14.

Context of and Expectations for the Education of Students with Intellectual Disability

There are a number of educational practices that evidence the impact of strengths-based, supports-focused models of disability. Before examining these practices, however, it is important to establish the context in which students are educated and the expectations for students within that context. Most of the analysis pertaining to inclusive education has been at the classroom level for obvious reasons. Increasingly, however, the lens for quality educational experiences has widened to emphasize schoolwide applications, such as Positive Behavior Interventions and Supports (PBIS; Chapter 13) and Tier-1 instruction in multitiered systems of supports (Chapter 12), and it is that schoolwide context that is important if we are to achieve high-quality educational supports for students with intellectual disability.

Schoolwide Integrated Framework for Transformation

In 2012, the US Department of Education, Office of Special Education Programs, funded a multisite technical assistance center to implement the Schoolwide Integrated Framework for Transformation (SWIFT) model, and collect data to demonstrate the degree to which the framework is doable, replicable, sustainable, scalable, and results in highly valued outcomes for all students, including students with the most extensive support needs. The SWIFT Center is currently working with 64 schools in 16 districts in five states. The SWIFT framework integrates research on inclusive educational practices and critical features of systemic school reform (McCart, Sailor, Bezdek, & Satter, 2014). It provides a framework for schools, districts, and state education agencies to promote lasting and sustainable change. The framework includes five evidence-based domains that schools address through systematic reform to promote positive outcomes for all students: (a) administrative leadership, (b) multitiered systems of supports, (c) integrated educational framework, (d) family and community engagement, and (e) inclusive policy structure and practice. Research-based practices in each of these domains are covered in chapters throughout this text. The unique feature of the SWIFT framework is that it brings together these elements into a systematic framework for change that enables systemic reform at the district and school level that impacts classroom practices and student outcomes.

Researchers examining schools engaged in inclusive school reform have found that these features can be implemented by schools, changing the culture and leadership of schools and enabling students with the most extensive support needs to be included in the general education classroom and curriculum (Kurth, Lyon, & Shogren, 2015; Shogren, McCart, Lyon, & Sailor, 2015). Data is being collected in schools where SWIFT is being implemented to document how changes are made and the short and long-term impact on student outcomes, with preliminary findings suggesting significant positive impacts of the SWIFT framework at the school and student level (Sailor, 2015; Sailor & McCart, 2014).

Access to the General Education Curriculum

The 1997 amendments to the Individuals with Disabilities Education Act (IDEA) and their associated regulations included statutory and regulatory language intended to ensure that students with disabilities had 'access' to the general curriculum. Section 300.347(a)(3) required that the Individualized Education Program (IEP) of students with disabilities include the following.

> A statement of the special education and related services and supplementary aids and services to be provided to the child, or on behalf of the child, and a statement of the program modifications or supports for school personnel that will be provided for the child
>
> (i)   to advance appropriately toward attaining the annual goals;
> (ii)   to be involved and progress in the general curriculum;
> (iii)   to be educated and participate with disabled and non-disabled children.

In fact, as reflected in the language in part (ii) above, what IDEA required was that students with disabilities be involved with and show progress in the general curriculum. The term "access to the general curriculum" refers to this requirement for student involvement and progress. The general curriculum was defined in the regulations as referring to "the same curriculum as for nondisabled children" [34 CFR § 300.347(a)(1)(i)]. The intent of these access provisions was threefold, as described by US Department of Education officials: (a) that all students, including students with disabilities, would have access to a challenging curriculum; (b) that all students, including students with disabilities, would be held to high expectations; and (c) to align special education practice with accountability mechanisms emerging through school reform efforts.

The 2004 amendments to IDEA contained all of the original IDEA 1997 mandates and added several new requirements, including that schools ensure that the IEP team includes someone knowledgeable about the general education curriculum and that the team meet at least annually to address any lack of expected progress in the general education curriculum (these amendments also changed the term from *general curriculum* to *general education curriculum*). Finally, the regulations to IDEA 2004 (issued in June 2005) prohibited a student with a disability from being removed from the general education setting based solely upon needed modifications to the general education curriculum.

These "access to the general education curriculum" requirements were implemented to ensure that students with disabilities were not excluded from the accountability systems linked with the standards-based reform inherent in the No Child Left Behind Act (NCLB), and that Act required states to establish challenging academic content and student achievement standards that apply to all students, including students with intellectual disability. To that end, under NCLB, states could establish alternate achievement standards for students with the most significant cognitive disabilities. The Act does not define "students with the most significant disabilities" explicitly, but instead capped "the number of proficient and advanced scores based on alternate achievement standards included in annual yearly progress (AYP) decisions" to "1.0 percent of the number of students enrolled in tested grades" (US Department of Education, 2005). Thus, by default, students with the most significant cognitive disabilities refer to the lowest performing 1.0 percent of students in public schools. These students, in general, overlap with students who are receiving special education services under the categorical areas of intellectual disability, deaf-blindness, autism, and multiple disabilities. (It's important to note that the determination as to whether a student receives alternate assessments linked to the alternate achievement standards is an IEP team decision and not linked solely to disability labels. Not every student in these categorical areas will be eligible for alternate assessments.)

We include issues of access to the general education curriculum in the section pertaining to context and expectations because these requirements don't stipulate how or through what methods a student must be involved with and progress in the general education curriculum; they simply stipulate the expectation that students with disabilities will be involved with and progress in the general education curriculum. This has implications in several ways. First, it means that the general education curriculum is the starting point for discussions about a student's instructional program. It does not mean that students with intellectual disability do not receive instruction in traditional life skills or functional domains; IDEA continues to require that the IEPs of students with disabilities identify "other educational needs" that are important to the student.

Second, it means that the IEP itself becomes a document identifying the specially designed instruction (e.g., special education services) needed for students to gain access and progress in the general education curriculum, as well as identifying supplementary aids and services and related services that are needed to enable students to progress. Chapter 8 goes into depth with regard to developing IEPs that achieve this outcome. It is worth noting that this changes the nature of the IEP: In traditional, label-based programs, the IEP is, in fact, an alternative curriculum. Finally, the access to the general education curriculum language in IDEA has spurred the development of strategies, like UDL, that enable learners to succeed in core content instruction, as discussed in Chapters 19 and 20 in this text.

Strategies and Practices Emerging from Strengths-Based Supports Models of Disability

We turn from the context of learning to examine how practices in special education will or should look if we adhere to strengths-based, social-ecological models of disability that emphasize supports. Each is described here and, in greater detail, in subsequent chapters.

Assessment for Supports and Progress

Assessment and instruction go hand-in-hand. This has been the case for students with, for example, learning disabilities; models such as curriculum-based measurement and Response to Intervention use frequent assessment to determine progress and to modify dosage or type of instruction. In the lives of students with intellectual disability, assessment is less often formative and used to make instruction decisions than it is to determine eligibility and document areas of impairment. Such efforts remain part of how we understand intellectual disability, and Chapter 5 provides current best practice in evaluating intellectual functioning and adaptive behavior—but assessment within these new paradigms also must attend to student support needs to identify the supports a student can receive to succeed, and it must provide means to assess, formatively, process in learning.

Supports Intensity Scales and Supports Assessment

Chapter 6 provides information about the assessment of support needs using the Supports Intensity Scales (SIS), including a version for children and, for purposes of transition planning, a version for adults. Normed with children, adolescents, and young adults with intellectual disability, the SIS differ from traditional standardized assessments in that instead of measuring personal competence (as discussed in Chapter 3), the SIS measure the support needs of a student and identify areas in which the identification of supports is important. The question asked by support measures is not whether a student can or cannot be successful in a given endeavor—it is what type, intensity, duration, and frequency of supports would a person need to be successful. The presumption is one of competence, not incompetence.

Dynamic Learning Maps and Alternate Assessment

As noted, the impetus, or at least one impetus, for the 1997 IDEA access requirements was to ensure that students with disabilities were not excluded from accountability systems introduced through Improving America's Schools Act of 1994 and, by default, excluded from the school reform and improvement efforts initiated by that Act and, essentially, further marginalized. The process of implementing alternate assessments for the 1% of students who were eligible was, however, a hit or miss proposition over time; different states created differing alternate assessments, and alignment of these alternate assessments with the state assessments used by the other 99% was questionable, at best (Kleinert & Kearns, 2010). To address this, the US Department of Education, Office of Special Education Programs, funded two large-scale projects to develop innovative ways to assess learning for students with the most significant cognitive disabilities.

The Dynamic Learning Maps (DLM) project, more about which you will learn in Chapter 7, was one of the two projects funded. While addressing the need for a viable alternate assessment, the DLM process has focused beyond just the alternate assessment to develop an assessment system that harnesses the power of technology and UDL to enable students with more extensive support needs to demonstrate learning. The details about DLM will be discussed in Chapter 7; the point to make here, and the reason we mention it in the context and expectations section, is that the DLM model eschews traditional ideas of learning as sequential and proposes a means to assess learning for students with intellectual disability in a parallel, distributed-processing manner. The learning maps in the DLM model are based upon 'nodes,' which are skill-based targets identified from the literature, clusters of which represent essential elements in learning. Typically, learning tasks tended to be thought of sequentially: Students acquire skill/knowledge A, then B, then C, and so forth. A student who could not progress from A to B to C was not provided any additional instruction. In the DLM model, learning progresses in a manner best comparable to the way our brains work. Neurons form neural networks for which there are multiple paths to a common end. So too within a DLM model: If a student can't acquire skill/knowledge B (a *node* in DLM terminology), then there is an alternate path through node B1, B2, B3 or more that may provide alternate routes to the outcome desired.

Universal Design for Learning

Historically, content information—particularly in core academic areas—has been presented almost exclusively through print-based formats (textbooks, worksheets) and lectures. Students who cannot read well or who have difficulty with memory or attention do not have access to the content presented through these mediums and, thus, do not have the opportunity to learn that content. Applying principles of UDL to curriculum development by providing multiple means for presenting information and for students to respond to that information (as discussed in detail in Chapter 14) is an example of the social-ecological models' emphasis on modifying the environment or context—in this case the curriculum—to ensure a better fit between the student's capacities and that context. If a student cannot read print, provide the content in a different format that the student can access.

Orkwis and McLane (1998) defined UDL as "the design of instructional materials and activities that allows learning goals to be achievable by individuals with wide differences in their abilities to see, hear, speak, move, read, write, understand English, attend, organize, engage, and remember" (p. 9). UDL promotes flexibility in representing content (how instructional materials present the content), in presenting content (how educators and materials deliver content), and in demonstrating content mastery (how students provide evidence of their learning). Flexibility in the presentation and representation of content information can be achieved by providing information in a variety of formats, including text, graphics or pictures, digital and other media formats (audio or video, movies), or performance formats (plays, skits). The development of curricular materials in digital (electronic text) formats allows for the use of computers to provide multiple output formats. For example, using specially designed media players, electronic text can be converted to multiple output formats, including electronic Braille, digital talking-book format, and sign-language avatars, as well as allowing for output in multiple languages and allowing the user to modify features of the presentation, including font size and color and background color. Similarly, there are multiple ways that students can provide evidence of their learning, including written reports, exams, portfolios, drawings, performances, oral reports, videotaped reports, and other alternative means.

There are, as well, pedagogical or instructional modifications that can provide greater access to content information. For example, the use of graphic or advance organizers has been shown to improve the comprehension of students with disabilities. Both graphic and advance organizers are, in essence, flexible ways of presenting content information to students.

The use of UDL to drive curriculum design is a perfect example of the impact of functional models of disability to education. These modifications alter the context, in this case the actual curricular materials, to enable learners with a wide array of abilities and experiences to have access to content information—it improves the 'fit' between the student with disability and the curriculum through which content information is presented.

Educational and Assistive Technology

The focus on providing supports to promote a better fit between a student's capacities and the educational context also places greater emphasis on the use of educational and assistive technologies. Traditionally, the role of technology in 'special' education has been narrowly prescribed as of benefit only to students with more severe impairments who need some 'assistive' technology device, such as an augmentative communication device, to accommodate for that student's deficits. This was consistent with an understanding of disability that focused on fixing the person. Within a functional model and supports systems, however, the role of technology—including information, electronic, and assistive technologies—becomes critical to addressing not only the student's capacities, but the educational context. Computer-assisted instruction (CAI), for example, involves the use of computer-based technologies to perform a variety of instructional roles, from initial delivery of content information to drill and practice activities. Research supports the efficacy of CAI with students with and without disabilities, including students with more severe disabilities (Wehmeyer, Smith, Palmer, Stock, & Davies, 2004).

Finally, technology can play a meaningful role in promoting the inclusion of students with disabilities in general education classrooms. Assistive technologies, such as augmentative or alternative communication devices, provide alternative means for students with disabilities to interact with their peers without disabilities, as well as to participate in classroom learning activities. Many devices can promote peer interactions by providing a topic of conversation between the student with disability and a peer. Technology devices, like smartphones and tablets, are socially desirable and can facilitate social interactions as well as provide needed supports.

Multitiered Systems of Supports and Positive Behavior Interventions and Supports (PBIS)

Multitiered systems of supports (MTSS; see Chapter 12) and PBIS (Chapter 13) are overarching frameworks for thinking about supports, whether academic or behavioral, as a function of the current performance of students with disabilities. In traditional models, student difficulty with content (or behavior) was responded to by 'referring' students to progressively more restrictive, segregated environments in which, presumably, more attention could be brought to bear on the problem. Tiered interventions, such as MTSS and PBIS, view student difficulty as a signal to change something about the intervention or support (e.g., as per social-ecological models, change the context of environment).

Multitiered Systems of Supports

The MTSS framework has emerged from the convergence of tiered interventions to address academic (Response to Intervention) and behavioral (PBIS) needs, respectively. In an MTSS model, (a) all students receive high-quality, evidence-based, and universally designed instruction, taking into consideration their linguistic and cultural backgrounds, disabilities, and other learning needs (Tier 1); (b) some students who are not successful behaviorally or academically with only Tier-1 supports receive additional targeted instruction in addition to Tier-1 instruction (Tier 2); and (c) a few students who need the most intensive supports to succeed receive not only Tier-1 and -2 interventions, but more intensive, sometimes individualized, instruction and supports (Tier 3). As students move to more intensive levels (tiers) of support, they do not need to be removed from general education classes (Sailor, 2009). Interventions can be embedded within general education instruction and activities, maintaining opportunities for the benefits of inclusion.

These MTSS models provide a framework in which to implement evidence-based, system-wide practices to support a rapid response to academic, behavioral, and social instructional needs, with frequent data-based monitoring for instructional decision making and the use of evidence-based instruction; supports at varying levels of intensity; collaboration among professionals across disciplines (e.g., special and general education, speech, language, content areas); and strong parent, professional, and community partnerships (Sailor, 2009). The goal is to enable professionals within organizations to use problem-solving strategies to implement and evaluate the impact of interventions that have a high probability of success and promote access to challenging curriculum in academic and nonacademic areas that prepares students for the demands of society. Such models assume that all students receive their education in the general education classroom and curriculum, and that separate programs are unnecessary, as all students—with and without disabilities—will receive the supports needed to be successful.

Positive Behavior Interventions and Supports (BPIS)

The field of positive behavior supports is an area of intervention and treatment that has moved from emphasizing the person with a disability as the problem to be fixed to recognizing that treatment and intervention must focus on the social and environmental context and the interaction between that context and the individual's limitations. Positive behavior interventions and supports go all out, as it were, to change the environment to make the exhibition of problem behaviors irrelevant or counter-productive for the person. Positive behavior supports focus on two primary modes of intervention: altering the environment before a problem behavior occurs and teaching appropriate behaviors as a strategy for eliminating the need for problem behaviors to be exhibited (Carr et al., 2000).

Turnbull, Turnbull, Soodak, and Erwin (2006) discussed the impact of PBIS at several levels of activity that illustrate the interaction between personal capacity, the demands of the context, and providing supports as articulated in social-ecological models of disability. First, the approach recognizes that "a student's behavior is affected by the philosophies, policies, procedures, practices, personnel, organization and funding of education agencies and other human service agencies involved in the student's education" (Turnbull et al., 2006, p. 185). As such, the first level of intervention will necessarily focus on systems change, that being the process of changing those features of the agency or agencies. Included in such systemic efforts are service integration efforts that bring together a wide array of supports in a unified and easily accessible manner.

Second, as has been emphasized, PBIS emphasizes altering the environment. Turnbull et al. (2006) noted that such environments are usually altered by:

- making different life arrangements by building on student strengths and preferences, identifying student and family priorities, building social and friendship networks and promoting health and wellness;
- improving the quality of the student's physical environment, including increasing the predictability and stability of events in school building, minimizing noise and other irritants;
- making personal accommodations for students;
- making instructional accommodations for students.

(p. 185)

A third level of action for PBIS is to focus on skill instruction to enhance the possibility that students will act appropriately. Such activities can extend from teaching specific behavioral patterns or routines (how to behave in school hallways between classes) to instruction to promote general problem-solving and self-management skills.

Once again, the focus on positive behavior supports attempts to modify the context in which students learn, in this case school and classroom settings, to ensure a better fit for the student. There are both capacity building and context modification activities involved.

Self-Determination, Student-Directed Learning, and Personalized Learning

The field of education is moving to an era of personalized learning; that is clear. Within such a frame, there is an emphasis on the infusion of technology and repeated assessment to drive instruction, as well as a focus on student-directed learning and promoting student choice and self-determination. As discussed in greater detail in Chapter 16, promoting self-determination enables students with intellectual disability, in essence, to support their own learning. Research in that chapter illustrates that students with intellectual disability who are more self-determined achieve more positive school- and transition-related outcomes and are more likely to be involved in their own transition planning (also discussed in Chapters 10 and 11). There is a strong evidence base for the positive impact of teaching students with intellectual disability to self-direct learning through strategies such as self-monitoring and self-evaluation or antecedent cue regulation.

We have a sufficient, and still growing, literature base on both the importance of promoting self-determination and on methods, materials, and strategies to do so. Further, promoting self-determination is important to achieving inclusion and access to the general education curriculum. Component elements of self-determined behavior—such as goal setting, problem solving, or self-regulation—are found in virtually all state and local standards across multiple content areas, and it seems self-evident that students who are goal oriented, can address problems, and are self-regulated and self-directed will do better in the context of the general education curriculum. In the parlance of MTSS, promoting self-determination should be a Tier-1 instructional strategy for all students, and more intensive efforts to promote self-determination should be incorporated into Tier-2 efforts. Promoting self-determination is, at its core, an exercise in having high expectations and is a student's most natural support.

Third-Generation Inclusive Practices

Turnbull, Turnbull, Wehmeyer, and Shogren (2013) have suggested that the paradigm shift in how disability is understood, and the alignment of educational practices to this shift, as described in the previous sections, have led to a third generation of inclusive practices. The first generation of inclusive practices focused on changing prevailing educational settings for students with disabilities from separate, self-contained settings to the regular education classroom. First-generation inclusion was additive in nature; that is, resources and students were "added" to the general education classroom. The second generation of inclusive practices was more generative in nature, in that instead of focusing on moving students from separate settings to regular classroom settings, second-generation practices focused on improving practice in the general education classroom. Research and practice during this phase emphasized aspects of instructional practices that promoted inclusion, such as collaborative teaming and team teaching, differentiated instruction, developing family/school/community partnerships, and so forth.

The most salient characteristic of the third generation of inclusive practices is that the focal point for such efforts switches from advocacy and supports with regard primarily to where a student receives his or her educational program, which Turnbull et al. (2013) suggested was the focus of the first two generations of inclusive practices, to a focus on what the student is taught.

The third generation of inclusion presumes a student's presence in the general education classroom; instead of a focus on integration into the classroom, the emphasis is on the quality of the educational program in that setting. Nothing about the first or second generations of inclusion is either obsolete or unimportant. In fact, both remain critical to ensure high-quality educational programs for students with disabilities. The need to consider issues pertaining to third-generation inclusive practices is, in fact, an outcome of the success of these first two generations' efforts. That is, as more students with disabilities are educated and successfully supported in the general education classroom, the expectations for students have become higher and higher, such that we are at a point in the evolution of inclusive practices where we need to consider how we maximize participation in the general education classroom and progress in the general education curriculum.

Conclusions

The chapters that follow provide greater detail on research- and evidence-based practices in the education of students with intellectual disability. More so, however, the chapters provide a road map for educating students with intellectual disability in the context of strengths-based approaches to disability. This chapter and the three preceding it have made a case for adopting social-ecological models of disability when thinking about intellectual disability. In the second section, chapter authors examine measurement and assessment issues (Chapters 5, 6, and 7) and planning procedures (Chapter 8, 9, 10, and 11) that can provide information about and direction for strengths-based educational approaches. The third section examines school- and classroom-wide academic and behavioral supports, beginning with discussions of MTSS and PBIS (Chapter 12 and 13) and UDL (Chapter 14). This section continues with chapters that examine the importance of promoting friendships and peer interactions (Chapter 15) and promoting self-determination and goal attainment (Chapter 16). Chapter 17 provides an overview of the knowledge-base about educating students with intellectual disability in inclusive classrooms and Chapter 18 examines family supports and family–professional partnerships. Section three ends with an examination of practices to teach reading and literacy skills (Chapter 19) and math and science (Chapter 20) to students with intellectual disability. The fourth section of the text looks at education across the 'lifespan,' that is, from early intervention (Chapter 21) and elementary (Chapter 22), to middle (Chapter 23) and high school (Chapter 24). This final section concludes with a chapter examining transition to employment (Chapter 25) and a chapter that examines the growing opportunities in postsecondary education for students with intellectual disability (Chapter 26).

References

Carr, E. G., Horner, R. H., Turnbull, A. P., Marquis, J. G., McLaughlin, D. M., McAtee, M. L. . . . Doolabh, A. (2000). *Positive behavior support for people with developmental disabilities: A research synthesis.* Washington, DC: American Association on Mental Retardation.

Janney, R., & Snell, M. E. (2013). *Teachers' guides to inclusive practices: Modifying schoolwork* (3rd ed.). Baltimore: Paul H. Brookes.

Kleinert, H. L., & Kearns, J. F. (2010). *Alternate assessment for students with significant cognitive disabilities.* Baltimore: Paul H. Brookes.

Kurth, J., Lyon, K. J., & Shogren, K. A. (2015). Supporting students with severe disabilities in inclusive schools: A descriptive account from schools implementing inclusive practices. *Research and Practice for Persons with Severe Disabilities, 40,* 261–274.

Kurth, J. A., Morningstar, M. E., & Kozleski, E. (2014). The persistence of highly restrictive special education placements for students with low-incidence disabilities. *Research & Practice for Persons with Severe Disabilities, 39*(3), 227–239.

Luckasson, R., Borthwick-Duffy, S., Buntinx, W. H. E., Coulter, D. L., Craig, E. P. M., Reeve, A., . . . Tasse, M. J. (2002). *Mental retardation: Definition, classification, and systems of support* (10th ed.). Washington, DC: American Association on Mental Retardation.

McCart, A., Sailor, W., Bezdek, J., & Satter, A. (2014). A framework for inclusive educational delivery systems. *Inclusion, 2,* 252–264.

Orkwis, R., & McLane, K. (1998). A curriculum every student can use: Design principles for student access. *ERIC/OSEP Topical Brief, Fall, 1988.* Reston, VA: Council for Exceptional Children.

Sailor, W. (2009). *Making RTI work: How smart schools are reforming education through schoolwide response-to-intervention models.* San Francisco: Jossey-Bass.

Sailor, W. (2015). Advances in schoolwide inclusive school reform. *Remedial and Special Education, 36,* 94–99. doi: 10.1177/0741932514555021

Sailor, W., & McCart, A. (2014). Stars in alignment. *Research and Practice for Persons with Severe Disabilities, 39,* 55–64.

Shogren, K. A., McCart, A., Lyon, K. J., & Sailor, W. (2015). All means all: Building knowledge for inclusive schoolwide transformation. *Research and Practice for Persons with Severe Disabilities, 40,* 173–191.

Thompson, J. R., Buntinx, W., Schalock, R. L., Shogren, K. A., Snell, M. E., Wehmeyer, M. L. . . . Yeager, M. H. (2009). Conceptualizing supports and the support needs of people with intellectual disability. *Intellectual and Developmental Disabilities, 47,* 135–146.

Turnbull, A. P., Turnbull, H. R., Soodak, L. C., & Erwin, E. J. (2006). *Families, professionals and exceptionality: Positive outcomes through partnerships and trust.* Columbus, OH: Merrill/Prentice-Hall.

Turnbull, A. P., Turnbull, H. R., Wehmeyer, M. L., & Shogren, K. A. (2013). *Exceptional lives: Special education in today's schools* (7th ed.). Columbus, OH: Merrill/Prentice Hall.

US Department of Education (2005). *Alternate achievement standards for students with the most significant cognitive disabilities: Non-regulatory guidance.* Washington, DC: Author. Accessed online at https://www2.ed.gov/policy/elsec/guid/altguidance.pdf February 23, 2016.

Wehmeyer, M. L., Smith, S., Palmer, S., Stock, S., & Davies, D. (2004). Technology use by students with intellectual disabilities: An overview. *Journal of Special Education Technology, 19*(4), 7–22.

Part II
Eligibility, Assessment, and Educational Planning

5

Measuring Intellectual Functioning and Adaptive Behavior in Determining Intellectual Disability

Marc J. Tassé, Margaret H. Mehling

As described in Chapter 2, a multidimensional framework for understanding human functioning is increasingly being adopted in the intellectual disability field to understand the role of individualized supports in enhancing human functioning (Schalock et al., 2010). This multidimensional framework assumes that multiple domains influence the provision of individualized supports and outcomes, including intellectual functioning, adaptive behavior, health, participation, and context. Two of these domains, intellectual functioning and adaptive behavior, are the focus of this chapter.

These two domains are the focus of this chapter as there is consensus among two major professional organizations in the field—i.e., the American Association on Intellectual and Developmental Disabilities (AAIDD) and the American Psychiatric Association (APA)—regarding the role of these domains in making an intellectual disability determination. The AAIDD is an interdisciplinary professional society founded almost 140 years ago that has led the way in establishing the definition and terminology of intellectual disability. The AAIDD definition of intellectual disability has historically been adopted by the federal and all state governments as well as the APA's *Diagnostic and Statistical Manual for Mental Disorders* (DSM). The APA has been publishing the *DSM* since the late 1950s, which establishes clear diagnostic criteria for intellectual disability. Both organizations—AAIDD in its 11th edition of its *Terminology and Classification Manual* (see Schalock et al., 2010) and APA in its 5th edition of the DSM (DSM-5; see APA, 2013)—define intellectual disability as originating during the developmental period and being characterized by significant impairments in both intellectual functioning and adaptive behavior, where "significant impairments in adaptive behavior" is defined by the presence of conceptual, social, or practical skills that are approximately two standard deviations or more below the population mean.

AAIDD suggests that making a diagnosis of intellectual disability based on these three criteria (i.e., limitations in intellectual functioning, adaptive behavior, and onset during the developmental period) is not an end in and of itself, but is done to enable the identification of individualized supports needed to enhance human functioning. Thus, understanding the information that goes into the determination of the presence of intellectual disability is one step in the process of identifying the factors that may influence the individualized supports needed by students with intellectual disability to maximize their functioning across domains, including in the educational context.

In the following sections, we will review the important aspects of the constructs of intelligence and adaptive behavior. We will then discuss critical assessment elements and briefly review the available standardized assessment instruments for both constructs, highlighting critical information that emerges in the diagnostic process that can influence the provision of individualized supports.

Intellectual Functioning

The study of human intelligence is certainly among the most heavily researched phenomena in the field of psychology. Wasserman (2012) attributes the first attempts to systematically study intelligence and the brain within the field of phrenology in the early 1800s. The pioneering work of Francis Galton on the measurement of individual differences in sensory and motor reaction times in the late 1880s is often credited for advancing the scientific study of human intelligence (Greenwood, 2015). It was nonetheless the groundbreaking work of Frenchmen Alfred Binet and his associate Theodore Simon that resulted in the creation of the first norm-referenced standardized test of intelligence (Wasserman, 2012). The Binet-Simon scale was quickly translated into English by Henry H. Goddard, and was later revised by Lewis Terman at Stanford University and disseminated in the United States as the Stanford-Binet scale (now in its 5th edition; Roid, 2003).

Probably the best known and most widely accepted theory of intelligence is the general intelligence theory ("g") put forth by Spearman (1904). The Cattell-Horn-Carroll (CHC) theoretical model of intelligence is the probably the most widely used today (Flanagan & Kaufman, 2004). The CHC model includes two forms of intelligence: fluid intelligence (Gf) and crystalized intelligence (Gc). Fluid intelligence generally refers to abilities that involve reasoning, problem solving, or tapping cognitive abilities that are not encountered in school or everyday life (e.g., recognizing patterns, abstract reasoning, responding to novel situations). Crystallized intelligence involves using knowledge, experience, and acquired understanding (often learned in school) and includes vocabulary and general knowledge. Despite these two well-established theories of intelligence, and more than a century of scientific work in the area of intelligence, there is still no unanimity on a theory or definition of human intelligence (Conway & Kovacs, 2015; Goldstein, 2015). Although there may not be a unified theory of intelligence or definition of intelligence that all intelligence researchers endorse, both the AAIDD *Terminology and Classification Manual* (Schalock et al., 2010) and the DSM-5 (APA, 2013) have adopted a version of the consensus definition of the meaning and measurement of intelligence published by Gottfredson (1997):

> Intelligence is a very general mental capability that, among other things, involves the ability to reason, plan, solve problems, think abstractly, comprehend complex ideas, learn quickly and learn from experience. It is not merely book learning, a narrow academic skill, or test-taking smarts. Rather, it reflects a broader and deeper capability for comprehending our surroundings-"catching on," "making sense" of things, or "figuring out" what to do.
>
> *(p. 13)*

Assessing Intellectual Functioning

Despite the debate regarding a prevailing theory or the defining construct of human intelligence, using individually administered standardized tests of intelligence that have a comprehensive set of tasks and subtests with adequate national norms remains the recommended means of determining the first prong of the diagnostic criteria for intellectual disability. The use of the full-scale IQ score remains the best way to represent the construct of general intellectual functioning for the purpose of making a diagnosis of intellectual disability (McGrew, 2015; Schalock et al., 2010). "Significant deficit" in intellectual functioning is operationally defined as a standard score that is approximately two standard deviations below the population mean, with consideration of all sources of measurement error (APA, 2013; Schalock et al., 2010).

We do not have sufficient space in this chapter to review in depth all the available tests of intelligence that are adequately constructed, standardized, and normed for the purpose of evaluating intellectual functioning when making a determination of intellectual disability. We will present some salient descriptive information for the main tests that are appropriate, knowing that newer editions of these tests or new intelligences altogether may be developed and published subsequent to the publication of this chapter. Hence, this chapter does not have the pretense of being all encompassing.

Cognitive Assessment System

The Cognitive Assessment System, 2nd Edition (CAS2; Naglieri, Das, & Goldstein, 2014) is a standardized test of intelligence developed for use with children between the ages of 5 years and 18 years 11 months and is based on Luria's neuropsychological theory of cognitive abilities, which includes four interrelated cognitive abilities: planning (problem-solving strategies), attention (ability to regulate attention on relevant and irrelevant stimuli), simultaneous processing (ability to make sense/integrate different stimuli), and successive processing (ability to sequence and organize stimuli). The CAS2 yields five supplemental composite scores: Executive Function without Working Memory, Executive Function with Working Memory, Working Memory, Verbal Content, and Nonverbal Content. It contains a total of 13 subtests that can be administered in either an eight-subtest Core Battery or a 12-subtest Extended Battery. The Cognitive Assessment System – 2nd Edition (CAS2; Naglieri, Das, & Goldstein, 2014) yields a Full Scale IQ and standard scores for each of the four cognitive processing scales: Planning, Attention, Simultaneous, and Successive. Administration time to complete the CAS2 is approximately 60 minutes.

Kaufman Assessment Battery for Children

The Kaufman Assessment Battery for Children, 2nd Edition (KABC-II; Kaufman & Kaufman, 2004) is a multidimensional test of intellectual functioning for children and adolescents between the ages of 3 years 0 months and 18 years 11 months. The KABC-II is somewhat different from other standardized tests of intelligence in that its development was based on two distinct theoretical models: Luria's neuropsychological model (very similar to the conceptual model used by the CAS authors) and the CHC model. The user can choose to administer either the Luria Model core battery of items or the CHC Model core battery of items. The two theoretical models yield different global scores for intellectual functioning: the Luria-based model administration produces the Mental Processing Index (MPI) and the CHC approach yields the Fluid-Crystalized Index (FCI). The key difference between these two global scores is that the MPI (Luria's theory) excludes measures of acquired knowledge, whereas the FCI (CHC theory) includes measures of acquired knowledge (Lichtenberger & Kaufman, 2010). For this reason, we recommend the administration and use of the CHC model and use of the FCI global score over the Luria model and MPI scores as the best indicators of the person's general intellectual functioning for the purpose of making an intellectual disability determination. Depending on the choice of the examiner, different subtests are administered and subscales scores result. The KABC-II's five CHC-based factor scores are Crystallized Ability (Gc), Fluid Reasoning (Gf), Visual Processing (Gv), Long-term Storage and Retrieval (Glr), and Short-term Memory (Gsm). The average administration time for the KABC-II CHC-based assessment is approximately 70 minutes, whereas the total administration time for the Luria-based assessment is approximately 55 minutes.

Stanford-Binet Intelligence Scales

The Stanford-Binet Intelligence Scales, 5th Edition (SB5; Roid, 2003), was developed and normed to assess people across the age span including 2–85 years old. The SB5 is the most current and modern version of the original scale developed by Alfred Binet and Theodore Simon in 1905. It consists of

10 subtests that assess intellectual functioning and produce standard scores for Verbal IQ (VIQ), Nonverbal IQ (NCIQ), and Full Scale IQ (FSIQ). The SB5 also includes measures of five important dimensions of intellectual functioning: Fluid Reasoning, Knowledge, Quantitative Reasoning, Visual–Spatial Processing, and Working Memory. Administration time to complete the SB5 is approximately 60 minutes.

Wechsler Preschool and Primary Scale of Intelligence

The Wechsler Preschool and Primary Scale of Intelligence, 4th Edition (WPPSI-IV; Wechsler, 2012) is a standardized test of intelligence for preschoolers and young children between the ages of 2 years 6 months and 7 years 7 months. The WPPSI-IV consists of a total of 15 subtests with the number of subtests administered depending on the chronological age of the child being assessed. For example, children between the ages of 2 years 6 months and 3 years 11 months are administered seven subtests and children between the ages of 4 years 0 months to 7 years 7 months are administered all 15 subtests. WPPSI-IV scores can be interpreted from either a normative reference group or within-person perspective (Raiford & Coalson, 2014). The WPPSI-IV yields standard scores for six specific index scores: Verbal Comprehension Index, Visual Spatial Index, Fluid Reasoning Index (ages 4:0 to 7:7 only), Working Memory Index, Processing Speed Index (ages 4:0 to 7:7 only), and Vocabulary Acquisition Index. The WPPSI-IV also yields three global composite scores: Full Scale IQ, Nonverbal IQ, and General Ability Index. The use of the Full Scale IQ and interpretation using the norm-referenced comparison are the most appropriate and robust to use for the purposes of making an intellectual disability determination.

Wechsler Intelligence Scale for Children

The Wechsler Intelligence Scale for Children, 5th Edition (WISC-V) was developed and normed on a representative sample of children between the ages of 6 years 0 months and 16 years 11 months. The results from the WISC-V provide a total of 13 primary, ancillary, and complementary index scores. The five primary index scores that encompass the individual's intellectual functioning: Verbal Comprehension Index, Visual Spatial Index, Fluid Reasoning Index, Working Memory Index, and Processing Speed Index. The WISC-V results also yield a Full Scale IQ, which is a composite standard score that best represents the individual's general intellectual functioning. The average administration time is approximately 65 minutes to administer all 10 primary subtests required to obtain results on all five primary subtests and Full Scale IQ (Wechsler, 2014a).

Wechsler Adult Intelligence Scale

The Wechsler Adult Intelligence Scale, 4th Edition (WAIS-IV; Wechsler, 2008) is probably the most widely used standardized test of intelligence. It is the 4th edition of the intelligence test developed by David Wechsler, the first version of this test being the Wechsler-Bellevue Intelligence Scale (Wechsler, 1939). The WAIS-IV was developed and normed on individuals from 16 years 0 months to 90 years 11 months. The WAIS-IV yields standard scores across the following five indices: Verbal Comprehension Index, Perceptual Processing Index, Working Memory Index, Processing Speed Index, and Full Scale IQ (the same concept as a Composite IQ score). The Full Scale IQ is considered the valid measure of general intellectual functioning (Wechsler, 2008). The approximate time of administration of the scale's 10 core subtests ranges from 60 to 90 minutes.

Woodcock-Johnson

The Woodcock-Johnson, 4th Edition Tests of Cognitive Abilities (WJ-IV COG; Schrank, McGrew, & Mather, 2015) is an individually administered measure of intellectual functioning that was designed and normed for individuals across the age span (i.e., 2–90 years old). The WJ-IV was developed based on the CHC theory of intelligence. The Standard Battery consists of 10 tests and the Extended Battery has a total of 18 tests. Based on the administration of the 10-test Standard Battery, the WJ-IV yields three composite scores: Brief Intellectual Ability (BIA), Gf-Gc Composite, and General Intellectual Ability (GIA). The BIA score is computed based on only three tests; the Gf-Gc Composite is derived from the individual's performance on four tests; and the GIA is computed based on the individual's performance on seven tests and represents the better estimate of the individual's general intellectual functioning (Schrank, McGrew, & Mather, 2015). Total test administration time for the Extended Battery is approximately 75 minutes.

Measurement Error

The obtained score (e.g., full-scale IQ score or composite adaptive behavior score) from any standardized test is the test's approximate measure of the person's true ability on the construct assessed by said test. All standardized tests have measurement error embedded in the obtained scores that they yield. It is critical to interpret all obtained scores, even from the most robust and reliable standardized tests, while considering that test's reliability and all potential sources of measurement error. Relevant to the determination of intellectual disability, both the AAIDD *Terminology and Classification Manual* (Schalock et al., 2010) and the DSM-5 (APA, 2013) recommend the use of clinical judgment and consideration of all sources of measurement error when interpreting results from standardized tests. These potential sources of measurement error include standard error of measurement, age of the test's norms, and practice effects.

Standard Error of Measurement

The standard error of measurement (SEM) is computed by administering the test to a large representative population and computing the test's reliability coefficient, which can then be translated into an average error of measurement for the population (AERA, 2014). Generally, the SEM is computed and then used to create confidence intervals around the obtained standard scores (e.g., 90% or 95%). A confidence interval of 95% represents a level of statistical certainty based on the test's reliability coefficient that the assessed individual's "true score" falls within the given confidence surrounding the obtained score. Thus, a professional reporting on an assessed individual's obtained Full Scale IQ score of 70 on IQ test "X" might report that there is a 95% certainty that the assessed person's "true score" falls within the range of Full Scale IQ scores 66–77.

Schalock et al. (2010) recommended using a confidence interval of 95% certainty when reporting and interpreting obtained scores (on IQ or adaptive behavior tests), which generally represents a band of certainty of plus or minus two times the test's standard error of measurement around the obtained score.

Age of Test Norms

James Flynn established unequivocally that the US population's mean IQ score is increasing each year (Flynn, 1985). In fact, historical IQ data going as far back as 1930s indicates that this upward trend has been in existence and there appears to be no end in sight (Flynn, 1984, 2006). This increase in IQ scores is not limited to only US populations but also has been shown to be true in all industrialized countries who have population data on standardized IQ tests. This phenomenon was coined the "Flynn effect" and refers to the increase in IQ scores over time (i.e., about three Full Scale IQ points per decade). Hence, the Flynn effect raises potential challenges in the interpretation of IQ scores obtained on tests that have aging norms. For example, when interpreting an individual's obtained full-scale IQ score on standardized test of intelligence "X," which was normed 10 years prior to the date of administration, it would be expected to provide an unadjusted IQ score that would be inflated by approximately three points. This is so because we are using "old norms" (i.e., collected on a comparative/normative sample from 10 years ago) that do not factor in the established fact that the comparative sample's mean IQ has been increasing at a rate of 0.3 points per year, hence, 10 years × 0.3 = 3.0 IQ points. Kaufman (2010) aptly stated *"The point is that a person tested on an outdated test will earn spuriously high scores as each year goes by, and that amount of spuriousness amounts to about 3 [IQ] points per decade for Americans"* (p. 503). Both the AAIDD *Terminology and Classification Manual* (Schalock et al., 2010) and the DSM-5 (APA, 2013) state clearly that in cases where a test with aging norms is used as part of a diagnosis of intellectual disability, this potential source of error must be considered by the clinician when interpreting the results.

Several researchers have documented that the rise in IQ scores extends to the lower end of the normal curve and impacts persons in the "significant deficit" range (i.e., −2 standard deviations below the population mean). Ceci and Kanaya (2010) reported that data from school evaluations of children referred for an intellectual disability evaluation. These authors reported that the number of children identified with intellectual disability increased almost threefold when assessed on the newer/more recently normed WISC-III than in previous years when children evaluations relied on the older version and more outdated norms of the WISC-R.

Practice Effects

Practice effects refer to gains in IQ scores on tests of intelligence that result from a person being retested on the same instrument. Kaufman (1995) noted that practice effects can also occur when the same individual is retested on a similar instrument. Both the AAIDD *Terminology and Classification Manual* (Schalock et al., 2010) and the DSM-5 (APA, 2013) emphasize the importance of accounting for artificially increased IQ scores during the administration of the same IQ test to the same individual within a short period of time. The WISC-V *Technical and Interpretive Manual* (Wechsler, 2014b) presents test-retest data showing an increase in IQ scores when the WISC-V is readministered to the same group of children within a time interval ranging from one week to 12 weeks. The average increase in FSIQ from Time 1 to Time 2 was six points (Wechsler, 2014b, p. 65). This artificial increase of approximately six points on the obtained FSIQ is due to the readministration of the same IQ test to the same individual within a short period of time and is known as the "practice effect." The practice effect on the FSIQ can be as high as 15 points (see Kaufman, 1995).

Adaptive Behavior

Adaptive behavior has its roots in the field of intellectual disability. Adaptive behavior is defined as behavior that has been learned and is performed to meet society's expectation across living settings, including the home, school, work, and other community-based settings, in our respective culture, and for one's chronological age (Schalock et al., 2010). Hence, since society's demands and expectations of any individual generally increase with the passage from infancy, to childhood, and to adulthood, it is expected that we acquire and perform a more complex array of adaptive skills as we grow older. In other words, society expects different skills from a child than it does from an adult. AAIDD defines "adaptive behavior" as the collection of conceptual, social, and practical skills that have been learned by people to function in their everyday lives (Luckasson et al., 2002; Schalock et al., 2010). The three adaptive behavior domains have been defined as follows: (1) Conceptual Skills consist of communication skills, functional academics, and self-direction; (2) Social Skills consist of interpersonal skills, social responsibility, following rules, self-esteem, gullibility, naiveté, and avoiding victimization; and (3) Practical Skills consist of basic personal-care skills such as hygiene, domestic skills, and health and safety, as well as work skills.

Adaptive behavior is a required criterion of all diagnostic systems defining intellectual disability (see APA, 2000; Schalock et al., 2010; World Health Organization, 1992). As mentioned previously, AAIDD has led the field in establishing the definition and diagnostic criteria for intellectual disability for more than a century. Since its first definition of intellectual disability in 1905, AAIDD has revised its definition 10 times to reflect the changes in research and understanding of this condition. It was not, however, until the 5th edition of its diagnostic manual that AAIDD required the assessment of adaptive behavior as a criterion for defining intellectual disability.

APA has historically adopted the AAIDD definition and diagnostic criteria of what is now referred to as intellectual disability in its *Diagnostic and Statistical Manual of Mental Disorders.* The DSM first included adaptive behavior in its diagnostic criteria of intellectual disability in its 2nd edition (APA, 1968). In fact, in the DSM-2, APA actually refers the reader to the 1961 AAIDD definition of intellectual disability (see Heber, 1961) for a fuller definition of mental retardation (as the preferred term was at the time) (see p. 14; DSM-2). In fact, the text in the DSM-2 reads "*Mental retardation refers to subnormal general intellectual functioning which originates during the developmental period and is associated with impairment in either learning and social adjustment or maturation, or both*" (p. 14). This reads exactly the same as Heber's (1959) definition of adaptive behavior, which he described as maturation, learning, and social adjustment. Since the 2002 and 2010 editions of the AAIDD's *Terminology and Classification Manual,*, it has returned to the psychometrically supported framework of three adaptive behavior domains: Conceptual, Social, and Practical skills (see Luckasson et al., 2002; Schalock et al., 2010), originally proposed by Heber (1959).

Relationship Between Intellectual Functioning and Adaptive Functioning

One of the forefathers of intelligence testing used the concept of "adaptation" in his definition of "intelligence" (Binet & Simon, 1905). For a long time, the two concepts were intertwined—and they are sometimes still to this day. However, increasingly, the larger definition of intelligence is much more focused on mental capabilities and capacity, whereas adaptive behavior is much more focused on the actual performance of skills when needed and in response to societal demands and expectations. The definition of intelligence adopted by AAIDD (Schalock et al., 2010) comes from the existing consensus position of prominent intelligence researchers and is defined as follows:

> Intelligence is a very general mental capability that, among other things, involves the ability to reason, plan, solve problems, think abstractly, comprehend complex ideas, learn quickly and learn from experience. It is not merely book learning, a narrow academic or test-taking smarts. Rather, it reflects a broader and deeper capability for comprehending our surroundings—"catching on," "making sense" of things, or "figuring out" what to do.
>
> *(Gottfredson, 1997, p. 13)*

As constructs, intelligence and adaptive behavior are related but remain distinct from one another (Keith, Fehrmann, Harrison, & Pottebaum, 1987; McGrew & Bruininks, 1990). Thus, discrepancies in the measurement of intelligence and of adaptive behavior are to be expected. Not everyone with significant limitations in intellectual functioning will have commensurately limited adaptive behavior and, conversely, not everyone with significant limitations in adaptive behavior will have comparable significant limitations in intellectual functioning. Due to a wide range of measures for IQ and adaptive functioning, conducting research on children with intellectual disability and interpreting the results can be challenging. However, some studies have reported a low to moderate correlation between the measures (Harrison & Oakland, 2003; Sparrow, Ciccheti, & Balla, 2005). A much smaller number of studies (Carpentieri & Morgan, 1996) have demonstrated a high correlation, while others have demonstrated that a larger portion of the variance (35%) in adaptive functioning among adults with intellectual disability can be explained by environmental variables other than intellectual ability (21%; Hull & Thompson, 1980).

A number of studies have examined the changes in adaptive functioning among adults with developmental disabilities after deinstitutionalization (Felce, deKock, Thomas, & Saxby, 1986; Fine, Tangeman, & Woodard, 1990; Silverman, Silver, Sersen, Lubin, & Schwartz, 1986). Consistently, a meaningful positive change in adaptive functioning has been reported after moving from a more institutional living environment to a less restrictive community setting (Lakin, Larson, & Kim, 2011). In their review of the literature, which included 23 longitudinal studies between 1977 and 2010, Charlie Lakin and his colleagues reported that all but three studies documented adaptive behavior improvements when people moved to less restrictive community-based living arrangements. The increase in adaptive behavior was especially marked in the following areas: self-care, domestic skills, and social skills.

Research findings have tended to document higher correlation between these two constructs in people with severe to profound deficits in intellectual functioning than for those who present with milder impairments in intellectual functioning (Childs, 1982; Sattler 2002).

Information about changes in IQ and adaptive measures over time, and their relationship to each other, can be useful for diagnosing intellectual disability and should be considered in planning supports. Many questions, however, remain unanswered. IQ scores appear to be stable over time, yet this stability may differ across IQ levels. Changes in adaptive functioning have not been well studied, especially for children with intellectual disability. The general consensus in the field appears to be that the IQ and adaptive behavior constructs are distinct but continue to have a modest relationship. Thus, adaptive behavior is a construct that provides valuable information about the person's functioning that is not captured by measures of intellectual functioning.

Assessing Adaptive Behavior

Although the assessment of intellectual functioning has a longer history (e.g., the first standardized test was developed in 1905) than the measurement of adaptive behavior, standardized tests of adaptive behavior have progressed significantly since the first such scale was published, the Vineland Social Maturity Scale (Doll, 1936). The first version of the Vineland instrument consisted of items organized into six broad domains: self-help (general, dressing, and eating), self-direction, communication, socialization, motor skills, and work. Somewhat oddly, but perhaps reflective of the times, the 1936 Vineland scale had items such as *"Uses money providently"* and *"Disavows literal Santa Claus."* Doll (1953a) defined the construct of social competence as *"the functional ability of the human organism for exercising personal independence and social responsibility"* (see p. 10). Doll's vision of assessing "social competence" (what would later be called "adaptive behavior") remains ingrained in today's definition of adaptive behavior and associated standardized measures: "Our task was to measure attainment in social competence considered as habitual performance rather than as latent ability or capacity" (see Doll, 1953b, p. 5). This interpretation is consistent with AAIDD's current position that the assessment of adaptive behavior focuses on the individual's typical performance and not maximal ability (see Schalock et al., 2010; Schalock et al., 2012). This is a critical difference from the assessment of intellectual functioning, where we assess best or maximal performance.

According to Tassé et al. (2012), the main features in assessing adaptive behavior for the purpose of diagnosing intellectual disability include the following:

- assessment of the individual's typical behavior (and not maximal performance);
- assessment of the individual's present adaptive behavior;
- assessment of the individual's adaptive behavior in relation to societal expectation for his/her age group and culture;
- use of a standardized adaptive behavior scale that was normed on the general population;

- use of convergence of information;
- use of clinical judgment.

AAIDD has specified: *"For the purpose of making a diagnosis or ruling out ID [intellectual disability], a comprehensive standardized measure of adaptive behavior should be used in making the determination of the individual's current adaptive behavior functioning in relation to the general population, The selected measure should provide robust standard scores across the three domains of adaptive behavior: conceptual, social, and practical adaptive behavior"* (Schalock et al., 2010, p. 49). It is possible in some cases that the use of a standardized assessment instrument will not be possible. A standardized adaptive behavior scale is generally completed with information from a respondent who knows the person well. Tassé (2009) described the ideal respondents as individuals who have the most knowledge of the individual's everyday functioning across settings. Typically, these people are parents or caregivers because they have had the most opportunity to observe the assessed student in his/her everyday functioning. As the assessed person ages into adulthood, the list of ideal respondents might expand to include a spouse or roommate. Other individuals who may provide valuable adaptive behavior information include older siblings, grandparents, aunts/uncles, neighbors, teachers, coaches, employers, coworkers, friends, or other adults who may have had multiple opportunities over an extended period of time to observe the person in his/her everyday functioning in one or more contexts (e.g., home, leisure, school, work, community). Multiple adaptive behavior scales can be completed, but generally only one respondent is used to complete the entire scale, per administration procedures.

In the following section we will review four standardized adaptive behavior scales that are in wide use today. Some of these instruments have been normed on a representative sample of the general population, while others have been intentionally normed on a subpopulation of persons with intellectual and developmental disabilities. The former are generally better instruments when the reason for evaluation is to assess the person's adaptive behavior to rule-in or rule-out a diagnosis of intellectual disability. AAIDD has encouraged clinicians to avoid certain instruments that might be appropriate for intervention planning but may not necessarily be appropriate for diagnostic purposes: *"The potential user must employ adaptive behavior assessment instruments that are normed within the community environments on individuals who are of the same age grouping as the individual being evaluated"* (Schalock et al., 2010, p. 51. Measures normed on persons with intellectual disability or related developmental disability are perhaps helpful in identifying the person's ability level in relation to a target disability population and may nonetheless yield helpful programmatic adaptive behavior goals.

Adaptive behavior scales are used predominantly for two purposes. The first purpose is for assessing the person's adaptive behavior for the purposes of establishing planning goals for intervention and habilitation. The second purpose is to assess a person's adaptive behavior to determine whether there is a presence of significant deficits for the purpose of determining if the person meets criteria for a diagnosis of intellectual disability or developmental disability. Some instruments have been developed to attempt to serve both functions while other instruments focus on one aspect. We will briefly describe the following adaptive behavior instruments that are most suitable for use in assessing adaptive behavior for the purpose of determining intellectual disability: (1) Vineland Adaptive Behavior Scale—2nd Edition, (2) Adaptive Behavior Assessment System—3rd Edition, (3) Scales of Independent Behavior—Revised, and (4) Adaptive Behavior Diagnostic Scale.

Vineland Adaptive Behavior Scale

The Vineland Adaptive Behavior Scale—2nd Edition (Vineland-II; Sparrow, Cicchetti, & Balla, 2005) is probably the most frequently used comprehensive standardized adaptive behavior scale. It was first published as the Vineland Social Maturity Scale (Doll, 1936) and then revised by Sparrow, Balla, and Cicchetti (1984) as the Vineland Adaptive Behavior Scale. Vineland-II was developed to assess adaptive behavior in individuals from 0 through 90 years old. There are four evaluation forms within the Vineland-II:

- **Parent/Caregiver Rating Form** (0–90 years old): This form contains a total of 383 items and can be completed directly by the parent or caregiver, who rates the assessed individual's performance on each of the adaptive skill items on the form without needing the presence of a professional.
- **Teacher Form** (3–18 years old): This form contains a total of 223 items and uses a rating form format. It is completed directly by a teacher, who rates the assessed student's performance on each of the adaptive skill items.
- **Survey Form** (0–90 years old): This form contains the same 383 items found on the Parent/ Caregiver Rating Form but is administered to the respondent via a semi-structured interview with a professional. The *Survey Form Manual* (Sparrow et al., 2005) recommends using the semi-structured interview format for administration when the purpose of assessment is for diagnosis or to determine eligibility for services.
- **Expanded Interview Form** (0–90 years old): This form uses a semi-structured administration procedure similar to the Survey Form but containing 433 items. It is recommended for younger children (0–5 years old) and individuals with more significant limitations. It can provide a more refined assessment of basic adaptive skills and thus is more informative for planning of intervention goals. Respondents for the Expanded Interview forms are typically the assessed person's parents, caregivers, and on occasion their grandparents.

The four domain names of the Vineland-II—Communication, Socialization, Daily Living Skills, and Motor Skills (which is used only for children less than 6 years old)—do not align perfectly with the current tripartite model of adaptive behavior (Conceptual, Social, and Practical) used in diagnostic systems (e.g., AAIDD *Terminology and Classification Manual*, DSM-5). Tassé, Schalock, Balboni, Spreat, and Navas (2016) proposed the following alignment of the Vineland-II subscales with the existing tripartite model of adaptive behavior: Communication = Conceptual; Socialization = Social; and Daily Living Skills = Practical Skills.

The Vineland-II has an extensive and representative normative sample, a long track record of use, and strong psychometric properties. The structure of the Vineland-II provides standard scores with a mean of 100 and standard deviation of 15 for each of the four domains. Widaman (2010) in his review of the adaptive behavior instrument cautions that the Vineland-II might have some accuracy issues around the cutoff score range; however, despite this comment, Widaman recommends the Vineland-II as an adaptive behavior assessment instrument of choice when making high-stakes decisions.

Adaptive Behavior Assessment System

The Adaptive Behavior Assessment System—3rd Edition (ABAS-3; Harrison & Oakland, 2015) is the third edition of the ABAS, which was first published in 2000. The ABAS-3 is a comprehensive norm-referenced measure of adaptive behavior that can be used for multiple purposes, including (1) assisting in the diagnosis and classification of intellectual disability, developmental disabilities, learning disabilities, behavioral disorders, and emotional disabilities; (2) identifying functional limitations of individuals with conditions such as autism spectrum disorder, attention deficit/hyperactivity disorder, and Alzheimer disease; (3) documenting a person's eligibility for special education services, Social Security administration benefits, and placement for other types of interventions; (4) assisting with identifying and measuring progress towards adaptive behavior and daily functioning intervention goals; and (5) using it as an outcome measure in program evaluation and treatment studies. The ABAS-3 can be used to assess the adaptive behavior of individuals between the ages of 0 and 89 years. There are five distinct questionnaire forms for the ABAS-3:

- **Parent or Primary Caregiver Form** (0–5 years old): This form can be used to assess adaptive behavior of infants to preschoolers in the home and other community settings. The respondents for this form are generally the child's parents or other primary caregivers.
- **Teacher or Daycare Provider Form** (2–5 years old): This form can be used to assess the adaptive behavior of toddlers and preschoolers in a child-care, preschool and similar settings. The respondents for this form are generally the child's teachers, day-care or child-care aides, or other similar child-care or preschool personnel.
- **Parent Form** (5–21 years old): This form is used to assess the adaptive behavior of children to adults in the home and other community settings. The respondents for this form are generally the child's parents or other primary caregivers.
- **Teacher Form** (5–21 years old): This form is used to assess the adaptive behavior of children to adults in their school settings (K–12). The respondents for this form are generally the child's teachers, aides, and other school personnel.
- **Adult Form** (16–89 years old): This form is used to assess the adaptive behavior of adults in the home and across other community settings. The respondents for this form can be any number of individuals, including the person her- or himself, family members, work supervisors, peers, and others who are familiar with the individual's everyday functioning. There are separate normative tables for the Adult Form for self-ratings and ratings from third-party respondents.

Although the *User's Manual* (Harrison & Oakland, 2015) indicates that the administration time is approximately 15–20 minutes, the more realistic time of administration is probably closer to 30–40 minutes to complete the Adult Form. The ABAS-3 continues to be the only standardized adaptive behavior scale that provides norms for self-reported adaptive behavior when using the Adult Form.

The ABAS-3 yields standard scores (mean = 100; standard deviation = 15) for each of the three domains—Conceptual, Social, and Practical—as well as a standard General Adaptive Composite score, which combines information from all items and provides an overall estimate of the person's adaptive behavior. The ABAS-3 scoring also provides standard scores based on a mean = 10 and standard deviation = 3 across potentially all 11 adaptive skill areas: communication, functional academics, self-direction, leisure, social, community use, home/school living, health and safety, self-care, motor (only on forms for children < 6 years old), and work (ratings are obtained only when the assessed person has part-time or full-time employment). The standard scores for the 11 adaptive skill areas have intervention, treatment, and other similar clinical utility.

Since the ABAS-3 is a very recently published revision, few independent reliability and validity data have yet been released, although Harrison and Oakland (2015) report excellent psychometric properties. The internal consistency of the ABAS-3 General Adaptive Composite (GAC) ranges from 0.96 to 0.99 and from 0.85 to 0.99 for the adaptive behavior domains (Conceptual, Social, and Practical), yielding lean average standard error of measure (SEM) coefficients for the adaptive behavior domains and GAC.

Scales of Independent Behavior

The Scales of Independent Behavior—Revised (SIB-R; Bruininks, Woodcock, Weatherman, & Hill, 1996) is a revision of an earlier version of the SIB (Bruininks, Woodcock, Weatherman, & Hill, 1984). The SIB-R is a comprehensive standardized adaptive behavior scale that was standardized on a representative sample of individuals from the general population. It was developed for use with individuals from 3 months to 80+ years old and consists of three separate forms: Early Development Form

(3 months–8 years old), Full Scale (3 months–80 years old), and Short Form (3 months–80 years old). The Early Development Form and Short Form are comprised of subset of 40 items drawn from the full SIB-R instrument. The SIB-R may be administered using the structured interview or a checklist procedure where the respondent completes the questionnaire directly.

The SIB-R Full Scale contains two sections: adaptive behavior and problem behavior. The adaptive behavior section contains a total of 259 items. It yields a total standard score called Broad Independence and four domain scores: Motor Skills, Social Interaction and Communication Skills, Personal Living Skills, and Community Living Skills. The problem behavior section contains descriptions of eight distinct challenging behaviors rated for their frequency (0–5) and severity (0–4). The SIB-R requires approximately 60 minutes to complete and may be completed either as a rating scale directly by the respondent or via an interview between the respondent and the administrator. Although the reliability and validity psychometric data for the Comprehensive Form are adequate, the psychometric properties of the Short Form and Developmental Form are questionable (2001).

Adaptive Behavior Diagnostic Scale

The Adaptive Behavior Diagnostic Scale (ABDS) is the newest of existing standardized adaptive behavior scales on the market (Pearson, Patton, & Mruzek, 2016). This interview-based scale assesses the adaptive behavior of individuals between the ages of 2 to 21 years. The structure of the scale includes the three prevalent domains: Conceptual, Social, and Practical. The scale administration is structured according to these three domains; each domain consists of 50 discrete adaptive skills. The results obtained yield standard scores with a mean = 100 and standard deviation = 15 for each of the three domains as well as an overall Adaptive Behavior Index.

Having been recently released, there exists no independent psychometric evaluation of the ABDS. The authors (Pearson et al., 2016) report excellent psychometric properties, including internal consistency coefficients for all domain and overall index standard scores above 0.90. The authors also reported a sensitivity coefficient of 0.85 and a specificity coefficient of 0.99. A review of the scale and its user's manual supports the use of the ABDS for obtaining standardized adaptive behavior assessment information for the purpose of making an intellectual disability determination.

Nonstandardized Measures

In many cases, the use of a standardized measure of adaptive behavior is either not sufficient or not possible. This might be because there are no or too few respondents available to provide objective information on the assessed person's adaptive behavior, some of the respondents providing the adaptive information can provide only partial information, or the evaluator cannot ensure the proper administration of the instrument per test guidelines. In these instances, alternate sources of adaptive behavior information should be referenced as complementary or alternative sources of the person's adaptive behavior.

The *AAIDD Terminology and Classification Manual* (Schalock et al., 2010) and *AAIDD User's Guide* (Schalock et al., 2012) recommend using several of the following sources:

- school records;
- medical records;
- previous psychological evaluations;
- drivers and motor vehicle bureau records regarding driving skills;
- employment performance records;
- information from state or federal offices that might have eligibility information;

- informal interviews with individuals who know the person and had the opportunity to observe the person in the community, etc.

In any event, Schalock and his colleagues (2010) recommend that all evaluations of adaptive behavior follow these guidelines:

- Use multiple types and sources of information to obtain convergence of information regarding the individual's skills and limitations in comparison to same-age peers.
- Reasonable caution should always be used when weighing qualitative information obtained from respondents—especially in light of conflicting information.
- Clinical judgment should always guide the evaluation of the reliability of all respondents as well as possible sources of bias (positive or negative).
- All types of information should be reviewed and analyzed critically for accuracy and pertinence. One should also ascertain the comparison group when determining ability and limitations. For example, in some special education programs, a "C" grade denotes something very different in achievement level than a "C" grade granted in a regular education classroom.

(p. 48)

Although adaptive behavior is an important construct for the purpose of ruling-in or ruling-out a diagnosis of intellectual disability, it is by far a more important construct than intellectual functioning because of its value as an outcome measure. Adaptive behavior comprises what Henry Leland once referred to as the skills that make one "invisible" in society. Teaching adaptive skills to persons will equip them to better respond to the expectations of their community and society-at-large. These skills are translatable into better coping skills, consumer skills, social interaction, personal health care, hygiene, cooking and home-living skills, employment, etc. When Schalock and his colleagues (2010) assert the assumption/aspiration that "With appropriate personalized supports over a sustained period, the life functioning of the person with intellectual disability generally will improve" (p. 1), what they are talking about is the person's adaptive behavior. With proper intervention and supports, a person will learn and improve his/her ability to meet society's expectations. This is important because we can teach everyone with intellectual disability—no matter their level of intellectual impairment—new adaptive skills and thereby contribute to their improved independence and resulting quality of life.

Measurement Error

In the same way that standardized tests of intellectual functioning yield observed scores that should be interpreted with clinical judgment and consideration for all sources of measurement error, so do adaptive behavior scales. Observed scores should be interpreted within the accepted recommended practice (see Schalock et al., 2010) of 95% confidence interval or plus/minus two times the test's standard error of measurement. Unlike with performance on tests of intelligence, current research on adaptive behavior assessment results does not indicate a rise in obtained scores or significant inflation in results due to obsolescence of adaptive behavior test norms. Because of the nature of adaptive behavior assessment, practice effects are not an issue.

Summary

The two major diagnostic systems (AAIDD's *Diagnostic and Statistical Manual* and APA's DSM-5) are in alignment in defining intellectual disability by means of the presence of significant deficits in both intellectual functioning and adaptive behavior (as expressed in Conceptual, Social, and Practical Skills). Although neither of these systems requires that a formal diagnosis be made during the developmental period, one must establish that these deficits were present prior to the age of 18 years. An etiology that results in comparable functioning beyond the developmental period is excluded from this diagnostic category. A comprehensive evaluation and determination of intellectual disability requires clinical judgment (Schalock & Luckasson, 2014). Although individually administered standardized tests play a critical role in assessing a person's intellectual and adaptive functioning, results from standardized tests must be interpreted in conjunction with collateral sources of relevant records. Intellectual functioning and adaptive behavior are both important to understand when building individualized supports to enhance human functioning, and understanding the information that is collected during the diagnostic process can inform this process of planning for individualized supports.

References

American Educational Research Association, American Psychological Association, and the National Council on Measurement in Education. (2014). *Standards for educational and psychological testing.* Washington, DC: American Educational Research Association.

American Psychiatric Association (APA). (1968). *Diagnostic and statistical manual of mental disorders* (2nd ed.). Washington, DC: Author.

American Psychiatric Association (APA). (2000). *Diagnostic and statistical manual of mental disorders* (4th ed., text rev.). Washington, DC: Author.

American Psychiatric Association (APA). (2013). *Diagnostic and statistical manual of mental disorders* (5th ed.). Arlington, VA: American Psychiatric Publishing.

Binet, A., & Simon, T. (1905). Méthodes nouvelles pour le diagnostic du niveau intellectuel des anormaux. *L'Année Psychologique, 11,* 191–244.

Bruininks, R. H., Woodcock, R., Weatherman, R., & Hill, B. (1996). *Scales of independent behavior—revised.* Chicago, IL: Riverside.

Bruininks, R. H., Woodcock, R. W., Weatherman, R. F., & Hill, B. K. (1984). *Scales of independent behavior: Interviewer's manual.* Allen, TX: DLM Teaching Resources.

Carpentieri, S., & Morgan, S. B. (1996). Adaptive and intellectual functioning in autistic and nonautistic retarded children. *Journal of Autism and Developmental Disorders, 26,* 611–620.

Ceci, S. J., & Kanaya, T. (2010). "Apples and oranges are both round": Furthering the discussion on the Flynn effect. *Journal of Psychoeducational Assessment, 28,* 441–447.

Childs, R. E. (1982). A study of the adaptive behavior of retarded children and the resultant effects of this use in the diagnosis of mental retardation. *Education and Training of the Mentally Retarded, 17,* 109–113.

Conway, A. R., & Kovacs, K. (2015). New and emerging models of human intelligence. *Wiley Interdisciplinary Reviews: Cognitive Science, 6*(5), 419–426.

Doll, E. A. (1936). *The vineland social maturity scale.* Vineland, NJ: Vineland Training School.

Doll, E. A. (1953a). *Measurement of Social Competence.* Circle Pines, MN: American Guidance Service, Inc.

Doll, E. A. (1953b). *Measurement of Social Competence: A manual for the Vineland Social Maturity Scale.* Circle Pines, MN: American Guidance Service, Inc.

Felce, D., deKock, U., Thomans, M., & Saxby, H. (1986). Change in adaptive behavior of severely and profoundly mentally handicapped adults in different residential settings. *British Journal of Psychology, 77,* 489–501.

Fine, M. A., Tangeman, P. J., & Woodard, J. (1990). Changes in adaptive behavior of older adults with mental retardation following deinstitutionalization. *American Journal on Mental Retardation, 94,* 661–668.

Flanagan, D. P. & Kaufman, A. S. (2004). *Essentials of WISC-IV assessment.* New York: John Wiley & Sons.

Flynn, J. R. (1984). The mean IQ of Americans: Massive gains 1932 to 1978. *Psychological Bulletin, 95,* 29–51.

Flynn, J. R. (1985). Wechsler intelligence tests: Do we really have a criterion of mental retardation. *American Journal of Mental Deficiency, 90*(3), 236–244.

Flynn, J. R. (2006). Tethering the elephant: Capital cases, IQ, and the Flynn effect. *Psychology, Public Policy, and Law, 12,* 170–189.

Goldstein, S. (2015). The evolution of intelligence. In S. Goldstein, D. Panciotta, and J. A. Naglieri (Eds.), *Handbook of intelligence: Evolutionary theory, historical perspective, and current concepts* (pp. 3–7). New York: Springer.

Gottfredson, L. (1997). Mainstream science on intelligence: An editorial with 52 signatories, history, and bibliography. *Intelligence, 24,* 13–23.

Greenwood, J. D. (2015). Intelligence defined: Wundt, James, Cattell, Thorndike, Goddard, and Yerkes. In S. Goldstein, D. Panciotta, and J. A. Naglieri (Eds.), *Handbook of intelligence: Evolutionary theory, historical perspective, and current concepts* (pp. 123–126). New York: Springer.

Harrison, P. L., & Oakland, T. (2003). *Adaptive behavior assessment system, second edition: Manual*. San Antonio, TX: Harcourt Assessment.

Harrison, P. L. & Oakland, T. (2015). *Adaptive Behavior Assessment System, Third Edition (ABAS-3): Manual*. San Antonio, TX: Harcourt Assessment.

Heber, R. (1959). A manual on terminology and classification in mental retardation: A monograph supplement. *American Journal of Mental Deficiency, 64*, 1–111.

Heber, R. (1961). *A manual on terminology and classification in mental retardation* (Rev. ed.). Washington, DC: American Association on Mental Deficiency.

Hull, J. T., & Thompson, J. C. (1980). Predicting adaptive functioning of mentally retarded persons in community settings. *American Journal of Mental Deficiency, 85*, 253–261.

Kaufman, A. S. (1995). Practice effects. In Robert J. Sternberg (Ed.), *Encyclopedia of human intelligence* (pp. 828–833). New York: Simon & Schuster Macmillan.

Kaufman, A. S. (2010). Looking through Flynn's rose-colored scientific spectacles. *Journal of Psychoeducational Assessment, 28*, 494–505.

Kaufman, A. S., & Kaufman, N. L. (2004). *Kaufman assessment battery for children manual* (2nd ed.; KABC-II). Circle Pines, MN: American Guidance Service.

Keith, T. Z., Fehrmann, P. G., & Harrison, P., & Pottebaum, S. M. (1987). The relationship between adaptive behavior and intelligence: Testing alternative explanations. *Journal of School Psychology, 25*, 31–43.

Lakin, K. C., Larson, S. A., & Kim, S. (2011). *Behavioral outcomes of deinstitutionalization for people with intellectual and/or developmental disabilities: Third decennial review of US studies, 1977–2010*. Minneapolis, MN: Research and Training Center on Community Living, Institute on Community Integration, University of Minnesota.

Lichtenberger, E. O., & Kaufman, A. S. (2010). Kaufman assessment battery for children. In C. S. Clauss-Ehlers (Ed.), *Encyclopedia of cross-cultural school psychology* (2nd ed.; KABC-II, pp. 557–564). New York: Springer.

Luckasson, R., Schalock, R. L., Spitalnik, D. M., Spreat, S., Tassé, M., Snell, M. E., . . . Craig, E. M. (2002). *Mental retardation: Definition, classification, and systems of supports* (10th ed.). Washington, DC: American Association on Mental Retardation.

McGrew, K. S. (2015). Intellectual functioning. In E. Polloway (Ed.), *The death penalty and intellectual disability* (pp. 85–112). Washington, DC: American Association on Intellectual and Developmental Disabilities.

McGrew, K. S., & Bruininks, R. H. (1990). Defining adaptive and maladaptive behavior within a model of personal competence. *School Psychology Review, 19*, 53–73.

Naglieri, J. A., Das, J. P., & Goldstein, S. (2014). *Cognitive Assessment System* (2nd ed.; CAS2). Austin, TX: Pro-Ed.

Pearson, N. A., Patton, J. R., & Mruzek, D. W. (2016). *Adaptive behavior diagnostic scale: Examiner's manual*. Austin, TX: PRO-ED.

Raiford, S. E., & Coalson, D. L. (2014). *Essentials of WPPSI-IV assessment*. Hoboken, NJ: John Wiley & Sons, Inc.

Roid, G. H. (2003). *Stanford-Binet intelligence scales—fifth edition* (SB-5). Itasca, IL: Riverside Publishing.

Sattler, J. M. (2002). *Assessment of children: Behavioral and clinical applications* (4th Ed.). San Diego, CA: Jerome M. Sattler, Publisher.

Schalock, R. L., Borthwick-Duffy, S. A., Bradley, V. J., Buntinx, W. H. E., Coulter, D. L., Craig, E. M., . . . Yeager, M. H. (2010). *Intellectual disability: Diagnosis, classification, and systems of supports* (11th ed.). Washington, DC: American Association on Intellectual and Developmental Disabilities.

Schalock, R. L., & Luckasson, R. (2014). *Clinical judgment* (2nd Ed.). Washington, DC: American Association on Intellectual and Developmental Disabilities.

Schalock, R. L., Luckasson, R., Bradley, V., Buntinx, W. H. E., Lachapelle, Y., Shogren, K., . . . Wehmeyer, M. (2012). *User's guide to accompany the 11th edition of intellectual disability: Definition, classification, and systems of supports*. Washington, DC: American Association on Intellectual and Developmental Disabilities.

Schrank, F. A., McGrew, K. S., & Mather, N. (2015). *The WJ-IV Gf-Gc composite and its use in the identification of specific learning disabilities (Woodcock-Johnson IV assessment service bulletin No. 3)*. Rolling Meadows, IL: Riverside.

Silverman, W. P., Silver, E. J., Sersen, E. A., Lubin, R. A., & Schwartz, A. A. (1986). Factors related to adaptive behavior changes among profoundly mentally retarded physically disabled persons. *American Journal of Mental Deficiency, 90*, 651–658.

Sparrow, S. S., Balla, D. A., Cicchetti, D. V., (1984). *Vineland adaptive behavior scale: Interview edition, survey form manual*. Circle Pines, MN: American Guidance Services.

Sparrow, S. S., Cicchetti, D. V., & Balla, D. A. (2005). *Vineland–II: Vineland adaptive behavior scales* (2nd ed.). Minneapolis, MN: Pearson Assessments.

Spearman, C. (1904). "General intelligence," objectively determined and measured. *The American Journal of Psychology, 15*(2), 201–292.

Tassé, M. J. (2009). Adaptive behavior assessment and the diagnosis of mental retardation in capital cases. *Applied Neuropsychology, 16*, 114–123.

Tassé, M. J., Schalock, R. L., Balboni, G., Bersani, H., Borthwick-Duffy, S. A., Spreat, S., . . . Zhang, D. (2012). The construct of adaptive behavior: Its conceptualization, measurement, and use in the field of intellectual disability. *American Journal on Intellectual and Developmental Disabilities, 117*, 291–303.

Tassé, M. J., Schalock, R. L., Balboni, G., Spreat, S., & Navas, P. (2016). Validity and reliability of the diagnostic adaptive behavior scale. *Journal of Intellectual Disability Research, 60*, 80–88.

Wasserman, J. D. (2012). A history of intelligence assessment: The unfinished tapestry. In Dawn P. Flanagan & Patti L. Harrison (Eds.), *Contemporary intellectual assessment: Theories, tests, and issues* (3rd ed.) (pp 3-55). New York: Guilford Press.

Wechsler, D. (1939). *The measurement of adult intelligence.* Baltimore, MD: Williams & Bilkins.

Wechsler, D. (2008). *Wechsler adult intelligence scale* (4th ed.; WAIS-IV). San Antonio, TX: Pearson.

Wechsler, D. (2012). *Wechsler preschool and primary scale of intelligence* (4th ed.; WPPSI-IV). Bloomington, MN: Pearson Clinical Assessment.

Wechsler, D. (2014a). *Wechsler intelligence scale for children—fifth edition (WISC-V): Administration and scoring manual.* Bloomington, MN: Pearson Clinical Assessment.

Wechsler, D. (2014b). *Wechsler intelligence scale for children—fifth edition (WISC-V): Technical and interpretive manual.* Bloomington, MN: Pearson Clinical Assessment.

Widaman, K. F. (2010). Review of the vineland adaptive behavior scales, Second Edition. In R. A. Spies, J. F. Carlson, & K. F. Geisinger (Eds.), *The eighteenth mental measurements yearbook* (pp. 682–684). Lincoln: University of Nebraska Press.

World Health Organization. (1992). ICD-10 *Classifications of mental and behavioural disorder: Clinical descriptions and diagnostic guidelines.* Geneva: Author.

6

Measuring Support Needs and Supports Planning

James R. Thompson, Carolyn Hughes,
Virginia L. Walker, Stephanie N. DeSpain

In any chapter that is focused on issues of measurement, it is reasonable to begin by asking "Why should people in the intellectual disability field value efforts to measure a psychological construct such as support needs?" What is to be gained from investing time, energy, and resources into tools and/or processes that, upon completion, yield a number or a set of numbers? The answer is that assessing (i.e., collecting information) and measuring (i.e., quantification of information gathered from assessment) are a means to an end. The critical assumption on which all assessment activities are based is that the life experiences of students with intellectual disability can be improved if the decisions made by schools and planning teams are based on accurate and relevant information, and conversely, that the life experiences of students will suffer if decisions are made with incomplete or faulty information.

Because extraordinary support needs are the most salient difference between students with intellectual disability and the general population, there is no more important information to gather than that which provides insight into the pattern and intensity of support that students need. Furthermore, because the intellectual disability field is an applied field, there is no more important practice than identifying and arranging personalized supports that enhance the opportunities for children and young adults to meaningfully participate in their communities, including in the general education classroom and curriculum.

This chapter is about assessing and measuring the support needs of students with intellectual disability and related developmental disabilities, and how supports needs information can be used to inform decision making by planning team members. First, we present a conceptual model for understanding the contextual nature of supports in relation to personal competence and the demands of the settings and activities that constitute children and youth's daily lives. Next, strategies for identifying and implementing supports are discussed. The chapter concludes with a case study that illustrates how support needs assessment information can be used by planning teams to enhance opportunities for students with disabilities to lead meaningful lives as full participants in today's world.

Support Needs and a Social-Ecological Understanding of Disability

As has been discussed in earlier chapters of this book, a social-ecological conceptualization of disability (Schalock et al., 2010; World Health Organization, 2001) is increasingly recognized as a more useful (i.e., functional) approach to understanding disability, especially in terms of planning and decision making at the individual level. The major premise of a social-ecological conceptualization is that disability is best understood as a state of functioning characterized by a significant and chronic mismatch between a person's competencies and the demands of settings and activities in contemporary society. Understanding students with disabilities through a social-ecological lens draws attention to each student's unique support needs.

For a proponent of a social-ecological conceptual model of intellectual disability, the most important difference between students with intellectual disability and the general population is that students with disabilities need more supports (i.e., extraordinary support) in order to fully participate in culturally valued activities. Figure 6.1 shows the contextual nature of a social-ecological conceptualization and the essential role of supports in bridging the gap between limitations in personal competency and environmental demands. Students with intellectual disability experience a mismatch between their personal competencies and what is expected of them in community activities and settings (i.e., environmental demands). From a social-ecological perspective, the chronic mismatch leads to disability. The students' limitations in personal competency and the complexity of environmental demands are influences on the extent of the disability. Supports are resources and strategies that mitigate the person-environment mismatch. Each component of Figure 6.1 is reviewed in this section.

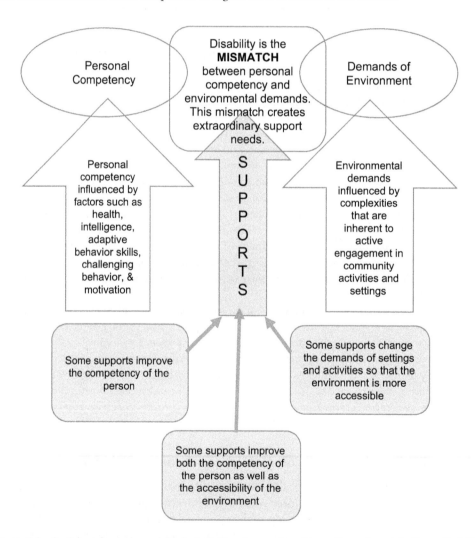

Figure 6.1 Social-ecological model of disability: Supports address the mismatch (i.e., disability) between personal competency and environmental demands

Personal Competence

Personal competence refers to the combination of abilities and skills that each person possesses. It is manifested as relative strengths and limitations. It is important to remember that each student with intellectual disability has a unique pattern of strengths and limitations. Individual differences in personal competence are self-evident: No two people are exactly the same. Because an extensive overview of concepts associated with personal competence was provided in Chapter 3, the information is not repeated here. For the purposes of this chapter, it is sufficient to point out that personal competence has a reciprocal relationship with support needs. In general, greater limitations in personal competence will be associated with more intense support needs.

Environmental Demands

Environmental demands are the other element of the person-environment mismatch. The complexity of the environment also has a reciprocal relationship with support needs: People need more intense supports when they participate in more complex environments. Therefore, when a person's support needs are the focus of assessment and planning efforts, it is critical to identify the expectations, challenges, and risks associated with daily life in community settings and activities, including the general education classroom and curriculum.

Environmental demands can be considered from two perspectives: the *general environment* and the *personal environment*. The *general environment* refers to the settings and activities of contemporary society. These are places and daily activities that are valued by the general population such as living in neighborhood homes, working at community jobs, learning in local schools as well as postsecondary educational institutions, shopping at local stores, and using services offered to the public such as banking services, postal services, and medical/health services.

At first consideration, there would seem to be tremendous diversity among the demands inherent within "general environments" in different locales. The available evidence, however, suggests that commonalities outweigh differences when it comes to assessing people's support needs. An instrument to measure people's support needs, the Supports Intensity Scale—Adult Version (SIS-A; Thompson et al., 2015), designed for youth and adults ages 16 to 64, and the Supports Intensity Scale—Children's Version (SIS-C; Thompson et al, 2016), designed for children ages 5 to 16, will be discussed in detail later in the chapter. But for now it is sufficient to point that the items included on the SIS-A and SIS-C are based on everyday life activities that take place in integrated, community environments, or the *general environment*. The SIS-A has been translated into 13 languages and used in 23 countries across Europe, Asia, Australia, and South America (AAIDD, 2013), and translations of the newly published SIS-C are under way. Published reports of translation teams suggest that there is a high degree of commonality in general environments no matter where one resides (Buntinx et al., 2008; Chou, Lee, & Chang, 2013; Cottini, Fedeli, Leoni, & Croce, 2008; Lamoureux-Hebert & Morin, 2009; Thompson & DeSpain, 2016; Verdugo, Arias, Ibanez, & Schalock, 2010). Therefore, although Rome, Italy may seem quite different from Rome, Georgia, in the United States, the people living in these two communities tend to engage in many of the same life activities and the environmental demands they encounter are similar. For instance, consider the fourth item on the Health and Safety Activities subscale of the SIS-A, *Obtaining health care services.* Although the health care systems in Italy and the United States have many differences, people in both countries need to obtain preventative and ongoing health care in order to maintain good physical and mental well-being. Activities such as a participating in a doctor's office visit, communicating with health care professionals, coordinating health care services, and getting prescriptions filled are common to people in both countries, and many people with intellectual and related developmental disabilities need support above and beyond what others in the general population require in order to do these activities.

It is important to stress that the general environment is *not* an activity, place, or program that is targeted solely to people with disabilities. By definition "specialized environments" (e.g., congregate residential settings, sheltered workshops, special schools) are not the same as integrated settings used by the general population. A norm-referenced measure of a person's support needs must be referenced to supports that are needed to participate in the general environment (i.e., the places and activities frequented by the general population). It is logically impossible to compare the pattern and intensity of people's support needs unless everyone's needs are considered in relation to the same types of settings and activities. Separate settings are, by definition, created to be alternatives to what is found in the general environment. Because they are special places with different demands/requirements for engagement, they simply are not suitable for norm-referenced measurement of support needs.

The *personal environment* is in contrast to the general environment because it refers to specific settings and activities in which individuals participate during the course of their everyday lives. Regardless of whether someone has a disability, each person has his or her own settings and activities that are unique from those of everyone else. Whereas "interacting with coworkers" is applicable to everyone who is employed and belongs under the umbrella of "general environment," for the person who has a job at a local furniture and appliance store, the personal environment entails interacting with the coworkers unique to that setting (e.g., Joe and Gabriella, who work alongside the person; Michaela, an employee in another department with whom there is frequent interaction; and the 25 other employees at the store, some who are long-time employees and others who have been employed only for a short time).

Table 6.1 illustrates the correspondence as well as the distinction between general and personal environments. The six general environment examples are for items on the SIS-A: One item was pulled from each subscale that comprises the norm-referenced portion of the scale. On the SIS-A, support needs are measured on intensity across three dimensions: Type of Support, Frequency of Support, and Daily Support Time. Table 6.1 reveals how one young woman's (Mary's) support needs were measured on the SIS-A for these six items.

A SIS-A and SIS-C assessments are complete when all items are scored, and at that point composite standard scores are generated. A composite standard score reveals the relative intensity of a person's overall support needs compared to other people with intellectual disability. Also, a completed SIS-A or SIS-C assessment provides a profile of a person's support needs. The SIS-A or SIS-C profile shows the relative intensity of support needs across the six "life activity" domains (i.e., subscales) of the scale (Thompson et al., 2015).

Table 6.1 shows several *personal environment* examples that were documented in one person's (i.e., Mary's) Individualized Support Plan (ISP). Each of the personal environment examples corresponds to a general environment item from the SIS-A. As is shown in Table 6.1, Mary is engaged in the "life activity" of housekeeping and cleaning because she has responsibilities related to cleaning in her family home. The actual supports that Mary needs for this area are minimal, but the intensity of support is beyond that which is needed by most other students in the population. It is important to note that in Mary's case, there are certain life activities where she needs considerably more support than most others from the general population (e.g., getting from place to place in her community), and other life activities where she does not need any extraordinary support (e.g., completing work tasks with acceptable quality on her job).

Table 6.1 also shows how information from a standardized assessment of support needs, such as the SIS-A or SIS-C, can inform individualized planning but is not sufficient to direct it. It is useful to know that Mary needs extra support in order to get from place to place in her community. Moving about the community without extraordinary support would put her at risk both emotionally (e.g., the anxiety that one experiences when lost) as well as physically (e.g., she could wander into a dangerous situation and be victimized). At the same time, the information from the SIS-A or SIS-C does not identify any specific, personalized supports that Mary requires in her daily life in regard to traveling within her local

Table 6.1 Supports to address the demands of the general environment and personal environment

General environment examples from SIS-A[a]	Supports identified on SIS-A[b]	Personal environment examples from ISP	Supports identified on ISP
A8—Housekeeping and cleaning	T = Monitoring F = At least once a day DST = Less than 30 minutes	Mary needs to work to keep her bedroom apartment clean.	On a weekly basis, Mary develops a checklist of "jobs" to be done each day; her mother checks on the condition of her bedroom daily and provide assistance if needed.
B1—Getting from place to place throughout the community (transportation)	T = Partial physical assistance F = At least once a day DST = 30 minutes to fewer than 2 hours	Mary walks or rides her bike to and from school and her job, but she needs someone to drive her (or accompany her using other transportation modes) to other places in the community.	Mary checks in with her family on her smart phone to indicate when she has left her home and when she has made it to work or school. Mary enjoys getting out for social events, going to the store, or visiting a different area of her town (e.g., mall), and her family/friends provide transportation.
C1—Learning health and physical education skills	T = Monitoring F = At least once a week DST = less than 30 minutes	Mary attends a Pilates and Core Strength class on Monday and Wednesday evenings.	Mary attends the class offered by the Park District, which has anywhere from six to 15 students. The instructor understands Mary's needs and monitors her participation a bit closer than the other students. Other students know Mary quite well, and provide her assistance as needed.
D6—Completing work-related tasks with acceptable quality	T = None F = None or less than monthly DST = None	Mary works part-time after school in the dietary services department of a assistive living center for senior citizens.	Mary works at a cafeteria at an assisted living center for senior citizens (her major duties include food preparation, seating diners, and bussing tables/cleaning up). Mary enjoys her work, has strong relationships with other cafeteria staff, and does not need support on her job beyond that which is provided to other workers.
E1—Taking medications	T = Verbal and gestural prompting F = At least once a day DST = Less than 30 minutes	Mary is in excellent health and does not take prescription medication regularly, but occasionally takes over-the-counter medication.	Mary cannot reliably discriminate one medication from another. Because medication is dangerous if taken in the wrong dosage, Mary's family and friends provide her with verbal directions when she wants to take a pain reliever or other over-the-counter medicine.
F8—Engaging in volunteer work	T = Verbal and gestural prompting F = At least once a day DST = Less than 30 minutes	Mary volunteers on Thursday in the late afternoon at the Humane Society.	Mary and a friend completed the Humane Society's volunteer training program several years ago, and they have been dependable volunteers ever since. They took to heart the message that volunteers need to do "fun" and "not so fun" jobs, and therefore make a point to clean the cat boxes and pick up dog poop in the "exercise yard" before interacting with the animals.

Note:
[a] Examples are from Section 2 of the SIS-A;
[b] Support dimensions on the SIS-A are: T = Type;
F = Frequency;
DST = Daily Support Time

community. Problem solving by Mary and her allies (i.e., people who care deeply about Mary and want to see her have a daily life that she finds to be fulfilling) is the only way to identify and arrange personalized supports. The fact that Mary is a "goer and doer" who likes to get out and about and has relative strengths in personal competency related to this area (she knows how to get to work and back by walking and biking, and how to operate a smart phone to check in with others) are among many factors that a planning team must consider when identifying and arranging her personalized supports.

Supports: The Bridge between Personal Competency and Environmental Demands

Once again, it is time to return to Figure 6.1. Between the ovals representing "Personal Competence" and "Demands of the Environment" is a box that indicates the mismatch between the two. The core concept of a social-ecological understanding of students with intellectual disability is that they experience a chronic mismatch between their personal competency and what is expected of them in community activities and settings (i.e., environments). As Figure 6.1 shows, the "chronic mismatch" creates "extraordinary support needs."

It is helpful to draw a distinction between *what supports do* (i.e., What is their purpose or function?) and *what supports are* (What is the nature of supports?). In terms of what supports do, supports have but one function: *to bridge the gap (i.e., address the mismatch) between personal competency and environmental demands.* Something that does not bridge the gap is by definition *not* a support even if it is intended to be a support. For example, there is a long history of adult service providers offering "prevocational training activities" in day activity centers and sheltered workshops. Although the programs were established with the best of intentions, these programs cannot be considered a "support" in terms of employment due to overwhelming evidence that they rarely provide a bridge to competitive employment (e.g., see Brickey, Campbell, & Browning, 1985; Cimera, 2011). Put another way, because prevocational programs do not address the mismatch between a person's competencies and the demands of employment settings and activities, they are not a support in terms of employment.

In regard to what supports *are,* a commonly cited definition is one that was first provided by Luckasson et al. (2002). Namely, supports are "resources and strategies that aim to promote the development, education, interests, and personal well-being of a person and that enhance individual functioning" (p. 151). Individualized (i.e., personalized) support planning must be based on careful consideration of people's goals and desires, their relative strengths as well as their relative limitations and vulnerabilities, and the demands inherent in the settings and activities in which they currently participate as well as those in which they would like to participate in the future. Effectively planning and arranging a system of supports for a person requires careful thought, creative problem solving, and an investment of time by members of a planning team. Moreover, it is work that is never "finished" because people's support needs change over time due to changes in the person and changes in the personal environment.

Figure 6.1 shows that supports "bridge the gap" between the person and environment through resources and strategies that (a) improve the competencies of people so they are better equipped to meet the demands of the environment, (b) change the environment so it is less demanding or better aligned with a person's competencies, or (c) do both (i.e., function to change the environment as well as to increase a person's competencies). Although assessing support needs and planning personalized supports has received considerable attention over the past 20 years since the publication of the 9th edition of the American Association on Intellectual and Developmental Disabilities's (AAIDD) terminology, definition, and classification manual (Luckasson et al., 1992), concepts that are clearly aligned with supports needs assessment and planning/delivery have been entrenched in the fields of special education and adult services since the earliest work in these areas was published. A brief overview of resources and strategies that increase personal competency, modify the environment to make it more accessible, and both increase competency and change the environment are provided next.

Supports to Enhance Personal Competency

The essence of education is to "change people;" that is, education should result in people becoming more competent as the result of acquiring new knowledge and skills. When people's skill sets and abilities increase, their proficiency in taking on the challenges of their environments improve, and the result is greater personal independence and functioning across a variety of settings and activities. Therefore, education is an important support in bridging the gap between environment demands and limitations in personal competency.

In the United States, the Individuals with Disabilities Education Act (IDEA) sets forth requirements regarding the education of all children with disabilities, specifying that planning teams (a) identify goals and objectives to target throughout the school year that address a child's specific support needs across relevant domains (e.g., academic, daily living); and (b) monitor and document a child's progress across targeted goals and objectives (Osborne & Russo, 2014). Although IDEA does not provide planning teams with clear guidelines in terms of instructional strategies that increase personal competence, researchers in fields associated with intellectual disability (e.g., special education, psychology) have identified effective teaching methods that planning teams should consider when engaged in supports planning (e.g., see Snell & Brown, 2011; Wehmeyer & Agran, 2005). Although not mandated by federal law, the continued education of adults with disabilities is of equal importance, as the opportunity to continue to grow and learn throughout adulthood is associated with a healthy lifestyle as well as a high quality of life (Kober, 2011).

As described in Chapter 3, people with intellectual disability have unique profiles of support needs based on their strengths and limitations in learning. A wide range of supports to improve learner abilities and skills across key education domains has resulted in positive outcomes for both adults and children. Learners with intellectual disability may benefit from instruction to improve social and communicative competence. For example, direct instructional approaches or peer-mediated strategies may be used to teach specific social interaction skills that promote the development and maintenance of relationships with typical peers in school, community, and vocational settings (Carter, Sisco, Chung, & Stanton-Chapman, 2010). Social Stories™ (Gray, 2000) or social narratives, have also been identified as potentially effective strategies to teach socially appropriate behavior and problem solving for individuals with intellectual disability (Test, Richter, Knight, & Spooner, 2011). Some learners with intellectual disability may exhibit communication impairments that limit social opportunities and, therefore, may require focused support to utilize communication systems that supplement or augment communication; these systems include, but are not limited to, sign language, speech-generating devices, or picture-based systems (Snell et al., 2010). For instance, Stoner et al. (2006) found that five adults with intellectual disability acquired functional communication skills after receiving instruction in the Picture Exchange Communication System (PECS; Bondy & Frost, 1993, 1994).

Because learners with intellectual disability are less likely to develop skills as a result of incidental or observational learning, more explicit and systematic methods have been utilized to teach academic, daily living, and vocational skills. Specifically, people with intellectual disability tend to benefit when complex tasks are broken down into smaller steps (e.g., task analysis) and instruction on each step is provided. Systematic prompting and prompt fading (e.g., time delay, least-to-most prompting), feedback, and reinforcement also contribute to more effective and efficient skill acquisition, as children and adults with intellectual disability benefit from consistency and immediacy when developing skills. There is also evidence suggesting that technology, often paired with components of systematic instruction, may be viable support to promote skill acquisition and self-management (Douglas, Ayres, & Langone, 2015; Scott, Collins, Knight, & Kleinert, 2013; Wehmeyer et al., 2006). For example, Scott et al. (2013) taught three college-aged students with intellectual disability to utilize a portable electronic device (i.e., an Apple iPod) with video modeling and auditory prompting to withdraw independently money from an ATM. More recently, Douglas et al. (2015) found that four students were able to successfully utilize grocery lists on an Apple iPhone to participate in grocery shopping skills.

Once a learner with intellectual disability has acquired a skill, it is unlikely that he or she will automatically generalize the skill to novel conditions. For instance, a student who learns to change clothes for a physical education class may not successfully generalize the skill to the community environment in which she or he is expected to change clothes before swimming at the community pool. Therefore, planning teams need to identify and implement specific teaching strategies that promote skill generalization (e.g., teaching functional skills, teaching across authentic environments with authentic materials, utilizing multiple exemplars; see Horner, McDonnell, & Bellamy, 1986; Westling & Floyd, 1990). The critical point is that instruction is a "support" when it results in increasing a person's competence and therefore lessens the person-environment mismatch.

Supports to Make the Environment More Accessible and Welcoming

Because supports bridge the gap between the limitations in personal functioning and environmental demands, anything that increases the capacity of the environment to fully include a person (i.e., mitigates the demands of settings or activities) is as much of a support as something that increases the competency of the person. For many years planning teams have focused efforts on changing the environment in some way (i.e., through altering the physical structure of the setting, adapting materials, or modifying performance expectations) in order to promote greater participation in community settings. The importance of identifying and providing supports that modify the environment in some way, shape, or form to make it more accessible has also been a cornerstone of federal legislation and regulations. In summarizing the legal requirements of the current US special education law (i.e., IDEA), Wrights Law (http://www.wrightslaw.com/) reported "the Act requires the IEP team to determine, and the public agency to provide, the *accommodations, modifications, supports, and supplementary aids and services*, needed by each child with a disability to successfully be involved in and progress in the general curriculum, achieve the goals of the IEP, and successfully demonstrate his or her competencies in State and district-wide assessments" (*emphasis added,* para. 11). In terms of service systems and legal protections for adults, since 1990, the Americans with Disabilities Act has required US employers to provide reasonable accommodations to employees with disabilities as well as required "public accommodations" (i.e., places open to all members of the public, such as places providing lodging, dining, recreation, transportation, education) to be accessible (United States Department of Justice Civil Rights Division, 2015).

Oftentimes, the terms "accommodations," "adaptations," and "modifications" are used interchangeably, while in other contexts (especially legal ones) these terms have very specific meanings. For the purposes of this chapter, we use these the term "environmental accommodation," generally, to refer to any adjustments to the environment that allow greater and more meaningful participation by a person with a disability. The concept is applicable to both adults and children. For example, allowing a student who does not have strong reading skills to take a multiple-choice history exam orally is an environmental accommodation because the environment for testing has been changed in order to allow the child to demonstrate knowledge of historical information covered on the test. Lowering file cabinets for an office worker who uses a wheelchair is also an example of an environmental accommodation (the environment has been adapted so the office worker can do the job). An example of performance accommodation would be providing a writing prompt to a high school student with intellectual disability that is consistent with the student's comprehension level, but is different from the more advanced writing prompt provided to most of the other students. This accommodation is a way to provide the student with access to the general education curriculum.

In addition to the personalized approaches to environmental accommodations that were discussed earlier, there are many examples of strategies that focus on understanding and addressing environmental demands. These include *ecological assessments* (where skills needed by a particular individual in his or her current and future environments are identified), *functional behavior assessments* (where data are collected on environmental factors that may influence problem behavior; see Watson, Gable, &

Greenwood, 2011), and *embedded accommodations* where instructional accommodations are planned in advance of implementing classroom instructional activities (see Horn & Banerge, 2009). In recent years there has been a particularly strong interest in researching new approaches to arranging supports that promote access to the general education curriculum. For example, Marino et al. (2014) investigated how a middle school science curriculum could be supplemented with video games and alternative print-based texts to more closely align with Universal Design for Learning (UDL) guidelines in order to accommodate the needs of students with disabilities.

Supports that Make the Environment More Accessible and Enhance Personal Competency

In practice, there are many cases where a certain support, or combination of supports, function to bridge the person-environment mismatch by both changing the person and changing the environment. An example can be found by returning to Table 6.1 and examining how Mary has learned to use her smart phone. When the smart phone was first given to Mary she did not know how to use it, and teaching her how to use the phone was a very important support. As a result of this instruction, as she developed competency in operating a variety of applications, including the GPS/Maps feature. She is competent in entering an address or landmark (and she has several important addresses saved on her phone); then following the "blinking dot" and audio GPS directions that her phone provides. This has made it much easier for her to navigate the streets of her town (previously, she had to rely on street signs and asking for verbal directions from others, and this did not work well for her).

So Mary has developed new competencies in using her phone, which has reduced the person-environment mismatch. However, the environment has changed as well because of the presence of a smart phone. The phone enables Mary to be easily located, and assistance can be provided to her very quickly if she needs it. Her phone is set up to always have the "Find My Friends" application turned on, and this application allows her to constantly share her location with family members who can immediately find out where she is if she becomes lost and hasn't checked in with them as scheduled. Of course, Mary can also contact her family or friends through the phone when she feels she needs help or has a question. Before the "Find My Friends" application on Mary's phone, others could not be exactly sure where she was in the community if she found herself in a vulnerable situation.

Therefore, the introduction of new technology (i.e., the smart phone) has changed Mary's environment in a very big way. Traveling by herself in the community no longer presents an untenable risk. The smart phone has also changed the environment in smaller ways. For instance, Mary uses her phone to determine how much an item costs in a store by using it to read bar codes and indicate the prices. Again, the environment previously required that she read a price tag or ask a store clerk for information on the price of items, a process that was not terribly efficient for her and one that she found stressful. Her phone has also changed the environment by providing her with reminders throughout the day, which she finds far more effective and efficient than consulting paper reminders and checklists. She can also use her phone to record class lectures and set reminders to do homework and other activities.

A Supports Planning Process

Figure 6.2 shows a supports assessment and planning process that has continually evolved since it was first presented in an article reporting pilot data on the SIS-A (i.e., Thompson et al., 2002) nearly 15 years ago. This current version calls for five conversations. The "five conversations" were previously called "five components," but "conversations" is a better term because it emphasizes that planning supports is not an episodic event, but rather an ongoing dialogue. Moreover, it is a dialogue that requires problem solving and decision making in response to changing life conditions and needs for support.

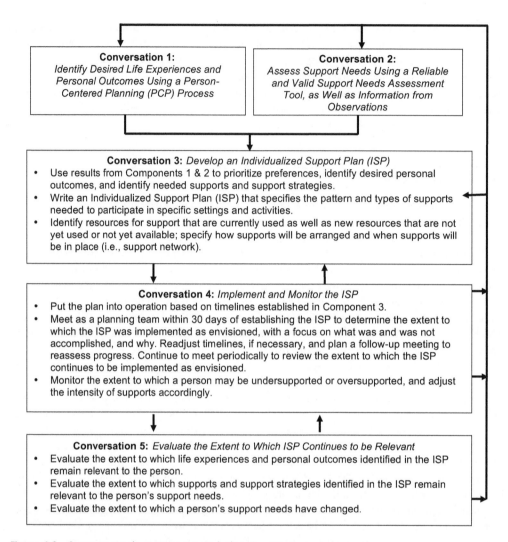

Figure 6.2 Support needs assessment and planning process

Conversation 1—Identify Desired Life Experiences and Personal Outcomes

The goal of Conversation 1 is to come up with a unified vision among planning team members as to what would constitute a good life for a person. We recommend that person-centered planning (PCP) processes be used to achieve this goal. Definitions and descriptions of person-centered planning vary. The common theme among definitions/descriptions, however, is that PCP processes place the wants and needs of people with intellectual and developmental disabilities at the center of the supports they receive and there is a deliberate effort to avoid getting distracted by the traditions, needs, and limitations of formal service systems. Additionally, PCP processes require the participation of the student with the disability, involve a facilitator that leads (but does not direct) group discussion and problem solving, focus on long-term goals and aspirations (it is not annual planning), and typically requires several group meetings that occur over time (e.g., a month) (Holburn, Gordon, & Vietze, 2007; O'Brien, O'Brien, & Mount, 1997; O'Brien, Pearpoint, & Kahn, 2010; Smull & Sanderson, 2009; Wells & Sheehey, 2012).

O'Brien et al. (1997) recounted how "person-centered planning grew as a voluntary commitment among interested people" (p. 482) and expressed concern that some of the newer planning processes that claim to be PCP are too formalized and inflexible. They argue that a looser structure is more conducive to getting people to creatively problem solve and "think outside the box." There is, however, no research demonstrating that one PCP approach is better than another, and in fact there is only limited research showing the efficacy of PCP processes in general (Claes, Van Hove, Vandevelde, van Loon, & Schalock, 2010; Holburn, 2002; Holburn, Jacobson, Schwartz, Flory, & Vietz, 2004; Robertson et al., 2007). Perhaps the value of PCP has more to do with the skills and commitment of planning team members than which particular process is used.

Although research findings supporting PCP processes may be limited, the logic underlying PCP processes would seem to be unassailable. As the late Yogi Berra said, "If you don't know where you are going, you might wind up someplace else" (New York Post, 2015, para. 10). PCP processes provide a means to identify desired life conditions, experiences, and opportunities, and such major decisions about life defy rigidly structured meetings that are quickly completed. Conversation 1 should identify discrepancies between "what is" and "what could be," as well as aspects of the student's life that are most important to maintain and to change. Thus, Conversation 1 requires the consideration and discussion of personal priorities. In the planning process shown in Figure 6.2, the most critical outcome of Conversation 1 is consensus among planning team members on what a good life for the person would entail, as well as a commitment to make the vision a reality.

Conversation 2—Assess Support Needs

Conversation 2 involves an assessment of support needs such as is completed through a supports needs assessments scale, although informal assessments of support needs (direct observations and anecdotal logs) can supplement the scale. A structured support needs assessment provides useful information to the planning team when developing actionable plans, and also assures that a person's support needs are comprehensively considered.

Descriptions and research findings on eight support needs assessment scales have been published since the early 2000s, but the extent and quality of information on the eight scales varies considerably. Descriptions and a short summary of research findings underlying each scale are provided next. Thompson and DeSpain (2016) provide a more detailed analysis of the technical evidence supporting each scale.

Care and Needs Scale (CANS)

This scale was developed in Australia for use with people with Traumatic Brain Injury. It is completed through a structured interview where information on 24 items is gathered. Each item is rated on a 1–8 scale (larger numbers indicate greater levels of support need). The results provide a profile of support needed in relation to the items. Criterion-related validity findings showed that CANS scores were correlated with two measures of functional outcome. In terms of construct validity, logistic regression analyses were used to investigate the extent to which the CANS distinguished people who were "independent" from people requiring some level of support. Statistically significant differences on the CANS scores were found among subgroups with different levels of support needs (Tate, 2004).

Checklist of Child Characteristics (CCC)

This scale was developed in the Netherlands for children with profound and multiple disabilities. A respondent who knows the child being assessed completes a checklist in regard to the type of support needed. A completed assessment provides a support profile that indicates the types of support necessary for education and care. The only research findings that are available reveal the scale's reliability (as measured by internal consistency alphas) was acceptable (Tadema, Vlaskamp, & Ruijssenaars, 2007).

I-CAN

This scale was created and field tested in Australia, and was designed to be used with people with intellectual disability and related developmental disabilities (but it can be used with other disability populations). It is completed through a structured interview that includes four Health and Well Being (HWB) domains and six Activities and Participation (A&P) domains. Items are rated for support according to both frequency (from 0 = never through 5 = constant support throughout the day) and level of support (from 0 = none through 5 = total physical assistance from one or two people). Information on health conditions and behaviors requiring support, changes in support needs, and preferences are also collected over the course of completing the scale. The results provide a profile of support needed across multiple support domains (Riches, Parmenter, Llewellyn, Hindmarsh, & Chan, 2009a, 2009b).

Research findings on the I-CAN show strong interrater and test-retest reliability on most of the subscales and good criterion-related validity with the Inventory for Client and Agency Planning (ICAP, an adaptive behavior scale; Riches et al., 2009a, 2009b). In terms of construct validity, correlations with Quality of Life Measures were mixed (rs ranged from 0.15 to 0.57) and stepwise multiple regression analyses showed I-CAN scores predicted 40% of daytime support hours and 27% of paid 24-hour support (Riches et al., 2009b). Additionally, positive correlations were found between a classification algorithm that was based on I-CAN scores and clinical judgment regarding the level of support a person needed (Arnold, Riches, & Stancliffe, 2014).

Need of Support and Service Questionnaire (NSSQ)

The NSSQ was designed for use with people with mental-health disorders requiring psychiatric services in Sweden, but its authors indicate that it could be used with any population. A structured interview is used to complete 33 items distributed across three areas: (1) socio-demographic information and present living situation, (2) need of support in activities of daily living, and (3) need of service provided by the public health and social service sector. A completed assessment provides a profile of support needs. Data were collected to evaluate the scale's reliability and criterion-related validity. Findings showed Kappas of 0.68 and 0.80 in regard to test-retest and interrater reliability respectively. Moderate to low correlations were found for sections of the NSSQ and a section of the Global Assessment of Functioning (GAF) scale and Social and Occupational Functioning Assessment Scale (SOFAS; Jansson, Wennstrom, & Wiesel, 2005).

North Carolina—Support Needs Assessment Profile (NC-SNAP)

This was the first support needs scale to appear in the professional literature. It was developed and field tested in North Carolina, and was designed for use with people with intellectual and developmental disabilities. The scale is very short compared to other support needs scales, with only 11 items, each of which is scored on a five-point scale in three support domains (Daily Living, Health Care, and Behavioral). The NC-SNAP can be scored using either interview or direct observation, and results categorize people into one of five support intensity levels. The NC-SNAP showed relatively good interrater reliability (r = 0.73), and in terms of construct validity, the NC-SNAP had higher correlations with support levels determined by jurisdictional staff than either the ICAP or the Developmental Disabilities Profile (DDP; Hennike, Myers, Realon, & Thompson, 2006).

Service Need Assessment Profile (SNAP)

The SNAP was developed and field tested in Australia, and was intended for use with "different disability types and levels of severity" (Harries, Guscia, Kirby, Nettelbeck, & Taplin, 2005, p. 393). It is completed through interview and includes 29 items that are divided across five domains. A completed assessment provides a profile of support needed in relation to the 29 items (Harries et al., 2005). Guscia, Harries, Kirby, & Nettelbeck (2006) reported test-retest reliability coefficients ranging from 0.86 to 0.97, and interrater coefficients ranged from 0.61 to 0.91 (depending on the disability population). In terms of criterion-related validity, the SNAP had strong correlations with the Supports Intensity Scale—Adult (SIS-A; $r = 0.79$) and ICAP ($r = 0.78$), and a somewhat weaker correlation with staff estimates of support needs ($r = 0.60$)

Supports Intensity Scales (Adult and Child)

There are two versions of the Supports Intensity Scale: the adult version (SIS-A; Thompson et al., 2015) normed on ages 16–64, and the child version (SIS-C; Thompson et al., 2016) normed on ages 5–16. Both versions were developed in the United States and field tested throughout North America, with the SIS-A originally published in 2004 and the SIS-C published in 2016. The SIS-A and SIS-C are the only support needs assessment tools that provide norm-referenced scores. The published findings regarding their psychometric properties far exceed those of any other support needs assessment scale.

Both instruments are completed through a structured interview, and it is required that at least two people who know the person being assessed very well be interviewed. The SIS-A and SIS-C were designed for use with people with intellectual and related developmental disabilities, although the scales have been used with other disability populations. The standardization samples on which the standard scores are based, however, have included only people with intellectual and related developmental disabilities, so the norm scores are not valid in regard to other disability groups. The standardized portions of both scales consist of items that reflect everyday life activities, and each is rated against three support dimensions (frequency, type, and daily support time). Each dimension is scored on a five-point scale

The SIS-A has three sections. Section 1 (32 items) provides measures of support needs due to exceptional medical conditions and challenging behavior, but data from this section does not provide standard scores. Section 2 is the normed-referenced portion of the scale. It includes 49 items that are spread across six subscales (Home Living, Community Living, Lifelong Learning, Employment, Health and Safety, and Social Activities). Section 3 concerns supports needed for protection and advocacy (P&A) activities. Section 3 was originally part of Section 2, but was removed from the norm-referenced section due to poor interrater-reliability findings from data that were collected during the original field test of the instrument. Subsequent investigations, however, have shown that the interrater reliability and other psychometric indicators are quite strong for the P&A scale. It is now apparent that the P&A scale provides every bit as valid a measure of support needs as do the subscales comprising Section 2, and it is likely that the P&A subscale will be reinserted into the standardized portion of the SIS-A in a future revision (Shogren et al., 2014).

The SIS-A has been translated into 13 languages and used in 23 countries across North and South America, Europe, Asia, and Australia. The psychometric indicators for the translated scales have been highly consistent, and in some cases, better than the original English version (see Bossaert et al., 2009; Buntinx et al., 2008; Cottini et al., 2008; Chou et al., 2013; Claes, Van Hove, van Loon, Vandevelde, & Schalock, 2009; Lamoureux-Hebert & Morin, 2009; Morin & Cobigo, 2009; Ortiz, Rio, Rodriguez, & Robaina, 2010; Verdugo et al., 2010).

The SIS-C (Thompson et al., 2016) has been developed more recently, but several articles on its psychometric properties have already been published or accepted for publication (Seo et al., 2015;

Shogren et al., 2015; Shogren et al., in press; Thompson et al., 2014; Thompson et al., 2016). In contrast to the SIS-A, the SIS-C has only two sections. Section 1 does not produce standard scores, but provides measures of support needs associated with exceptional medical (19 items) and behavioral (14 items) needs. Section 2 is comprised of 61 items and is divided into seven subscales (Home Life, Community and Neighborhood, School Participation, School Learning, Health and Safety, Social, and Advocacy Activities) that produce norm-referenced, standard scores for each subscale (support needs profile) as well as a composite score (the Support Needs Index, or SNI score). The standard scores indicate the relative intensity of a child's support needs in relation to a representative sample of children with intellectual or developmental disabilities of the same age (Thompson et al., 2016).

Research findings from the SIS-A and SIS-C show that both scales have strong reliability and validity (Thompson et al., 2015; Thompson et al., 2016). Additionally, factor analyses studies have confirmed the subscale structure of both scales (Thompson et al., 2015; Viriyangkura, 2014) and structural equation modeling procedures have confirmed score comparability across the two assessments (Seo et al., 2015).

Conversation 3—Develop an Individualized Support Plan (ISP)

Conversation 3 is the plan of action. Here is where information from Conversation 1 (the unified vision for the person's life) and Conversation 2 (an accurate and thorough understanding of the person's needs for support) are considered, and an "optimistically realistic" actionable plan is created and launched. Settings and activities in which the person will be involved during a typical week are specified, environmental modifications and activity accommodations are thought through, and personalized supports are unambiguously identified. Additionally, it is critical to explicitly identify people who are responsible for arranging supports and to specify target dates for implementation. A vague plan where people are not accountable for following through on commitments is no better (and perhaps worse) than no plan at all. As was alluded to earlier, developing and carrying out support plans is difficult work and there should be no illusions regarding the commitment of time and energy that is required.

Planning team members should strive for "optimistically realistic" plans that address a person's key priorities and specify actions that can logically lead to desired outcomes. In the professional literature in the field of intellectual and developmental disabilities there is little guidance in terms of determining parameters for providing support. Although slogans such as "do whatever it takes" may be a good way to encourage planning teams to guard against a path of least resistance and settle for unimpressive outcomes, the reality of a world with finite resources is that that priorities need to be established and choices need to be made. If everything is a priority, then by definition nothing is a priority. The ISP should be an ambitious, but workable, plan for action that is driven by a manageable number of priorities.

Conversation 4—Implement and Monitor the ISP

The arrows in Figure 6.2 go back and forth between Conversations 3 and 4. This is to acknowledge that ISPs may not proceed exactly as intended. Monitoring implementation is critically important because there will likely be unforeseen challenges that need to be addressed, and supports will need to be adjusted over time. Modifying plans in response to new information is part and parcel of a good support system, and planning team members must accept that change is inevitable. Hopefully it is the rare case where an initial plan proves to be widely off-base, but even if that happens there is no shame in trying something ambitious and having it not work out. There is shame, however, in not making adjustments to a support plan that is clearly not meeting a person's needs.

One important aspect of monitoring involves holding team members accountable for commitments that are made. Did people follow through with their portion of the plan? If not, why? Was it due to lack of effort or changing circumstances, or was the plan simply not as workable as people thought it would be? Time spent on planning is wasted if people are content to make promises they do not intend, or do not know how, to keep. The planning process pictured in Figure 6.2 will not work unless there is as strong a commitment to monitoring the implementation of the plan as there was in developing it in Conversation 3.

Another aspect of monitoring involves judging the suitability of the intensity of supports that have been put into place. Attempting to arrange a system of support so that a person is not "undersupported" or "oversupported" is a challenge with which many planning teams struggle. On one hand, one may want to err on the side of providing "too much support" because people with intellectual disability are a vulnerable population. On the other hand, like most others, people with intellectual disability tend to want supports that are as unobtrusive as possible.

The professional literature associated with the field of "college student development" can provide guidance in regard to evaluating if people are under- or oversupported. In his classic "Theory of Challenge and Support" Sanford (1962) argued that college students thrive when they experience an appropriate balance of support and challenge. He identified four situations: (a) situations where students experience *too much challenge* and *too little support* will likely lead to feelings of high anxiety, defensiveness, and discouragement; (b) conversely, situations where students experience *too little challenge* and *too much support* are also not ideal, as they will feel bored with their education, have little sense of urgency to learn and excel, and will stagnate; (c) receiving *too little support* and *too little challenge* is also to be avoided, as students in this situation are prone to disengage from their activities as they see little point in making an effort to stretch themselves; but, finally (d) the desirable condition is for students to be *highly challenged* as well as *highly supported*, as these students tend to be the most ambitious, most engaged, and most stimulated by their education, and they also show the maximal amount of growth.

Although Sanford was concerned with first-semester college freshmen and the support he was referring to was focused on academic supports on a college campus, the prospect of monitoring the reactions of students with intellectual disability as a means to gaining insight into the alignment of their support needs and the supports they receive is relevant to the field of intellectual and developmental disabilities. On one hand, when people show evidence of being stimulated by their activities and excited about their opportunities, it may be a good indication that their supports are well aligned with their support needs. On the other hand, students who are highly anxious may not be getting enough support. Conversely, those who tend to be habitually bored and apathetic may be oversupported. For the purpose of this chapter, the critical point is that monitoring should be more than just determining if people followed through with their responsibilities for the ISP. Monitoring should include efforts to evaluate the extent to which the intensity of support that students receive is aligned with the intensity of their needs.

Conversation 5—Evaluation

The last conversation is an evaluation of the continued relevance of supports that are being provided through the lens of personal outcomes. By evaluating a student's general happiness, satisfaction, and the extent to which the students finds their life conditions and experiences to be meaningful, insight can be obtained regarding the usefulness of the supports that are being provided through the ISP. This is not an evaluation of the implementation of the plan or the suitability of specific supports. Rather, the focus of Conversation 5 is on whether or not the support plan continues to be relevant to a student's desired life experiences and needs. People's preferences and support needs can and do change over time, and there are some supports that may be great at one point in time but may not be needed or wanted at another. For children, adolescents, and young adults it can be safely assumed that their interests and goals will change in important ways within a relatively short time span; a 10 year old's interests are quite different from a 13 year old's; a 13 year old's are very different from those of someone who is 16, and so on. However, adults can also want different things at different times of life, and Conversation 5 is intended to prevent people from falling into too much of a rut where opportunities to explore new personal horizons are limited.

Therefore, the function of Conversation 5 is to determine whether a person's life is going the way he or she wants, and what aspects, if any, need to be considered for major changes. Quality of Life measures Sanford (1962) such as the Personal Outcomes Scale (POS; van Loon, Van Hove, Schalock, & Claes, 2008) are useful to initiate Conversation 5, and should be scheduled periodically (e.g., once every couple years) as a means to assess how a person feels about how his or her life is going, as well as the impressions of others who know the person well. The POS, for instance, is structured to allow for comparisons between the impressions of a person and the impressions of important people in his or her life. Results from Conversation 5 may or may not prompt a return to Conversations 1 and 2 (i.e., initiating a new PCP process and reassessing support needs). It would seem wise, however, to initiate a new PCP process and complete a comprehensive assessment of support needs at least once every five years, even in cases where Conversation 5 suggests that people are quite satisfied with their life conditions, experiences, and how their needs for support are addressed.

Case Study in Support Needs Assessment and Planning

The final section of this chapter will present a case study that illustrates the supports needs assessment and planning process shown in Figure 6.2. Although this case study is fictional, it is based loosely on people we have known and our experiences with them.

Angie Wadkins

Background

Angie is a 16-year-old sophomore at Eisenhower High School. She has a diagnosis of intellectual disability and cerebral palsy. She has received physical therapy services throughout her life and under typical conditions she walks with good strength, balance, and coordination and moves about her environment freely. Her gait, however, remains affected by cerebral palsy (she walks somewhat bent-kneed and on her toes) and she must take extra care when the weather is poor (e.g., sidewalks are icy). She received much of her education in a special education classroom during her early school years, but has been included mostly in general education classes since the fourth grade.

Currently, she takes five courses at her high school that are attended by students in the general education program during her school day, has a free "study hall" period where she can either go to the school library or attend a supervised study hall, a lunch period, and a "resource period" where she meets 1:1 with a special education teacher who is also her Individualized Education Program (IEP) case manager. The activities during the 1:1 resource period vary from day to day. There are days when she receives counseling, guidance, and instruction in terms of self-determination and her long-term goals, plans, and support needs (described later); days when she is provided direct assistance on studying for an upcoming test; days when she receives direct assistance on completing a course assignment; and still other days when the focus is on organizing her materials and thoughtfully planning for events and assignments that are on the horizon.

Angie has far exceeded the academic achievement expectations that professionals had communicated to her family when she first entered an early childhood special education program as a 3 year old. Although she has made steady academic progress throughout her school career, her proficiency in academic skills lags behind the vast majority of her typically functioning peers in important ways. Currently, reading material written above an eighth-grade reading level is difficult for her to comprehend. Her writing is at a much lower level than her reading. Her spoken language, however, is a relative strength. She has the ability to complete computation problems (i.e., addition, subtraction, multiplication, division), but almost always uses a calculator for anything other than the most basic operations. Although she has difficulty with mental arithmetic, she has demonstrated a relatively strong understanding of certain higher order mathematic concepts such as estimation and ratio/proportion. Her teachers consistently report that she pays attention in class and understands the main ideas expressed during class presentations and class discussions. Angie has earn passing grades so far in high school, but the curriculum gets increasingly demanding every year and state law requires that she achieve a certain score on her state's standardized "exit test" in order to receive a diploma. Angie's long-term memory and retention of information is good.

Angie's family has been a tremendous source of support for her, and she has a very close relationship with her parents and siblings (she is the youngest child). She is friendly with peers and adults. Peers view her as nonthreatening, and except for the occasional bully, she and most of her peers get along with one another quite well. Compared to many teenagers, Angie is not as concerned with peer attention and popularity, and she is not easily influenced by peer pressure and or vulnerable to peer manipulation. Most peers and adults would state that Angie can be quite charming as she projects a genuineness that people appreciate and she laughs with others easily. However, there is one problem behavior that suggests a certain degree of social immaturity: She cries rather easily over small matters, and she tends to continue crying as long as there are people are around her who are willing to express sympathy.

Angie's IEP case manager initiated the support needs assessment and planning process shown in Figure 6.2. Here is a summary of how the five conversations were approached and what was learned.

Conversation 1—Identify Desired Life Experiences and Personal Outcomes

At the beginning of the school year, the IEP case manager (special education teacher) discussed with Angie and her parents the aims of PCP. Neither Angie nor her parents were keen on adhering to a published PCP process such as Planning Alternative Tomorrows with Hope (PATH) and MAPS (see Chapter 11 for a definition; O'Brien et al., 2010) or the Picture Method (Holburn et al., 2007); they didn't like the idea of group meetings/discussions and using flip charts to document conversations and decisions. They were, however, excited about the prospect of the case manager facilitating Angie's exploration of future goals and learning skills leading to self-determination over the course of several months by using some of the 1:1 meeting time that was built into Angie's school schedule. All were in strong agreement that future goals and plans would be most meaningful if Angie felt an ownership of them.

Angie's IEP case manager not only borrowed materials and ideas from several published resources (e.g., *Who's Future is it Anyway? A Student Directed Transition Planning Process* by Wehmeyer et al., 2004), but she and Angie came up with their own ideas as well. The result was a book that included text and pictures, which documented her goals for the remaining years of high school as well as after graduation, her thoughts on her relative strengths, areas she needed to improve, and her support needs. Also included were the thoughts of others, and well as critical milestones that she hoped to achieve along the way. The title of the book was *Dr. Who Takes Angie into the Future* (Angie is a *Dr. Who* fan and enjoyed using the *Dr. Who* imagery.)

Five goals were identified in the process of creating the book. The first three were related to her education and career plans: (1) graduate from high school, (2) attend a local community college in the Office Assistant preparation program, and upon completion perhaps pursue the more demanding Administrative Assistant training program where she could earn an Associates degree, and (3) secure employment as an office assistant in a company where there were opportunities for job security and advancement. The other two goals were related to her home and social life. She wanted to (4) continue to live at home for the foreseeable future, but someday wanted her own apartment or house and

(5) keep in contact and have fun with high school friends after graduation, as well as make new friends (although discussing and setting social goals were not a big priority for her). Upon completing her book, Angie shared it with family members, as well as with friends and teachers whom she trusted and with whom she had a strong relationship.

Conversation 2—Assess Support Needs

This conversation was simultaneous with Conversation 1 and proved to be emotionally difficult and stressful at certain times. Whereas Angie eagerly embraced envisioning future plans and setting goals during Conversation 1, she was not initially comfortable exploring her support needs as she felt that such discussions highlighted her weaknesses and areas of life where she did not measure up to her peers. The IEP case manager was sensitive to Angie's feelings and took care to respect how far Angie was willing to go in terms of taking an honest look at her support needs on any given day. Despite the challenges, however, the case manager, Angie's parents, and Angie all agreed that that thoughtfully assessing and discussing support needs not only enabled others to better understand Angie, but more importantly also helped her to achieve a much better understanding of herself. The case manager had too much respect for Angie to superficially gloss over Angie's needs for extra supports.

The SIS-A was used to measure support needs, since Angie was 16 and focused on planning for her future postschool. The case manager first interviewed Angie as the respondent, and then Angie served as the SIS-A interviewer and interviewed her parents and older sister (whom she adores) as respondents. The teacher and Angie reviewed the results from these two interviews, and the two came to consensus on the scoring: On some items, Angie acknowledged that she needed more support than she had initially identified as the interview respondent. On other items, however, Angie stuck to her guns and concluded that her parents and sister were overestimating the assistance she needed.

In addition to increasing Angie's overall self-awareness about her needs for extra support that most other people do not need, Angie and her case manager chose to closely investigate academic supports needed in high school and community college. Angie and her case manager took a morning field trip away from high school to visit the community college and meet with staff at the college's Disability Services Office. They specifically discussed Angie's support needs in relation to supports the Disability Services Office could provide, and clarified what Angie would need to do to assure she was provided the supports she needed. Other strategies for success that Angie may wish to consider were also discussed. For example, Angie learned that she did not have to be a full-time student, and that many students found taking a somewhat lighter load was the best way for them to be successful in the Office Assistant program.

Conversation 3—Develop an Individualized Support Plan (ISP)

Angie did not need a separate ISP document, because as a student covered under the Individual with Disabilities Education Act (IDEA), Angie was entitled to an IEP as well as an Individualized Transition Plan (ITP). In Angie's *Dr. Who Takes Angie into the Future* book, supports were identified in common sense, user-friendly language, and this information was transferred into the more formal planning documents used by the school district. Here are supports that were identified (some of which had been in place prior to initiating the planning process and some which had not):

1. Peer tutoring in high school for certain assignments completed in the classroom (e.g., labs). A peer will work with Angie on in-class assignments to assure all aspects of the assignments are completed in a timely fashion and that Angie has full access to the learning opportunities associated with each assignment. The IEP case manager and the general education teachers will share responsibility for selecting the peer tutors (there will be a different one for each class), provide

tutors with some brief training and direction on working with Angie, and monitor their work (intervening when needed).

2. A calendar application (app) will be purchased for Angie's smart phone. The application is designed specifically for students who have difficulty keeping track of their assignments and responsibilities; it is not only more comprehensive, but more user-friendly than the calendar apps that come embedded in smart phones. The case manager will help Angie install the special app, teach her how to use it, and monitor Angie's use of it. The intent is for Angie to use the app as an organizational and memory aid.

3. Adapt assigned reading by highlighting key information to make reading assignments more accessible. Each content area teacher will work with the case manager to use a yellow highlighter to indicate the parts of reading assignments that are crucial for her to focus on, and conversely, which parts of the assigned reading should be ignored unless she is particularly motivated or has extra time to read.

4. Create different examination questions (and/or select a subset) for classroom tests that reflect the individualized learning expectations for Angie (which are different from those for others in the class). Content teachers will create and prepare Angie's tests, but the case manager will be available for consultation and problem solving as needed.

5. For any essay test, allow Angie to answer orally. Content teachers will conduct the examinations outside of classroom hours, possibly during Angie's free "study hall" period, her resource period, her lunch period, or just before or after school. The case manager will assist in making arrangements for Angie to take oral tests.

6. Provide Angie with tutoring, which involves more explicit instruction than is offered in the classroom, during her resource period. The case manager will provide this instruction, but the general education teachers will be available for consultation especially in regard to content.

7. Angie will work with the case manager and the school work coordinator to identify possible summer jobs and/or work experiences that involve office work. The goal is for Angie to gain practical experience as an office worker as well as to have a basis for determining if working in an office continues to be work that is aligned with her interests.

8. Angie and the case manager will identify "college visit" days for her junior and senior year so that she can more fully explore opportunities at the community college as well as to establish dialogue with the Disability Services Office to determine the extent to which supports she uses in high school might be arranged or modified at the community college. Lists of questions will be developed in advance of the visits.

9. Angie and the case manager will work with the high school guidance counselor to identify and arrange reasonable accommodations for the state's standardized exit test on which a passing score is needed for graduation. The case manager will support Angie in preparing for the test.

Conversation 4—Implementing and Monitoring the Plan

To monitor implementation, the IEP case manager and Angie will review the support plan during the first week of every month, and Angie will report conclusions from the review to her parents. The following questions will guide the monitoring:

1. Did people do what they said they would do in relation to the timeline of tasks that was documented in the *Dr. Who Takes Angie into the Future* book? Why or why not? Do any of the tasks or timelines need to be changed?

2. Are the supports that Angie receives working as intended? Are there any supports that need to be changed because she no longer needs them, or (conversely) that are not useful/powerful enough to enable her to reach her goals? Does Angie need any additional or new supports?

Conversation 5—Evaluation

Conversation 5 will focus on whether Angie's preferences and support needs have changed in important ways since the support plan was developed. This conversation will also occur once per month in a very straightforward way. Angie will be asked to evaluate her plans and indicate whether the plans continue to be relevant to her future goals and needs. If Angie communicates reservations about the plans for several months in a row, it would serve as a trigger to revisit Conversations 1 and 2 in earnest to determine if a different direction is warranted. Conversation 5 will be more focused after Angie completes some work experiences and future visits to the community college. The case manager will encourage Angie to evaluate whether office work continues to be something that she feels that she would enjoy and would be successful at, and if the course of study at the community college is still of interest to her.

Should alternative ideas emerge, they will need to be considered thoughtfully and in light of certain realities (e.g., deciding not trying to graduate from high school is not an option; all jobs have some downsides; paid work is not always going to be enjoyable). Obviously, thoughtfully developed plans such as the one developed with Angie should not be abandoned abruptly without careful thought, but the fact that Angie is still only 16 years old needs to be recognized. The interests of young adults do change, and no high school student should feel as if he or she is locked into a plan that was developed at an earlier time.

Conclusion

"Knowledge Through Measurement" was a motto that the physicist Heike Onnes placed over each of his laboratory doors to remind students that a key to understanding something was to be able to measure it (APS, 2015). Modern life would be quite different if there were no meaningful measures of important concepts in the physical world. For instance, if there were no reliable ways to measure temperature, then people would need to rely on vague concepts such as hot, cold, lukewarm, and so on. The ability to precisely determine how relatively hot or cold something is has been essential to advances in fields as diverse as transportation, health care, and food preparation.

Although the physical sciences are different from the social sciences in important ways, the same logic is applicable in terms of advancing research and practice in an applied field. The concept of support needs is increasingly recognized as perhaps the most important construct in the field of intellectual and developmental disabilities (see Schalock et al., 2010), and accurately measuring it is essential to moving the field forward. Although much progress has been made in developing scales to assess people's support needs during the past 15 years, support needs assessment and measurement are still in their infancy, particularly for children and youth in the school context. Hopefully, procedures and measures will become increasingly advanced in the coming years. It is not inconceivable that more sophisticated support needs assessment tools could eventually be suitable for purposes of diagnosis and classification in order to more fully align professional practices with a social-ecological understanding of people with disabilities.

Assessing and measuring support needs, however, ultimately makes sense only if information is produced that is useful in identifying, planning, and arranging personalized supports that result in richer life experiences and expanded opportunities for students with disabilities. In this chapter we presented a systematic planning process that can be used to develop "optimistically realistic," unambiguous plans of action. The case study of Angie Wadkins illustrates how such a process could work with a young woman who is preparing for the transition from school to adult life.

References

American Association on Intellectual and Developmental Disabilities (AAIDD; 2013). International SIS Use. Retrieved from http://aaidd.org/sis/international#.Vmm87cpUyXQ

American Physical Society (APS; 2015). APS News—This month in Physics History, April 1911: Onnes begins work on superconductivity. Retrieved from https://www.aps.org/publications/apsnews/200704/history.cfm

Arnold, S. R. C., Riches, V. C., & Stancliffe, R. J. (2014). I-CAN: The classification and prediction of support needs. *Journal of Applied Research in Intellectual Disabilities, 27*, 97–111. doi: 10.1111/jar.12055

Bondy, A. S., & Frost, L. A. (1993). Mands across the water: A report on the application of the picture-exchange communication system in Peru. *The Behavior Analyst, 16*, 123–128.

Bondy, A. S., & Frost, L. A. (1994). The picture exchange communication system. *Focus on Autistic Behavior, 9*, 1–9.

Bossaert, G., Kuppens, S., Buntinx W., Molleman, C., Van den Abeele, A., & Moes, B. (2009). Usefulness of the Supports Intensity Scale (SIS) for persons with other than intellectual disabilities. *Research in Developmental Disabilities, 30*, 1306–1316.

Brickey, M.P., Campbell, K. M., & Browning, L. J. (1985). A five year follow-up of sheltered workshop employees placed in competitive jobs. *Mental Retardation, 23*, 67–73.

Buntinx, W., Croce, L., Ekstein, Y., Giné, C., Holmes, S., Lamoureux-Hébert M. . . . Verdugo, M. A. (2008). International implementation of the Supports Intensity Scale. In R. L. Schalock, J. R. Thompson, & M. J. Tassé (Eds.), *AAIDD SIS White Paper Series* (pp. 1–20). Washington, DC: American Association on Intellectual and Developmental Disabilities.

Carter, E. W., Sisco, L. G., Chung Y., & Stanton-Chapman, T. L. (2010). Peer interactions of students with intellectual disabilities and/or autism: A map of the intervention literature. *Research and Practice for Persons with Severe Disabilities, 35*, 63–79.

Chou, Y. C., Lee, Y. C., & Chang, S. C. (2013). Evaluating the Supports Intensity Scale as a potential assessment instrument for resource allocation for persons with intellectual disability. *Research in Developmental Disabilities: A Multidisciplinary Journal, 34*, 2056–2063.

Cimera, R. E. (2011). Does being in sheltered workshops improve the employment outcomes of supported employees with intellectual disabilities? *Journal of Vocational Rehabilitation, 25*, 21–27. doi: 10.3233/JVR-2011-0550

Claes, C., Van Hove, G., Vandevelde, S., van Loon, J., & Schalock, R. L. (2010). Person-centered planning: Analysis of research and effectiveness. *Intellectual and Developmental Disabilities, 48*(6), 432–453.

Claes, C., Van Hove, G., van Loon, J., Vandevelde, S., & Schalock, R. L. (2009). Evaluating the inter-respondent (consumer vs. staff) reliability and construct validity (SIS vs. Vineland) of the Supports Intensity Scale on a Dutch sample. *Journal of Intellectual Disability Research, 53*, 329–338. doi: 10.1111/j.1365-2788.2008.01149.x

Cottini, L., Fedeli, D., Leoni, M., & Croce, L. (2008). *SIS Supports Intensity Scale: Assessment the intensity of need support, handbook.* Brescia: Vannini Editore.

Douglas, K. H., Ayres, K. M., & Langone, J. (2015). Comparing self-management strategies delivered via an iPhone to promote grocery shopping and literacy. *Education and Training in Autism and Developmental Disabilities, 20*, 446–465.

Gray, C. (2000). *The new social storybook* (Illustrated ed.). Arlington, TX: Future Horizons, Inc.

Guscia, R., Harries, J., Kirby, N., & Nettelbeck, T. (2006). Rater bias and the measurement of support needs. *Journal of Intellectual & Developmental Disability, 31*, 156–160. doi: 10.1080/13668250600876459

Harries, J., Guscia, R., Kirby, N., Nettelbeck, T., & Taplin, J. (2005). Support needs and adaptive behaviors. *American Journal on Mental Retardation, 110*(5), 393–404.

Hennike, J. M., Myers, A. M., Realon, R. E., & Thompson, T. J. (2006). Development and validation of a needs-assessment instrument for persons with developmental disabilities. *Journal of Developmental and Physical Disabilities, 18*, 201–217. doi: 10.1007/s10882-006-9012-x

Holburn, S. (2002). How science can evaluate and enhance person-centered planning. *Research and Practice for Persons with Severe Disabilities, 27*, 250–260.

Holburn, S., Gordon, A., & Vietze, P. M. (2007). *Person-centered planning made easy: The PICTURE method.* Baltimore, MD: Paul H. Brookes.

Holburn, S., Jacobson, J. W., Schwartz, A. A., Flory, M. J., & Vietz, P. M. (2004). The Willowbrook futures project: A longitudinal analysis of person-centered planning. *American Journal on Mental Retardation, 109*, 63–76.

Horn, E. & Banerge, R. (2009). Understanding curriculum modifications and embedded learning opportunities in the context of supporting all children's success. *Language, Speech, and Hearing Services in Schools, 40*, 406–415. doi: 0161–1461/09/4004–0406

Horner, R. H., McDonnell, J. J., & Bellamy, G. T. (1986). Teaching generalized skills: General case instruction in simulation and community settings. In R. H. Horner, L. H. Meyer, & H. D. Fredericks (Eds.), *Education of Learners with Severe Handicaps: Exemplary Service Strategies* (pp. 289–314). Baltimore, MD: Brookes.

Jansson, L., Wennstrom, E., & Wiesel, F. A. (2005). The need of support and service questionnaire (NSSQ): A brief scale to assess needs in clients with long-term mental disabilities. *Nordic Journal of Psychiatry, 59*, 465–472. doi: 10.1080/08039480500360716

Kober, R. (Ed.) (2011). *Enhancing the quality of life of people with intellectual disabilities.* New York: Springer.

Lamoureux-Hebert, M., & Morin, D. (2009). Translation and cultural adaptation of the Supports Intensity Scale in French. *American Journal on Developmental Disability, 114*, 61–66. doi: 10.1352/2009.114.

Luckasson, R., Coulter, D., Polloway, E., Reiss, S., Schalock, R., Snell, M. . . . Stark, J. A. (1992). *Mental retardation: Definition, classification and systems of supports* (10th ed.). Washington, DC: American Association on Mental Retardation.

Luckasson, R., Borthwick-Duffy, S., Buntinx, W., Coulter, D., Craig, E., Reeve, A., . . . Tassé, M. (2002). *Mental retardation: Definition, classification, and systems of supports* (10th ed.). Washington, DC: American Association on Mental Retardation.

Marino, M. T., Gotch, C., Israel, M., Vaquez, E., Basham, J. D., & Becht, K. (2014). UDL in the middle school science classroom: Can video game and alternative text heighten engagement and learning for students with learning disabilities? *Learning Disability Quarterly, 37,* 87–99. doi: 10.1177/0731948713503963

Morin, D., & Cobigo, V. (2009). Reliability of the Supports Intensity Scale (French version). *Intellectual and Developmental Disabilities, 47,* 24–30.

New York Post. (2015). 35 of Yogi Berra's Most Memorable Quotes. Retrieved from http://nypost.com/2015/09/23/35-of-yogi-berras-most-memorable-quotes/

O'Brien, C. L., O'Brien, J., & Mount, B. (1997). Person-centered planning has arrived . . . or has it? *Mental Retardation, 35,* 480–484.

O'Brien, J., Pearpoint, J., & Kahn, L. (2010). *The PATH and MAPS handbook: Person-centered ways to build community.* Toronto, Canada: Inclusion Press.

Ortiz, M. C., Rio, C. J., Rodriguez, M., & Robaina, N. (2010). Applicability of the Spanish version of the Supports Intensity Scale (SIS) in the Mexican population with severe mental illness. *Revista Latino-Americana de Enfermagaem, 18,* 975–982.

Osborne, A. G., & Russo, C. J. (2014). *Special education and the law: A guide for practitioners.* Thousand Oaks, CA: Corwin Press.

Riches, V. C., Parmenter, T. R., Llewellyn, G., Hindmarsh, G., & Chan, J. (2009a). I-CAN: A new instrument to classify support needs for people with disability: Part I. *Journal of Applied Research in Intellectual Disabilities, 22,* 326–339. doi: 10.1111/j.1468–3148.2008.00466.x

Riches, V. C., Parmenter, T. R., Llewellyn, G., Hindmarsh, G., & Chan, J. (2009b). The reliability, validity and practical utility of measuring supports using the I-CAN instrument: Part II. *Journal of Applied Research in Intellectual Disabilities, 22,* 340–353. doi: 10.1111/j.1468–3148.2008.00467.x

Robertson, J., Emerson, E., Hatton, C., Elliott, J., McIntosh, B., Swift, P., . . . Joyce, T. (2007). Person-centered planning: Factors associated with successful outcomes for people with intellectual disabilities. *Journal of Intellectual Disability Research, 51,* 232–243. doi: 10.1111/j.1365–2788.2006.00864.x

Sanford, N. (1962). Developmental status of the entering freshman. In N. Sanford (Ed.), *The American College: A Psychological and Social Interpretation of the Higher Learning* (pp. 253–282). New York: Wiley.

Schalock, R. L., Borthwick-Duffy, S., Bradley, V. J., Buntinx, W. H. E., Coulter, D. L., Craig, E. M., . . . & Yeager, M. H. (2010). *Intellectual disability: Definition, classification, and systems of supports* (11th ed.). Washington, DC: American Association on Intellectual and Developmental Disabilities.

Scott, R., Collins, B., Knight, V., & Kleinert, H. (2013). Teaching adults with moderate intellectual disabilities ATM use via the iPod. *Education and Training in Autism and Other Developmental Disabilities, 48,* 190–199.

Seo, H., Shogren, K. A., Wehmeyer, M. L., Hughes, C., Thompson, J. R., Little, T. D., & Palmer, S. P. (2015). Exploring shared measurement properties and score comparability between two version of the Supports Intensity Scale. *Career Development and Transition for Exceptional Individuals, 38*(3), 1–11. doi: 10.1177/2165143415583499

Shogren, K. A., Seo, H., Wehmeyer, M. L., Thompson, J. R., Hughes, C., Little, T. D., & Palmer, S. B. (2015). Support needs of children with intellectual and developmental disabilities: Age-related implications for assessment. *Psychology in the Schools, 52,* 874–891. doi: 10.1002/pits.21863

Shogren, K. A., Thompson, J. R., Wehmeyer, M., Chapman, T., Tassé, M. J., & McLaughlin, C. A. (2014). Reliability and validity of the supplemental protection and advocacy scale of the Supports Intensity Scale. *Inclusion, 2,* 100–109, doi: 10.1352/2326–6988-2.2.125

Shogren, K. A., Wehmeyer, M. L., Seo., H., Thompson, J. R., Schalock, R. L., Hughes, C., . . . Palmer, S. B. (in press). Examining the reliability and validity of the Supports Intensity Scale—Children's version in children with autism and intellectual disability. *Focus on Autism and Other Developmental Disabilities.* doi: 10.1177/1088357615625060

Smull, M. W., & Sanderson, H. (2009). *Essential lifestyle planning for everyone.* Annapolis, MD: The Learning Community.

Snell, M. E., Brady, N., McLean, L., Ogletree, B. T., Siegel, E., Sylvester, L., . . . Sevcik, R. (2010). Twenty years of communication intervention research with individuals who have severe intellectual and developmental disabilities. *American Journal on Intellectual and Developmental Disabilities, 115,* 364–380.

Snell, M. E., & Brown, F. (Eds.) (2011). *Instruction for students with severe disabilities.* Upper Saddle River, NJ: Merrill/Prentice-Hall.

Stoner, J. B., Beck, A. R., Bock, S. J., Kosuwan, K., Hickey, K., & Thompson, J. R. (2006). The effectiveness of the picture exchange communication system with nonspeaking adults. *Remedial and Special Education, 27,* 154–165.

Tadema, A. C., Vlaskamp, C., & Ruijssenaars, W. (2007). The validity of support profiles for children with profound multiple learning difficulties. *European Journal of Special Needs Education, 22,* 147–160. doi: 10.1080/08856250701269440

Tate, R. L. (2004). Assessing support needs for people with traumatic brain injury: The care and needs scale (CANS). *Brain Injury, 18,* 445–460. doi: 10.1080/02699050310001641183

Test, D. W., Richter, S., Knight, V., & Spooner, F. (2011). A comprehensive review and meta-analysis of the social stories literature. *Focus on Autism and Other Developmental Disabilities, 26,* 49–62.

Thompson, J. R., Bryant, B. B., Schalock, R. L., Shogren, K. A., Tassé, M. J., Wehmeyer, M. L., . . . Rotholz, D. A. (2015). *Supports Intensity Scale—Adult version user's manual.* Washington, DC: American Association on Intellectual and Developmental Disabilities.

Thompson, J. R., & DeSpain, S. N. (2016). Community support needs. In N. N. Singh (Ed.), *Handbook of Evidence-based Practices in Intellectual and Developmental Disabilities* (pp. 137–168). New York: Springer.

Thompson, J. R., Hughes, C., Schalock, R. L., Silverman, W., Tassé, M. J., Bryant. B., . . . Campbell, E. M. (2002). Integrating supports in assessment and planning. *Mental Retardation, 40,* 390–405. doi: 10.1352/0047–6765(2002)040

Thompson, J. R., Wehmeyer, M. L., Hughes, C., Shogren, K. A., Little, T. D., Copeland, S. R., . . . Tassé, M. J. (2016). *Supports Intensity Scale—Children's version user's manual.* Washington, DC: American Association on Intellectual and Developmental Disabilities.

Thompson, J. R., Wehmeyer, M. L., Hughes, C., Shogren, K. A., Palmer, S. B., & Seo, H. (2014). The Supports Intensity Scale—children's version. *Inclusion, 2,* 140–149. doi: 10.1352/2326–6988–2.2.140

United States Department of Justice Civil Rights Division. (2015). Information and Technical Assistance on the Americans with Disabilities Act. Retrieved from http://www.ada.gov/

van Loon, J., Van Hove, G., Schalock, R. L., & Claes, C. (2008). *Personal outcomes scale: A scale to assess an individual's quality of life.* Middleburg, The Netherlands, Stichting Arduin and Gent, Belgium: University of Gent.

Verdugo, M., Arias, B., Ibanez, A., & Schalock, R. L. (2010). Adaptation and psychometric properties of the Spanish version of the Supports Intensity Scale (SIS). *American Association on Intellectual and Developmental Disabilities, 115,* 496–503. doi: 10.135/1944–7558–115.6.496

Viriyangkura, Y. (2014). Understanding the support needs of people with intellectual and related disabilities through cluster analysis and factor analysis of statewide data (Doctoral dissertation). Retrieved from ISU ReD: Research and eData http://ir.library.illinoisstate.edu/cgi/viewcontent.cgi?article=1074&context=etd

Watson, S. M. R., Gable, R., & Greenwood, C. R. (2011). Combining ecobehavioral assessment, functional assessment, and response to intervention to promote more effective classroom instruction. *Remedial and Special Education, 32,* 334–344. doi: 10.1177/0741932510362219

Wehmeyer, M. L., & Agran, M. (Eds.) (2005). *Mental retardation and intellectual disabilities: Teaching students using innovative and research-based strategies.* Washington, DC: American Association on Mental Retardation.

Wehmeyer, M. L., Lawrence, M., Kelchner, K., Palmer, S. B., Garner, N., & Soukup, J. (2004). *Who's future is it anyway? A student-directed transition planning process.* Lawrence, KS: Beach Center on Disability and Kansas University Center on Developmental Disabilities.

Wehmeyer, M. L., Palmer, S. B., Smith, S. J., Parent. W., Davies, D. K., & Stock S. (2006). Technology use by people with intellectual and developmental disabilities to support employment activities: A single-subject design meta analysis. *Journal of Vocational Rehabilitation, 24,* 81–85.

Wells, J. C., & Sheehey, P. H. (2012). Person-centered planning: Strategies to encourage participation and facilitate communication. *Teaching Exceptional Children, 44*(3), 32–39.

Westling, D. L., & Floyd, J. (1990). Generalization of community skills: How much training is necessary? *Journal of Special Education, 23,* 386–406.

World Health Organization. (2001). *The international classification of functioning, disability and health.* Geneva, Switzerland: Author.

7

Alternate Assessment

Meagan Karvonen, Shawnee Wakeman, Neal Kingston

Alternate assessment is one of the most rapidly evolving elements of the educational system for students with significant cognitive disabilities,[1] which include students with intellectual disability, in the United States. Originally conceived as a means to include all students in large-scale assessments for accountability, alternate assessments have changed considerably since their inception around 1990. These changes have been driven by shifting policies and improvements in assessment design. The relationship between alternate assessments and research-based classroom practices for students with intellectual disability has been a tenuous one at best, although recent developments are promising. This chapter provides an overview of the history of alternate assessment and a description of students who participate in the assessments. It then describes some of the challenges associated with design and use of alternate assessments based on alternate achievement standards (AA-AAS). The chapter follows by identifying research-based practices impacted by AA-AAS and providing suggestions for strengthening the link between AA-AAS and classroom practices. Finally, it highlights two new alternate assessment systems and describes their implications for improving instruction and outcomes for students with significant cognitive disabilities, including students with intellectual disability.

Historical Overview

Alternate assessments are used in states' large-scale academic assessment systems and their results are reported and used for accountability purposes. States may have a variety of purposes for or intended uses of alternate assessments, such as monitoring student achievement and progress, and guiding instruction (Elliott & Roach, 2007; Marion & Perie, 2009). The history of the policies that have guided alternate assessments is well documented (e.g., Rigney, 2009).

The earliest large-scale alternate assessment was implemented in Kentucky in 1990 as an outgrowth of its Reform Act of 1990 (Quenemoen, 2008). At about the same time, Maryland also implemented an alternate assessment program. But it was only with the Individuals with Disabilities Education Act reauthorization of 1997 (IDEA) that alternate assessments specifically designed for students with disabilities who could not meaningfully participate in large-scale, general education assessments (even with appropriate accommodations) became a common component of state assessment systems. Along with the requirement that all students with disabilities have access to the general curriculum, all states were challenged to design assessments for this population by the year 2000 that accurately measured what students knew. A goal of including alternate assessment results in accountability systems was that decision makers would consider *all* students when making decisions about resource allocation to improve educational programming (Ysseldyke & Olsen, 1997). Little was known about how to develop alternate assessments or the likely impact of the requirement to assess this population (Browder et al., 2003). Many states' alternate assessments focused on functional skills that were prominent in the curriculum in the 1990s (Thompson & Thurlow, 2001).

A few years later, No Child Left Behind (NCLB, 2002) required states to report annually on the academic achievement of all students in reading/language arts and mathematics, adding science by 2007. Alternate assessments were required to be aligned to the state's content and achievement standards, and their results were to be reported along with the results from general education assessments. Many states developed alternate content standards or curriculum frameworks that identified academic expectations for students with significant cognitive disabilities. These were based on chronologically appropriate grade-level general education content standards, but reduced in depth and/or breadth to provide access for this population.

"Alternate assessments" became "alternate assessments based on alternate achievement standards" after new regulations in 2003 required that the assessments be "aligned with the State's academic content standards; promote accesses to the general curriculum; and reflect professional judgment of the highest achievement standards possible" (34 C.F.R. S200.1(d)(1)-(3)). Subsequently, nonregulatory guidance (US Department of Education, 2005) prevented states from assigning a large number of low-achieving students with disabilities to alternate assessments by imposed a 1% cap on the percentage of students who could be counted as proficient on alternate assessments. This cap reinforced the importance of holding all students with disabilities to high expectations and reserving alternate assessments as a way for students with the most significant cognitive disabilities to demonstrate their academic achievement.

Students Participating in AA-AAS

The Individualized Education Program (IEP) team makes the decision on whether a student with a disability participates in AA-AAS or a general education assessment with accommodations as needed. Eligibility tends to be determined by holistic evaluation of the student's cognitive abilities and instructional needs, not by disability label. Students with intellectual disability may participate in AA-AAS or in general education assessments; IQ is not a sufficient indicator to assign a student to either AA-AAS or general education assessment. Many states provide guidelines to support IEP teams' decision making. But who are students with "the most significant cognitive disabilities"?

There have been efforts across the years to describe students who have participated in AA-AAS (e.g., Kearns, Towles-Reeves, Kleinert, Kleinert, & Thomas, 2011; Nash, Clark, & Karvonen, 2015; Towles-Reeves, Kearns, Kleinert, & Kleinert, 2009). Based on data from 2015 AA-AAS administrations, students with intellectual disability comprise 32% (Dynamic Learning Maps [DLM], 2016) to 45% (Thurlow, Wu, Quenemoen, & Towles, 2016) of students who participate in AA-AAS. The two other most common labels are autism (25% DLM, 2016; 27% Thurlow et al., 2016) and multiple disabilities (20% DLM 2016; 15% Thurlow et al., 2016).

More relevant to eligibility decision making is information about students' academic skills. For example, Towles-Reeves et al. (2009) surveyed teachers in three states regarding the learning characteristics of the students who participated in the AA-AAS using the Learner Characteristics Inventory (LCI) and found that most students who participate in the AA-AAS use symbolic language to communicate, and many can read basic sight words and do computational procedures with or without a calculator. These findings were supported by later surveys from Kearns et al. (2011).

Additional information highlights students' support needs and instructional experiences. For example, in a 2013 census of more than 40,000 students identified by their teachers as being eligible for AA-AAS (Nash et al., 2015), 19% use an Augmentative and Alternative Communication (AAC) device, 7% are also blind or have low vision, and 5% are also deaf or hard of hearing. One-third (33%) have a health or care issue that interferes with instruction or assessment.

AA-AAS participants also have varied complexity and modes of communication. For example, in one study, an estimated 76% of students use speech to meet their expressive communication needs (Nash et al., 2015). Of the 24% of students who do not, 71% combine three or more words according to grammatical rules. The remaining 29% use only one or two words at a time. Students who use symbols or signs instead of speech tend to use only one or two at a time. Among students who do not yet have speech, sign language, or AAC, nearly half (48%) use conventional gestures or vocalizations to communicate intentionally, 14% use only unconventional vocalizations, gestures, or body movements to communicate intentionally, and 38% exhibit behaviors that are not intentionally communicative but may be interpreted by others as such. In a survey of teachers in seven states, 88% of students who took AA-AAS could follow one- or two-step directions independently or with cues (Kearns et al., 2011).

Challenges

In attempts to be responsive to shifting legislative requirements, states' alternate assessment systems have undergone frequent changes (Cameto et al., 2009; Thompson, Johnstone, Thurlow, & Altman, 2005). Each source of policy guidance forced stakeholders to consider and address questions around eligibility for participation in the assessments, curricular priorities identified for instruction and assessment, and best instructional practices for teaching academic content to the population. At the same time, those who designed AA-AAS refined the assessment systems to support valid interpretations and uses of assessment results.

Eligibility

The US Department of Education (2005) permitted up to 1% of students with the most significant cognitive disabilities to be *considered proficient* when assessed with AA-AAS. With the Every Student Succeeds Act of 2015 (ESSA), the cap is now set to allow up to 1% of students to *participate* in AA-AAS. Legislation and nonregulatory guidance have not specified who qualifies as a student with the most significant cognitive disability. States developed their own definitions and provided guidelines to IEP teams to evaluate student eligibility for participation in AA-AAS (Thompson et al., 2005). Research conducted on states' descriptions of participation guidelines revealed 12 types of guidelines (Musson, Thomas, Towles-Reeves, & Kearns, 2010). The majority of states mentioned significant cognitive impairments (72%) and the role of the IEP team in determining whether a student was eligible to participate in AA-AAS (56%). Other categories included adaptive skills, criteria based on the student's instructional needs, and educators' evaluation that the student was unable to participate in the regular assessment. Specific disability labels were infrequently included in participation guidelines (14%). In 2012 two multistate consortia developed eligibility criteria that emphasize three criteria: (a) the student has a significant cognitive disability, (b) the student is working on an academic curriculum based on extended content standards, and (c) the student requires direct instruction and extensive supports to make progress in academics. Teams are cautioned against making decisions based on factors such as excessive absences; sensory or motor disabilities; or language, cultural, or economic differences.

With these multiple guidelines, it is not surprising that some educators make decisions based on subjective interpretation of students' characteristics within the context of local expectations and accountability systems. These decisions may lead educators to assign students with more mild impairments to AA-AAS. For example, Cho and Kingston (2013) found that some teachers of students with mild impairments who nonetheless assigned them to the alternate assessment did so because they felt a child needed a read-aloud accommodation that was not available on the general or modified assessment. Others did so simply because their personal definition of "significant cognitive disability" was based on low academic achievement.

Decisions about eligibility may be most difficult when considering students with high achievement on alternate assessments or very low achievement on general assessments. In an analysis of student assignment to general or alternate assessments during a three-year span, Saven, Anderson, Nese, Farley, and Tindal (2016) found that 12% of a third-grade cohort and 9% of a sixth-grade cohort did not consistently participate in alternate or general assessments in all three years.

Curricular Priorities

Curricular priorities for students with disabilities tend to reflect a broad range of topics including academic, functional, therapeutic, behavior, and postsecondary transition. With the IDEA 1997 requirement to provide access to the general curriculum, this concept has been interpreted in various ways (Ryndak, Moore, Orlando, & Delano, 2008–2009). For example, to some access means participation in inclusive settings (i.e., context), and to others it means access to academic content. Others have advocated for both of these and emphasized the importance of holding students to high expectations so they can make progress in the general education curriculum (Ryndak et al., 2008–2009; Wehmeyer, 2006a).

Alternate assessments have brought an increased emphasis on academics-aligned grade level content standards. How academics fit into curricular priorities for individual students depends in part on educator views of the value of academics for students with significant cognitive disabilities. There has been a tendency to see academics as an additional demand, competing with the other priorities (Hunt, McDonnell, & Crockett, 2012).

In the early years of alternate assessment, it is not surprising that teachers questioned the value of academics for students with severe disabilities (Agran, Alper, & Wehmeyer, 2002). Even 10 years after the IDEA 1997 requirement that all students have access to the general curriculum, there was evidence that teachers prioritized a narrow range of academic content, best aligned with functional academics, as the enacted academic curriculum (Karvonen, Wakeman, Browder, Rogers, & Flowers, 2011). Students with stronger use of symbolic communication had access to a broader array of academic content (Karvonen, Flowers, & Wakeman, 2013b). But even more recently, there is evidence that some teachers still replace academic instruction with functional skills instruction during academic classes in order to meet requirements of academic instruction and are still skeptical about the value of academic instruction for students with significant cognitive disabilities, believing that AA-AAS requirements infringe on professional judgment about curricular priorities (Timberlake, 2016).

Recently, guidance from the US Office of Special Education and Rehabilitative Services (US Department of Education, 2015) outlined that IEPs, even for those students who participate in the AA-AAS, must be aligned with the state's academic content standards from the grade in which the student is enrolled. The guidance went on to recommend that if a significant gap occurs between the academic content standard and the student's present level of performance, the IEP goals should be "sufficiently ambitious to help close the gap" (p. 5) and include specialized instruction. While the guidance does not prevent the inclusion of functional, social, and behavioral goals, it does dictate that IEPs must address academic content based upon the content standards of the student's assigned grade level. Given this clarity, it is anticipated there will be an increase in the alignment between the content standards and curricular priorities for students who take the AA-AAS.

Instructional Practice

Although many states have created extended content standards or curricular frameworks to help teachers translate grade-level academic content into higher expectations for students with significant cognitive disabilities, these documents are not sufficient to support academic instruction. Even when teachers see value in providing general curriculum access to students with significant cognitive disabilities, they face barriers to implementation, including lack of materials, lack of collaboration with general educators, and a view of instruction that separates activities devoted to IEP goals, content standards, and the content on AA-AAS (Petersen, 2016). In a survey of more than 400 special education teachers in three states, Karvonen, Wakeman, Flowers, and Moody (2013) found that teachers did not consistently report using content standards to design instruction or plan for what to teach next when a student had learned a concept.

Another barrier has been research on effective instruction in academic content for students with significant cognitive disabilities. However, there is growing body of research in this area (Browder, Spooner, Ahlgrim-Delzell, Harris, & Wakeman, 2008; Browder, Wakeman, Spooner, Ahlgrim-Delzell, & Algozzine, 2006). One question is whether instructional strategies that have proven effective with this population of students in other contexts (e.g., functional curricula) could also be effective when teaching challenging academic content. While many instructional strategies have been utilized and been effective in changing student outcomes with this population, such as embedded instruction (e.g., Jameson, Walker, Utley, & Maughan, 2012; Riesen, McDonnell, Johnson, Polychronis, & Jameson, 2003), task analytic instruction (e.g., Browder, Trela, & Jimenez, 2007; Courtade, Browder, Spooner, & DiBiase 2010), and prompting strategies (e.g., Skibo, Mims, & Spooner, 2011; Waugh, Fredrick, & Alberto, 2009), research syntheses on the use of these practices in academic instruction are limited. Browder, Ahlgrim-Delzell, Spooner, Mims and Baker (2009) applied quality indicators of research to determine that time delay was an effective instructional practice in the teaching of picture and sight word recognition for students with moderate to severe disabilities. Spooner, Knight, Browder, and Smith (2012) also applied quality indicators of research to identify task analytic instruction as well as time delay as evidence based in teaching academic content to students with severe disabilities. Erickson, Hanser, Hatch, and Sanders (2009) provided a systematic literature review on the components of comprehensive literacy instruction for students with significant intellectual disability.

Assessment Design

Over the years, common alternate assessment designs have included portfolios, checklists, and performance assessments. In a 2009 survey, Altman et al. (2010) found that 25 states reported using a portfolio or body of evidence, 23 used performance tasks, eight used multiple-choice responses, and seven reported their AA-AAS was in revision.

There are trade-offs in the various alternate assessment designs (see Hess, Burdge, & Clayton, 2011 for an overview). For example, performance tasks support standardized administration and allow for more evidence (multiple items) across a broader range of academic content, but the design of the tasks may leave some students with no way of demonstrating content knowledge. Portfolios, with content identified and evidence selected by the teacher, are flexible and tend to allow more accessibility supports—yet they are at risk of losing their connection to academic content standards and repeating the same skills for the student in every grade, thereby limiting the student's ability to demonstrate growth across years. Without supporting evidence, checklist ratings can be highly subjective and difficult to corroborate. Also, academic content on a checklist type of AA-AAS may be perceived as inaccessible for some students (Goldstein & Behuniak, 2012).

In a survey of teachers who participated in an early alternate assessment system, Kleinert, Kennedy, and Kearns (1999) found that teachers believed the use of their portfolio-based alternate assessment improved instructional programming, helped students assess their own performance, and increased student access to augmentative communication systems. However, in another study of teacher perceptions, Restorff, Sharpe, Abery, Rodriguez, and Kim (2012) found that most teachers did not perceive a change in student performance due to participation in alternate assessment, though among teachers who did perceive change it was in the positive direction. In a similar survey of administrator perceptions, Towles-Reeves, Kleinert, and Anderman (2008) found principal perceptions in the two participating states to be positive.

Another common challenge with AA-AAS design is the scoring systems. With portfolio approaches, scoring may be holistic or have several dimensions that are evaluated with a rubric.

Performance tasks and multiple choice formats provide raw scores, but still tend to be reported as total performance for a subject. Rubric-based scoring systems have historically included criteria outside the student's control, such as participation in general education settings and alignment to content standards (Thompson et al., 2005). More recently, Cameto et al. (2009) reviewed AA-AAS scoring systems and summarized four scoring criteria: (a) accuracy of student response ($n = 45$ states), (b) amount of independence ($n = 39$ states), (c) generalization across settings ($n = 23$ states), and (d) amount of progress ($n = 13$ states).

Assessment Results: Interpretation and Uses

As mentioned previously, common intended uses of AA-AAS are within accountability systems (i.e., to inform decisions about resource allocation to support effective educational programing) to inform instruction (though some would question the use of year-end assessments to inform instruction). Valid inferences about student results require that the scores reflect students' actual knowledge and skills. Yet if teachers limit students' academic instruction, AA-AAS scores may reflect students' lack of opportunity to learn what is assessed, rather than their lack of achievement of content that was taught to them.

From an accountability perspective, results for small groups (e.g., fewer than five students in a school) are not reported due to concerns that individuals may be identifiable. When this happens, students with significant cognitive disabilities may unintentionally be "hidden" when resource decisions are made based on large-scale assessment results. High proficiency rates (Karvonen, Flowers, & Wakeman, 2013a), lack of vertical scales, and variation from year to year in student assignment to alternate and general assessment (Saven et al., 2016) all make it difficult to document student growth across grades. Finally, when results are expressed in performance levels for the entire subject (e.g., "proficient") rather than specific content, this information is of little use to IEP teams. As a result, AA-AAS scores have historically not been very useful when evaluating students' present levels of academic performance and planning educational goals and strategies.

Research-Based Practices

There are several research-based practices that have the potential to support improved outcomes for students with significant cognitive disabilities who participate in the AA-AAS. We define "improved outcomes" as those associated with the goal of preparing students who take AA-AAS to be ready for postsecondary opportunities including education, employment, and community involvement. To meet this goal, students would be held to high expectations each year, with increasing expectations across grade levels. Aligned educational systems, universal design for learning (UDL), data-based decision making, inclusion, and self-determination are strategies that have a direct relationship with students' academic outcomes.

Aligned Educational System

Students with intellectual disability have the best opportunity for positive AA-AAS outcomes and long-term growth in academic knowledge and skills when their educational programs reflect alignment of content standards, instruction, and assessment. IEP priorities should support student learning in the general curriculum. Given the history of curricular priorities and tendency to teach a narrow range of academics with limited complexity (Karvonen et al., 2011), this is one area with potential for big impact.

An aligned educational system means that academics are not fragmented or repetitive each year. Teachers design instruction that embeds academics in meaningful contexts so that academics integrate with, rather than compete with, other curricular priorities. It also requires teachers to have both deep academic content expertise and knowledge of instructional strategies. Research evidence exists supporting markedly different instructional paradigms (e.g., Browder et al., 2006; Erickson et al., 2009).

Earlier, we described evidence that some AA-AAS–eligible students do not yet have intentional or symbolic expressive communication systems and some have limited symbolic systems. The greatest potential to help this subgroup of students be successful in the academic curriculum is through instruction to help them develop communication systems that allow them to show what they know and can do on AA-AAS. Kleinert, Kearns, and Kleinert (2010) identified four steps to facilitate communication competence for students with significant disabilities: (a) reviewing the students' current intention and forms of expression, (b) collecting student observation and family interview data, (c) reviewing information, and (d) developing a system. In an example specific to academic instruction, Erickson and Karvonen (2014) outlined strategies for supporting students who are preintentional or presymbolic communicators in literacy instruction aligned with the Common Core State Standards (CCSS, http://www.corestandards.org/).

Positive AA-AAS outcomes have been associated with teachers' time spent on professional development in academics and with teacher self-reports that academic resources such as content standards and general education teachers at their school are influential (Karvonen, Wakeman, et al., 2013).

Accessibility and Universal Design for Learning

Large-scale academic assessments in the United States started with Horace Mann in the 1850s when he introduced standardized testing as an educational reform in the Boston school system. While this standardization movement had the good intent of reducing favoritism in the granting of high school diplomas, over time it became clear that standardization could put up barriers, especially for students with disabilities. To remove these barriers, in the latter half of the 20th century test publishers developed systems of accommodations to allow students to demonstrate their knowledge and skills. Accommodations were developed after the test was designed and were applied as exceptions to the typical test administration. In contrast, designing assessments within an accessibility framework means starting with the design process to minimize barriers. As an example, allowing extra time for a student with a documented medical need would be an accommodation, while providing all students as much time as they need to respond fully to all test questions would an example of universal design for assessment (UDA) that maximizes one aspect of accessibility.

UDA has its roots in the principles of UDL (Rose & Meyer, 2002), which are clearly reflected in the practices that promote accessibility. In their UDL guide, the Council for Exceptional Children (2005) linked the IDEA 1997 description of access to an education without barriers for all students directly to the concept of UDL. In order for the student to be able to show what he or she knows and can do, he or she must first be able to access the content of the assessment and be able to demonstrate a response. Rose, Meyer, and Hitchcock (2005) suggested three essential qualities of curricular materials developed under the principles of UDL: The curriculum is designed to (a) provide multiple representations of content, (b) provide multiple options for expression, and (c) provide multiple options for engagement. Such qualities can also be used when designing assessments and must be considered when designing AA-AAS in particular.

Although principles of UDA were used in alternate assessments from the early part of the 21st century, Burdge, Clayton, Denham, and Hess (2010) formalized a framework to support student learning that can be applied during both instruction and assessment design. First, the authors suggest reflecting on how the content and materials are presented to the student: Can the student use the information in the format in which it is presented? Does the student understand the language, symbols, and graphics used? Next, consider how the student is expected to and is able to interact with the materials and show what he or she knows. How will the student understand the directions within the task and then make a response? Finally, consider the student's interests and needs. Is the assessment delivered in a setting that reduces distraction or limits sensory input? When is the assessment being delivered (e.g., delivering the assessment during a child's recess or break time can increase frustration and reduce concentration)? The use of this framework can reduce barriers and increase accessibility for all students.

Assessment designers can promote accessibility in multiple ways. For example, Wehmeyer (2006b) described several examples for how materials and response options can be better tailored to reduce barriers and provide multiple methods for students to demonstrate their understanding. Wehmeyer also described how such designs can be applied with students with severe disabilities (Wehmeyer, 2006a).

There is some evidence that suggests interventions grounded in UDL principles have benefits for students with significant intellectual disability (e.g., Coyne, Pisha, Dalton, Zeph, & Cook Smith, 2012; Roberts, Park, Brown, & Cook, 2011). There is a research base regarding the application of UDL during instruction and assessment designed for students with disabilities (Rao, Ok, & Bryant, 2014), but there is limited information about the impact of such planning on student outcomes.

Use of Data for Instructional Decision Making

AA-AAS are useful for accountability in that they provide a broad, summative understanding of students' knowledge and skills—but most are designed to capture that information at a single point in time. A combination of formative and summative measures provides a more complete picture of students' knowledge, skills, and abilities over time. Researchers have outlined the need for other valid measures (e.g., interim, benchmark, formative assessments) within a year to document student progress and inform teacher decision making (Heritage, 2010; Herman, Osmundson, & Dietel, 2010). However, standardized assessments for interim or benchmark evaluation of progress for students with significant cognitive disabilities are not available. Instead, teachers typically rely on self-designed data-collection tools and curriculum-based measures to monitor student progress. Browder, Spooner, and Jimenez (2011) describe two specific methods for collecting data that can be used for academic goals: task analytic and discrete trial. Task analysis involves the use of a defined sequence of responses needed to complete an activity (e.g., steps to complete a science experiment or write a paragraph). There is a great deal of research using a task analytic approach and data collection method to measure student progress (e.g., Browder, Lee, & Mims, 2011; Courtade et al., 2010; DiPipi-Hoy & Jitendra, 2004; Jimenez & Staples, 2015).

Discrete trial tools for data collection may also be called "repeated trial." Many examples in research exist for the use of discrete trial data collection methods to determine academic progress (e.g., Jameson et al., 2012; Mechling, Gast, & Krupa, 2007; Swain, Lane, & Gast, 2015). Data can be collected in a discrete trial format during naturally occurring times (e.g., during calendar or in a textbook to identify a number), embedded in an academic lesson (e.g., identifying numbers for measurement purposes within a science experiment), or given in a massed trial format (e.g., identifying numbers on flash cards).

The use of ongoing data-based decision efforts within a classroom as well as more standardized assessment efforts at designated points in time helps teachers determine progress and remaining expectations toward academic targets—but teachers need strategies to collect and evaluate data, and time to do so. Opportunities to collaborate on data interpretation include data review teams and professional learning communities. These groups can also be powerful resources to help a teacher identify the reasons for observed performance and brainstorm changes in instructional strategies where needed.

There are benefits for students when teachers use performance data to make ongoing instructional changes (e.g., Hager & Slocum, 2005; Quenemoen, Thurlow, Moen, Thompson, & Blount Morse, 2004). Although direct evidence on the use of data to support instruction aligned to AA-AAS is limited, teacher training on data evaluation and decision making has been associated with higher AA-AAS scores (Browder, Karvonen, Davis, Fallin, & Courtade-Little, 2005).

Inclusion

With the shift toward general curriculum access comes the opportunity for students with significant cognitive disabilities to be included in general education settings. When students are included with their peers, they have the opportunity to become part of that learning community (Ryndak et al., 2008–2009). Soukup, Wehmeyer, Bashinski, and Bovaird (2007) found that percent of time spent in the general education classroom was associated with greater access to the general curriculum for students with intellectual disability or autism. Roach and Elliott (2006) found a direct relationship between access to the general curriculum (including time spent in a general education classroom) and student performance on the AA-AAS. Unfortunately, estimates of the number of AA-AAS participants who are served in separate classrooms or schools nationwide range from 80% (Nash et al., 2015) to 93% (Kleinert, Towles-Reeves, Quenemoen, Thurlow, & Fluegge, 2015). Separate settings may also hinder teacher efforts to provide appropriate academic instruction, if they are isolated from general education teachers and grade-level materials and other resources (Petersen, 2016). Separate settings also make it difficult to take advantage of natural supports such as peers.

There are research-based practices found to be successful with students with moderate to severe intellectual disability in a general education environment. Hudson, Browder, and Wood (2013) conducted a literature review to identify instructional practices that have an evidence base for promising use with students with significant cognitive disabilities in general education classrooms. The authors found that of the 17 studies that met the criteria for quality research, 10 used embedded trial instruction (many times in combination with systematic instructional strategies); two used systematic instructional prompting strategies (i.e., system of least prompts; constant time delay); and three used peer-delivered supports or cues and feedback. One study used embedded teacher-delivered statements not in a trial format, and the final study used constant time delay. As many of these strategies are evidenced based, with extensive research support for use with students with significant cognitive disabilities, their use in a general education classroom with a clear focus on academic content standards can lead to positive outcomes on the AA-AAS.

Instruction to promote student self-determination in inclusive settings may also support students with intellectual disability in achieving their academic goals. For example, Palmer, Wehmeyer, Gipson, and Agran (2004) applied the Self-Determined Learning Model of Instruction with students during their instruction in language arts, science, and social studies. Most of the students (19 of 22) received academic instruction in inclusive settings. Students demonstrated statistically significant improvements in their planning and problem-solving skills.

Current State of AA-AAS

More recently, the emphasis on college and career readiness, including states' adoption of more rigorous academic content standards such as the CCSS, has once again impacted academic expectations and alternate assessments for students with significant cognitive disabilities. Newly developed assessments are designed to address previous shortcomings and challenges within the historic AA-AAS systems. States and multistate consortia have developed new alternate assessments based on AA-AASs that consider the unique needs of the population while reliably capturing student progress. Two new alternate assessments, the Dynamic Learning Maps Alternate Assessment (DLMAA) system and the National Center and State Collaborative Alternate Assessments (NCSCAA), introduce new possibilities.

DLMAA

The DLMAA is based on a set of guiding principles chosen to prioritize student learning first while meeting all requirements for usage in an accountability system. A brief description of some of the most important principles are as follows. Further details are provided in Kingston, Karvonen, Bechard, and Erickson (in press).

Fine-grained learning maps can guide instruction and assessment. A learning map is a variant of a learning progression, but while learning progressions typically contain a single sequential pathway, learning maps typically denote multiple pathways. Most of the research support regarding the use of learning maps is theoretical in nature and more empirical evidence is needed. One example of such a study is Yin et al. (2008), which yielded mixed results. However, a follow-up study by Furtak et al. (2008) found that students whose teachers used information from the learning progression along with instructional strategies that provided informational feedback had learning gains.

The DLMAA learning maps are based on research literature on students' development of conceptual understandings and are periodically refined through statistical modeling of response patterns. The DLM Professional Development system (http://dlmpd.com) features modules organized to develop teachers' conceptual understanding of instruction in groups of academic content called "conceptual areas." Each module builds teacher capacity to teach content that is organized within the learning map.

For each assessed content standard (called an "Essential Element"), teachers have access to small map segments that show the relationships between skills assessed at each level of complexity. These maps help teachers identify current instructional targets for individual students and show the various pathways by which students may reach the grade-level expectation in the content standard. A DLMAA is comprised of a series of testlets, each of which contains an engagement activity and a few items. For each Essential Element, testlets are available at several levels of complexity to provide students with content that is accessible so they can provide independent (unprompted) responses.

A subset of particularly important map nodes, called Essential Elements, provides useful organizational structure to teachers. Prima facie the use of curriculum standards appears to make sense. Having a knowledge of a goal makes it easier to work toward that goal. This is the widely held belief behind the standards movement (e.g., Kingston & Reidy, 1997). There is some correlational evidence of the influence of content standards on AA-AAS outcomes (e.g., Karvonen, Wakeman, et al., 2013) but we are aware of no experimental research on the relationship for this population. However, in a general education study, Harris, Penuel, DeBarger, D'Angelo and Gallagher (2014) used an experimental design with sixth-grade science classrooms in 42 schools and showed that students of teachers trained in the use of the Framework for K–12 Science Education had 0.2 standard deviations–higher achievement than students of teachers who taught the same material based on a science textbook.

Instructionally embedded assessments designed to be instructionally relevant provide teachers with models of good instructional activities. It has long been believed (and anecdotally supported) that when faced with high-stakes accountability tests teachers will teach to the structure of the test. Studies of teaching to the test conclude that it leads to adoption of ineffective teaching approaches (Sacks, 2000) and a reduction of time spent on higher-order skills (Herman, 1992). Moreover, improvements in test scores do not generalize to other measures (Shepard, 2000).

To combat the potential negative effects of teaching to tests not designed to be taught to, DLMAA testlets are designed to be relevant for instruction. Engagement activities (which are not scored) provide relevant contexts, activate prior knowledge, and prepare students for the cognitive demands of the items. Each testlet takes 5 to 15 minutes to complete.

Short, instructionally embedded assessments reinforce instruction and provide teachers and students with feedback they can use to improve learning. The results of the instructionally embedded assessments are validated in a year-end component. Strong evidence exists that appropriate use of formative assessment will lead to at least modest improvement in student learning (Kingston & Nash, 2011). Other writers claim higher effect sizes when formative assessment is properly implemented (Black & Wiliam, 1998).

In the DLMAA system, teachers who use instructionally embedded assessments can work within the test blueprint to choose the Essential Element and level of complexity of each testlet to be assigned to a student. This flexibility is designed to allow teachers to think about meaningful instructional objectives for the student during the year, relative to the grade level expectation in the Essential

Element. Throughout the year, the teacher can retrieve a progress report that shows student mastery of skills for each Essential Element. Summative score reports at the end of the year provide evidence of student mastery of skills for each Essential Element as well as summaries of performance on groups of related Essential Elements and in the subject overall.

The DLMAA incorporates several promising practices described earlier in this chapter:

- Consistent with principles of UDL, the content of the Essential Element and the learning map represent students' conceptual understandings and skills. Neither limit the ways in which students may demonstrate what they know. Testlets are carefully constructed to minimize barriers to accessibility, and alternate forms are available when needed.
- Within the routine of standardized test administration, teachers have discretion to use flexibility in how they present content and how students indicate their responses.
- Assessments are delivered via computer or tablet and there are few constraints on the settings in which assessments may be administered.

More information about DLMAA is available at http://dynamiclearningmaps.org/.

NCSCAA

The National Center and State Collaborative (NCSC) approach to the AA-AAS is designed around a system of curriculum, instruction, and assessment. The content of the NCSCAA is based upon a prioritized set of the CCSS. These standards, in consideration with hypothesized learning progressions, result in articulated Core Content Connectors (CCCs), each being a teachable and assessable part of the content (NCSC, 2014, May). The CCCs focus on the big ideas within each content area from third grade through high school.

Extensive support—instructional resources and professional development—is part of the NCSC comprehensive system. NCSC (2013) created a diagram and description of the resources including the plans to both understand the content and plan instruction. All resources and materials designed within NCSC regarding what and how to teach can be found at the NCSC Wiki (https://wiki.ncscpartners. org). The instructional resources support teachers in two ways: First, resources are available to increase teacher understanding of unfamiliar content; and second, curriculum resources are designed that are aligned to the prioritized content reflected within the AA-AAS that serve as models for how to teach academic content. Curriculum resources include units of instruction planned with principles of UDL for inclusive practice as well as scripted resources incorporating research and evidence-based practices (described previously) for students who have little to no experience or knowledge of critical priority concepts.

NCSC used components of evidence centered design (ECD) to develop the AA-AAS. ECD permitted developers to methodically vary the complexity of items across and within content standards. It also provided the opportunity for NCSC to support its conceptual model to create an assessment system that showcased content aligned to the CCSS and created tasks giving consideration to the characteristics of students with significant cognitive disabilities and how they demonstrate what they know and can do. Content experts used design patterns and task templates from specifications provided by NCSC to develop items. The NCSCAA is administered to students in grades 3–8 and 11, English language arts (ELA) and mathematics, in the spring each year. NCSC (2014, November) describes its AA-AAS:

> There are approximately 30 items per assessment that cover approximately 10 CCCs. Most of the assessment items are selected response (multiple choice). However, writing is assessed by asking students to construct a response in one of a variety of ways, including through the use of picture

symbols or written responses developed with graphic organizers, dictating a response, and use of Augmentative and Alternative Communication (AAC) and Assistive Technology devices.

(p. 2, question 9)

Items are available at four tiers of complexity. The complexity tier of items administered to each student is based on a prescreening tool completed by the teacher. While the testing time is expected to be between 1.5–2 hours for each assessment (mathematics and ELA), it is permissible to complete the test over a period of days as based upon student need. A stopping rule is triggered if a student does not make a response to four consecutive items. The test is designed to be delivered via a computer using open-source technology, but can be delivered in alternate formats (paper and pencil) as determined by the IEP team based upon the needs of each individual student.

"The assessment contains many built-in supports that allow students to use materials they are most familiar with and communicate what they know and can do as independently as possible" (NCSC, 2015, p. 1). These include:

- Reduced passage length for the ELA reading passages;
- Pictures and other graphics to help students understand what they read (or what is read to them);
- Models for students to use during the ELA and mathematics tests;
- Common geometric shapes and smaller numbers on the mathematics tests; and
- The option to have the entire test read aloud.

The NCSCAA score reports include performance levels, scale scores, and descriptive information. Performance level descriptors (PLD) are written at four levels to describe what a student knows and is able to do within each content area at each grade level. Score reports are created at the district, school, and individual student levels. Examples of score reports and performance level descriptors are provided to each state within the Guide for Score Report Interpretations (e.g., South Carolina, http://ed.sc.gov/tests/middle/scncsc/ncsc-guide-for-score-report-interpretation-2015/).

The NCSCAA incorporates several promising practices described earlier in this chapter, including the following.

- NCSCAA was conceptualized and designed to be an aligned educational system—not simply an assessment.
- Instructional resources and supports are available that are directly aligned to reflect the assessment priorities and provide students with the opportunity to learn complex content using research-based and evidence-based practices.
- Consistent with principles of UDL, the use of ECD during item development increases accessibility within the item tiers. Considerations for the sensory needs of students are highlighted in the administration manual.
- Test administrators have choices based upon student need for mode of item delivery (i.e., computer or paper and pencil).

The NCSC system is described at http://ncscpartners.org/.

Future Directions

In this chapter we have described several promising strategies for promoting academic achievement for students with significant cognitive disabilities who are eligible to take AA-AAS. Where possible, these strategies are based on evidence. The field of alternate assessment is still relatively new, and the understanding of access to the general curriculum for students with significant cognitive disabilities is still evolving. At this point, much of the evidence about practices associated with AA-AAS outcomes is still based on correlational research, perceived influences, and findings borrowed from general curriculum access research for a broader range of students with disabilities. Rigorous implementation research on AA-AAS implementation and student outcomes is still on the horizon. The new multi-state assessments—DLMAA and NCSCAA—bring the potential to overcome previous challenges in AA-AAS design research.

The overall purpose of an assessment system is to improve outcomes for students (Hager & Slocum, 2005). Along with more rigorous implementation research that can inform future practice, additional research is needed on the consequences of the new AA-AAS and their use within educational programs that incorporate research-based practices such as aligned instruction, universal design, and data-based decision making. Documenting the use and impact of these systems and practices on students' long-term outcomes will allow policy makers to determine whether AA-AAS fulfills the purpose of providing students access to, and maximizing their progress in, the general curriculum.

Note

1. Because the term "students with the most significant cognitive disabilities" is used in federal legislation as it pertains to eligibility for alternate assessment, this chapter will use the term (or derivations thereof).

References

Agran, M., Alper, S., & Wehmeyer, M. (2002). Access to the general curriculum for students with significant cognitive disabilities: What it means to teachers. *Education and Training in Mental Retardation and Developmental Disabilities, 37*, 123–133.

Altman, J. R., Lazarus, S. S., Quenemoen, R. F., Kearns, J., Quenemoen, M., & Thurlow, M. L. (2010). *2009 survey of states: Accomplishments and new issues at the end of a decade of change*. Minneapolis, MN: University of Minnesota, National Center on Educational Outcomes. Retrieved from http://www.cehd.umn.edu/NCEO/OnlinePubs/StateReports/2009_survey_of_states.htm

Black, P., & Wiliam, D. (1998). Inside the black box: Raising standards through classroom assessment. *Phi Delta Kappan, 80*(2), 139–144.

Browder, D. M., Ahlgrim-Delzell, L., Spooner, F., Mims, P., & Baker, J. N. (2009). Using time delay to teach literacy to students with severe developmental disabilities. *Exceptional Children, 75*, 343–364. doi: 10.1177/001440290907500305

Browder, D. M., Karvonen, M., Davis, S., Fallin, K., & Courtade-Little, G. (2005). The impact of teacher training on state alternate assessment scores. *Exceptional Children, 71*, 267–282.

Browder, D. M., Lee, A., & Mims, P. (2011). Using shared stories and individual response modes to promote comprehension and engagement in literacy for students with multiple, severe disabilities. *Education and Training in Autism and Developmental Disabilities, 46*, 339–351.

Browder, D. M., Spooner, F., Ahlgrim-Delzell, L., Flowers, C., Algozzine, R., & Karvonen, M. (2003). A content analysis of the curricular philosophies reflected in states' alternate assessments. *Research and Practice for Persons with Severe Disabilities, 28*, 165–181.

Browder, D. M., Spooner, F., Ahlgrim-Delzell, L., Harris, A., & Wakeman, S. Y. (2008). A meta-analysis on teaching mathematics to students with significant cognitive disabilities. *Exceptional Children, 74*, 407–432.

Browder, D. M., Spooner, F., & Jimenez, B. (2011). Standards-based individualized education plans and progress monitoring. In D. M. Browder & F. Spooner (Eds.), *Teaching students with moderate and severe disabilities* (pp. 42–91). New York: Guilford Press.

Browder, D. M., Trela, K., & Jimenez, B. (2007). Training teachers to follow a task analysis to engage middle school students with moderate and severe developmental disabilities in grade-appropriate literature. *Focus on Autism and Other Developmental Disabilities, 22*, 206–219. doi: 10.1177/10883576070220040301

Browder, D. M., Wakeman, S., Spooner, F., Ahlgrim-Delzell, L., & Algozzine, B. (2006). Research on reading for students with significant cognitive disabilities. *Exceptional Children, 72*, 392–408.

Burdge, M., Clayton, J., Denham, A., & Hess, K. K. (2010). Ensuring access: A four step process for accessing the general curriculum. In H. L. Kleinert & J. F. Kearns (Eds.), *Alternate assessment for students with significant cognitive disabilities* (pp. 109–147). Baltimore, MD: Brookes.

Cameto, R., Knokey, A. M., Nagle, K., Sanford, C., Blackorby, J., Sinclair, B., & Riley, D. (2009). *National profile on alternate assessments based on alternate achievement standards: A report from the national study on alternate assessments* (NCSER 2009–3014). Menlo Park, CA: SRI International. Retrieved from http://ies.ed.gov/ncser/pdf/20093014.pdf

Cho, H., & Kingston, N. M. (2013). Why IEP teams assign low performers with mild disabilities to the alternate assessment based on alternate achievement standards. *Journal of Special Education, 47*, 162–174.

Council for Exceptional Children. (2005). *Universal design for learning: A guide for teachers and education professionals.* Arlington, VA: Author.

Courtade, G. R., Browder, D. M., Spooner, F., & DiBiase, W. (2010). Training teachers to use an inquiry-based task analysis to teach science to students with moderate and severe disabilities. *Education and Training in Autism and Developmental Disabilities, 45*, 378–399.

Coyne, P., Pisha, B., Dalton, B., Zeph, L. A., & Cook Smith, N. (2012). Literacy by design: A universal design for learning approach for students with significant intellectual disabilities. *Remedial and Special Education, 33*, 162–172. doi: 10.1177/0741932510381651

DiPipi-Hoy, C., & Jitendra, A. (2004). A parent-delivered intervention to teach purchasing skills to young adults with disabilities. *The Journal of Special Education, 38*, 144–157.

Dynamic Learning Maps. (2016). *Technical report for the 2014–15 operational administration of the Dynamic Learning Maps Alternate Assessment System.* Lawrence, KS: Author.

Elliott, S. N., & Roach, A. T. (2007). Alternate assessments of students with significant disabilities: Alternative approaches, common technical challenges. *Applied Measurement in Education, 20*, 301–333. doi: 10.1080/08957340701431385

Erickson, K., Hanser, G., Hatch, P., & Sanders, E. (2009). *Research-based practices for creating access to the general curriculum in reading and literacy for students with significant intellectual disabilities.* Chapel Hill, NC: University of North Carolina at Chapel Hill, Center for Literacy and Disability Studies. Retrieved from http://www.ccsso.org/documents/2009/research_based_practices_reading_2009.pdf

Erickson, K., & Karvonen, M. (2014, July). *College and career readiness instruction and assessment for pre-intentional and pre-symbolic communicators.* Presentation at the annual conference of the US Department of Education Office of Special Education Programs (OSEP) Project Directors, Washington, DC.

Every Student Succeeds Act of 2015. Pub. L. No. 114–95.

Furtak, E. M., Ruiz-Primo, M. A., Shemwell, J. T., Ayala, C. C., Brandon, P., Shavelson, R. J., & Yin, Y. (2008). On the fidelity of implementing embedded formative assessments and its relation to student learning. *Applied Measurement in Education, 21*, 360–389.

Goldstein, J., & Behuniak, P. (2012). Assessing students with significant cognitive disabilities on academic content. *Journal of Special Education, 46*, 117–127. doi: 10.1177/0022466910379156

Hager, K. D., & Slocum, T. A. (2005). Using alternate assessment to improve educational outcomes. *Rural Special Education Quarterly, 24*, 54–59.

Harris, C. J., Penuel, W. R., DeBarger, A., D'Angelo, C., & Gallagher, L. P. (2014). *Curriculum materials make a difference for next generation science learning: Results from year 1 of a randomized controlled trial.* Menlo Park, CA: SRI International.

Heritage, M. (2010). *Formative assessment: Making it happen in the classroom.* Thousand Oaks, CA: Corwin.

Herman, J. L. (1992). What research tells us about good assessment. *Educational Leadership, 49*(8), 74–78.

Herman, J. L., Osmundson, E., & Dietel, R. (2010). *Benchmark assessments for improved learning* (AACC Report). Los Angeles, CA: University of California. Retrieved from https://www.cse.ucla.edu/products/policy/R2_benchmark_report_Herman.pdf

Hess, K., Burdge, M., & Clayton, J. (2011). Challenges to developing and implementing alternate assessments based on alternate achievement standards (AA-AAS). In M. Russell & M. Kavanaugh (Eds.), *Assessing students in the margins: Challenges, strategies, and techniques* (pp. 171–213). Charlotte, NC: Information Age Publishing.

Hudson, M. E., Browder, D. M., & Wood, L. A. (2013). Review of experimental research on academic learning by students with moderate and severe intellectual disability in general education. *Research and Practice for Persons with Severe Disabilities, 38*, 17–29. doi: 10.2511/027494813807046926

Hunt, P., McDonnell, J., & Crockett, M. A. (2012). Reconciling an ecological curricular framework focusing on quality of life outcomes with the development and instruction of standards-based academic goals. *Research and Practice for Persons with Severe Disabilities, 37*, 139–152.

Individuals with Disabilities Education Act of 1997. 120 USC. §1400 et seq.

Jameson, I. M., Walker, R., Utley, K., & Maughan, R. (2012). A comparison of embedded total task instruction in teaching behavioral chains to massed one-on-one instruction for students with intellectual disabilities: Accessing general education settings and core academic content. *Behavior Modification, 36*, 320–340.

Jimenez, B. A., & Staples, K. (2015). Access to the common core state standards in mathematics through early numeracy skill building for students with significant intellectual disability. *Education and Training in Autism and Developmental Disabilities, 50*, 17–30.

Karvonen, M., Flowers, C., & Wakeman, S. (2013a, April). *An exploration of methods for measuring academic growth for students with significant cognitive disabilities.* Paper presented at the 2013 annual meeting of the American Educational Research Association. April 27–May 1, 2013. San Francisco, CA.

Karvonen, M., Flowers, C., & Wakeman, S. (2013b). Factors associated with access to the general curriculum for students with intellectual disability. *Current Issues in Education, 16*(3), 10. Retrieved from http://cie.asu.edu/ojs/index.php/cieatasu/article/view/1309

Karvonen, M., Wakeman, S. Y., Browder, D. M., Rogers, M. A. S., & Flowers, C. (2011). *Academic curriculum for students with significant cognitive disabilities: Special education teacher perspectives a decade after IDEA 1997.* Retrieved from ERIC database. (ED521407).

Karvonen, M., Wakeman, S. Y., Flowers, C., & Moody, S. (2013). The relationship of teachers' instructional decisions and beliefs about alternate assessments to student achievement. *Exceptionality, 21*, 238–252. doi: 10.1080/09362835.2012.747184

Kearns, J. F., Towles-Reeves, E., Kleinert, H. L., Kleinert, J. O., & Thomas, M. K. K. (2011). Characteristics of and implications for students participating in alternate assessments based on alternate academic achievement standards. *Journal of Special Education, 45*, 3–14.

Kingston, N. M., Karvonen, M., Bechard, S., & Erickson, K. (in press). *The philosophical underpinnings and key features of the Dynamic Learning Maps Alternate Assessment. Teachers College Record (Yearbook), 118*, 140311.

Kingston, N. M., & Nash, B. (2011). Formative assessment: A meta-analysis and a call for research. *Educational Measurement: Issues and Practice, 30*, 28–37.

Kingston, N. M., & Reidy, E. (1997). Kentucky's accountability and assessment systems. In J. Millman (Ed.), *Grading teachers, grading schools: Is student achievement a valid evaluation measure?* (pp. 191–209) Thousand Oaks, CA: Corwin Publishers.

Kleinert, H., Kennedy, S., & Kearns, J. (1999). Impact of alternate assessments: A statewide teacher survey. *Journal of Special Education, 33*, 93–102.

Kleinert, H., Towles-Reeves, E., Quenemoen, R., Thurlow, M., & Fluegge, L. (2015). Where students with the most significant cognitive disabilities are taught: Implications for general curriculum access. *Exceptional Children, 81*, 312–328.

Kleinert, J. O., Kearns, J. F., & Kleinert, H. L. (2010). Students in the AA-AAS and the importance of communication competence. In H. L. Kleinert & J. F. Kearns (Eds.), *Alternate assessment for students with significant cognitive disabilities* (pp. 41–73). Baltimore, MD: Brookes.

Marion, S. F., & Perie, M. (2009). An introduction to validity arguments for alternate assessments. In W. D. Schafer & R. W. Lissitz (Eds.), *Alternate assessments based on alternate achievement standards: Policy, practice, and potential* (pp. 113–126). Baltimore, MD: Paul H. Brookes.

Mechling, L. C., Gast, D. L., & Krupa, K. (2007). Impact of SMART board technology: An investigation of sight word reading and observational learning. *Journal of Autism and Developmental Disorders, 37*, 1869–1882. doi: 10.1007/s10803-007-0361-9

Musson, J., Thomas, M., Towles-Reeves, E., & Kearns, J. (2010). An analysis of state alternate assessment participation guidelines. *Journal of Special Education, 44*, 67–78.

Nash, B., Clark, A. K., & Karvonen, M. (2015). *First contact: A census report on the characteristics of students eligible to take alternate assessments.* Lawrence, KS: University of Kansas, Center for Educational Testing and Evaluation.

National Center and State Collaborative. (2013). *Explanation of the NSCS instructional resources diagram.* Retrieved March 7, 2016 from http://ncscpartners.org/Media/Default/PDFs/Resources/Parents/NCSC-Diagram-and-explanation-9-10-13.pdf

National Center and State Collaborative. (2014, May). *The NCSC model for a comprehensive system of curriculum, instruction, and assessment.* Retrieved March 7, 2016 from http://ncscpartners.org/Media/Default/PDFs/Resources/Parents/parentdocs/NCSC%20Model%20for%20a%20Comprehensive%20System%20of%20Curriculum%20Instruction%20and%20Assessment%205-12-14%20.pdf

National Center and State Collaborative. (2014, November). *Frequently asked questions: NCSC alternate assessment based upon alternate achievement standards.* Retrieved March 1, 2016 from http://ncscpartners.org/Media/Default/PDFs/Resources/Parents/parentdocs/Summary%20of%20NCSC%20Frequently%20Asked%20Questions%20regarding%20the%20Alternate%20Assessment%20%20%202011-24-14.pdf

National Center and State Collaborative. (2015). *NCSC assessment policies.* Retrieved March 1, 2016 from http://ncscpartners.org/Media/Default/PDFs/Resources/Parents/NCSCAssessmentPolicies082415.pdf

No Child Left Behind Act of 2001 (2002). Pub. L. No. 107–110, 115 Stat. 1425.

Palmer, S. B., Wehmeyer, M. L., Gipson, K., & Agran, M. (2004). Promoting access to the general curriculum by teaching self-determination skills. *Exceptional Children, 70*, 427–439. doi: 10.1177/001440290407000403

Petersen, A. (2016). Perspectives of special education teachers on general education curriculum access: Preliminary results. *Research and Practice for Persons with Severe Disabilities, 41,* 19–35. doi: 10.1177/1540796915604835

Quenemoen, R. (2008). *A brief history of alternate assessments based on alternate achievement standards (Synthesis Report 68).* Minneapolis, MN: University of Minnesota, National Center on Educational Outcomes. Retrieved from http://www.cehd.umn.edu/NCEO/TopicAreas/AlternateAssessments/altAssessResources.htm

Quenemoen, R., Thurlow, M. L., Moen, R., Thompson, S., & Blount Morse, A. (2004). *Progress monitoring in an inclusive standards-based assessment and accountability system (Synthesis Report 53).* Minneapolis, MN: University of Minnesota, National Center on Educational Outcomes. Retrieved from http://education.umn.edu/NCEO/OnlinePubs/Synthesis53.html

Rao, K., Ok, M. W., & Bryant, B. R. (2014). A review of research on universal design educational models. *Remedial and Special Education, 35,* 153–166. doi: 10.1177/0741932513518980

Restorff, D., Sharpe, M., Abery, B., Rodriguez, M., & Kim, N. K. (2012). Teacher perceptions of alternate assessments based on alternate achievement standards: Results from a three-state survey. *Research and Practice for Persons with Severe Disabilities, 37,* 185–198.

Riesen, T., McDonnell, J., Johnson, J. W., Polychronis, S., & Jameson, M. (2003). A comparison of constant time delay and simultaneous prompting within embedded instruction in general education classes with students with moderate to severe disabilities. *Journal of Behavioral Education, 12,* 241–259.

Rigney, S. L. (2009). Public policy and the development of alternate assessments for students with cognitive disabilities. In W. D. Schafer & R. W. Lissitz (Eds.), *Alternate assessments based on alternate achievement standards: Policy, practice, and potential* (pp. 41–60). Baltimore, MD: Paul H. Brookes.

Roach, A. T., & Elliott, S. N. (2006). The influence of access to general education curriculum on alternate assessment performance of students with significant cognitive disabilities. *Educational Evaluation and Policy Analysis, 28,* 181–194.

Roberts, K. D., Park, H. J., Brown, S., & Cook, B. (2011). Universal design for instruction: A systematic review of empirically based articles. *Journal of Postsecondary Education and Disability, 24*(1), 5–15.

Rose, D. H., & Meyer, A. (2002). *Teaching every student in the digital age.* Alexandria, VA: ASCD. Retrieved from http://www.cast.org/teachingeverystudent/ideas/tes/

Rose, D. H., Meyer, A., & Hitchcock, C. (2005). *The universally designed classroom: Accessible curriculum and digital technologies.* Cambridge, MA: Harvard Education Press.

Ryndak, D. L., Moore, M. A., Orlando, A. M., & Delano, M. (2008–2009). Access to the general curriculum: The mandate and role of context in research-based practice for students with extensive support needs. *Research and Practice for Persons with Severe Disabilities, 34,* 199–213. doi: 10.2511/rpsd.33.4.199

Sacks, P. (2000). Predictable losers in testing schemes. *School Administrator, 57*(11), 6–9.

Saven, J. L., Anderson, D., Nese, J. F. T., Farley, D., & Tindal, G. (2016). Patterns of statewide test participation for students with significant cognitive disabilities. *Journal of Special Education, 49,* 209–220. doi: 10.1177/0022466915582213

Shepard, L. (2000). The role of assessment in a learning culture. *Educational Researcher, 29*(7), 4–14.

Skibo, H., Mims, P., & Spooner, F. (2011). Teaching number identification to students with severe disabilities using response cards. *Education and Training in Autism and Developmental Disabilities, 46,* 124–133.

Soukup, J. H., Wehmeyer, M. L., Bashinski, S. M., & Bovaird, J. A. (2007). Classroom variables and access to the general curriculum for students with disabilities. *Exceptional Children, 74,* 101–120. doi: 10.1177/001440290707400106

Spooner, F., Knight, V., Browder, D., & Smith, B. (2012). Evidence-based practice for teaching academics to students with severe developmental disabilities. *Remedial and Special Education, 33,* 374–387. doi: 10.1177/0741932511421634

Swain, R., Lane, J. D., & Gast, D. L. (2015). Comparison of constant time delay and simultaneous prompting procedures: Teaching functional sight words to students with intellectual disabilities and autism spectrum disorder. *Journal of Behavioral Education, 24,* 210–229.

Thompson, S. J., Johnstone, C. J., Thurlow, M. L., & Altman, J. R. (2005). *2005 State special education outcomes: Steps forward in a decade of change.* Minneapolis, MN: University of Minnesota, National Center on Educational Outcomes. Retrieved from http://www.cehd.umn.edu/NCEO/OnlinePubs/2005StateReport.htm

Thompson, S. J., & Thurlow, M. (2001). *2001 State special education outcomes: A report on state activities at the beginning of a new decade.* Minneapolis, MN: University of Minnesota, National Center on Educational Outcomes. Retrieved from http://education.umn.edu/NCEO/OnlinePubs/2001StateReport.html

Thurlow, M. L., Wu, Y., Quenemoen, R. F., & Towles, E. (2016, January). *Characteristics of students with significant cognitive disabilities: Data from NCSC's 2015 assessment* (NCSC Brief No 8). Minneapolis, MN: University of Minnesota, National Center and State Collaborative.

Timberlake, M. T. (2016). The path to academic access for students with significant cognitive disabilities. *Journal of Special Education, 49,* 199–208. doi: 10.1177/0022466914554296

Towles-Reeves, E., Kearns, J., Kleinert, H., & Kleinert, J. (2009). An analysis of the learning characteristics of students taking alternate assessments based on alternate achievement standards. *Journal of Special Education, 42,* 241–254.

Towles-Reeves, E., Kleinert, H., & Anderman, L. (2008). Alternate assessments based on alternate achievement standards: Principals' perceptions. *Research and Practice for Persons with Severe Disabilities, 33,* 122–133.

US Department of Education. (2005, August). *Alternate achievement standards for students with the most significant cognitive disabilities: Non-regulatory guidance.* Retrieved from http://www2.ed.gov/admins/lead/account/saa.html

US Department of Education, Office of Special Education and Rehabilitative Services. (2015, November 16). *Dear colleague letter.* Washington, DC: Author.

Waugh, R. E., Fredrick, L. D., & Alberto, P. A. (2009). Using simultaneous prompting to teach sounds and blending skills to students with moderate intellectual disabilities. *Research in Developmental Disabilities, 30,* 1435–1447. doi: 10.1016/j.ridd.2009.07.004

Wehmeyer, M. L. (2006a). Beyond access: Ensuring progress in the general education curriculum for students with severe disabilities. *Research and Practice for Persons with Severe Disabilities, 31,* 322–326. doi: 10.1177/154079690603100405

Wehmeyer, M. L. (2006b). Universal design for learning, access to the general education curriculum and students with mild mental retardation. *Exceptionality, 14,* 225–235. doi: 10.1207/s15327035ex1404_4

Yin, Y., Shavelson, R. J., Ayala, C. C., Ruiz-Primo, M. A., Brandon, P., Furtak, E. M., . . . Young, D. B. (2008). On the impact of formative assessment on student motivation, achievement, and conceptual change. *Applied Measurement in Education, 21,* 335–359.

Ysseldyke, J. E., & Olsen, K. R. (1997). *Putting alternate assessments into practice: What to measure and possible sources of data (Synthesis Report No. 28).* Minneapolis, MN: University of Minnesota, National Center on Educational Outcomes. Retrieved from http://education.umn.edu/NCEO/OnlinePubs/Synthesis28.htm

8

Individualized Education Programs to Promote Access to the General Education Curriculum for Students with Intellectual Disability

Michael L. Wehmeyer, Suk-Hyang Lee

Since 1997, federal law regulating the provision of special education and related services has contained language that requires that the Individualized Education Programs (IEPs) of all students receiving special education services promote and ensure "access to the general education curriculum." We will discuss in greater detail what this means subsequently, and other chapters in this text discuss instructional strategies to promote the acquisition of skills related to core content areas (reading, math, science, etc.)—content areas at the heart of the access mandates. This chapter, like others in this section, focuses on the educational planning process and how IEP teams can ensure that students with intellectual disability receive the special education, supplementary aids and services, and related services that will enable them to be involved with and progress in the general education curriculum.

Federal Requirements for the Education of Students with Disabilities

It is worth taking some time to overview what, exactly, the Individuals with Disabilities Act (IDEA) requires with regard to the education of students with disabilities, in general, and with regard to access to the general education curriculum, specifically, beginning with how special education is understood in the law. Special education is defined (and, we should note, has always been defined) in the Regulations to IDEA as "specially designed instruction, at no cost to the parents, to meet the unique needs of a child with a disability" [IDEA Regulations Part 300, Subpart A, Sec. 300.39(a)(1)]. "Specially designed instruction" is defined as "adapting, as appropriate to the needs of an eligible child under this part, the content, methodology, or delivery of instruction" [IDEA Regulations Part 300, Subpart A, Sec. 300.39(b)(3)]. Such adaptations to content, methodology, or delivery of instruction are intended to (a) address the unique needs of the child that result from the child's disability, and (b) to ensure access of the child to the general education curriculum, so that the child can meet the educational standards within the jurisdiction of the public agency that apply to all children [IDEA Regulations Part 300, Subpart A, Sec. 300.39(b)(3)(i)(ii)].

Let's pause for a moment to be clear about what is intended. Special education is specially designed instruction. It is not a place and it is not an adjective to describe a student. It refers to adaptations to content, methodology, or delivery of instruction to meet the unique needs of the child to ensure that he or she can meet the educational standards within schools that apply to all children.

IDEA also mandates the provision of related services, defined as:

> . . . transportation and such developmental, corrective, and other supportive services as are required to assist a child with a disability to benefit from special education, and includes speech-language pathology and audiology services, interpreting services, psychological services, physical and occupational therapy, recreation, including therapeutic recreation, early identification and assessment of disabilities in children, counseling services, including rehabilitation counseling, orientation and mobility services, and medical services for diagnostic or evaluation purposes. Related services also include school health services and school nurse services, social work services in schools, and parent counseling and training.
>
> *[IDEA Regulations Part 300, Subpart A, Sec. 300.34(a)]*

Again, let's be clear about what IDEA intends: Related services are to be provided as necessary to assist a child with a disability to benefit from special education. In 1982, the US Supreme Court ruled in Board of Education of the Hendrick Hudson Central School District v. Rowley (Rowley, 1982, p. 458) that, in essence, an "appropriate" education (as in a free, appropriate public education, or FAPE) was one from which a student with a disability might reasonably derive benefit. The decision set two criteria for determining if a school has met its obligations under IDEA to provide FAPE:

> First, has the [school] complied with the procedures of the Act? And second, is the individualized education program developed through the Act's procedures reasonably calculated to enable the child to receive educational benefits?
>
> *(Rowley, 1982, pp. 206–207 as cited in Yell, Katsiyannis, & Hazelkorn, 2007)*

Yell and colleagues (2007), in analyzing the Rowley decision on its 25th anniversary, observed that as IDEA was reauthorized subsequent to Rowley, and particularly in the access to the general education curriculum mandates in the 1997 and 2004 reauthorizations, the standard for reasonable benefit has been changed and that "[in] the 25 years since the Rowley decision, the major purpose of IDEA has shifted from providing access to educational services to providing *meaningful and measurable* programs for students with disabilities" (p. 12).

So, the emphasis on reasonable benefit from special education (as per the related services definition) has to be considered with regard to meaningful and measurable progress in the general education curriculum.

One last definition before examining the IDEA "access to the general education curriculum" mandates themselves more closely is that of supplementary aids and services. The IDEA defines supplementary aids and services as:

> aids, services, and other supports that are provided in regular education classes, other education-related settings, and in extracurricular and nonacademic settings, to enable children with disabilities to be educated with nondisabled children to the maximum extent appropriate in accordance with Sec. 300.114 through 300.116."
>
> *[IDEA Regulations Part 300, Subpart A, Sec. 300.42]*

Sections 300.114 through 300.116 referred to in this definition refer to the so-called Least Restrictive Environment (LRE) requirements (Sec. 300.114), the continuum of alternative placements language (Sec. 300.115), and the placement requirements (300.116). Sec. 300.114 requires that each public agency must ensure that "(i) To the maximum extent appropriate, children with disabilities, including children in public or private institutions or other care facilities, are educated with children who are nondisabled; and (ii) Separate classes, separate schooling, or other removal of children with disabilities from the regular educational environment occurs only if the nature or severity of the disability is such that education in the regular classes with the use of supplementary aids and services cannot be achieved satisfactorily" [IDEA Regulations Part 300, Subpart A, Sec. 300.114(a)(2)(i)(ii)].

In Chapter 1 we discussed the historical context with regard to the LRE, the continuum, and placement components of IDEA. Clearly, IDEA still allows placement outside the context of the regular classroom. But, just as the 1997 and 2004 reauthorizations of IDEA have (as per Yell et al., 2007) changed the expectations for the education of learners with disabilities to emphasize meaningful, measurable progress, we would argue that innovations in instruction and changes brought about by changing understandings of disability have changed expectations for where a student is educated, as identified in Chapter 4 and the third generation of inclusive practices. Simply put, we are at a point in time when students with disabilities, including students with intellectual disability, can receive specially designed instruction in typical classroom settings, and—with the use of supplementary aids and services and related services—can succeed in those settings.

In many ways, ensuring such success begins with the IEP team. It is important that IEP team members understand what is expected with regard to access to the general education curriculum and how such expectations change the nature of the IEP. Chapter 4 provided the statutory language in IDEA pertaining to the access to the general education curriculum. The 1997 reauthorization required that the IEP of students with disabilities include:

> A statement of the special education and related services and supplementary aids and services to be provided to the child, or on behalf of the child, and a statement of the program modifications or supports for school personnel that will be provided for the child
>
> (i)   to advance appropriately toward attaining the annual goals;
> (ii)   to be involved and progress in the general curriculum;
> (iii)   to be educated and participate with disabled and non-disabled children
>
> *[Section 300.347(a)(3)]*

First, note that the expectation is not just access, but, in fact, *involvement with and progress in* the general education curriculum (the 2004 amendments changed the term from "general curriculum" to "general education curriculum"). The IDEA regulations define the "general education curriculum" as "the same curriculum as for nondisabled children." The IEP must include information about special education and related services and supplementary aids and services to be provided to the child that will enable that child to be involved with and progress in the general education curriculum and to be educated with his or her nondisabled peers.

A November 2015 Office of Special Education Programs (OSEP) "Dear Colleague" letter (https://www2.ed.gov/policy/speced/guid/idea/memosdcltrs/guidance-on-fape-11–17–2015.pdf) makes it clear that these expectations still exist:

> The Department interprets "the same curriculum as for nondisabled children" to be the curriculum that is based on a State's academic content standards for the grade in which a child is enrolled. This interpretation, which we think is the most appropriate reading of the applicable regulatory language, will help to ensure that an IEP for a child with a disability, regardless of the nature or severity of the disability, is designed to give the child access to the general education curriculum based on a State's academic content standards for the grade in which the child is enrolled, and includes instruction and supports that will prepare the child for success in college and careers. This interpretation also appropriately harmonizes the concept in the IDEA regulations of "general education curriculum (i.e., the same curriculum as for nondisabled children)," with the ESEA statutory and regulatory requirement that the same academic content standards

must apply to all public schools and children in the State, which includes children with disabilities.

And, with regard to implementation of this interpretation, the OSEP memo stated:

Based on the interpretation of "general education curriculum" set forth in this letter, we expect annual IEP goals to be aligned with State academic content standards for the grade in which a child is enrolled. This alignment, however, must guide but not replace the individualized decision-making required in the IEP process. In fact, the IDEA's focus on the individual needs of each child with a disability is an essential consideration when IEP Teams are writing annual goals that are aligned with State academic content standards for the grade in which a child is enrolled so that the child can advance appropriately toward attaining those goals during the annual period covered by the IEP. In developing an IEP, the IEP Team must consider how a child's specific disability impacts his or her ability to advance appropriately toward attaining his or her annual goals that are aligned with applicable State content standards during the period covered by the IEP. For example, the child's IEP Team may consider the special education instruction that has been provided to the child, the child's previous rate of academic growth, and whether the child is on track to achieve grade-level proficiency within the year.

In addressing the needs of students with the most significant cognitive disabilities, the OSEP memo stated:

The Department recognizes that there is a very small number of children with the most significant cognitive disabilities whose performance must be measured against alternate academic achievement standards, as permitted in 34 CFR §200.1(d) and §300.160(c). As explained in prior guidance, alternate academic achievement standards must be aligned with the State's grade-level content standards. The standards must be clearly related to grade-level content, although they may be restricted in scope or complexity or take the form of introductory or pre-requisite skills. This letter is not intended to limit a State's ability to continue to measure the achievement of the small number of children with the most significant cognitive disabilities against alternate academic achievement standards, but rather to ensure that annual IEP goals for these children reflect high expectations and are based on the State's content standards for the grade in which a child is enrolled.

In a case where a child's present levels of academic performance are significantly below the grade in which the child is enrolled, in order to align the IEP with grade-level content standards, the IEP Team should estimate the growth toward the State academic content standards for the grade in which the child is enrolled that the child is expected to achieve in the year covered by the IEP. In a situation where a child is performing significantly below the level of the grade in which the child is enrolled, an IEP Team should determine annual goals that are ambitious but achievable. In other words, the annual goals need not necessarily result in the child's reaching grade-level within the year covered by the IEP, but the goals should be sufficiently ambitious to help close the gap. The IEP must also include the specialized instruction to address the unique needs of the child that result from the child's disability necessary to ensure access of the child to the general curriculum, so that the child can meet the State academic content standards that apply to all children in the State.

Chapter 7 discusses innovation in alternate assessment, but we include this (lengthy) information from OSEP to emphasize the point that for all students, including students with intellectual disability who may have more extensive support needs, the federal law holds high expectations for student involvement with and progress in the general education curriculum. For many students with intellectual disability, the IEP has been an alternate curriculum, describing goals that students would work on that were outside the general education curriculum. The expectation now is that the IEP provide information with regard to special education services, related services, and supplementary aids and services that will enable students to progress in the general education curriculum. IDEA still requires that the educational programs of students with disabilities include goals related to students' "other educational needs that result from the child's disability," but it is clear that the starting point for the IEP team is the general education curriculum. In a subsequent section, we describe a process that IEP teams can follow to meet these requirements. First, though, we examine the research pertaining to access and students with intellectual disability.

Research on Access to the General Education Curriculum and Students with Intellectual Disability

In this section, we examine research investigating the degree to which students with intellectual disability have access to the general education curriculum, and factors impacting such access. This is not an examination of whether students can learn core content (Chapters 19 and 20) or whether students can learn in inclusive settings (Chapter 17), but research on the degree to which students have access to grade-level content and instruction and factors that mediate that outcome. Browder and colleagues (2007) provided a definition of the concept of grade-level content access:

> To be linked to grade-level standards, the target for achievement must be academic content (e.g., reading, math, science) that is referenced to the student's assigned grade based on chronological age. Functional activities and materials may be used to promote understanding, but the target skills for student achievement are academically focused. The alternate expectation for achievement may focus on prerequisite skills or some partial attainment of the grade level, but students should still have the opportunity to meet high expectations, to demonstrate a range of depth of knowledge, to achieve within their symbolic level, and to show growth across grade levels or grade bands.
>
> (p. 11)

Certainly, students with intellectual disability have had instruction in academic content in the past, and, as Wehmeyer, Field, Doren, Jones, and Mason (2004) noted, there is often considerable overlap between the general education curriculum (as defined by content and student achievement standards) and some important traditional "special education" instructional areas. For example, most state and local content and student achievement standards across multiple content areas contain language pertaining to component elements of self-determined behavior, such as goal setting, problem solving, and decision making, the promotion of which is an important component of the educational programs with intellectual disability (Chapter 16). What is unique, really, about this is the grade-level content focus—and does such a focus matter? Roach and Elliott (2006) conducted a study examining the influence of access to the general education curriculum by students with significant cognitive disabilities (including a focus on grade-level content instruction) on the performance of these students on a state alternate assessment in reading, language arts, and math. Roach and Elliott found that students who had greater access to the general education curriculum, increased time in the general education classroom, and academic goals on their IEP performed better on reading, language arts, and math assessments. Similarly, Kleinert and colleagues(2015) found that students who took the alternate assessment and were served in inclusive settings had greater expressive communication and reading and math skills.

So, to what degree do students with intellectual disability have such access? Wehmeyer, Lattin, Lapp-Rincker, and Agran (2003) observed 33 students with intellectual disability in naturally occurring classroom contexts from 120 to 240 minutes each to examine if they were involved in tasks related to the general education curriculum. Overall, students were observed to be either working on the same task as peers or on a task related to a different standard or benchmark for 70% of intervals. There was variability by level of impairment. Students with limited support needs were engaged in a task linked to a standard in 87% of intervals, while students with more extensive support needs were doing so 55% of the time. Students served in the general education classroom were observed working on tasks linked to a grade-level standard in 90% of intervals, while students served primarily in self-contained settings engaged in tasks related to a standard in only 50% of the observations intervals. Further, students with intellectual disability were working on a task linked to an IEP in 22% of the intervals, provided accommodations to work on a task linked to a standard 5% of the time, and were working on an adapted task 3% of the time. Moreover, there were significant differences in inclusive versus self-contained settings in a number of areas. Students served in inclusive settings were significantly more likely to be working on a task linked to a standard. Students educated primarily in self-contained settings were significantly more likely to be working on a task linked to a standard below grade level or on a task not linked to a standard, and to be working on a task linked to an IEP objective.

Soukup, Wehmeyer, Bashinski, and Bovaird (2007) examined access to activities that could be linked to district standards in social studies and science for 19 elementary students with intellectual disability. In 61% of intervals students' activities could be linked to a grade level standard, and in an additional 20% of intervals activities could be linked to an off-grade level standard. However, when examined based on how much time the student spent in the general education classroom, 83% of intervals for students in a high inclusion group and 93% of intervals for students in a moderate inclusion group could be linked to grade level standards, while not one of the intervals for students in the self-contained classroom were linked to grade-level standards (groups did not differ by level of impairment).

Lee, Wehmeyer, Palmer, Soukup, and Little (2008) used the same computer-based recording system utilized by Soukup and colleagues (2007) to examine the impact of promoting self-determination on student access to the general education. These observations occurred exclusively in a general education classroom, and in almost 80% of intervals students with disabilities were working on grade-level standards (compared to 93% of the time for peers without disabilities). In another 18% of intervals, students with disabilities were working on an off-grade level standard. In only 26% of the intervals was an IEP goal addressed, and it was suggested by Lee and colleagues (2008) that this was because students' IEPs were not well-aligned with the general education curriculum. Similarly, Matzen, Ryndak, and Nakao (2010) conducted structured interviews and classroom observations comparing instructional activities for three students with significant cognitive disabilities in both general education and self-contained classrooms and found that in general education contexts, students were disproportionately exposed to grade-level academic content, while during instruction in self-contained settings they were not.

These studies suggest, on one hand, that students receiving their education in self-contained settings tend to work on IEP goals that are not focused on grade-level, general education curriculum content. Students educated in the general education classroom, on the other hand, have frequent opportunities to work on tasks linked to grade-level standards. What the studies do not provide is information on why this is the case, though clearly teacher expectations play some role. Agran, Alper, and Wehmeyer (2002) surveyed teachers working with students with extensive and pervasive support needs about their perception of the access requirements as they applied to their students. When asked if they thought access to the general education curriculum was important, 75% of teachers agreed to some degree, though 63% of them indicated that they felt this was more important for students with high-incidence disabilities. The largest proportion (37%) of respondents in the Agran and colleagues (2002) study indicated that students were receiving an educational program developed wholly outside the context of the general curriculum. Nearly three quarters (75%) of respondents indicated that students with disabilities were evaluated exclusively by criteria stipulated in the IEP. A more recent study by Kleinert et al.

(2015) examined the degree to which students who took the alternate assessment across 15 states had access to general education settings. The researchers found that more than 90% of students were still served in self-contained classrooms, separate schools, or home settings, while only 7% were educated in the general education classrooms.

Dymond, Renzaglia, Gilson, and Slagor (2007) interviewed teachers working with students with and without disabilities to examine how they understood how issues of access to the general education curriculum might apply to students with significant cognitive disabilities. Eighty percent of respondents identified core content issues with regard to what they interpreted access to the general education curriculum to mean. General education teachers most frequently defined access for students with extensive and pervasive support needs as instruction in core content areas in the general education classroom using the same curriculum and materials provided to students without disabilities. Special educators, however, defined it as having access to an adapted curriculum that was "relevant and meaningful to the student and addresses individual student needs and interests" (p. 11). Timberlake (2016) interviewed 33 special educators about their decision making when promoting access to the general education curriculum for students with significant cognitive disabilities, finding that special education teachers feel isolated when making decisions about promoting academic access and significant barriers within general education classrooms.

Lee, Soukup, Little, and Wehmeyer (2009) studied student and teacher variables that predicted student access to the general education curriculum, finding that student engagement in behaviors that competed with learning (e.g., disruptive behavior, talking, inattention, etc.) interacted with the difficulty of the task and teacher instructional behavior (questioning, talking, reading aloud) and teacher management behavior (questioning, discipline, prompting) to predict access scores. Increased task difficulty predicted increased teacher management behavior, decreased teacher instructional behavior, and increased student competing behavior. Lee and colleagues (2009) pointed to the absence of appropriate supports (accommodations, adaptations) for students to succeed as mediating this sequence of behaviors, an issue that has been found in other studies. Lee, Wehmeyer, Soukup, and Palmer (2010) examined whether curriculum modifications predicted adaptive or maladaptive behaviors in general education settings for students with intellectual disability and determined that when students were engaged in tasks linked to an on- or off-grade standard without the support of any curriculum modification, they were more likely to be engaged in behaviors that competed with active engagement, but when engaged with standards and provided any type of curriculum modifications, were likely to be engaged in academically beneficial responses.

In addition to teacher, supports, and student factors, the IEPs of students with intellectual disability far too often fail to identify core content instruction. Karvonen and Huynh (2007) examined the IEPs of students with extensive support needs in the content areas of language arts and math, and found few IEP goals pertaining to either domain. When such goals were present, they tended to not be focused on grade-level content, but instead on 'functional' math skills that have made up traditional alternate curricular areas—like telling time or using a calendar—that are misunderstood as something different, not differentiated, from the general education curriculum (Trela & Jimenez, 2013).

Finally, research clearly establishes that instructional practices can improve access to the general education curriculum for students with intellectual disability. Lee and colleagues (2008) showed, using a randomized-control trial design, that students with intellectual disability who were provided instruction to promote skills leading to self-determination improved their access to the general education curriculum, a result echoed in a second randomized control trial by Shogren, Palmer, Wehmeyer, Williams-Diehm, and Little (2012). Agran, Wehmeyer, Cavin, and Palmer (2010) showed that teaching students with intellectual disability self-monitoring skills improved engagement in the general classroom and promoted access to the general education curriculum. In addition, the result of a meta-analysis on 15 single-subject research studies examining the efficacy of the Self-Determined Learning Model of Instruction (SDLMI) as an intervention for students with disabilities indicated that promoting self-determination using the SDLMI was effective in enabling students to attain goals related to the general education curriculum as well as transition-related goals (Lee, Wehmeyer, & Shogren, 2015). Spooner, Baker, Harris, Ahlgrim-Delzell, and Browder (2007) identified instructional strategies that have been shown to enhance student engagement and, as such, should promote access to the general education curriculum, including applying Universal Design for Learning (UDL) principles to promote student access to content (and, thus, involvement with and progress in the general education curriculum), peer-support interventions, and promoting self-determination. Spooner, Dymond, Smith, and Kennedy (2006) showed that training teachers to apply UDL principles changed their lesson planning in ways that would promote access.

Spooner, Knight, Browder and Smith (2012) documented evidence-based practices for teaching academic skills across content areas to students with severe developmental disabilities including time delay, task-analytic instruction, and systematic prompting and feedback. Jimenez and Staples (2015) showed that systematic early numeracy skill instruction was effective for three students with significant intellectual disability in gaining grade-aligned 4th- and 5th-grade Common Core math skills as well as proficiency of early numeracy skills. Systematic instruction can also be paired with assistive technology to promote access. Spooner, Kemp-Inman, Ahlgrim-Delzell, Wood, and Davis (2015) demonstrated the impact of using portable technology such as an iPad2 paired with systematic instruction to promote generalization and listening comprehension skills of students with severe disabilities. As such, there is a growing body of work suggesting that, with individualized and systematic instruction, students with extensive and pervasive support needs can access grade-level standards (Cusing, Clark, Carter, & Kennedy, 2005; Erickson & Davis, 2015; Hunt, McDonnell, & Crockett, 2012; Olson, Roberts, & Leko, 2015). Research is clear that students who are educated in the general education setting have greater access to the general education curriculum and that there are multiple strategies that can promote such access, but that too often the types of supports students need to succeed are not in place. Returning to the prior discussion, then, these findings suggest that IEP teams need strategies to identify special education services, supplementary aids and services, and related services that would enable students with intellectual disability to succeed. The final section of this chapter details such a model.

Designing IEPs to Promote Access to the General Education Curriculum for Students with Intellectual Disability

IDEA requires that the educational program of students with disabilities be designed to address the unique needs of students. Individualization is a hallmark of special education practice. Too often in the past, however, the IEP has become an alternative curriculum when, as has been discussed, it is clear from IDEA regulations that it should be a plan to identify goals, modifications, and strategies needed to enhance, not replace, the general education curriculum (Nolet & McLaughlin, 2000). Figure 8.1 provides a process that IEP teams can use to achieve the dual purposes of promoting access to the general education curriculum and ensuring that students' other educational needs are still addressed (Wehmeyer, Lance, & Bashinski, 2002).

The planning process in this model begins with the general education curriculum and student unique learning needs. The 2004 amendments to IDEA required that the IEP team include someone knowledgeable about the general education curriculum. As with the definition forwarded by Browder and colleagues (2007), it is clear that the general education curriculum is that which is derived from grade-level state and local standards and includes, at the least, core academic content areas. Increasingly, those standards are reflected in the Common Core Standards. Of course, educational planning of any type relies on assessment information, and the IEP team should have information gathered from such assessments of student capacity in the general education curriculum as well as prior instructional experiences. The IEP team also gathers information about other educational needs that may not (though

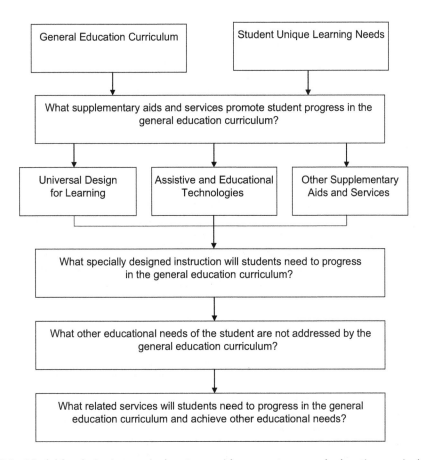

Figure 8.1 Model for designing curriculum to provide access to general education curriculum

at this point, the team is only gathering information about these other educational needs) be included in the general education curriculum.

Then, IEP teams are guided through the process by asking and answering four questions. The first such question is "What supplementary aids and services promote student progress in the general education curriculum?" As noted previously, IDEA defines supplementary aids and services as "aids, services, and other supports that are provided in general education classes or other education-related settings to enable children with disabilities to be educated with non-disabled children to the maximum extent appropriate." Such supplementary aids and supports include modifications to the curriculum or the classroom (room or seating arrangement), extended time to complete tasks, extended school year services, assistive and educational technology, a paraprofessional or notetaker, and other accommodations to promote regular classroom participation. Issues pertaining to UDL come into play here, with IEP teams considering how to modify the presentation or representation of content information or student's responses to the content (discussed previously) to promote student access and progress.

Next, teams ask "What specially designed instruction will students need to progress in the general education curriculum?" Again, as discussed previously, IDEA defines "special education" as "specially designed instruction." The IEP team should consider those instructional strategies that will be needed for students to be involved with and progress in the general education curriculum, many of which are discussed in later chapters in this text. After IEP teams have considered supplementary aids and services and specially designed instruction that would enable students to engage with the general education curriculum, they should then consider "What other educational needs of the student are not addressed by the general education curriculum?" Using strategies such as curriculum mapping and curriculum overlay, teams can identify where, in the context of the typical day within the school, students can address these other educational needs. Finally, the team should consider "What related services will students need to progress in the general education curriculum and achieve other educational needs?"

Summary

The context within which the education of students with intellectual disability are educated has changed from the early years of P.L. 94–142. IDEA sets high expectations that all students, including students with intellectual disability, will be educated with their nondisabled peers and provided the supports and modifications needed for them to be involved with and progress in the general education curriculum. Subsequent chapters in this text provide information on critical features of promoting such access to the general education curriculum, from UDL (Chapter 14), to promoting self-determination (Chapter 16) and inclusion (Chapter 17), to teaching core content areas (Chapters 19 and 20). Such efforts begin, however, with an IEP that promotes high expectations and not an alternative curriculum.

References

Agran, M., Alper, S., & Wehmeyer, M. (2002). Access to the general curriculum for students with significant disabilities: What it means to teachers. *Education and Training in Mental Retardation and Developmental Disabilities, 37*, 123–133.

Agran, M., Wehmeyer, M., Cavin, M., & Palmer, S. (2010). Promoting active engagement in the general education classroom and access to the general education curriculum for students with cognitive disabilities. *Education and Training in Autism and Developmental Disabilities, 45*, 163–174.

Browder, D.M., Wakeman, S.Y., Flowers, C., Rickelman, R.J., Pugalee, D., & Karvonen, M. (2007). Creating access to the general curriculum with links to grade-level content for students with significant cognitive disabilities: An explication of the concept. *The Journal of Special Education, 41*, 2–16.

Cusing, L.S., Clark, N.M., Carter, E.W., & Kennedy, C.H. (2005). Access to the general education curriculum for students with significant cognitive disabilities. *Teaching Exceptional Children, 38*, 6–13.

Dymond, S.K., Renzaglia, A., Gilson, C.L., & Slagor, M.T. (2007). Defining access to the general curriculum for high school students with significant cognitive disabilities. *Research and Practice for Persons with Severe Disabilities, 32*, 1–15.

Erickson, J., & Davis, C.A. (2015). Providing appropriate individualized instruction and access to the general education curriculum for learners with low-incidence disabilities. *International Perspectives on Inclusive Education, 5*, 137–158.

Hunt, P., McDonnell, J., & Crockett, M.A. (2012). Reconciling an ecological curricular framework focusing on quality of life outcomes with the development and instruction of standards-based academic goals. *Research and Practice for Persons with Severe Disabilities, 37*, 139 152.

Jimenez, B.A., & Staples, K. (2015). Access to the common core state standards in mathematics through early numeracy skill building for students with significant intellectual disability. *Education and Training in Autism and Developmental Disabilities, 50*, 17–30.

Karvonen, M., & Huynh, H. (2007). Relationship between IEP characteristics and test scores on an alternate assessment for students with significant cognitive disabilities. *Applied Measurement in Education, 20*, 273–300.

Kleinert, H., Towles-Reeves, E., Quenemoen, R., Thurlow, M., Fluegge, L., Weseman, L., & Kerbel, A. (2015). Where students with the most significant cognitive disabilities are taught: Implications for general curriculum access. *Exceptional Children, 81*, 312–328.

Lee, S.H., Soukup, J.H., Little, T.D., & Wehmeyer, M.L. (2009). Student and teacher variables contributing to access to the general education curriculum for students with intellectual and developmental disabilities. *Journal of Special Education, 43*, 29–44.

Lee, S.H., Wehmeyer, M.L., Palmer, S.B., Soukup, J.H., & Little, T.D. (2008). Self-determination and access to the general education curriculum. *The Journal of Special Education, 42*, 91–107.

Lee, S.H., Wehmeyer, M.L., & Shogren, K.A. (2015). The effect of instruction with the Self-Determined Learning Model of Instruction on students with disabilities: A meta-analysis. *Education and Training in Autism and Developmental Disabilities, 50*, 237–247.

Lee, S.H., Wehmeyer, M.L., Soukup, J.H., & Palmer, S.B. (2010). Impact of curriculum modifications on access to the general education curriculum for students with disabilities. *Exceptional Children, 76*, 213–233.

Matzen, K., Ryndak, D., & Nakao, T. (2010). Middle school teams increasing access to general education for students with significant disabilities. *Remedial and Special Education, 31*, 287–304.

Nolet, V., & McLaughlin, M. (2000). *Accessing the general curriculum.* Thousand Oaks, CA: Corwin Press.

Olson, A.J., Roberts, C.A., & Leko, M.M. (2015). Teacher-, student-, and peer-directed strategies to access the general education curriculum for students with autism. *Intervention in School and Clinic, 51*, 37–44.

Roach, A.T., & Elliott, S.N. (2006). The influence of access to general education curriculum on alternate assessment performance of students with significant cognitive disabilities. *Educational Evaluation and Policy Analysis, 28*, 181–194.

Rowley (1982). Board of Education of the Hendrick Hudson Central School District v. Rowley.

Shogren, K., Palmer, S., Wehmeyer, M.L., Williams-Diehm, K., & Little, T. (2012). Effect of intervention with the self-determined learning model of Instruction on access and goal attainment. *Remedial and Special Education, 33*, 320–330.

Soukup, J.H., Wehmeyer, M.L., Bashinski, S.M., & Bovaird, J. (2007). Classroom variables and access to the general education curriculum of students with intellectual and developmental disabilities. *Exceptional Children, 74*, 101–120.

Spooner, F., Baker, J.N., Harris, A.A., Ahlgrim-Delzell, L., & Browder, D.M. (2007). Effects of training in Universal Design for Learning on lesson plan development. *Remedial and Special Education, 28*, 108–116.

Spooner, F., Dymond, S.K., Smith, A., & Kennedy, C.H. (2006). What we know and need to know about accessing the general curriculum for students with significant cognitive disabilities. *Research and Practice for Persons with Severe Disabilities, 31*, 277–283.

Spooner, F., Kemp-Inman, A., Ahlgrim-Delzell, L., Wood, L., & Davis, L. (2015). Generalization of literacy skills through portable technology for students with severe disabilities. *Research and Practice for Persons with Severe Disabilities, 40*, 52–70.

Spooner, F., Knight, V.F., Browder, D.M., & Smith, B.R. (2012). Evidence-based practice for teaching academics to students with severe developmental disabilities. *Remedial and Special Education, 33*, 374–387.

Timberlake, M.T. (2016). The path to academic access for students with significant cognitive disabilities. *Journal of Special Education, 49*, 199–208.

Trela, K., & Jimenez, B.A. (2013). From different to differentiated: Using "ecological framework" to support personally relevant access to general curriculum for students with significant intellectual disabilities. *Research and Practice for Persons with Severe Disabilities, 38*, 117–119.

Wehmeyer, M.L., Field, S., Doren, B., Jones, B., & Mason, C. (2004). Self-determination and student involvement in standards-based reform. *Exceptional Children, 70*, 413–425.

Wehmeyer, M.L., Lance, G.D., & Bashinski, S. (2002). Promoting access to the general curriculum for students with mental retardation: A multi-level model. *Education and Training in Mental Retardation and Developmental Disabilities, 37*, 223–234.

Wehmeyer, M.L., Lattin, D., Lapp-Rincker, G., & Agran, M. (2003). Access to the general curriculum of middle-school students with mental retardation: An observational study. *Remedial and Special Education, 24*, 262–272.

Yell, M.L., Katsiyannis, A., & Hazelkorn, M. (2007). Reflections on the 25th anniversary of the US Supreme Court's decision in Board of Education v. Rowley. *Focus on Exceptional Children, 39*(9), 1–12.

9

Planning for Other Educational Needs and Community-Based Instruction

David W. Test, Fred Spooner, Debra Holzberg,
Colleen Robertson, Luann Ley Davis

Introduction

One of the purposes of the Individuals with Disabilities Education Act (IDEA, 2004) is to ensure that all children with disabilities receive a free, appropriate public education that will prepare them for further education, employment, and independent living [34CFR 300.1(a)] [20USC.1400(d)(1)(A)]. Part of this "free, appropriate" education is an Individualized Education Program (IEP). According to IDEA (2004):

> An IEP must include a statement of measurable annual goals, including academic and functional goals designed to meet the child's disability to enable the child to be involved in and make progress in the general curriculum and to meet each of the child's *other educational needs* [italics added] that result from the child's disability.
>
> *[34CFR§300.347(a)(2)]*

This chapter is designed to overview the planning needed for "other educational needs" and community-based instruction. The problem is that "other educational needs" is not specifically defined in IDEA; however, guidance from the US Department of Education states:

> Thus, if a child's unique needs require goals that address the child's present levels of educational performance in *nonacademic* [italics added] areas of instructional need, such as behavioral skills, communication and language skills, self-determination skills, job-related skills, independent living skills, or social skills, the statement of present levels of educational performance in the child's IEP should provide information regarding the child's present levels of educational performance in those areas.
>
> *(US Department of Education, Office of Special Education and Rehabilitative Services, 2000)*

As a result, since it appears that "other educational needs" relate to "nonacademic" areas, this chapter will focus on planning to help students with intellectual disability achieve their "other educational needs" or "functional" IEP goals.

While IDEA (2004) does not define "functional," in the comments section of the IDEA (2004) rules and regulations, it states:

> It is not necessary to include a definition of "functional" in these regulations because we believe it is a term that is generally understood to refer to skills or activities that are not considered academic or related to a child's academic achievement. Instead, "functional" is often used in the context of routine activities of everyday living.
>
> *(Federal Register, 2006, p. 46661)*

Based on this guidance, it might be expected that "functional" has been clearly defined by the field. But as you can probably guess by now, this is not the case. The field has many different names and definitions (although the definitions are fairly similar) including "adaptability skills" (Mithaug, Martin, & Agran, 1987), "life skills" (Cronin, 1996), and "daily living skills" (Storms, O'Leary, & Williams, 2000). Because of this we chose to use the definition of "life skills instruction" from the position paper of the Division for Career Development and Transition (Clark, Field, Patton, Brolin, & Sitlington, 1994) that states it includes "personal responsibility, social competence interpersonal relationships, health (physical and mental), home living, employability, occupational awareness, job skills, recreation and leisure skills, consumer skills, and community participation" (p. 126).

Given that IDEA requires "other educational needs" be included in a student's IEP, and the field has had a definition of "functional" skills since at least 1987, one might expect students with disabilities to be well-prepared for life after high school. But postschool outcome data indicate they are not. For example, data from the National Longitudinal Transition Study-2 (NLTS-2; Newman et al., 2011) gathered on students with disabilities who have been out of high school for eight years, indicate the following outcomes: (a) only 28.7% had ever enrolled in postsecondary education; (b) while 76.2% had been in paid employment, at the time of the interview, only 38.8% were currently employed, the average wage was $7.90 per hour, and only 48.6% had any benefits (this resulted in 93.4% having an annual income of $25,000 or less); (c) only 36.3% were living independently, 10.5% were married, and 25.3% had at least one child; (d) in terms of financial management, 42% had a savings account, 29% had a checking account, and 19.4% had a credit card; and (e) in terms of community engagement after high school, 58.1% indicated seeing friends outside of work weekly, 18.9% volunteered, and 36.6% belonged to a community group.

Clearly, if we are to improve the postschool outcomes of students with intellectual disability, we need to ensure each student receives the best educational services possible, which includes daily access to instructional practices based on the best research evidence available. The purpose of this chapter is to provide an overview of strategies for planning for other education needs and community-based instruction derived from research-based practices including planning for (a) determining what to teach, (b) how to teach these skills, and (c) how to assess student learning.

Determining What to Teach

Determining what to teach should be based on an individual student's preferences, strengths, and needs in both current and future settings. To do this requires assessing both students and environments to determine what other educational needs must be addressed.

Considerations for Selecting Appropriate Skills

Spooner and Test (1994) described six considerations (derived from Falvey, 1986; Fredericks & Brodsky, 1994) for selecting appropriate skills. The six considerations include the criterion of ultimate functioning, criterion of next environment, criterion of immediate environment, functionality, chronological age-appropriateness, and reflection of transition.

The criterion of ultimate functioning represents the dynamic, growing, and specific group of factors each individual must possess in order to function as completely and independently in socially, vocationally, and domestically integrated adult community environments (Brown, Nietupski, & Hamre-Nietupski, 1976). In other words, skills such as taking care of one's personal hygiene needs, dressing oneself, and preparing basic meals facilitate autonomy and foster greater self-efficacy.

The second consideration is the criterion of next environment, which examines the skills necessary for a child to function in the subsequent environment. For example, it would be important to work on independent toileting skills for a student transitioning from preschool to kindergarten. A student transitioning from high school to the workplace might need to know how to use public transportation.

The criterion of immediate environment is exactly what it suggests. It looks at skills necessary for the student to function in each of his or her current environments. In essence, it looks at the skills students need—both academic and nonacademic—to function in their current environment. It does not make sense to teach a student in fourth grade how to use public transportation in order to reach a work site; however, it does make sense to teach that student how to ride the school bus with his or her peers.

Functionality, the fourth component, is a more pragmatic perspective. While similar to the criterion of ultimate functioning, it hones in on specific skills and asks, "If the student is not able to perform the skill him- or herself, will someone else need to do that task for him or her?"

Next, it is important to consider the chronological age-appropriateness of skills and materials. Chronological age-appropriate skills are those that reflect the activities performed by their same-age peers without disabilities; in other words, chronological age-appropriateness refers to socially valid skills. For example, although Maya was a 17-year-old student, she often came to school in clothing more appropriate for a second grader (i.e., a My Little Pony T-shirt). Imagine the look on Maya's classmates' faces when, as a high school junior, she provided her classmates with an accounting of what the Easter bunny brought her. Clearly, these behaviors were not age appropriate. Ryndak, Alper, Hughes, and McDonnell (2012) suggest a relationship between students with significant disabilities in inclusive classrooms who have appropriate social skills services and postschool employment success.

The final consideration, reflection of transition, must demonstrate careful planning for the student's next environment in order to prepare the student for transition from secondary education into their next setting (i.e., work, postsecondary education). Factors to consider are transportation to and from the student's workplace or postsecondary educational setting; skills needed for independent living, including household tasks like laundry, cooking, and cleaning; health care needs; personal hygiene needs; and employment preparation skills (Spooner & Test, 1994; Test & Spooner, 1996).

Assessing Students

Although the term "assessment" has many different applications in education, researchers frequently use the more encompassing term "transition assessment" when referring to life skills assessment. According to the Division on Career Development and Transition (DCDT) of the Council for Exceptional Children, transition assessment refers to the

> . . .ongoing process of collecting data on the individual's needs, preferences, and interests as they relate to the demands of current and future working, educational, living, and personal and social environments. Assessment data serve as the common thread in the transition process and form the basis for defining goals and services to be included in the Individualized Education Program (IEP).
>
> (Sitlington, Neubert, & Leconte, 1997, p. 70–71)

The process encompasses two elements: life skills assessment and environmental or ecological assessment. Life skills assessments can be formal or informal—but, in either case, they must consider student choice through interest inventories, student conference, and parent input, and they must include the selection of appropriate skills. Formal life skills assessments include norm-referenced tests. In other words, formal assessments have been tested across a wide group of individuals and have been determined to be both reliable and valid means of gathering information on student performance (Spooner & Test, 1994).

Informal life skills assessments are excellent for gathering information about the student's functional skills and interests. They are usually more individualized, are typically developed by individuals working with students (i.e., teachers, transition coordinators), are not standardized (or norm-referenced), and are used to collect a large range of information in a variety of settings. Practitioners may use the following informal assessments: observations, checklists, surveys, rating scales, and interviews (student and parent).

Assessing the Environment

Returning to the six considerations mentioned at the beginning of the section, we look at assessing the environment. Each aspect (i.e., criterion of ultimate functioning, criterion of next environment, criterion of immediate environment, functionality, chronological age-appropriateness, reflection of transition) takes into account the needs of students in either the current or next environment. It is important to evaluate the student's skills relative to each environment. In other words, we must take into account what is needed in each environment and how that compares to the student's skills. In order to accomplish this objective, practitioners often conduct an ecological assessment.

An ecological assessment is a comprehensive, collaborative process in which data are collected about how a student currently functions in a variety of settings and includes ecological inventories, functional assessments, family interviews and collaborative planning processes, and person-centered planning (Brown et al., 1979; Hunt, McDonnell, & Crockett, 2012; Welch, 1994). In other words, an ecological assessment looks at the skills an individual needs in order to be successful in a personal environment (e.g., kindergarten general education classroom, middle school physical education class, workplace, restaurant).

The first part of the ecological assessment, the ecological inventory, is a list of life skills needed by the student in settings in which she or he currently functions or in which she or he will function in the future (Browder & King, 1987; Fredericks & Brodsky, 1994). The second part, the functional assessment, includes an assessment of the student's knowledge and skills followed by a determination of the skills the student needs in order to complete a particular task or goal (Fredericks & Brodsky, 1994). Together, teachers, parents, and students determine possible future residential and vocational placement settings for the student. The necessary skills for success in those placements are determined. The student's current and future placement settings are evaluated to determine the prerequisite skills needed. Then, the student's existing set of skills is compared to the skills needed to determine if and what gaps are present and what needs to be taught. Once a list of needed skills is generated, individual instructional goals are prioritized for the student.

Two levels (age ranges) underscore the functional assessment: the primary level and the secondary level. The primary level should have the following goals, predicated on the idea that communication and socialization are key skills for every individual: communication, self-help skills, motor skills/recreation, and academics/functional academics. When assessing older students (i.e., secondary level), it is imperative to examine potential future environments. At the secondary level, practitioners work with parents and students to determine the student's postschool environment. Four critical domains and skills are evaluated for students transitioning to the next environment (secondary level): social skills, independent living skills, leisure skills, and vocational and work skills (Fredericks, 1990; Fredericks & Brodsky, 1994).

Social skills encompass communication and independent living skills such as hygiene, transportation, food preparation, and time management. Leisure skills are important, as they are a way for students to integrate into the community and are seen as a key to a student's independence. Vocational and work skills refer to skills needed for a specific task such as stocking shelves or folding clothes. Additionally, associated skills may include skills from other domains such as social skills or independent living (Fredericks & Brodsky, 1994).

Family interviews and collaborative planning processes help determine what needs to be taught and the order in which it should be taught. Not only are the current needs considered, but it is imperative that future needs are considered, particularly with students in secondary education settings. Finally, person-centered planning empowers individuals to take an active role in planning their future and is an important aspect of student self-determination.

Planning how to Teach Students' Other Educational Needs

Planning how to teach students with intellectual disability their other educational needs involves several factors. The purpose of this section is to provide an overview of the key aspects in this planning process. First, who will provide the instruction (e.g., special education teacher, paraprofessional, job coach)? Second, where will instruction take place (e.g., simulated in the classroom, in the natural environment, or a combination of both)? Next, how will skills be taught (e.g., using total task/whole task chaining, constant time delay [CTD], video modeling)? Lastly, how will you plan to train for generalization to a range of community-based environments?

Who Will Provide the Instruction?

Teaching students with intellectual disability functional life skills such as riding a city bus to access a postsecondary college campus, a job, or a grocery store is an example of a priority skill that could help students with intellectual disability gain more independence in their life. Deciding who will provide the instruction depends upon staff content knowledge and whether they have the necessary skills to deliver the instruction. Additionally, liability or safety concerns also may be factors (e.g., paraprofessional without proper training to administer Diastat working with a student with intellectual disability with a history of seizures in a community-based setting). The IEP team needs to decide based upon knowledge, rapport, and staffing logistics (e.g., a paraprofessional clocks out at 2:00 pm and an in vivo training ends at 2:30 pm). The most appropriate person to implement the instructional opportunities is the special educator, paraprofessional, or job coach.

Special Educator

School district policies vary by state, but liability and safety concerns would warrant the lead teacher (special educator), rather than the paraprofessional, providing the initial instruction and follow-up probes in the community setting. For instance, Mechling and O'Brien (2010) taught three high school students with mild to moderate intellectual impairment how to request a specific stop on a bus route. The student's special educator taught each student one-on-one using a simulated, computer-based video instruction format to successfully teach the skill. Familiar landmarks such as Target were displayed as attentional cues to help students notice their stop was coming up. Generalization probes were later conducted in vivo, and all three students' skills transferred to the natural environment.

Paraprofessional

Day to day in special education classrooms, teachers rely upon paraprofessionals (for a variety of reasons, including, but not limited to, student-to-teacher ratios, IEP meetings or trainings that occur during the instructional day, or teacher absences) to share the load and work with students to address both their academic and functional needs. Lane, Carter, and Sisco (2012) surveyed 223 paraprofessionals regarding their roles in promoting skills leading to self-determination among K–12 students with high-incidence disabilities. Although paraprofessionals were not responsible for introducing new material to students, results revealed the quality and impact of their instruction was equally as valid as the licensed teachers'. Many paraprofessionals have years of classroom experience and are integral members of the teaching team, especially when valued as collaborative partners and provided with adequate guidance and training.

Job Coach

Assisting students with intellectual disability to prepare for their lives after they complete high school may include preparation for supported employment opportunities. Stocking groceries in a supermarket or hanging clothes for display in a department store are examples of supported employment tasks that a job coach could train a student to perform. Job coaches bridge the gap between special educators and employment supervisors. A job coach can assess the work environment to gauge the requisite skills needed for a student to perform the job and also the unique social demands involved. Employers may worry about prompt-dependent employees who require extra time and attention to complete tasks. Cihak, Kessler, and Alberto (2008) conducted a study with four high school students with intellectual disability using a handheld prompting device to complete vocational tasks (i.e., food prep in a restaurant, stocking items in a grocery store, and hanging garments in a department store). Results showed students were more independent, less reliant on external prompts, and completed their assigned tasks with fewer errors using the handheld device. A job coach can additionally help a student navigate unforeseen social situations that typically arise in work environments (e.g., questions about weekend plans or being asked for directions).

How Will Instruction Be Delivered?

Once the IEP team determines who the most relevant or skilled staff member is to teach the student, the next step is to decide how instruction will be delivered. The following section will discuss one-on-one vs. small group instruction. In order to maximize the conditions for a student to acquire new functional life skills, consideration of student instructional grouping needs to be addressed. Teaching discrete, chained skills can be taught via one-on-one instruction with less distraction for the student or via small group instruction with students working on similar goals. Referring back to the results of the assessments designed to elicit information regarding a student's needs, preferences, and interests, as well as the demands of the environmental context, will dictate the best mode of delivering instruction. Additional considerations include the total class size and number of support staff available.

One-on-One

Direct instruction involving the special educator or person in charge of teaching a specific skill and the student alone is commonly referred to as one-on-one or individual instruction. Recently, Hua, Morgan, Kaldenberg, and Goo (2012) found that it was beneficial to teach young adults with intellectual disability how to calculate gratuities for restaurant bills using one-on-one instructional methods. This could be viewed as an expansion upon the work of Test, Howell, Burkhart, and Beroth (1993) using the "one more than" technique as a strategy for counting money to make purchases by enabling students with intellectual disability to calculate percentages for the purpose of tipping.

An obvious advantage of one-on-one instruction resides in the undivided, personalized attention the student receives from the instructor. Typically students demonstrate higher rates of on-task behavior when taught one-on-one (Logan, Bakeman, & Keefe, 1997). The instructor can more aptly redirect off-task behavior, provide prompts specific to the student's unique learning needs, and often move through the material more efficiently in regards to time.

Disadvantages to one-to-one instruction include staffing, high student-to-teacher ratios, and budgetary constraints that may prohibit this form of teaching when other students are simultaneously in need of instructional time and attention. Additionally, in reference to helping students increase their independence for postsecondary life experiences, consistent one-on-one support is neither a realistic nor sustainable long-term solution.

One-on-one instruction may be utilized most effectively during initial skill acquisition, then faded as the student gains independence and skill mastery. Small group instruction is an appropriate option when students have similar community-based needs (e.g., preparing a meal or making a purchase) and are otherwise homogeneous in their functional and intellectual abilities.

Small Group Instruction

Definitions of small group instruction vary by exact number yet typically range from two to five students to each staff member conducting training. Reid and Favell (1984) discussed the spaced-trial format in which the teacher presents stimulus materials sequentially to each student in the small group. In a review of more than 50 studies addressing functional life skills curricula to enhance postschool outcomes for students with disabilities, Alwell and Cobb (2009) concluded that more research is needed to determine the optimum methods and settings for teaching life skills.

Before IDEA and No Child Left Behind (NCLB) were mandated, Collins, Gast, Ault, and Wolery (1991) discussed the advantages of small group instruction for students with moderate to severe intellectual impairment. Logic dictates these benefits would naturally extend to most students with or without disabilities. First, staff can work with multiple students at once. Students can be actively engaged simultaneously, making effective use of staffing resources and instructional time. Additionally, students can benefit by learning functional and social skills from their peers.

Potential drawbacks of small group instruction can include variations in teaching style among instructors. For instance, one special education teacher may use well-honed systematic instructional practices, prompting strategies, and behavior-chaining procedures while another instructor may not be as adept using these teaching techniques. Inequities in instructional presentation between the small groups can lead to disparities in skill acquisition for students.

Once staffing and grouping decisions have been made, the mode of instructional delivery needs to be determined.

Where Will Instruction Take Place?

Although it seems logical that other educational need skills would be best taught in the environment in which the student would naturally use the skill, budgetary issues (e.g., transportation, personnel, community-based instructional expenses) and scheduling logistics (e.g., staffing and interference with other school activities or therapy sessions) may limit instruction in the natural environment. As a result, the IEP team needs to decide if instruction will occur through classroom simulations or in vivo in the natural environment, or a combination.

Using Simulated Settings

A simulated setting can be defined as a pretend or close approximation of the natural environment (e.g., restaurant, bank, grocery store) where the skill is to be used. Mechling, Pridgen, and Cronin (2005) suggest that when teaching using simulations, it is important to replicate the materials and stimuli found in the natural setting as much as possible to promote skill generalization. Given advances in technological devices, teaching using video-based formats is becoming more common and accessible. Computer-based video instruction, video prompting, and video modeling teaching strategies will be discussed in the next section.

Using a simulated setting has the advantage of reducing the need for scheduling community-based outings. The use of well-constructed simulations eliminates the burden of financial constraints, staffing coverage, parental permission paperwork, and transportation. For example, Mechling and O'Brien (2010) conducted a study teaching three students with intellectual disability to utilize a public bus route using computer-based video instruction relying solely on video simulations and found students were able to generalize the skills learned without community-based instruction included. One clear benefit of teaching a student using a simulated setting is the ability to provide multiple opportunities or teaching trials.

In contrast, simulations have the potential disadvantage of not adequately preparing students for the unpredictable nature of experiences in the natural environment. For instance, a classroom simulation involving making a store purchase may omit the social nuances of different store clerks' personalities, credit card payment machine prompts, and unfamiliar questions. Additionally, simulations are only as valid as the functional results they produce. If a student is able to score 100% during each teaching trial in the classroom practicing how to go through a lunch line but cannot generalize these skills to the school cafeteria, how valid is the data if the skill is not useful in vivo?

Natural Environments

Herrygers, Clark, Crosland, and Deschênes (2009) suggest in vivo teaching involves training in relevant natural community settings (home, school, work) to develop and assist the generalization of relevant skills to appropriate settings and people. Ideally, students would have unlimited opportunities to acquire functional life skills in their communities.

The advantage of teaching in the natural environment equates to preparing students for the uncertain nature of real-life situations. To adequately prepare students for real-life situations, opportunities to learn and utilize functional life skills need to occur in the setting where they will ultimately be used, in the natural environment. Kelley, Test, and Cooke (2013) recently found that college-age students with intellectual disability were able to navigate a college campus successfully using picture prompts on an iPod device to locate their desired destinations in vivo. This approach is additionally significant in that the students with intellectual disability utilized iPods, which are unobtrusive and similar in size and design to commonplace smartphones their same-age peers would likely use on a college campus.

Disadvantages of instruction in the natural environment involve (a) thorough logistical planning, (b) time out of the classroom, (c) appropriate staffing, (d) safety considerations, (e) transportation, and (f) financial expenses. Additionally, teaching in the natural environment may limit the number of naturally occurring instructional opportunities (e.g., placing an order at a restaurant equals one teaching trial).

Using a Combination of Simulated and Natural Environments

Browder and Spooner (2011) discussed the benefit of a hybrid approach combining classroom simulations and instruction in the natural environment to increase the likelihood of skill acquisition, mastery, and generalization. Morse and Schuster (2000) taught 10 elementary-age students with moderate intellectual impairment using a combination of classroom-based instructional simulations and in vivo teaching to effectively teach grocery shopping skills. Half of the students learned how to locate grocery items during the classroom simulation using picture symbols on a storyboard, while the other half of the students learned in vivo using CTD.

There are pros and cons of both approaches to negotiate. The ultimate goal lies in providing students the best instructional opportunities to promote skill generalization in the natural environment based upon predetermined wants and needs revealed from their ecological assessments and postsecondary life goals.

Once the who, how, and where of instruction are decided, the next question is, what evidence-based teaching strategies will be used to facilitate skill acquisition?

How Will Instruction Be Delivered?

Over the years, research and evidence-based strategies to teach functional life skills have been validated as effective practices both in and outside of the classroom, including (a) total task chaining, (b) CTD, (c) computer-based video instruction including video prompting and video modeling, and (d) training individuals with intellectual disability to generalize the skills learned to other environments, people, and materials.

Total Task Chaining

Total task chaining or whole task presentation is defined as a variation of forward chaining because the student is provided instruction on each step of the task analysis chain from beginning to end during each instructional session (Cooper, Heron, & Heward, 2007; Spooner, 1984). Similarly, Browder and Spooner (2011) describe total task presentation as a form of task analysis chaining procedure that instructs an individual through each step from the beginning until a designated level of mastery is achieved. Hammond, Whatley, Ayres, and Gast (2010) conducted a study with three students with moderate intellectual impairment using a total task chaining procedure to teach the students how to effectively access leisure activities independently (e.g., watching a movie, listening to music, and looking at photos on an iPod). Additionally, Ayres, Maguire, and McClimon (2009) taught three students with intellectual disability using a total task format to successfully set a table, make soup, and prepare a sandwich.

The benefit of total task or whole task presentation lies in that the student moves from the first step in chain to the last step during every training opportunity. McDonnell and McFarland (1988) refer to total task presentation as "concurrent chain training" and note that students with severe intellectual disability were taught how to use laundromat washers and dryers more efficiently and maintained their skills better than when taught using forward chaining procedures. The benefit is that every step in the chain is attempted until the task is completed.

Constant Time Delay

Snell and Gast (1981) define CTD as a near-errorless systematic procedure in which a stimulus prompt is paired with a second prompt occurring at a set delay point (e.g., typically 3 to 5 seconds) until "stimulus control is shifted from the prompt to the task request and materials" (p. 4). Browder and Spooner (2011) further clarify that "constant time delay, after several rounds at a zero delay, the stimulus is presented, and the instructor waits a predetermined amount of time (e.g., 4 seconds) before the controlling prompt is provided" (p. 106). Collins, Karl, Riggs, Galloway, and Hager (2010) highlight the importance of embedding real-life, functional skills such as grocery shopping and preparing a meal into classroom instructional opportunities using CTD. Recently, Seward, Schuster, Ault, Collins, and Hall (2014) used CTD for five high school students with moderate to severe intellectual impairment to teach them solitaire card games as a leisure activity and found CTD to be an effective instructional strategy.

Computer-Based Video Instruction (CBVI), Video Prompting, and Video Modeling

Recent research has shown computer-based instruction including video prompting and/or video modeling to be effective teaching tools for students with a range of intellectual impairments.

The ease, portability, and affordable aspect of computer-based instructional methods (e.g., including handheld smartphone, or iPod or iPad technology) are making this teaching tool more commonplace. CBVI admittedly takes on many forms, as Ayres et al. (2009) note, yet central to the technique involves the use of prerecorded video prompts or models that allow students to watch and practice target behaviors that typically simulate functional, community-based skills (e.g., using a debit machine or ordering at a fast-food restaurant). Ramdoss et al. (2012) reviewed 50 studies involving individuals with intellectual disability incorporating computer-based interventions (CBI) to promote daily living skills and noted that CBI is a promising approach.

Video prompting is described by Franzone and Collet-Klingenberg (2008) as separating a skill into components and recording steps with pauses where the learner attempts one step before viewing later steps. This can be accomplished with someone else serving as the model or with the learner. Mechling and Gustafson (2009) conducted a comparison study with static picture prompts and video prompting involving six students with moderate intellectual impairment performing cooking skills. Results indicated that all six students demonstrated higher rates of accuracy with the cooking tasks when provided video prompting over static picture prompts alone.

Video modeling is defined as "a mode of teaching that uses video recording and display equipment to provide a visual model of the targeted behavior or skill" (Franzone & Collet-Klingenberg, 2008, p. 2). Mechling, Ayres, Foster, and Bryant (2013) studied the effects of custom-made video models vs. commercially made video models with young adults with moderate intellectual impairment for cooking foods such as pancakes and mashed potatoes. The results demonstrate that all students exhibited higher performance when preparing the recipes with the custom-made videos.

How Will You Train for Generalization?

Ultimately, effective instructional practices should be planned to prepare students with the other educational needs skills that prepare them to be as successful as possible in their lives after graduation, living independently, securing employment, and/or enrolling in postsecondary educational opportunities. Whether functional life skills are taught in a simulated setting using CBVI or in vivo using total task or CTD procedures, special educators' time is well spent when planning includes clear organization and attention to how their training opportunities can maximize the potential for student success in natural environments independently. Educators' long-range goals for students ought to be designed to promote greater levels of independence, which includes planning for generalization and skill maintenance over time. Neidert, Dozier, Iwata, and Hafen (2010) reiterate the importance of teaching students with intellectual disability using natural reinforcers, using a sufficient number of exemplars, training for a variety of unknown conditions, and training using stimuli that is likely to be present in other settings so students can experience the best outcomes. Stokes and Baer (1977), in their classic piece on training for generalization, outline nine strategies for promoting generalization. Of these nine strategies, three consistently appear in the research literature: (a) introducing natural contingencies, (b) training multiple exemplars, and (c) programming common stimuli.

Introducing Natural Contingencies

Stokes and Baer (1977) define natural contingencies or reinforcers as "teaching behaviors that will be reinforced in the student's natural environment" (p. 167). Copper et al. (2007) expand on this definition and add "a naturally existing contingency of reinforcement (or punishment) that operates independent of the practitioner's efforts" (p. 623). Mechling et al. (2005) conducted a study with three high school students with moderate intellectual impairment, teaching them how to order meals at a variety of fast-food restaurants (e.g., Wendy's, McDonald's, and Hardees). Students were taught using computer-based video models of task-analyzed steps and constant time procedures to place their orders and pay for their meals. The natural contingency or natural reinforcers for these students were receiving their desired food choices (i.e., reward or reinforcement for ordering correctly) in a timely manner. In effect, these students learned to provide the accurate target behavior—ordering their food—and received the naturally occurring and reinforcing contingency, their preferred meals.

Training Multiple Exemplars

Training multiple exemplars is based directly on Stokes and Baer's (1977) seminal article on generalization discussing training sufficient exemplars and was translated into layperson's terms by Spooner and Test (1994) suggesting that the behavior be trained in a number of settings and/or/with several different instructors. In a study conducted with three middle school students with autism and intellectual disability, Ayres et al. (2009) used CBVI to teach the students how to make sandwiches, prepare soup, and set a table using a chained task procedure and modified least-to-most prompting system. The research team varied the locations (e.g., home, classroom, school cafeteria), materials (e.g., different brands and flavors of soup; types of meats and cheeses), and combined teacher and computer-based prompts. These variations embedded multiple exemplars and aided students in promoting skill generalization across a range of locations, materials, and conditions successfully to their natural settings. One parent later commented that her son corrected her when she placed the napkin on the wrong side of the plate.

Programming Common Stimuli

Programming common stimuli is defined as making the training setting comparable to the natural environment (Spooner & Test, 1994; Stokes & Baer, 1977). Programming common stimuli involves including typical features of the generalization setting into the instructional setting. Given these parameters for training for generalization, special educators need to attempt to replicate the most salient features of the natural environment by using real materials and situations. Stock, Davies, Wehmeyer, and Palmer (2008) conducted a study to teach 22 adolescents and young adults with intellectual disability to use cellphones to send and receive phone calls and increase socialization with their peers. The phones were set up with a specially designed software program called Pocket ACE (Accessible Communication Enabler) that allowed participants to locate their contacts using a picture-based address book. The research team used common, unobtrusive cellphones similar to standard smartphones used by many people in the mainstream population. Adaptations such as this demonstrate that a specific plan for skill acquisition and generalization was incorporated to promote participant independence and success across natural environments and situations.

The examples mentioned lend credence to the efficacy of proper planning for student success in natural environments by embedding generalization strategies into instructional opportunities. Thorough planning (e.g., determining who, where, how, and what steps to promote generalization) is critical for ensuring the best outcomes for students with intellectual disability and their other educational needs beyond the classroom. Effective instructional practices, for either functional or academic tasks, require accurate assessment and data collection, which will be discussed next.

Planning How to Assess Student Learning

Assessment is more than simply administering tests and interpreting results. Unlike formal testing, assessment is much broader, being conceptualized as a systematic process for gathering information (or data) for use in making diagnostic, legal, educational, and postschool decisions. The main difference is that data collected during the assessment process are centered on content and individual performance, rather than formal norm-based testing with comparisons to other students. Planning for, and administering assessments, is critical to effectively and successfully provide services to students with intellectual disability. Assessments are used to determine what to teach based on a student's current level of functioning on a specific task, to monitor his or her ongoing progress towards a goal, and to determine if a skill is maintained over time and generalized to novel situations.

Determining and planning the who, how, and when of assessment is dependent on the purpose of the assessment and the specific identified goals for each individual student. Assessment can provide professionals with information needed to give direction to instruction and enable teachers to adequately monitor student progress to make timely adjustments to instruction as needed. We must always start with the end in mind: Target the goal and provide sound evidence-based assessments and progress monitoring that will ensure students with intellectual disability meet goals and are successful. Students with intellectual disability often present unique challenges; however, Donnellan (1984) suggested teachers should make the "least dangerous assumption" by assuming all students can learn. It is important to choose assessments and data collection strategies that are as least intrusive as possible yet provide adequate data to determine instructional effectiveness. In planning for assessments and data collection, four questions should be considered: (a) Who will conduct the assessments? (b) How will they be conducted? (c) When and how often should assessments be given? and (d) How will the data from the assessment be collected?

Who Conducts the Assessments and How Will They Be Conducted?

Teachers, related service providers, and students can all play active roles in assessment. Teachers and related service providers can use assessment for progress monitoring for students with intellectual disability (Browder, 1987; Fredericks & Brodsky, 1994). Students can use assessment to increase their independence by gaining the skills necessary to monitor and regulate their own performance through self-monitoring and self-recording.

Teachers and Related Service Providers

There is a broad range of informal teacher assessments and procedures that can be used to assess the effects of instruction on other educational needs. Teacher-administered assessments include work sample assessments, task analysis, portfolio assessments, functional assessments, and criterion-referenced assessments. All of these informal assessments can be considered when planning to assess the effects of teacher instruction by monitoring student progress.

WORK SAMPLE ASSESSMENTS

In a work sample assessment, the teacher collects samples of the student's work to identify areas that the student has made progress on and areas that will need further remediation and instruction. By reviewing the student's work samples, a teacher can identify patterns or trends in a student's errors and determine where instructional methods need to be altered, as well as what is working successfully to replicate that instructional method in areas of need. A work sample assessment can include anything from collecting mock timecards, whose purpose is to increase a student's punctuality, that indicate at what time a student arrived and left, to collecting log-in sheets that include the number of times over a certain period that a student was able to successfully log into the computer independently.

TASK ANALYSIS

A task analysis can be used as *both* an assessment strategy, and an instructional strategy. A task analysis involves the teacher, or other related service provider, breaking a complex task or skill into smaller, teachable steps. The teacher can then monitor a student's progress based on the number of steps completed independently and correctly each day by creating a graph to provide a visual display of growth. This also allows the teacher to make timely adjustments to the task analysis by adding, altering, or omitting steps depending on the students' ability.

PORTFOLIOS

A portfolio assessment includes collecting student work products that are used to demonstrate skill improvement over time for a student's specified objectives and goals. This strategy is one of the most widely used as it allows teachers to collect artifacts to demonstrate growth that students would have completed anyhow without additional instruction or assessment methods required by the teacher. Portfolios can display students' efforts, progress, and achievements in an organized and structured way. Individualized items reveal a student's goals, interests, and abilities in various curricular and community-based areas. Portfolios can include a collection of multiple artifacts of a student's work or performances that pertain to each of the students' goals (Kearns, Burdge, Clayton, Denham, & Kleinert, 2006). For example, an anecdotal record in the portfolio that shows how the student is progressing toward a goal (e.g., notes on a student's first attempt at opening the lock on their school locker, until they are able to successfully unlock it independently). Such items often reveal many aspects of learning, thinking, and performance. By compiling and discussing portfolios together, teachers and students can make instructional decisions. Each portfolio parallels classroom and community-based activities that can lead to new activities based on each student's progress and interests. Portfolios are meaningful to students as they enable students to take an active role in evaluating their own work and progress. Although this strategy is widely accepted, teachers and other related service providers using this assessment strategy need to ensure that the artifacts collected are consistent with the specific instructional objectives and goals identified for each individual student.

TEACHER-MADE CRITERION-REFERENCED ASSESSMENTS

These assessments provide teachers and related service personnel with information on how well a student is performing. Criterion-referenced tests, a type of test introduced by Glaser (1962) and Popham and Husek (1969), also are known as domain-referenced tests, competency tests, basic skills tests, mastery tests, performance tests or assessments, authentic assessments, and objective-referenced tests. In this strategy, the instructor sets the specific criteria that will serve as the standard for what each student is expected to do or know, with the scoring set to allow comparisons to these benchmarks (e.g., student will attend to a task for 15 minutes; teacher will track student's progress toward this set criterion). These assessments allow teachers to interpret what an individual can do without considering the performance of others. They are designed to measure the results of instruction and each student's individual performance on a specific behavioral or instructional objective because they compare a student's individual skill mastery to a specific criterion set by the teacher. These assessments allow the teacher to determine the individual needs and abilities to aid in the selection of areas to target in intervention, allowing instructional goals and approaches to be specifically created for each student.

Student Self-Instruction and Self-Recording

Students with intellectual disability also can actively participate in assessing their instructional progress through self-monitoring and self-graphing. By doing so, students are able to experience greater independence and self-determination by guiding themselves through tasks and recording their own data. Research has shown students who are more self-determined when they leave high school achieve more positive employment, independent living, and quality-of-life outcomes than do their peers with intellectual disability who are less self-determined (Wehmeyer & Palmer, 2003; Wehmeyer & Schwartz, 1997).

A major component of self-determination is the ability to self-monitor one's behavior (Wehmeyer, Gragoudas, & Shogren, 2006). Self-monitoring occurs when a student assesses his or her own behavior to determine whether the desired behavior occurred and then records the occurrence or nonoccurrence of the behavior (Lee, Palmer, & Wehmeyer, 2009; Lienemann & Reid, 2006). The use of self-monitoring has several benefits for students, including (a) increasing self-reliance, (b) decreasing overreliance on external sources (e.g., teacher, paraprofessional), (c) increasing instructional time, and (d) improving overall quality of life (Lee et al., 2009; Wehmeyer, Hughes, Agran, Garner, & Yeager, 2003). Students can use checklists, task analyses, and/or self-graphing (with or without picture cues or sight words) to monitor and assess their own progress.

CHECKLISTS

The use of a checklist can foster greater independence and build students' self-monitoring skills. A checklist outlining the students' daily routine can assist students in organizing their day, reduce dependence on teacher directives, and increase their independence. Adding a sight word in place of a sentence can serve as a prompt for students who are emerging readers. For students who are currently nonreaders, the addition of a picture cue to each item on the checklist can assist in helping them identify each item on the list independently. As a student becomes familiar with the schedule, the teacher can fade (or remove) the picture cues and enable the student to enrich his or her sight word base. Students can review their checklist at the end of the day and track their own progress towards independently completing each of the items by graphing them (e.g., in a notebook, on poster-board on the wall). Teachers also can collect data on each student's independent use of the checklist and use that information to target instruction, and indicate demonstrated strengths and needs. Checklists can be used to assess the mastery of a variety of types of skills, including safety, food preparation, mobility, leisure, and community activities. A checklist for safety skills might include items such as avoiding strangers, asking for help, using a cellphone, and using a seat belt (Browder, 2001).

TASK ANALYSIS

Students also can monitor their own progress by using a task analysis. Although the teacher or other related service provider may need to create the task analysis and provide instruction to the student on how to perform each of the individual steps of a chained task, the goal is that, over time, the student will use the steps of the task analysis to complete the task independently. The number of steps to include depends on the ability level of the student. The student can count the number of steps completed correctly and independently, then graph them to create a visual of his or her own growth (e.g., steps to independently open a carton of milk). The end result is that as the student masters each step, the teacher can reduce the number of steps until the student no longer needs the task analysis and can independently perform the task. Table 9.1 is an example of a basic-step task analysis using picture cues. The picture cues make it easy for nonreaders to use the task analysis as a self-monitoring checklist.

SELF-GRAPHING

Another strategy that students can use independently to assess their own progress towards learning a new skill is self-graphing. A self-graphing task analysis is presented in an upside-down format. The first step is located at the bottom of the page with each additional step in the chain placed on top. Step numbers are placed in columns to the right of each written step and as the learner completes each task, the correctly performed step is marked over with an "X." When the student has completed

Table 9.1 Basic skills task-analysis with picture cues for mowing the grass

Skill or Task To Be Completed		+/–	+/–	+/–	+/–	Comments
1. Get out the mower.						
2. Start the mower.						
3. Depress the lever.						
4. Push mower in straight line from edge of lawn to edge of lawn.						
5. Repeat passes of mower from edge to edge until all yard is mowed.	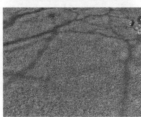					

6. Turn mover off.

7. Empty grass catcher bag from mower into a garbage bag.

8. Set garbage bag on street curb.

9. Clean and put mower away.

Table 9.2 Self-graphing task analysis for accessing a website

Steps Date:	08/19	08/20	08/21	08/22	08/23		
10. Move the cursor with the mouse to the website of choice and click the mouse.	10	10	10	10	10	10	10
9. Hit the "enter" button on the keyboard.	9	9	9	✗	9	9	9
8. Type in the search topic of interest using the keyboard.	8	8	8	8	8	8	8
7. Left click using the mouse in the Google search box.	7	7	7	7	7	7	7
6. Move the cursor with the mouse to the Google search box.	6	6	6	⑥	6	6	6
5. Double click the Internet Explorer icon.	5	5	⊗	✗	5	5	5
4. Move the cursor using the mouse until it points to the Internet Explorer icon.	4	⊗	✗	✗	4	4	4
3. Place hand on the mouse.	⊗	✗	✗	✗	3	3	3
2. Press the monitor power button.	✗	✗	✗	✗	2	2	2
1. Press the computer power button.	✗	✗	✗	✗	1	1	1

the task, the numbers of X's are totaled, and the number of correct steps is circled on that column. Table 9.2 gives an example of a self-graphing task analysis for accessing a website. For example, the student completed three steps independently correct on August 19, then four steps the next day, then five steps, and six steps independently correct on the last date that data was collected. When the correct number of steps is circled and connected with a line, a performance graph is created. The self-graphing strategy makes data collection and instructional decision making simpler as a graph is created as the data is collected, and is a simple way for students to get immediate feedback on their performance to self-monitor their own progress.

When and How Often Should Assessment Be Given?

Simply stated, student learning needs to be assessed as often as necessary for a teacher to be able to evaluate student progress on acquiring, maintaining, and generalizing skills. Daily assessments can be used for tasks such as navigating from one place to another, increasing a student's time on task, or tracking punctuality. Teachers, related service providers, and students do not need to record every response that is made; the use of intermittent probes can be highly effective in evaluating the effects of instruction. As a basic guideline, (a) after specific goals have been targeted for a student, and prior to instruction, an assessment should be conducted to establish a baseline or starting point of what the student knows before instruction; (b) during acquisition, conduct at least one data collection probe for each day of instruction for each new skill being taught, and (c) when a skill is mastered (e.g., performed correctly three times in a row independently) move to probing one time per week; finally, (d) after three weekly probes, move to monthly probes.

Table 9.3 Assessment categories, who administers, and examples

Categories	Administration	Examples
Work Sample Assessment	Teacher or other related service provider	Samples of student's ability to sew on a button
Task Analysis	Student, teacher, or other related service provider	List of steps to purchase a movie ticket online
Portfolio Assessment	Teacher or other related service provider	Collection of recipes that student has independently prepared, with anecdotal notes
Functional Assessment	Teacher or other related service provider	Correctly measuring laundry soap according to the directions to wash a load of clothing
Criterion-Referenced Assessment	Student, teacher, or other related service provider	Correctly count coins to $1.00 using quarters or dimes
Checklists	Student, teacher, or other related service provider	Complete all household chores prior to playing a video game

Periodic probes can be used to determine what skills students have mastered and maintained, as well as what skills still need remediation. Periodic probes should be taken when teaching skills that practicality does not allow to be observed on a daily basis (e.g., ordering food at a restaurant, going swimming, using a work timeclock, responding appropriately to emergency situations). Using periodic probes also alleviates the issues of trying to provide instruction and collect data at the same time. The idea is to collect sufficient data to allow for student progress to be determined and instructional decisions to be made. As you can see, assessments are one of the most essential tools for teachers, related service providers, and students. When properly developed and interpreted, assessments can create better understanding of what and how students are learning. Table 9.3 provides some basic samples of the categories of assessments, who administers them, and examples of the type of information that can be collected.

Summary

Instructional planning for other educational needs and community-based instruction for students with intellectual disability requires the use of a range of resources and strategies. Understanding what to teach, how to teach, and how to assess student learning by utilizing evidence-based practices provides a solid foundation for successful planning. The range of resources of what to teach, combined with tools and strategies for how to teach and assess student learning and teacher instruction, is extensive. Thoughtful and comprehensive planning will not only benefit students, but also can benefit teachers and related service providers. Utilizing the range of available tools and strategies will allow for flexibility that will allow for individualization to meet a student's needs.

Arranging for ongoing progress monitoring using assessments can allow educators to effectively monitor their own instructional effectiveness and student learning. It can provide timely feedback to gauge and adjust student mastery of targeted skills. Most importantly, it will help students with intellectual disability increase their independence and improve their own performances for greater postschool success.

References

Alwell, M., & Cobb, B. (2009). Functional life skills curricular interventions for youth with disabilities: A systematic review. *Career Development for Exceptional Individuals, 32,* 2, 82–93.

Ayres, K. M., Maguire, A., & McClimon, D. (2009). Acquisition and generalization of chained tasks taught with computer based video instruction to children with autism. *Education and Training in Developmental Disabilities, 44,* 493–508.

Browder, D. M. (1987). *Assessment of individuals with severe handicaps: An applied behavior approach to life skills assessment.* Baltimore, MD: Paul H. Brookes.

Browder, D. M. (2001). *Curriculum and assessment for students with moderate and severe disabilities.* New York: Gilford Press.

Browder, D. M., & King, D. (1987). Comprehensive assessment for longitudinal curriculum development. In D. M. Browder (Ed.), *Assessment of individuals with severe handicaps: An applied behavior approach to life skills assessment* (pp. 25–53). Baltimore, MD: Paul H. Brookes.

Browder, D. M., & Spooner, F. (2011). *Teaching students with moderate and severe disabilities.* New York: Guilford Press.

Brown, L., Bronston, M. B., Hamre-Nietupski, S., Pumpiam, I., Certo, N., & Gruenewald, L. (1979). A strategy for developing chronological-age-appropriate and functional curricular content for severely handicapped adolescents and young children. *Journal of Special Education, 13,* 81–90.

Brown, L., Nietupski, J., & Hamre-Nietupski, S. (1976). Criterion of ultimate functioning. In M. A. Thomas (Ed.), *Hey, don't forget about me! Education's investment in the severely, profoundly, and multiply handicapped* (pp. 2–15). Reston, VA: Council for Exceptional Children.

Cihak, D. F., Kessler, K., & Alberto, P. A. (2008). Use of a handheld prompting system to transition independently through vocational tasks for students with moderate and severe intellectual disabilities. *Education and Training in Developmental Disabilities, 43,* 102–110.

Clark, G. M., Field, S., Patton, J. R., Brolin, D. E., & Sitlington, P. L. (1994). Life skills instruction: A necessary component for all students with disabilities: A position statement of the Division of Career Development and Transition. *Career Development for Exceptional Individuals, 17,* 125–134.

Collins, B. C., Gast, D. L., Ault, M. J., & Wolery, M. (1991). Small group instruction: Guidelines for teachers of students with moderate to severe handicaps. *Education and Training in Mental Retardation, 26,* 18–32.

Collins, B. C., Karl, J., Riggs, L., Galloway, C. C., & Hager, K. D. (2010). Teaching core content with real-life applications to secondary students with moderate and severe disabilities. *Teaching Exceptional Children, 43*(1), 52–59.

Cooper, J. O., Heron, T. E., & Heward, W. L. (2007). *Applied behavior analysis.* Upper Saddle River, NJ: Pearson/Merrill-Prentice Hall.

Cronin, M. E. (1996). Life skills curricula for students with learning disabilities: A review of the literature. *Journal of Learning Disabilities, 29,* 53–68.

Donnellan, A. M. (1984). The criterion of the least dangerous assumption. *Behavioral Disorders, 9,* 141–150.

Falvey, M. A. (1986). *Community-based curriculum: Instructional strategies for students with severe handicaps.* Baltimore, MD: Paul H. Brookes.

Federal Register 71 (156) Monday, August 14, 2006, page 46661.

Franzone, E., & Collet-Klingenberg, L. (2008). *Overview of video modeling.* Madison, WI: The National Professional Development Center on Autism Spectrum Disorders, Waisman Center, University of Wisconsin.

Fredericks, B. (1990). Education for the child with Down syndrome. In S. Pueschel (Ed.), *Parent's guide to Down syndrome* (pp. 179–212). Baltimore, MD: Paul H. Brookes.

Fredericks, B., & Brodsky, M. (1994). Assessment for a functional curriculum. In E. C. Cipani & F. Spooner (Eds.), *Curricular and instructional approaches for persons with severe disabilities* (pp. 31–49). Boston, MA: Allyn & Bacon.

Glaser, R. (Ed.). (1962). *Training research and education.* New York: Columbia University Press.

Hammond, D. L., Whatley, A. D., Ayres, K. M., & Gast, D. L. (2010). Effectiveness of video modeling to teach iPod use to students with moderate intellectual disabilities. *Education and Training in Autism and Developmental Disabilities, 45,* 525–538.

Herrygers, J., Clark, H. B., Crosland, K., & Deschênes, N. (2009). *In-vivo teaching: Strategies for teaching relevant skills to transition-age youth and young adults.* Tampa, FL: National Network on Youth Transition for Behavioral Health.

Hua, Y., Morgan, B. S. T., Kaldenberg, E. R., & Goo, M. (2012). Cognitive strategy instruction for functional mathematical skill: Effects for young adults with intellectual disability. *Education and Training in Autism and Developmental Disabilities, 47,* 345–358.

Hunt, P., McDonnell, J., & Crockett, M. A. (2012). Reconciling an ecological curricular framework focusing on quality of life outcomes with the development and instruction of standards-based academic goals. *Research and Practice for Persons with Severe Disabilities, 37,* 139–152.

Individuals with Disabilities Education Improvement Act (IDEA) of 2004, Public Law No. 108–446, 20 USC. 1400, H. R. 1350.

Kearns, J., Burdge, M. D., Clayton, J., Denham, A. P., & Kleinert, H. L. (2006). How students demonstrate academic performance in portfolio assessment. In D. M. Browder & F. Spooner (Eds.), *Teaching language arts, math, & science to students with significant cognitive disabilities* (pp. 277–293). Baltimore, MD: Paul H. Brookes.

Kelley, K. R., Test, D. W., & Cooke, N. L. (2013). Effects of picture prompts delivered by a video iPod on pedestrian navigation. *Exceptional Children, 79*, 459–474.

Lane, K. L., Carter, E. W., & Sisco, L. (2012). Paraprofessional involvement in self-determination instruction for students with high-incidence disabilities. *Exceptional Children, 78*, 237–251.

Lee, S., Palmer, S. B., & Wehmeyer, M. L. (2009). Goal setting and self-monitoring for students with disabilities: Practical tips and ideas for teachers. *Intervention in School and Clinic, 44*, 139–145.

Lienemann, T., & Reid, R. (2006). Self-regulated strategy development for students with learning disabilities. *Teacher Education and Special Education, 29*, 3–11.

Logan, K. R., Bakeman, R., & Keefe, E. B. (1997). Effects of instructional variables on engaged behavior of students with disabilities in general education classrooms. *Exceptional Children, 63*, 481–497.

McDonnell, J., & McFarland, S. (1988). A comparison of forward and concurrent chaining strategies in teaching laundromat skills to students with severe handicaps. *Research in Developmental Disabilities, 9*, 177–194.

Mechling, L. C., Ayres, K. M., Foster, A. L., & Bryant, K. J. (2013). Comparing the effects of commercially available and custom-made video prompting for teaching cooking skills to high school students with autism. *Remedial and Special Education, 34*, 371–383.

Mechling, L. C., & Gustafson, M. (2009). Comparison of the effects of static picture and video prompting on completion of cooking related tasks by students with moderate intellectual disabilities. *Exceptionality, 17*, 103–116.

Mechling, L. C., & O'Brien, E. (2010). Computer-based video instruction to teach students with intellectual disabilities to use public bus transportation. *Education and Training in Autism and Developmental Disabilities, 45*, 230–241.

Mechling, L. C., Pridgen, L. S., & Cronin, B. A. (2005). Computer-based video instruction to teach students with intellectual disabilities to verbally respond to questions and make purchases in fast food restaurants. *Education and Training in Developmental Disabilities, 40*, 47–59.

Mithaug, D., Martin, J. E., & Agran, M. (1987). Adaptability instruction: The goal of transitional programming. *Exceptional Children, 53*, 500–505.

Morse, T. E., & Schuster, J. W. (2000). Teaching elementary students with moderate intellectual disabilities how to shop for groceries. *Exceptional Children, 66*, 273–288.

Neidert, P. L., Dozier, C. L., Iwata, B. A., & Hafen, M. (2010). Behavior analysis in intellectual and developmental disabilities. *Psychological Services, 7*, 103–113.

Newman, L., Wagner, M., Knokey, A. M., Marder, C., Nagle, K., Shaver, D., . . . Schwarting, M. (2011). *The post-high school outcomes of young adults with disabilities up to 8 years after high school: A Report from the National Longitudinal Transition Study-2 (NLTS2)* (NCSER Publication No. 2011–3005). Menlo Park, CA: SRI International. Retrieved from www.nlts2.org/reports/

Popham, W. J., & Husek, T. R. (1969). Implications of criterion-referenced measurement. *Journal of Educational Measurement, 6*, 1–9.

Ramdoss, S., Lang, R., Fragale, C., Britt, C., O'Reilly, M., Sigafoos, J., . . . Lancioni, G. E. (2012). Use of computer-based interventions to promote daily living skills in individuals with intellectual disabilities: A systematic review. *Journal of Developmental and Physical Disabilities, 24*, 197–215.

Reid, D. H., & Favell, J. E. (1984). Group instruction with persons who have severe disabilities: A critical review. *The Journal of the Association for Persons with Severe Handicaps, 9*, 167–177.

Ryndak, D. L., Alper, S., Hughes, C., & McDonnell, J. (2012). Documenting impact of educational contexts on long-term outcomes for students with significant disabilities. *Education and Training in Autism and Developmental Disabilities, 47*, 127–138.

Seward, J., Schuster, J. W., Ault, M. J., Collins, B. C., & Hall, M. (2014). Comparing simultaneous prompting and constant time delay to teach leisure skills to students with moderate intellectual disability. *Education and Training in Autism and Developmental Disabilities, 49*, 381–385.

Sitlington, P. L., Neubert, D. A., & Leconte, P. J. (1997). Transition assessment: The position of the division of career development and transition. *Career Development for Exceptional Individuals, 20*(1), 69–79.

Snell, M. E., & Gast, D. L. (1981). Applying time delay procedure to the instruction of the severely handicapped. *The Journal of the Association for the Severely Handicapped, 6*, 3–14.

Spooner, F. (1984). Comparisons of backward chaining and total task presentation in training severely handicapped persons. *Education and Training of the Mentally Retarded, 19*, 15–22.

Spooner, F., & Test, D. W. (1994). Domestic and community living skills. In E. C. Cipani & F. Spooner (Eds.), *Curricular and instructional approaches for persons with severe disabilities* (pp. 149–183). Boston, MA: Allyn and Bacon.

Stock, S. E., Davies, D. K., Wehmeyer, M. L., & Palmer, S. B. (2008). Evaluation of cognitively accessible software to increase independent access to cellphone technology for people with intellectual disability. *Journal of Intellectual Disability Research, 52*(12), 1155–1164.

Stokes, T. F., & Baer, D. M. (1977). An implicit technology of generalization. *Journal of Applied Behavior Analysis, 10*, 349–367.

Storms, J., O' Leary, E., & Williams, J. (2000). *Transition requirements: A guide for states, districts, schools, universities and families.* Eugene, OR: University of Oregon, Western Regional Resource Center.

Test, D. W., Howell, A., Burkhart, K., & Beroth, T. (1993). The one more than technique as a strategy for counting money for individuals with moderate mental retardation. *Education and Training in Mental Retardation, 28*, 232–241.

Test, D. W., & Spooner, F. (1996). Community-based training as an instructional support. In D. Browder (Series Ed.), *Innovations* (No. 6, pp. 1–34). Washington, DC: American Association on Mental Retardation.

US Department of Education, Office of Special Education and Rehabilitative Services (2000). A guide to the individualized education program. Retrieved from http://www2.ed.gov/parents/needs/speced/iepguide/index.html

Wehmeyer, M. L., Gragoudas, S., & Shogren, K. (2006). Self-determination, student involvement, and leadership development. In P. Wehman (Ed.), *Life beyond the classroom* (4th ed., pp. 41–69). Baltimore, MD: Paul H. Brookes.

Wehmeyer, M. L., Hughes, C., Agran, M., Garner, N., & Yeager, D. (2003). Student-directed learning strategies to promote the progress of students with intellectual disability in inclusive classrooms. *International Journal of Inclusive Education, 7*, 415–428.

Wehmeyer, M. L., & Palmer, S. B. (2003). Adult outcomes for students with cognitive disabilities three years after high school: The impact of self-determination. *Education and Training in Developmental Disabilities, 38*, 131–144.

Wehmeyer, M. L., & Schwartz, M. (1997). Self-determination and positive adult outcomes: A follow-up study of youth with mental retardation or learning disabilities. *Exceptional Children, 63*, 245–255.

Welch, M. (1994). Ecological assessment: A collaborative approach to planning instructional interventions. *Intervention in School and Clinic, 29*, 160–164, 183.

10

Transition Planning

James E. Martin, Amber E. McConnell

The Individuals with Disabilities Education Act of 2004 (IDEA 2004) established transition educa-tion as a fundamental component of secondary education for students with disabilities of transition age (Kohler & Field, 2003). Transition planning provides Individualized Education Program (IEP) teams the opportunity to develop students' postschool and annual transition goals and transition services that support the achievement of those goals, including postsecondary community-based support linkages to facilitate transition from school to adult life. This process enables transition-age youth with intellectual disability and their families to explore and create meaningful plans depicting what students need to learn now for postschool education, employment, and independent living in an iterative annual process. As the IEP team learns students' interests, skills, needs, desires, and avail-able community postschool supports and services, postschool goals and supporting transition services become more focused.

To explain transition planning, first this chapter will review federal legal foundations establishing minimum transition planning requirements. Second, an effective method to conduct transition plan-ning with a focus on completing transition sections of students' IEPs will be explained. Third, and last, the major points made in this chapter will be summarized and implications for practice will be discussed.

Legal Foundation

IDEA 2004 provides the minimal legal transition planning requirements. This section will (a) present the purpose of special education, (b) discuss the age when school-provided transition planning must begin, (c) discuss required and optional IEP transition planning team members, and (d) review required transition planning components.

Purpose of Special Education

Federal special education law succinctly defines the purpose of special education as providing edu-cation and services to meet the needs of students with IEPs to prepare them for post–high school employment, further education, and independent living (Wright & Wright, 2011). To fulfill this purpose, IEPs of transition-age youth with intellectual disability must describe where students would like to work, learn, and live after high school. These statements are called "postsecondary goals." The process of determining postsecondary goals and related transition services drives the transition planning process and the IEP for secondary students (Kochhar-Bryant, Shaw, & Izzo, 2009).

Transition Age

Federal law determines when transition planning must begin based on student age, and this age has fluctuated over time (Flexer & Baer, 2013). The Individuals with Disabilities Education Act of 1990 (IDEA 1990) first mandated transition planning for students 16 years old and older. The Individuals with Disabilities Education Act of 1997 (IDEA 1997) changed the required transition planning age to 14. The Individuals with Disabilities Education Act of 2004 (IDEA 2004) returned the starting transition planning age to 16. States may require more stringent requirements than stated in IDEA 2004. Recognizing benefits of earlier transition planning, including higher employment rates for students with intellectual disability (Cimera, Burgess, & Bedesem, 2014), the majority of states require an earlier transition planning age, with most of these states beginning transition planning at age 14 (Martin & McConnell, 2011).

IEP Transition Team

For students of transition age with intellectual disability, the IEP team consists, at a minimum, of six required team members (Wright, Wright, & O'Connor, 2010). First, students of transition age must be invited to attend their IEP meeting. Second, parents or guardians of students with intellectual disability are invited. Third, at least one special education teacher serves on the IEP team. Fourth, if the student receives general education services, at least one general education teacher who provides IEP-specified education to the student must attend the meeting. Fifth, the school district representative, typically an assistant principal, counselor, or special education supervisor, knowledgeable about district resources and general education curriculum, must be a part of the team. Sixth, representatives from agencies who may provide funding or services for postschool needs or desires must be invited to the meeting.

Educators and parents may invite others who have unique student knowledge or expertise to attend the IEP meeting and assist with transition planning. For instance, parents may want to invite a grandparent, family friend, advocate, or a professional specialist, such as a Board Certified Behavior Analyst. Educators may want to invite a counselor from the state vocational rehabilitation services office or a representative of a community-based supported employment program. With parental permission, students may want to invite a best friend, or a community job coworker.

Age of Majority

When students with disabilities reach the age of majority, which typically is 18 years (Age of Majority, 2016), all educational rights previously held by parents transfer to students (as occurs for all students). The Board of Directors of the Council for Exceptional Children Division on Autism and Developmental Disabilities (formerly the Division on Mental Retardation and Developmental Disabilities) supports the transfer of rights to students and suggests that prior to this occurring, students need to be taught and provided opportunities to become self-determined (Lindsey, Wehmeyer, Guy, & Martin, 2001). In addition, simply because a student turns 18, that does not mean that his or her parents cannot continue to be involved in the IEP meetings. For example, students with intellectual disability who are 18 years old or older and who want parents to continue to represent their rights at IEP meetings can, according to Wright and Wright (2011), write a signed and dated statement appointing their parents as educational representatives and bring them to the IEP meeting.

Some students may have a legal guardian, which means that a court has appointed a person to assume some or all rights that otherwise would go to the student (Millar, 2003; Millar & Renzaglia, 2002). Millar and Renzaglia (2002) examined guardianship decisions and found an almost equal split between guardians being granted all or only a few rights. If guardians have been granted only a few rights, the remaining rights belong to the person with a disability. Irrespective of guardianship status, students need to be taught to use their rights and provided opportunities to practice doing so (Lindsey et al., 2001) and to engage in supported decision making.

Required Transition Planning Components

IDEA 2004 stipulates minimum transition planning components to be included in the IEPs of transition-aged students. To measure compliance with IDEA 2004 educational requirements, the US Department of Education requires each state to evaluate 20 special education performance indicators (US Department of Education, 2015). Indicator-13, which is the transition planning indicator, measures the

> percent of youth with IEPs aged 16 and above with an IEP that includes appropriate measurable postsecondary goals that are annually updated and based upon an age appropriate transition assessment, transition services, including courses of study, that will reasonably enable the student to meet those postsecondary goals, and annual IEP goals related to the student's transition services needs. There also must be evidence that the student was invited to the IEP team meeting where transition services are to be discussed and evidence that, if appropriate, a representative of any participating agency was invited to the IEP team meeting with the prior consent of the parent or student who has reached the age of majority.
>
> *(Part B SPP/APR Indicator Measurement Table, n.d., p. 13)*

Educators may use a locally developed measurement tool or the National Secondary Transition Technical Assistance Center (NSTTAC) Indicator-13 Checklist (Transition Planning, n.d.) available from the National Technical Assistance Center on Transition (NTACT), which the US Department of Education's Office of Special Education Programs (OSEP) approved in 2006 (Gaumer-Erickson, Noonan, Brussow, & Gilpin, 2014). To measure Indicator-13 compliance, typically the IEP case manager will answer each Indicator-13 question listed in Table 10.1 with a "yes" or "no" response. To be

Table 10.1 Indicator-13 questions

Indicator-13 Checklist	Circle Yes or No	
Are there *measurable postsecondary goals* in the areas of education or training, employment, and when appropriate, independent living?	Yes	No
Are postsecondary goals *updated annually*?	Yes	No
Is there evidence the measureable goals were based on age-appropriate *transition assessments*?	Yes	No
Are there *annual IEP goals* related to student's transition services needs?	Yes	No
Are there *transition services* in the IEP that will reasonably enable the student to meet his or her postsecondary goals?	Yes	No
Do the transition services include *course of study* that will reasonably enable the student to meet his or her postsecondary goals?	Yes	No
Is there evidence that the *student was invited* to the IEP team meeting where transition services were discussed?	Yes	No
If appropriate, is there evidence that a *representative of any participating agency* was invited to the IEP team meeting with the prior consent of the parent (or student who has reached age of majority)?	Yes	No
Mark YES if the IEP meets all of the Indicator-13 requirements. If one or more items were marked "no," circle no.	Yes	No

Note. The NSTTAC Indicator-13 Checklist served as the source for the questions in this table. The original Indicator-13 Checklist can be found at this NTACT website: http://www.transitionta.org/sites/default/files/transitionplanning/NSTTAC_ChecklistFormA.pdf.

in compliance with IDEA 2004 transition planning requirements, all Indicator-13 questions for each transition-aged youth's IEP must be answered with a "yes." One "no" answer will make the IEP out of compliance with IDEA 2004 transition planning requirements.

The Transition Planning Process

Indicator-13 components define the required minimal transition planning components that must be included and aligned in the IEPs of transition-aged students to facilitate students attaining their postsecondary goals (Baer & Martin, 2013). This section will examine the eight required Indicator-13 transition components (transition assessment, measurable postsecondary goals, annual transition goals, transition services, courses of study, student involvement in the IEP, relevant agency representative invited to IEP meeting, and measurable postsecondary goals) and describe the transition planning processes needed to address Indicator-13 requirements. But first, a note about student input into the transition planning process: IDEA 2004 emphasizes the importance of students of transition age providing input into transition-planning discussions. A student's support needs must be considered in determining the most appropriate ways to gather information on preferences and interests to inform the transition planning process. Depending on the student's support needs, information can also be gathered from other people in the student's life, including family members and friends.

Transition Assessment

The NSTTAC Indicator-13 Checklist (Transition Planning, n.d.) item for transition assessment is: Is there evidence the measureable goals were based on age-appropriate transition assessments?

Transition assessments used within meaningful transition planning discussions lead students, families, and other IEP team members from postschool uncertainty to a well-developed transition plan to attain postsecondary goals (Leconte, 2006). IDEA 2004 uses the phrase "transition assessments," and the word "assessments" means the results from two or more transition assessments need to be used annually to identify students' strengths, needs, and interests, followed by writing transition goals (Neubert & Leconte, 2013). The Council for Exceptional Children's Division on Career Development and Transition (DCDT) asserts

> transition assessment is an ongoing process of collecting information on the youth's needs, strengths, preferences, and interests as they relate to measurable postsecondary goals and the annual goals that will help facilitate attainment of postsecondary goals.
>
> *(Neubert & Leconte, 2013, p. 74)*

Transition Assessments

Special educators and other IEP team members will need a range of transition assessments from which appropriate assessments will be selected for each transition-aged youth. Numerous listings of transition assessments—such as the *Age Appropriate Transition Assessment Toolkit* (NSTTAC, 2013), or those described at the OU Zarrow Center website (Zarrow Center, 2016)—provide the names of transition assessments and how they can be obtained. Some listings are organized by formal or informal assessments. Others cluster assessments by outcome domains, including further education, employment, and independent living. Unfortunately, many of these listings do not describe how the assessments were developed or for whom the assessments are intended, nor do they present supporting validity evidence. This means users need to examine available materials, including technical manuals and assessment websites, to determine suitability for particular students.

Importance of Validity and Reliability Evidence

When educators use assessment results to make important educational decisions, the *Standards for Educational and Psychological Testing* (AERA, APA, & NCME, 2014) indicate educators should use well-developed assessments that have ample validity evidence supporting use of the results. The most important task that IEP teams for transition-aged students need to accomplish is to identify student transition strengths, needs, and interests, and develop postsecondary goals and supporting IEP transition services sections. To do this, IEP teams need results from well-developed assessments with appropriate validity data supporting their use. Thus, IEP teams need to consider facts about the various transition assessments and determine whether the assessments are sufficiently validated for use in developing IEPs for students of transition age.

Questions to Select Transition Assessments

The following set of questions may assist special educators in selecting transition assessments for use with transition-aged students with intellectual disability.

- What is the purpose of this assessment? Does this purpose meet my needs?
- For whom is the assessment designed?
- Is this assessment designed to assess high school students with intellectual disability?
- How were the assessment items developed?
- Does the assessment address what the IEP team needs to know?
- Are the results presented in an understandable manner that can be used to create annual transition goals and summarize results in the IEP?
- If multiple versions of this assessment exist, will parents and the student's support be able to complete this assessment?
- Do results vary based on student gender, race or ethnicity, or family economic status?
- Does other validity evidence support using the results of this assessment?

Educators will need a reasonable response for most of these, and perhaps other questions, before considering an assessment well-developed and having ample validity evidence to support using the results for transition-planning discussions and decision making.

Because the IDEA 2004 transition assessment requirement is still fairly recent, only a few well-developed transition assessments designed specifically for transition-age students with disabilities exist (Zarrow Center, 2016). Due to the shortage, many educators use transition assessments that are not designed for the students they teach, that are not well-developed, or that lack the most basic validity evidence supporting use of their results. When faced with using these inferior assessments, special educators need to interpret results with caution and acknowledge this during transition-planning discussions.

Placing Results into the IEP

Special educators summarize the results of transition assessments in students' IEPs, but where the results are written depends upon the IEP form being used. On some IEP forms, transition assessment results are summarized—and strengths, needs, and interests written—in a specific IEP transition section. On other IEP forms, transition assessment results are added to the Present Level of Academic and Functional Performance section alongside other assessment results and listings of strengths and needs. Some IEP forms require transition assessment results to be placed within both locations. Several IEP forms provide ample space to write the transition assessment results, while others do not. Certain IEP forms require results, strengths, and needs written in sentences, while other IEP forms request bulleted

Table 10.2 Example summary of transition assessment results section

Assessments	Summary of Results
Repeated Pictorial Card Choice with Try-Outs Doing Selected Jobs	After repeated choice selections and job try-outs over the past four months, Adrian chose in rank order the following jobs: (1) body shop technician, (2) car shop lube technician, and (3) car shop transport driver.
Transition Assessment and Goal Generator (TAGG) ; Martin et al., 2015)	Blake, his dad, and his special education teacher completed the TAGG, a norm-referenced transition assessment with research-based items known to be associated with postschool employment and education. Compared to similar students, Blake's overall results were in the average range. His scores indicate greatest strengths in the areas of Disability Awareness and Employment. TAGG scores indicate the greatest needs in the areas of Student Involvement in the IEP, Goal Setting and Attainment, and Strengths and Limitations.
Transition Planning Inventory-2 (TPI-2; Patton & Clark, 2014)	Jose, his mother, and his special education teacher completed the TPI-2 in April. All three agreed his greatest strengths were in community involvement and usage, and interpersonal relationships, and his greatest needs were in independent living skills. His mom rated Jose low in personal money management; Jose and the teacher both provided low scores in the further education and training area.

Example Student Strengths and Needs Sections	
Strengths	**Needs**
Disability Awareness	Goal setting and attainment
Employment Skills (punctual, complete tasks in quality manner, accepts supervisor feedback, works well with others)	Active engagement and participation in IEP meeting and transition planning discussions
Community Involvement	Independent living skills, identified from TPI-2
Interpersonal Relationships	Personal money management

lists. The point is, transition assessment results must be included in the IEP somewhere, with the exact location dependent upon the format of the IEP form schools use. Table 10.2 provides example transition assessment summaries and lists of strengths and needs identified through transition assessments.

Measurable Postsecondary Goals

The NSTTAC Indicator-13 Checklist (Transition Planning, n.d.) items for measurable postsecondary goals are:

- Are there measurable postsecondary goals that cover education or training, employment, and (as needed) independent living?
- Are postsecondary goals updated annually?

At least annually, students and their IEP teams use results from transition assessments to assist in developing or revising postsecondary goals. Postsecondary goals set the direction for the secondary IEP and represent what students want to attain after completing high school. Grigal, Hart, and Migliore (2011) examined IEPs and discovered those of transition-aged youth with intellectual disability contained many more postsecondary sheltered and supported employment goals than postsecondary education or competitive employment goals, despite the importance of promoting postsecondary education or competitive employment. Interestingly, they found only one type of postsecondary goal predictive of individuals with intellectual disability working postschool, and those postsecondary goals addressed students with intellectual disability attending two- or four-year college programs.

Needed and Optional Postsecondary Goals

IDEA 2004 requires two postsecondary goals be included in the IEPs of transition-aged students, addressing (a) further education and (b) employment. Independent living postsecondary goals need to be included only when required by the state, district, or deemed necessary by the IEP team. By law, if independent living is not deemed necessary, then it does not need to be addressed during transition planning discussions nor included in students' IEPs (Wright & Wright, 2011).

BEST PRACTICE SUGGESTIONS

All students with intellectual disability will live somewhere after completing high school: Specifying a planned living location begins the dialogue among IEP team members to determine independent living and other skills students need to learn, and the supports needed for living in the community. Thus, discussing and writing independent living goals into IEPs *should not be dismissed* simply because this is an optional goal. Instead, best practice suggests discussing results of independent living transition assessments and living options with the IEP team. Then, based upon needs, and student and family desires, the team can decide whether to include within the IEP an independent living postsecondary goal, at least one annual transition goal, and related transition services.

Questions Students Need to Answer to Provide Input into Postsecondary Goals

After discussing transition assessment results with teachers and family, students need to annually answer three questions to develop postsecondary goals. Answers to these questions will most likely change over the years as students learn and refine their interests, skills, and needs, and discover available community support options.

1. Where do I want to live after completing high school?
2. What type of work do I want to do after completing high school?
3. How do I want to learn to do my job after completing high school?

Writing Postsecondary Goals

Begin writing postsecondary goals with the phrase "After graduating from high school . . . ," "Upon completion of high school . . . , " or "After leaving high school . . . ." Postsecondary goals should identify specific further education, employment, and independent living outcomes. If postsecondary goals answer the question "Where will the student work, learn, and live (if needed) after high school?" the goals are measureable and comply with IDEA 2004 requirements.

Some IEP forms require one combined further education, employment, and independent living postsecondary goal, while others request one postsecondary goal for each outcome area. Both methods of writing postsecondary goals can be appropriate.

EXAMPLES OF COMBINED GOALS FOR FURTHER EDUCATION, EMPLOYMENT, AND INDEPENDENT LIVING

The following examples demonstrate how to write combined postsecondary goals for students with differing levels of support needs.

- After graduating from high school, Hunter will live with his parents while attending the dental assistant program at Riverside Career Technology Center, and will then work at a local dentist's office.
- After completing high school, Kayla will live at home with her mother, and with needed supports will audit child care classes at the Riverside Career Technology Center, and then will volunteer at Early Horizons preschool daycare program.
- After finishing high school, John will live in a small local home with supports, and with training and support from a job coach, he will operate a home-based balloon business.

COMPLIANCE CHECK QUESTIONS

To check whether postsecondary goals are measureable and address postschool further education, employment, and independent living goals, ask the following questions. If each question has a meaningful answer matching the student's interests, skills, and needs, consider the postsecondary goals acceptable.

- Where will the student learn?
  - Hunter will learn at the Career Technology Center.
  - Kayla will learn at the Career Technology Center.
  - John will learn from a job coach.
- Where will the students work or volunteer?
  - Hunter will work at the dentist's office.
  - Kayla will volunteer at the daycare center.
  - John will work at his home-based balloon business.
- Where will the students live?
  - Hunter will live at his parents' home.
  - Kayla will live at her parents' home.
  - John will live in a small group home.

Will educators be held responsible if students do not attain postsecondary goals? Many factors—including the job market, student and family decisions, and available supports—determine whether postsecondary goals can be attained. Most, if not all of these factors, are beyond the ability of educators to influence, although the role of educators is to provide the instruction and supports needed to maximize the potential for success.

Annual Transition Goals

The NSTTAC Indicator-13 Checklist (Transition Planning, n.d.) item for annual transition goals is: Are there annual IEP goals related to student's transition services needs?

Annual measurable transition goals identify skills students need to learn to attain their postsecondary goals, as described in the previous section. The IEP team uses identified transition needs and postsecondary goals to develop each annual transition goal. According to NSTTAC's Enhanced Form B Indicator-13 Checklist (NSTTAC I-13, 2012), at least one annual transition goal is required in the IEP for each further education and employment postsecondary goal. If an independent-living postsecondary goal also exists in the IEP, at least one annual transition goal addressing independent living is also required.

Importance

Annual goals are not mere statements of passing a class with a certain grade or even enrolling in a class. Annual goals are critical skills students will learn and master throughout the year, and attaining these goals should make a difference in the student's life. Benz, Lindstrom, and Yovanoff (2000) found transition-aged students with intellectual and other disabilities who attained four or more annual transition goals were twice as likely to graduate from high school as students with IEPs who completed fewer or no transition goals. These same students who attained four or more annual transition goals were four times more likely to be employed and/or involved in further education after leaving high school.

Best Practice Suggestions

Postsecondary goals often change from year to year, and initial research suggests few students actually attain stated postsecondary goals after graduation (Steele, Konrad, & Test, 2005). Consider building annual transition goals using academic and nonacademic generalizable skills associated with or predictive of the most postschool further education or employment outcomes. To identify students' generalizable behavior needs, use the online Transition Assessment and Goal Generator (TAGG) developed by Martin, Hennessey, McConnell, Terry, and Willis (2015), following guidelines provided by the *Standards for Educational and Psychological Testing* (AERA et al., 2014).

The TAGG's constructs and items derive from research-identified behaviors associated with postschool further education and employment (McConnell et al., 2013), ample validity evidence exists (Hennessey, Terry, Martin, McConnell, & Willis, 2016; McConnell, Martin, & Hennessey, 2015; McConnell, Martin, Herron, & Hennessey, 2016), and results predict postschool further education and employment of former high school students with disabilities, including those with intellectual disability (Burnes, Martin, Terry, & Hennessey, 2016). The TAGG's result profile provides a written results summary and lists of strengths and needs, all of which can be copied and pasted directly into students' IEPs.

Writing Annual Transition Goals

Annual transition goals describe what the student will learn within an academic year to facilitate attaining postsecondary goals. Each annual goal consists of three crucial components:

> *Condition.* The materials and environment necessary for the goal to be completed.
> *Behavior.* The action that can be directly observed and monitored.
> *Criterion.* How much, how often, or to what extent the behavior must occur to demonstrate that it has been achieved.

Merging Transition Goals and Academic Standards

Transition planning and education can be incorporated into the general curriculum, and annual goals can be aligned with state academic standards (Wehmeyer, 2002). Addressing transition needs through core curriculum is a way to teach transition education skills while preparing students for end-of-instruction achievement tests. Educators can infuse transition-related content through essays, reports, and stories into English standards to simultaneously prepare students for chosen careers while teaching required achievement skills (Konrad & Test, 2007; McConnell, Little, & Martin, 2015). The following examples demonstrate how annual transition goals can be connected to general academic standards and alternative academic standards, while addressing the need for learning generalized skills associated with postschool outcomes.

EXAMPLES OF ANNUAL TRANSITION GOALS

When connecting annual transition goals to general academic standards, the goals might look like this:

- *For Language Arts Grade 12 Writing & Grammar.* Emily will write an essay to compare and contrast two careers in the field of computer technology. She will include salary, benefits, and required educational training, and describe which career is better suited for her strengths and abilities, with 85% accuracy for grammar and usage.
- *For Financial Literacy.* Given instruction in a high school financial literacy class, Tyler will demonstrate balancing and reconciling a household budget and checkbook to include car payment, fuel, insurance, and monthly expenditures, with 100% accuracy.

When writing goals linked to alternative achievement standards specific to postschool outcomes, a postsecondary employment goal might state: After graduation from high school, John will live at home with his parents, and with the support and training of a job coach, he will develop and operate a home-based balloon business. The associated annual transition goal for John might then read: John will participate in on-the-job training at Party Galaxy to learn how to properly inflate 30 balloons with 100% accuracy for three consecutive trials. Further, short-term objectives for this annual transition goal might read: (a) While completing an on-the-job training at Party Galaxy, John will correctly attach 10 balloons onto the inflator with 100% accuracy for three consecutive trials; (b) while completing on-the-job training at Party Galaxy, John will inflate 10 balloons for 3 to 5 seconds, remove them from the inflator, and tie the balloon with a ribbon for three consecutive trials.

Transition Services

The NSTTAC Indicator-13 Checklist (Transition Planning, n.d.) item for transition services is: Are there transition services in the IEP that will reasonably enable the student to meet his or her postsecondary goals?

Transition services provide coordinated activities to improve the academic and functional achievement of the young adult with an IEP to facilitate successful movement from high school to adult life (Kochhar-Bryant, 2009). A unique relation exists between annual transition goals and transition services. Annual transition goals identify skills that students will learn to facilitate postsecondary goal attainment, while transition services enable students to attain the skill to facilitate postsecondary goal attainment.

IDEA 2004 identifies six types of transition services that, at a minimum, IEP teams may use to specify the type of transition education students receive to facilitate attaining annual transition goals. According to Simmons, Bauder, and Flexer (2013), the IEP team arranges the following transition services for each student based upon his or her unique transition needs, interests, skills, and annual goals.

- *Instruction:* Teaching specific transition-related skills in both formal and informal educational settings and in the community.
- *Related Services:* Physical therapy, social work assistance, speech-language therapy, school health assistance, rehabilitation counseling, and other services that support developing skills leading toward attaining postsecondary goals.
- *Community Experiences:* Opportunities to learn skills and experience events outside the classroom in the greater community. This includes job shadowing, tours of postsecondary educational facilities, community work experiences, recreational experiences, volunteerism, and learning to use community resources.

- *Development of Employment and Other Postschool Adult-Living Goals:* Developing additional post-secondary and annual goals through career exploration activities, self-awareness and self-advocacy efforts, and vocational experiences.
- *Acquisition of Daily Living Skills (when appropriate):* Creating opportunities at school and in the community to learn skills to live independently or with support. These skills include housekeeping, medication self-management, transportation and mobility, self-advocacy and self-awareness, and becoming an active community member.
- *Functional Vocational Evaluation:* When typical transition assessments are not appropriate for students with intellectual disability, more practical and community-based functional assessments are needed. Functional vocational evaluation includes situational assessments at actual job sites and use of checklists and other tools that assess student interests and skills.

Best Practice Suggestions

NTACT researchers reviewed the research literature to identify evidence-based transition education practices to facilitate student attainment of education, employment, and independent living post-secondary goals (Effective Practices Matrix, 2015). Evidence-based practices are those with a strong record of success established by rigorous quality research. The NTACT website (http://www.transitionta.org/evidencepractices) lists numerous evidence-based strategies and provides in-depth practice description.

Who Implements Transition Services?

The roles of people (i.e., family members, physical therapists, the students themselves) responsible for implementing transition services need to be listed alongside each coordinated activity, which typically is linked to a specific annual transition goal. As long as the IEP case manager coordinates all activities, almost any responsible person can implement transition services. For instance, the student's mother could be responsible for taking her child to visit a college experience program. A coworker at a community job site could evaluate a student's on-the-job performance. The student could be responsible for completing job applications.

Courses of Study

The NSTTAC Indicator-13 Checklist (Transition Planning, n.d.) item for courses of study is: Do the transition services include courses of study that will reasonably enable the student to meet his or her postsecondary goal(s)?

IDEA 2004 requires the IEP of each transition-aged student include courses of study. The NSTTAC Indicator-13 Checklist considers courses of study to be a "multi-year description of coursework from the student's current to anticipated exit year designed to help achieve the student's desired post-school goals," and the courses of study need to "align with students' postsecondary goals" (NSTTAC I-13, 2012, p. 3).

Best transition-planning practice for each student with intellectual disability ensures courses of study align with other IEP transition sections and include (a) classes matching the requirements for a specific type of diploma or exit certificate; (b) classes teaching work skills, independent living skills, and those needed to prepare for planned further education; and (c) classes associated with anticipated extended-year summer programs. To manage courses of study, each year students' case managers, along with the student whenever possible, review and match courses of study with transcripts to determine if students enrolled, dropped, or earned passing grades, and if there are issues, move or assign other courses, and revise as postsecondary goals change and annual transition goals are attained.

Begin Early, if Needed

State-provided scholarships for students to attend postsecondary education experience programs or matriculate into formal postsecondary educational programs at community colleges, career technology centers, or four-year colleges often require set courses and early applications. The IEP team should consider these entry requirements and include them in middle school IEPs coordinated activities to complete applications and courses of study to meet scholarship and entry requirements, and to learn needed behaviors.

Continuing High School Through Age 21

Students with intellectual disability may continue their high school education through the age of 21 if extra time is needed to complete the secondary education program designed by the IEP team. If extra years are needed, it is best practice to build the courses of study to depict courses year-by-year up to the expected completion date. It is best to create the extended courses of study as early as possible to demonstrate the long-term intent of the IEP team extending secondary education through the age of 21.

Student Involvement in the IEP

The NSTTAC Indicator-13 Checklist (Transition Planning, n.d.) item for student involvement in the IEP is: Is there evidence the student was invited to the IEP meeting where transition services were discussed?

Students of transition age must be invited to attend their IEP transition meetings (NSTTAC I-13, 2012). IDEA 2004 implies that when students with disabilities are in attendance at IEP meetings, to the maximum extent possible, they are to share their thoughts and opinions during transition planning discussions, and their input will be viewed equally with that provided by other IEP team members.

Invitation

Most schools use a formal Notification of Meeting form to invite IEP team members. The Indicator-13 requirements for what must be included on a student's invitation are minimal. Per NSTTAC's Indicator-13 Checklist instructions, the Notice of Meeting sent to students must have been signed by an educator and dated before the scheduled IEP meeting (NSTTAC I-13, 2012). The Notification of Meeting sent to parents, unlike the student invitation, must include at least four items: (a) a statement indicating transition planning will be discussed, (b) a statement indicating the student will be invited to attend the meeting, (c) the student's name must be listed among the participants attending the meeting, and (d) names or roles of agency staff that may be responsible for paying or providing transition services will be listed. A Notification of Meeting will be addressed to students 18 years old or older, and it should include the four points described with regard to parent invitations.

STUDENTS WRITE AND DELIVER INVITATION TO IEP MEETINGS

An opportunity to demonstrate student engagement and ownership of the IEP process occurs when students create and personally deliver invitations to attend IEP meetings to IEP team members. Instead of using the legal-looking official Notification of Meeting form, students could use, for example, a party invitation website to create invitations. Students can choose the design for these informal invitations; then include all needed information, including the date, time, and location of the IEP meeting, and a statement that transition planning issues will be discussed. Some educators will ask students to include the official Notification of Meeting in the envelope as well.

After printing, students can personally deliver the invitations to those who need to attend the IEP meetings and others whom the student and parents wish to invite. As long as parents provide permission for students that are 18 years old or younger, students may invite their best friend or other important people in their life to their IEP meetings.

IF STUDENTS DO NOT ATTEND OR DO NOT PARTICIPATE DURING IEP MEETING

If students decline the invitation and do not attend the IEP meeting, or attend but do not participate in transition-planning discussions, the meeting can continue under the condition that prior to the IEP meeting team members obtained information from students regarding postschool interests, skills, and needs.

INVITATIONS DO NOT EQUAL PARTICIPATION

Many students attend IEP meetings without receiving instruction in the IEP meeting process and what to do at the meetings (Martin, Marshall, & Sale, 2004). Too often, these students do not know why the meeting is taking place, do not understand the meaning of words being spoken, do not know what to do, and sadly, if they do talk during the IEP meeting, many students believe no one actually listened to them or wanted to hear from them (Lehman, Bassett, & Sands, 1999; Powers, Turner, Matuszewski, Wilson, and Loesch, 1999). Surveys and observational studies support student opinions gathered through qualitative means. Martin, Van Dycke, Greene et al. (2006) directly observed secondary IEP meetings and discovered at educator-directed IEP meetings that students talked on average 3% of the time, and students indicated they did not know the reason for the meeting nor did they understand their role.

Best Practice Hints

To avoid students becoming token IEP team members if they are invited to attend their IEP meetings, students need to be taught what to do at IEP transition meetings and provided opportunities to engage in transition-planning discussions. Chapter 11 discusses person-centered and student-directed transition planning. Read this chapter to learn effective practices to obtain meaningful input from students, and how to increase student involvement and leadership of IEP meetings. In brief, teaching students to become actively involved in their IEP meetings and providing opportunities for them to implement what they learned has been identified as effective transition practice (Effective Practices Matrix, 2015). Active student engagement in the IEP meeting planning discussions increases students' skills leading to self-determination (Martin, Van Dycke, Christensen et al., 2006; Seong, Wehmeyer, Palmer, & Little, 2015) and predicts postschool education and employment outcomes (Burnes et al., 2016).

Relevant Agency Representative Invited to IEP Meeting

The NSTTAC Indicator-13 Checklist (Transition Planning, n.d.) item for relevant agency representative invited to IEP meeting is: If appropriate, is there evidence that a representative of any participating agency was invited to the team meeting with the prior consent of the parent or student?

If transition services provided or paid for by nonschool agencies or programs will be discussed or planned during the IEP meeting, representatives of these programs need to be invited to attend the transition IEP meeting to participate in planning discussions (NSTTAC I-13, 2012). However, before the outside agency representatives can be invited, parent or student consent (if over age of majority) will need to be obtained.

The duration for the consent for an agency representative to attend a student's IEP meeting can be for one specific IEP meeting, or it may last up to a year. The signed consent form must be in writing and kept in the student's confidential file.

Conclusion and Summary

The 2005 National Longitudinal Transition Study-2 indicated only 60% of youth with intellectual disability have any type of employment, and 81% of this population are in nonwork settings with little hope of ever making minimum wage (Butterworth et al., 2013). Without proper transition planning and education for students with intellectual disability, graduation from high school does not lead to the further education, employment, or independent living that the IDEA legislation intends. With reports of adults with intellectual disability being twice as likely to be fired or laid off from their jobs as their same-aged peers (Newman, Wagner, Cameto, & Knokey, 2009), transition skills are extremely important for this population. With IDEA 2004 regulations and additional implementation of evidence-based transition practices, there is a shifting paradigm to high expectations for students.

Transition planning provides the last opportunity schools have to fulfill the purpose of special education, which is to prepare students for postsecondary education, employment, and independent living. Transition planning provides students the opportunity to obtain skills and supports needed to achieve their postschool dreams. Students with intellectual disability may need more time to develop these skills and supports, thus transition planning needs to begin as early as possible—which is why the majority of states mandate transition planning earlier than the federal age of 16.

Prince, Plotner, and Yell (2014) discovered, after studying district court transition-planning decisions, educators must implement ample and effective Indicator-13 compliant practices to avoid costly due process and court cases and prepare students to attain their postschool goals. These researchers recommend IEP teams use practices that address Indicator-13, and suggest that doing so enhances IEP teams' effectiveness and demonstrates the spirit of IDEA 2004 transition requirements. Specifically, Prince et al. (2014) suggest IEP teams (a) maximize student engagement in the transition planning process by teaching students concepts and skills to become actively engaged in IEP discussions and provide opportunities for students to become involved during actual IEP meetings; (b) examine results from repeated use of well-developed transition assessments that have ample supporting validity evidence; (c) align all parts of IEPs to focus on attaining students' postsecondary goals; and (d) identify in IEPs who will implement listed coordinated activities.

References

Age of majority. (2016). Retrieved from http://minors.uslegal.com/age-of-majority/

American Educational Research Association, American Psychological Association, & National Council on Measurement in Education (AERA, APA, NCME). (2014). *Standards for educational and psychological testing.* Washington, DC: American Psychological Association.

Baer, R., & Martin, J. (2013). Developing postsecondary goals. In R. Flexer, R. Baer, P. Luft, & T. Simmons (Eds.), *Transition planning for secondary students with disabilities* (4th ed., pp. 124–150). Upper Saddle River, NJ: Pearson.

Benz, M. R., Lindstrom, L., & Yovanoff, P. (2000). Improving graduation and employment outcomes of students with disabilities: Predictive factors and student perspectives. *Exceptional Children, 66,* 509–529. doi: 10.1177/001440290006600405

Burnes, J. J., Martin, J. E., Terry, R., & Hennessey, M. N. (2016). *Establishing predictive validity: Predicting postsecondary education and employment outcomes using the TAGG.* Manuscript submitted for publication.

Butterworth, J., Hall, A. C., Smith, F. A., Migliore, A., Winsor, J., Domin, D., & Sulewski, J. (2013). *State data: The national report on employment services and outcomes.* Boston, MA: University of Massachusetts Boston, Institute for Community inclusion.

Cimera, R. E., Burgess, S., & Bedesem, P. L. (2014). Does providing transition services by age 14 produce better vocational outcomes for students with intellectual disability? *Research and Practice for Persons with Severe Disabilities, 39,* 47–54. doi: 10.1177/1540796914534633

Effective Practices Matrix. (2015). Retrieved from http://www.transitionta.org/sites/default/files/effectivepractices/EP_Matrix_print_12_4_2015.pdf

Flexer, R. W., & Baer, R. M. (2013). Transition legislation and models. In R. W. Flexer, R. M. Baer, P. Luft, & T. J. Simmons (Eds.), *Transition planning for secondary students with disabilities* (pp. 22–45). Boston, MA: Pearson.

Gaumer-Erickson, A. S., Noonan, P. M., Brussow, J. A., & Gilpin, B. J. (2014). The impact of IDEA Indicator 13 compliance on postsecondary outcomes. *Career Development and Transition for Exceptional Individuals, 37*, 161–167. doi: 10.1177/2165143413481497

Grigal, M., Hart, D., & Migliore, A. (2011). Comparing the transition planning, postsecondary education, and employment outcomes of students with intellectual and other disabilities. *Career Development and Transition for Exceptional Individuals, 34*, 4–17. doi: 10.1177/0885728811399091

Hennessey, M. N., Terry, R., Martin, J. E., McConnell, A. E., & Willis, D. M. (2016). *Validating the Transition Assessment and Goal Generator (TAGG): Factor structure and basic psychometric properties.* Manuscript submitted for publication.

Kochhar-Bryant, C. A. (2009). Federal legislation, research, and state initiatives advance transition services. In C. A. Kochhar-Bryant & G. Greene (Eds.), *Pathways to successful transition for youth with disabilities: A development process* (pp. 106–161). Upper Saddle River, NJ: Pearson.

Kochhar-Bryant, C. A., Shaw, S., & Izzo, M. (2009). *What every teacher should know about transition and IDEA 2004* (pp. 31–38). Upper Saddle River, NJ: Pearson.

Kohler, P., & Field, S. (2003). Transition-focused education. *The Journal of Special Education, 37*, 174–183.

Konrad, M., & Test, D. (2007). Effects of GO 4 IT. . .NOW! strategy instruction on the written IEP goal articulation and paragraph-writing skills of middle school students with disabilities. *Remedial and Special Education, 28*, 277–291. doi: 10.1177/07419325070280050301

Leconte, P. J. (2006). The evolution of career, vocational, and transition assessment: Implications for the summary of performance. *Career Development and Transition for Exceptional Individuals, 29*, 114–124. doi: 10.1177/08857288060290020301

Lehman, J. P., Bassett, D. S., & Sands, D. J. (1999). Students' participation in transition-related actions: A qualitative study. *Remedial and Special Education, 20*, 160–169. doi: 10.1177/074193259902000307

Lindsey, P., Wehmeyer, M. L., Guy, B., & Martin, J. E. (2001). Age of majority and mental retardation: A position statement of the Division on Mental Retardation and Developmental Disabilities. *Education and Training in Mental Retardation and Developmental Disabilities, 36*, 3–15.

Martin, J. E., Hennessey, M. N., McConnell, A. E., Terry, R., & Willis, D. (2015). *Transition assessment and goal generator.* Norman, OK: Board of Regents of The University of Oklahoma. Retrieved from https://tagg.ou.edu/tagg/

Martin, J. E., Marshall, L. H., & Sale, P. (2004). A 3-year study of middle, junior high, and high school IEP meetings. *Exceptional Children, 70*, 285–297.

Martin, J. E., & McConnell, A. (2011). *National profile of state mandated age requirements for transition planning.* Poster presentation at the 16th CEC's Division on Career Development and Transition Conference, Kansas City, MO.

Martin, J. E., Van Dycke, J. L., Christensen, W. R., Greene, B. A., Gardner, J. E., & Lovett, D. L. (2006). Increasing student participation in IEP meetings: Establishing the self-directed IEP as an evidenced-based practice. *Exceptional Children, 72*, 299–316. doi: 10.1177/001440290607200303

Martin, J. E., Van Dycke, J. L., Greene, B. A., Gardner, J. E., Christensen, W. R., Woods, L. L., & Lovett, D. L. (2006). Increasing student participation in IEP meetings: Establishing the self-directed IEP as an evidenced-based practice. *Exceptional Children, 72*, 299–316. doi: 10.1177/001440290607200303

McConnell, A. E., Little, K., & Martin, J. E. (2015). Transition planning and writing instruction: The effects of a brief intervention. *British Journal of Special Education, 42*, 87–111. doi: 10.1111/1467-8578.12071

McConnell, A. E., Martin, J. E., Herron, J. P., & Hennessey, M. N. (2016). The influence of gender on non-academic skills associated with post-school employment and further education. *Career Development and Transition for Exceptional Individuals.* doi:10.1177/2165143416629629

McConnell, A. E., Martin, J. E., Juan, C. Y., Hennessey, M. N., Terry, R., El-Kazimi, N., Pannells, T., & Willis, D. (2013). Identifying non-academic behaviors associated with post-school employment and education. *Career Development and Transition for Exceptional Individuals, 36*, 174–187. doi: 10.1177/2165143412468147

McConnell, A. E., Martin, J. E., & Hennessey, M. N. (2015). Indicators of postsecondary employment and education for youth with disabilities in relation to GPA and general education. *Remedial and Special Education, 36*, 327–336. doi: 10.1177/0741932515583497

Millar, D. S. (2003). Age of majority, transfer of rights and guardianship: Considerations for families and educators. *Education and Training in Developmental Disabilities, 38*, 378–397.

Millar, D. S., & Renzaglia, A. (2002). Factors affecting guardianship practices for young adults with disabilities. *Exceptional Children, 68*, 465–484. doi: 10.1177/001440290206800404

National Secondary Transition Technical Assistance Center (NSTTAC). (2013). *Age appropriate transition assessment toolkit* (3rd ed.). Charlotte, NC: Author.

National Technical Assistance Center on Transition Indicator 13 Checklist: Form B Enhanced for Professional Development [NSTTAC I-13]. (2012). Retrieved from http://www.transitionta.org/sites/default/files/transitionplanning/Indicator%2013%20Filled%20Example.pdf

Neubert, D. A., & Leconte, P. J. (2013). Age-appropriate transition assessment: The position of the Division on Career Development and Transition. *Career Development and Transition for Exceptional Individuals, 36*, 72–83. doi: 10.1177/2165143413487768

Newman, L., Wagner, M., Cameto, R., & Knokey, A. M. (2009). *The post-high school outcomes of youth with disabilities up to 4 years after high school: A Report from the National Longitudinal Transition Study-2 (NLTS2)* (NCSER 2009–3017). Menlo Park, CA: SRI International.

Part B SPP/APR indicator/measurement table. (n.d.). Retrieved from https://www2.ed.gov/policy/speced/guid/idea/bapr/2014/2014-part-b-measurement-table.pdf

Patton, J. R. & Clark, G. M. (2014). *Transition Planning Inventory-Second Edition (TPI-2)*. Austin, TX: Pro-Ed.

Powers, L. E., Turner, A., Matuszewski, J., Wilson, R., & Loesch, C. (1999). A qualitative analysis of student involvement in transition planning. *The Journal for Vocational Special Needs Education, 21*, 18–26.

Prince, A. M. T., Plotner, A. J., & Yell, M. L. (2014). Postsecondary transition and the courts: An update. *Journal of Disability Policy Studies, 25*, 41–47. doi: 10.1177/1044207314530469

Seong, Y., Wehmeyer, M. L., Palmer, S. B., & Little, T. D. (2015). Effects of the Self-Directed IEP on self-determination and transition of adolescents with disabilities. *Career Development and Transition for Exceptional Individuals, 38*, 132–141. doi: 10.1177/2165143414544359

Simmons, T., Bauder, D., & Flexer, R. (2013). Collaborative transition services. In R. Flexer, R. Baer, P. Luft, & T. Simmons (Eds.), *Transition planning for secondary students with disabilities* (pp. 176–198). Boston, MA: Pearson.

Steele, R. B., Konrad, M., & Test, D. W. (2005). An evaluation of IEP transition components and post-school outcomes in two states. *The Journal for Vocational Special Needs Education, 27*, 4–18.

Transition Planning. (n.d.). Retrieved from http://www.transitionta.org/transitionplanning

US Department of Education. (2015). *Part B state performance plans (SPP) letters and annual performance report (APR) letters*. Retrieved from http://www2.ed.gov/fund/data/report/idea/partbspap/allyears.html#skipnav2

Wehmeyer, M. L. (2002). Transition and access to the general education curriculum. In C. A. Kochhar-Bryant & D. S. Bassett (Eds.), *Aligning transition and standards-based education: Issues and strategies* (pp. 25–41). Arlington, VA: Council for Exceptional Children.

Wright, P. W. D., & Wright, P. D. (2011). *Special education law* (2nd ed.). Hartfield, VA: Harbor House Law Press.

Wright, P. W. D., Wright, P. D., & O'Connor, S. W. (2010). *All about IEPs: Answers to frequently asked questions about IEPs*. Hartfield, VA: Harbor House Law Press.

Zarrow Center for Learning Enrichment. (2016). Retrieved from http://www.ou.edu/content/education/centers-and-partnerships/zarrow.htm

11

Person-Centered and Student-Directed Planning

Karrie A. Shogren, Michael L. Wehmeyer, James R. Thompson

This chapter will introduce person-centered planning, an approach to engage in individualized program and supports planning in the intellectual disability field that has been demonstrated through research to have positive impacts on outcomes (Claes, Van Hove, Vandevelde, van Loon, & Schalock, 2010). We will provide an overview of the history, purpose, and key components of person-centered planning. We will then discuss student-directed planning, differentiating it from person-centered planning and highlighting curricula to promote student involvement in educational and transition planning. Finally, we will discuss how person-centered and student-directed planning can be merged to promote valued outcomes in the context of education and transition planning for students with intellectual disability.

Person-Centered Planning

Person-centered planning emerged in the intellectual disability field in the mid-1980s (Holburn & Vietze, 2002) as a systematic approach to planning focused on developing an "understanding of the needs of the person with disabilities and not the system that serves them" (Seabrooks-Blackmore & Williams, 2013, p. 91). Person-centered planning operationalizes the values associated with the normalization movement, the social-ecological model of disability, and promoting self-determination (Claes et al., 2010), which have been described in other chapters in this text (see Chapters 1–4). The emphasis on person-centered planning approaches is ensuring that the focus is on the person with a disability when identifying valued life outcomes (e.g., where to live, work, learn, and play) and creating systems of support that actualize these outcomes, rather than allowing currently available services to dictate what is possible and what are "reasonable" goals for the future. As Wehmeyer (2002) described it, person-centered planning processes "share common beliefs and attempt to put those shared beliefs into a planning framework" (p. 56). As such, person-centered planning approaches involve changes at the organizational level (e.g., within education and service systems) as well as the level of how planning for the future is conducted (Schwartz, Holburn, & Jacobson, 2000).

Key Components

As will be described in subsequent sections, there are multiple approaches to person-centered planning that have been introduced in the intellectual disability field; however, there is general consensus with regard to the key values that define person-centeredness across approaches. For example, Schwartz et al. (2000) worked to build a definition of person-centeredness and standards associated with person-centered planning by working with a group of people with disabilities and those who supported them who engaged in person-centered planning. Eight "hallmarks" of a person-centered approach were identified:

1. The person's activities, services, and supports are based upon his or her dreams, interests, preferences, strengths, and capacities.
2. The person and people important to him or her are included in lifestyle planning, and have the opportunity to exercise control and make informed decisions.
3. The person has meaningful choices, with decisions based on his or her experiences.
4. The person uses, when possible, natural and community supports.
5. Activities, supports, and services foster skills to achieve personal relationships, community inclusion, dignity, and respect.
6. The person's opportunities and experiences are maximized, and flexibility is enhanced within existing regulatory and funding constraints.
7. Planning is collaborative, recurring, and involves an ongoing commitment to the person.
8. The person is satisfied with his or her relationships, home, and daily routine.

(p. 238)

Schwartz et al. (2000) further operationalized each of eight hallmarks of person-centered planning approaches, identifying indicators that could be used to rate whether or not the hallmarks were present in person-centered planning processes as implemented. The goal was that by defining these key characteristics, high-quality person-centered planning could be supported across organizations, and research could be conducted on the impact of person-centered planning on outcomes, as this is the primary goal of engaging in a person-centered planning process.

Person-Centered Planning Approaches

A number of approaches to person-centered planning have been introduced in the intellectual disability field. Some of the more commonly used and researched include Group Action Planning (GAP; see Turnbull et al., 1996), Essential Lifestyles Planning (ELP; see Smull & Harrison, 1992), MAPS (see Vandercook, York, & Forest, 1989), Personal Futures Planning (PFP; see Mount & Zwernik, 1988), and Planning Alternative Tomorrows with Hope (PATH; see Pierpoint, O'Brien, & Forest, 1995). We will describe each of these approaches, briefly, in the following sections.

Group Action Planning (GAP)

GAP was developed by Turnbull et al. (1996) to enable people with cognitive and multiple disabilities to be more actively involved in planning and decision-making about their lives. Turnbull et al. identified the following key characteristics of GAP:

1. Actively invite people who can be helpful to participate in a reciprocal and interdependent manner.
2. Create a context of social connectedness and caring among all participants.
3. Foster dynamic and creative problem solving fueled by great expectations.
4. Continuously affirm and celebrate the progress that is being made.

The GAP process has been used during planning for the transition from school to adult life for adolescents with extensive support needs and their families. One of GAP's unique features is an "action group" formed to support people with intellectual disability to express, practice, and benefit from their developing skills leading to self-determination that they learn as a function of engaging in the GAP process (Turnbull et al., 1996). These action groups form the planning and decision-making team that works with the student to plan for his or her future. The student's role in the process varies according to student preferences, but he or she is actively involved in developing goals for the action plan. Thus, the capacity enhancement process is linked directly to planning activities. Like most person-centered planning processes, the action group assembled in the GAP process meets frequently and the meetings are convened in comfortable, nonthreatening environments with an emphasis on community inclusion and participation.

GAP has been more fully described in other sources (Turnbull & Turnbull, 1996) and has been implemented with youth and young adults from Hispanic backgrounds and their families (Blue-Banning, Turnbull, & Pereira, 2000). In focus groups with families and professionals participating in the process, the family members felt that GAP enabled parents to share responsibilities for meeting their children's needs and enhanced communication and relationships among team members. However, participants also brought up concerns related to navigating differences in cultural preferences and understandings of decision-making processes. The findings suggest benefits of GAP, but also the need to further examine how to enhance benefit for professionals and to consider culturally responsive practices and their role in enhancing person-centered planning.

Essential Lifestyles Planning (ELP)

ELP was developed by Smull and Harrison (1992) at the University of Maryland nearly 30 years ago as part of a deinstitutionalization project involving adults with intellectual disability who had been designated as "not ready for the community" due to a variety of reasons (e.g., failures at previous community placements, significant challenging behaviors). Smull and Harrison believed the traditional approach to deinstitutionalization, characterized by finding a community service provider with an opening, sending the person to the new setting, and then trying to figure out how to make the placement successful (all of which was done with little input from the person with the disability)— contributed to the problems that people were experiencing when moving out of institutions. According to Smull and Harrison:

> Most human service systems develop programs and put people into them. We are suggesting a system that starts with individuals and builds services around them. People need to be provided with settings where their essential lifestyle choices are met. If this can be done, the lives of people with disabilities will improve dramatically and the problems of the services system will be significantly reduced.
>
> *(p. 1)*

Although ELP emerged out of the Smull and Harrison (1992) deinstitutionalization project, Smull and Sanderson (2009) have more recently described ELP as an approach to "life coaching" that is applicable to everyone. Moreover, they report it is "being used with children and families, with people who have mental health issues, with older people, and with people who have drug and alcohol issues" (p. 5). ELP can include the types of group discussions and problem solving that are common to many person-centered planning approaches, but in ELP more emphasis is placed on ongoing conversations involving the ELP facilitator, the person with the disability, and those who love and care about the person with the disability (e.g., relatives, friends, direct support staff).

The impact that the facilitator has on the value of an ELP process is difficult to overstate, as the process requires a facilitator who has strong communication skills and displays a high level of commitment. Listening skills are the most important communication skills for the ELP facilitator to possess. Much emphasis is placed on listening closely to people with disabilities in order to find out what is important to them. Also emphasized is communicating what has been learned in a manner that is very clear to the person with the disability and easily understood by those who are in a position to provide support to the person (Smull & Sanderson, 2009).

Another key feature of ELP is learning what health, safety, and risk means to both the person with the disability and to those who know and care about the person. Facilitators and planning teams are encouraged to find a balance between "what is important *to*" and "what is important *for*" a person. Problem solving is stressed, and those involved in ELP are reminded to focus on what is possible, not simply on what is traditional or readily available (Smull & Sanderson, 2009).

ELP has multiple stages that are circular (not linear) because the work of planning is recognized as being ongoing (i.e., it is never finished; plans are always going to need to be refined based on implementation issues, anticipated and unanticipated outcomes, and changing circumstances). ELP stages have been described as a "learning wheel" to reflect the focus placed on continuous listening and learning from experiences. The stages include: (1) investing time in answering the question "What do we need to learn?" so that the information that is sought is clearly identified, and the approaches that will be used to gather information are well thought through; (2) gathering information through a series of conversations where ideas are discussed, considered, and reconsidered; (3) developing a plan of action based on the conversations from the prior stage; (4) implementing the plan; and (5) continuing the learning process by collecting information on what parts of the plan do and do not work well, documenting what is learned through learning logs, and using learning logs to guide changes as a person's life experiences evolve (Smull, 2000; Smull & Sanderson, 2009)

MAPS

MAPS started out as an acronym for the McGill Action Planning System (see Vandercook et al., 1989), taking its name from McGill University where the approach was developed during the 1980s. It later became an acronym for Making Action Plans (see Holburn & Vietze, 2002), and now is simply known as MAPS (see O'Brien, Pearpoint, & Kahn, 2012; Wells & Sheehey, 2012). Despite the name changes, the approach has remained the same.

According to Wells and Sheehey (2012), MAPS can be divided into three phases: Preparation, Meetings, and Follow-Up. However, there is nothing that prohibits subdividing the process further. For example, the Preparation phase could be subdivided into selecting the team members/participants and arranging meeting logistics (i.e., establishing the date, time, and place for the meeting, ordering refreshments and supplies for the meeting). As the names of the phases suggest, the Preparation phase refers to activities that prepare participants for a series of meetings. The Meetings phase typically involves two to three meetings (each lasting a couple hours) and culminates with the creation of a plan. The Follow-Up phase includes any meeting or activity with the purpose of evaluating the implementation or continued suitability of the plan.

MAPS has been used most often as a person-centered planning approach with children, but it could be used during any age of life. Participants include the person with a disability, his or her family and friends, and relevant professionals (in the case of schools this would include both special and general education teachers). MAPS proponents have repeatedly stressed the importance of including same-age peers (Vandercook et al., 1989; Wells & Sheehey, 2012) in the meetings.

The following questions/goals drive the Meetings phase:

1. What is the person's history? (Hear the story.)
2. What is your dream for the individual? (Honor the dream.)
3. What is your nightmare? (Recognize the nightmare.)
4. Who is the person? (Name.)
5. What are the person's strengths, gifts, and abilities? (Name the person's gifts.)
6. What are the person's needs? (See what it takes to receive gifts.)

7. What would the person's ideal day at school look like? (Agree on action.)
8. What must be done to make it happen? (Agree on action.)

Questions 1–6 are typically covered during the first meeting, and subsequent meetings are used to address questions 7 and 8. MAPS calls for a facilitator to lead the discussion and assure that everyone has the opportunity to contribute. Also, there is a recorder who documents the discussions using markers and flip charts—both text and pictures are used to document information (O'Brien et al., 2012; Wells & Sheehey, 2012)

Personal Futures Planning (PFP)

Mount (1990) is credited with creating the PFP approach, and perhaps due to the popularity of her approach it is not uncommon to find people using the phrase "futures planning" as a synonym for any person-centered planning processes. Nevertheless, PFP is a distinct approach. It has special focus on promoting meaningful relationships with others and discovering new opportunities for participation in community life. PFP involves four frameworks/phases: Exploring Commitment, Discovering Opportunities, Finding New Directions, and Taking Action.

Exploring Commitment is the phase where the facilitator meets with the person with the disability who is the focus of the planning effort. Among other things, the facilitator develops a "relationship map" with the person where the facilitator identifies key people in the person's life and the nature of these relationships. The Discovering Opportunities phase involves the facilitator meeting with a small group (including the focus person and those with whom he or she has the closest relationships): the "relationship map" is refined and several other maps are created. These include the "places map" (pattern of current daily life), "background map" (overview of the person's life experiences), "preferences map" (personal preferences, gifts, interests, and dislikes/things to avoid), "dreams map" (personal dreams and desires for the future), "hopes and fears map" (perspectives on opportunities for the future, fears, and obstacles), "choices map"(how decisions are made in life, need for personal assistance), "health issues map" (conditions that affect health), and "respect map" (barriers to community acceptance) (Mount, 1990).

The next phase, Finding New Directions, involves considering all of the maps that were developed during the prior phase and gathering people together who are central to the person in order to (1) develop a plan for implementation and (2) assure that people make commitments to take action. The final phase, Taking Action, is focused on implementing the plan. Assuring that people follow through on their commitments and remain involved in implementing the plan is stressed during this phase (Mount, 1990).

Although PFP is a distinct approach, Mount (1990) advocated for infusing personal futures planning into other planning activities and has been skeptical of efforts to make PFP overly standardized. For example, some of the "maps" described earlier are optional. In one sense, PFP is very flexible person-centered planning approach because planning teams are encouraged to select parts of it that meet their needs, perhaps to supplement other planning activities in which they are involved. According to Mount, "If these meeting formats and tools get in the way, *don't use them*. Adapt the ideas to fit each situation, but don't get lost in the trees and miss the opportunity to help people find their way out of the forest" (p. 31).

Planning Alternative Tomorrows with Hope (PATH)

Pierpoint et al. (1995) introduced PATH and refer to the planning team members who participate in the process as "Pathfinders." Consistent with several other person-centered planning approaches, PATH calls for investing time and effort in group meetings where Pathfinders engage in problem solving. There are concerted efforts made to not allow "system-centered" thinking to restrict people's creativity or imagination. Graphic displays play a critical role in PATH, and similar to MAPS it is helpful to have a recorder in addition to a group facilitator. The driving question underlying PATH is "What can happen because of you and your allies that will make your life better and build your community" (J. O'Brien et al., 2012, p. 63).

PATH begins with a visioning process where the focus is on what a person's life would look like if his or her hopes and dreams were fully realized, and ideal supports were in place. This collective vision of an ideal future is known as the "North Star." Once the North Star is established, the planning process moves backwards to the current day, and Pathfinders eventually are charged with specifying what should be done "right now" when people leave the meeting (O'Brien et al., 2012). PATH is focused on linking life activities, opportunities, and experiences, using the following steps:

1. Locate the North Star—a person's long-range hopes and dreams are articulated.
2. Generate a Vision of a Positive Possible Future—the focus is on the near future (e.g., 1–2 years later) and describing what life will be like for the person.
3. Describe the Now—here the person's current reality is described so that everyone has a good picture of what the person's life is like today.
4. Invite Enrollment—the discrepancy between "the now" and the "positive possible future' is analyzed; additional people who could help bridge the gap between "what is" and "what could be" are identified, and strategies for recruiting these people into the process are developed.
5. Decide to Get Stronger—this step is about what the group needs to do that will keep them strong and sustained for the difficult work that lies ahead.
6. Identify Bold Steps—this step is a return to the "backward thinking process" where intermediate steps to reach the "Positive Possible Future" are identified.
7. Organize the Month's Work—in this step the backward-thinking process gets more specific, and definitive plans are made to reach the first intermediate "bold step" identified previously.
8. Agree to Next Steps—here, the actions get very specific; exactly what people are going to do upon leaving the meeting are identified (e.g., make a phone call).

(O'Brien et al., 2012)

Research on Person-Centered Planning

It has been suggested that the loose structure (i.e., flexible guidelines, roles for people that are not clearly defined) of person-centered planning processes is the key to allowing people to creatively problem solve. However, because of the lack of standardization and the uniqueness of every person and planning team, some have argued that it is it very hard to investigate the efficacy of person–centered planning using research methods associated with the social sciences (Evans, 2002; C. L. O'Brien, O'Brien, & Mount, 1997). Others, however, have argued that rigorous scientific investigation of person-centered planning processes is possible if key variables and procedures of a person-centered process are defined, and data are collected on fidelity of implementation and outcomes (Holburn & Vietze, 2002).

Two empirical studies of person-centered planning processes have investigated the impact of person-centered planning. Holburn, Jacobson, Schwartz, Flory, and Vietz (2004) investigated the experiences of 20 people with intellectual disability and challenging behavior who were moving from an institutional setting to a community home. They followed these 20 people over two and a half years, collecting data four times at eight-month intervals. When compared to a matched control group of people who received conventional planning services provided by the state of New York, the 20 people who received person-centered planning experienced significantly better quality of life and other outcomes (greater autonomy, choice making, engagement in daily activities, relationships with others, and personal satisfaction). The researchers also found positive outcomes for people on the planning/transition teams, and concluded that "person-centered planning procedures enhanced team roles, commitment to a vision, and both identification and solution of barriers to community living" (p. 70).

Robertson et al. (2006) and Robertson et al. (2007) reported similar findings in England from a two-year study of 93 people with intellectual disability, ages 16–68 years. After trained facilitators implemented person-centered planning, follow-up data showed that people with intellectual disability who participated in person-centered planning had increased social networks, expanded contact with family and friends, increased participation in community-based activities, and increased choice making. The researchers cautioned, however, that although most people showed significantly improved life experiences and conditions, some experienced more limited benefits. In exploring possible reasons for the varied results, the researchers found that participants with concurrent mental health issues and emotional or behavioral support needs were less likely to benefit. This suggests the need for more research that focuses on the best ways to support people with these types of needs in person-centered processes. Relatedly, the skills and dedication of the facilitators had a marked influence on the success of the process.

Claes et al. (2010) conducted a review of the research on person-centered planning, specifically focusing on identifying articles that evaluated the outcomes and effectiveness of person-centered planning. They identified 15 articles and found that there was no universal definition of person-centered planning adopted in all the articles. They also found that many articles combined person-centered planning with other approaches, such as functional assessment and positive behavior support or later life planning. The majority of articles met criteria for methodological rigor, and studies examined an array of outcomes, including changes in frequency of challenging behavior, increases in social networks and community involvement, as well as increased involvement of people with disabilities and their family members in visioning for the future. Overall, the findings across studies suggested person-centered planning led to improvements in social networks and greater involvement in community and group activities. Some studies looked at factors related to implementation of key elements of person-centered planning and found that promoting the active involvement of the person with a disability and their team in the process were critically important and led to increased communication and development of a vision for the future. Other studies, however, did not find significant impacts on outcomes like employment and wages; while still other studies suggested the need for more focus on supporting engagement of people from culturally diverse communities. Overall, the lack of definitional consensus introduced issues in understanding the impact of person-centered planning on outcomes, as it was not clear across studies if the hallmarks of person-centered planning were implemented. This body of research also focused on person-centered planning in the adult context, primarily, although the studies that combined person-centered planning with functional assessment tended to focus on younger children and their families. One study (Miner & Bates, 1997), did focus on the use of the PFP model with transition-age youth with disabilities and their families to specifically increase the involvement of family members in the Individualized Education Program (IEP) meeting, finding that parents spoke more when PFP was used, but that there was not more of a focus on postschool issues in the discussions, which was another target of the process.

Student-Directed Education and Transition Planning

The previous section described person-centered planning, its key components, approaches to person-centered planning, and current research. As described in the previous sections, many of the person-centered planning approaches and research in the field specifically address issues related to supporting children and adolescents with intellectual disability. For example, GAP specifically focuses on promoting self-determination of transition-age youth through action teams that also focus on building supports and social networks for family members who are providing support. In addition, there is general consensus in the field that education and transition planning for students with disabilities should embody the key components of person-centeredness described previously. However, promoting student involvement in education and transition planning has a broader history, and differing approaches have emerged to enable student-directed planning. Wehmeyer (2002) argued that person-centered planning processes and student-directed or self-directed planning processes differ, not in the values undergirding the process—which share considerable overlap—but in the priority assigned to those values. Wehmeyer noted:

> To some degree, the ingredients to these two processes are the same, but they are mixed differently, with varying proportions of each value reflected in each respective process. For example, in person-centered planning, both currently and historically, there has been a greater emphasis on the role of significant others in plan making than exists in student-directed planning, while student-directed planning processes have placed greater emphasis on building student capacity to set or track goals or make decisions then has person-centered planning.
>
> *(p. 57)*

Wehmeyer elaborated that merging person-centered approaches with student-directed approaches where the values, processes, and intent of each process are included has the best probability of promoting valued outcomes for students. Part of this merging will involve addressing issues of student and family involvement in the planning process as well as building connections among families, the student, professionals, natural supports, and other members of the team; there are examples of doing this, such as GAP. Having high expectations, setting and developing action plans for going after goals, and problem solving when barriers are encountered will all be part of this blended approach. In the following sections, we describe the history and components of student-directed planning, and in the final section we describe approaches to bring together person-centered and student-directed approaches.

History and Key Components of Student-Directed Planning

The 1990 amendments to the Individuals with Disabilities Education Act (IDEA) were the first to emphasize "student involvement" in transition planning, stating that transition services should be based on student interests and preferences. This language has been interpreted to emphasize the role of student self-determination and student-directed planning. Self-determination is discussed in greater depth in Chapter 16, and the skills associated with self-determination such as goal setting, problem solving, decision making, and self-advocacy are critical to promoting student involvement and student-directed planning. However, the focus on student involvement emphasizes the need to enhance the role of the student in planning processes relevant to their lives, making these processes "student-directed." And, through learning to engage in self-determined action, students can take on leadership roles during their educational planning processes. Wehmeyer and Ward (1995) suggested that the student involvement language places the intent and spirit of the IDEA in line with other movements in the disability field, such as those that shaped the emergence of person-centered planning, including normalization, community inclusion, consumer choice, and social-ecological models of understanding disability.

When promoting student involvement in education planning it is important to note that student involvement, decision making, and instruction can take many forms. This can range from students generating their own IEP goals and objectives, to tracking their progress on self-selected goals or objectives, to running their own IEP meeting. It is important to emphasize that it is not what the student does in the meeting that is critical, but instead the degree to which the student is an equal partner in and, to the greatest extent possible, in control of his or her planning. Students with extensive support needs can be involved in their educational program every bit as much as students with less severe impairments. Students with severe disabilities may need more intense and differing supports than students with less intensive support needs, but this is not the criteria by which student involvement should be judged. Instead it's the degree to which students are causal agents—that is, the person that makes things happen in his or her educational planning—that is what defines student involvement. Another way to say this is that all students can engage in self-direction of their education planning; the manner in which they do this and the supports they need to do so will vary.

Approaches to Student-Directed Planning

Although student involvement can take many forms, as described previously, several approaches to promote student direction in educational planning have been developed in the special education field to meet the student involvement mandates of IDEA. Many of these emerged from funding provided by the US Department of Education after the introduction of the student involvement mandates to develop strategies to support students in developing skills associated with self-determination that would enable them to take active roles in their education and transition planning. We review some of the more commonly utilized strategies and research approaches in the following sections.

ChoiceMaker Self-Determination Transition curriculum and Program

The *ChoiceMaker Self-Determination Transition* curriculum (Martin & Marshall, 1995) was developed to promote student self-determination, and the *Self-Directed IEP* lessons that are components of *ChoiceMaker* explicitly focus on promoting student self-direction in the IEP process by teaching students to lead their IEP meetings. The *ChoiceMaker* curriculum consists of three sections: (1) *Choosing Goals,* (2) *Expressing Goals,* and (3) *Taking Action.* Each section contains from two to four teaching goals and numerous teaching objectives. The *Choosing Goals* lessons focus on teaching students the skills and personal information needed to articulate their interests, skills, limits, and goals across one or more self-selected transition areas. The *Self-Directed IEP* lessons (in a separate section) enable students to learn the leadership skills necessary to lead their IEP meetings and publicly disclose their interests, skills, limits, and goals identified through the *Choosing Goals* lessons. Rather than be passive participants at their IEP meetings, students learn to lead their meetings, with appropriate supports. These lessons teach students strategies for performing 11 steps that are associated with leading one's own planning meeting (see Table 11.1 for a list of the steps). The *Expressing Goals* section involves

Table 11.1 Eleven steps for leading the IEP meeting from the self-directed IEP process (Martin, Marshall, Maxson, & Jerman, 1996)

1. Begin the meeting by stating the purpose.
2. Introduce everyone.
3. Review past goals and performance.
4. Ask for others' feedback.
5. State your school and transition goals.
6. Ask questions if you don't understand.
7. Deal with differences in opinion.
8. State the support you will need.
9. Summarize your goals.
10. Close meeting by thanking everyone.
11. Work on IEP goals all year.

communicating goals, and *Taking Action* involves developing and implementing a plan for achieving actions. The *Taking Action* materials enable students to learn how to break their long-range goals into specific goals. Students learn how to: (1) set a standard for goal performance, (2) devise a means to get performance feedback, (3) identify what motivates them to do it, (4) identify the strategies they will use, (5) recruit needed supports, and (6) create a schedule for implementation and attainment.

Next S.T.E.P.: Student Transition and Educational Planning

Another student-directed transition-planning program is the *Next S.T.E.P* curriculum (Halpern et al., 1995), which provides education materials for multiple stakeholders including students, teachers, and family members. The goal is to enable students to become motivated to engage in transition planning, self-evaluate transition needs, identify and select transition goals and activities, assume responsibility for conducting their own transition planning meeting, and monitor the implementation of their transition plans. The curriculum consists of 16 lessons, clustered into four instructional units, that are designed to be delivered to students in 50-minute class periods. Each lesson includes teacher and student materials, videos, guidelines for involving parents and family members, and a process for tracking student progress. Unit 1 (*Getting Started*) includes two lessons that introduce and provide an overview of transition planning. It is intended to enable students to understand the transition-planning process and to motivate them to participate. Unit 2 (*Self-Exploration and Self-Evaluation*) includes six lessons that focus on student self-evaluation. Students work through activities that identify unique interests, strengths, and weaknesses in various adult-outcome oriented areas. At the end of this unit, students complete the student form of the *Transition Skills Inventory*, a 72-item rating instrument assessing how well the student is doing in four transition areas: (1) personal life; (2) jobs; (3) education and training; and (4) living on one's own. The student's self-evaluations in these areas are combined with similar evaluations by his or her teacher and a family member to form a basis for future transition-planning activities. Students are encouraged to discuss differences of opinion between the teacher or family member evaluations and their own self-evaluation and to resolve these discrepancies either before or during the transition-planning meeting.

Unit 3 (*Developing Goals and Activities*) includes five lessons regarding transition goal identification in the four areas on the *Transition Skills Inventory*. Students identify their hopes and dreams, then select from a range of potential goals in each area, narrowing the total set of transition goals to four or five that they prefer. In addition, students choose activities that will help them pursue the goals they have selected. Unit 4 (*Putting a Plan into Place*) includes three lessons preparing students for their transition-planning meeting. The lessons emphasize the implementation of their plan, and teachers and support teams work with students to ensure that they monitor their progress and, if necessary, make adjustments.

The Self-Advocacy Strategy for Education and Transition Planning

Van Reusen, Bos, Schumaker, and Deshler (1994) developed a strategy that teaches self-advocacy skills and is designed to enhance student motivation and enable students to gain a "sense of control and influence over their own learning and development" (p. 1). Students progress through a series of lessons focusing on seven instructional stages. Stage 1, *Orient and Make Commitments*, broadly introduces education and transition planning meetings and how participation can increase student power and control in this process. Stage 2, *Describe*, defines and provides detailed information about transition and education meetings and the advantages students experience if they participate. In this stage the "I PLAN" steps of student participation are introduced. These steps provide a simple framework that students can use to guide their participation in planning meetings.

In Stage 3, *Model and Prepare*, the teacher models the I PLAN steps. Students complete an inventory, which is Step 1 in the I PLAN process, that results in information they can use at their conference. Stage 4 is *Verbal Practice*, during which students are asked questions to make sure they know what to do during each step of the I PLAN strategy. Students then verbally rehearse each step. In Stage 5, *Group Practice and Feedback*, students participate in a simulated planning meeting in which they receive feedback from the teacher and other students. Stage 6, *Individual Practice and Feedback*, allows each student to meet independently with the teacher for practice, feedback and, eventually, mastery. The student and instructor work together to improve areas of self-identified need and engage in another simulated conference. Stage 7, *Generalization,* is intended to generalize the I PLAN strategy to actual conferences. This stage has three phases: (1) preparing for and conducting the planning conference, (2) preparing for other uses of the strategy, and (3) preparing for subsequent conferences.

TAKE CHARGE for the Future

TAKE CHARGE for the Future (Powers et al., 1996) is a student-directed, collaborative model to promote student involvement in educational and transition planning. The model is an adaptation of a validated approach, referred to as *TAKE CHARGE*, that promotes the self-determination of youth with and without disabilities (Powers et al., 1998). *TAKE CHARGE* uses four primary components: skill facilitation, mentoring, peer support, and parent support. For example, *TAKE CHARGE* introduces youth to three major skills areas that one needs to take charge of in one's life: achievement skills, partnership skills, and coping skills. Youth involved in the *TAKE CHARGE* process are matched with successful adults of the same gender who experience similar challenges and share common interests, and are involved in peer support activities throughout (Powers, Sowers, et al., 1996). Parent support is provided via information, technical assistance, and written materials.

TAKE CHARGE uses the same set of core strategies to enable learners with disabilities to participate in a planning meeting. Students use instructional materials and coaching to identify their transition goals, to organize and conduct transition planning meetings, and to achieve their goals through the application of problem solving, self-regulation, and partnership strategies. Concurrently, youth participate in self-selected mentorship and peer-support activities to increase their transition-focused knowledge and skills, and to build social networks to enable success. This element of *TAKE CHARGE* shares commonalities with person-centered planning approaches. Students' parents are also provided with information and support to promote their capacities for active involvement in transition planning.

Whose Future Is It Anyway?

Whose Future Is It Anyway? (Wehmeyer et al., 2004) was developed to enable students with intellectual disability to direct their transition-planning process. This curriculum consists of 36 sessions introducing students to the concept of transition and transition planning. Student learn about (1) self- and disability-awareness, (2) making decisions about transition-related outcomes, (3) identifying and securing community resources to support transition services, (4) writing and evaluating transition goals and objectives, (5) communicating effectively in small groups, and (6) developing skills to become an effective team member, leader or self-advocate.

The materials are student-directed in that they are written for students as end users. The level of support needed by students to complete activities varies a great deal: Some students with difficulty reading or writing may need one-on-one support to progress through the materials; others can complete the process independently. The materials make every effort to ensure that students retain control while at the same time receiving the support they need to succeed. Additionally, an electronic version of the curriculum has been developed that embeds features of universal design to promote even greater student self-direction in interacting with the materials (Wehmeyer & Palmer, 2011).

Section 1 (*Getting to Know You*) introduces the concept of transition and educational planning, provides information about transition requirements in IDEA, and enables students to identify who has attended past planning meetings, who is required to be present at meetings, and who they want involved in their planning process. They are introduced to four primary transition outcome areas (employment, community living, postsecondary education, and recreation and leisure); activities throughout the curriculum focus on these four areas. Students identify their unique characteristics, including their abilities and interests. Students then learn to identify their unique learning needs resulting from their disability.

In Section 2 (*Making Decisions*), students learn a simple problem-solving process by working through each step in the process to make a decision about a potential living arrangement, and then applying the process to make decisions about the three other transition outcome areas. Section 3 (*How to Get What You Need, Sec. 101*) enables students to locate community resources identified in previous planning meetings that are intended to provide supports in each of the transition outcome areas. Section 4 (*Goals, Objectives and the Future*) enables students to apply a set of rules to identify transition-related goals and objectives that are currently on their IEP or transition-planning form, evaluate these goals based on their own transition interests and abilities, and develop additional goals to take to their next planning meeting. Students learn what goals and objectives are, how they should be written, and ways to track progress on goals and objectives.

Section 5 (*Communicating*) introduces effective communication strategies for small group situations, like the transition-planning meetings. Students work through sessions that introduce different types of communication (verbal, body language, etc.) and how to interpret these communicative behaviors, the differences between aggressive and assertive communication, how to effectively negotiate and compromise, when to use persuasion, and other skills that will enable them to be more effective communicators during transition planning meetings. Section 6 (*Thank You, Honorable Chairperson*), the final section, enables students to learn types and purposes of meetings, steps to holding effective meetings, and roles of the meeting chairperson and team members. Students are encouraged to work with school personnel to take a meaningful role in planning for and participating in the meeting.

Beyond High School

Beyond High School (Wehmeyer, Garner, Yeager, Lawrence, & Davis, 2006) was developed to focus on promoting student involvement in 18–21 services for young adults with intellectual disability who remain eligible for educational services through the age of 22. *Beyond High School* teaches students to establish short- and long-term goals based on their own preferences, abilities, and interests. In Stage 1 of the model, students are involved in targeted instruction teaching them to self-direct planning and decision making specific to the transition process. Next, students are taught to self-direct the transition goal setting, action planning, and program implementation process using the *Self-Determined Learning Model of Instruction*, described in greater depth in Chapter 16. Once students learn this self-regulated learning process, they apply the first part of the *Self-Determined Learning Model of Instruction* ("What is my goal?") to identify goals in key transition areas, including employment, independent living, recreation and leisure, and postsecondary education.

Stage 2 of the model involves convening a student-directed, person-centered planning meeting that brings together stakeholders to work with the student to refine goals, as needed, to support the student as he or she implements the second phase of the *Self-Determined Learning Model of Instruction* ("What is my plan?"). This meeting is not intended to be the mandated IEP meeting, although these activities certainly can occur at an IEP meeting. Instead, the meeting bears a closer resemblance to person-centered planning process in which stakeholders come together on a more frequent basis to identify hopes and dreams, to identify natural supports, and so forth. However, the meeting varies from traditional person-centered planning meetings in that it is intended to be the student's meeting. The teacher or person-centered planning facilitator should support the student to present the goals he or she has generated. In addition, these student goals provide the foundation for the meeting's purpose and direction. Other stakeholders are encouraged to help the student refine the goals, more clearly define the goals, or identify objectives to reach the goals, but not to criticize or replace the goals. These goals will form only a subset of the total goals on a student's IEP, but the intent is that students have a forum to discuss their goals and gather the support of parents, family members, teachers, and others to make those goals achievable. This is also an opportune time to consider how each stakeholder can support and contribute to the student's efforts to attain those goals.

In Stage 3 (the final stage of the model), the student, with supports identified from Stage 2, implements the plan, monitors his or her progress in achieving the goal, and evaluates the success of the plan, making revisions to the goal or the plan as warranted. This is accomplished using the strategies and questions comprising the third phase of the *Self-Determined Learning Model of Instruction*.

Research on Student-Directed Planning

Test et al. (2004) conducted an extensive review of the literature pertaining to student involvement, and determined that students across disability categories can be successfully involved in education and transition planning, and that a number of programs, including those mentioned subsequently, are effective in increasing student involvement. With regard to the specific curricula mentioned previously, a wide array of research over a 20-year period has suggested the power of the various curricula. Powers et al. (2001) conducted a control-group study and found that the *TAKE CHARGE* materials positively impacted student involvement. More recently, Powers et al. (2012) examined a modified version of *TAKE CHARGE, My Life*, in a longitudinal, randomized control trial with youth with disabilities in foster care and found significant positive impact on student involvement and postschool outcomes.

Van Reusen and Bos (1994) found that the Self-Advocacy Strategy led to enhanced student motivation and participation. Wehmeyer et al. (2006) demonstrated the benefits of *Beyond High School* for students with intellectual disability served in 18–21 programs. Martin et al. (2006) conducted a randomized trial control group study of the *Self-Directed IEP* components of the *ChoiceMaker* curriculum and found that students with disabilities who received instruction using *Self-Directed IEP* (a) attended more IEP meetings; (b) increased their active participation in the meetings; (c) showed more leadership behaviors in the meetings; (d) expressed their interests, skills, and support needs across educational domains; and (e) remembered their IEP goals after the meeting at greater rates than did students in the control group, who received no such instruction. Seong, Wehmeyer, Palmer, and Little (2015) conducted another randomized-trial placebo-control group study of *Self-Directed IEP*, finding that instruction using the process resulted in enhanced self-determination and transition knowledge of students exposed to *Self-Directed IEP*.

Wehmeyer, Palmer, Lee, Williams-Diehm and Shogren (2011) conducted a randomized-trial, placebo-control group design study of the WFA curriculum and found that instruction using the WFA process resulted in significant, positive differences in self-determination when compared with a placebo-control group, and that students who received instruction gained transition knowledge and skills. Lee et al. (2011) conducted another randomized-trial study of the impact of the WFA process both with and without the use of technology, and determined significant gains in skills leading to self-determination and transition knowledge and skills as a function of instruction with WFA. Overall, research has consistently suggested that students with intellectual disability can learn skills that enable them to be actively involved and self-direct their educational planning meetings.

Person-Centered, Student-Directed Approaches

As discussed in the previous sections, there is considerable overlap between the values of person-centered planning and student-directed planning approaches. There are distinctions, however, in terms of who is seen as responsible for making the plan, and setting and directing the goal attainment process.

Key, however, to providing special education supports and services is promoting student involvement, self-determination, and self-direction. Thus, it is critical that the person for whom the planning and the supports to enable the attainment of goals are being designed should be the one directing the planning. It is important to not confuse self-direction, self-determination, and independence. These are not equivalent terms. A person can be self-determined—making or causing things to happen in his or her life—without being independent in the process. All of us rely on supports, and supports can be structured to enable self-determination and self-direction. Thus, bringing together student-directed approaches with person-centered planning strategies and values—as some of the curricula and approaches described in the previous sections do—allows for people with intellectual disability, including people with extensive and pervasive support needs, to benefit by acting in a self-directed manner with an interdependent system of support. This will enable the vision—and plan for achieving the vision for the future—to be guided by the student with a disability, with support from his or her family and social networks.

Critical to enabling this process, then, is to focus on involving all stakeholders (student, family, educators, natural supports) in the visioning process but focusing on enabling the student to direct this process. The entire person-centered planning team can then be involved in supporting the identification and implementation of strategies to achieve the student's vision. GAP, *TAKE CHARGE,* and *Beyond High School* each embed elements of self-directed planning, family involvement, and person-centered planning. Using one of these approaches—or considering ways to merge other person-centered planning approaches with student-directed curricula—will enable the valued outcomes of self-determination, family empowerment, and comprehensive systems of support that enable valued postschool outcomes to occur for students with intellectual disability.

References

Blue-Banning, M. J., Turnbull, A. P., & Pereira, L. (2000). Group Action Planning as a support strategy for Hispanic families: Parent and professional perspectives. *Mental Retardation, 38*(3), 262–275.

Claes, C., Van Hove, G., Vandevelde, S., van Loon, J., & Schalock, R. L. (2010). Person-centered planning: Analysis of research and effectiveness. *Intellectual and Developmental Disabilities, 48*, 432–453.

Evans, I. M. (2002). Trying to make apple pie an independent variable: Comment on how science can evaluate and enhance person-centered planning. *Research and Practice for Persons with Severe Disabilities, 27*, 265–267.

Halpern, A. S., Herr, C. M., Wolf, N. K., Lawson, J. D., Doren, B., & Johnson, M. D. (1995). *NEXT S.T.E.P.: Student transition and educational planning.* Eugene, OR: University of Oregon.

Holburn, S., Jacobson, J. W., Schwartz, A. A., Flory, M. J., & Vietz, P. M. (2004). The Willowbrook futures project: A longitudinal analysis of person-centered planning. *American Journal on Mental Retardation, 109,* 63–76.

Holburn, S., & Vietze, P. M. (Eds.). (2002). *Person-centered planning: Research, practice, and future directions.* Baltimore, MD: Paul H. Brookes Publishing Co.

Lee, Y., Wehmeyer, M. L., Palmer, S. B., Williams-Diehm, K., Davies, D. K., & Stock, S. E. (2011). The effect of student-directed transition planning with a computer-based reading support program on the self-determination of students with disabilities. *The Journal of Special Education, 45,* 104–117. doi: 10.1177/0022466909358916

Martin, J. E., & Marshall, L. H. (1995). ChoiceMaker: A comprehensive self-determination transition program. *Intervention in School and Clinic, 30,* 147–156.

Martin, J. E., Marshall, L. H., Maxson, L., & Jerman, P. (1996). *Self-directed IEP* (2nd ed.). Longmont, CO: Sopris West.

Martin, J. E., van Dycke, J. L., Christensen, W. R., Greene, B. A., Gardner, J. E., & Lovett, D. L. (2006). Increasing student participation in IEP meetings: Establishing the self-directed IEP as an evidenced-based practice. *Exceptional Children, 72,* 299–316.

Miner, C., & Bates, P. (1997). The effect of person centered planning activities on the IEP/transition planning process. *Education and Training in Developmental Disabilities, 32,* 105–112.

Mount, B. (1990). *Making futures happen: A manual for facilitators of Personal Futures Planning.* St. Paul, MN: Governor's Council on Developmental Disabilities.

Mount, B., & Zwernik, K. (1988). *It's never too early, It's never too late: A booklet about personal futures planning for persons with developmental disabilities, their families and friends, case managers, service providers, and advocates.* St. Paul, MN: Metropolitan Council.

O'Brien, C. L., O'Brien, J., & Mount, B. (1997). Person-centered planning has arrived . . . or has it? *Mental Retardation, 35,* 480–484.

O'Brien, J., Pearpoint, J., & Kahn, L. (2012). *The Path and MAPS handbook: Person-centered ways to build community.* Toronto, Canada: Inclusion Press.

Pierpoint, J., O'Brien, J., & Forest, M. (1995). *PATH: A workbook for planning positive possible futures* (2nd ed.). Toronto, Ontario: Inclusion Press.

Powers, L. E., Geenen, S., Powers, J., Pommier-Satya, S., Turner, A., Dalton, L., . . . Swand, P. (2012). My life: Effects of a longitudinal, randomized study of self-determination enhancement on the transition outcomes of youth in foster care and special education. *Children and Youth Services Review, 34,* 2179–2187.

Powers, L. E., Sowers, J., Turner, A., Nesbitt, M., Knowles, E., & Ellison, R. (1996). TAKE CHARGE! A model for promoting self-determination among adolescents with challenges. In L. E. Powers, G. H. S. Singer, & J. Sowers (Eds.), *On the road to autonomy: Promoting self-competence in children and youth with disabilities* (pp. 69–92). Baltimore, MD: Paul H. Brookes.

Powers, L. E., Turner, A., Westwood, D., Loesch, C., Brown, A., & Rowland, C. (1998). TAKE CHARGE for the future: A student-directed approach to transition planning. In M. L. Wehmeyer & D. J. Sands (Eds.), *Making it happen: Student involvement in education planning, decision making and instruction* (pp. 187–210). Baltimore: Paul H. Brookes.

Powers, L. E., Turner, A., Westwood, D., Matuszewski, J., Wilson, R., & Phillips, A. (2001). TAKE CHARGE for the Future: A controlled field-test of a model to promote student involvement in transition planning. *Career Development for Exceptional Individuals, 24,* 89–103.

Robertson, J., Emerson, E., Hatton, C., Elliott, J., McIntosh, B., Swift, P., . . . Joyce, T. (2006). Longitudinal analysis of the impact and cost of person-centered planning for people with intellectual disabilities in England. *American Journal on Mental Retardation, 111,* 400–416.

Robertson, J., Emerson, E., Hatton, C., Elliott, J., McIntosh, B., Swift, P., . . . Joyce, T. (2007). Person-centered planning: Factors associated with successful outcomes for people with intellectual disabilities. *Journal of Intellectual Disability Research, 51,* 232–243. doi: 10.1111/j.1365-2788.2006.00864.x

Schwartz, A. A., Holburn, S. C., & Jacobson, J. W. (2000). Defining person-centeredness: Results of two consensus methods. *Education and Training in Mental Retardation and Developmental Disabilities, 35,* 235–249.

Seabrooks-Blackmore, J., & Williams, G. (2013). Transition planning: Planning strategies. In M. L. Wehmeyer & K. W. Webb (Eds.), *Handbook of transition for youth with disabilities* (91–101). Arlington, VA: Council for Exceptional Children.

Seong, Y., Wehmeyer, M. L., Palmer, S. B., & Little, T. D. (2015). Effects of the Self-Directed IEP on self-determination and transition of adolescents with disabilities. *Career Development and Transition for Exceptional Individuals, 38,* 132–141. doi: 10.1177/2165143414544359

Smull, M. (2000). *Listen, learn, act.* Annapolis, MD: Support Development Associates.

Smull, M., & Harrison, S. B. (1992). *Supporting people with severe reputations in the community.* Arlington, VA: NASMRPD.

Smull, M., & Sanderson, H. (2009). *Essential lifestyle planning for everyone.* Annapolis, MD: The Learning Community.

Test, D. W., Mason, C., Hughes, C., Konrad, M., Neale, M., & Wood, W. M. (2004). Student involvement in individualized education program meetings. *Exceptional Children, 70*(4), 391–412.

Turnbull, A. P., Blue-Banning, M. J., Anderson, E. L., Turnbull, H. R., Seaton, K. A., & Dinas, P. A. (1996). Enhancing self-determination through group action planning. In D. J. Sands & M. L. Wehmeyer (Eds.), *Self-determination across the lifespan: Independence and choice for people with disabilities* (pp. 237–256). Baltimore: Paul H. Brookes.

Turnbull, A. P., & Turnbull, H. R., III. (1996). Group action planning as a strategy for providing comprehensive family support. In L. K. Koegel, R. L. Koegel, & G. Dunlap (Eds.), *Positive behavioral support: Including people with difficult behavior in the community.* (pp. 99–114). Baltimore, MD, US: Paul H Brookes Publishing.

Vandercook, T., York, J., & Forest, M. (1989). The McGill Action Planning System (MAPS): A strategy for building the vision. *Journal of the Association for Persons with Severe Handicaps, 14,* 205–215.

Van Reusen, A. K., & Bos, C. S. (1994). Facilitating student participation in individualized education programs through motivation strategy instruction. *Exceptional Children, 60,* 466–475.

Van Reusen, A. K., Bos, C. S., Schumaker, J. B., & Deshler, D. D. (1994). *The self-advocacy strategy for education and transition planning.* Lawrence, KS: Edge Enterprises, Inc.

Wehmeyer, M. L. (2002). The confluence of person-centered planning and self-determination. In S. Holburn & P. M. Vietze (Eds.), *Person centered planning: Research, practice, and future directions* (pp. 51–69). Baltimore, MD: Paul H. Brookes Publishing Co.

Wehmeyer, M. L., Garner, N., Yeager, D., Lawrence, M., & Davis, A. K. (2006). Infusing self-determination into 18–21 services for students with intellectual or developmental disabilities: A multi-stage, multiple component model. *Education and Training in Developmental Disabilities, 41*, 3–13.

Wehmeyer, M. L., Lawrence, M., Kelchner, K., Palmer, S. B., Garner, N., & Soukup, J. H. (2004). *Whose future is it anyway? A student-directed transition planning process.* Lawrence, KS: Kansas University Center on Developmental Disabilities.

Wehmeyer, M. L., & Palmer, S. B. (2011). *Whose future is it?* Verona, WI: Attainment Company.

Wehmeyer, M. L., Palmer, S. B., Lee, Y., Williams-Diehm, K., & Shogren, K. (2011). A randomized-trial evaluation of the effect of whose future is it anyway? On self-determination. *Career Development for Exceptional Individuals, 34*, 45–56. doi: 10.1177/0885728810383559

Wehmeyer, M. L., & Ward, M. J. (1995). The spirit of the IDEA mandate: Student involvement in transition planning. *The Journal for Vocational Special Needs Education, 17*, 108–111.

Wells, J. C., & Sheehey, P. H. (2012). Person-centered planning: Strategies to encourage participation and facilitate communication. *Teaching Exceptional Children, 44*(3), 32–39.

Part III

Schoolwide and Classroomwide Academic and Behavioral Supports

12

Multitiered Systems of Supports

Karrie A. Shogren, Michael L. Wehmeyer,
Kathleen Lynne Lane, Carol Quirk

Multitiered Systems of Supports (MTSS) are defined by their emphasis on the provision of high-quality supports for all students across multiple domains (i.e., academic, behavioral, social-emotional), with increasingly specialized supports for students who need them in a particular domain at a particular point in time. As such, MTSS models provide a framework that can be utilized to support all students, including students with intellectual disability, to access high-quality educational opportunities. MTSS models are consistent with functional, strengths-based approaches to understanding intellectual disability (see Chapter 2) as they emphasize (a) providing all students with access to research-based supports across critical domains (i.e., academic, behavioral, and social-emotional); (b) identifying additional supports students need to be successful; and (c) systematically implementing more intensive interventions and supports to address those specific needs. In this chapter, we will provide an overview of the history of MTSS and their relationship to other approaches that focus on the provision of high-quality support to all students, such as positive behavior support (PBS) and response to intervention (RtI). We will then introduce a Comprehensive, Integrated, Three-Tiered (Ci3T) model of prevention that brings together RtI for academics, PBS for meeting students' behavioral needs, and a validated curriculum to teach core social skills (e.g., conflict-resolution skills, character, or bullying-prevention skills). Finally, we will discuss emerging directions within the context of MTSS for students with intellectual disability, with an emphasis on applications that have the potential to enhance the inclusion of and access to the general education curriculum for students with intellectual disability and to embed issues related to self-determination in the context of MTSS.

Emergence of Multitiered Systems of Supports

Within the intellectual disability field, the introduction of the supports model (Thompson et al., 2009) has led to a growing emphasis of the role of comprehensive systems of supports for students with intellectual disability. As further described in Chapter 3, the supports model defines systems of supports as the "planned and integrated use of individualized support strategies and resources that encompass the multiple aspects of human performance in multiple settings" (Schalock et al., 2010, p. 106) and is based in a social-ecological model of disability. The focus for all people, but particularly for students with intellectual disability, is understanding disability as a mismatch between personal competencies and environmental demands that creates a need for supports. The supports model recognizes that all people have support needs, but that because of mismatches between personal competencies and environmental demands, some people need more intense supports. Students with intellectual disability tend to have more intense support needs in domains related to learning and participation in educational contexts than the general population as a function of the mismatches they experience.

Supports are defined as any "resources and strategies that aim to promote the development, education, interests, and personal well-being of a person and enhance individual functioning" (Schalock et al., 2010, p. 175). For students with intellectual disability in the education context, supports can encompass a wide array of resources and strategies that promote learning and participation (Schalock et al., 2012). It is critical, however, to recognize that supports can involve environmental restructuring to reduce environmental mismatches as well as personalized supports that provide targeted instruction and assistance specific to each student's needs. Many supports that promote environmental restructuring, or universal supports, lead to changes in the environment that benefit all students, including students with intellectual disability, by reducing the mismatches between environmental demands and personal capacities. Thus, the notion of universal supports, or those that proactively support all people, are a natural part of a system of support for students with intellectual disability. Essentially by designing the environment, including both the learning environment and the physical environment, to be maximally accessible to all, students with intellectual disability benefit (as do all students) and more specialized and personalized supports are provided only as necessary after universal supports have been implemented. Universal design (Connell et al., 1997) and Universal Design for Learning (UDL; Hall, Meyer, & Rose, 2012) emphasize how physical and learning environments, products, and materials can be structured to ensure access for all members of society, including students with intellectual disability. For example, UDL emphasizes providing multiple means of representing content, expressing learning, and promoting student engagement. If information is presented in multiple forms (e.g., print based, audio, visual) this provides greater access for students who may not have strengths in one form (e.g., print based) but can meaningfully engage with visual representations of content.

MTSS are functional and strengths-based, and they incorporate concepts related to the supports model, universal design, and UDL, along with other concepts related to instructional design and data-based decision making. MTSS models are unique in that they address multiple domains relevant to the provision of a high-quality education for all students, including those that need more intensive supports. The starting point in MTSS is high-quality universally designed instruction for all students, with increasingly specialized interventions only as necessary after universal supports are in place (Greenwood, Kratochwill, & Clements, 2008; Lane, Menzies, Oakes, & Kalberg, 2012). Within education, PBS and RtI models use the systems of supports framework; the MTSS framework merges academic and behavioral models into a system. Some integrated models such as the Ci3T model are emerging to address academics, behavior, and social emotional development. The intent of such blended models is to meet students' multiple needs in these areas as needed in the education system. In the following sections, we will briefly review PBS and RtI models as these are foundational to emerging MTSS models, then introduce the Ci3T model.

Positive Behavior Support (PBS)

A more extensive discussion of PBS is provided in Chapter 13, but it is important to highlight that, while PBS emerged initially from research on effective strategies to eliminate problem behavior of students with disabilities by redesigning environments and providing learning supports for positive behavior (Carr et al., 2002), the relevance of environmental redesign and learning supports for positive behavior were quickly recognized as relevant for all students, and the benefits for students with intellectual and developmental disabilities heightened when the focus was on a tiered approach to supporting all students that started with universal interventions. Tiered systems of PBS (Sugai & Horner, 2010) focus on providing universal supports for all students, with increasingly specialized and differentiated interventions for groups of students and individual students, based on data that identify the context and motivation for problem and pro-social behavior. Specifically, PBS is often organized into a three-tier model, with Tier 1 representing universal supports; Tier 2, group or low-intensity supports (e.g., classroom-level supports or social skill groups for a targeted group of students); and Tier 3, individualized or high-intensity supports (e.g., functional assessment-based interventions; Lane, Oakes, & Cox, 2011). Research has suggested a strong and positive impact of PBS on students' behavioral outcomes when implemented school-wide and state-wide (Bohanon et al., 2006; Muscott, Mann, & LeBrun, 2008; Sugai & Horner, 2010).

Response to Intervention (RtI)

RtI models have emerged that focus on academic supports for students. Some RtI models focus on the identification of students with learning disabilities (Hale et al., 2010), while others have a broader focus and address issues of universal academic supports, with increasingly specialized interventions for students who have more intense learning needs. The latter approach, called "problem-solving RtI" (Sailor, 2009), is more closely aligned with the MTSS framework described in this chapter. Problem-solving RtI approaches use student performance data to make instructional decisions and tiered systems to systematically design and offer research-based interventions to promote all students' academic progress. As with PBS, the starting point is Tier 1, or universal supports (i.e., high-quality, evidence-based instruction for all students), with more intensive supports provided only after effective Tier 1 strategies are attempted with fidelity (Lane et al., 2007).

It is important to note that tiered systems of supports in the PBS or RtI models are not directly linked with special education services or program modifications that are needed as a result of a particular disability. All students, including students with intellectual disability, should participate in universal Tier-1 instruction and intervention systems. Accommodations or modifications specific to a student's disability can be provided in that context. A tiered intervention system has rules for entry and exit from interventions that are applied based on the student progress and performance, and not on the label or type of disability. In a comprehensive tiered system of supports, additional interventions are provided as Tier 2 based on data regarding the student's performance and response to Tier 1, and more intensely in Tier 3 based on data regarding the student's performance and response to Tier 2. Tier 2 and Tier 3, or more intensive supports, are not equivalent to special education supports and services. Students with and without disabilities can and should access Tier-3 supports, based on instructional need. Further, more intensive tiered supports are provided in addition to Tier-1 supports; all students should participate in the universal instruction made available within a grade or school with Tier-2 or -3 supports offered at other times of the day.

Unfortunately, there is not yet a large research base on the application of MTSS to students with intellectual disability, particularly in the area of academic supports. Most research in this domain has focused on students with high-incidence disabilities, such as learning disabilities (Koutsoftas, Harmon, & Gray, 2009; Pyle & Vaughn, 2012). Thus, further research is needed that explores effective strategies to include and research the outcomes of students with intellectual disability in MTSS models. Further, work on implemented RtI and PBS has often operated separately within school systems, without integrating supports for academics and behavior as well as other important educational domains such as social-emotional development, and postschool and transition outcomes.

Comprehensive, Integrated, Three-Tiered (Ci3T) Model

As described previously, many school systems across the country have focused on systemic approaches for preventing and responding to learning and behavioral support needs using PBS and RtI. In recent years, an increased emphasis has been placed on developing integrated approaches to meet students' academic, behavioral, and social needs in a comprehensive manner, rather than having separate teams and structures for addressing each domain (Lane, Menzies, Ennis, & Oakes, 2015; McIntosh, Chard,

Boland, & Horner, 2006). This shift toward integrated models is rapidly becoming a national priority. In fact, Michael Yudin (Assistant Secretary for the Office of Special Education and Rehabilitation of the US Department of Education) gave a compelling keynote address at the 2014 National PBS Leadership Conference during which he urged educators to "pay as much attention to students' social and behavioral needs as we do academics." In this section, we describe a model that systematically integrates these domains, the Ci3T model (Lane, Oakes, Lusk, Cantwell, & Schatschneider, in press; McIntosh & Goodman, 2015).

The Ci3T model—and other frameworks that work to integrate supports for learning, behavior, and other domains—retains a data-informed approach to providing a continuum of supports according to individual students' needs. It also provides a collaborative, resource-efficient model to support all students, including students with intellectual disability. Ci3T is a model of prevention that blends RtI practices for reading and math, PBS, and teaching of validated social skills curriculum designed as one unified system (Lane et al., in press).

As with other tiered systems, the Ci3T model features graduated continuum of instruction and supports: Tier 1 for all students (primary prevention), Tier 2 for some students (secondary prevention), and Tier 3 for a few students (tertiary prevention). As part of this data-informed model, a range of data is collected and examined. First, stakeholders' views of each level of prevention (Tier 1, 2, and 3) are collected and examined to obtain feedback on the social significance of the goals, the social acceptability of the procedures, and the social importance of the effects or outcomes (Wolf, 1978). It is important to assess social validity regularly—even during the Ci3T building process—as we have learned that schools' social validity scores during the training process actually predict how well Tier-1 components are implemented during the first year of implementation (Lane et al., 2009). Second, treatment integrity data are collected to examine the extent to which each level of prevention is implemented as planned (Gresham, 1989). Information on the integrity of Tier-1 practices is critical as we certainly do not want to indicate a student is not responding to primary prevention efforts without knowing the universal components are being implemented with adequate integrity (e.g., 80%). Third, data are collected regarding students' performance to determine responsiveness to school-wide efforts using academic and behavior screening tools (Lane et al., 2012) and Tier-2 and Tier-3 supports using progress monitoring tools as they are more sensitive to change. The Ci3T model is firmly grounded in the notion that it is important to consider students' multifaceted needs by examining multiple sources of data in tandem. In the Ci3T model, data collected as part of regular school practices such as academic screeners (e.g., AIMSweb; Pearson Education, 2008), behavior screeners (e.g., Student Risk Screening Scale; Drummond, 1994; Lane, Oakes, Carter, Lambert, & Jenkins, 2013), office discipline referrals (ODRs), and attendance (e.g., absenteeism and tardies) are examined at regular intervals to inform instruction at each level of prevention.

Primary Prevention

All students participate in primary prevention efforts, including students receiving special education services. This level of prevention includes three domains: (a) academic, including instruction in core academic curriculum according to state and district standards; (b) behavioral, including participation in a school-wide PBS framework, and (c) social, including instruction in social skills using a validated curriculum to address a district-identified focus area (e.g., skills leading to self-determination, bullying prevention, character education; Lane et al., 2012).

For the academic domain, roles and responsibilities are defined in the Ci3T blueprint for all stakeholders (e.g., teachers, students, parents, and administrators) to support core curricula being implemented with integrity and accessed by all students. Teachers provide instruction in core academic content areas with integrity, differentiating instruction (process, content, and products) to allow all students to benefit from the instructional experience. As part of Tier-1 practices all teachers are empowered with research-based strategies such as increasing opportunities to respond and incorporating instructional choice to maximize engagement and assist students in learning academic content (Simonsen, Fairbanks, Briesch, Myers, & Sugai, 2008). Teachers are often expected to communicate daily with parents using a web-based system to facilitate home–school partnerships. Students may be asked to bring required materials to class and engage in a range of tasks offering their best effort. Parents may be asked to support existing attendance policies, support homework completion, and monitor student progress on the web-based system.

The behavioral domain includes a PBS framework—not a curriculum—that subscribes to an instructional approach to behavior. Faculty and staff collaborate to establish school-wide expectations (e.g., respect, responsibility, and best effort) for each common area in the school (e.g., classrooms, hallways, lunch room). Teachers provide explicit instruction in expectations, offering multiple opportunities for students to practice and receive reinforcement for meeting expectations. By having one set of expectations, one universal reinforcer (e.g., PBS tickets), and involving all adults in the building, students are able to receive feedback and reinforcement from multiple sources. This programming for generalization is particularly important for students who require more trials to meet mastery (e.g., students with intellectual disability).

The school-site team adopts an evidence-based social skills curriculum with attention to issues of effectiveness and feasibility to address district priorities. For example, if behavior screening and ODR data suggest students are struggling with interpersonal skills, the team may select the Social Skills Improvement System—Classwide Intervention Program (Elliott & Gresham, 2007), which provides instruction in 10 top social skills. The Ci3T blueprint would include defined roles and responsibilities for stakeholders for the selected curriculum to support high-integrity implementation.

For each domain, treatment integrity data are examined to determine implementation and social validity data are reviewed to secure stakeholders' views. These programmatic measures are reviewed in addition to student performance on academic and behavior screening measures to (a) examine overall performance of the school as a whole, (b) determine teacher-delivered interventions (e.g., increasing opportunity to respond) if screening data suggest more than 20% of students in a class are struggling, and (c) connect students to Tier-2 and -3 supports if primary prevention efforts implemented with integrity are insufficient (Oakes, Lane, Cantwell, & Royer, 2016).

Secondary Prevention

Secondary or Tier-2 supports are provided for students who need additional instruction or assistance because they are encountering difficulties with acquisition (cannot complete problems), fluency (have trouble doing problems), or performance (won't do problems) (Elliott & Gresham, 2007). Such supports include research- and evidence-based interventions such as small group instruction, repeated reading groups to support fluency goals, or social skills instruction for students with common acquisition deficits. Such supports can also include low-intensity programs such as the Check-In Check-Out program (Crone, Hawken, & Horner, 2010), behavior contracts (Downing, 2002), and self-management strategies (Mooney, Ryan, Uhing, Reid, & Epstein, 2005). They can also be integrated, such as using a self-monitoring intervention for those students in Tier-2 reading groups who score below benchmark in reading according to AIMSweb data and who also have higher-than-average impulsivity and inattentiveness according to the Strengths and Difficulties Questionnaire (SDQ; Goodman, 2001) behavior screening subscale. In this example, students might have a self-monitoring form that is used to support active participation in their reading group to ensure they are accessing this supplemental support. An estimated 10–15% of the student body will need secondary prevention efforts, recognizing these are additive in nature and should not be viewed as substitutes for primary prevention efforts.

Each Ci3T blueprint includes Tier-2 intervention grids to make these extra supports transparent and accessible to all stakeholders. These grids include the name of the support; a description; inclusion criteria (using screening data and other data collected as part of regular school practices on all students); data to monitor implementation, stakeholders' views, and student progress; and exit criteria. Such grids facilitate communication between teachers, parents, and students and make the expectation clear that additional supports available and are intended to assist all students in achieving school success (see Lane et al., 2015 for examples).

Tertiary Prevention

Tertiary or Tier-3 supports are intensive, individualized interventions typically needed for 3–5% of students with the most intensive support needs (Lane et al., in press). Examples include functional assessment–based interventions (Kern & Manz, 2004), wraparound services (Eber et al., 2009), and highly intensive reading instruction (Denton, Fletcher, Anthony, & Francis, 2006). Such supports are used to provide targeted and highly intensive instruction to address the needs of students who have not reached the expected performance level for their age and grade, even with small group/Tier-2 supports. For example, an elementary student scoring in the extremely elevated risk category on the BASC^2 Behavior and Emotional Screening Scales (BASC^2 BESS; Kamphaus & Reynolds, 2008), who is also frequently engaging in disruptive behavior when interacting with peers according to ODR data, and whose behavior has not made significant improvements through low-intensity behavior interventions, may benefit from an individualized functional assessment-based intervention program to improve social interactions and reduce disruptive behavior. As with primary and secondary efforts, treatment integrity, social validity, and student performance on target and replacement behavior are monitored.

Ci3T: Visioning for the Future

All movement between prevention phases is data informed, with a goal of meeting students' multiple needs in an efficient, effective manner that capitalizes on the existing expertise of school personnel. As part of the Ci3T model, general and special education teachers, instructional coaches, counselors, administrators, and the like collaborate to support student success. The Ci3T blueprint defines dedicated roles and responsibilities for faculty and staff, administrators, and parents, as well as students, to ensure transparency and clarity (see Lane, Oakes, Jenkins, Menzies, & Kalberg, 2014 for a sample Ci3T blueprint). For example, the Ci3T model builds in regularly scheduled professional learning opportunities for district and school-site teams as well as faculty and staff to learn and become fluent in core components such as validated social skills curriculum for all students (e.g., Positive Action) and dedicated team time to review data to assess integrity, review stakeholder input, and examine student performance to inform instruction.

George Sugai's (2013) closing keynote address at the Northeast PBIS Network Leadership Forum emphasized the importance of integrating academic and behavioral domains. He described a vision for carefully crafted blended models that would include school-wide instruction in social skills using validated curricula, strategies, and practices. This information and these skill sets have the potential to provide foundational skills for all students that could then be practiced during academic instructional activities (e.g., cooperative learning groups) and in other noninstructional activities (e.g., during lunch, visiting during transitions). This facilitates the even loftier goals of establishing a positive, productive, safe school climate.

By learning social skills and self-determined behaviors in a blended model, the entire student body has common language systems and opportunities to acquire and build fluency in many "soft skills." These skills are needed to facilitate successful instructional experiences and interpersonal skills in school (Walker, Ramsey, & Gresham, 2004) as well as successful experiences beyond the school setting in the community and later in employment (Lane, Oakes, & Menzies, 2014).

To date, randomized control trials (RCTs) examining the efficacy of integrated models have not been conducted (Lane et al., in press). However, RCTs have established the efficacy of many features of this model. For example, RCTs have been conducted demonstrating the impact of core reading programs (Fuchs, Fuchs, & Compton, 2010), PBS frameworks (Bradshaw, Waasdorp, & Leaf, 2012), and social-skills curricula (e.g., Positive Action; Flay & Allred, 2003). In addition, there are numerous studies to show that when the Ci3T model is implemented with fidelity, schools implementing it experience shifts in risk over time, and that behavior-screening scores in these schools predict important student outcomes such as grade point averages, course failures, ODRs, suspensions, reading performance, and social skills performance (Oakes, Lane, Cox, & Messenger, 2014).

As discussed previously, there are several benefits to the Ci3T model of prevention that are detailed elsewhere (Lane et al., 2014). To summarize, such models provide a framework for addressing students' multiple needs in a transparent manner that enables professionals to collaborate in a data-driven model to effectively and efficiently meet students' individual needs.

First, the Ci3T model offers an integrated approach to addressing the academic, behavioral, and social needs of all students in a way that honors the transactional nature of these skill sets. It is not surprising that strong interpersonal, organizational, and problem-solving skills facilitate positive academic success for students. By examining students' success and challenges in academic, behavioral, and social domains, educators can better serve students by quickly connecting them to relevant and effective supports.

Second, these models offer a structure for allowing school-site personnel to work collaboratively to support all students' success. These data-driven models enable the school community to determine shared visions for a cascade of supports and enhance communication and collaboration between all stakeholders. By developing a Ci3T blueprint, stakeholders who utilize this document facilitate transparency and build efficiencies for meeting students' individual needs. Explicitly listing the full scope of roles and responsibilities at Tier 1 as well as Tier-2 and -3 supports elucidates the message of "we do what is necessary" for students to succeed, which is very consistent with the equity work taking place in many schools. This also creates a frame for focusing professional development activities to ensure all faculty, staff, and parents have assistance in meeting their defined roles and responsibilities regarding implementation and evaluation. The introduction of academic and behavior screening removes unnecessary pressures placed on teachers who have previously been asked to make subjective decisions as to which students may benefit from more intensive supports. In the Ci3T model, data drive the decision-making process as teachers and other school-site personnel meet regularly to review screening data to ensure equal and timely access to appropriate, research-based strategies.

Finally, schools are required to have procedures in place to determine eligibility for special education services (Individuals with Disabilities Education Act, 2004). The Ci3T model may prove useful in addressing this charge as the model includes a systematic approach to monitoring student performance for each level of prevention. If each level of prevention is implemented with integrity and the desired changes are not achieved for a given student, then a referral to a multidisciplinary team to consider special education eligibility determination may be in order. It is important to note that a tiered system of support is not intended to serve as a special education pipeline; however, the data on student performance gathered within this framework can provide supplementary information to inform the process of disability identification.

As such, the Ci3T model of prevention offers a blueprint to meet students' multiple needs; support collaboration between general and special education communities; enable equal access to academic, behavioral, and social-emotional supports; and facilitate inclusive educational services. It may hold particular promise for supporting students with intellectual disability as it creates a common culture for all educators: assuming responsibility for all students and educating all students within a common school-wide framework. By creating classrooms that use research-based strategies to support engagement (opportunity to respond, instructional choice), common expectations through the entire school,

school-wide social competencies, and common language systems in each domain, schools develop a context that is clear and facilitates the generalization of knowledge and skills taught. This is particularly important for students who may be otherwise challenged to build fluency in these areas. The Ci3T model provides a blueprint for special education teachers to "(a) retain the skill sets needed to serve students identified with special needs and (b) refine the skill sets needed to serve as collaborators with the general education community to prevent the development of learning and behavior problems and respond more effectively to existing instances of these concerns" (Lane et al., 2013, p. 24).

Emerging Directions and Applications of Tiered Systems

As described in the previous sections, systems of support for academics and behavior are increasingly being merged, with added emphasis on addressing all domains that are critical for promoting positive outcomes for students. Despite the lack of research specific to the inclusion of students with intellectual disability in tiered models, there is clearly an alignment between the theoretical basis of the supports model in the intellectual disability field and tiered systems in education. A particular area of overlap is the emphasis on universal supports linked to the general education classroom and curriculum. Within the intellectual disability field, a fundamental assumption of the supports model is that the reference environment (for determining if there is a mismatch between personal competencies and environmental demands) is the environment in which a student would be expected to function if they did not have a disability (i.e., the age-appropriate general education classroom and the teaching opportunities and focus of instruction in that classroom). When students are taught within the grade-level curriculum, there is an increased likelihood that they will acquire those skills and when students are taught learning strategies and behavioral expectations alongside their nondisabled peers, the expectation for performance at or close to grade level is raised.

Tiered Systems, Inclusion and Access to the General Education Curriculum

"Inclusion" is not a place, nor is it an outcome. To be included is a process that requires intentional consideration and planning for all students to be valued members of their school community, who participate in their grade-level curriculum in a meaningful way and are successful in learning skills to become contributing members of their communities. When it occurs for one student, but not all students, it is hard to say that the school is "inclusive." But when the school systematically creates inclusive organizational structures (schedule, collaborative planning time, professional training) and student learning opportunities (an expectation for participation in all parts of school life, language that refers to students as equally important members of the student body, unique planning structures for unique situations), then the school is moving toward the practice of being inclusive.

Turnbull, Turnbull, Wehmeyer, and Shogren (2016) described the movement to include students with disabilities in the general education classroom and curriculum as occurring in three waves. The first wave or generation focused on addressing the question of "where" to provide educational services and supports. This generation of practice focused primarily on getting students with intellectual disability into inclusive environments, ensuring students were in age- and grade-appropriate placements alongside nondisabled peers. This phase, while focused on promoting access to the classroom, did not heavily emphasize participating in the general education curriculum that was designed for all students. The thinking at the time was that proximity to students without disabilities promoted positive social behavior.

Experiences with proximity to other students and the general education curriculum showed us that, in fact, students with intellectual disability could learn curricular content to an extent that was not expected. The second wave or generation adopted an additive model of inclusive practice, focusing on, in addition to "where," the "how" of inclusion, or how to ensure meaningful inclusion in the classroom through teaching arrangements like co-teaching, differentiation, collaborative planning and teaming, and family–professional partnerships. While such practices potentially benefit all students, they were instituted primarily to promote the learning of students with disabilities within the general education setting, rather than considering the implementation of these practices for the benefit of all students, including those without disabilities who had more targeted and intensive support needs. Research has unequivocally demonstrated the benefits of inclusion for students with intellectual disability (Ryndak, Jackson, & White, 2013), such as enhanced opportunities to interact socially with peers, enhanced task engagement, improved skills acquisition, enhanced social competence, and enhanced access to the general education curriculum, and for students without disabilities, who realize socially valued outcomes as well as have access to resources and supports that promote success for all students (Carter & Kennedy, 2006; Shogren, Gross, et al., 2015). Thus, inclusive practices shifted in focus from placement to learning and promoted a change in how adults worked together to create an inclusive culture. The challenge remained that the implementation of high-quality instruction for students with intellectual disability remained at the mercy of the particular set of teachers working together in a classroom, and students with intellectual disability were often left out of that conversation.

The third wave or generation of inclusive practices is more closely aligned with the emphasis in tiered models on a school-wide approach to designing educational instruction systems that integrate supports for academics, behavior, and related domains, with specialized instruction for students with intellectual disability provided in the general education classroom and, in particular, in the general education curriculum. The emphasis is on *all* students: a school-wide framework that designs increasingly more intensive interventions and supports considers all learners. Specialized instruction, the special education service that addresses the student's unique IEP goals, can be provided within each and any tier of intervention. The third generation of inclusive practices focuses on the total education program: where, how, and what students are being taught. Third-generation inclusive practices emphasize environmental modifications, universal supports, differentiation based on the students participating in a given class, and high-quality instruction for all; thus there is a natural fit between third-generation inclusive education practices and tiered systems of support. Third-generation practices have shifted the focus from individual classrooms to school-wide planning for the provision of high-quality and responsive instruction for all students, with more intensive instruction provided to students who have additional support needs. The notion is that all students, including students with intellectual disability, benefit when the curriculum and instructional practices are designed from the start to accommodate the wide variety of learners who are expected to attend the school. For students who present unique or extensive support needs, planning for meeting those needs in school settings where they participate in instructional and social activities alongside their nondisabled peers becomes the norm. Furthermore, communication, social interaction, and social acceptance, as well as academic participation, are part of the planning process.

Further work is needed to systematically integrate and conduct research on the integration of tiered systems and the participation of students with intellectual disability in those models. Work on Ci3T provides a start for these endeavors; however, further research is needed. McCart, Sailor, Bezdek, and Satter (2014) describe, for example, a model for merging PBS, RtI, and inclusive practices, and associate these practices with equity and access for all students, including those with the most significant support needs. The School-Wide Integrated Framework for Transformation (SWIFT) model focuses on five school-wide educational domains: administrative leadership, multitiered systems of support, integrated educational framework, family and community engagement, and inclusive policy structures and practices (McCart et al., 2014). As such, this model embeds tiered systems in a broader school reform model that promotes the merging of district-, school-, and student-level supports and evidence-based practices. Sailor (2015) emphasizes movement from "one size fits all" models to broader MTSS and Ci3T models that address school-wide applications of evidence-based practices with an emphasis on universal design and collaborative teaching, as well as blending funding to unify programs and addressing issues related to the implementation and scaling up of effective practices, to promote equity for all students. Further research is needed to bring together, and research the impacts of, models of school reform that integrate these components to support all students in being successful.

Tiered Systems and Self-Determination

Work is needed to ensure that constructs that have been emphasized in the intellectual disability field, and have relevance for all students, are integrated into these models. Researchers have, for example, suggested the importance of integrating self-determination into tiered systems with a specific focus on developing a tiered approach to supporting all students to develop skills leading to self-determination, with increased supports for students based on need (Shogren, Wehmeyer, & Lane, in press). While research on self-determination and its importance in promoting postschool outcomes has primarily been conducted in the disability field (Shogren, Palmer, Wehmeyer, Williams-Diehm, & Little, 2012; Shogren, Plotner, Palmer, Wehmeyer, & Paek, 2014; Shogren, Wehmeyer, Palmer, Rifenbark, & Little, 2015; Wehmeyer et al., 2012), researchers are increasingly suggesting that skills leading to self-determination and actions are relevant for all students, and that by promoting self-determination for all students, students with intellectual disability will benefit from universal supports (Shogren, Wehmeyer, & Lane, in press; Shogren, Wehmeyer, Palmer, Forber-Pratt, et al., 2015; Shogren, Wehmeyer, Palmer, et al., in press). Thus, developing tiered supports for the development of self-determination and embedding these supports in integrated models in addition to academic, behavior, and social-emotional supports is an emerging direction that has the potential to promote valued outcomes for all students.

Chapter 16 provides an overview of research-based practices to promote self-determination, with a focus on research in the intellectual disability field. Researchers have suggested, however, the potential of interventions such as the Self-Determined Learning Model of Instruction (Wehmeyer, Palmer, Agran, Mithaug, & Martin, 2000)—which is a model of instruction that enables teachers to support students to engage in a self-regulated problem-solving process in service of educational goals—as a tiered intervention with all students learning the critical skills associated with problem solving, goal setting, and self-regulation of behavior as a Tier-1 intervention, with increasing supports for students that target specific skills and outcomes (e.g., intensive instruction on decision-making, problem-solving, or self-advocacy skills) at the group or individual level, based on need (Shogren, Wehmeyer, & Lane, in press). Such interventions have the potential to benefit all students, including students with intellectual disability, as well as to further enhance the educational domains and outcomes targeted by comprehensive tiered systems. Promoting self-determination has documented benefits associated not only with transition outcomes, but also with school-based academic outcomes, including enhanced access to the general education curriculum (Lee, Wehmeyer, Soukup, & Palmer, 2010; Shogren et al., 2012). Further, teachers tend to perceive students as having more capabilities when they are engaged in the process of setting goals and taking action toward their goals (Shogren et al., 2014). As such, and given the importance of self-regulation, problem solving, and goal setting for all students, particularly as these outcomes are targeted in learning standards in core academic areas for all students (Council of Chief State School Officers & National Governors Association, 2011; National Council of Teachers of Mathematics (NCTM), 2000; Wehmeyer, Field, Doren, Jones, & Mason, 2004), self-determination is a natural fit in efforts to promote positive outcomes for all students. Given the growing emphasis in MTSS and models such as Ci3T on integrating tiered systems of supports that address the multiple domains that impact student learning, it is logical to explore the integration of self-determination into such models in future research and practice.

Conclusions

For students with intellectual disability to achieve the goals of IDEA, including equality of opportunity, full participation, independent living, and economic self-sufficiency, it is critical that they have access to challenging academic content combined with effective systems of support that promote success in all domains of education. As described previously, MTSS provides a framework for promoting access to evidence-based practices and supports for all students, within increasing supports as necessary for students. This aligns with the focus on building a total education program that promotes inclusion and access to the general education curriculum for students with disabilities that focuses on where, how, and what students are being taught. All students, including students with intellectual disability, need access to high-quality instruction delivered through MTSS models, as well as opportunities to learn and apply skills that enable them to become self-determined learners. As tiered models continue to develop to address students' social-emotional needs (e.g., Ci3T), it will be critical that supports for participation in the general education classroom *and* supports for learning in the general education curriculum are provided for all students. Identifying supports for participation and learning requires the adoption of a social-ecological model to promote success through the identification of needed supports, and the provision of these supports at the universal level, with increasingly specialized supports provided only as needed and selected based on principles of data-based decision making. Identifying support needs based on the demands of the environment and the curriculum, and the personal competencies of the students, makes it possible to design and deliver supports that are maximally relevant to the classroom and curriculum and build on universal supports provided through tiered systems and enhanced self-determination.

References

Bohanon, H., Fenning, P., Carney, K. L., Minnis-Kim, M. J., Anderson-Harriss, S., Mortoz, K. B., . . . Pigott, T. D. (2006). Schoolwide application of positive behavior support in an Urban High School: A case study. *Journal of Positive Behavior Interventions, 8*, 131–145. doi: 10.1177/10983007060080030201

Bradshaw, C. P., Waasdorp, T. E., & Leaf, P. J. (2012). Effects of school-wide positive behavioral interventions and supports on child behavior problems. *Pediatrics, 130*, e1136–e1145. doi: 10.1542/peds.2012-0243

Carr, E. G., Dunlap, G., Horner, R. H., Koegel, R. L., Turnbull, A. P., Sailor, W., . . . Fox, L. (2002). Positive behavior support: Evolution of an applied science. *Journal of Positive Behavior Interventions, 4*, 4–16, 20.

Carter, E. W., & Kennedy, C. H. (2006). Promoting access to the general curriculum using peer support strategies. *Research and Practice for Persons with Severe Disabilities, 31*, 284–292.

Connell, B. R., Jones, M., Mace, R., Mueller, J., Mullick, A., Ostroff, E., . . . Vanderheiden, G. (1997). The principles of universal design. Retrieved from http://www.ncsu.edu/ncsu/design/cud/about_ud/udprinciplestext.htm

Council of Chief State School Officers, & National Governors Association. (2011). *Common core state standards.* Washington, DC: Authors.

Crone, D. A., Hawken, L. S., & Horner, R. H. (2010). *Responding to problem behavior in schools: The behavior education program* (2nd ed.). New York: Guilford Press.

Denton, C. A., Fletcher, J. M., Anthony, J. L., & Francis, D. J. (2006). An evaluation of intensive intervention for students with persistent reading difficulties. *Journal of Learning Disabilities, 39*, 447–466.

Downing, J. A. (2002). Individualized behavior contracts. *Intervention in School and Clinic, 37*, 168–172.

Drummond, T. (1994). *The Student Risk Screening Scale (SRSS).* Grants Pass, OR: Josephine County Mental Health Program.

Eber, L., Hyde, K., Rose, J., Breen, K., McDonald, D., & Lewandowski, H. (2009). Completing the continuum of schoolwide positive behavior support: Wraparound as a tertiary-level intervention. In W. Sailor, G. Dunlap, G. Sugai, & R. H. Horner (Eds.), *Handbook of positive behavior support* (pp. 671–703). New York: Springer.

Elliott, S. N., & Gresham, F. M. (2007). *Social skills improvement system: Classwide intervention program guide.* Bloomington, MN: Pearson Assessments.

Flay, B. R., & Allred, C. G. (2003). Long-term effects of the Positive Action program. *American Journal of Health Behavior, 27*, S6.

Fuchs, L. S., Fuchs, D., & Compton, D. (2010). Rethinking response to intervention at middle and high school. *School Psychology Review, 39*, 22–28.

Goodman, R. (2001). Psychometric properties of the Strengths and Difficulties Questionnaire (SDQ). *Journal of the American Academy of Child and Adolescent Psychiatry, 40,* 1337–1345. doi: 10.1097/00004583-200111000-00015

Greenwood, C. R., Kratochwill, T. R., & Clements, M. (Eds.). (2008). *Schoolwide prevention models: Lessons learned in elementary schools.* New York: Guilford Press.

Gresham, F. M. (1989). Assessment of treatment integrity in school consultation and prereferral intervention. *School Psychology Review, 18,* 37–50.

Hale, J., Alfonso, V., Berninger, V., Bracken, B., Christo, C., Clark, E., . . . Yalof, J. (2010). Critical issues in response-to-intervention, comprehensive evaluation, and specific learning disabilities identification and intervention: An expert white paper consensus. *Learning Disability Quarterly, 33*(3), 223–236. doi: 10.1177/073194871003300310

Hall, T. E., Meyer, A., & Rose, D. (2012). *Universal design for learning in the classroom: Practical applications.* New York: Guilford.

Individuals with Disabilities Education Act, as amended in 2004, 20 USC. § 1400 et seq.

Kamphaus, R. W., & Reynolds, C. R. (2008). *Behavior and emotional screening system—behavioral and emotional screening system.* Bloomington, MN: Pearson.

Kern, L., & Manz, P. (2004). A look at current validity issues of school-wide behavior support. *Behavioral Disorders, 30,* 47–59.

Koutsoftas, A. D., Harmon, M. T., & Gray, S. (2009). The effect of tier 2 intervention for phonemic awareness in a response-to-intervention model in low-income preschool classrooms. *Language, Speech, and Hearing Services in Schools, 40,* 116–130. doi: 10.1044/0161-1461(2008/07-0101)

Lane, K. L., Kalberg, J. R., Bruhn, A. L., Driscoll, S. A., Wehby, J. H., & Elliott, S. (2009). Assessing social validity of school-wide positive behavior support plans: Evidence for the reliability and structure of the Primary Intervention Rating Scale. *School Psychology Review, 38,* 135–144.

Lane, K. L., Menzies, H. M., Ennis, R. P., & Oakes, W. P. (2015). *Supporting behavior for school success: A step-by-step guide to key strategies.* New York: Guilford Press.

Lane, K. L., Menzies, H. M., Oakes, W. P., & Kalberg, J. R. (2012). *A comprehensive, integrated three-tier model to meet students' academic, behavioral, and social needs.* Washington, DC: American Psychological Association.

Lane, K. L., Oakes, W. P., Carter, E. W., Lambert, W., & Jenkins, A. (2013). Initial evidence for the reliability and validity of the Student Risk Screening Scale for Internalizing and Externalizing Behaviors at the middle school level. *Assessment for Effective Intervention, 39,* 24–38. doi: 10.1177/1534508413489336

Lane, K. L., Oakes, W. P., & Cox, M. (2011). Functional assessment-based interventions: A university-district partnership to promote learning and success. *Beyond Behavior, 20,* 3–18.

Lane, K. L., Oakes, W. P., Jenkins, A., Menzies, H. M., & Kalberg, J. R. (2014). A team-based process for designing Comprehensive, Integrated, Three-Tiered (CI3T) Models of Prevention: How does my school-site leadership team design a CI3T model? *Preventing School Failure, 58,* 129–142. doi: 10.1080/1045988X.2014.893976

Lane, K. L., Oakes, W. P., Lusk, M. E., Cantwell, E. D., & Schatschneider, C. (in press). Screening for intensive intervention needs at the secondary level: Directions for the future. *Journal of Emotional and Behavioral Disorders.* doi: 10.1177/1063426615618624

Lane, K. L., Oakes, W. P., & Menzies, H. M. (2014). Comprehensive, Integrated, Three-Tiered (CI3T) Models of Prevention: Why does my school—and district—need an integrated approach to meet students' academic, behavioral, and social needs? *Preventing School Failure, 58,* 121–128. doi: 10.1080/1045988X.2014.893977

Lane, K. L., Rogers, L. A., Parks, R. J., Weisenbach, J. L., Mau, A. C., Merwin, M. T., & Bergman, W. A. (2007). Function-based interventions for students who are nonresponsive to primary and secondary prevention efforts: Illustrations at the elementary and middle school levels. *Journal of Emotional and Behavioral Disorders, 15,* 169–183. doi: 10.1177/10634266070150030401

Lee, S. H., Wehmeyer, M. L., Soukup, J., & Palmer, S. B. (2010). Impact of curriculum modifications on access to the general education curriculum for students with disabilities. *Exceptional Children, 76,* 213–233.

McCart, A., Sailor, W., Bezdek, J., & Satter, A. (2014). A framework for inclusive educational delivery systems. *Inclusion, 2,* 252–264.

McIntosh, K., Chard, D. J., Boland, J. B., & Horner, R. H. (2006). Demonstration of combined efforts in school-wide academic and behavioral systems and incidence of reading and behavior challenges in early elementary grades. *Journal of Positive Behavior Interventions, 8,* 146–154.

McIntosh, K., & Goodman, S. (2015). *Integrating multi-tiered systems of support: Blending RTI and PBIS.* New York: Guilford Press.

Mooney, P., Ryan, J. B., Uhing, B. M., Reid, R., & Epstein, M. H. (2005). A review of self-management interventions targeting academic outcomes for students with emotional and behavioral disorders. *Journal of Behavioral Education, 14*(3), 203–221. doi: 10.1007/s10864-005-6298-1

Muscott, H. S., Mann, E. L., & LeBrun, M. R. (2008). Positive behavioral interventions and supports in New Hampshire: Effects of large-scale implementation of schoolwide positive behavior support on student discipline and academic achievement. *Journal of Positive Behavior Interventions, 10*(3), 190–205. doi: 10.1177/1098300708316258

National Council of Teachers of Mathematics (NCTM). (2000). *Principles and standards for school mathematics.* Reston, VA: NCTM.

Oakes, W. P., Lane, K. L., Cantwell, E. D., & Royer, D. J. (2016). Installing systematic screening for behavior in K–12 settings: Practical considerations and recommendations. *Manuscript in Preparation.*

Oakes, W. P., Lane, K. L., Cox, M., & Messenger, M. (2014). Logistics of behavior screenings: How and why do we conduct behavior screenings at our school? *Preventing School Failure, 58,* 159–170. doi: 10.1080/1045988X.2014.895572

Pearson Education. (2008). *AIMSWeb.* San Antonio, TX: Author.

Pyle, N., & Vaughn, S. (2012). Remediating reading difficulties in a response to intervention model with secondary students. *Psychology in the Schools, 49,* 273–284.

Ryndak, D., Jackson, L. B., & White, J. M. (2013). Involvement and progress in the general curriculum for students with extensive support needs: K–12 inclusive education research and implications for the future. *Inclusion, 1,* 28–49. doi: 10.1352/2326-6988-1.1.028

Sailor, W. (2009). *Making RtI work: How smart schools are reforming education through schoolwide response-to-intervention models.* San Francisco: Jossey-Bass.

Sailor, W. (2015). Advances in schoolwide inclusive school reform. *Remedial and Special Education, 36,* 94–99. doi: 10.1177/0741932514555021

Schalock, R. L., Borthwick-Duffy, S., Bradley, V., Buntix, W. H. E., Coulter, D. L., Craig, E. P. M., . . . Yeager, M. H. (2010). *Intellectual disability: Definition, classification, and systems of support* (11th ed.). Washington, DC: American Association on Intellectual and Developmental Disabilities.

Schalock, R. L., Luckasson, R., Bradley, V., Buntinx, W., Lachapelle, Y., Shogren, K. A., . . . Wehmeyer, M. L. (2012). *User's guide for the 11th edition of intellectual disability: Diagnosis, classification and systems of support.* Washington, DC: American Association on Intellectual and Developmental Disabilities.

Shogren, K. A., Gross, J. M. S., Forber-Pratt, A. J., Francis, G. L., Satter, A. L., Blue-Banning, M., & Hill, C. (2015). The perspectives of students with and without disabilities on inclusive schools. *Research and Practice for Persons with Severe Disabilities, 40,* 243–260. doi: 10.1177/1540796915583493

Shogren, K. A., Palmer, S. B., Wehmeyer, M. L., Williams-Diehm, K., & Little, T. D. (2012). Effect of intervention with the self-determined learning model of instruction on access and goal attainment. *Remedial and Special Education, 33,* 320–330. doi: 10.1177/0741932511410072

Shogren, K. A., Plotner, A. J., Palmer, S. B., Wehmeyer, M. L., & Paek, Y. (2014). Impact of the Self-Determined Learning Model of Instruction on teacher perceptions of student capacity and opportunity for self-determination. *Education and Training in Autism and Developmental Disabilities, 49,* 440–448.

Shogren, K. A., Wehmeyer, M. L., & Lane, K. L. (in press). Embedding interventions to promote self-determination within multi-tiered systems of supports. *Exceptionality.*

Shogren, K. A., Wehmeyer, M. L., Palmer, S. B., Forber-Pratt, A., Little, T. J., & Lopez, S. J. (2015). Causal agency theory: Reconceptualizing a functional model of self-determination. *Education and Training in Autism and Developmental Disabilities, 50,* 251–263.

Shogren, K. A., Wehmeyer, M. L., Palmer, S. B., Forber-Pratt, A., Little, T. J., & Seo, H. (in press). Preliminary validity and reliability of scores on the self-determination inventory: Student report version. *Career Development and Transition for Exceptional Individuals.*

Shogren, K. A., Wehmeyer, M. L., Palmer, S. B., Rifenbark, G. G., & Little, T. D. (2015). Relationships between self-determination and postschool outcomes for youth with disabilities. *Journal of Special Education, 53,* 30–41. doi: 10.1177/0022466913489733

Simonsen, B., Fairbanks, S., Briesch, A., Myers, D., & Sugai, G. (2008). Evidence-based practices in classroom management: Considerations for research to practice. *Education and Treatment of Children, 31,* 351–380. doi: 10.1353/etc.0.0007

Sugai, G. (2013). *Keynote address.* Paper presented at the North East Positive Behavior Support Conference, Cromwell, CT.

Sugai, G., & Horner, R. (2010). Schoolwide positive behavior supports: Establishing a continuum of evidence-based practices. *Journal of Evidence-Based Practices for Schools, 11,* 62–83.

Thompson, J. R., Bradley, V., Buntinx, W. H. E., Schalock, R. L., Shogren, K. A., Snell, M. E., . . . Yeager, M. H. (2009). Conceptualizing supports and the support needs of people with intellectual disability. *Intellectual and Developmental Disabilities, 47*(2), 135–146.

Turnbull, A. P., Turnbull, H. R., Wehmeyer, M. L., & Shogren, K. A. (2016). *Exceptional lives* (8th ed.). Columbus, OH: Merrill/Prentice Hall.

Walker, H. M., Ramsey, E., & Gresham, F. M. (2004). *Antisocial behavior in school: Evidence-based practices* (2nd ed.). Belmont, CA: Wadsworth.

Wehmeyer, M. L., Field, S., Doren, B., Jones, B., & Mason, C. (2004). Self-determination and student involvement in standards-based reform. *Exceptional Children, 70*, 413–425.

Wehmeyer, M. L., Palmer, S. B., Agran, M., Mithaug, D. E., & Martin, J. E. (2000). Promoting causal agency: The self-determined learning model of instruction. *Exceptional Children, 66*, 439–453.

Wehmeyer, M. L., Shogren, K. A., Palmer, S. B., Williams-Diehm, K., Little, T. D., & Boulton, A. (2012). Impact of the self-determined learning model of instruction on student self-determination: A randomized-trial placebo control group study. *Exceptional Children, 78*, 135–153.

Wolf, M. M. (1978). Social validity: The case for subjective measurement or how applied behavior analysis is finding its heart. *Journal of Applied Behavior Analysis, 11*, 203–214.

Yudin, M. (2014). *PBIS: Providing opportunity*. Paper presented at the National PBIS Leadership Forum: PBIS Building Capacity & Partnerships to Enhance Educational Reform, Rosemont, IL.

13

Positive Behavior Supports for Students with Intellectual Disability

Glen Dunlap, Donald Jackson, Ashley Greenwald

Problem behaviors constitute perhaps the greatest impediment to the delivery of effective educational services. This is the case for students of all ages. When a student engages in persistent problem behaviors, it is extremely difficult to provide meaningful instruction regardless of the student's age, developmental status, or classroom placement. Problem behaviors are defined as any repeated pattern of responding that interferes with the learning or social interaction of the student or the student's classmates. Typical topographies include tantrums (e.g., crying, falling on the floor, screaming), physical and verbal aggression, stereotypic behavior (e.g., repetitive body rocking, finger flipping), self-injury (e.g., head banging), and property destruction, as well as excessive withdrawal and refusal to cooperate with instruction and group activities. Not all students with intellectual disability engage in problem behaviors. However, for those who do, their presence can be a very serious concern.

For the past 20 years or so, the preferred, research-based approach for addressing problem behaviors has been positive behavior support (PBS), which is often referred to in school settings as positive behavior interventions and supports (PBIS). PBS is a broad approach for supporting people in developing adaptive behavior and an improved quality of life while reducing the occurrence of problem behavior (Carr et al., 2002; Dunlap, Kincaid, & Jackson, 2013; Sailor, Dunlap, Sugai, & Horner, 2009). PBS can be applied at multiple levels of implementation. It can be used in a focused manner to resolve serious problem behaviors of individuals, and it can be used in the form of classroom–wide and school–wide applications in order to promote desired patterns of behavior and prevent the occurrence of problems (Sailor et al., 2009).

The purpose of this chapter is to provide a description of PBS with an emphasis on its use with students with intellectual disability. The majority of the chapter will be devoted to the use of PBS with individual students (Brown, Anderson, & DePry, 2015), and this means that the focus will be on problem behaviors that are not resolved effectively with high-quality classroom or school-wide strategies. It is acknowledged that many problem behaviors can be addressed effectively with careful group instruction, clear expectations, ample reinforcement for desired behavior, comprehensible routines, and other evidence-based procedures. However, some behaviors are so well-established that they are resistant to group or low-intensity interventions. This chapter is largely devoted to the form of PBS that is individualized, assessment-based (using functional behavioral assessments), and sufficiently intensive so that it can be (and has been demonstrated to be) effective with the most persistent and severe problem behaviors (Dunlap & Carr, 2007).

The first part of the chapter provides a definition of PBS and a description that includes its development from earlier forms of behavior management. The social and procedural foundations of PBS will be presented as will a summary of systemic structures that have made possible the dissemination of the

PBS technology. The second part of the chapter offers a description of the process and the strategies of the individualized PBS approach. The chapter concludes with a brief synopsis of existing research that makes PBS an evidence-based practice.

Definition and Terminology

Due to the rapid expansion of PBS, a functional definition of the approach has been adjusted as new levels of implementation have been adopted. Initially the entire focus was on individualized interventions, and definitions tended to include the process of functional behavioral assessment (Horner et al., 1990); however, this particular type of individualized assessment is not pertinent for group applications. In an effort to build a unified definition that would be relevant for the current breadth of PBS, Kincaid and colleagues (2016) proposed a new definition:

> PBS is an approach to behavior support that includes an ongoing process of research-based assessment, intervention, and data-based decision making focused on building social and other functional competencies, creating supportive contexts, and preventing the occurrence of problem behaviors. PBS relies on strategies that are respectful of a person's dignity and overall well-being and that are drawn primarily from behavioral, educational and social sciences, although other evidence-based procedures may be incorporated. PBS may be applied within a multitiered framework at the level of the individual and at the level of larger systems (e.g., families, classrooms, schools, social service programs and facilities).

It is important to note that this definition emphasizes core principles that have distinguished PBS since its inception: (1) an integration of empirically valid technology with values related to human dignity; (2) data-based accountability; (3) an emphasis on skill building and quality of life, with a secondary priority on reducing problem behaviors; and (4) an appreciation of contributions from multiple disciplines.

As is the case with the definition, the terms that have been applied to the PBS approach have caused some confusion. Prior to 1990, the most common term used to describe PBS was "nonaversive behavior management." Subsequently, authors and program developers have used PBS variations including "positive behavioral support," "positive behavior supports," "positive behavior support," and "positive behavior interventions and supports." In a recent essay, Dunlap, Kincaid, Horner, Knoster, and Bradshaw (2014) asserted that the best term for the broad field of PBS is "positive behavior support." Among the arguments put forth was that this term could be parsed in two ways, both of which convey the essence of the approach: First, the term can be read as "support" for "positive behavior," which emphasizes the PBS priority of building and strengthening a person's competencies; and second, the term can also be read as using "positive" as an adjective for "behavior support," thereby emphasizing that the supports and interventions are respectful and strength-based, rather than punitive. The essay also acknowledged that PBIS is a legitimate term, introduced in the 1999 legislative stature that amended the Individuals with Disabilities Education Act, which describes the use of PBS in schools (note: in this chapter, we have elected to use "positive behavior support" to refer to the full breadth of PBS). Other terms are useful for describing additional categories of PBS applications. For example, program-wide positive behavior support (PW-PBS) is commonly used to refer to PBS in early childhood programs.

Historical and Foundational Perspectives

PBS emerged from two major developments in the mid-to-late 1980s—the disability rights movement and the burgeoning discipline of applied behavior analysis—and it was precipitated by a crisis involving both of these developments. The crisis involved the increasing use of aversive stimuli to suppress patterns of unwanted (problem) behavior. The aversive stimuli included painful, humiliating, and stigmatizing events such as slapping, applications of water mist or hot pepper sauce, and contingent electric shock with a cattle prod. The behaviors in question were usually very serious acts that presented imminent health risks to the person and/or to others (e.g., physical aggression and self-injury such as violent head banging and self-biting). But sometimes aversive consequences were used to reduce seemingly mild infractions along the lines of "self-stimulatory" stereotypes (head weaving, body rocking) and non-compliance. Importantly, the procedures were almost always used to control the behaviors of people with severe to profound intellectual disability who had limited to no ability to communicate, and they were used in segregated settings such as hospitals, private clinics, and self-contained special education programs. Although aversive conditioning strategies were legitimized through hundreds of scientific journal publications, they were not the kinds of interventions that would be tolerated in public. By the mid-1980s, the utilization of aversive stimuli had raised the ire of advocates and a major movement was created to prohibit the use of such strategies (Guess, Helmstetter, Turnbull, & Knowlton, 1987).

One reason that aversives were controversial is that they were incompatible with tenets of the growing disability rights movement. This movement was part of the broader civil rights movement and was based on core principles that all people, including people with disabilities, should be treated with dignity, allowed and encouraged to participate in the mainstream of their schools and communities, and be treated in all contexts with the same respect that is accorded all other human beings. Disability rights advocates contributed significantly to initiatives to close institutions and establish community-based residential options (deinstitutionalization), promote educational inclusion, encourage options for supported employment and, in general, focus the goals of service provision on the all-important quest for improved quality of life. In this respect, the disability rights movement provided the first essential foundation for the development of PBS.

The use of pain and stigmatizing interventions violated core principles of the disability rights movement, as did the obvious fact that the use of aversives was impossible in the everyday, inclusive world of education, commerce, and family life. The crisis of "aversive behavior management" was brought to the attention of policy makers and the broader professional arena and, as a result, great pressure was exerted to end the use of aversive procedures and find alternatives that would be both effective and acceptable (see Dunlap, Sailor, Horner, & Sugai, 2009; Lucyshyn, Dunlap, & Freeman, 2015 for extended discussions).

An explanation for the popularity of aversive strategies lies in the dominant position that contingency management occupied in the armamentarium of behavior modification. Procedures for decreasing the occurrence of undesirable behaviors very largely consisted of (1) positive reinforcement for desired behaviors—including differential reinforcement of other behaviors (DRO); (2) withholding of reinforcement for targeted problem behaviors (extinction); and (3) if necessary, punishment for instances of problem behavior. The punishment could be time out from positive reinforcement or it could be the application of painful or noxious stimuli. If an interventionist relied heavily or exclusively on contingency management, a problem arose when typical reinforcers (e.g., praise) and punishers (e.g., a mild reprimand) failed to produce effects. In cases of such persistent problems, the strength of the contingencies was often increased so that tangible or edible reinforcers were used and more disagreeable punishers were employed. This cycle led to the use of increasingly extreme stimuli. In general, extreme contingencies were demonstrated to be effective in suppressing problem behavior (and, thus, empirical studies were often published in professional journals); however, the effects were invariably short term and limited to the very specific context in which they were implemented. Maintenance and generalization did not occur with aversive procedures.

Applied Behavior Analysis

The second essential foundation for positive behavior support is applied behavior analysis (ABA). By the 1970s and 1980s, ABA was recognized as the primary approach for education and behavior modification for people with disabilities. ABA was extraordinarily successful in deploying basic, scientific laws of behavior to create instructional strategies that led to huge advances in education (e.g., Sulzer & Mayer, 1975), and research on ABA principles and practices were being rapidly disseminated through periodicals such as the *Journal of Applied Behavior Analysis*. Unfortunately, by the mid-1980s, vital conceptual and technological advances were not always manifested in practice. As a result, behavior modification, for the most part, continued to be limited to variants of contingency management, in spite of pivotal findings from ABA researchers in the areas of functional equivalence (Carr, 1977), functional analysis and functional assessment (Iwata, Dorsey, Slifer, Bauman, & Richman, 1982; Lennox & Miltenberger, 1989), functional communication training (Carr & Durand, 1985), and stimulus control (Luiselli & Cameron, 1998). Despite the research in ABA that supported the use of teaching and differential reinforcement of replacement behaviors, much of ABA applications continued to be centered on the manipulation of contingencies alone, resulting in the regrettable by-product of aversive control to manage problem behaviors of people with severe disabilities and extreme behavior problems.

PBS was developed principally by applied researchers and advocates who were deeply influenced by ABA and who were aligned with the scientific and pragmatic traditions of ABA (Dunlap, 2006; Lucyshyn et al., 2015). Spurred by the crisis surrounding aversives, a number of authors produced writings in the mid-1980s that articulated alternatives to punishment-oriented strategies and that served as early iterations of "nonaversive behavior management" and, eventually, PBS. Most notably, Luanna Meyer and Ian Evans (Evans & Meyer, 1985; Meyer & Evans, 1989) emphasized an educational orientation; Gary LaVigna and Anne Donnellan (1986) described a variety of reinforcement-based procedures; and Robert Gaylord-Ross (1980) articulated a decision model for using positive strategies to resolve serious problem behaviors. Meanwhile, behaviorally oriented researchers published findings that showed how assessment-based interventions could reduce problem behavior simply by teaching children to communicate requests for functionally equivalent outcomes (Carr & Durand, 1985; Horner & Budd, 1985), and how assessments could also identify antecedent variables that could be manipulated to decrease occurrences of problems (Touchette, MacDonald, & Langer, 1985). In short, ABA was finding strategies that could potentially make the use of aversive consequences unnecessary and irrelevant. It was the germ of these early studies, along with the essential conceptual and procedural groundwork, that served as the basis for PBS, and it is noteworthy that ABA continues to be the primary ingredient in PBS (Dunlap, 2006; Dunlap, Carr, Horner, Zarcone, & Schwartz, 2008; Lewis, 2015).

In 1987, the US Department of Education provided funding for a "Rehabilitation Resource and Training Center on Community-Referenced, Nonaversive Behavior Management" (the name of which was soon changed to the RRTC on Positive Behavior Support) that was conducted for 15 years by a consortium of researchers and trainers who sought to establish a research-based technology of PBS sufficient to produce rapid, durable, and generalized changes in problem behavior while facilitating improvements in quality of life. At this time, the focus of PBS was still on people of all ages with intellectual and developmental disabilities and severe problem behavior. Members of the consortium published an article in 1990 that first introduced the term "PBS" and laid out a vision for a comprehensive new approach to behavior support (Horner et al., 1990). The authors presented nine themes that helped define the PBS approach: (1) an emphasis on lifestyle change, (2) functional analysis, (3) multicomponent interventions, (4) manipulation of ecological and setting events, (5) emphasis on antecedent manipulations, (6) teaching adaptive behavior, (7) building environments with effective consequences, (8) minimizing the use of punishers, and (9) distinguishing emergency procedures from proactive programming. It is fair to say that this 1990 article signaled the establishment of the PBS approach.

In the early 1990s, the procedures and process of PBS were applied with additional populations, including students with mild and moderate intellectual impairment, young children with and at risk for disabilities, and students with emotional and behavioral disorders (Bambara, Dunlap, & Schwartz, 2004; Lucyshyn et al., 2015). PBS interventions were introduced to additional populations in the late 1990s and the first decade of the 21st century. Dissemination of the PBS approach was bolstered by the publication of additional research, practical manuals on functional assessment and assessment-based interventions, and textbooks, as well as websites and conferences. In 1999, the *Journal of Positive Behavior Interventions* began publishing new research and perspectives on PBS; and in 2003 an international organization, The Association for Positive Behavior Support, was formed (Knoster, Anderson, Carr, Dunlap, & Horner, 2003).

A major development that transformed PBS occurred around the turn of the century when PBS researchers and program developers described a new, multitiered approach to PBS. This development was inspired by the need for strategies that could effectively prevent (rather than simply intervene with) the emergence of serious problem behaviors and by the presence of previous work that had documented the effectiveness of positive strategies with larger units of analysis, such as classrooms (Colvin & Lazar, 1997; Lewis & Sugai, 1999). Adopting the multitiered framework popularized in the field of public health (see Walker et al., 1996), the approach known as school-wide positive behavior support (SW-PBS) was created. SW-PBS is comprised of evidence-based practices at three levels of intensity: universal (or primary prevention) strategies for the entire school population, targeted (or secondary) strategies for specific high-risk portions of the school population, and individualized (or tertiary) interventions that usually involve relatively intensive, assessment-based PBS procedures (Sugai et al., 2000). The logic of multitiered systems of support is that efforts to build a preventative, positive school culture, with evidence-based practices at all levels of the continuum, can substantially reduce the need for more intensive procedures, even for those students with the most intense needs (Freeman et al., 2006). With ongoing funding from the Office of Special Education Programs (US Department of Education), the Technical Assistance Center on Positive Behavioral Interventions and Supports (see www.pbis.org) has provided information, training, technical assistance, and resources for many thousands of schools across the country.

Building Capacity to Implement PBS

If PBS interventions are to be helpful for students and others with intellectual disability, mechanisms must be established to disseminate information and to build local capacity to implement the procedures. Providers who carry out the interventions and who guide others to implement them must be trained adequately so that the PBS process and the specific assessment and intervention procedures can be implemented with fidelity. Although there were many preservice and in-service initiatives developed to deliver training in PBS, an important step toward this objective was taken by the RRTC on Positive Behavior Support in the late 1980s and early 1990s. The training agenda of the RRTC was comprised largely of an effort to establish a capacity for training and dissemination within selected states so that state training teams could deliver comprehensive training on PBS for local providers, including teachers, therapists, families, administrators, and any other personnel involved with developing and implementing services for people with disabilities and problem behaviors.

The effort to establish state training teams began with the development of a training curriculum. Led by Dr. Jacki Anderson, the initial curriculum created by the RRTC consisted of 10 days of training on foundations, learning principles, person-centered planning (PCP), functional assessment, data-based decision making, and all aspects of the development and implementation of behavior support plans (Anderson, Albin, Mesaros, Dunlap, & Morelli-Robbins, 1993; Anderson, Russo, Dunlap, & Albin, 1996; Dunlap et al., 2000). In the years during which the RRTC was establishing states' capacities (roughly between 1988 and 2002), a total of 26 states participated in the training and created their own mechanisms for funding, training, and dissemination. Over time, state training teams adapted the curriculum to meet the needs of their particular constituencies. Often the training was shortened and many versions were created to address the needs of educators, families, job coaches, and residential support providers. One example of a state's development in building capacity to disseminate PBS is described in Box 13.1.

Box 13.1 Building Capacity to Implement Positive Behavior Support: PBS-Nevada

Nevada is a geographically diverse state with 110,567 square miles of Great Basin desert, high forested and desert mountains, and urban areas. It is the 7th largest state in the United States, and the 35th most populous, with about 2.8 million people. Eighty percent of the state is considered rural or frontier, with 11 of Nevada's 17 counties having population densities under five people per square mile. In comparison, 88% of the population lives in the Las Vegas and Reno areas. Nevada's population growth rate has been the highest or near-highest in the nation for many years, while its funding of schools and disability services typically ranks near the bottom.

Despite these problems, momentum grew starting in the 1990s for community-based support options for people with intellectual disability, including people with challenging behavior. During that same period, a few practitioners were beginning to incorporate PBS into their practices for addressing problem behaviors at the individual and systems levels, and in 1999 a consortium was formed between Nevada's developmental services system, the Nevada Department of Education, the University of Nevada, Reno's (UNR) Center for Excellence in Disabilities (NCED), and several key private disability agencies for the purpose of submitting an application to join the RRTC on Positive Behavior Support (see description, this chapter). The application was successful, and the timing could not have been better. This new partnership with a national network of PBS practitioners and researchers, along with the recent passage of anti-aversive treatment laws in Nevada, created a foundation for establishing a framework for building PBS capacity on a statewide basis.

As a condition of participating in the RRTC project, Nevada identified a state training team consisting of 10 to 12 professionals and parents from diverse settings around the state. State team members (and their home agencies) made a minimum three-year commitment that included receiving comprehensive training in PBS and then providing frequent workshops around the state. National PBS experts from the RRTC project demonstrated the in-service model, and supplied detailed curricula, articles, and technical assistance over ensuing years. Most operational costs, including travel and release time, were embedded within stakeholder budgets, which promoted important system buy-in and longitudinal change. The project, named PBS-Nevada, was initially operated through the state's Sierra Regional Center and the Washoe Ability Resource Center, a regional disability agency, both located in northern Nevada. In 2004, the project moved to its current home at University of Nevada, Reno's Center for Excellence in Disabilities.

People of all ages with intellectual disability and problem behavior in need of a behavior support plan (focus people) were identified, and the training was provided to the family members, school or agency staff, and other professionals and friends who were involved in the focus person's support. Using the team-based training model, each focus person's support team attended as a group, with three to five teams typically being trained at a time. In all, these early training workshops involved 60 hours of in-class time broken into five two-day blocks as well as completion of related activities between sessions. In the years following the initial rollout, the 10-day workshop structure was used to conduct in-depth PBS training in Reno, Las Vegas, Elko, Winnemucca, Carson City, and elsewhere.

As the process of building a sustainable state-level structure for PBS in-service proceeded, the growth of interest in and capacity with the PBS planning and intervention approach did not go unnoticed by stakeholders and decision makers. The project received the endorsement of the Nevada Commission on Mental Health and Development Services, and requests were received to provide training in child and family services, mental health, and other areas. Importantly, PBS was identified as a key intervention strategy in government documents, and legislation was passed identifying PBS as one of three disability service areas eligible to compete for grants made possible through Nevada's share of funds from the states' master settlement with tobacco companies. Since 2002, these dollars and a small annual grant from disability services have provided the primary support for the work of PBS-Nevada. Other sources of support included tuition or fee-for-service contracts and contributions of staff time, small grants, funds for travel, and training space from various local and state agencies.

PBS-Nevada built interest and understanding about PBS through presentations to parent and advocacy groups, professional associations, school and agency staff meetings, state advisory committees, and legislative hearings. Nevada's three regional centers actively participated in building and sustaining the PBS-Nevada project, and in ensuring that their staff and related private provider staff learned PBS and embedded its processes in their daily work with families and people with intellectual disability. Assistance was provided to practitioners from agencies or schools who conducted their own PBS workshops after they had participated in a comprehensive workshop themselves. PBS staff and collaborators wrote policy revisions for some agencies to ensure systemic support for PBS services. Training in individual PBS was provided to school faculty and school districts, usually on a fee-for-service basis. Over the years, PBS-Nevada and leading school-wide experts from the national PBIS technical assistance center provided school-wide PBS training and follow-up support to administrators and staff from Washoe (Reno area), Clark (Las Vegas area), and a few smaller county school districts with the goal of establishing school-wide PBS. Although these efforts were only moderately successful at the time, they provided a foundation for the initiation of a large state-wide, multiyear project funded in 2015.

Although the project's primary focus on family and in-service staff training and technical assistance did not change, the format and process for delivering these services went through a number of revisions. A significant change came with the transition to a three-tiered model in which the intensity of the services was tailored to the interests of participants and the severity of presenting problems. Tier 1 included training on universal prevention strategies, using positive behavior support. Tier-2 training consisted of more targeted, specialized strategies on topics such as "picky eaters," "Teaching effective communication," "Successful routines and transitions," and "potty pros." Tier 3 involved more comprehensive, individualized, function-based training including "Addressing challenging behaviors" and "prevent-teach-reinforce comprehensive" (for educators utilizing the specialized PTR model). Addressing challenging behavior was delivered in five sessions, and interspersed with home consultation visits.

As capacity in PBS grew, PBS-Nevada was able to rely more heavily on local expertise, and a series of training activities are now coordinated and provided through three regional offices. The staff of all regions includes at least one Board Certified Behavior Analyst, and some classes are provided in Spanish. PBS-Nevada participates in the activities of the Association for Positive Behavior Support and the national Positive Behavioral Interventions & Supports Technical Assistance Center, and benefits from consultations with leading PBS experts. The Nevada APBS Network sponsors various activities to increase PBS awareness. PBS-Nevada is now a part of Nevada's PBIS Technical Assistance Center, which also includes a state-wide, federally funded school climate transformation project, fee-for-service activities, and services focused on juvenile justice, autism, aging, court-mandated parent training, and school mental health. Other affiliated projects include a Nevada early childhood partnership and a research project on the Prevent Teach Reinforce for Young Children model.

The remainder of this chapter addresses two important considerations: the actual process and procedures of individual PBS and the research that supports its efficacy. We emphasize that the PBS process is described as it would be implemented to support people with the most severe and persistent problem behaviors. It is acknowledged that many problem behaviors are not terribly intractable and that less extensive and rigorous procedures might be sufficient. In some cases, for example, it might not even be necessary to conduct a functional assessment, to implement an assessment-based intervention plan, or to rely on a complete PBS support team. However, we have found that it is generally worse to do less than is necessary than to do more. When people with intellectual disability have problem behaviors that compromise their learning and their social opportunities, it is vital to do everything possible to eliminate such problems and promote avenues to improved behavioral adaptation and quality of life. Similarly, much of the research that is described later in the chapter was focused on relatively extreme problems that could not be resolved with less precise or intensive strategies.

The Process of Individual PBS

The process of individual PBS occurs on a continuum of complexity and intensity determined by the needs of the person. Within this continuum, the practitioner should assume that each person engages in a unique behavioral repertoire and has specific preferences, dislikes, and learning histories. All of these variables contribute to the development of the target behavior and hence, should influence the behavior support plan. As such, it is important that prior to plan development, people who know the focus person well are brought together in a team process to share information. Once all seemingly relevant information is gathered regarding the person, the PBS process can begin and the practices can be attuned to needs and context.

The question of whether or not someone is actually implementing PBS is common. One major misconception is that the use of positive reinforcement, or rewarding appropriate behavior, means that PBS is being used. In actuality, PBS for individuals is a multicomponent process inclusive of a team approach, PCP, goal setting, functional assessment, a multicomponent behavior plan, data-based decision making, and fidelity measures, all with the aim of reducing problem behavior, increasing skills, and overall, enhancing the person's quality of life (Dunlap & Carr, 2007).

Teams are likely to begin a PBS process following a crisis situation and intend to solve the problem immediately. It is not uncommon that these teams formed around a crisis are hoping for a "quick fix" solution to a problem behavior, making them potentially resistant to allocating so much time to the development of each component within PBS. While concerns regarding time commitments and the realities of limited resources may be quite valid, team members must understand that developing effective and long-lasting interventions requires a systemic process that takes time (Bambara & Kunsch, 2015). The team must be thoughtful about balancing the investment of resources with the urgency of the circumstances and find a timeline that will work for them and the person they are supporting.

The actual process for individual PBS is composed of five key elements: teaming, goal setting, assessment, intervention, and data-based decision making. Each phase may vary in length based on the unique needs of the person, including the setting, staffing, and intensity of the situation. A number of manualized approaches to individual PBS interventions are available to teachers and other professionals supporting people with problem behaviors (e.g., Dunlap, Iovannone, et al., 2010). The following section provides detailed information on the progression of the major foundations involved in individualized PBS.

Teaming

Teaming is the process in which a team of people is formed to support a focus person and complete the steps of the individual PBS process. The primary purpose of a team is to share information, address concerns, and engage in a collaborative process of behavior intervention planning to support the focus person. The emphasis on teaming is integral to PBS and provides an important framework for the success and sustainability of the intervention. While some members of the team may find it frivolous to dedicate so much time to teaming, there are many factors that contribute to the success of the team process, including selecting the vital members of the team, developing collaborative work styles and communication, and selecting roles and responsibilities.

The size and composition of the team is determined by the needs and circumstances of the focus person. Generally, the team should be comprised of people who interact with the focus person on a regular basis as well as the professionals who will be responsible for implementing and evaluating the intervention. Key members of the team generally include the focus individual's parents or primary caregivers along with a teacher or job coach who spends a great deal of time with the person and is intimately aware of the problem behaviors. Other related service providers or paraprofessionals may be invited to join the team with the intention of consistency of supports across environments. Another key member of the team is a person with extensive knowledge of behavior principles such as a behavior analyst, behavior specialist, social worker, counselor, or psychologist. If the intervention is aimed at supporting a person in a school or community setting, an administrator from the school or community setting should have representation on the team to address policy issues and make sure that the appropriate resources are available to allocate to the implementation and sustainability of the plan. The focus person, or the person the team is supporting, might also be invited to participate in goal setting and other team meetings, supporting self-determination and PCP.

A final component to teaming is the development of roles and responsibilities within a team. One of the challenges in the teaming process is fostering collaboration between professionals from multiple disciplines. While for a small team this may not be an issue, large teams are often comprised of many related service providers (e.g., speech pathologist, occupational therapist, behavior analyst, physical therapist) who need to establish criteria and expectations for the operation of the team. Therefore the expectations for the team should be set during the first meeting and ought to be carried out through the implementation and data-based decision-making stages of the plan. The primary roles needed on a team include a facilitator to schedule and conduct the meetings; an agenda planner to come up with a meeting agenda and keep the meetings on-track and productive; and an action plan recorder, or a person who is responsible for compiling the steps completed, the future actions needed, and the results of each stage. With all of these teaming matters addressed, the structure will now be in place to ensure effective and efficient use of team resources.

Goal Setting and Data Collection

The primary purpose of goal setting is to identify the problem behaviors that pose barriers to the person's participation in society and the target behaviors that will improve the person's quality of life. In other words, this is the step where the team decides which behaviors to decrease and which to increase. The team should consider what the short-term goals would be, such as what can be achieved within weeks through a behavior intervention plan, and what long-term goals might be, such as academic productivity and enhancement of social interactions and the establishment of friendships.

As an example of goal setting, we consider a middle school student named Kenneth who engages in aggressive behavior to have his needs met. The team confirms that Kenneth hits students and teachers when he wants to interact. The short-term goals for Kenneth may include reducing hitting behavior and using appropriate forms of communication to interact with others (more on selection of replacement behaviors following the assessment phase). A long-term or broad goal that may be identified for Kenneth is his being able to appropriately interact with peers and make friends.

An important component of goal setting is to clearly identify the short-term goal target behaviors such that everyone on the team agrees upon the behavior. The behaviors should be defined using observable and measurable terms, allowing anyone implementing the plan to clearly identify both the target behaviors for reduction and acquisition. In the example of Kenneth, the term "aggressive behavior" is quite vague and could be interpreted differently depending on the individual reading the behavior plan. For example, the speech therapist may be looking at moderate hitting, but the parents may be so used to Kenneth's hitting that they are looking at a full body attack. In this regard, it is important for the team to generate appropriate operational definitions for each behavior that will be tracked.

A critical step at this stage of the PBS process is to select a measurement system for monitoring behavior change. The measurement system must include ways to track both the problem behavior for reduction and the target behavior for acquisition. When developing a system of data collection, the team should consider contextual fit, meaning the feasibility of data collection given the existing resources. The following questions should be considered: Who will collect the data? When will the data be collected? and How often will the data be reviewed, and by whom? If an adequate data collection system is put into place, the team should be able to answer the following questions when reviewing data: Is the problem behavior decreasing? Is the replacement behavior increasing? Are the intervention strategies effective? Are the goals of the intervention being met? and Are modifications needed for this plan? Data collection should begin immediately to collect baseline (comparison) data prior to intervention.

Assessment

A behavioral assessment is conducted to determine the purpose of a particular behavior. The Functional Behavior Assessment (FBA) is a main component of any individual PBS plan. The information gathered through an FBA will help the team determine the function or purpose of a problem behavior; the setting events that make a behavior more likely to occur; the antecedents that immediately precede and trigger the behavior; and the people, places, and things that are typically in the environment when the problem behavior occurs and does not occur.

Decades of research have demonstrated a functional relationship between behavior (appropriate or inappropriate) and the social and physical environment (e.g., Doggett, Edwards, Moore, Tingstrom, & Wilczynski, 2001; Iwata, Dorsey, Slifer, Bauman, & Richman, 1982/1994; Sasso et al., 1992). In identifying the "function" of behavior, the team is actually identifying the reinforcing variables that are maintaining that behavior. The prevailing socially-mediated maintaining variables for problem behavior are to gain social attention, get access to preferred items or activities, or to escape work or nonpreferred demands.

There are two types of FBA procedures that are used in PBS: descriptive and indirect functional assessment. A descriptive FBA uses direct observation of the person in a natural environment. Antecedent-Behavior-Consequence (ABC) data collection is commonly used to record occurrences of the target problem behavior. ABC recording involves continuous recording in which all occurrences of the problem behavior are recorded for a period of time. The ABC data allows the team to look for patterns in the data by recording the target behavior incident and what happened immediately before the behavior (the antecedent) and what immediately followed the behavior (the consequence). A thorough ABC analysis will also include description of setting events, or variables that are present that make the behavior more likely to occur. A second type of FBA is the indirect functional assessment, which uses interviews, existing records reviews (where applicable), and checklists and other questionnaires from persons who are familiar with the person and the problem behavior. This type of FBA is called "indirect" because it does not incorporate direct observation of the behavior but rather gathers the information from persons who are most familiar with the behavior across environments. A thorough amount of information should be provided in the indirect assessment regarding the conditions in which behavior is more likely (setting events) and less likely to occur. While each type of assessment has its benefits and limitations, which are beyond the scope of this chapter, it is recommended to use both direct and indirect FBA measurements whenever possible (O'Neill et al., 1997).

Conducting a full FBA can be summarized as a four-step process (Cooper, Heron, & Heward, 2007). The first step is to gather information on the problem behavior through indirect assessments such as questionnaires to the primary caregivers. The second step is to use the information gathered in the indirect assessment to formulate a hypothesis statement about the purpose of the problem behavior, why it occurs, when it occurs, and under what environmental circumstances it is most and least likely to occur. The third step is to confirm this hypothesis through direct observation of the problem behavior, using a descriptive FBA procedure. In the fourth step, interventions should be selected based on the identified and confirmed function of the problem behavior.

Intervention

A Behavior Intervention Plan (BIP) should be written following the assessment and should be comprehensive in nature, addressing support strategies for three major purposes: (1) prevention of the problem behavior, (2) identification of a replacement behavior, and (3) consequence strategies for maintaining the appropriate behavior and extinguishing the problem behavior. In general, each of the three areas of the BIP should have at least one intervention strategy identified, and each strategy should have a step-by-step implementation plan outlined by the team, a plan for training and technical assistance on the strategies must be specified, and there should be some way to measure fidelity of implementation (e.g., Dunlap, Carr et al., 2010). The hypothesis statement needs to be referenced when working on intervention planning, as it will provide insight into what environmental changes and supports should be provided.

Prevention strategies are often the easiest to implement, and should be identified and attempted prior to more complex interventions. In selecting a prevention strategy for the BIP, teams ought to consider the antecedent component of the FBA. In other words, the team needs to identify what environmental events evoke, or trigger, the problem behavior. In addition, the team should be able to describe the environmental conditions in which the problem behavior is least likely to occur. For example, if we know that Susan engages in problem behavior during her morning routine while getting ready for work and we know that she has a much easier time following routines in the evening, we might consider making some modifications to the morning routine. The team may have identified certain setting events that contribute to Susan's problem behaviors, such as the behaviors being more likely to occur when Susan has stayed up late at night and is tired, or when Susan has not had anything to eat first. Some prevention strategies that the team might select include making sure that Susan has had adequate sleep each night and that she begins her morning by eating breakfast. By making these minor preventative modifications to Susan's day, the team can expect to see a decrease in problem behavior.

Selecting a replacement behavior is perhaps the most important component of the PBS plan because the focus on teaching appropriate pro-social skills should always be at the forefront of any behavioral intervention. The replacement behavior is a functionally equivalent behavior that is taught to replace the problem behavior but still allows the individual to have his or her needs met. The functional relationship determined in the FBA allows for the planning of a replacement behavior or teaching intervention that is specific to the function of the behavior and not necessarily the topography (Cooper, Heron, & Heward, 2007). In selecting a replacement behavior, the team should consider the relevancy of the behavior with regard to the person's natural environment, the ease with which the person can learn the behavior, and the response effort with which the person will need to perform the new appropriate behavior. Stated simply, the replacement behavior needs to be socially appropriate, quick to learn, and easy to perform. In the event that a behavior is multiply maintained, or is found to have multiple functions or purposes, the team will need to select a replacement behavior to correspond with each identified function.

In selecting consequence strategies, the team should refer to the data collected during the FBA on the maintaining consequences of the problem behavior. It is important that the team uses the identified reinforcing consequence to reinforce the replacement behavior instead of the problem behavior, rendering the person's problem behavior ineffective. For example, if the function of Joe's pencil throwing has historically been to get out of doing work and the team has identified a replacement behavior of asking for a "break," Joe should be given a break contingent upon "break" and instructed to continue working if he throws pencils. In this scenario, "break" is being reinforced with escape from work and pencil throwing is placed on escape extinction, in a behavioral process known as "differential reinforcement." The potency of reinforcers may change over time, so the team should be prepared to change and enhance consequences, as necessary.

Data-Based Decision Making

The data-based decision-making process is the final step in creating an individual PBS plan. While it is arguably the most important part, it is often neglected as it can become overwhelming if not carefully planned for. In this step, the team will establish a system for ongoing data collection on the identified target behaviors as well as a way to monitor the fidelity of implementation. This collected data will be used for progress monitoring, or the evaluation of success or lack thereof following the implementation of the behavior support plan. Data-based decision making is critical to the success of the plan, and it is important to continue data collection prior to (baseline), during (implementation), and beyond (maintenance) the initial stages of implementation. This comprehensive approach to progress monitoring and data-based decision making ensures sustainability and effectiveness of interventions, as well as efficient use of time and resources.

The first consideration in the data-based decision-making process is to determine a method and a procedure for data collection for both the problem behavior and the replacement behavior. In selecting a data collection methodology, the topography and frequency of the behavior need to be considered. Some considerations include whether the behavior is high rate (meaning that it happens frequently throughout the day), if the behavior has a particularly long or short duration, and how intense the behavioral episode is. Contextual fit and who will be responsible for documentation should also be a consideration in selecting a format for data collection. Data can be collected in a variety of ways, including event recording, in which each individual episode of behavior is recorded, or using a time sample, where behavior is recorded over a predetermined and consistent interval of time. If the contextual fit dictates that behavior cannot be regularly recorded throughout the day (i.e., there are not enough people readily available for ongoing data collection), a perceptual rating scale may be considered in which data is collected once at the end of a day by a consistent observer who provides a quantitative summary of the daily behavior.

Once data are collected for a specified amount of time, the team should convene in regularly scheduled data meetings to review the data and make data-based decisions. Visual analysis is a standard way to interpret data in a PBS model; therefore someone on the team should be assigned to the task of graphing the data prior to each data meeting. Within the first two weeks of implementation, the team should compare the baseline data, or preintervention data, to the postintervention data to determine if the plan is working. If the plan is working and the behavior is improving, this does not mean that the problem has been fixed and the plan is no longer necessary, but rather there should be a focus around maintenance of the BIP. If the plan does not appear to be resulting in significant behavior change, the team should evaluate the fidelity of plan implementation, if the resources allocated to the interventions are sufficient, and whether the training provided to support persons and caregivers was adequate, and perhaps also revisit the assessment to ensure that the interventions selected still correspond to the function of the behavior. Evaluation meetings to review data should occur regularly so that modifications to the plan can be made.

Research Evidence on PBS

Since the mid-1980s, the volume of studies on PBS assessment and intervention strategies for people with intellectual disability has grown to include strong empirical data on many of the major tenets and procedural variables in the PBS approach. Other aspects remain ripe for further development

(Dunlap & Carr, 2007). In the following section, the current status of PBS research with participants who have intellectual disability is summarized. More extensive reviews are available and we refer readers to Brown, Anderson, and DePry (2015); Carr and colleagues (1999); and Dunlap and Carr (2007).

Assessment and Planning in PBS

Preintervention assessments in PBS are concerned with variables related to (1) the function of problem behaviors, (2) larger lifestyle issues and preferences, and (3) the fit of the plan with the implementation setting. Decades of research are available on the process of functional behavioral assessment and functional analysis (a critical subset of FBAs, involving controlled experimental manipulations). Since an FBA is typically conducted in natural settings, the results can have strong external validity and relevance for intervention planning. Indeed, reviews of the literature have found conclusively that interventions based on an FBA, identifying the factors that maintain problem behavior, are much more likely to be effective than interventions that are not (Carr et al., 1999; Ingram, Lewis-Palmer, & Sugai, 2005).

In recent research examining ways to make FBAs more practical and usable, Loman and Horner (2014) found that typical change agents with brief training could use basic FBA procedures to accurately identify the function of problem behaviors. Since clearly determining (or confirming) the function of behavior may require more rigorous examination, other researchers are developing an adapted functional analysis procedure that has been effectively implemented in applied settings (Lambert, Bloom, & Irvin, 2012; Rispoli et al., 2015). It can also be important to assess other contextual or distal factors that might influence the occurrence of problem behaviors. To get at this information, Carr, Ladd, and Schulte (2008) empirically validated a contextual assessment inventory for identifying variables such as physical, social, task-related, or biological factors.

The use of PCP and the related process of wraparound are commonly used in PBS as a means of assessing larger lifestyle issues and preferences that may be enhanced by PBS interventions and support (Carr et al., 2002). Some data are available regarding the fidelity of implementation of these procedures, and there are exemplars of how PCP and wraparound can be beneficial in ensuring that the lifestyle preferences of students with disabilities are met within programs such as school-wide PBS (Freeman et al., 2006; Freeman et al., 2015). Overall, however, the research on the influence of wraparound and PCP on the personal outcomes of people with intellectual disability has shown only moderate results, and there is a need for more rigorous evidence-based research (Claes, Van Hove, Vandevelde, Van Loon, & Schalock, 2010).

Finally, measuring contextual fit—or contextual appropriateness of intervention plans with respect to the values, skills, priorities, and overall context of the implementation setting—has long been considered important and is emphasized in a growing body of literature (McIntosh, Lucyshyn, Strickland-Cohen, & Horner, 2015). A few studies have yielded data supporting the hypothesis that behavior change is more likely to occur when treatment planning includes assessing and considering contextual variables (contextual fit) compared to when a prescriptive approach is taken (e.g., Moes & Frea, 2000). However, one analysis of published research on behavior support implemented by families found that most studies did not measure or report on family ecology or family perspectives (McLaughlin, Denney, Snyder, & Welsh, 2012). Overall, there are limited data regarding the validity of contextual fit assessments and the impact they have on PBS plan implementation or effectiveness.

Intervention Strategies in PBS

Although a variety of methods might be included in the PBS assessment and planning stages of support plan development, their purpose is always to inform the design of interventions that will reliably prevent problem behavior from occurring. Broadly, PBS interventions involve two types of strategies:

instructional and environmental design. Instructional methods focus on building competencies that will render problem behavior unnecessary or irrelevant. It is generally acknowledged that teaching, guidance, and reinforcement of selected skills—using well-designed curricula in all relevant activities and settings—will effectively reduce problem behaviors (Ferro, Foster-Johnson, & Dunlap, 1996; Lucyshyn, Dunlap, & Freeman, 2015). The process of replacing a problem behavior with a desirable alternative that serves the same communicative function (functional communication training, or FCT), is a widely used intervention strategy with an expansive array of research, applications, and procedural manuals (Durand, 2012; Durand, 2015). FCT is an extremely well-established procedure and has been a cornerstone practice of PBS since its inception (Carr & Durand, 1985). Nevertheless, it can be noted that research does not yet address why some parents and teachers experience barriers in implementing FCT, nor does it delineate variables that might limit effective FCT implementation (Durand, 2015).

Another type of instructional strategy has to do with developing coping or self-control skills, such as relaxation, social skills, and ways of tolerating delays of gratification. In particular, a good deal of PBS research testifies to the effectiveness of self-monitoring and self-management procedures, including strategies that children with intellectual disability can use to modify or regulate their own behavior (e.g., Koegel, Harrower, & Koegel, 1999). However, self-management strategies are still underused, and more research is necessary to understand the barriers to incorporating these strategies in individual and school-wide PBS systems (Agran, 2015).

The second category of intervention strategies, environmental design, includes the removal or presentation of a broad array of antecedent or contextual (setting event) variables (Kern & Clarke, 2005). Modifications of events or stimuli that immediately precede problem behavior include pacing/sequencing of instructions and modifying the difficulty of tasks. Ways of altering contextual variables could include enriching the environment by incorporating preferred stimuli (e.g., opportunities for making choices throughout the day; McIntosh et al., 2015), and enhancing interpersonal relationships (Magito McLauglin & Carr, 2005), to mention a few. There is great deal of research in support of such individualized antecedent manipulations, using a wide variety of stimuli to produce efficient and substantial behavior change (Loman & Sanford, 2015; Luiselli, 2006), although durable effects are unlikely unless they are combined with other components in a comprehensive plan.

The literature on multicomponent PBS interventions, as described earlier in this chapter, is growing and offers examples of how support plans can be effective in typical settings when carefully designed and implemented (e.g., Albin & Todd, 2015; De Pry & Esparaza Brown, 2015). A few studies show the results of long-term implementation (e.g., Dunlap, Carr et al., 2010; Jensen, McConnachie, & Pierson, 2001). However, we have limited knowledge about some aspects of larger-scale delivery of support technology, including systems variables related to sustainability; how best to address the quality-of-life needs of family members; and how typical support persons in typical physical, activity, and social contexts can implement and maintain PBS interventions (Dunlap & Carr, 2007).

Research on Models of PBS Implementation

The development of standardized, evidence-based PBS models for tertiary intervention in specific settings is providing the means for adoption of PBS strategies on a larger scale. PBS models provide a complete package of practices to ensure the host environment will support the full implementation and sustainability of the program when used by typical practitioners in applied settings. In addition to employing basic intervention components with a substantial empirical foundation, a number of these programs have conducted group comparison studies using randomized controlled trials. PBS models found in the literature include the "First Step to Success Program" (Carter & Horner, 2009; Sprague & Perkins, 2009), a variation on the now classic "Teaching-Family Model" (De Wein & Miller, 2009), the "Prevent-Teach-Reinforce" (PTR) model (Dunlap, Iovannone et al., 2010; Iovannone et al., 2009; Strain, Wilson, & Dunlap, 2011), the "Positive Family Intervention" model (Durand, Hieneman,

Clarke, Wang, & Rinaldi, 2013), and "Prevent-Teach-Reinforce Model for Young Children" (PTR-YC) (Dunlap, Wilson, Strain, & Lee, 2013; Dunlap, Lee, Joseph, & Strain, 2015). The PTR-YC model, for example, presents standardized, evidence-based practices backed by extensive research in a complete package and in such a way as to enhance the feasibility and fidelity of implementation when used by typical practitioners of early childhood care and education (Dunlap et al., 2015).

Summary

Over the course of the past 20 years, PBS has become the preferred approach for addressing problem behaviors of children and adults with intellectual disability and problem behaviors. This has occurred because PBS is founded on a firm conceptual and procedural foundation, based largely on the practical science of applied behavior analysis, and because the PBS process accounts for the individuality of participants' characteristics and settings. Research has shown the strategies and tactics to be effective in a large number of circumstances. Although all elements of the PBS process can be improved through innovation and applied investigation, it is clear that PBS, when implemented with fidelity, can contribute significantly to the quality of life of people affected by intellectual disability.

References

Agran, M. (2015). Strategies for self-management. In F. Brown, J.L. Anderson, & R.L. De Pry (Eds.), *Individual positive behavior support: A standards-based guide to practices in school and community settings* (pp. 333–346). Baltimore, MD: Paul H. Brookes Publishing Co.

Albin, R.W. & Todd, A.W. (2015). Application of a multi-element positive behavior interventions and supports plan for Alie, an elementary student with intellectual disabilities. In F. Brown, J.L. Anderson, & R.L. De Pry (Eds.), *Individual positive behavior support: A standards-based guide to practices in school and community settings* (pp. 463–480). Baltimore, MD: Paul H. Brookes Publishing Co.

Anderson, J., Albin, R., Mesaros, R., Dunlap, G., & Morelli-Robbins, M. (1993). Objectives and processes of comprehensive training in community-referenced behavior management. In J. Reichle & D. Wacker (Eds.), *Communicative approaches to the management of challenging behavior* (pp. 363–406). Baltimore: Paul H. Brookes.

Anderson, J.L., Russo, R., Dunlap, G., & Albin, R.W. (1996). A team training model for building the capacity to provide positive behavioral supports in inclusive settings. In L.K. Koegel, R.L. Koegel, & G. Dunlap (Eds.), *Positive behavioral support: Including people with difficult behavior in the community* (pp. 467–490). Baltimore, MD: Paul H. Brookes Publishers.

Bambara, L., Dunlap, G., & Schwartz, I. (Eds.) (2004). *Positive behavior support: Critical articles on improving practice for individuals with severe disabilities.* Austin, TX: Pro-Ed and TASH.

Bambara, L.M. & Kunsch, C. (2015). Effective teaming for positive behavior support. In F. Brown, J.L. Anderson, & R.L. DePry (Eds.), *Individual positive behavior supports* (pp. 47–70). Baltimore, MD: Paul H. Brookes.

Brown, F., Anderson, J.L., & DePry, R.L. (Eds.), (2015). *Individual positive behavior supports: A standards-based guide to practices in school and community-based settings.* Baltimore, MD: Paul H. Brookes.

Carr, E.G. (1977). The motivation of self-injurious behavior: A review of some hypotheses. *Psychological Bulletin, 84,* 800–816.

Carr, E.G., Dunlap, G., Horner, R.H., Koegel, R.L., Turnbull, A.P., Sailor, W., . . . Fox, L. (2002). Positive behavior support: Evolution of an applied science. *Journal of Positive Behavior Interventions, 4,* 4–16.

Carr, E.G. & Durand, V.M. (1985). Reducing behavior problems through functional communication training. *Journal of Applied Behavior Analysis, 18,* 111–126.

Carr, E.G., Horner, R.H., Turnbull, A.P., Marquis, J.G., Magito McLaughlin, D., McAtee, M.L., . . . Braddock, D. (1999). *Positive behavior support for people with developmental disabilities.* Washington, DC: American Association on Mental Retardation.

Carr, E.G., Ladd, M.V., & Schulte, C.F. (2008). Validation of the contextual assessment inventory for problem behavior. *Journal of Positive Behavior Interventions, 10,* 91–104.

Carter, D.R. & Horner, R.H. (2009). Adding function-based behavioral supports to first step to success: Integrating individualized and manualized practices. *Journal of Positive Behavior Interventions, 11,* 22–34.

Claes, C., Van Hove, G., Vandevelde, S., van Loon, J., & Schalock, R. (2010). Person-centered planning: Analysis of research and effectiveness. *Intellectual and Developmental Disabilities, 48,* 432–453.

Colvin, G. & Lazar, M. (1997). *The effective elementary classroom: Managing for success.* Longmont, CO: Sopris West.

Cooper, J.O., Heron, T.E., & Heward, W.L. (2007). *Applied behavior analysis* (2nd ed.). Upper Saddle River, NJ: Pearson.

De Pry, R.L. & Esparaza Brown, J. (2015). Developing a multielement behavior support plan for a middle school student from a diverse background with significant behavioral challenges. In F. Brown, J.L. Anderson, & R.L. De Pry (Eds.), *Individual positive behavior support: A standards-based guide to practices in school and community settings* (pp. 447–462). Baltimore, MD: Paul H. Brookes Publishing Co.

De Wein & Miller, L.K. (2009). The teaching-family model: A program description and its effects on the aggressive behaviors and quality of life of two adults with intellectual disabilities. *Journal of Positive Behavior Interventions, 11,* 235–251.

Doggett, A.R., Edwards, R.P., Moore, J.W., Tingstrom, D.H., & Wilczynski, S.M. (2001). An approach to functional assessment in general education classroom settings. *School Psychology Review, 30,* 313–328.

Dunlap, G. (2006). The applied behavior analytic heritage of PBS: A dynamic model of action-oriented research. *Journal of Positive Behavior Interventions, 8,* 58–60.

Dunlap, G., & Carr, E.G. (2007). Positive behavior support and developmental disabilities: A summary and analysis of research. In S.L. Odom, R.H. Horner, M. Snell, & J. Blacher (Eds.), *Handbook of developmental disabilities* (pp. 469–482). New York: Guilford Publications.

Dunlap, G., Carr, E.G., Horner, R.H., Koegel, R.L., Sailor, W., Clarke, S., . . . Fox, L. (2010). A descriptive, multi-year examination of positive behavior support. *Behavioral Disorders, 35,* 259–293.

Dunlap, G., Carr, E.G., Horner, R.H., Zarcone, J.R., & Schwartz, I. (2008). Positive behavior support and applied behavior analysis: A familial alliance. *Behavior Modification, 32,* 682–698.

Dunlap, G., Hieneman, M., Knoster, T., Fox, L., Anderson, J., & Albin, R. (2000). Essential elements of in-service training in positive behavior support. *Journal of Positive Behavior Interventions, 2,* 22–32.

Dunlap, G., Iovannone, R., Wilson, K., Kincaid, D., Christiansen, K., Strain, P., & English, C. (2010). *Prevent-Teach-Reinforce: A school-based model of positive behavior.* Baltimore, MD: Paul H. Brookes.

Dunlap, G., Kincaid, D., & Jackson, D. (2013). Positive behavior support: Foundations, systems, and quality of life. In M. Wehmeyer (Ed.), *The Oxford handbook of positive psychology and disability* (pp. 303–316). New York: Oxford University Press.

Dunlap, G., Kincaid, D., Horner, R.H., Knoster, T., & Bradshaw, C. (2014). A comment on the term "Positive behavior support." *Journal of Positive Behavior Interventions, 16,* 133-136.

Dunlap, G., Lee, J.K., Joseph, J.D., & Strain, P. (2015). A model for increasing the fidelity and effectiveness of interventions for challenging behaviors: Prevent-teach-reinforce for young children. *Infants & Young Children, 28,* 3–17.

Dunlap, G., Sailor W., Horner, R.H., & Sugai, G. (2009). Origins and history of positive behavior support. In W. Sailor, G. Dunlap, G. Sugai, & R. H. Horner (Eds). *Handbook of positive behavior support* (pp. 3-16). New York: Springer.

Dunlap, G., Wilson, K., Strain, P., & Lee, J.K. (2013). *Prevent-teach-reinforce for young children: The early childhood model of individualized positive behavior support.* Baltimore, MD: Paul H. Brookes.

Durand, V.M. (2012). Functional communication training to reduce challenging behavior. In P. Prelock & R. McCauley (Eds.), *Treatment of autism spectrum disorders: Evidence-based intervention strategies for communication & social interaction* (pp. 107–138). Baltimore, MD: Paul H. Brookes Publishing Co.

Durand, V.M. (2015). Strategies for functional communication training. In F. Brown, J.L. Anderson, & R.L. De Pry (Eds.), *Individual positive behavior support: A standards-based guide to practices in school and community settings* (pp. 385–396). Baltimore, MD: Paul H. Brookes Publishing Co.

Durand, V.M., Hieneman, M., Clarke, S., Wang, M., & Rinaldi, M. (2013). Positive family intervention for severe challenging behavior I: A multisite randomized clinical trial. *Journal of Positive Behavior Interventions, 15,* 133–143.

Evans, I.M. & Meyer, L.H. (1985). *An educative approach to behavior problems: A practical decision model for interventions for severely handicapped learners.* Baltimore: Paul H. Brookes Publishing Co.

Ferro, J., Foster-Johnson, L., & Dunlap, G. (1996). Relation between curricular activities and problem behaviors of students with mental retardation. *American Journal on Mental Retardation, 101,* 184–194.

Freeman, R., Eber, L., Anderson, C., Irvin, L., Horner, R., Bounds, M., & Dunlap, G. (2006). Building inclusive school cultures using school-wide PBS: Designing effective individual support systems for students with significant disabilities. *Research and Practice in Severe Disabilities, 31,* 4–17.

Freeman, R., Enyart, M., Schmitz, K., Kimbrough, P., Matthews, K., & Newcomer, L. (2015). Integrating and building on best practices in person-centered planning, wraparound, and positive behavior support to enhance quality of life. In F. Brown, J.L. Anderson, & R.L. De Pry (Eds.), *Individual positive behavior support: A standards-based guide to practices in school and community settings* (pp. 241–257). Baltimore, MD: Paul H. Brookes Publishing Co.

Gaylord-Ross, R. (1980). A decision model for the treatment of aberrant behavior in applied settings. In W. Sailor, B. Wilcox, & L. Brown (Eds.), *Methods of instruction for severely handicapped students* (pp. 135–158). Baltimore: Paul H. Brookes.

Guess, D., Helmstetter, E., Turnbull, H.R., & Knowlton, S. (1987). *Use of aversive procedures with persons who are disabled: An historical review and critical analysis.* Seattle: The Association for Persons with Severe Handicaps.

Horner, R.H. & Budd, C.M. (1985). Acquisition of manual sign use: Collateral reduction of maladaptive behavior, and factors limiting generalization. *Education and Training of the Mentally Retarded, 20,* 39–47.

Horner, R.H., Dunlap, G., Koegel, R.L., Carr, E.G., Sailor, W., Anderson, J., . . . O'Neill, R.E. (1990). Toward a technology of "nonaversive" behavioral support. *Journal of the Association for Persons with Severe Handicaps, 15,* 125–132.

Ingram, K., Lewis-Palmer, T., & Sugai, G. (2005). Function-based intervention planning: Comparing the effectiveness of FBA function-based and non-function-based intervention plans. *Journal of Positive Behavior Interventions, 7,* 224–236.

Iovanonne, R., Greenbaum, P.E., Wang, W., Kincaid, D., Dunlap, G., & Strain, P. (2009). Randomized control trial of the prevent-teach-reinforce (PTR) tertiary intervention for students with problem behavior. *Journal of Emotional and Behavioral Disorders, 17,* 213–225.

Iwata, B.A., Dorsey, M.F., Slifer, K.J., Bauman, K.E., & Richman, G.S. (1982/1994). Toward a functional analysis of self-injury. *Journal of Applied Behavior Analysis, 27,* 197–209.

Jensen, C.C., McConnachie, G., & Pierson, T. (2001). Long-term multicomponent intervention to reduce severe problem behavior: A 63-month evaluation. *Journal of Positive Behavior Interventions, 3,* 225–236.

Kern, L. & Clarke, S. (2005). Antecedent and setting event interventions. In L. Bambara & L. Kern (Eds.), *Individualized supports for students with problem behaviors: Designing positive behavior plans* (pp. 201–236). New York: Guilford Press.

Kincaid, D., Dunlap, G., Kern, L., Lane, K., Brown. F, Bambara, L., Fox, L., &, Knoster, T. (2016). Positive Behavior Support: A proposal for updating and refining the definition. *Journal of Positive Behavior Interventions, 18,* 69-73.

Knoster, T., Anderson, J., Carr, E.G., Dunlap, G., & Horner, R.H. (2003). Emerging challenges and opportunities: Introducing the association for positive behavior support. *Journal of Positive Behavior Interventions, 5,* 183–186.

Koegel, L.K., Harrower, J.K., & Koegel, R.L. (1999). Support for children with developmental disabilities in full inclusion classrooms through self-management. *Journal of Positive Behavioral Interventions, 1,* 26–34.

Lambert, J.M., Bloom, S.E., & Irvin, J. (2012). Trial-based functional analysis and functional communication training in an early childhood setting. *Journal of Applied Behavior Analysis, 45,* 579–584.

LaVigna, G.W. & Donnellan, A.M. (1986). *Alternatives to punishment: Nonaversive strategies for solving behavior problems.* New York: Irvington Press.

Lennox, D.B. & Miltenberger, R.G. (1989). Conducting a functional assessment of problem behavior in applied settings. *Journal of the Association for Persons with Severe Handicaps, 14,* 304–311.

Lewis, T. (2015). Applied behavior analysis as a conceptual framework for understanding positive behavior support. In F. Brown, J. Anderson, & R. DePry (Eds.), *Individual positive behavior supports: A standards-based guide to practices in school and community-based settings* (pp. 107–122). Baltimore, MD: Paul H. Brookes Publishing.

Lewis, T.J. & Sugai, G. (1999). Effective behavior support: A systems approach to pro-active school-wide management. *Focus on Exceptional Children, 31,* 1–24.

Loman, S. & Horner, R.H. (2014). Examining the efficacy of a basic functional behavioral assessment training package for school personnel. *Journal of Positive Behavior Interventions, 16,* 18–30.

Loman, S.L. & Sanford, A.K. (2015). Antecedent strategies to change behavior. In F. Brown, J.L. Anderson, & R.L. De Pry (Eds.), *Individual positive behavior support: A standards-based guide to practices in school and community settings* (pp. 123–145). Baltimore, MD: Paul H. Brookes Publishing Co.

Lucyshyn, J.M., Dunlap, D., & Freeman, R. (2015). A historical perspective on the evolution of positive behavior support as a science-based discipline. In F. Brown, J.L. Anderson, & R.L. De Pry (Eds.), *Individual positive behavior support: A standards-based guide to practices in school and community settings* (pp. 3–25). Baltimore, MD: Paul H. Brookes Publishing Co.

Luiselli, J.K. (2006). *Antecedent assessment & intervention: Supporting children & adults with developmental disabilities in community settings.* Baltimore, MD: Paul H. Brookes Publishing Co.

Luiselli, J.K., & Cameron, M.J. (Eds.) (1998). *Antecedent control: Innovative approaches to behavioral support.* Baltimore, MD: Paul H. Brookes.

Magito McLauglin, D. & Carr, E.G. (2005). Quality of rapport as a setting event for problem behavior: Assessment and intervention. *Journal of Positive Behavior Interventions, 7,* 68–91.

McIntosh, K., Lucyshyn, J.M., Strickland-Cohen, K., & Horner, R.H. (2015). Building supportive environments. In F. Brown, J.L. Anderson, & R.L. De Pry (Eds.), *Individual positive behavior support: A standards-based guide to practices in school and community settings* (pp. 401–415). Baltimore, MD: Paul H. Brookes Publishing Co.

McLaughlin, T.W., Denney, M.K., Snyder, P.A., & Welsh, J.L. (2012). Behavior support interventions implemented by families of young children: Examination of contextual fit. *Journal of Positive Behavior Interventions, 14,* 87–97.

Meyer, L. H., & Evans, I. M. (1989). *Nonaversive interventions for problem behaviors: A manual for home and community.* Baltimore: Paul H. Brookes.

Moes, D.R. & Frea, W.D. (2000). Using family context to inform intervention planning for the treatment of a child with autism. *Journal of Positive Behavior Interventions, 2*, 40–46.

O'Neill, R.E., Horner, R.H., Albin, R.W., Sprague, J.R., Storey, K., & Newton, J.S. (1997). *Functional assessment and program development for problem behavior: A practical handbook.* Pacific Grove, CA: Brooks/Cole Publishing.

Rispoli, M., Burke, M.D., Hatton, H., Ninci, J., Zaini, S., & Sanchez, L. (2015). Training head start teachers to conduct trial-based functional analysis of challenging behavior. *Journal of Positive Behavior Interventions, 17*, 235–244.

Sailor, W., Dunlap, G., Sugai, G., & Horner, R. (Eds.) (2009). *Handbook of positive behavior support.* New York: Springer.

Sasso, G.M., Reimers, T.M., Cooper, L.J., Wacker, D., Berg, W., Steege, M., Kelly, L., & Allaire, A. (1992). Use of descriptive and experimental analyses to identify the functional properties of aberrant behavior in school settings. *Journal of Applied Behavior Analysis, 25*, 809–821.

Sprague, J. & Perkins, K. (2009). Direct and collateral effects of the first step to success program. *Journal of Positive Behavior Interventions, 11*, 208–221.

Strain, P.S., Wilson, K., & Dunlap, G. (2011). Prevent-teach-reinforce: Addressing problem behaviors of students with autism in general education classrooms. *Behavioral Disorders, 36*, 160–171.

Sugai, G., Horner, R.H., Dunlap, G., Hieneman, M., Lewis, T.J., Nelson, C.M., . . . Wilcox, B. (2000). Applying positive behavior support and functional behavioral assessment in schools. *Journal of Positive Behavior Interventions, 2,* 131–143.

Sulzer, B. & Mayer, G.R. (1975). *Behavior modification procedures for school personnel.* Hindsdale, Ill.: Dryden Press.

Touchette, P.E., MacDonald, R.F., & Langer, S.N. (1985). A scatter plot for identifying stimulus control of problem behavior. *Journal of Applied Behavior Analysis, 18*, 343–351.

Walker, H.M., Horner, R.H., Sugai, G., Bullis, M., Sprague, J.R., Bricker, D., & Kaufman, M.J. (1996). Integrated approaches to preventing antisocial behavior patterns among school-age children and youth. *Journal of Emotional and Behavioral Disorders, 4*, 194–209.

14

The Role of Technology in Implementing Universal Design for Learning

Loui Lord Nelson, Mindy Johnson

Technology, the kind that requires power, is becoming more and more apparent within classrooms (Purcell, Heaps, Buchanan, & Friedrich, 2013). Studies demonstrate the power of technology as a support for the inclusion of students with intellectual disability in general education settings so they can achieve positive academic, social, communication, and functional outcomes (Coyne, Pisha, Dalton, Zeph, & Smith, 2012; Knight, Wood, Spooner, Browder, & O'Brien, 2015). But technology alone, whether powered or not (i.e., low/no tech), does not establish a learning environment that supports all learners. That requires thoughtful design and planning, which can occur through the use of the universal design for learning (UDL) framework, as illustrated in Box 14.1.

Box 14.1

Ms. Jones's 5th-grade classroom is buzzing with activity. The students are working on a social studies lesson that requires them to discover land and water routes used by early settlers of North America and share what they discover with one another. This unit is designed to last one week and has students seeking information from a variety of sources, completing maps to show the routes, gaining new vocabulary, gathering information about their chosen explorers, and deciding how they want to share their newly learned information with their peers. The work is guided by an overall rubric so the students can monitor their progress and the quality of their products.

Ms. Jones's class includes a variety of students, including students who qualify for Title I, gifted and talented services, and special education services, including two students with intellectual disability. There are also multiple cultures represented as well as languages. The varying levels of support needed by this complex and diverse group of students used to stymie Ms. Jones, but this year she began utilizing UDL to design her lessons and, more importantly, her environment. She has come to realize that all of her students are unique learners.

Ms. Jones's thinking has shifted from believing all students learn the same way to knowing all students have different learning needs based on context. If she offers her students a variety of ways to learn throughout her lessons and within her environment, they can all have the opportunity to be more successful. She knows all of her students enter her classroom having experienced life and learning in different ways and she wants to use those differences to her and her students' advantage. This means

---

establishing an environment where students have the ability to access information in a variety of ways, build on their capacity to plan and stick with the project, accurately demonstrate the knowledge or skills they have gained, and find meaning and purpose in their learning.

For example, Ms. Jones used to think that using her interactive whiteboard to show students examples of historical events or people was enough to help them access the information they needed. After all, they were seeing and hearing the information at the same time and sometimes there was a video—students always liked the video. She also thought that the interactive whiteboard was a great way to hold their attention. But as she began to learn more about UDL she understood that by giving her students more opportunities to explore the information on their own and in a variety of ways, sometimes independently and sometimes collaboratively, could lead to their learning being deeper and more meaningful.

To ensure she is meeting the needs of her students with disabilities, including her two students with intellectual disability, Ms. Jones turns to the building's special education teacher, Mr. Marcus. While Mr. Marcus cannot be in Ms. Jones's classroom the entire day, he meets with Ms. Jones weekly to go over her lesson plans and activities for the following week and suggests strategies and tools that meet the accommodations and modifications described in the Individualized Education Program (IEPs) of the students in her class. What Ms. Jones has discovered through her work with UDL is that the suggestions Mr. Marcus makes for her students with disabilities are often helpful for many of the students in her classroom. Some of those strategies and tools include technologies, both low and high tech.

Ms. Jones's school has recently acquired an online program that each student can log into and use for many of their reading, science, and social studies assignments. Most of her students, including those with disabilities, use this program. It has features such as built-in text-to-speech with synchronized highlighting that allows her students with low decoding skills to listen to the words as they read, a built-in dictionary that provides relevant definitions of terms the students click or tap on, and often has alternate versions of reading assignments or passages geared toward the same content at different reading levels so students can have access to the same content without the barrier of text that is beyond their current reading level. Ms. Jones also knows these tools are appreciated and used by her students with limited English skills as well as her students who struggle with finding a personal connection with the history topics covered in her classroom. However, some of her students prefer to use paper textbooks or articles from magazines, and still others like to find additional resources through the school's media center. Students who choose lower-tech options understand that they may need to take additional steps such as finding definitions for unknown words from a dictionary or asking the media center specialist if there is an audio recording of the paper resource, if needed. Regardless of the tools her students use, Ms. Jones and Mr. Marcus maintain focus on the instructional goal and find ways to scaffold their students' skill development through the available resources whether high tech or low tech.

For one lesson within her unit she has written the goal, "Students will describe the paths early settlers used to explore North America," and she cannot wait to see all of the creative ways her students will show what they know. Some of her students experience physical differences that make writing on paper maps an impossible task, so she turns to an online map making program that her students who use toggle switches can also manipulate. She already knows many of her other students will want to use the online version rather than the paper maps, but she also knows that she has students who will want to get their hands dirty and create salt-dough relief maps. These options are available because she placed them within the design of the lesson and the learning environment and planned ahead with her assessment of the goal by creating a rubric that allows for the different options in how students create their maps.

Most importantly, Ms. Jones recognizes that by reducing the barriers some students face in gaining access to information and skills, she can maintain high expectations for what students can accomplish. She does not need to limit the use of these tools to certain students because she knows that the design of her lesson is based on the outcomes she wants her students to experience and the standards set by the curriculum. Students will use these tools to produce evidence of their learning. They will not merely access the information; they will do something with it. Through her use of the UDL framework, Ms. Jones has designed an environment and a unit where she can expect her students to produce work that demonstrates growth and understanding.

This chapter introduces UDL and its implementation, then describes how UDL and technology can be used to educate all learners. Focusing on all learners enables meaningful steps to be taken to promote the thoughtful, meaningful, and purposeful inclusion of learners with intellectual disability in the general education classroom and curriculum. The term *learner* is used throughout the chapter, rather than the term *student*. Leaders in the field of UDL, including Meyer, Rose, and Gordon (2014), have shifted to the use of *learner* because this term recognizes that learning takes place in all settings, whether individuals are in or out of the classroom. Though this chapter focuses on UDL as a guide for lesson and environment design and technology as a support within classroom environments and lessons, there is the potential to limit our thinking and perceptions of the children and youth we teach when we consider them to only be students rather than people who experience and influence the world as learners. Thus, the word *learner* will be used throughout the chapter.

The Foundations of UDL

The origins of UDL came from a desire to make learning accessible to learners with disabilities. Using research from the fields of neuroscience, brain science, and the research sciences of education, educational psychology, and special education, the founders of the Center for Applied Special Technology, now known as CAST, applied for a grant to design tools using Apple IIe® computers to support learners with significant disabilities. The outcomes for the project were very positive. Learners demonstrated greater capabilities and abilities than had been previously seen. Some learners were expressing knowledge and skills no one knew they had. Others were gaining and using knowledge more quickly than had been seen previously (Meyer, Rose, & Gordon, 2014). For example, a young boy with cerebral palsy was able to use a single switch to communicate his answers to academic questions; prior to this, the young man had no way of demonstrating his knowledge other than through yes, no, or set answers. When he was able to take control of how he responded, he was able to demonstrate more complex learning (Meyer, Rose, & Gordon, 2014).

The work the team did during this project showed that learners with disabilities needed more ways to access information and demonstrate their knowledge. The researchers believed that these learners had capabilities beyond what had been assumed. To ensure this kind of support could be made available to other learners, the CAST staff knew they needed to establish a structure or framework others could utilize. By reviewing the research and identifying the latest findings in learning and best practices in education, educational psychology, and learning sciences, CAST researchers began to identify the foundations of UDL.

This initial work was published in the seminal book, *Teaching Every Student in the Digital Age: Universal Design for Learning* (2002). Though some of that text is now outdated because what we understand about the brain and learning has moved forward, this influential book increased UDL's trajectory of influence. One of the most influential components was CAST's identification of the UDL framework.

Building the UDL Framework

The UDL framework was created to make the concepts underlying UDL more accessible. The overarching structure of UDL includes three principles that came from the work of two key researchers. The first researcher was Lev Vygotsky, a Russian psychologist who described the three prerequisites of learning as: "Engagement with the learning task; recognition of the information to be learned; and, strategies to process that information" (Meyer, Rose, & Gordon, 2014, p. 55). The second was Benjamin Bloom, who described three educational objectives related to cognitive, psychomotor, and affective learning. The work from both researchers aligned with the information CAST was compiling from neuroscience to develop the UDL framework.

The framework was further defined by including three neural networks. Neural networks are the connections our brains make while performing a task. As researchers have come to understand more about how the brain works, scientists have grouped neural networks into categories, including affective, recognition, and strategic networks. While there are other networks utilized in our daily lives, CAST determined that the affective, recognition, and strategic networks (a) coincided with the seminal work of Lev Vygotsky and Benjamin Bloom, and (b) provided the strongest link to learning (Rose & Meyer, 2002). CAST also recognized the need to use language that was easily recognizable to those outside of the brain sciences. Thus, they established the three principles of UDL: engagement, representation, and action and expression. These three principles align with the three neural networks and communicate the meaning of each neural network. Figure 14.1 describes the three neural networks and the associated UDL principles.

The three UDL principles are further clarified in the UDL guidelines developed by CAST and shown in Figure 14.2. For each of the three principles, guidelines are provided for how educators can implement the principle in their lessons and environments. Each of the nine guidelines begins with the phrase, "provide options for," and points educators toward strategies for designing accessible lessons and environments. Under each of the guidelines are checkpoints that provide further clarity on the application of the principles and guidelines.

When educators purposefully use the guidelines and checkpoints, they create learning environments and experiences that enable all students to become purposeful, motivated, resourceful, knowledgeable, strategic, and goal-directed learners (CAST, 2011). Educators should consider the entire set of guidelines when designing the learning environment and lessons, and Box 14.2 provides an example of how an educator can apply specific guidelines to their classroom.

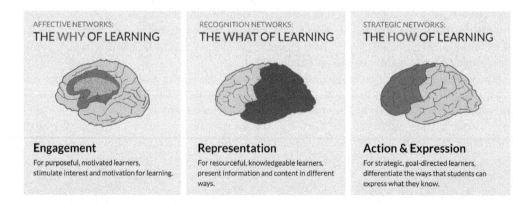

Figure 14.1 Aligning brain networks, the principles of UDL, and their meanings

Universal Design for Learning Guidelines

Provide Multiple Means of **Engagement** *Purposeful, motivated learners*	Provide Multiple Means of **Representation** *Resourceful, knowledgeable learners*	Provide Multiple Means of **Action & Expression** *Strategic, goal-directed learners*
Provide options for self-regulation + Promote expectations and beliefs that optimize motivation + Facilitate personal coping skills and strategies + Develop self-assessment and reflection	**Provide options for comprehension** + Activate or supply background knowledge + Highlight patterns, critical features, big ideas, and relationships + Guide information processing, visualization, and manipulation + Maximize transfer and generalization	**Provide options for executive functions** + Guide appropriate goal-setting + Support planning and strategy development + Enhance capacity for monitoring progress
Provide options for sustaining effort and persistence + Heighten salience of goals and objectives + Vary demands and resources to optimize challenge + Foster collaboration and community + Increase mastery-oriented feedback	**Provide options for language, mathematical expressions, and symbols** + Clarify vocabulary and symbols + Clarify syntax and structure + Support decoding of text, mathematical notation, and symbols + Promote understanding across languages + Illustrate through multiple media	**Provide options for expression and communication** + Use multiple media for communication + Use multiple tools for construction and composition + Build fluencies with graduated levels of support for practice and performance
Provide options for recruiting interest + Optimize individual choice and autonomy + Optimize relevance, value, and authenticity + Minimize threats and distractions	**Provide options for perception** + Offer ways of customizing the display of information + Offer alternatives for auditory information + Offer alternatives for visual information	**Provide options for physical action** + Vary the methods for response and navigation + Optimize access to tools and assistive technologies

Figure 14.2   Universal design for learning guidelines

Implementing the UDL Framework

Box 14.2

Mr. Harmondie, an 8th-grade educator, has set a learning goal for his students: "Students will compare and contrast the settings of two stories." In his instruction, he wants to recruit the interest of his students per the principle of engagement (see Figure 14.2). He uses two checkpoints related to this guideline to promote interest and engagement. First, he provides students with a selection of stories from which to choose but also lets them bring in books or stories from home that are their favorites (to optimize choice and autonomy). Second, the stories he selects are based on the backgrounds and current interests of his students (to optimize relevance, value, and authenticity).

He also uses the guideline of "provide options for perception" under the principle of representation and the checkpoint of "offer ways of customizing the display of information" in his learning environment. Mr. Harmondie knows some of his students require support in decoding, so he ensures that the stories he suggests are available digitally. Students are also allowed to bring in digital texts. He also knows several of his students will likely need scaffolding to help them identify the pieces to compare and contrast. He looks to the UDL guidelines under representation and sees "provide options for comprehension" and the suggestion that he "highlight patterns, critical features, big ideas, and

---

relationships." This motivates him to create a grid that any student can use to investigate stories. It guides students to identify the setting from each story, use descriptive language to describe each of those settings, and investigate their descriptions to look for similarities and differences in the two settings. He also provides sentence starters, general outline suggestions, and other tools that support writers who are comparing and contrasting information. All of these tools are available to all of his students. Mr. Harmondie knows that when students learn to identify their needs and have access to the supports they need, they move toward becoming expert learners.

In this example, Mr. Harmondie's decisions are purposeful and tie directly back to UDL principles and guidelines. He knows why he chose to design his lesson the way he did and can be confident that as he uses the UDL guidelines to design his learning environment and lessons, he will establish an inclusive environment that more readily supports all of his students' learning needs. Mr. Harmondie also understands how to always link his selection of the guidelines and checkpoints to the goal of the lesson. There will be occasions when not all of the guidelines are necessary or appropriate for a single lesson, but there will also be occasions where more than one guideline or checkpoint under a guideline is used (Nelson, 2014; Novak, 2014). To understand which guidelines and checkpoints align with the goal, educators should get to know the definitions behind the framework by using approachable online resources such as www.udlcenter.org and books by Meyer Rose, and Gordon (2014), Nelson (2014), Novak (2014), and Ralabatte (2015). In addition, educators should "start small" (Nelson, 2014, p. xi), focus on the guidelines and checkpoints that align with their current teaching practices, and begin in a way that is comfortable to them and their students.

Designing Lessons Using UDL

Educators routinely engage in lesson planning. Lesson planning involves teachers identifying what curriculum standards need to be met, determining the goals for the lesson to teach the curriculum standards, gathering their planning materials, deciding on an assessment, and writing the actual lesson plan. UDL provides a framework for educators to look more closely at the four different components that create a lesson: goals, methods, materials, and assessment.

The goal of the lesson is written to identify what topic or skill will be taught. It does not, however, identify how the topic or skill will be taught or a specific way learners will demonstrate their knowledge. Returning to the scenario about Ms. Jones's unit in Box 14.1, a non-UDL designed goal would have read: "Learners will create salt dough maps to show the paths settlers used to explore North America." The UDL-designed goal would read: "Students will describe the paths early settlers used to explore North America."

The UDL-designed goal leaves open how learners will demonstrate their knowledge and broadens the materials they can use. They can use salt dough, online programs, paper, or other map tools of choice to demonstrate their knowledge. In addition, the goal does not limit the learners to demonstrating their knowledge through the use of maps. The teacher can provide options outside of map development where learners can express how settlers explored North America. By writing the goal in this way and providing these options, educators spend less time figuring out which mode is the best for which learner; rather, learners build their executive skills by choosing the mode that suits them best and working through the completion of that map.

Second, through the use of UDL, the assessment design recognizes the variety of needs present within the classroom. Some modifications might be necessary for learners with intellectual or physical disabilities to complete the activity (e.g., the online map-generating program that can be used with a switch device), but the overall design of the lesson and the assessment is flexible enough that these accommodations are a natural extension accessible to all learners (i.e., all learners have access to the online map-generating program).

Finally, by providing a variety of options and understanding the desired outcome for the learners (as determined by the goal), the teacher lowers the risk of inadvertently putting in place "construct-irrelevant" barriers. The *construct* is the design of the lesson and assessments that are based on the goal. A construct-irrelevant barrier would be an assignment, activity, or assessment (i.e., an assessment question or design) that pulls learners away from the central learning or the outcome. For example, having all of the learners write a paper about the settlers would be a construct-irrelevant barrier. Many learners with intellectual disability, and some of their peers, would likely struggle with the assignment because the assigned task (i.e., writing) would limit their ability to express their knowledge, whereas these same learners might be successful expressing their knowledge about the settlers using a different mode. In line with the discussion about flexibility, educators must watch for construct-irrelevant barriers introduced in lesson plans and goals, be they technology tools, assignments, or assessments.

Designing the Environment

UDL suggests teachers shift from the act of planning to the act of designing. Specifically, teachers should plan not only the lesson but also the environment (Nelson, 2014). The environment in which learners learn is a crucial part of their experience. The environment includes the layout of the room, the resources available to the learners (e.g., books, seating options, digital tools, writing utensils, etc.), and the interactions between the learner and peers as well as the interactions between the learner and the teacher. The environment is not only a place filled with tactile objects, but there are also systems in place that communicate certain messages to learners. Those messages are delivered via classroom rules, daily operations (e.g., how the classroom is run), and communication patterns (e.g., consistent comments that occur daily to guide or redirect learners). The implementation of the lesson occurs within the environment; therefore, the design of this environment directly impacts the outcomes of the lesson.

Borrowing from the fields of architecture (Connell et al., 1997) and industrial design (Holm, 2006), when we design a lesson or environment, we create a plan that integrates the aesthetic and functional components of an environment. UDL builds on this concept, considering how the environment impacts learners' emotional connection to learning as well as the learners' access, both physical and cognitive, to resources, information, and skill acquisition. UDL provides guidance in how to design lessons and environments to meet these needs.

Variability

Another foundational element of UDL is variability (Meyer, Rose, & Gordon, 2014). Neuroscientists have helped us understand that there are billions of neurons in our brains. These neurons connect when we learn new information or we connect new learning to current understanding. The way those connections are made, though, are unique and those unique connections make us all unique learners. Just as we would never expect everyone in a road race to wear the same-sized running shoe and then run their best races, we should not expect all learners to learn the same way and then experience their best outcomes (Rose, 2012). We should not expect Person A to learn new information or a new skill the exact same way Person B learns that information. Due to life experiences, Person A will always walk into a learning environment with different background information and experiences than Person B. If we add in factors such as disability, socioeconomic status, and culture, we can begin to see how differently each learner will connect to learning.

A second dynamic related to variability is unpredictable variability (Meyer, Rose, & Gordon, 2014). While variability refers to the needs we predict our learners will have (e.g., some students have higher support needs while others have lower support needs when completing a task), unpredictable variability refers to the everyday occurrences that affect learning and teaching. These can range from the loss of Internet connection to a fight on the playground that affects the mood in the classroom. As educators become more familiar with UDL, they can mentally sort through their on-hand tools and strategies and choose which are appropriate for the context and lesson.

Expert Learner

As stated earlier, the initial goal of UDL was to make learning accessible to learners with disabilities. That goal has widened to making learning accessible to all. When learning is made accessible through the implementation of the UDL framework, students move toward becoming expert learners. An expert learner is motivated and finds purpose in his or her learning, is knowledgeable and resourceful during the process of learning, and is strategic and goal directed throughout the process of learning (CAST, 2011).

These skill sets are learned and cannot be acquired when the environment does not actively promote them. This means that learners need consistent opportunities to identify and find purpose and meaning in what they are learning. They must be shown how learning connects back to their lives and then encouraged to seek their own examples of those connections. Beyond the typical, "When am I ever going to use this?" question, all learners need to be supported to wonder how their day-to-day interactions with peers will impact their lives. Teachers can support and guide students to see connections and identify meaning and purpose.

Learners also need to have opportunities to identify and use different resources so they can own their knowledge. When we constantly place resources in learners' hands and then have them regurgitate what they have read or heard, we are denying them opportunities to explore and identify what resources serve them best and how they can apply acquired knowledge. Learners need to be provided a variety of resources from which to choose (even if that variety starts with two resources) so they can begin to investigate their needs, strengths, and preferences.

Finally, all learners need to be strategic in their thinking and actions. It does not matter the type of task or activity that learners are engaged in, they have to be strategic in their thinking. What will be their first step? Are there steps they can skip, or do they need to take them all? Do they need to add in any steps to complete the task successfully? Similarly, learners need to be goal-directed in their daily lives. Whether they are solving math problems or planning a social event for the weekend, they need to understand what they can accomplish in a set amount of time, what steps they need to take to accomplish a larger goal, and how to identify when they have reached their goal. Combined, these components demonstrate the actions of an expert learner.

UDL and Technology

Because technology was such an integral part of the conception of UDL, people often think that the two are inexorably linked. It is true that technology tools, with their potential for flexibility and accessibility, can make implementing the UDL framework much more efficient and in some cases more effective. However, the UDL framework itself does not require access to technology (Rose, Gravel, & Domings, 2012). In the next sections, however, ways that technology tools can be used to support UDL implementation are described, with an emphasis on both low- and no-tech options as well as high-tech options. The emphasis is on elucidating the concepts of UDL and how they can be applied in an environment without or with digital technology access and infrastructure.

What Is Technology?

> Technology is just a tool. In terms of getting the kids working together and motivating them, the teacher is the most important.
>
> (Bill Gates, founder of Microsoft, 1997, cited in Knowles, 1999)

When we think of technology in the classroom, we often think of computers plugged into the wall at the corner of the room, a laptop on a teacher's desk, an LCD projector shining slide shows onto a screen, or a cart containing tablets that are so popular they can be scheduled only every two months. But technology can be the pencil a learner uses to write down the steps in solving a math problem or the chalkboard at the front of the classroom where the teacher writes homework assignments and the week's planner. Technology does not need to plug into the wall to be transformative, but we do need to understand its role.

Technology can be defined as a tool used to solve a particular problem. The pencil solved a problem of insufficient working memory: We needed a way to record and save things to show others or use later. The chalkboard solved a problem of communication: We needed a way to convey information to a large group and refer to it visually over time. What problems do computers solve? Are we using them to solve already-solved problems? Are we using them to solve those problems more efficiently and effectively? Or are we using them to transform our practice, engage our learners in new ways, give our learners opportunities to express and act on what they know using the strengths of the medium, and represent our content and our process in ways that recognize the variability of the learners to whom we are responsible?

Januszewski and Molenda (2008) define the concept of educational technology as "the study and ethical practice of facilitating learning and improving performance by creating, using, and managing appropriate technological processes and resources" (p. 141). In the classroom of the 21st century, we think of educational technology hardware as devices we plug into the wall, and educational technology as digital technologies used to enhance learning. For our purposes in this chapter, when we discuss educational technology we are referring to digital technologies (hardware and software) used in educational contexts.

Variability in Access to Technology

Classrooms can have no digital devices, a few digital devices, or a digital device for each learner and teacher. Connectivity can also vary within classrooms, with some districts developing robust wireless Internet infrastructures and others able to connect to the Internet only at specific portals in each building. With initiatives like Bring Your Own Device (BYOD; see Burns-Sardone, 2014) and one-to-one laptop or tablet programs (Penuel, 2006) where every learner has access to their own device, connectivity is becoming increasingly essential to a technology-rich learning environment. As cloud-based resources and tools become more ubiquitous in our everyday lives, schools are scrambling to meet the demand for faster and more connections while at the same time addressing issues of equity among learner populations—and though digital technology can certainly help support learners, often in a highly efficient way, many of the features and tools can be implemented in a low-tech or no-tech way.

For example, it is quite convenient to find an online reading program with a built-in glossary that highlights particular vocabulary terms and provides just-in-time definitions with the click of a mouse or a tap of a tablet screen. A similar type of functionality can be achieved with glossary term definitions on individual notecards and highlighted terms on a paper copy of the reading assignment. The low-tech version of this functionality certainly requires a bit more work on the educator and/or learner's part, but it may be worth the extra steps if the learner benefits from this functionality and a technology-rich equivalent is not available.

A technology-rich classroom does not require a digital, Internet-connected device for every learner, nor does it require constant use of digital technologies or a paperless environment. A technology-rich classroom utilizes the technology available to maximize learning and minimize barriers to that learning. Technology is integrated into learners' and teachers' daily activities, just as the pencil and the chalkboard.

As we move toward true digital technology integration in our classrooms, as more educators transform their practice to take full advantage of the promise and flexibility of digital technology, we think less about the tools and apps themselves and more about the goals of our instruction and how the digital tools can support and enhance learning.

Educational Technology with Purpose

Educators often ask questions such as, "Which app will work best for my students with intellectual disability?" There are several problems with this question, beginning with the focus on a specific app. In the field of digital technology, apps, software, and even hardware change, evolve, and become obsolete over relatively short periods of time. Tools that were popular and useful one year may be seen as old and defunct the next. Refocusing the question on features of tools, capabilities of tools, and supports within tools helps circumvent the digital expiration date of the latest and greatest educational technology and helps bring the focus back to the instructional goal. The other problem with this question is the assumption that all learners with a specific disability label learn the same way and have the same needs. Depending on the instructional goal, different supports and scaffolds may be beneficial regardless of special education category or lack of one.

A rephrased and more purposeful question might be, "We're reading *Call of the Wild* in our 6th-grade language arts class. What types of tools and features should I look for in a digital reader to support vocabulary knowledge and access to background information as my students read?" With the question phrased in this way, we know that the teacher is working on reading comprehension (vocabulary and background knowledge) and we can recommend features and supports such as a glossary or dictionary, the ability to highlight and gather words and phrases for later reference and discussion, access to historical references for other background information, and text-to-speech tools for reading fluency since decoding was not mentioned as an instructional goal for this task. In this manner, educators can seek out tools and apps that either have these features built in or can cobble together a suite of apps and tools that provide reading supports learners can choose to use as they read.

Assistive Technology and Educational Technology

Though assistive technology is often seen as separate from educational technology, an educational technology tool to one learner may be seen as an assistive technology tool to another. Assistive technologies typically provide the learner with physical or intellectual access to content, communication, or learning environments, while educational technologies tend to focus on skills practice and application, content management, and content creation. It is easy to recognize the overlap when looking at the purpose of a particular tool. For example, a learner with low vision may consider text-to-speech tools as an assistive technology and this may be identified as such in his or her IEP. An educator may also choose to install text-to-speech tools on classroom devices so that any learner can access those supportive tools at any time as an educational technology. In other words, what is necessary to some may be helpful to all, which is a core assumption in UDL. In fact, assistive technologies are highlighted in the UDL guidelines (CAST, 2011) under the principle of providing multiple means of action and expression.

There are several thorough and supportive resources about assistive technology, including the *QIAT Community's Quality Indicators for Assistive Technology: A Comprehensive Guide to Assistive Technology Services* (QIAT Leadership Team, 2015). This research-based resource defines eight areas important to the development and delivery of assistive technology services, including consideration of assistive technology needs, assessment of assistive technology needs, assistive technology in the IEP, assistive technology implementation, evaluation of effectiveness of assistive technology, assistive technology in transition, administrative support for assistive technology, and assistive technology professional development. In the following sections, we will discuss educational technologies that may be considered assistive to some learners and special considerations required for assistive technology acquisition and integration within the IEP team.

Instructional Applications of UDL

In the following three sections, we will explore three topics with relation to UDL in instructional settings: communication, functional learning, and academics. The first section discusses the importance of communication options for learners with intellectual disability and how technology can support options for communication within the UDL framework. The second section focuses on functional learning, including executive functions and strategies required to become a functional learner. This section also includes examples of supporting executive function skills through technology tools. The final section discusses academic learning and the types of technology supports and scaffolds available to facilitate inclusion within a typical academic curriculum.

It is important to note, as Rose, Hasselbring, Stahl, and Zabala (2005) remind us:

> While providing accessible spaces and materials is often essential to learning, it is not sufficient. Success requires that the components of pedagogy—the techniques, methods, scaffolds, and processes that are embedded in classrooms and curricula—are also accessible, and that the measure of their success is learning.
>
> *(p. 509)*

In other words, true inclusion in a UDL learning environment requires planning and design beyond access to content (accessibility, in a traditional sense). It requires the belief that all learners are capable and willing to learn and there must be intentionally designed learning experiences that honor this belief. Designing our goals, assessments, methods, and materials with this ideal in mind transforms how we see learners and how learners see themselves. It is how our learning environments become learning communities.

Communication

For an environment to serve the purpose of education, that environment must provide learners the opportunity to communicate with educators and peers. The purpose of communication can range from the educator sharing information with the learners to the learners expressing their knowledge or the skills gained. This bidirectional communication enables and facilitates learning. The communication modes might be verbal, nonverbal, involve technology, or not involve technology. Communication modes in the classroom can include speaking, singing, punctuated vocalizations (e.g., a short burst of sound), facial expressions, hand gestures, body movement, overall body language, tapping an icon, pressing a button with an assigned message, or pointing to a specific picture. Regardless of the mode used, communication is a mandatory component of any learning environment because an effective learning environment establishes a community of learners—and communication is the cornerstone of building that community.

The utilization of UDL to design the learning environment is crucial when considering communication. This is because all learners vary in how they communicate and vary in the way they communicate within different environments and with different people. For example, while a learner might be interested in using his or her tablet to make requests in one classroom, he or she might not even take the tablet out of the bag in the other classroom, preferring to use gestures, facial expressions, and vocalizations. As with any learner, these preferences need to be honored and expected. This is an example of predictable variability related to communication; when it comes to designing lessons, the construction of the goal is where to begin.

As discussed within the section on UDL, the goal of the lesson determines the design of the lesson. Once that goal has been determined, the educator can return to the UDL guidelines and begin to explore the best options that allow all of the learners to communicate their current and learned knowledge and skills. When the goal is written without the means (e.g., "Students will describe the paths early settlers used to explore North America"), the educator now has the flexibility necessary to provide each learner the options necessary to communicate. For some learners, that will mean writing and speaking. For others, that might mean the use of assistive technology. If a specific type of communication is required within the standard, educators can scaffold the means used and support the learners in achieving that goal. From this point, the educator can select tools and resources that provide learners the opportunity to communicate their growth. The following sections addressing functional learners and academics include scenarios that demonstrate how a lesson can be designed to provide the opportunity for communication between peers and with the teacher, thus establishing a healthy learning community.

Functional Learning

Developing skills to become functional learners is a crucial component to becoming both self-sufficient and a member of the community. Today we support learners with intellectual disability as they acquire these skills as an integrated part of daily instruction, but that was not always the case.

In the 1970s, students with intellectual disability often were often educated using curricula based on discrete stages of human development rather than the age-based learning their peers in general education experienced. The belief was these students advanced through developmental stages on their way to adulthood and there was a sequence to these stages. The outcome was that students with intellectual disability often received instruction typically reserved for infants or very young children (Brown et al., 1979). A subsequent backlash emerged against those curricula as parents and professionals recognized that the curricula were not age appropriate.

Advocates encouraged an instructional shift that emphasized functional skills. Skills such as cooking, shopping, personal care, the use of public transportation and housekeeping were seen as necessary within the home, work, and community environments (Brown, Branston, Hamre-Nietupski, Pumpian, Certo, & Gruenewald, 1979). Instruction focused on activities and skill building related to the actions and activities of their same-aged peers. For example, learners who had been working on their fine motor skills by sorting buttons practiced that same fine motor skill by identifying and sorting coins with the goal of purchasing their favorite soda or coffee at a restaurant. Key to the design of these experiences was the process of skill delineation—breaking down the overall task and understanding what skills were necessary to participate in this task (Belmore & Brown, 1978). Preferably, learners were to participate in as much of the activity as possible. Instead of an all-or-nothing campaign where learners were allowed to participate only if they could complete the task independently, learners were supported to participate as independently as possible throughout the entire process (Belmore & Brown, 1978). This mindset was crucial for the next step of the inclusion movement.

The inclusion movement of the 1990s brought an additional emphasis on academic inclusion (Freeman & Alkin, 2000), social inclusion (Juvonen & Bear, 1992), and self-determination (Wehmeyer, 1996, 1997). The 2000s brought the age of academic standards and accountability (Browder et al., 2007), a new frontier that pushed educators to consider another aspect of functional skills: what skills students needed to engaging the process of learning. Learners, including those with intellectual disability, needed supports and opportunities to improve their executive functioning.

Executive functioning is our ability to organize and act on information (Morin, 2015). Goal identification, follow-through on that goal, and the use of problem solving are all a part of executive functioning—and those skills are a part of successfully implementing functional skills. Each of those subcategories fall under the term "working memory," which is our ability to "store and manipulate information in our mind for brief periods of time" (Alloway, 2010, p. 448). The ability to be flexible and plan are also part of our working memory (Alloway, 2010). To successfully implement functional skills, learners—including those with intellectual disability—need to be supported to strengthen and utilize their executive functioning skills.

The UDL framework is grounded in providing scaffolding for executive functioning skills, which are essential to becoming expert learners. Using the framework enables educators to design lessons and activities focused on executive functioning skills, building in the supports learners need to be successful.

For example, a learner goal might be, "travel independently from home to the grocery store using public transportation." If an educator focuses on "providing options for executive functions" from the UDL guidelines and the related checkpoints (see Figure 14.2), the following options could be embedded in the lesson:

- Break down the larger task into smaller, more manageable steps. For example, the learner may decide to create a to-do list or set of directions to follow as the journey is made, offloading the working memory effort required to hold these steps in one's memory for long periods of time. This can be accomplished jointly with the learner with the teacher using a scaffolded process. The emphasis might be on using high-tech tools, low- or no-tech tools, or a combination of these. Tools that support list creation and management, geolocation-triggered reminders, mapping programs that integrate with public transportation schedules, and wearable GPS devices require significant access to Internet-connected technology but may be highly useful. However, paper lists and a pen or pencil can also be used to keep track of the steps in the process and have the added benefit of being a backup if the high-tech gadgets fail.

- Allow the learner to choose which type of public transportation to use based on availability (bus, subway, train or light rail, or a combination) and scaffold the decision-making process. Part of using public transportation requires careful forethought about scheduling, time management, and ease of access. There may be several different available options to get from Point A to Point B, but which is most efficient? Which type of transportation will arrive at the time needed? Which type of transportation is most enjoyable and comfortable? Online tools such as maps integrated with public transportation timetables and apps that alert riders to arriving vehicles and delays, and low-tech tools such as videos that show the different options for public transportation and paper lists of the pros and cons of each type of transportation can assist in the decision-making process.

- Practice the steps of the process, gradually releasing scaffolds as the learner becomes more independent. Learners at different stages and levels of practice with using public transportation or navigating independently require different levels of scaffolding from physical guidance and in-person monitoring or prompting to fully independent navigation with the assistance of symbol or image reminder lists at each juncture of the journey. Creating videos and photographs during practice runs can provide the material needed when the learner becomes more independent and requires only visual reminders or steps. Hand-held devices can capture and display these videos and photographs, while integration with an online Boardmaker program can create image- and video-oriented schedules accessed through the same device. With little or no technology, a similar visual schedule can be created through paper Boardmaker programs or printed photographs taped in sequence on a piece of plain paper.

Through the use of high- and low/no-tech tools partnered with the UDL framework, educators can establish a learning environment that supports learners with intellectual disability as they gain the skills necessary to participate in their communities as well as our accountability and standards driven settings.

Box 14.3 provides an example of how a student, Diego, utilizes several technology tools to support executive functioning and facilitate functional skills while working in groups. The educators in the scenario, Ms. Jones and Mr. Marcus, have chosen tools that support and scaffold the skills Diego struggles with, using the principle of action and expression as guidance. For example, Diego uses a to-do list app to keep track of and monitor his progress through the salt dough recipe and constructing the salt dough map. He uses the timer to facilitate reminders for turn taking during the mixing process. He uses his tablet to take photos and videos to document the process and has the option to review these artifacts later if he's asked to do a project like this again. Through these technology tools, Diego is a participating member of his class, engaging and demonstrating his learning alongside his classmates.

Box 14.3

Ms. Jones's students are busy working on their projects showing the paths early settlers used as they explored North America. Diego, one of her students with intellectual disability, has chosen to partner with two nondisabled peers to create a salt dough map. Diego needs support with directions and task completion during projects such as this and often has difficulty remembering to take turns when working in small groups.

Ms. Jones gathers groups who have chosen to create salt dough maps together to help them organize their materials. She has some students cut cardboard and construction paper, some mix and measure paints, some gather other materials like toothpicks and popsicle sticks from the classroom cupboard to divide evenly among the groups, and some help measure and mix the salt dough recipe. She asks Diego if he would help the group follow the recipe and measure the ingredients. She has preloaded the steps of the recipe onto his tablet in a cross-platform app that many of her learners use to keep track of assignments, projects, schedules, and activities.

Diego uses his tablet's built-in text-to-speech application to help read each step of the recipe out loud. After reading the step, another student chooses the correct measuring cup, and Diego fills and levels off the ingredient and dumps it into the mixing bowl. After each step is complete, Diego taps the step on his tablet to complete it and directs the text-to-speech application to read the next step out loud. When all of the ingredients have been added, the students take turns mixing the dough for one minute each. Diego uses the built-in timer application on his tablet to make sure each student has an equal chance to mix.

Back in his group, Diego again uses the app to follow the directions for creating the salt map and discusses the proper placement of the flags and markers to indicate significant stops the explorers made on their journeys. He documents his group's work by using his tablet to take photos of the map in progress, and at the end records a video as the students in the group explain their map and what they learned.

Academics

More learners with intellectual disability are included in the general education environment than ever before (McLeskey, Landers, Williamson, & Hoppey, 2012). However, as clarified by Wehmeyer (2009) and restated by Kurth, Lyon, and Shogren (2015), it is not the physical placement that is most important—it is the quality of the supports provided. Both technology and UDL can play a role in providing those quality supports.

Advancements in how technology can be used to scaffold learning (King-Sears, Swanson, & Mainzer, 2011; MacArthur, Ferretti, Okolo, & Cavalier, 2001; Strangman & Dalton, 2005) along with the implementation of UDL (Dalton & Proctor, 2007; King-Sears, 2009; Pisha & Coyne, 2001; Wehmeyer, Smith, Palmer, Davies, & Stock, 2004) have provided strategies to offer quality supports for learners with intellectual disability in inclusive classrooms.

For example, in a study by Coyne, Pisha, Dalton, Zeph, and Smith (2012), the researchers demonstrated how the use of a technology-based universal design for learning approach, Learning by Design (LBD) along with multimedia e-books, improved the reading achievement of learners with intellectual disability. In this study, nine teachers and 16 learners with intellectual disability focused on phonemic awareness, phonics, comprehension, fluency, and vocabulary. All of the teachers participated in a day-long workshop to enhance their knowledge of best- and evidence-based practices related to the five reading areas as well as strategies for teaching students with intellectual disability. Five of those teachers received additional training on software packages and LBD. The software packages included e-books from two different sources and a set of interactive games and exercises. Each of these software packages were designed utilizing UDL. On average, and after controlling for their initial reading achievement, the LBD group made significant gains in comprehension in comparison to the control group. The study provided outcome data demonstrating both strong literacy outcomes related to UDL-designed approaches to literacy through the intentional use of technology designed using UDL.

Another study by Knight, Wood, Spooner, Browder, and O'Brien (2015) investigated the use of a technology-based tool designed utilizing the UDL guidelines to teach science content to learners with Autism Spectrum Disorder (ASD). *Book Builder* ™, a free, electronic text (eText) platform created by CAST, provides teachers the ability to create e-Texts that include supports learners might need to decode and comprehend the information including pictures, graphics, voice, and hyperlinks to a glossary. The platform includes virtual coaches, visually presented as avatars, which allow teachers to include scaffolded prompts that can either provide text or include a voice that reads the text. The e-Texts are entirely developed by teachers and can either be made public or kept private. The pilot study evaluated whether science content, including vocabulary, literal comprehension, and application questions delivered via *Book Builder* ™ would be beneficial to learners with ASD. Stakeholders included the classroom teacher and four learners. Overall, *Book Builder* ™ was found to be a helpful tool and it increased the learners' science knowledge. An important outcome to the study was the finding that the intentional use of the virtual coaches within *Book Builder* ™ was important for learner comprehension. The specific coaching provided via this tool enabled teachers to support the decoding and comprehension needs of their learners in ways that best suited the learners' needs.

When developing lessons and learning environments, it is important to consider each UDL principle (see Table 14.1). For example, researchers have identified how important emotions are in relation to our learning. Immordino-Yang and Damasio (2007) demonstrated a connection between how learners feel at the moment of instruction and/or within a learning environment and learning outcomes. This simple aspect of the affective networks (i.e., the neural networks behind the principle of engagement) undeniably shifts educators to consider how learners feel when learning and within the environment. Building honest friendships, participating in collaborative work groups and partnerships, as well as a sense of belonging, are important for any learner, including learners with intellectual disability (Carter, Moss, Hoffman, Chung, & Sisco, 2011). This, in combination with support to enable learners to learn academically, can lead to significant and positive outcomes for learners. Learners need to know that they will have the opportunity to learn, that they will have the tools provided to them to learn, and they will be supported by their peers and educators as they explore learning with technologies new to them.

The principles of representation and action and expression tend to be recognized more easily by educators. Because representation focuses on how educators portray, describe, and guide learners in their comprehension of material and concepts, many educators feel comfortable with the principle. As the principle did for Ms. Jones in the Box 14.1, it enables educators to plan for the fact that not all learners learn information in the same way. In addition, learners' abilities to demonstrate their knowledge and skills will vary. Incorporating the principle of expression provides educators and learners with different tools and pathways to explore as they come to know themselves as functional learners. Time management, organization, and goal development and achievement are woven into the principle. All three principles have a place within every lesson and learning environment. Educators are encouraged to use tools developed by CAST (www.cast.org) to support their implementation of UDL.

Box 14.4 shows the potential of planning with all three principles in mind. Because reading decoding is not part of the goal for Ms. Jones's assignment, Ling makes full use of the text-to-speech supports built into the online program, eliminating the barrier she might face in accessing content at a reading level above her current one. Providing multiple means of representing the content allows Ling and her peers to engage in learning in a personalized way. Having access to multiple ways of expressing her knowledge, Ling is not limited by making a map or drawing a picture to show that she has met the goal. As a burgeoning expert learner, she knows that she will be able to express her knowledge best in a visual representation, choosing a creative tool to create a comic strip as her mode of expression, and medium that is highly engaging for her. She also understands that her visual representation may require additional explanation for some. Instead of facing another barrier if she had been required to write an explanation, she uses her ability to verbally explain her comic to others while also inviting them to respond to her work in the same manner. Taking full advantage of strengths, scaffolding challenges, and encouraging high expectations for all learners in the classroom, educators can use the tools to support all the learners through the UDL framework.

Box 14.4

Ling, another learner with intellectual disability in Ms. Jones's class, is also working on her project to show the paths early settlers used to explore North America. Ling has chosen to work independently with some assistance from Terry, the paraprofessional who helps out in Ms. Jones's classroom. Ling has significant challenges with reading and writing, but has a keen interest in visual arts and design. In fact, Ling is the class expert on using online tools to create images and other visual designs and is often called upon to help learners who want to try out these visual composition tools.

Ling spends some independent time reading about the early settlers and their journeys in the online program her class uses. She utilizes the text-to-speech functionality built into the program to help her maintain pace with her classmates and ensure that her decoding challenges do not prevent her from understanding the content of the reading assignment. She discovers that the stories of the early settlers remind her of some of her favorite adventure comics and games. She tells Terry about her idea, and they decide that creating a series of comic strips could be a great way to show the different paths the settlers took as they were exploring North America.

Terry has recently discovered an online tool for creating comic strips and story boards, and introduces it to Ling. Immediately, Ling starts manipulating the characters and creating scenery for her comic strips. She also frequently returns to the reading assignment and makes sure her comic strips accurately reflect the information she's learned. She asks Terry to type in the dialogue and descriptions to fill out her comic strips.

After the comics are completed, Ling decides to upload the final products to another tool that allows her to provide a spoken commentary for each comic strip. She invites her classmates to view and also comment on her project and enjoys the great feedback she receives from her peers and teachers.

Conclusion

Technologies, especially those which are high tech, are continuously being updated, designed, or cycled out. That fact drives the need to use a framework like UDL to choose what tools and resources best support students as they work to achieve the goal and demonstrate their knowledge and/or skills. Tools that support all learners, including those with intellectual disability, can and do have additional scaffolding that enables information to be delivered in an individualized way. Research is linking instructional strategies and tools with the implementation of each of the UDL principles, showing a positive impact on student learning.

Emerging technologies such as virtual and augmented reality, and 3D printing, are still in their infancies, and existing, research-based classroom applications show the impact of high- and low-tech supports for learning. As educators are selecting tools—technology and otherwise—to support the implementation of UDL it is critical to ground decision making in the goals of lessons and address variability. UDL is a framework and not a simple checklist of to-do's; it is that very flexibility that allows educators to use their professional knowledge, skills, and wisdom to create rich learning environments where all students are welcomed and can become expert learners.

References

Alloway, T. P. (2010). Working memory and executive functioning profiles of individuals with borderline intellectual functioning. *Journal of Intellectual Disability Research, 54*, 448–456. doi: 10.1111/j.1365-2788.2010.01281.x

Belmore, K., & Brown, L. (1978). A job skill inventory strategy for use in a public school vocational training program for severely handicapped potential workers. In N. G. Haring & D. Bricker (Eds). *Teaching the severely handicapped, vol. III* (pp. 223–262). Seattle: American Association for the Education of the Severely/Profoundly Handicapped.

Browder, D. M., Wakeman, S. Y., Flowers, C., Rickelman, R. J., Pugalee, D., & Karvonen, M. (2007). Creating access to the general curriculum with links to grade-level content for students with significant disabilities: An explication of the concept. *The Journal of Special Education, 41*, 2–16.

Brown, L., Branston, M. B., Hamre-Nietupski, S., Pumpian, I., Certo, N., & Gruenewald, L. (1979). A strategy for developing chronological-age-appropriate and functional curricular content for severely handicapped adolescents and young adults. *The Journal of Special Education, 13*(1), 81–90.

Burns-Sardone, N. (2014). Making the case for BYOD instruction in teacher education. *Issues in Informing Science and Information Technology, 11*, 191–210.

Carter, E., Moss, C. K., Hoffman, A., Chung, Y., & Sisco, L. (2011). Efficacy and social support of peer support arrangements for adolescents with disabilities. *Exceptional Children, 78*, 107–125.

CAST. (2011). *Universal design for learning guidelines version 2.0.* Wakefield, MA: Author.

Connell, B. R., Jones, M., Mace, R., Mueller, J., Mullick, A., Ostroff, E., . . . Vanderheiden, G. (1997). *The principles of universal design.* Retrieved from: http://www.ncsu.edu/ncsu/design/cud/about_ud/udprinciplestext.htm

Coyne, P., Pisha, B., Dalton, B., Zeph, L. A., & Smith, N. C. (2012). Literacy by design: A universal design for learning approach for students with significant intellectual disabilities. *Remedial and Special Education, 33*, 162–172.

Dalton, B., & Proctor, C.P. (2007). Reading as thinking: Integrating strategy instruction in a universally designed digital literacy environment. In D.S. McNamara (Ed.), *Reading comprehension strategies: Theories, interventions, and technologies* (pp. 421–440). Mahwah, NJ: Lawrence Erlbaum Associates.

Freeman, S. F., & Alkin, M. C. (2000). Academic and social attainments of children with mental retardation in general education and special education settings. *Remedial and Special Education, 21*(1), 3–26.

Holm, Ivar. (2006). *Ideas and beliefs in architecture and industrial design: How attitudes, orientations and underlying assumptions shape the built environment.* Oslo: Arkitektur- og designhøgskolen i.

Immordino-Yang, M.H., & Damasio, A. (2007). We feel, therefore we learn: The relevance of affective and social neuroscience to education. *Mind, Brain, and Education, 1*(1), 3–10. doi: 10.1111/j.1751-228X.2007.00004.x

Januszewski, A., & Molenda, M. (Eds.). (2008). *Educational technology: A definition with commentary.* New York: Routledge.

Juvonen, J., & Bear, G. (1992). Social adjustment of children with and without learning disabilities in integrated classrooms. *Journal of Educational Psychology, 84*, 322–330.

King-Sears, P. (2009). Universal design for learning: Technology and pedagogy. *Learning Disability Quarterly, 32*(4), 199–201.

King-Sears, M. E., Swanson, C., & Mainzer, L. (2011). Technology and literacy for adolescents with disabilities. *Journal of Adolescent & Adult Literacy, 54,* 569–578. doi: 10.1598/JAAL.54.8.2

Knight, V. F., Wood, C. L., Spooner, F., Browder, D. M., & O'Brien, C. P. (2015). An exploratory study using science etexts with students with autism spectrum disorder. *Focus on Autism and Other Developmental Disabilities, 30,* 86–99. doi: 10.1177/1088357614559214

Knowles, E. (1999). *The Oxford dictionary of quotations.* Retrieved from https://books.google.com/books?id= o6rFno1ffQoC

Kurth, J. A., Lyon, K. J., & Shogren, K. A. (2015). Supporting students with severe disabilities in inclusive schools a descriptive account from schools implementing inclusive practices. *Research and Practice for Persons with Severe Disabilities, 40,* 261–274.

MacArthur, C. A., Ferretti, R. P., Okolo, C. M., & Cavalier, A. R. (2001). Technology applications for students with literacy problems: A critical review. *The Elementary School Journal, 101,* 273–301.

McLeskey, J. Landers, E., Williamson, P., & Hoppey, D. (2012). Are we moving toward educating students with disabilities in less restrictive settings? *The Journal of Special Education, 46*(3), 131–140.

Meyer, A., Rose, D. H., & Gordon, D. (2014). *Universal design for learning: Theory and practice.* Wakefield, MA: CAST Publications.

Morin, A. (2015). *Understanding executive functioning issues.* Retrieved from: https://www.understood.org/en/ learning-attention-issues/child-learning-disabilities/executive-functioning-issues/understanding-executive-functioning-issues

Nelson, L. L. (2014). *Design and deliver: Planning and teaching using universal design for learning.* Baltimore: Paul H. Brookes Publishing Co.

Novak, K. (2014). *UDL Now! A teacher's Monday-morning guide to implementing common core standards using universal design for learning.* Wakefield, MA: CAST Professional Publishing.

Penuel, W. R. (2006). Implementation and effects of one-to-one computing initiatives: A research synthesis. *Journal of Research on Technology in Education, 38,* 329–348. doi: 10.1080/15391523.2006.10782463

Pisha, B., & Coyne, P. (2001). Smart from the start: The promise of universal design for learning. *Remedial & Special Education, 22*(4), 197–203.

Purcell, K., Heaps, A., Buchanan, J., & Friedrich, L. (2013). *How teachers are using technology at home and in their classrooms.* Washington, DC: Pew Research Center. Retrieved from: http://pewInternet.org/Reports/2013/ Teachers-and-technology

QIAT Leadership Team. (2015). *Quality indicators for assistive technology: A comprehensive guide to assistive technology services.* Wakefield, MA: CAST Professional Publishing.

Ralabatte, P. (2015). *Your UDL lesson planner: The step-by-step guide for teaching all learners.* Baltimore: Paul H. Brookes Publishing Co.

Rose, T. (2012). *Todd rose: Variability matters.* Retrieved from: https://www.youtube.com/watch?v=8WClnVj CEVM

Rose, D., & Meyer, A. (2002). *Teaching every student in the digital age.* Alexandria, VA: ASCD.

Rose, D., Hasselbring, T. S., Stahl, S., & Zabala, J. (2005). Assistive technology and universal design for learning: Two sides of the same coin. In D. Edyburn, K. Higgins, & R. Boone (Eds.). *Handbook of special education technology research and practice* (pp. 507–518). Whitefish Bay, WI: Knowledge by Design.

Rose, D. H., Gravel, J. W., & Domings, Y. (2012). Universal design for learning "unplugged": Applications in low-tech settings. In T. E. Hall, A. Meyer, & D. H. Rose (Eds.). *Universal design for learning in the classroom: Practical applications* (pp. 120–134). New York: Guilford Press.

Strangman, N., & Dalton, B. (2005). Using technology to support struggling readers: A review of the research. In D. L. Edyburn, K. Higgins, & R. Boone (Eds.). *Handbook of special education technology research and practice* (pp. 545–569). Whitefish Bay, WI: Knowledge by Design.

Wehmeyer, M. (1996). Student self-report measure of self-determination for students with cognitive disabilities. *Education and Training in Mental Retardation and Developmental Disabilities, 31,* 282–293.

Wehmeyer, M. (1997). Self-determination as an educational outcome: A definitional framework and implications for intervention. *Journal of Developmental and Physical Disabilities, 9,* 175–209.

Wehmeyer, M. L. (2009). Autodeterminacion y la tercera generacion de la practices de inclusion [Self-determination and the third generation of inclusive practices]. *Revista de Educacion [Journal of Education], 349,* 45–67.

Wehmeyer, M. L., Smith, S. J., Palmer, S. B., Davies, D. K., & Stock, S. (2004). Technology use and people with mental retardation. *International Review of Research in Mental Retardation, 29,* 291–337.

15

Supporting the Social Lives of Students with Intellectual Disability

Elizabeth E. Biggs, Erik W. Carter

Schools are thoroughly social settings. From the moment students arrive on campus to their departure for home, children and youth spend substantial time in the influential company of peers, educators, and other school staff. Indeed, the social interactions taking place in classrooms, hallways, clubs, cafeterias, courtyards, and other areas of the school are what many students look forward to most about going to school each day. Casual conversations, collaborative projects, and time spent with friends often are at the center of what makes school enjoyable. Likewise, the absence of strong social connections can make school a lonely, anxious, and unengaging place for students. Supporting students socially is an essential aspect of providing a strong and well-rounded education.

This chapter addresses key considerations and promising pathways for supporting the social development of children and youth with intellectual disability throughout the school day. Our particular accent is on the relationships students have with their same-age peers within and beyond the classroom. We begin by addressing the importance of promoting social relationships alongside other academic, behavioral, and other educational outcomes. To highlight the necessity of well-planned intervention efforts, we address the paucity of peer relationships in the lives of many students with intellectual disability. We then discuss seven important elements that set the occasion for relationships to develop among students with and without disabilities. Drawing upon these seven elements, we review research-based practices for strengthening the social competence and peer relationships of students with intellectual disability. We conclude with recommendations for research and practice aimed at fostering rich and satisfying social lives for students with intellectual disability.

The Power of Peer Relationships

Relationships are at the heart of what enables people to flourish. Indeed, decades of research and scores of studies converge around this very simple statement: Social relationships matter immensely in the lives of children and youth (e.g., Donlan, Lynch, & Lerner, 2015; Rubin, Bukowski, & Laursen, 2009). Relationships with family members and caring professionals are absolutely essential, but it is the powerful place of peers that we will consider centrally in this chapter. In almost any school, the lives of hundreds of students intersect in the array of activities and settings that comprise the school day. Through their interactions with peers—within and beyond the classroom—students learn important skills leading to self-determination in addition to social, communication, academic, and other life skills. They encounter ideas, values, and norms that shape their understanding of their world and themselves. The friendships they form provide a sense of companionship, emotional support, validation, and intimacy that can enhance their well-being.

Spending time together brings students a sense of satisfaction and personal enjoyment that makes going to school fun (or at least tolerable).

For all of these same reasons, peer relationships should hold a central place in the education and development of children and youth with intellectual disability (Carter & Brock, 2016; Kersh, Corona, & Siperstein, 2013). Interactions with peers offer a rich context for the acquisition of new skills, provide access to natural supports, and promote growth and learning. This is particularly true when students spend substantial time in the company of peers who do not have similar disabilities in inclusive classrooms, clubs, and other school activities. When occasional interactions evolve into friendships and other supportive relationships, a deeper sense of belonging and membership can accrue. Not surprisingly, thriving socially is central to most conceptualizations of quality of life (Verdugo, Schalock, Keith, & Stancliffe, 2005) and influences overall well-being (Biggs & Carter, 2016; Umberson & Montez, 2010). Put simply, having friends one can count on—people who miss you when you are not there—contributes to a strong sense of belonging.

The Social Relationships of Children and Youth with Intellectual Disability

Most descriptive studies suggest students with intellectual disability miss out on the numerous social interaction and relationship opportunities existing throughout a typical school day. Observational research within inclusive classrooms and other school settings indicate social interactions with peers may take place infrequently apart from active efforts to connect students (e.g., Carter, Hughes, Guth, & Copeland, 2005; Cutts & Sigafoos, 2001; Hughes et al., 1999; Kennedy, Shukla, & Fryxell, 1997). For example, Carter, Sisco, Brown, Brickham, and Al-Khabbaz (2008) reported that the social interactions of students enrolled in inclusive middle and high school classrooms were quite variable and usually involved a narrow range of one or two classmates. Moreover, peer interactions were not observed during one quarter of all class periods. Likewise, Chung, Carter, and Sisco (2012b) found that students with intellectual disability who used augmentative and alternative communication (AAC) and were enrolled in inclusive elementary and middle school classrooms interacted almost entirely with support staff rather than peers. Indeed, low or absent levels of social interaction consistently characterize the baseline phases of intervention studies focused on improving social outcomes across both special or general education settings (see reviews by Carter, Sisco, Chung, & Stanton-Chapman, 2010; Chung, Carter, & Sisco, 2012a; Hughes, Kaplan et al., 2012).

Studies describing the peer relationships of students with intellectual disability also highlight themes of isolation and inconsistent social participation (Tipton, Christensen, & Blacher, 2013; Webster & Carter, 2010, 2013). Two nationally representative studies provide broad perspectives on social relationships in the United States at the elementary and secondary levels. According to parents surveyed as part of the National Longitudinal Transition Study-2, 16% of youth with intellectual disability (ages 13–17) never saw friends outside of school, 42% never or rarely received phone calls from friends, and 25% had not been invited to other youth's social activities during the past year (Wagner, Cadwallader, Garza, & Cameto, 2004). A similar portrait emerged among younger students (ages 6–13). According to parents surveyed in the Special Education Elementary Longitudinal Study, 17% of children with intellectual disability never visited with friends outside of school, 50% rarely or never received telephone calls from friends, and 20% had not been invited to other children's social activities in the past year (Wagner et al., 2002). Studies in other countries reflect similar patterns (see review by Petrina, Carter, & Stephenson, 2014).

Although peer relationships can be limited, adult relationships often hold a very prominent place in the lives of students with intellectual disability. The social circles of students with intellectual disability—particularly students with more extensive support needs—are often dominated by professionals rather than peers (e.g., friends, classmates, teammates, and other acquaintances; see Figure 15.1).

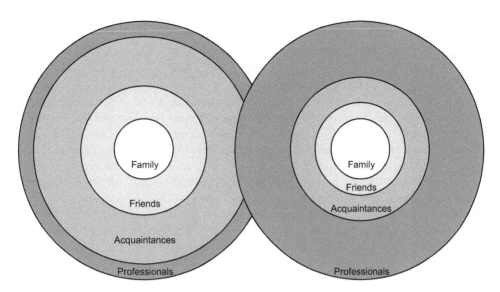

Figure 15.1 Examples of the social affiliations of students with intellectual disability who are well-connected with peers (left) or whose relationships are heavily dominated by professionals (right)

For example, 97% of paraprofessionals regularly provide one-to-one instruction (Carter, O'Rourke, Sisco, & Pelsue, 2009), and these staff report spending an average of 86% of their time in close proximity to the students with intellectual disability whom they are supporting (Giangreco & Broer, 2005). Special education teachers are intimately involved in students' educational lives throughout the school day (Brock & Schafer, 2015; Kurth, Morningstar, & Kozleski, 2014), as are a constellation of related service providers (e.g., occupational therapists, physical therapists, speech-language pathologists). These adult relationships are essential to students' learning and success in school—but concerns have been raised about the extent to which professional involvement can inadvertently hinder social connections with peers (Giangreco, 2010).

We would emphasize these descriptive findings should not be interpreted to imply that limited social interactions and relationships are intrinsic to having intellectual disability. Social outcomes for students in these studies are quite variable: While some students are socially isolated, others are quite well connected. Such variability suggests outcomes are impacted as much by the absence of opportunities and supports for building strong social connections within the school day as they are from the disability-related challenges students experience. Likewise, as we address later in this chapter, relatively simple educational practices have been shown to produce a fairly large impact on the social-related outcomes of students with intellectual disability.

Creating Contexts for Social Connections

Peer relationships can be quite complex. They form and falter, deepen and dissolve, for a host of reasons—some predictable, others unanticipated. Although facilitating friendships requires more flexibility than formula, much is now known about the contexts that set the occasion for interactions to occur and friendships to form among students with and without intellectual disability. In this section, we highlight seven important elements that may substantially increase the likelihood that students with and without intellectual disability will develop positive relationships with one another within schools (Carter & Brock, 2016; Carter, Huber, & Biggs, 2015). Each of these elements may represent a key consideration in the design and delivery of school-based interventions.

Presence

Among the most prevalent barriers to interactions among students with and without intellectual disability is the limited extent to which these students spend time together in the same settings and activities during the school day. Stated simply, interactions cannot take place if students are not in the same places, at the same times, and doing the same things. Yet, educational service delivery models in most schools provide students limited involvement in general education classrooms. For example, only 17% of students with intellectual disability and 3% of students on the alternate assessment have their primary placement in general education classrooms alongside classmates without similar disabilities (Kleinert et al., 2015; US Department of Education, 2014). Even when enrolled in general education classes, students with disabilities may be gone from the classroom as much as 20% of the period—arriving late, leaving early, or inconsistently attending (Chung et al., 2012b; Feldman, Carter, Asmus, & Brock, 2016). Likewise, involvement in extracurricular and other formal school activities can be quite limited for secondary school students with disabilities (Kleinert, Miracle, & Sheppard-Jones, 2007; Schnorr, 1990). A requisite starting point for fostering relationships involves ensuring students have sufficient opportunities to participate in shared activities with others in their school.

Proximity

Even within integrated settings, students with intellectual disability may be on the peripheries of ongoing activities, often even physically apart from their peers. Carter et al. (2005) found proximity of peers to be an influential factor in the occurrence and quality of peer interaction among high school students with and without intellectual disability. Students cannot converse or collaborate if they are nowhere near one another. Chung et al. (2012b) found that even when elementary students with disabilities were enrolled in general education classes, they were not in close proximity to any of their classmates during 41% of the class period. Among high school students with severe disabilities enrolled in general education classrooms, Feldman et al. (2016) found that students were not in proximity to any of their classmates during 58% of the class period. For example, students may have been sitting next to a paraprofessional instead of alongside peers, working at a separate table with other students with disabilities, or gone from the classroom. Efforts to include students socially must attend to students' course schedules, as well as who they are close to within instructional or other activities.

Reliable Communication

Enjoyable, ongoing peer interactions are predicated on students having a reliable form of communication. Yet, a sizable percentage of students with severe disabilities do not have a reliable and understandable mode of communication (Kearns, Towles-Reeves, Kleinert, Kleinert, & Thomas, 2011). For students with intellectual disability who use AAC, it is important that communication systems are in working condition and readily available. Chung et al. (2012b) found that elementary and middle school students who had AAC devices were not in close proximity to their device 60% of the time when enrolled in inclusive classrooms. Moreover, communication systems must include vocabulary content that is appropriate across a range of contexts, including for interacting socially with peers. For example, Chung and Carter (2013) worked with educational teams to identify content for the speech-generating devices of middle school students with intellectual disability that could be used to converse with peers during different types of class activities (e.g., whole-group discussions, small-group projects, lab activities, down time).

Common Connections

Friendships are usually forged on the basis of shared interests, backgrounds, or experiences. Efforts to connect students with and without disabilities on the basis of these commonalities may create opportunities for new friendships to emerge. Approaches can include inviting the involvement of peers who have specific hobbies, entertainment preferences, or other personal interests in common with the focus student; designing activities that incorporate the student's interests; having school staff highlight shared interests; supporting the involvement of students with intellectual disability in clubs or teams focused on things they enjoy; or helping students with intellectual disability develop age-appropriate interests and talents (Asmus et al., in press; Causton-Theoharis & Malmgren, 2005; Koegel, Kim, Koegel, & Schwartzman, 2013). Unless students discover common connections, lasting relationships are unlikely to develop and may dissolve when external contingencies to spend time together are removed.

Valued Roles

The types of relationships that develop among students are likely influenced by the extent to which shared activities involve reciprocal, valued roles of all students. When students with intellectual disability are consistently the recipients of support and instruction from their peers—or have only peripheral involvement in inclusive activities—they may come to be viewed primarily in terms of their deficits or differences (Burns, Storey, & Certo, 1999; Van der Klift & Kunc, 2002). While this may reinforce negative stereotypes, ensuring instead that students with intellectual disability have valued roles within activities may enable peers to see them in light of their strengths, talents, and contributions (Wolfensberger, 2007). Examples of high-status involvement within inclusive activities might include having a leadership role, serving within inclusive volunteer projects, or being assigned interdependent responsibilities within class activities (Carter, Swedeen, Walter, Moss, & Hsin, 2011; Carter, Swedeen, & Moss, 2012).

Relevant Information

The awareness and attitudes of peers may affect their receptivity toward spending time and developing friendships with students with intellectual disability. Limited knowledge about disabilities, uncertainty about how to interact with someone who has complex communication needs or behavioral challenges, or questions about someone's capabilities can make peers reluctant to initiate interactions or pursue relationships. In some cases, providing accurate and relevant information can ensure peers feel confident and competent in their interactions. Broader efforts to equip peers in these areas have incorporated targeted curricula, media, personal contact, and/or simulations (Lindsay & Edwards, 2013). This type of peer training is often successful when it occurs within individualized interventions, focuses on specific information about the student with whom peers will be spending time, and highlights the expectations of a particular activity (Carter et al., 2016). In other words, broader disability awareness efforts may not have the same impact on relationship formation as more individualized and targeted information.

Sufficient Support

The roles of special educators, paraprofessionals, and other school staff can either help or hinder the development of positive peer relationships for students with intellectual disability (Broer, Doyle, & Giangreco, 2005; Russel, Allday, & Duhon, 2015). As students enter adolescence, the persistent presence of adults can limit peer interactions and shared learning opportunities, as well as lead to greater stigmatization (Carter, Sisco et al., 2008; Rutherford, 2012; Tews & Lupart, 2008). At the same time, the facilitative role of staff can be instrumental in creating connections among students and supporting active participation (Asmus et al., in press; Feldman & Matos, 2013). Striking the appropriate balance between providing just enough adult support to promote participation—but not too much to stifle the development of relationships—is an important consideration within any intervention effort.

Evidence-Based and Promising Interventions

The remainder of this chapter focuses on strategies and interventions for supporting social interactions and peer relationships among students with and without intellectual disability. We highlight educational practices that are both feasible to implement and have some evidence of efficacy in the peer-reviewed literature.

Inclusive Educational Experiences

Shared activities over a sustained period of time provide the most fertile context for both social interactions and peer relationships. For students with intellectual disability, limited involvement in inclusive settings—such as classrooms, cafeterias, and clubs—is among the most pervasive barrier to strong social connections. When students attend classes, eat lunch, and travel the hallways with a very narrow set of schoolmates (i.e., only other students with intellectual disability), it is not surprising that their friendship circles remain limited. Increasing students' involvement in inclusive school activities increases their opportunities to meet, work alongside, and interact with a wider range of peers. Indeed, studies comparing social interactions across special education and general education classrooms consistently favor more inclusive settings (see Freeman & Alkin, 2000; Jackson, Ryndak, & Wehmeyer, 2008).

However, it is important to emphasize that inclusive educational experiences are characterized by much more than location and student composition. It is common to see students with intellectual disability who are enrolled in general education classrooms sitting in separate areas from their peers, working exclusively alongside paraprofessionals, or participating in entirely different curricular activities than their classmates without disabilities (Carter, Sisco et al., 2008; Soukup, Wehmeyer, Bashinski, & Bovaird, 2007). A focus on increasing presence and proximity must be accompanied by an investment in thoughtful planning and individualized supports aimed toward full and active participation.

Social and Communication Skills Training

Many students with intellectual disability experience social or communication challenges that can limit the quantity and quality of their social interactions with peers. Strengthening the social and communicative competence of students can be an important focus of school-based intervention efforts. Although numerous strategies for teaching these skills to students have been shown effective (see reviews by Carter et al., 2010; Snell et al., 2010), a particular challenge involves promoting the broad use of these skills across people and places. Teaching social and communication skills in isolated settings or involving only adults in instruction can hinder the extent to which students acquire and generalize these skills across the school day and with multiple peers. More widespread and sustained use of new skills may be promoted by involving multiple people in providing instruction and reinforcement, engaging peers as communication partners, teaching skills across settings, and embedding instruction into naturally occurring contexts. Likewise, the social-related goals of students with intellectual disability should not be crafted too narrowly. The forms and functions of communication taking place with peers can be quite diverse. Equipping students with the breadth of skills they will need to interact with peers across activities (e.g., from social- to academic-focused contexts) and settings (e.g., classrooms, cafeterias, hallways, buses) is an essential part of building communicative competence (Downing, Peckham-Hardin, & Hanreddy, 2015). To illustrate, we highlight several possible areas of intervention focus.

Social Amenities

Being able to greet others, extend a compliment, communicate gratitude, offer an apology, and excuse oneself are important social conventions in school and elsewhere. Such behaviors are not the same as sustained social interactions, but they are integral to being perceived well by others and initiating conversations (Hughes et al., 2012). These social amenities can involve both verbal and nonverbal communication such as smiles, glances, head nods, gestures, or verbalizations. These behaviors can be taught throughout the day through prompting, modeling, or reinforcement (Downing et al., 2015).

Conversational Skills

Participating in ongoing conversations with peers requires a variety of diverse skills: Initiating, making comments, taking turns, maintaining focus on a topic, and asking questions are just a few examples. Multiple approaches exist for teaching these skills—individually and in combination. For example, communication books can be used to help students with and without verbal speech to ask partner-focused questions or to increase the number of conversational turns (Hughes et al., 2011; Hunt, Alwell, & Goetz, 1991). Likewise, modeling strategies can be used to teach children to use AAC to initiate inter-actions with peers (Johnston, Nelson, Evans, & Palaolo, 2003) or make comments about storybooks (Binger, Kent-Walsh, Ewing, & Taylor, 2010).

Social Skills

Successful social interactions often require understanding complex social behaviors marked by situationally specific rules. Limited understanding or use of these social behaviors can impact students' interactions with peers as well as the stability of their friendships. Some students may benefit from instruction focused on skills such as using eye contact, understanding nonverbal behavior and communication, or managing one's behavior. Effective social skills instruction often involves providing direct information about social guidelines, situations, or behaviors that otherwise may be unspoken. In addition, such training may involve chaining complex tasks, coaching and prompting, modeling, taking advantage of opportunities for practice and rehearsal, and providing positive feedback or reinforcement. Social skills can be taught individually or in groups involving other students (with or without disabilities). Social skills groups involve a small number of students and an adult instructor who meet regularly to participate in a structured lesson involving modeling and opportunities for practice, discussion, and individualized feedback on a specific skill (Reichow, Steiner, & Volkmar, 2013). Within both individual and group approaches, various approaches can be used to present, model, and teach specific social behaviors. For example, video modeling involves having students watch peers model a targeted social behavior (Shukla-Mehta, Miller, & Callahan, 2010), and individualized social-focused scripts can help students learn about and practice needed social skills (Test, Richter, Knight, & Spooner, 2010).

Adult Facilitation and Fading Supports

The prominence of professionals in the lives of students with intellectual disability can be either an asset or a liability when it comes to creating social connections. For preschool and elementary students, the presence of a special educator or paraprofessional can be a draw for peers; in middle and high school, the opposite may be true. Across grade levels, school staff should take active steps to facilitate connections between students with intellectual disability and their peers (Rosetti & Goessling, 2010). In some cases, this facilitation may be open and direct. For example, a special education teacher might structure integrated play activities, assign collaborative tasks, or organize a peer group (e.g., Chung & Carter, 2013; Hunt, Alwell, Farron-Davis, & Goetz, 1996). In other cases, this facilitation may be more subtle and embedded within existing activities. For example, paraprofessionals might model positive and respectful interactions, redirect interactions toward other students, highlight interests and experiences students have in common, explain unconventional behaviors, or provide needed information to students (e.g., Brock & Carter, 2016; Causton-Theoharis & Malmgren, 2005). Table 15.1 includes

Table 15.1 Example facilitation strategies to promote social interactions and relationships

Strategy	Examples
Prompt physical proximity	Teacher says to a student: "Brian, do you want to join the group with Paul and Mary for the activity?"
	Paraprofessional says to a peer: "Sarah, maybe you could sit here with Beth for lunch."
Prompt social interactions	Teacher points to a symbol on a student's augmentative communication device: "Can you ask Greg what he did this weekend?"
	Teacher says to a peer: "Would you be willing to introduce Allie to everyone else in the group?"
	Paraprofessional says to a peer: "How about asking Michelle what she thought about the activity when she is done?"
Redirect interactions to the student with intellectual disability	Paraprofessional says to a peer: "That book is for Anita. You can give it to her."
	Teacher says to a peer: "Instead of asking me what Mark is working on, you could ask him directly."
Highlight similarities between students	Paraprofessional says to a peer: "Elise saw that movie too! Maybe you two can talk about what you thought of it."
	Teacher says to a student: "I heard that Paul is a huge wrestling fan. Maybe you can ask him about it."
Prompt academic interactions	Paraprofessional says to a peer: "Can you read the paragraph and talk about it with Mike?"
	Teacher says to a student: "Perhaps you could tell Katie the answers with your iPad and she can write them down for you."
Reinforcing interactions	Paraprofessional says to a student and peer while they work together on a project: "You two are doing great!"
	Teacher gives a student a discreet thumbs-up when he starts a conversation with a peer.
Checking in with students	Paraprofessional says to a student: "How did it go working with Mark and Amy on the group project?"
	Paraprofessional says to a peer who is working with a student: "Looks like you might be unsure about what to do next. Is there something I can do to help?"
Provide information to help support interactions	Paraprofessional says to a peer: "When Matt does not respond right away, it may be because he is looking for the right things to say with his communication device. If you wait a little, he will answer."
	Teacher says to a peer: "When Trey touches your hair like that it is his way of saying he is glad to see you. You can let him know you prefer a fist bump instead."

examples of social facilitation strategies used by educators and other school staff as part of broader intervention packages.

Paraprofessionals and special educators can actively facilitate social interactions in these ways, even as they fade their close proximity and direct support to students with intellectual disability. School staff should strive to promote as much independence as possible for students, while also ensuring they have sufficient support to remain involved in ongoing interactions and learning with peers (Hunt, Doering, Maier, & Mintz, 2009). This might involve adopting a continuum of supports, in which staff determine whether students can participate in activities on their own, with peers, or with additional supports (e.g., self-management strategies, technology, adaptations) before introducing occasional or continuous support from an educator or paraprofessional.

Peer Awareness and Interaction Training

The attitudes, knowledge, and skills peers bring to their encounters with students with intellectual disability can influence whether and how relationships develop. For example, some peers may be uncertain of how to converse with someone who has limited speech, is reluctant to spend time with someone who engages in unfamiliar behaviors, or is unsure how best to support someone during different class activities. Such uncertainty often leads to avoidance. Providing peers with information and guidance related to their interactions and shared activities with students with disabilities can positively impact their motivation and competence. This peer training often precedes or accompanies the peer-mediated interventions described later in this chapter (e.g., peer support arrangements, peer networks, peer partner programs). Although few studies have isolated the impact of this component of packaged social interventions (Carter et al., 2010), targeted training is designed to address prevailing peer-related barriers in schools.

The focus of training provided to peers can vary widely based on the characteristics of the students with whom peers will be spending time, the roles peers will play in these shared activities, and the contexts in which students will spend time together. Table 15.2 displays examples of topics that have been incorporated into peer-focused trainings within the intervention literature. The formats for delivering this training have included whole-class lessons, small-group meetings, individualized instruction and modeling, or a combination of all three (e.g., Hunt et al., 2009; Kent-Walsh & McNaughton, 2005). Peers can be taught a variety of interaction strategies. For example, high school students learned to sustain conversations with their classmates by asking questions and using a communication book (Hughes et al., 2011); young children have learned to approach their schoolmates with disabilities during recess to ask them to play (Kasari, Rotheram-Fuller, Locke, & Gulsrud, 2011); and middle school students have learned how to initiate interaction with a classmate who used a speech-generating device (Chung & Carter, 2013).

Table 15.2 Potential discussion topics when equipping peers to provide ongoing support

- Introduce the student and adult facilitator.
- Discuss the goals of the peer-mediated intervention.
- Share the reasons for involving peers in supporting the student with a disability.
- Learn what motivated peers to become involved in this way.
- Explain the importance of confidentiality and respectful language.
- Provide background on the student's interests, strengths, and preferences.
- Highlight interests, experiences, or other commonalities shared by peers and the student.
- Address specific expectations for peers as they support the student.
- Describe, model, and practice communication, social, and other support strategies.
- Explain and demonstrate the student's AAC system, if applicable.
- Share ideas for conversation topics and alternate modes of communication.
- Provide examples of how to provide encouragement and feedback appropriately.
- Explore ways that peers and the student might connect with each other during other times of the day and outside of school.
- Give guidance on when peers should seek assistance from the adult facilitator.
- Solicit ideas from peers for involving the student in class or other school activities.
- Address any questions or concerns the peers have about their involvement.

Broader informational and awareness presentations have also been widely used in schools (Leigers & Myers, 2015). These approaches involve providing general information about particular disabilities (e.g., autism, Down syndrome) or various disability-related issues (e.g., school inclusion, accessibility) to improve knowledge about and attitudes toward people with disabilities (e.g., Rillotta & Nettelbeck, 2009). Although these awareness efforts can have a place in schools, actual interactions may be more likely to take place when peers receive individualized information about a particular student. For example, providing general information about people with Down syndrome may dispel prevailing myths and assumptions among peers. However, teaching peers about how a particular student uses an AAC system to communicate, showing them how to use wait time when asking questions, demonstrating how to offer choices during class activities, and providing examples of conversation topics based on the student's interests may better prepare them to work with the student within an extracurricular or class activity.

Peer Support Arrangements

A peer support arrangement is an evidence-based intervention for increasing social interactions and shared learning among students with intellectual disability and their peers in inclusive elementary, middle, and high school classrooms. These individualized interventions involve equipping one or more peers to provide social and academic support to their classmate with disabilities under the guidance of an educator or paraprofessional. Peers participate in an initial training to learn more about their classmate and the supports they will be providing in the classroom. Throughout the remainder of the semester, the students work together while receiving any needed support and facilitation from special education staff. As appropriate, the special education staff fades back their individualized support over time and shifts to a broader classroom-based support role. The efficacy and social validity of these interventions have been demonstrated in a range of academic and elective courses for students with a range of support needs (e.g., Brock & Carter, 2016; Carter et al., 2016; Carter, Moss, Hoffman, Chung, & Sisco, 2011). Although peer support arrangements are highly individualized interventions, they include several core components.

Developing a Peer Support Plan

A student's educational team begins by identifying social, communication, and other learning goals that could be addressed within the general education classroom. For example, goals might focus on initiating interactions with peers, asking and answering questions, sharing information, or contributing within a collaborative group. A written peer support plan is crafted to identify how students will participate in various aspects of the class (e.g., arriving to class, large-group lectures, small-group activities, independent seat work, noninstructional times), the roles peers will play in supporting this participation, and the facilitation strategies paraprofessionals or educators will employ. As shown in Table 15.3, peers can provide a broad range of social, academic, and other supports throughout the semester. The educational team carefully considers which strategies to include in the support plan to ensure they benefit the focus student, are feasible for peers to implement while completing their own work, and fit well within the activities and expectations of the class.

Inviting and Equipping Peers

Once a written plan is crafted, peers are invited and prepared for their roles. A wide range of peers can be effective in these roles. For example, peers who are struggling academically can benefit themselves from their involvement. When selecting peers from within the same classroom, educators might consider peers who (a) indicate they want to participate, (b) have consistent attendance and will remain

Table 15.3 Example social, academic, and other supports peers might provide to their classmates

---

Social-Related Supports
- Introduce their classmate to others.
- Model and teach social skills.
- Give advice or provide emotional support.
- Encourage their classmate to interact with others in the class.
- Initiate conversation with their classmate during transitions or breaks in instruction.
- Provide reinforcement for social interaction and communication.
- Encourage their classmate to use his or her AAC system.

Academic-Related Supports
- Paraphrase lectures or class discussions by highlighting the key points and concepts.
- Share books, worksheets, or other class materials.
- Review course content with their classmate.
- Share notes or help their classmate complete guided notes.
- Invite their classmate to work together on a group assignment.
- Work with their classmate in cooperative group activities.
- Write down answers to a worksheet or assignment that their classmate gives orally or with an augmentative communication device.
- Read a section of an assignment or textbook out loud with their classmate.
- Help their classmate be motivated by encouraging them.
- Assist their classmate to keep his or her materials organized.

Other Supports
- Walk with each other from one class to the next.
- Remind their classmate how to follow classroom rules or routines.
- Prompt or model the use of an augmentative communication device.
- Talk about the class schedule and what will happen next.
- Help their classmate manage his or her own behavior.

---

involved throughout the semester, (c) have good interpersonal skills and a willingness to learn, (d) have interests or experiences in common with the student, (e) are likely to receive guidance well from the educator or paraprofessional, and (f) have had positive interactions with the student in the past. When appropriate, educators should solicit the preferences of the student with intellectual disability about which classmates to invite. Interested peers attend an initial meeting—typically 40–60 minutes in length—designed to orient them to their roles as a peer partner. The training session addresses the specific information peers will need to be effective in their roles, such as relevant background about their classmate with a disability, specific strategies outlined in the written plan, and guidance on when and how to seek assistance (Carter, Cushing, & Kennedy, 2009).

Providing Ongoing Support

After the orientation meeting, the student and peers begin sitting together, and peers begin using the strategies they learned to work collaboratively with their classmate with intellectual disability. During the first few class periods, an educator or paraprofessional is close by to model support strategies and offer needed guidance. As students gain experience working together, the adult shifts to a more facilitative role—still encouraging interactions, but fading his or her close proximity. The facilitator may prompt peers or the student with the disability by providing specific directions (e.g., "Can you sit next to Brian and share your notes during the lecture?"), reinforce students for working well together (e.g., "You two are making great progress on your report!"), share information students need to work in more effective or enjoyable ways (e.g., "When Matt does not respond to you immediately, it may not be because he does not hear you, but because he is looking for the right symbols on his communication device. You can give him more time to respond."), introduce needed accommodations or modifications to a particular activity (e.g., "Instead of doing the whole worksheet, Patrice can focus on the top section."), and check in to see how the relationship is developing. The type and intensity of support and guidance staff provide will depend on the characteristics of the student, the confidence and capabilities of peers, and the context of the class.

Peer Networks

Peer networks are individualized interventions focused on promoting peer interaction and social connections outside of the classroom and during noninstructional times of the day. These individualized interventions involve forming a cohesive group that meets both formally and informally around shared activities across an entire semester or school year (Carter et al., 2013). Groups typically involve three to six peers and a student with intellectual disability. Peer network meetings can take place in the cafeteria at lunch, on the playground at recess, in an empty classroom during an advisory period, or during extracurricular or after-school events. During each meeting, students engage in a mutually enjoyable activity (e.g., playing a game, eating a meal, doing a service project, engaging in a leisure activity). In addition, students plan ways to connect with one another at other times throughout the week outside of formal meetings. For example, students might walk with one another to a class, hang out during a break, eat lunch together, attend a club meeting, or get together outside of school. The efficacy and social validity of these interventions have been demonstrated across school levels and students (e.g., Gardner et al., 2014; Hochman, Carter, Bottema-Beutel, Harvey, & Gustafson, 2015; Koegel et al., 2012; Mason et al., 2014).

As with peer support arrangements, an adult facilitator organizes and supports peer networks. Their responsibilities include inviting peers to participate, organizing the group, holding an initial orientation meeting for all students, implementing facilitation strategies to promote enjoyable interactions during the meetings, encouraging students to connect outside of formal meetings, and fading back support as the group coalesces and students take increasing responsibility for organizing future activities. Any staff within the school can serve in this role. Adults who already have strong relationships with a broad cross-section of students without disabilities at the school—such as a coach, club leader, general educator, school counselor, or special educator—can be especially effective at organizing and leading such a group.

Peer Partner Programs

Peer partner programs are formalized efforts to create a more welcoming and inclusive school culture. They differ from peer networks and peer support arrangements in their focus on creating opportunities for *groups* of students with and without intellectual disability to spend time with one another during or beyond the school day. These formal efforts are referred to by a variety of names (e.g., peer buddy programs, peer partner clubs), but share in common the structuring of regular interaction opportunities for students under the guidance of special education staff (Hughes & Carter, 2008). For example, some schools offer course credit to peers to free them up one period a day to spend time with students with intellectual disability in special education classrooms. Other schools have created social-oriented clubs involving students with and without disabilities that meet weekly or monthly for social- and/or service-focused activities. The scope of peer partner programs can also vary—some programs are led by a single teacher on behalf of his or her caseload; others are collaborative endeavors that extend across classrooms. Although rigorous evaluations of these programs have not been conducted, their feasibility and social validity have led to their adoption in numerous schools (Carter &

Pesko, 2008; Copeland et al., 2004). Additional research is needed to examine how they impact the social interaction and long-term relationships among participating students.

The Roles of Professionals in Fostering Connections

Although this chapter focuses on fostering social interactions and relationships among students with intellectual disability and their peers, the relationships students have with adults can provide an indispensable pathway for meeting this goal. In this section, we address the ways in which educators and others might each spur and support relationships from their professional positions. A team-based, school-wide commitment is paramount to providing students the opportunities and instruction they need to forge strong friendships throughout their schooling.

Special Educators

Among all school staff, special educators typically assume the most prominent role in the design and delivery of special education services for students with intellectual disability. They are intimately familiar with their students' social-related goals and arrange the instruction, experiences, and supports students will need to accomplish those goals. From this position, special educators can consider whether students' entire individualized education programs (IEPs) include sufficient social opportunities. Their roles may include carrying out relevant assessments; planning social-related instruction; coordinating data collection across settings; training paraprofessionals to assume facilitative roles; arranging peer-mediated interventions in partnership with general educators and club leaders; training peers; promoting access to inclusive classrooms, extracurriculars, and other school activities; and communicating with families.

General Educators

General educators are chiefly responsible for delivering rigorous and relevant instruction to all of their students. In doing so, they can actively promote shared learning opportunities for students with and without intellectual disability in their classrooms. They can also work to create a classroom culture characterized by cooperation, full participation, and belonging. From this leadership position, they are able to design collaborative learning activities; evaluate the extent to which students with disabilities are interacting socially with their classmates; encourage peers to reach out socially to students with disabilities; collaborate with special educators to provide accommodations and modifications that enable meaningful participation; and work with paraprofessionals to ensure they are promoting, rather than hindering, students' social participation and learning. When peer support arrangements are implemented within the inclusive classroom, general educators can help identify peer partners, contribute to orientation activities, and support students as they work together. Beyond the classroom, general educators often serve as leaders of clubs, athletic teams, and other extracurricular activities. In these roles, they can actively encourage and support the involvement of students with intellectual disability.

Paraprofessionals

Paraprofessionals have an increasing presence in schools around the world (Giangreco, Carter, Doyle, & Suter, 2010). Indeed, more special education paraprofessionals are now employed by schools in the United States than certified special education teachers (US Department of Education, 2014). Many play an active and extensive role in supporting the IEPs of students with intellectual disability—within both special and general education settings. When supporting students with intellectual disability in inclusive classrooms, paraprofessionals can actively facilitate social connections with other classmates, monitor peer support arrangements, ensure students are participating actively in all learning activities, collect data on social and learning progress, collaborate with general and special educators to carry out well-planned supports, and look for opportunities to fade back direct support when it is not needed. In other settings, paraprofessionals may be involved in modeling and reinforcing appropriate social skills, recruiting and supporting the involvement of peers, and carrying out individualized interventions.

Related Service Providers

Related service providers bring specialized expertise to the education of students with intellectual disability. Each can also play a role in expanding opportunities for—or reducing barriers to—social interactions and peer relationships. A speech-language pathologist can ensure students learn critical social and communication skills needed within peer interactions, as well as enable students to use their AAC device fluently across settings. A physical therapist can design treatments and supports to ensure students with physical impairments have access to the full range of school activities. Behavior analysts can design interventions that diminish challenging and stereotypical behaviors that hinder interactions with peers or participation in inclusive activities. Occupational therapists can share ideas for technological and other adaptations that enable students to participate more fully in shared activities with peers. The collaborative involvement of all members of an interdisciplinary IEP team substantially increases the opportunities and supports students will have to build their social competence and connections.

School Administrators

School administrators set the priorities for a school and have an influential role in service delivery models for students with intellectual disability. Attitudes of administrators toward the inclusion of students with intellectual disability vary widely, as does their commitment to inclusive practices (Praisner, 2003; Waldron, McLeskey, & Redd, 2011). These school leaders can play an important role in creating a welcoming and inclusive school culture; prioritizing social relationships alongside academic outcomes; promoting the enrollment of students with intellectual disability in classrooms, clubs, and other school activities; creating opportunities for school staff to carry out collaborative planning and teaching; providing professional development on inclusive practices for all school staff; and encouraging other school staff to play a role in facilitating social connections.

Other School Staff

Other school staff can support opportunities for students with and without intellectual disability to spend time together in supportive ways that foster friendships. School counselors, bus drivers, cafeteria staff, librarians, recess monitors, and other members of a school community also spend considerable time with students throughout the school day. It is these out-of-classroom contexts that so often provide the richest opportunities for social connections among students. For example, school counselors and social workers are well connected to peers throughout the school who might be invited to participate in peer networks or peer partner programs. Bus drivers, cafeteria monitors, and staff on recess duty can ensure the interactions among students during these unstructured times are safe, positive, and enjoyable.

Families

Collaboration with families is an essential element of efforts to promote social connections that extend beyond the school day and over time. Parents can provide school teams with information about their children's strengths, interests, and out-of-school activities that could provide the basis for connections and conversations with peers. Likewise, schools can keep parents informed about activities taking place outside of school so transportation can be arranged. Parents also want to know about the relationships their children are having at school, their involvement in everyday school activities, and the skills they should teach and reinforce at home to promote greater social competence.

Moving Forward in Research and Practice

Strengthening the social interactions and peer relationships of students with intellectual disability has been a longstanding focus of both research and practice throughout the history of federally mandated special education services (Carter, Bottema-Beutel, & Brock, 2014). Although many students with intellectual disability are thriving socially in schools around the world, many others still have few opportunities to meet, learn alongside, and develop lasting friendships with others in their schools. We conclude this chapter by highlighting several pathways through which research and practice might serve to elevate the social outcomes of children and youth with intellectual disability.

First, four types of barriers often coalesce to limit social participation in schools (see Figure 15.2). These barriers include: (a) the social and communication skill challenges of students with intellectual disability (student-focused barriers); (b) the knowledge, attitudes, and intentions of peers (peer-focused barriers); (c) the avenues through which adults support the participation of students with intellectual disability (support-focused barriers); and (b) the limited opportunities students with and without intellectual disability have to encounter one another during the school day (opportunity barriers). Combining intervention efforts in ways that collectively address these barriers may hold the most promise for improving social outcomes in schools. Future research is needed to explore how the various interventions described in this chapter might work in tandem to address social-related barriers on a school-wide basis. To date, most studies have focused narrowly on the impact of individual interventions on a small number of students. Broader application and integration of these interventions should be a key focus of research.

Second, assessing the social dimensions of the lives of students is a complex endeavor. The published literature reports a constellation of measures that could each provide useful insights into the social lives of students with intellectual disability—initiations, responses, reciprocity, affect, interaction quality, social contacts, social status, friendships, and many others. But each individual measure provides only a narrow vantage point into this multifaceted construct. Practitioners should be intentional about assessing social outcomes and selecting measurement approaches that provide a clear understanding of their students' social-related needs, experiences, and progress in a given setting. Ongoing data collection using socially valid measures is essential to ensuring students are making progress in

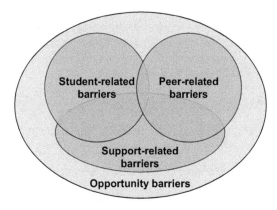

Figure 15.2 Illustration of the multiple barriers that coalesce to limit social opportunities for students with intellectual disability in school

an area so vital to their well-being and success in school. Likewise, researchers should ensure they are incorporating a portfolio of measures that will provide a fuller picture of how students and their peers are being impacted by specific intervention efforts (Bogenschutz et al., 2015). The current literature focuses most heavily on discrete interaction outcomes (e.g., initiations, responses, interactions). Much more should be learned about the type and quality of the peer relationships that form through different types of intervention efforts.

Third, the social relationships of students are influenced by myriad factors, including context and culture. The types of interactions that take place—and are valued most—can vary widely from one setting or activity to the next. For example, the conversations taking place in the cafeteria are usually quite different from those carried out in the classroom; the relationships that form during a group assignment may look quite different from those students develop when they are part of the same athletic team or fine arts group. Likewise, culture can shape where, when, and how students spend time together in a particular school; influence views about disability and inclusion; and impact students' views on intervention approaches and support models. Practitioners should strive to understand how students at their school view and navigate their relationships with peers, as well as the ways in which different types of interactions and interventions might be perceived across settings. Unfortunately, few studies have addressed the intersection of disability, culture, and social relationships. Additional research is needed to explore how cultural considerations should inform the design and delivery of school-based interventions.

Fourth, friendships usually emerge from repeated interactions over time. For practitioners, this reinforces the importance of planning beyond episodic encounters of peers (e.g., a single social activity, volunteer experience, or class project) and instead creating avenues through which students with and without intellectual disability can spend sustained time together over multiple weeks, months, or semesters (e.g., inclusive service-learning projects, shared extracurricular club involvement, enrollment in shared classes). For researchers, this emphasizes the need for more focused study of those factors contributing to peer relationships that sustain—and even deepen—over time. The long-term impact of the intervention approaches described in this chapter has received scant attention. For example, Carter et al. (2016) found that 40% of high school classmates who participated in peer support arrangements were still considered friends of the focus student with severe disabilities one year later. Future research should incorporate a longer time frame for data collection to better capture how friendships might form and fade as a result of social-focused interventions.

Social relationships are of central importance in the lives of children and youth with intellectual disability—just as they are for all students. Educators can play an active role in providing students with disabilities the instruction, supports, and opportunities they need to develop positive and satisfying relationships with their peers. The considerations and approaches described in this chapter hold considerable promise for enhancing the social lives and learning of students with intellectual disability in inclusive schools. Such a goal is not only important for students with disabilities, but it also ensures other students in the school have the opportunity to meet, benefit from, and enjoy the friendships they form with important members of their school community.

References

Asmus, J. A., Carter, E. W., Moss, C. K., Born, T. L., Vincent, L. B., Lloyd, B. P., & Chung, Y. (in press). Social outcomes and acceptability of two peer-mediated interventions for high school students with severe disabilities: A pilot study. In *Inclusion*.

Biggs, E. E., & Carter, E. W. (2016). Quality of life for transition-age youth with autism or intellectual disability. *Journal of Autism and Developmental Disorders, 46,* 190–204. doi: 10.1007/s10803-015-2563-x

Binger, C., Kent-Walsh, J., Ewing, C., & Taylor, S. (2010). Teaching educational assistants to facilitate the multisymbol message productions of young students who require augmentative and alternative communication. *American Journal of Speech-Language Pathology, 19,* 108–120.

Bogenschutz, M., Amado, A., Smith, C., Carter, E. W., Copeland, M., Dattilo, . . . Walker, P. (2015). National goals for social inclusion for people with IDD. *Inclusion, 3,* 211–218. doi: 10.1352/2326-6988-3.4.211

Brock, M. E., & Carter, E. W. (2016). Efficacy of teachers training paraprofessionals to implement peer support arrangements. *Exceptional Children, 82,* 354–371. doi: 10.1177/0014402915585564

Brock, M. E., & Schafer, J. M. (2015). Location matters: Geographic location and educational placement of students with developmental disabilities. *Research and Practice for Persons with Severe Disabilities, 40,* 154–164.

Broer, S. M., Doyle, M. B., & Giangreco, M. F. (2005). Perspectives of students with intellectual disabilities about their experiences with paraprofessional support. *Exceptional Children, 71,* 415–430.

Burns, M., Storey, K., & Certo, N. J. (1999). Effects of service learning on attitudes towards students with severe disabilities. *Education and Training in Mental Retardation and Developmental Disabilities, 34,* 58–65.

Carter, E. W., Asmus, J., Moss, C. K., Amirault, K. A., Biggs, E. E., Bolt, D., . . . Wier, K. (2016). Randomized evaluation of peer supports arrangements to support the inclusion of high school students with severe disabilities. *Exceptional Children, 82,* 209–233. doi: 10.1177/0014402915598780

Carter, E. W., Asmus, J., Moss, C. K., Cooney, M., Weir, K., . . . Fesperman, E. (2013). Peer network strategies to foster social connections among adolescents with and without severe disabilities. *Teaching Exceptional Children, 46*(2), 51–59.

Carter, E. W., Bottema-Beutel, K., & Brock, M. E. (2014). Social interactions and friendships. In M. Agran, F. Brown, C. Hughes, C. Quirk, & D. Ryndak (Eds.), *Equity and full participation for individuals with severe disabilities: A vision for the future* (pp. 197–216). Baltimore, MD: Paul H. Brookes.

Carter, E. W., & Brock, M. E. (2016). Promoting social competence and peer relationships. In F. Brown, J. McDonnell, & M. E. Snell (Eds.), *Instruction of students with severe disabilities* (8th ed., pp. 371–403). Upper Saddle River, NJ: Merrill.

Carter, E. W., Cushing, L. S., & Kennedy, C. H. (2009). *Peer support strategies: Improving all students' social lives and learning.* Baltimore, MD: Paul H. Brookes.

Carter, E. W., Huber, H., & Biggs, E. E. (2015). The importance of peers as communication partners. In J. E. Downing, A. Hanreddy, & K. Peckham-Hardin (Eds.), *Teaching communication skills to students with severe disabilities* (3rd ed., pp. 233–258). Baltimore, MD: Paul H. Brookes.

Carter, E. W., Hughes, C., Guth, C., & Copeland, S. R. (2005). Factors influencing social interaction among high school students with intellectual disabilities and their general education peers. *American Journal on Mental Retardation, 110,* 366–377.

Carter, E. W., Moss, C. K., Hoffman, A., Chung, Y., & Sisco, L. G. (2011). Efficacy and social validity of peer support arrangements for adolescents with disabilities. *Exceptional Children, 78,* 107–125.

Carter, E. W., O'Rourke, L., Sisco, L. G., & Pelsue, D. (2009). Knowledge, responsibilities, and training needs of paraprofessionals in elementary and secondary schools. *Remedial and Special Education, 30,* 344–349.

Carter, E. W., & Pesko, M. J. (2008). Social validity of peer interaction intervention strategies in high school classrooms: Effectiveness, feasibility, and actual use. *Exceptionality, 16,* 156–173.

Carter, E. W., Sisco, L. G., Brown, L., Brickham, D., & Al-Khabbaz, Z. A. (2008). Peer interactions and academic engagement of youth with developmental disabilities in inclusive middle and high school classrooms. *American Journal on Mental Retardation, 113,* 479–494.

Carter, E. W., Sisco, L. G., Chung, Y., & Stanton-Chapman, T. (2010). Peer interactions of students with intellectual disabilities and/or autism: A map of the intervention literature. *Research and Practice for Persons with Severe Disabilities, 35,* 63–79.

Carter, E. W., Swedeen, B., & Moss, C. K. (2012). Engaging youth with and without significant disabilities in inclusive service experiences. *Teaching Exceptional Children, 44*(5), 46–54.

Carter, E. W., Swedeen, B., Walter, M. J., Moss, C. K., & Hsin, C. T. (2011). Perspectives of young adults with disabilities on leadership. *Career Development for Exceptional Individuals, 34,* 57–67.

Causton-Theoharis, J. N., & Malmgren, K. W. (2005). Increasing peer interactions for students with severe disabilities via paraprofessional training. *Exceptional Children, 71,* 431–444.

Chung, Y., Carter, E. W., & Sisco, L. G. (2012a). A systematic review of interventions to increase peer interactions for students with complex communication challenges. *Research and Practice for Persons with Severe Disabilities, 37,* 271–287.

Chung, Y., Carter, E. W., & Sisco, L. G. (2012b). Social interaction of students with severe disabilities who use augmentative and alternative communication in inclusive classrooms. *American Journal on Intellectual and Developmental Disabilities, 117,* 349–367. doi: 10.1352/1944-7558-117.5.349

Chung, Y. C., & Carter, E. W. (2013). Promoting peer interactions in inclusive classrooms for students who use speech-generating devices. *Research and Practice for Persons with Severe Disabilities, 38,* 94–109.

Copeland, S. R., Hughes, C., Carter, E. W., Guth, C., Presley, J., Williams, C. R., & Fowler, S. E. (2004). Increasing access to general education: Perspectives of participants in a high school peer support program. *Remedial and Special Education, 26,* 342–352.

Cutts, S., & Sigafoos, J. (2001). Social competence and peer interactions of students with intellectual disability in an inclusive high school. *Journal of Intellectual and Developmental Disability, 26*, 127–141.

Donlan, A. E., Lynch, A. D., & Lerner, R. M. (2015). Peer relationships and youth development. In E. P. Powers, G. J. Geldhof, S. K. Johnson, L. J. Hilliard, R. M. Hershberg, J. V. Lerner, & R. M. Lerner (Eds.), *Promoting positive youth development* (pp. 121–136). New York: Springer.

Downing, J. E., Peckham-Hardin, K. D., & Hanreddy, A. (2015). Teaching a wide range of communication skills beyond requesting. In J. E. Downing, A. Hanreddy, & K. D. Peckham-Hardin (Eds.), *Teaching communication skills to students with severe disabilities* (3rd ed., pp. 163–188). Baltimore, MD: Paul H. Brookes.

Feldman, E. K., & Matos, R. (2013). Training paraprofessionals to facilitate social interactions between children with autism and their typically developing peers. *Journal of Positive Behavior Interventions, 15*, 169–179.

Feldman, R., Carter, E. W., Asmus, J., & Brock, M. E. (2016). Presence, proximity, and peer interactions of adolescents with severe disabilities in general education classrooms. *Exceptional Children, 82,* 192–208. doi: 10.1177/0014402915585481

Freeman, S. F., & Alkin, M. C. (2000). Academic and social attainments of children with mental retardation in general education and special education settings. *Remedial and Special Education, 21*, 3–26.

Gardner, K., Carter, E. W., Gustafson, J. R., Hochman, J. M., Harvey, M. N., Mullins, T. S., & Fan, H. (2014). Effects of peer networks on the social interactions of high school students with autism spectrum disorders. *Research and Practice for Persons with Severe Disabilities, 39*, 100–118.

Giangreco, M. F. (2010). One-to-one paraprofessionals for students with disabilities in inclusive classrooms: Is conventional wisdom wrong? *Intellectual and Developmental Disabilities, 48*, 1–13.

Giangreco, M. F., & Broer, S. M. (2005). Questionable utilization of paraprofessionals in inclusive schools: Are we addressing symptoms or causes? *Focus on Autism and Other Developmental Disabilities, 20*, 10–26.

Giangreco, M. F., Carter, E. W., Doyle, M. B., & Suter, J. C. (2010). Supporting students with disabilities in inclusive classrooms: Personnel and peers. In R. Rose (Ed.), *Confronting obstacles to inclusion: International responses to developing inclusive schools* (pp. 247–263). London, UK: Routledge.

Hochman, J. M., Carter, E. W., Bottema-Beutel, K., Harvey, M. N., & Gustafson, J. R. (2015). Efficacy of peer networks to increase social connections among high school students with and without autism. *Exceptional Children, 82*, 96–116.

Hughes, C., & Carter, E. W. (2008). *Peer buddy programs for successful secondary school inclusion.* Baltimore, MD: Paul H. Brookes.

Hughes, C., Golas, M., Cosgriff, J., Brigham, N., Edwards, C., & Cashen, K. (2011). Effects of a social skills intervention among high school students with intellectual disabilities and autism and their general education peers. *Research and Practice for Persons with Severe Disabilities, 36*, 46–61.

Hughes, C., Kaplan, L., Berstein, R., Boykin, M., Reilly, C., Brigham, N., . . . Harvey, M. (2012). Increasing social interaction skills of secondary school students with autism and/or intellectual disability: A review of the literature. *Research and Practice for Persons with Severe Disabilities, 37*, 288–307.

Hughes, C., Rodi, M. S., Lorden, S. W., Pitkin, S. E., Derer, K. R., Hwang, B., & Cai, X. (1999). Social interactions of high school students with mental retardation and their general education peers. *American Journal on Mental Retardation, 104*, 533–544.

Hunt, P., Alwell, M., Farron-Davis, F., & Goetz, L. (1996). Creating socially supportive environments for fully included students who experience multiple disabilities. *Journal of the Association for Persons with Severe Handicaps, 21*, 53–71.

Hunt, P., Alwell, M., & Goetz, L. (1991). Establishing conversational exchanges with family and friends: Moving from training to meaningful communication. *The Journal of Special Education, 25*, 305–319.

Hunt, P., Doering, K., Maier, J., & Mintz, E. (2009). Strategies to support the development of positive social relationships and friendships for students who use AAC. In G. Soto & C. Zangari (Eds.), *Practically speaking: Language, literacy, and academic development for students with AAC needs* (pp. 247–264). Baltimore, MD: Paul H. Brookes.

Jackson, L. B., Ryndak, D. L., & Wehmeyer, M. L. (2008). The dynamic relationship between context, curriculum, and student learning: A case for inclusive education as a research-based practice. *Research and Practice for Persons with Severe Disabilities, 33*, 175–195.

Johnston, S., Nelson, C., Evans, J., & Palaolo, K. (2003). The use of visual supports in teaching young children with autism spectrum disorder to initiate interactions. *Augmentative and Alternative Communication, 19*, 86–103.

Kasari, C., Rotheram-Fuller, E., Locke, J., & Gulsrud, A. (2011). Making the connection: Randomized controlled trial of social skills at school for children with autism spectrum disorders. *Journal of Child Psychology and Psychiatry, 53*, 431–439.

Kearns, J. F., Towles-Reeves, E., Kleinert, H. L., Kleinert, J. O., & Thomas, M. K. (2011). Characteristics of and implications for students participating in alternate assessments based on alternate academic achievement standards. *The Journal of Special Education, 45*, 3–14.

Kennedy, C. H., Shukla, S., & Fryxell, D. (1997). Comparing the effects of educational placement on the social relationships of intermediate school students with severe disabilities. *Exceptional Children, 64*, 31–47.

Kent-Walsh, J., & McNaughton, D. (2005). Communication partner instruction in AAC: Present practices and future directions. *Augmentative and Alternative Communication, 21*, 195–204.

Kersh, J., Corona, L., & Siperstein, G. (2013). Social well-being and friendship of people with intellectual disability. In M. Wehmeyer (Ed.), *The Oxford handbook of positive psychology and disability* (pp. 60–81). New York: Oxford University Press.

Kleinert, H. L., Miracle, S., & Sheppard-Jones, K. (2007). Including students with moderate and severe intellectual disabilities in school extracurricular and community recreation activities. *Intellectual and Developmental Disabilities, 45*, 46–55.

Kleinert, H., Towles-Reeves, Quenemoen, R., Thurlow, M., Fluegge, L., Weseman, L., & Kerbel, A. (2015). Where students with the most significant cognitive disabilities are taught: Implications for general curriculum access. *Exceptional Children, 81*, 312–328.

Koegel, R. L., Fredeen, R., Kim, S., Danial, J., Rubinstein, D., & Koegel, L. (2012). Using perseverative interests to improve inter-actions between adolescents with autism and their typical peers in school settings. *Journal of Positive Behavior Interventions, 14*, 133–141.

Koegel, R., Kim, S., Koegel, L., & Schwartzman, B. (2013). Improving socialization for high school students with ASD by using their preferred interests. *Journal of Autism and Developmental Disorders, 43*, 2121–2134.

Kurth, J. A., Morningstar, M. E., & Kozleski, E. B. (2014). The persistence of highly restrictive special education placements for students with low-incidence disabilities. *Research and Practice for Persons with Severe Disabilities, 39*, 227–239.

Leigers, K. L., & Myers, C. T. (2015). Effect of duration of peer awareness education on attitudes toward students with disabilities: A systematic review. *Journal of Occupational Therapy, Schools, & Early Intervention, 8*, 79–96.

Lindsay, S., & Edwards, A. (2013). A systematic review of disability awareness interventions for children and youth. *Disability and Rehabilitation, 35*, 623–646.

Mason, R., Kamps, D., Turcotte, A., Cox, S., Feldmiller, S., & Miller, T. (2014). Peer mediation to increase communication and interaction at recess for students with autism spectrum disorders. *Research in Autism Spectrum Disorders, 8*, 334–344.

Petrina, N., Carter, M., & Stephenson, J. (2014). The nature of friendship in children with autism spectrum disorders: A systematic review. *Research in Autism Spectrum Disorders, 8*, 111–126.

Praisner, C. L. (2003). Attitudes of elementary school principals toward the inclusion of students with disabilities. *Exceptional Children, 69*, 135–145.

Reichow, B., Steiner, A. M., & Volkmar, F. (2013). Cochrane review: Social skills groups for people aged 6 to 21 with autism spectrum disorders (ASD). *Evidence-Based Child Health, 8*, 266–315.

Rillotta, F., & Nettelbeck, T. (2009). Effects of an awareness program on attitudes of students without an intellectual disability towards persons with an intellectual disability. *Journal of Intellectual and Developmental Disability, 32*, 19–27.

Rosetti, Z. S., & Goessling, D. P. (2010). Paraeducators' roles in facilitating friendships between secondary students with and without autism spectrum disorders or developmental disabilities. *Teaching Exceptional Children, 42*(6), 64–70.

Rubin, K. H., Bukowski, W. M., & Laursen, B. (Eds.). (2009). Handbook of peer interactions, relationships, and groups. New York: Guilford Press.

Russel, C. S., Allday, R. A., & Duhon, G. J. (2015). Effects of increasing distance of a one-on-one paraprofessional on student engagement. *Education and Treatment of Children, 38*, 193–210.

Rutherford, G. (2012). In, out or somewhere in between? Disabled students' and teacher aides' experiences of school. *International Journal of Inclusive Education, 16*, 757–774.

Schnorr, R. F. (1990). "Peter? He comes and goes. . .": First graders' perspectives on a part-time mainstream student. *Journal of the Association for Persons with Severe Handicaps, 15*, 231–240.

Shukla-Mehta, S., Miller, T., & Callahan, K. J. (2010). Evaluating the effectiveness of video instruction on social and communication skills training for children with autism spectrum disorders: A review of the literature. *Focus on Autism and Other Developmental Disabilities, 25*, 23–36.

Snell, M. E., Brady, N., McLean, L., Ogletree, B. T., Siegel, E., Sylvester, L. . . . Sevcik, R. (2010). Twenty years of communication intervention research with individuals who have severe intellectual and developmental disabilities. *American Journal on Intellectual and Developmental Disabilities, 115*, 364–380.

Soukup, J. H., Wehmeyer, M. L., Bashinski, S. M., & Bovaird, J. A. (2007). Classroom variables and access to the general curriculum for students with disabilities. *Exceptional Children, 74*, 101–120.

Test, D. W., Richter, S., Knight, V., & Spooner, F. (2010). A comprehensive review and meta-analysis of the Social Stories literature. *Focus on Autism and Other Developmental Disabilities, 26*, 49–62.

Tews, L., & Lupart, J. (2008). Student with disabilities' perspectives of the role and impact of paraprofessionals in inclusive education settings. *Journal of Policy and Practice in Intellectual Disabilities, 5*, 39–46.

Tipton, L. A., Christensen, L., & Blacher, J. (2013). Friendship quality in adolescents with and without an intellectual disability. *Journal of Applied Research in Intellectual Disabilities, 26*, 522–532.

Umberson, D., & Montez, J. K. (2010). Social relationships and health: A flashpoint for health policy. *Journal of Health and Social Behavior, 51*, S54-S66.

US Department of Education. (2014). *Data on the education of students with disabilities*. Washington, DC: Author. Available from http://www.ideadata.org

Van der Klift, E., & Kunc, N. (2002). Beyond benevolence: Supporting genuine friendship in inclusive schools. In J. S. Thousand, R. A. Villa, & A. I. Nevin (Eds.), *Creativity and collaborative learning: The practical guide to empowering students, teachers, and families* (pp. 21–28). Baltimore, MD: Paul H. Brookes Publishing.

Verdugo, M. A., Schalock, R. L., Keith, K. D., & Stancliffe, R. J. (2005). Quality of life and its measurement: Important principles and guidelines. *Journal of Intellectual Disability Research, 49*, 707–717.

Webster, A. A., & Carter, M. (2010). Characteristics of relationships between children with developmental disabilities and peers in an inclusive setting. *Australasian Journal of Special Education, 34*, 61–78.

Webster, A. A., & Carter, M. (2013). A descriptive examination of the types of relationships formed between children with developmental disability and their closest peers in inclusive school settings. *Journal of Intellectual and Developmental Disability, 38*, 1–11.

Wagner, M., Cadwallader, T. W., Garza, N., & Cameto, R. (2004). Social activities of youth with disabilities. *NLTS2 Data Brief, 3*(1), 1–4.

Wagner, M., Cadwallader, T. W., Marder, C., Newman, L., Garza, N., & Blackorby, J. (2002). *The other 80% of their time: The experiences of elementary and middle school students with disabilities during their nonschool hours*. Menlo Park, CA: SRI International.

Waldron, N. L., McLeskey, J., & Redd, L. (2011). Setting the direction: The role of the principal in developing an effective, inclusive school. *Journal of Special Education Leadership, 24*, 51–60.

Wolfensberger, W. (2007). Social role valorization news and reviews. *The SRV Journal, 2*(2), 70–80.

16

Self-Determination
and Goal Attainment

Karrie A. Shogren, Michael L. Wehmeyer

Self-determination is widely recognized as a valued outcome of education (Mazzotti, Rowe, Cameto, Test, & Morningstar, 2013; Wehman, 2012), and promoting the self-determination of children and youth with intellectual disability has emerged as best practice (Test et al., 2009), in large part because of the established relationship between enhanced self-determination and postschool outcomes (Shogren, Wehmeyer, Palmer, Rifenbark, & Little, 2015; Wehmeyer & Palmer, 2003; Wehmeyer & Schwartz, 1997). Enhancing self-determination is also consistent with emerging models of understanding disability that emphasize person-environment fit and strengths-based approaches (see Chapter 2; see also Shogren, 2013). Instructional strategies and supports have been developed and demonstrated to be efficacious in promoting self-determination in education contexts (Algozzine, Browder, Karvonen, Test, & Wood, 2001; Wehmeyer, Palmer, Shogren, Williams-Diehm, & Soukup, 2013), and this chapter will provide an overview of the self-determination construct, assessment strategies to identify instructional needs related to self-determination, and research-based strategies to promote self-determination and goal attainment.

What Is Self-Determination?

"Self-determination" refers to the determination of one's own fate or course of action or the rights of nations or groups of people to autonomy and self-governance (American Heritage Dictionary of the English Language, 2000). The personal use of the term has a long history in the field of philosophy and, more recently, in the fields of psychology and disability. Within the field of philosophy, the term is linked with the philosophical doctrine of determinism. Determinism holds that all action, including human behavior, is in some ways caused, either by the self or by external forces. Philosophers like John Locke introduced a soft-determinism perspective that held that human action can be both caused and free, with a person (the agent) having the freedom to act (or not act) as one chooses, although action itself may be influenced by environmental factors.

As psychology emerged as its own discipline in the early 20th century, the doctrine of determinism was adapted to develop a science of personality development. For example, Angyal (1941) described the development of autonomy or the capacity to engage in self-governance vs. other-governance, as a critical developmental milestone. Thus, self-determination came to describe actions undertaken by a person that were self-caused vs. other-caused. Motivational psychologists also began to use "self-determination" to describe the innate psychological needs that humans have to be autonomous and to feel competence and relatedness to others (Deci & Ryan, 1985, 2002), and emphasized ways that the environment could be structured to meet these needs.

Within the disability field, the term "self-determination" was first used by Bengt Nirje (1972) in a book on the normalization principle (Wolfensberger, 1972). Nirje's chapter was titled "The Right to Self-Determination" and drew on understandings of self-determination as a personal construct referring to the right to self-governance. Unfortunately, Nirje's early application of the construct of self-determination did not exert an influence on the special education field until almost 20 years later, when then US Department of Education, Office of Special Education Programs (OSEP) identified the promotion of self-determination as an area in need of research and model development in secondary transition services, largely in response to the poor outcome data of students, particularly students with intellectual disability moving from school to the adult world (Blackorby & Wagner, 1996). This, in combination with data suggesting that youth and adults with intellectual disability had restricted opportunities to make choices and participate in decisions about their lives (Houghton, Bronicki, & Guess, 1987), led to OSEP funding more than 25 model demonstration projects on self-determination theory development, assessment, and intervention between 1990 and 1996 (Ward & Kohler, 1996). Concurrently, the collective use of the term (i.e., the rights of nations or groups of people to autonomy and self-governance) exerted influence on the disability rights and the self-advocacy movements (Dybwad & Bersani, 1996; Wehmeyer, Bersani, & Gagne, 2000). The disability rights and self-advocacy movements have shaped the availability of opportunities for children and youth with intellectual disability to learn and express self-determination. The focus of this chapter will be on the personal use of the term in the field of special education to define self-determination and development instructional strategies and supports to enable young people with intellectual disability to become self-determining.

Frameworks for Self-Determination and Instructional Design

Emerging from the OSEP model demonstration projects described previously, several frameworks were developed to guide understandings of self-determination and efforts to promote its development in the field of special education (Abery, 1994; Field & Hoffman, 1994; Mithaug, 1996; Powers et al., 1996; Wehmeyer, Abery, Mithaug, & Stancliffe, 2003). Our work to promote self-determination, and the framework that guides our presentation of relevant interventions and supports for self-determination in this chapter was based on a functional model of self-determination (Wehmeyer, 1999, 2003b) developed through the early OSEP projects, that has recently been reconceptualized as Causal Agency Theory (Shogren, Wehmeyer, Palmer, Forber-Pratt et al., 2015). Causal Agency Theory and the functional model of self-determination are rooted in understandings of determinism and autonomy from philosophy and psychology, emphasizing the ability of all people—including people with disabilities—to make or cause things to happen in their lives, rather than others (or other things) making them act in certain ways, while also acknowledging the impact of environmental factors. The functional model and Causal Agency Theory assume that self-determination cannot be defined by a specific list of behaviors, but instead is defined by the function that self-determined action serves for the person. Specifically, self-determined action involves acting in ways that lead to causal agency. In 1996, Wehmeyer, Kelchner, and Richards published an empirical evaluation of the functional model of self-determination that demonstrated its viability, based on the function of actions caused by the person.

Causal Agency Theory

Building on the basis of the functional model of self-determination, but recognizing that a complex construct like self-determination evolves over time as research is conducted that impacts definitions and understandings of human action, Causal Agency Theory was introduced as a reconceptualization of the functional model. The primary reasons for the reconceptualization were related to emerging understandings of disability, human functioning, and strengths-based approaches from social-ecological models of disability and the field of positive psychology (see Chapter 2).

As in the functional model, Causal Agency Theory views self-determination as a general psychological construct that falls under broader theories of human agentic behavior, which adopt the perspective that people are active contributors to, or *agents* of, their behavior. In this context, we define self-determination as a

> ... dispositional characteristic manifested as acting as the causal agent in one's life. Self-determined *people* (i.e., causal agents) act in service to freely chosen goals. Self-determined *actions* function to enable a person to be the causal agent is his or her life.
>
> *(Shogren, Wehmeyer, Palmer, Forber-Pratt et al., 2015, p. 258)*

Central to this definition is the notion that self-determination is an enduring characteristic of a person (i.e., a dispositional characteristic) that can be measured and that develops over time as people experience environmental contexts that enhance the development of the essential characteristics of self-determined action. The process of goal generation and attainment is key to the development of the essential characteristics of self-determined action.

Essential Characteristics of Self-Determined Action

We posit three essential characteristics of self-determined action—volitional action, agentic action, and action-control beliefs—that are defined by several component constructs and elements (see Table 16.1). These essential characteristics refer not to specific actions performed or to the beliefs that drive action, but to the *function* the action serves for the individual; that is, whether the action enabled the person to act as a causal agent. The first essential characteristic, volitional action, refers to people making conscious choices based on their preferences. Conscious choice implies intentionality; self-determined actions are intentionally conceived, deliberate acts that occur without direct external influence. When people act volitionally, they act in a self-initiated manner that is autonomous and they are able to cause things to happen in their lives.

Table 16.1 Essential characteristics, component constructs, and component elements of self-determination

Essential Characteristics	Component Constructs	Component Elements
Volitional Action	Autonomy Self-initiation	• Choice-making skills • Decision-making skills • Goal-setting skills • Problem-solving skills • Planning skills
Agentic Action	Self-regulation Self-direction Pathways thinking	• Self-management skills (self-monitoring, self-evaluation, etc.) • Goal-attainment skills • Problem-solving skills • Self-advocacy skills
Action-Control Beliefs	Psychological empowerment Self-realization Control expectancy Agency beliefs Causality beliefs	• Self-awareness • Self-knowledge

The second essential characteristic is agentic action. Acting agentically refers to self-directed action in the service of a goal. When people are engaged in self-determined action, they can identify pathways that will lead to specific ends to cause desired change. Identifying pathways is a proactive, purposive process and therefore, agentic actions are self-regulated. Self-determined people are able to self-direct progress toward personally chosen goals, and when encountering barriers and opportunities, respond purposively. The final essential characteristic, action-control beliefs, represents beliefs that support and enable self-determined people to engage in volitional and agentic action. There are three types of action-control beliefs: beliefs about the link between the self and the goal (control expectancy, "When I want to do ____, I can"); beliefs about the link between the self and the means for achieving the goal (capacity beliefs, "I have the capabilities to do _____"); and beliefs about the utility or usefulness of a given means for attaining a goal (causality beliefs, "I believe my effort will lead to goal achievement" vs. "I believe other factors—luck, access to teachers or social capital—will lead to goal achievement"). Positive action-control beliefs function to enable a person to act with self-awareness and self-knowledge in an empowered, goal-directed manner. People with strong action-control beliefs have a sense of personal empowerment; they believe they have what it takes to achieve freely chosen goals.

Component Elements of Self-Determined Action

To develop and express the essential characteristics and component constructs of self-determined action, it is critical and children and youth learn skills and attitudes associated with self-determined action, have opportunities to use these skills and attitudes in supportive contexts, and access appropriate supports and accommodations that enable the expression of these skills and attitudes. There are several interrelated skills and attitudes, referred to as "component elements of self-determined action," that can be taught and supported, and that enable the development of volitional and agentic action and action-control beliefs. These skills and attitudes include making choices and expressing preferences, solving problems, making decisions, setting and attaining goals, engaging in self-managing and self-regulating action, self-advocating, and acquiring self-awareness and self-knowledge.

How Is Self-Determination Assessed?

As described previously, self-determination is understood as a dispositional characteristic that develops over time, and is influenced by environmental factors. As such, self-determination can be assessed, individual variation identified, and more importantly for the purposes of this chapter, the impact of contextual factors including instruction and opportunities to promote self-determination evaluated. Through the OSEP model demonstration projects, described previously, assessments of self-determination were developed. Two of the more widely used measures will be described subsequently, The Arc's *Self-Determination Scale* and the *AIR Self-Determination Scale*. Finally, a new measure of self-determination that is currently under development, the *Self-Determination Inventory System*, will be described. Each of these measures has been used in research and practice with students with intellectual disability.

The Arc's Self-Determination Scale *(SDS)*

The SDS (Wehmeyer & Kelchner, 1995) is a 72-item self-report measure based on the functional model of self-determination forwarded by Wehmeyer and colleagues (Wehmeyer, 2003a; Wehmeyer, Kelchner, & Richards, 1996). A total of 148 points are available on the scale, with higher scores indicating higher levels of self-determination. An overall score, as well as subscale scores for the four essential characteristics of self-determined behavior identified in the functional model of self-determination—autonomy, self-regulation, psychological empowerment, and self-realization—can be calculated. The

SDS was developed and normed with 500 adolescents with intellectual and learning disability and shown to have adequate reliability and validity for use in this population (Wehmeyer, 1996). Subsequent research (Shogren et al., 2008) has verified the theoretical structure of the SDS, namely that there are four related but distinct subscales (autonomy, self-regulation, psychological empowerment, and self-realization) that define a higher-order construct of self-determination. The SDS has been used extensively in the published literature to provide a measure of overall self-determination and its essential characteristics to document contextual factors (i.e., disability label, environmental opportunities) that impact relative self-determination, as well as the outcome of the implementation of interventions and supports to promote the development of self-determination.

The AIR Self-Determination Scale (AIR)

The second validated assessment of self-determination, used widely with students with disabilities, including intellectual disability, is the AIR (Wolman, Campeau, Dubois, Mithaug, & Stolarski, 1994). The AIR differs from SDS in that it measures student capacity and opportunity for self-determination. It also includes both a student self-report version, like SDS, as well as an educator and parent version. The AIR-Student version has 24 questions and yields capacity and opportunity subscale scores. The capacity subscale consists of questions pertaining to things that students do related to self-determination ("Things I Do" subscale) and how students feel about performing these self-determined behaviors ("How I Feel" subscale). The opportunity subscale consists of questions regarding students' perceptions of their opportunities to perform self-determined behaviors at home and at school. The parent and educator versions parallel the structure of the student version.

The AIR was developed and validated with 450 students with and without disabilities in California and New York (Wolman et al., 1994). It was demonstrated to have adequate reliability and validity in the measurement of capacity and opportunity for self-determination (see Wolman et al., 1994 for details). Other research (Shogren et al., 2008) has confirmed the theoretical structure of the AIR (i.e., two related subscales—capacity and opportunity—that contribute to a higher-order construct of self-determination). This research also confirmed that while the AIR and the AIR-Student are related ($r = .50$), they measure distinct aspects of the construct. The SDS measures a student's levels of overall self-determination, while the AIR-Student focuses on both capacity and opportunities that might influence self-determination. Thus, the two measures serve different purposes, and educators can select the purpose that aligns best with their instructional outcomes.

Self-Determination Inventory System

Given changes in understandings of disability and human agentic theories, Shogren and colleagues (in press) are in the initial stages of validating a new system of measuring self-determination, the *Self-Determination Inventory System*, based on Causal Agency Theory. Given that Causal Agency Theory is a reconceptualization of the functional model of self-determination, the *Self-Determination Inventory* (SDI) includes items from the SDS, but expands assessment to include domains associated identified by Shogren et al. (2015) pertaining to Causal Agency Theory (discussed previously). Field testing of the *Self-Determination Inventory-Student Report* and a parallel version for educators and parents, the *Self-Determination Inventory-Other Report* is ongoing with students with and without disabilities, including a large sample of students with intellectual disability. The SDI-Student is being developed and validated with students with and without disabilities to reflect the importance of self-determination for all students as well as the need for assessment systems that can be used in general education classrooms with all students, including students with intellectual disability. Initial pilot testing of the tool suggests that it has strong measurement properties in students with and without disabilities, and that the theoretical structure of Causal Agency Theory can be meaningfully assessed (Shogren et al., in press). Thus, the SDI will provide another measure that can be used by educators to understand and support the development of self-determination. The SDI-Student Report version includes an online and paper and pencil version, and the online version will provide immediate reports to students and those who support them on the results of the assessment and links to instructional materials.

Research-Based Practices to Promote Self-Determination and Goal Attainment

As described previously, Causal Agency Theory holds that causal agents act in service to freely chosen goals, and that the skills and attitudes that enable causal agency develop over time, enabling the expression of the essential characteristics of self-determined action. The skills and attitudes, or component elements of self-determined action, therefore, are the level at which instruction can occur. After gathering assessment data, educators and others who support students with intellectual disability can implement instruction targeting these skills and attitudes, listed in Table 16.1, which include making choices and expressing preferences, solving problems, engaging in making decisions, setting and attaining goals, self-managing and self-regulating action, self-advocating, and acquiring self-awareness and self-knowledge. Educators can provide instruction related to each of these skills and attitudes, create opportunities in the learning environment and school community for the expression and use of these skills and attitudes, and provide supports to students to enable them to engage in self-determined action. Students with intellectual disability may need more intensive supports for learning and participation than students without disabilities or with other disability labels, but a wide and growing body of research suggests that students with intellectual disability can learn and use these skills to become causal agents.

Teaching the Component Elements of Self-Determination

Researchers have shown that students with disabilities can learn the skills associated with self-determination (Algozzine et al., 2001) and that teaching these skills can lead to enhanced academic and transition outcomes. Teaching skills leading to self-determination such as choice making, problem solving, and self-management skills augments the curriculum by providing students with strategies to set goals related to academic and transition or postschool outcomes, to solve problems encountered in the process of working toward those goals, and to monitor and evaluate progress toward goals, and towards critical skills for academic and life success (Wehmeyer, Lance, & Bashinski, 2002).

Algozzine et al. (2001) conducted a meta-analysis of single-subject design research and a second meta-analysis of group design studies from any study that had attempted to teach skills related to component elements of self-determination (e.g., choice making, decision making, problem solving, goal setting and attainment, self-advocacy, etc.). Algozzine and colleagues found that when students with disabilities were provided instruction to promote the component elements of self-determination, they were able to learn, use, and apply these skills. For students with intellectual disability, the majority of research on teaching the component elements of self-determination has focused on teaching and creating opportunities for choice making and the use of self-management skills, including promoting antecedent cue regulation, self-monitoring, and self-evaluation strategies.

Choice making (e.g., the expression of a preference between two or more options) has received considerable attention in the literature on self-determination. In large part this was due to a large body of research suggesting that that people with intellectual disability had restricted opportunities to make choices (Dunlap et al., 1994; Houghton et al., 1987; Stancliffe, 1995; Wehmeyer & Bolding, 1999, 2001), and the negative impact this had both on behavior and development, suggesting the importance of teaching and creating opportunities for these skills in childhood and adolescence. For example, Wehmeyer and Metzler (1995) found that people with intellectual disability experienced significantly fewer choice opportunities pertaining to where they lived and worked, what leisure activities they enjoyed, who they spent time with, and so forth. Stancliffe and Wehmeyer (1995) found that choice opportunities varied for people with intellectual disability as a function of where a person lived, with people with intellectual disability who lived in their communities having significantly more choice opportunities than did people with intellectual disability living in congregate settings.

Research has shown, however, that when students with disabilities are provided opportunities to make choices, reductions in problem behavior and increases in adaptive behaviors are observed (Shogren, Faggella-Luby, Bae, & Wehmeyer, 2004). Additionally, creating opportunities to learn and practice choice-making skills can contribute to the development of other component elements of self-determined action. Choice opportunities can and should be infused through the school day. Students can be provided opportunities to choose within or between instructional activities. They can also choose with whom they engage in a task, where they engage in an activity, and if they complete an activity. To teach choice-making skills, picture cues or objects can be used to teach students to choose between two or more activities, with the selection of an activity followed immediately by performance of the activity, with the complexity of the choice increased over time.

Self-Management

To teach and create opportunities for the development of self-management skills, educators can teach multiple self-management skills, beginning with antecedent cue regulation strategies, which involve the use of visual cues—such as photographs, illustrations, or line drawings of steps in a task—that support students to complete an activity that consists of a sequence of tasks. Instead of visual cues, audio cues can also be used that involve prerecorded directions that students listen to. Technologies such as smart phones and tablet computers provide a means to provide audio and visual cues. Researchers have found that students can learn to complete tasks independently using these supports, including complex academic and transition-related tasks (Davies, Stock, & Wehmeyer, 2002; Mechling & O'Brien, 2010).

Self-monitoring involves teaching students to observe whether they have performed a targeted behavior; researchers have shown that students with intellectual disability can learn and apply self-monitoring skills to enhance engagement in academic environments (Agran et al., 2005; Cihak, Wright, & Ayres, 2010; Gilberts, Agran, Hughes, & Wehmeyer, 2001; Hughes et al., 2002) as well as to learn and apply work-related skills (Nittrouer, Shogren, & Pickens, 2016; Woods & Martin, 2004). Self-evaluation and self-reinforcement involve teaching the student to compare his or her performance, typically documented through self-monitoring, with a desired goal or outcome and to administer consequences to themselves (e.g., verbally telling themselves they did a good job). Self-reinforcement allows students to provide themselves with reinforcers that are accessible, immediate, and aligned with their preferences. Researchers have found that self-management interventions can be learned and generalized across settings, and that they can lead to changes in targeted behaviors (Lee, Simpson, & Shogren, 2007; Wood, Fowler, Uphold, & Test, 2005).

Promoting Student Involvement in Education and Transition Planning

Researchers have also developed and evaluated ways to promote self-determination by enabling student engagement and involvement in education and transition planning. Such instruction targets self-advocacy and other component elements of self-determination related to goal setting and attainment in the context of transition and education planning. A number of instruction programs and packages have been developed. Test et al. (2004) reviewed the literature on student involvement, documenting that teaching these skills led to increased student engagement and participation in education and transition planning. A number of interventions have been developed to teach these skills, and in the

261

following sections we will describe three curricula developed and/or evaluated with students with intellectual disability.

Whose Future Is It Anyway? (WFA; Wehmeyer et al., 2004) is a student-directed process to support students with intellectual disability to learn skills that enable them to meaningfully participate in transition-planning meetings during middle or high school. The WFA process consists of 36 sessions introducing students to the concept of education and transition planning. The WFA curriculum is set up to enable students to self-direct instruction related to (1) self- and disability-awareness; (2) making decisions about transition-related outcomes; (3) identifying and securing community resources to support transition services; (4) writing and evaluating transition goals and objectives; (5) communicating effectively in small groups; and (6) developing skills to become an effective team member, leader, or self-advocate.

Section 1 (Getting to Know You) introduces the concept of transition and educational planning; provides information about transition requirements in the Individuals with Disabilities Education Act (IDEA); and enables students to identify who has attended past planning meetings, who is required to be present at meetings, and who they want involved in their planning process. Later, students are introduced to four primary transition outcome areas (employment, community living, postsecondary education, and recreation and leisure). Activities throughout the process focus on these transition outcome areas. The remainder of the sessions in this first section discuss the topic of disability and disability awareness. Students identify their unique characteristics, including their abilities and interests. Students then identify unique learning needs related to their disability. Finally, students identify their unique learning needs resulting from their disability.

In the second section (Making Decisions), students learn a simple problem-solving process by working through each step in the process to make a decision about a potential living arrangement and then applying the process to making decisions about the three other transition outcome areas. The third section (How to Get What You Need, Sec. 101) enables students to locate community resources identified in previous planning meetings that are intended to provide supports in each of the transition outcome areas. The fourth section (Goals, Objectives, and the Future) enables learners to apply a set of rules to identify transition-related goals and objectives that are currently on their Individualized Education Program (IEP) or transition-planning form, evaluate these goals based on their own transition interests and abilities, and develop additional goals to take to their next planning meeting. Students learn what goals and objectives are and how they should be written, as well as ways to track progress on goals and objectives.

The fifth section (Communicating) introduces effective communication strategies for small-group situations, such as the transition-planning meetings. Students work through sessions that introduce different types of communication (e.g., verbal, body language) and how to interpret these communicative behaviors, the differences between aggressive and assertive communication, how to effectively negotiate and compromise, when to use persuasion, and other skills that will enable them to be more effective communicators during transition planning meetings. The final section (Thank You, Honorable Chairperson) enables students to learn types and purposes of meetings, steps to holding effective meetings, and roles of the meeting chairperson and team members. Students are encouraged to work with school personnel to take a meaningful role in planning for and participating in the meeting.

The materials are student directed in that they are written for students as end-users. The level of support needed by students to complete activities varies a great deal. Some students with difficulty reading or writing need one-to-one support to progress through the materials; others can complete the process independently. The materials make every effort to ensure that students retain this control while at the same time receiving the support they need to succeed. Students are encouraged to work on one session per week during the weeks between their previous transition planning meeting and the next scheduled meeting. The final two sessions review the previous sessions and provide a refresher for students as they head into their planning meeting.

Wehmeyer and Lawrence (1995) conducted a field test of WFA, documenting that students who went through the process had increased self-determination, self-efficacy, and greater involvement in their meetings. Wehmeyer, Palmer, Lee, Williams-Diehm, and Shogren (2011) conducted a larger randomized-trial design to study the impact of intervention with the WFA process on self-determination and transition knowledge and skills. They found that when students received WFA (vs. typical transition planning instruction), they showed significantly higher self-determination as well as transition knowledge and skills. Similarly, Lee et al. (2011) conducted a randomized-trial study of the impact of the WFA process both with and without the use of technology to support student engagement, and again found that WFA led to significant gains in self-determination and transition knowledge and skills.

Another curricula that has demonstrated efficacy students with intellectual disability is *The Self-Directed IEP* (SDIEP), which is one component of the *ChoiceMaker Self-Determination Transition Curriculum* (Martin & Marshall, 1995). The SDIEP teaches students leadership skills to self-direct their IEP meeting. Students learn 11 steps, including stating the purpose of the meeting, introducing meeting attendees, reviewing their past goals and progress, stating new transition goals, summarizing goals, and closing the meeting by thanking attendees. Martin et al. (2006) conducted a randomized trial control group study of the SDIEP and determined that students who received instruction using the SDIEP (1) attended more IEP meetings; (2) increased their active participation in the meetings; (3) showed more leadership behaviors in the meetings; (4) expressed their interests, skills, and support needs across educational domains; (5) and remembered their IEP goals after the meeting at greater rates than did students in the control group, who received no such instruction. Seong, Wehmeyer, Palmer, and Little (in press) conducted another randomized-trial placebo control group study of the SDIEP, finding that instruction using the process resulted both in enhanced transition skills, as well as enhanced self-determination.

TAKE CHARGE for the Future (Powers et al., 1996) is another curriculum that promotes student direction in educational and transition planning. *TAKE CHARGE* includes four primary components to promote enhanced students involvement: (1) skill facilitation, (2) mentoring, (3) peer support, and (4) parent support. The process introduces youth to three major skills areas needed to take charge in one's life: (1) achievement skills, (2) partnership skills, and (3) coping skills. Youth involved in the *TAKE CHARGE* process are matched with successful adults of the same gender who experience similar challenges, share common interests, and are involved in peer support activities throughout (Powers et al., 1998). Students are provided self-help materials and coaching to identify their transition goals; to organize and conduct transition planning meetings; and to achieve their goals through the application of problem solving, self-regulation, and partnership management strategies. Concurrently, youth participate in self-selected mentorship and peer support activities to increase their transition-focused knowledge and skills. Their parents are also provided with information and support to encourage their sons' or daughters' active involvement in transition planning. Powers et al. (2001) conducted a field test of the curriculum, and found that implementation led to significant increases in student involvement. In a large randomized-trial study that specifically targeted youth in foster care who were receiving special education services, including students with intellectual disability, Powers et al. (2012) found a significant impact of the implementation of the curriculum that continued for one year postschool on self-determination and quality of life. Youth who were exposed to the curriculum were also significantly more likely to utilize transition services, complete high school, obtain employment, and live in the community.

Promoting Goal Attainment and Self-Determination

In the previous sections, we described ways to teach the component elements of self-determination and to promote student involvement in education and transition planning. In addition to these critical domains, it is important to focus more broadly on promoting goal identification and attainment, as these are critical elements in Causal Agency Theory, which defines self-determined *people* as those who act in service of freely chosen goals. Further, in a narrative metasynthesis of the literature pertaining to efforts to promote the self-determination of students with disabilities, Cobb, Lehmann, Newman-Gonchar, and Alwell (2009) found that there were greater effects of multicomponent interventions to promote self-determination, or interventions that addressed multiple component elements of self-determination simultaneously.

One multicomponent intervention developed to teach self-regulated problem-solving skills in service to a goal is the Self-Determined Learning Model of Instruction (SDLMI) (Wehmeyer, Palmer, Agran, Mithaug, & Martin, 2000). The SDLMI is based on the component elements of self-determination and goal-direct action, the process of self-regulated problem solving, and research on student-directed learning. It is appropriate for use with students with and without disabilities across a wide range of content areas, and can be individualized to the unique needs of students with intellectual disability. In the following sections, we will discuss the SDLMI and its implementation as well as research demonstrating its impact on student outcomes.

Self-Determined Learning Model of Instruction (SDLMI)

The SDLMI is a model of instruction, which is defined as "a plan or pattern that can be used to shape curriculums (long-term courses of study), to design instructional materials, and to guide instruction in the classroom and other settings" (Joyce & Weil, 1980, p. 1). Effective teachers typically use multiple models of teaching to support unique and diverse characteristics of learners within the classroom. However, many of the most common models of teaching tend to be teacher directed. To promote self-determination and casual agency, alternative models are needed that are student directed, such as the SDLMI. Implementation of the model consists of a three-phase instructional process. Each instructional phase presents a problem that the student solves by posing and answering a series of four *Student Questions* per phase. The students learn the questions, make them their own, and apply them to reach self-selected goals. Each student question is also linked to a set of *Teacher Objectives* that provides teachers with guidance on what they are trying to support each student to achieve in answering the questions. Each instructional phase includes a list of *Educational Supports* that teachers can use to enable students to self-direct learning. This process is depicted in Figure 16.1 (Wehmeyer, Agran, Palmer, & Mithaug, 1999; Wehmeyer, Shogren, et al., 2003).

The student questions in the model are meant to direct the student through a problem-solving sequence in any content domain—academic, social, behavioral, transition. In generating a solution to the problem posed in each phase, students learn to lead themselves through the phases of the SDLMI (set a goal, take action, adjust goal or plan) Teachers implementing the model teach students to solve the sequence of problems to construct a means-ends chain—a causal sequence—that moves them from where they are (an actual state of not having their needs and interests satisfied) to where they want to be (a goal state of having those needs and interests satisfied). Students are learning how to self-regulate their actions to reduce or eliminate the discrepancy between what they want or need and what they currently have or know. As mentioned previously, this process can be applied to academic, social, behavioral, or any other valued educational or live domain.

Each of the three phases has four questions that students work through, and the four questions differ from phase to phase, but represent identical steps in the problem-solving sequence. That is, students answering the questions must: (1) identify the problem, (2) identify potential solutions to the problem, (3) identify barriers to solving the problem, and (4) identify consequences of each solution. These steps are the fundamental steps in any problem-solving process and they form the means-end problem-solving sequence represented by the *Student Questions* in each phase.

Because the model itself is designed for teachers to implement, the language of the *Student Questions* are, intentionally, not written to be understandable by every student, nor does the model assume

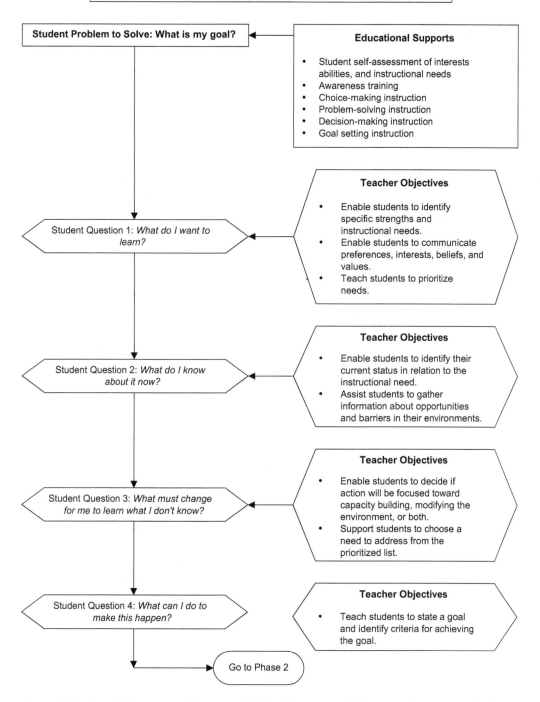

Figure 16.1   The Self-Determined Learning Model of Instruction (Wehmeyer, Shogren, et al., 2003)

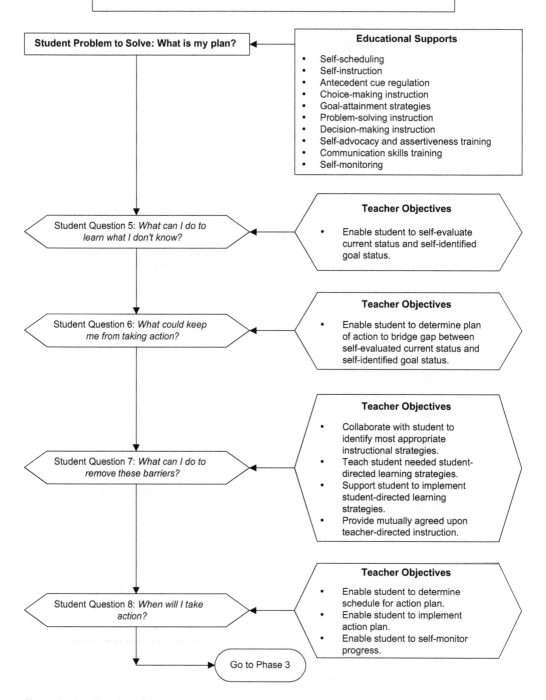

Phase 2: Take Action

Student Problem to Solve: What is my plan?

Educational Supports

- Self-scheduling
- Self-instruction
- Antecedent cue regulation
- Choice-making instruction
- Goal-attainment strategies
- Problem-solving instruction
- Decision-making instruction
- Self-advocacy and assertiveness training
- Communication skills training
- Self-monitoring

Student Question 5: *What can I do to learn what I don't know?*

Teacher Objectives

- Enable student to self-evaluate current status and self-identified goal status.

Student Question 6: *What could keep me from taking action?*

Teacher Objectives

- Enable student to determine plan of action to bridge gap between self-evaluated current status and self-identified goal status.

Student Question 7: *What can I do to remove these barriers?*

Teacher Objectives

- Collaborate with student to identify most appropriate instructional strategies.
- Teach student needed student-directed learning strategies.
- Support student to implement student-directed learning strategies.
- Provide mutually agreed upon teacher-directed instruction.

Student Question 8: *When will I take action?*

Teacher Objectives

- Enable student to determine schedule for action plan.
- Enable student to implement action plan.
- Enable student to self-monitor progress.

Go to Phase 3

Figure 16.1 (Continued)

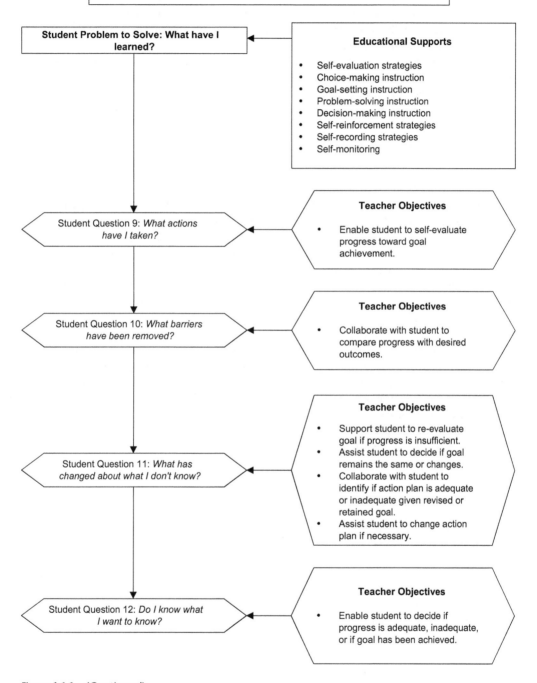

Figure 16.1   (Continued)

that students have life experiences that enable them to fully answer each question. The *Student Questions* are written in first-person voice in a relatively simple format, with the intention that they are the starting point for discussion between the teacher and the student. Some students will learn and use all 12 questions as they are written. Other students will need to have the questions rephrased to be more understandable. Still other students, due to the intensity of their instructional needs, may have the teacher paraphrase the questions for them.

The first time a teacher uses the model with a student or a group of students, the initial step in the implementation process is to read the question with or to the student, discuss what the question means, and then, if necessary, change the wording to enable that student to better understand the intent of the question. Such wording changes must, however, be made such that the problem-solving intent of the question remains intact. For example, changing *Student Question 1* from "What do I want to learn?" to "What is my goal?" changes the nature of the question. The *Teacher's Objectives* associated with each student question provide direction for teachers regarding the intent of the questions.

The *Teacher Objectives* provide the objectives that a teacher will be trying to accomplish by implementing the model. In each instructional phase, the objectives are linked directly to the *Student Questions*. These objectives can be met by utilizing strategies provided in the *Educational Supports* section of the model. The *Teacher Objectives* provide teachers with a road map to assist the teacher in enabling students to solve the problem stated in the student question. For example, regarding the first *Student Question* ("What do I want to learn?") *Teacher Objectives* linked to this question comprise the activities in which students should be engaged in order to answer this question. In this case, the activities involve enabling students to identify their specific strengths and instructional needs; to identify and communicate preferences, interests, beliefs, and values; and to prioritize their instructional needs. As teachers use the model, it is likely that they can generate more objectives that are relevant to the question, and they are encouraged to do so.

The emphasis in the model on the use of instructional strategies and educational supports that are student directed provides another means of teaching students to teach themselves. As important as this is, however, not every instructional strategy implemented will be student directed. The purpose of any model of teaching is to promote student learning and growth. There are circumstances in which the most effective instructional method or strategy for achieving a particular educational outcome will be a teacher-directed strategy. Students who are considering what plan of action to implement to achieve a self-selected goal can recognize that teachers have expertise in instructional strategies and take full advantage of that expertise.

Research on the Impact of the SDLMI

Wehmeyer and colleagues (2000) conducted an initial field test of the model with 21 teachers of students with disabilities, including intellectual disability, demonstrating the viability of the model for enabling students to engage in goal setting and attainment. The field test suggests that after receiving instruction with the SDLMI, students made progress on their goals, and that a large percentage of students made more progress than their teacher expected on their goals. Agran, Blanchard, and Wehmeyer, (2000) and McGlashing, Agran, Sitlington, Cavin, and Wehmeyer (2003) examined the efficacy of the SDLMI for students with severe disabilities using single-case designs and demonstrated that the SDLMI was effective in enabling students to set and make progress in education and employment-related goals.

In a series of larger, randomized-control trial studies, the impact of the SDLMI on self-determination, goal attainment, and access to the general education curriculum has been demonstrated. Lee, Wehmeyer, Palmer, Soukup, and Little (2008) examined the impact of the SDLMI on access to the general education curriculum for 45 students with intellectual or learning disabilities who were randomly assigned to receive instruction with the SDLMI, or continue with current instruction. Students in the treatment group learned and implemented the SDLMI to set and attain goals related to core content areas in the general education classroom. Classroom observations using momentary time-sampling software (Access CISSAR) were conducted, as were data on student goal attainment using the Goal Attainment Scaling (GAS) process. Results from this small sample provided preliminary support for the impact of the SDLMI on self-determination, access to the general education curriculum, and academic goal attainment for students in the treatment group. Wehmeyer et al. (2012) expanded these findings, conducting a group-randomized, modified equivalent control group design study of the efficacy of the SDLMI to promote self-determination with 312 high school students with intellectual disability or learning disabilities. There were significant differences in self-determination after two years of intervention between the control and treatment group. As an outcome of the same study, Shogren, Palmer, Wehmeyer, Williams-Diehm, and Little (2012) examined the impacts of the SDLMI on academic and transition goal attainment and access to the general education curriculum, and found that students in the treatment group had greater academic and transition attainment and greater access to the general education curriculum, even as instruction occurred in self-contained or resource rooms, not general education classrooms. Shogren, Plotner, Palmer, Wehmeyer, and Paek (2014) also examined the impact of the SDLMI on teacher views of student capacity and opportunity for self-determination and found that when teachers were trained and supported to implement the SDLMI (vs. teachers continuing in control group), there were significant increases in their views of student capacity and opportunities on the AIR. Shogren et al. (2015) conducted a follow-up study of students involved in another randomized control trial intervention to promote self-determination, which included the SDLMI (Wehmeyer, Shogren, et al., 2012). Self-determination status when exiting school predicted more positive employment outcomes one year after school (and employment status one year predicted employment status two years after school) in addition to community access at year one and two.

A variation of the SDLMI has been developed called the *Self-Determined Career Development Model* (SDCDM; Wehmeyer, Lattimore, et al., 2003). The SDCDM includes slightly modified student questions, facilitator objectives, and education supports while retaining the same self-regulated problem solving process to promote goal setting and attainment targeted to career development and employment goals for youth and adults with disabilities. Through all phases, participants engage in activities that enable them to set a job or career goal, develop a plan to meet that goal, and adjust their plan (if needed) to meet that goal. In addition to the questions, each phase also contains a list of objectives that serve as guidelines for facilitators. That is, the list of objectives provides facilitators with a means to accurately gauge what is being taught and what the person should be learning. Each phase also has a list of employment supports that facilitators may use if they find they need additional instructional methods for the participant. Wehmeyer, Lattimore, and colleagues (2003), in a pilot study of the SDCDM, found it had a significant impact on self-determination and career goals. Ongoing work is under way to further evaluate the impact of the SDCDM on self-determination, employment, and goal attainment.

Conclusion

Researchers have shown that when interventions supporting self-determination are systematically implemented in schools, changes in student self-determination result (Wehmeyer et al., 2013; Wehmeyer et al., 2012) that are linked to enhanced school and postschool outcomes (Shogren, Palmer, Wehmeyer, Williams-Diehm, & Little, 2012; Shogren, Wehmeyer, Palmer, Rifenbark, et al., 2015). The importance of self-determination is increasingly being discussed as a valued outcome for all students, including students with intellectual disability (Shogren, Wehmeyer, & Lane, in press). For example, research is emerging that focuses on embedding self-determination in multitiered systems of supports (see Chapter 12) and providing a range of supports for all students to learn and apply skills leading to self-determination, with individualized and more intensive supports for students who need them. This emphasis is emerging given the research that suggests that self-determination promotes not only the attainment of valued academic, social, and behavioral outcomes, but it also emphasizes the importance of transition and postschool outcomes—a critical focus for students with intellectual disability. The emerging base of evidence-based practices to promote self-determination creates an opportunity for the implementation of research-based practices in schools to support self-determination and other valued outcomes.

References

Abery, B. H. (1994). A conceptual framework for enhancing self-determination. In M. F. Hayden & B. H. Abery (Eds.), *Challenges for a service system in transition: Ensuring quality community experiences for persons with developmental disabilities* (pp. 345–380). Baltimore: Paul H. Brookes.

Agran, M., Blanchard, C., & Wehmeyer, M. L. (2000). Promoting transition goals and self-determination through student self-directed learning: The self-determined learning model of instruction. *Education & Training in Mental Retardation & Developmental Disabilities, 35*(4), 351–364.

Agran, M., Sinclair, T., Alper, S., Calvin, M., Wehmeyer, M. L., & Hughes, C. (2005). Using self-monitoring to increase following-direction skills of students with moderate to severe disabilities in general education. *Education and Training in Developmental Disabilities, 40*(1), 3–13.

Algozzine, B., Browder, D., Karvonen, M., Test, D. W., & Wood, W. M. (2001). Effects of interventions to promote self-determination for individuals with disabilities. *Review of Educational Research, 71*, 219–277. doi: 10.3102/00346543071002219

American heritage dictionary of the English language. (2000). (4th ed.). Boston: Houghton Mifflin Company.

Angyal, A. (1941). *Foundations for a science of personality.* Cambridge, MA: Harvard University Press.

Blackorby, J., & Wagner, M. (1996). Longitudinal postschool outcomes of youth with disabilities: Findings from the National Longitudinal Transition Study. *Exceptional Children, 62*, 399–413.

Cihak, D. F., Wright, R., & Ayres, K. M. (2010). Use of self-modeling static-picture prompts via a handheld computer to facilitate self-monitoring in the general education classroom. *Education and Training in Autism and Developmental Disabilities, 45*(1), 136–149.

Cobb, R. B., Lehmann, J., Newman-Gonchar, R., & Alwell, M. (2009). Self-determination for students with disabilities: A narrative metasynthesis. *Career Development for Exceptional Individuals, 32*, 108–114. doi: 10.1177/0885728809336654

Davies, D. K., Stock, S. E., & Wehmeyer, M. L. (2002). Enhancing independent task performance for individuals with mental retardation through use of a handheld self-directed visual and audio prompting system. *Education and Training in Mental Retardation and Developmental Disabilities, 37*(2), 209–218.

Deci, E. L., & Ryan, R. M. (1985). *Intrinsic motivation and self-determination in human behavior.* New York: Plenum.

Deci, E. L., & Ryan, R. M. (Eds.). (2002). *Handbook of self-determination research.* Rochester, NY: University of Rochester Press.

Dunlap, G., dePerczel, M., Clarke, S., Wilson, D., Wright, S., White, R., & Gomez, A. (1994). Choice making to promote adaptive behavior for students with emotional and behavioral challenges. *Journal of Applied Behavior Analysis, 27*(3), 505–518.

Dybwad, G., & Bersani, H., Jr. (1996). *New voices: Self-advocacy by people with disabilities.* Cambridge, MA: Brookline Books.

Field, S., & Hoffman, A. (1994). Development of a model for self-determination. *Career Development for Exceptional Individuals, 17*, 159–169.

Gilberts, G. H., Agran, M., Hughes, C., & Wehmeyer, M. L. (2001). The effects of peer delivered self-monitoring strategies on the participation of students with severe disabilities in general education classrooms. *Journal of the Association for Persons with Severe Handicaps, 26*(1), 25–36.

Houghton, J., Bronicki, G. B., & Guess, D. (1987). Opportunities to express preferences and make choices among students with severe disabilities in classroom settings. *Journal of the Association for Persons with Severe Handicaps, 12*(1), 18–27.

Hughes, C., Copeland, S. R., Agran, M., Wehmeyer, M. L., Rodi, M. S., & Presley, J. A. (2002). Using self-monitoring to improve performance in general education high school classes. *Education and Training in Mental Retardation and Developmental Disabilities, 37*(3), 262–272.

Joyce, B., & Weil, M. (1980). *Models of teaching* (2nd ed.). Englewood Cliffs, NJ: Prentice Hall.

Lee, S. H., Simpson, R. L., & Shogren, K. A. (2007). Effects and implications of self-management for students with autism: A meta-analysis. *Focus on Autism and Other Developmental Disabilities, 22*, 2–13.

Lee, S. H., Wehmeyer, M. L., Palmer, S. B., Soukup, J. H., & Little, T. D. (2008). Self-determination and access to the general education curriculum. *The Journal of Special Education, 42*(2), 91–107.

Lee, Y., Wehmeyer, M. L., Palmer, S. B., Williams-Diehm, K., Davies, D. K., & Stock, S. E. (2011). The effect of student-directed transition planning with a computer-based reading support program on the self-determination of students with disabilities. *The Journal of Special Education, 45,* 104–117. doi:10.1177/0022466909358916

Martin, J. E., & Marshall, L. H. (1995). ChoiceMaker: A comprehensive self-determination transition program. *Intervention in School and Clinic, 30,* 147–156.

Martin, J. E., van Dycke, J. L., Christensen, W. R., Greene, B. A., Gardner, J. E., & Lovett, D. L. (2006). Increasing student participation in IEP meetings: Establishing the self-directed IEP as an evidenced-based practice. *Exceptional Children, 72,* 299–316.

Mazzotti, V. L., Rowe, D. A., Cameto, R., Test, D. W., & Morningstar, M. E. (2013). Identifying and promoting transition evidence-based practices and predictors of success: A position paper of the division on career development and transition. *Career Development and Transition for Exceptional Individuals, 36*(3), 140–151. doi: 10.1177/2165143413503365

McGlashing-Johnson, J., Agran, M., Sitlington, P., Cavin, M., & Wehmeyer, M. L. (2003). Enhancing the job performance of youth with moderate to severe cognitive disabilities using the self-determined learning model of instruction. *Research and Practice for Persons with Severe Disabilities, 28*(4), 194–204.

Mechling, L., & O'Brien, E. (2010). Computer-based video instruction to teach students with intellectual disabilities to use public bus transportation. *Education and Training in Autism and Developmental Disabilities, 45,* 230–241.

Mithaug, D. E. (1996). *Equal opportunity theory.* Thousand Oaks, CA: Sage.

Nirje, B. (1972). The right to self-determination. In W. Wolfensberger (Ed.), *Normalization: The principle of normalization in human services* (pp. 176–193). Toronto: National Institute on Mental Retardation.

Nittrouer, C. L., Shogren, K. A., & Pickens, J. (2016). Using a collaborative process to develop goals and self-management interventions to support young adults with disabilities in the workplace. *Rehabilitation, Research, Policy and Education, 30,* 110–128. doi:10.1891/2168-6653.30.2.110

Powers, L. E., Geenen, S., Powers, J., Pommier-Satya, S., Turner, A., Dalton, L., . . . Swand, P. (2012). My life: Effects of a longitudinal, randomized study of self-determination enhancement on the transition outcomes of youth in foster care and special education. *Children and Youth Services Review, 34,* 2179–2187.

Powers, L. E., Sowers, J., Turner, A., Nesbitt, M., Knowles, E., & Ellison, R. (1996). TAKE CHARGE! A model for promoting self-determination among adolescents with challenges. In L. E. Powers, G. H. S. Singer, & J. Sowers (Eds.), *On the road to autonomy: Promoting self-competence in children and youth with disabilities* (pp. 69–92). Baltimore, MD: Paul H. Brookes.

Powers, L. E., Turner, A., Westwood, D., Loesch, C., Brown, A., & Rowland, C. (1998). TAKE CHARGE for the future: A student-directed approach to transition planning. In M. L. Wehmeyer & D. J. Sands (Eds.), *Making it happen: Student involvement in education planning, decision making and instruction* (pp. 187–210). Baltimore: Paul H. Brookes.

Powers, L. E., Turner, A., Westwood, D., Matuszewski, J., Wilson, R., & Phillips, A. (2001). TAKE CHARGE for the Future: A controlled field-test of a model to promote student involvement in transition planning. *Career Development for Exceptional Individuals, 24,* 89–103.

Seong, Y., Wehmeyer, M. L., Palmer, S. B., & Little, T. D. (in press). Effects of the Self-Directed IEP on self-determination and transition of adolescents with disabilities. In *Career development and transition for exceptional individuals.*

Shogren, K. A. (2013). A social-ecological analysis of the self-determination literature. *Intellectual and Developmental Disabilities, 51,* 496–511. doi: 10.1352/1934-9556-51.6.496

Shogren, K. A., Faggella-Luby, M., Bae, S. J., & Wehmeyer, M. L. (2004). The effect of choice-making as an intervention for problem behavior: A meta-analysis. *Journal of Positive Behavior Interventions, 6*(4), 228–237.

Shogren, K. A., Palmer, S. B., Wehmeyer, M. L., Williams-Diehm, K., & Little, T. D. (2012). Effect of intervention with the self-determined learning model of Instruction on access and goal attainment. *Remedial and Special Education, 33,* 320–330. doi: 10.1177/0741932511410072

Shogren, K. A., Plotner, A. J., Palmer, S. B., Wehmeyer, M. L., & Paek, Y. (2014). Impact of the Self-Determined Learning Model of Instruction on teacher perceptions of student capacity and opportunity for self-determination. *Education and Training in Autism and Developmental Disabilities, 49,* 440–448.

Shogren, K. A., Wehmeyer, M. L., & Lane, K. L. (in press). Embedding interventions to promote self-determination within multi-tiered systems of supports. In *Exceptionality.*

Shogren, K. A., Wehmeyer, M. L., Palmer, S. B., Forber-Pratt, A., Little, T. J., & Lopez, S. J. (2015). Causal agency theory: Reconceptualizing a functional model of self-determination. *Education and Training in Autism and Developmental Disabilities, 50,* 251–263.

Shogren, K. A., Wehmeyer, M. L., Palmer, S. B., Forber-Pratt, A., Little, T. J., & Seo, H. (in press). Preliminary validity and reliability of scores on the self-determination inventory: Student report version. In *Career development and transition for exceptional individuals*.

Shogren, K. A., Wehmeyer, M. L., Palmer, S. B., Rifenbark, G. G., & Little, T. D. (2015). Relationships between self-determination and postschool outcomes for youth with disabilities. *Journal of Special Education, 53*, 30–41. doi: 10.1177/0022466913489733

Shogren, K. A., Wehmeyer, M. L., Palmer, S. B., Soukup, J. H., Little, T. D., Garner, N., & Lawrence, M. (2008). Understanding the construct of self-determination: Examining the relationship between the Arc's Self-Determination Scale and the AIR Self-Determination Scale. *Assessment for Effective Intervention, 33*, 94–107. doi: 10.1177/1534508407311395

Stancliffe, R. J. (1995). Assessing opportunities for choice-making: A comparison of self- and staff reports. *American Journal on Mental Retardation, 99*(4), 418–429.

Stancliffe, R., & Wehmeyer, M. L. (1995). Variability in the availability of choice to adults with mental retardation. *The Journal of Vocational Rehabilitation, 5*, 319–328.

Test, D. W., Fowler, C. H., Richter, S. M., White, J., Mazzotti, V., Walker, A. R., . . . Kortering, L. (2009). Evidence-based practices in secondary transition. *Career Development for Exceptional Individuals, 32*, 115–128. doi: 10.1177/0885728809336859

Test, D. W., Mason, C., Hughes, C., Konrad, M., Neale, M., & Wood, W. M. (2004). Student involvement in individualized education program meetings. *Exceptional Children, 70*(4), 391–412.

Ward, M. J., & Kohler, P. D. (1996). Promoting self-determination for individuals with disabilities: Content and process. In L. E. Powers, G. H. S. Singer, & J. Sowers (Eds.), *On the road to autonomy: Promoting self-competence in children and youth with disabilities* (pp. 275–290). Baltimore: Paul H. Brookes.

Wehman, P. (2012). *Life beyond the classroom: Transition strategies for young people with disabilities* (5th ed.). Baltimore, MD: Paul H. Brookes Publishing Co.

Wehmeyer, M. L. (1996). Student self-report measure of self-determination for students with cognitive disabilities. *Education and Training in Mental Retardation and Developmental Disabilities, 31*, 282–293.

Wehmeyer, M. L. (1999). A functional model of self-determination: Describing development and implementing instruction. *Focus on Autism and Other Developmental Disabilities, 14*, 53–61. Retrieved from http://www.proedinc.com

Wehmeyer, M. L. (2003a). A functional theory of self-determination: Definition and categorization. In M. L. Wehmeyer, B. Abery, D. E. Mithaug, & R. Stancliffe (Eds.), *Theory in self-determination: Foundations for educational practice* (pp. 174–181). Springfield, IL: Charles C. Thomas Publishing Company.

Wehmeyer, M. L. (2003b). A functional theory of self-determination: Model overview. In M. L. Wehmeyer, B. Abery, D. E. Mithaug, & R. Stancliffe (Eds.), *Theory in self-determination: Foundations for educational practice* (pp. 182–201). Springfield, IL: Charles C. Thomas Publishing Company.

Wehmeyer, M. L., Abery, B., Mithaug, D. E., & Stancliffe, R. (2003). *Theory in self-determination: Foundations for educational practice*. Springfield, IL: Charles C. Thomas Publishing Company.

Wehmeyer, M. L., Agran, M., Palmer, S. B., & Mithaug, D. (1999). *A teacher's guide to implementing the self-determined learning model of instruction: Adolescent version*. Lawrence, KS: Beach Center on Disability, University of Kansas.

Wehmeyer, M. L., Bersani, H., Jr., & Gagne, R. (2000). Riding the third wave: Self-determination and self-advocacy in the 21st century. *Focus on Autism and Other Developmental Disabilities, 15*, 106–115.

Wehmeyer, M. L., & Bolding, N. (1999). Self-determination across living and working environments: A matched-samples study of adults with mental retardation. *Mental Retardation, 37*, 353–363.

Wehmeyer, M. L., & Bolding, N. (2001). Enhanced self-determination of adults with intellectual disability as an outcome of moving to community-based work or living environments. *Journal of Intellectual Disability Research, 45*, 371–383.

Wehmeyer, M. L., & Kelchner, K. (1995). *The Arc's Self-Determination Scale*. Arlington, TX: The Arc National Headquarters.

Wehmeyer, M. L., Kelchner, K., & Richards, S. (1996). Essential characteristics of self-determined behavior of individuals with mental retardation. *American Journal on Mental Retardation, 100*, 632–642.

Wehmeyer, M. L., Lance, G. D., & Bashinski, S. (2002). Promoting access to the general curriculum for students with mental retardation: A multi-level model. *Education and Training in Mental Retardation and Developmental Disabilities, 37*(3), 223–234.

Wehmeyer, M. L., Lattimore, J., Jorgensen, J., Palmer, S. B., Thompson, E., & Schumaker, K. M. (2003). The self-determined career development model: A pilot study. *Journal of Vocational Rehabilitation, 19*, 79–87.

Wehmeyer, M. L., & Lawrence, M. (1995). Whose future is it anyway? Promoting student involvement in transition planning. *Career Development for Exceptional Individuals, 18*, 69–83.

Wehmeyer, M. L., Lawrence, M., Kelchner, K., Palmer, S. B., Garner, N., & Soukup, J. H. (2004). *Whose future is it anyway? A student-directed transition planning process*. Lawrence, KS: Kansas University Center on Developmental Disabilities.

Wehmeyer, M. L., & Metzler, C. A. (1995). How self-determined are people with mental retardation? *The National Consumer Survey. Mental Retardation, 33,* 111–119.

Wehmeyer, M. L., & Palmer, S. B. (2003). Adult outcomes for students with cognitive disabilities three-years after high school: The impact of self-determination. *Education and Training in Developmental Disabilities, 38,* 131–144.

Wehmeyer, M. L., Palmer, S. B., Agran, M., Mithaug, D. E., & Martin, J. E. (2000). Promoting causal agency: The self-determined learning model of instruction. *Exceptional Children, 66,* 439–453.

Wehmeyer, M. L., Palmer, S. B., Lee, Y., Williams-Diehm, K., & Shogren, K. (2011). A randomized-trial evaluation of the effect of whose future is it anyway? On self-determination. *Career Development for Exceptional Individuals, 34,* 45–56. doi: 10.1177/0885728810383559

Wehmeyer, M. L., Palmer, S. B., Shogren, K. A., Williams-Diehm, K., & Soukup, J. H. (2013). Establishing a causal relationship between interventions to promote self-determination and enhanced student self-determination. *Journal of Special Education, 46,* 195–210. doi: 10.1177/0022466910392377

Wehmeyer, M. L., & Schwartz, M. (1997). Self-determination and positive adult outcomes: A follow-up study of youth with mental retardation or learning disabilities. *Exceptional Children, 63,* 245–255.

Wehmeyer, M. L., Shogren, K. A., Palmer, S., Garner, N., Lawrence, M., Soukup, J., . . . Kelly, J. (2003). *The self-determined learning model of instruction: A teacher's guide*. Lawrence, KS: Beach Center on Disability, University of Kansas.

Wehmeyer, M. L., Shogren, K. A., Palmer, S. B., Williams-Diehm, K., Little, T. D., & Boulton, A. (2012). Impact of the self-determined learning model of instruction on student self-determination: A randomized-trial placebo control group study. *Exceptional Children, 78,* 135–153.

Wolfensberger, W. (1972). *Normalization: The principle of normalization in human services*. Toronto: National Institute on Mental Retardation.

Wolman, J., Campeau, P., Dubois, P., Mithaug, D., & Stolarski, V. (1994). *AIR self-determination scale and user guide*. Palo Alto, CA: American Institute for Research.

Wood, W. M., Fowler, C. H., Uphold, N., & Test, D. W. (2005). A review of self-determination interventions with individuals with severe disabilities. *Research and Practice for Persons with Severe Disabilities, 30,* 121–146. doi: 10.2511/rpsd.30.3.121

Woods, L. L., & Martin, J. E. (2004). Improving supervisor evaluations through the use of self determination contracts. *Career Development for Exceptional Individuals, 27*(2), 207–220. doi: http://dx.doi.org/10.1177/088572880402700206

17

Educating Students in Inclusive Classrooms

Jennifer Kurth, Susan Marks, Jody Bartz

Introduction

The Individuals with Disabilities Education Improvement Act (IDEA) of 2004 requires students with disabilities be provided a free, appropriate public education in the least restrictive environment (LRE). The LRE mandate of IDEA has increasingly emphasized that students, regardless of the severity of their disability, be educated to the maximum extent appropriate in the LRE with their peers without disabilities. IDEA further states that separate schooling or removal of students from regular educational environments should occur only if the nature or severity of the disability is such that education in those settings cannot be achieved even with the use of supplementary aids and services. Yet, despite the preference expressed in IDEA for education in general education settings, most students with intellectual disability continue to spend most of their day in segregated classrooms. In this chapter we first review the historical context and the evolving view of the LRE for students with disabilities. We then spend the second half of the chapter reviewing the evidence base for inclusive education, particularly for students with intellectual disability.

Historical Background and the Evolution of Inclusive Practices

Implied in the LRE mandate is a continuum of services for students with disabilities, ranging from hospitals, to homebound instruction, to self-contained schools, to self-contained classrooms, to resource rooms, to inclusive education programs. Inherent in the idea of a continuum is that the appropriate placement for any student can be found somewhere along that continuum, and that more intensive supports are provided in more restrictive settings along the continuum (Taylor, 1988). The further assumption of a continuum of LRE placements as it has been implemented has been, "not whether people with disabilities should be restricted, but to what extent" (Turnbull, 1981, p. 17).

Marginalization and exclusion are thus normative experiences for students with the most significant support needs, including those with intellectual disability. This is both an historic and contemporary fact. Only since 1975, with the passage of the Education of All Handicapped Children Act (PL94–142), have schools been mandated to provide education services to this specific group of students. Immediately after passage of the law, debate ensued as to the most appropriate education for students with intellectual disability. For some in the field, it was simply assumed that students with intellectual disability could not be "expected to profit from a program of normalization that emphasized the traditional goals of education, nor can they be expected to take on a self directed role in society" (Burton & Hirshoren, 1979a, p. 599). Further, some reiterated that given the inaccessibility of public schools, negative reactions of nondisabled peers, and the caretaking programming needs of students with disabilities, a free and appropriate education is best provided in environments with care-taking capacities such as institutions, separate schools, and in the family home (Burton & Hirshoren, 1979b). In contrast, Brown and his colleagues (1977) advanced the notion that the "educational service delivery models used for severely handicapped students [sic] must closely approximate the best available educational service delivery models used for nonhandicapped students [sic]" (p. 197).

The debate about placement practices became more intense with the inclusion movement of the 1990s, which split special educators into those who favored large-scale placement of students with intellectual disability in general education classes from those who viewed such placements as largely inappropriate (Fuchs & Fuchs, 1994; Kauffman, Bantz, & McCullough, 2002; Kavale & Forness, 2000). Advocates of segregated special education settings have suggested that instruction should occur outside of general education for purposes of skill remediation (Fuchs, Fuchs, & Stecker, 2010), for providing a different curriculum (Ayres, Lowrey, Douglas, & Sievers, 2011), and for providing individualized, responsive, supportive instruction (Kauffman et al., 2002). Meanwhile, advocates of inclusive educa-tion have noted the failure of self-contained settings to deliver beneficial instructional environments and supports (Causton-Theoharis, Theoharis, Orsati, & Cosier, 2011), the profound importance of the general education context in providing learning opportunities and access to the core curriculum (Jackson, Ryndak, & Wehmeyer, 2008–2009), and growing research support documenting positive student learning outcomes in these settings (Dessemontet & Bless, 2013).

Many of the earlier arguments in support of inclusive education and in support of segregated edu-cation have continued into the present day. Although there has been increasing support for inclusive placements for students with intellectual disability, the field has experienced difficulty with moving forward, largely because the views for many have remain unchanged.

Evolution of Inclusive Practices

The move towards inclusive education began with the passage of PL 94–142, with the focus con-tinuing to grow over the ensuing 40 years. These evolving practices have been characterized as generations of inclusive education (Wehmeyer, 2009). The first generation of inclusive research and advocacy emerged with PL 94–142 and focused on gaining physical access to schools (Wehmeyer, 2009). Inclusive education was additive in nature—that is, resources and students were added to gen-eral education (Wehmeyer, 2009). The second generation of inclusive education was more generative in nature, focusing on improving practices such as collaborative teaching, differentiated instruction, and family partnerships as a means towards greater opportunities for inclusive education (Wehmeyer, 2009). Finally, the current third generation of inclusive education presumes students with intellectual disability are placed in general education classrooms, and the focus is on maximizing student partici-pation and progress in this setting (Wehmeyer, 2009). Practices such as self-determination, universal design for learning, schoolwide positive behavior supports, and flexible instruction characterize this generation of inclusive education. Each generation of inclusive education has been informed by the previous generation, and in reality, the practices and needs of a particular setting may reflect earlier generations based on the specific school's stage in their adoption of inclusive practices. As can be seen in schools today, individual classrooms will vary and exemplify features from each of the generations of inclusive education. Furthermore, the vision of inclusive education varies considerably amongst professionals in the field.

Towards a Definition of Inclusive Education

While researchers and advocates support the concept of inclusivity, IDEA has never explicitly defined 'inclusive education'; instead, the law relies on the principle of LRE. As researchers, educational team members, and others have struggled to conceptualize inclusive education, amount of time in general education has often been used as a proxy (Cosier & Causton-Theoharis, 2011). As a result, the use of the term 'inclusion' is frequently misapplied. For example, stating students "go to inclusion" for portions of the school day does not constitute being included, as students with disabilities are visiting a classroom, and not are included in the full day-to-day activities and social fabric of a class. Similarly, placing a student in general education without the range of supports and services needed for participation, access, and progress in the curriculum is not inclusive education. This may best be referred to as dumping a student in a classroom. Earlier views of inclusive education used the term 'mainstreaming.' However, this view of inclusion failed to lead to students with intellectual disability being truly included in the general education setting.

More recently, a consensus view of inclusive education is that it is best defined through indicators of practice (hence, a focus on the term 'inclusive education' or 'inclusive practices'), which range from physical placement to meaningful participation and outcomes. Thus, placing students with disabilities in the classroom and school he/she would attend if he/she did not have a disability merely is a first step towards inclusive education (Austin, 2001; Cook, 2001; Downing & Eichinger, 2008; Giangreco & Broer, 2005). The student must also have access to all of the supports and services he/she will need to participate fully in general education activities and curriculum (Burstein, Sears, Wilcoxen, Cabello, & Spagna, 2004; Downing & Eichinger, 2008; Mulvibill, Cotton, & Gyaben, 2004; Pivik, McComas, & LaFlamme, 2002). This indicator of inclusive education suggests that services will come to the student, rather than the student going to the services. In other words, proponents stress that special education is a set of services, not a place.

Inclusive education also embodies a philosophy of accepting, valuing, and respecting all students (Carrington & Elkins, 2002). Inclusive schools are accommodating to all learners (Thomson et al., 2003); the school facilities are accessible, as are curricula and activities. Inclusive education means that students with disabilities are full-time members of general education (Foreman, Arthur-Kelly, Pascoe, & King, 2004), not "visitors" who come in the class for certain activities and not others. Full membership extends beyond the classroom and onto the playground, lunchroom, and extra-curricular activities (Kleinert, Miracle, & Sheppard-Jones, 2007). Last, inclusive education means that each child, regardless of his/her learning style, pace, or preference, is provided a high-quality education with meaningful curriculum and effective teaching (Ferguson, 1995).

Myths About Inclusive Education

Despite evolving through multiple generations and improved indicators of inclusive education, most students with intellectual disability continue to be served in segregated self-contained classrooms (McLeskey, Waldron, Spooner, & Algozzine, 2014). In fact, some argue there has been a "regression. . . or resignation toward, a self-contained setting as a viable placement for students with severe disabilities" (Jackson, Ryndak, & Wehmeyer, 2008–2009, p. 176). One reason for continued restrictive placements of students with intellectual disability may relate to the myths about placement and needs of students with intellectual disability. In this section, we describe four of these common myths. As will be seen, these myths depict views from the first, second, and third generations of inclusive education.

Myth 1: Only Self-Contained Settings Can Provide the Types of Instruction that Students with Disabilities Require

A common myth prohibiting students with intellectual disability from being educated in inclusive settings is that these students require intensive services that can be provided in separate settings only (Mayton, Carter, Zhang, & Wheeler, 2014). For example, Mock and Kauffman (2002) argue a flaw in inclusive education is the assumption "that the normalizing influence of the general education classroom is more important and powerful than specialized, therapeutic interventions" (p. 214). Mock and Kauffman (2002) further argue educating students with disabilities in general education settings does not ensure that students will make progress or that teachers will be capable of providing effective instruction in these settings.

However, research has demonstrated that self-contained settings are not more effective than inclusive settings with regard to student outcomes. For example, a recent analysis of data from the NLTS-2 (a large-scale study of students with disabilities) found students with autism who had been educated in inclusive settings had no differences in outcome measures from those educated in self-contained settings, which included likelihood of going to college, high school dropout rates, and cognitive scores (Foster & Pearson, 2012). Findings such as these can be interpreted to mean that outcomes for students with disabilities are similar whether they are educated in self-contained or inclusive settings. Thus, there is no outcome benefit to self-contained educational settings. This is an important finding because IDEA requires that removal of students with disabilities from general education settings should be based on whether the student cannot be adequately educated in the general education setting.

Little empirical research has directly tested the hypothesis that intensive services can be provided only, or are more effective, in separate settings. In fact, some data (although generally not comparative) has found that such intensive services can be provided in the general education classroom. Additional research indicates that self-contained settings are no more "intensive" or "individualized" than inclusive settings. In fact, "effective teaching strategies and an individualized approach are the more critical ingredients in special education, and neither of these is associated solely with one particular environment" (Zigmond, 2003, p. 198). For example, the use of curricular modifications and embedded instruction have been effective in individualizing instruction for young children with disabilities in early childhood settings (Horn & Banerjee, 2009), and both strategies focus on intensity and individualization of instruction in inclusive settings.

Furthermore, research has indicated either favorable outcomes for inclusive education or no differences in outcomes when comparing outcomes for students with intellectual disability educated in inclusive and self-contained settings in a variety of valued-skill outcomes, including academic skills, social skills, adaptive behavior skills, and communication skills. In considering academic skills, Kurth and Mastergeorge (2012) examined the academic outcomes for students with autism and intellectual disability in inclusive and self-contained settings, and found that segregated settings are no more likely to offer intensive and systematic instruction than inclusive settings, and that students in inclusive settings obtained greater academic skills than those in self-contained settings. Similarly, Cosier, Causton-Theoharis, and Theoharis (2011) analyzed the relationship between time in general education and reading and math scores for 1,300 elementary school students with disabilities, including intellectual disability, finding more time in general education was associated with higher math and reading achievement scores. As for adaptive behavior skills, students with intellectual disability who were educated in self-contained settings were found to have no greater progress in developing adaptive behavior skills than students in inclusive settings (Dessemontet, Bless, & Morin, 2012). Finally, placement in inclusive settings has been associated with higher language scores than placement in self-contained settings for young children with severe disabilities (Rafferty, Piscitelli, & Boettcher, 2003).

Myth 2: Only Self-Contained Settings Can Provide the Qualified Instructors and Types of Experiences that Students with Disabilities Require

Those who support separate educational settings for students with intellectual disability often insist that the general education environment lacks the instructional capacity to support such students. Specifically, they argue general education teachers lack the training to teach students with intellectual disability, and that when students with intellectual disability are present they negatively impact the curriculum for all other students. Research supports, however, that with proper preparation, general education teachers can effectively deliver instruction to students with intellectual disability in general education settings without interfering with the instruction of all other students (Polychronis, McDonnell, Johnson, Riesen, & Jameson, 2004). For example, general education teachers delivered embedded instruction during regularly scheduled instructional activities, resulting in students learning sight words, requesting assistance, and identifying numerical concepts (Johnson & McDonnell, 2004). In a similar study using embedded instruction, general education teachers and paraprofessionals effectively taught students to answer questions from the science curriculum, to read functional sight words, and make requests using an augmentative and alternative communication (AAC) device (Johnson, McDonnell, Holzwarth, & Hunter, 2004). Furthermore, paraprofessionals can effectively teach skills to students with intellectual disability in general education settings (Brock & Carter, 2013) with sufficient preparation. For example, paraprofessionals taught adolescents to read and define vocabulary words (McDonnell, Johnson, Polychronis, & Riesen, 2002). Thus, both teachers and paraprofessionals in inclusive settings can implement high-quality, effective instruction without compromising the education of other students.

Relatedly, supporters of self-contained special education fear that inclusive education will require teachers to slow their pace of instruction or otherwise "water down" the curriculum (Kurth, Forber-Pratt, & Griswold, 2015). Others are concerned students with disabilities will require an inordinate amount of teacher time, thus interfering with the learning of all other students (Heller, Holtzman, & Messick, 1982). However, research related to the outcomes and experiences of students without disabilities in inclusive classrooms consistently finds these myths to be untrue. For example, students without disabilities made significantly greater progress in reading and math when served in inclusive settings (Cole, Waldron, & Majd, 2004). Others have found small positive to neutral outcomes in academic achievement for students without disabilities taught in inclusive classrooms (Kalambouka, Farrell, & Dyson, 2007; Ruijs, Van der Veen, & Peetsma, 2010).

Myth 3: Only Self-Contained Classrooms Provide the Curriculum Students with Intellectual Disability Require

This myth asserts students with intellectual disability require a different curricula than do students without disabilities—assuming that students with intellectual disability need a different instructional focus because they are not capable of learning the core academic content. For example, some have argued that inclusive education has shifted the focus from functional skills to a standards-based curriculum that is less meaningful and less individualized for students with intellectual disability (e.g., Ayres, Lowrey, Douglas, & Sievers, 2011). These authors argue that many general education topics, such as learning about the planets or reading Shakespeare's *Romeo and Juliet*, are simply teaching students with intellectual disability "useless knowledge and/or skills" (p. 17). They argue this type of instruction is meaningless, and limited instructional time should be refocused on prioritized areas such as independent living and functional skills for students with intellectual disability.

Yet, research documents students with intellectual disability are able to learn the core content, and therefore should be afforded the right to do so. For example, Browder, Wakeman, Spooner, Ahlgrim-Delzell, and Algozzine (2006) have demonstrated students with intellectual disability can learn reading skills. Similarly, students with severe disabilities have shown the ability to learn math skills (Browder, Spooner, Ahlgrim-Delzell, Harris, & Wakeman, 2008) and science skills (Courtade, Spooner, & Browder, 2007).

Inclusive education was also found to be feasible, in that students with intellectual disability can be taught to learn by observation in group instruction rather than only in one-on-one settings (Farmer, Gast, Wolery, & Winterling, 1991). Finally, studies demonstrate that academic performance in reading and math can be better achieved in inclusive settings (Cole et al., 2004). However, students with intellectual disability as a whole have less access to academic instruction than peers with high-incidence disabilities (e.g., learning disability), and continue to receive the majority of their instruction in special education classrooms (Bouck & Satsangi, 2015). This is contrary to the current view implied in IDEA that states all students with disabilities must have access to general education content.

Additionally, this assumption is flawed when viewed through the lens of the least dangerous assumption (Donnellan, 1984) and Schalock's quality-of life-framework (Schalock, 2000). As outlined by Courtade, Spooner, Browder, and Jiminez (2012), the premise of this assumption neglects to account for the right to educational opportunity for all students and the unknown potential of students with intellectual disability

Myth 4: Mainstreaming Is Sufficient for Providing Inclusive Experiences for Students with Intellectual Disability

As noted earlier, mainstreaming was the predominant view of the LRE for the past several decades. With mainstreaming, students with disabilities would attend only the general education classes for which they were either ready or would not require any additional supports to participate in the class. This view tended to focus on physical placement, resulting in students with intellectual disability attending certain classes deemed to not require any learning outcomes (i.e., art, PE, cooking, etc.). Supporters of inclusive education argue that physical placement is not inclusive education—instead, inclusive education is evidenced by memberships, relationships, and skills in general settings (Schwartz, 2000). Membership is about belonging to a group, with the idea that people in that group care about what happens to each other. Failure to adequately include students with intellectual disability often results in failure to form memberships. For example, Schnorr (1990) describes the experiences of Peter, a first grader with intellectual disability who spent a part of his day in the first-grade classroom. While he was physically present for some of the day, Peter's classmates were quick to note that he did not really belong in the classroom, as he did not have a mailbox, was allowed to color while they worked, and did not have a Valentine's Day envelope for the class party.

Relationships include friendships, helpee and helper interactions, acquaintances, and playmates. Unlike self-contained classrooms, which are often isolated and void of relationships (Kurth, Born, & Love, 2015), inclusive classrooms generally present the range of relationship opportunities described by Schwartz (Staub, Schwartz, Gallucci, & Peck, 1994). Finally, skills include the behavior, social, communication, and academic outcomes associated with inclusive education. As articulated, growing research continues to document the impact of inclusive education in skill development for students with intellectual disability. Thus, with these indicators of inclusive education in mind (relationships, memberships, and skills), it is apparent that simply visiting a general setting as is done in mainstreaming, or inviting students without disabilities to participate in activities in a special education setting as done in reverse-inclusive education, are not feasible and do not convey inclusive experiences.

A fifth common myth is that students with disabilities who are educated with their peers without disabilities in inclusive educational settings will not form 'true' or natural friendships (Heller et al., 1982). Rather, proponents of self-contained settings believe these settings allow students with disabilities to form friendships with one another, due to the similarities of children within these settings, which is unlikely, if not impossible, in general education settings. Research, however, bears out that inclusive settings are more effective at promoting social skills and social competence for students with intellectual and developmental disabilities than self-contained settings (Bellini, Peters, Benner, & Hopf, 2007). In fact, inclusive education is directly associated with gains in social competence for students with intellectual disability (Fisher & Meyer, 2002). In a series of interviews with key stakeholders (parents, teachers, and paraeducators), students educated in inclusive settings were reported to experience academic and social success (Downing & Peckham-Hardin, 2008). However, because students with greater difficulties with social skills are more likely to be placed in self-contained or other restrictive placements (Lauderdale-Littin, Howell, & Blacher, 2013), these students are at great risk of failing to develop social competence from schooling experiences.

Indicators of Quality Inclusive Education

One way to understand inclusive education is to examine what researchers have found to signify features of quality inclusive education. Advocates and researchers have proposed various indicators of quality inclusive education (e.g., Jorgensen, McSheehan, Schuh, & Sonnenmeier, 2012a). A number of research teams who have worked with schools and districts over the past decades have identified these indicators, based on their experiences of barriers and facilitators as they have sought whole-school and classroom level changes to increase inclusive placements for students with intellectual disability (Florida Inclusion Network, n.d.; Jorgensen, McSheehan, Schuh, & Sonnenmeier, 2012b; Maryland Coalition for Inclusive Education, n.d.). Here, we present indicators of quality inclusive education common among the tools developed by various research teams (i.e., general education class membership and full participation; quality supports to develop communicative competence; individualized supports and services within a multitiered system of support; progress monitoring; family, community, and school partnerships; futures planning, graduation, and transition to adult life; self-determination; resource allocation and funding; inclusive leadership), along with a description of each.

General Education Class Membership and Full Participation

Students with disabilities should be welcome members of the school community and have access to the full range of learning experiences, environments, and social networks offered to students without disabilities. Specifically, students should be full-time members of age-appropriate general education classes with natural proportions of students with and without disability (Ryndak, Jackson, & Billingsley, 2000). To achieve this outcome, students with intellectual disability should participate in a variety of inclusive curricular and extracurricular activities with same-aged peers (Kleinert et al., 2007). Further, students with intellectual disability should be provided multiple opportunities to form friendships and share a variety of social networks, including close friends, acquaintances, and paid relationships (e.g., teachers), thus mirroring the social networks of same-aged peers without disability. Students should not be removed from this setting to receive supports and services. Rather, supports (such as curricular accommodations) and service providers (such as occupational therapists) should come to the general setting (Giangreco, York, & Rainforth, 1989). Further, students with intellectual disability should arrive to and leave the setting at the same time as other students, and receive the same materials as students without disabilities, but with supports provided as necessary (e.g., physical supports, adapted materials, individualized grading plans, assistive technology). Students with intellectual disability should assume multiple and varied roles, including acting as a helper and being helped by peers without a disability (Carter, Cushing, & Kennedy, 2009) and participating in classroom instruction (e.g., whole class discussions, reading assignments) and extracurricular activities in similar manners and frequencies as those students without a disability, again, with supports provided as needed.

Quality Supports to Develop Communicative Competence

Students who may not communicate in ways commensurate to their same-age classmates should be provided reliable AAC and assistive technology supports so they can effectively communicate in academic and social situations with peers and educators. Because students who use AAC are less likely to access the general education environment (Kleinert et al., 2015) and the presence of a communication system is predictive of positive postschool outcomes (Kleinert et al., 2002), the need to develop communicative competence is particularly pressing. To achieve this, students must have access to their AAC device at all times, and the device should be updated regularly to reflect the interests and preferences of the student, as well as contain core vocabulary and content-specific academic and social vocabulary. Teachers must have strategies to assure access to literacy and communication instruction for AAC users (Ruppar, Dymond, & Gaffney, 2011). Lastly, students must have the support and ability to communicate their own thoughts, needs, opinions, wishes, and goals (Light & McNaughton, 2014).

Individualized Supports and Services Within a Multitiered System of Support

Students with disabilities should be provided culturally responsive and "only as special as necessary" (Giangreco, 1996) supports to enhance social and academic participation in the general education classroom. These supports and services would be conceptualized and delivered within a multitiered system of support (MTSS) framework in which academic failure is prevented by screening all students and providing supplemental supports to those students identified as at-need in general education activities (McCart, Sailor, Bezdek, & Satter, 2014). Further, instructional activities should be developed within a universally designed learning (UDL) framework, in which all classrooms and instruction are flexible and inclusive, providing alternatives and means of access for all students to learn (Rose & Meyer, 2000). UDL considers how to support the widest diversity of learners possible so that *all* children benefit (Cate, Diefendorf, McCullough, Peters, & Whaley, 2010).

Progress Monitoring

Members of educational teams should evaluate student learning in natural contexts and settings and use progress monitoring and formative strengths-based assessments to inform instruction and determine when intensive interventions are needed. Progress monitoring, which includes measuring student progress on individualized education program (IEP) goals and objectives, using this data to make timely and informed instructional decisions, should be done regularly (Etscheidt, 2006). As progress monitoring has been found to improve student motivation and teacher evaluation of the effectiveness of instruction (Luckner & Bowen, 2010), such practices should be incorporated into inclusive settings, activities, and assessments.

Family, Community, and School Partnerships

Students with disabilities should be provided quality inclusive educational experiences through equitable partnerships between families and schools. Inclusive schools engage in deliberate actions "to engage in reciprocal communication, exchange knowledge, participate in decision making, and create shared goals" (McCart, Sailor, Bezdek, & Satter, 2014, p. 258). Additionally, communication between school and community agencies should be welcoming, visible, purposeful, active, and positive with emphasis on sharing resources to strengthen the network of supports for students with disabilities (McCart et al., 2014).

Futures Planning, Graduation, and Transition to Adult Life

Students with disabilities should be provided opportunities to develop social skills, experience improved academic outcomes, and explore career and postsecondary options commensurate with their nondisabled peers. Students with intellectual disability should have in place a transition plan that is developed using principles of person-centered planning and should include choices for education, work, community living, leisure, and recreation (Miner & Bates, 1997). To prepare students with intellectual disability to assume these responsibilities, inclusive schools should involve students with intellectual disability in their IEP meetings (Martin et al., 2006; Mason, McGahee-Kovac, Johnson, & Stillerman, 2002).

Self-Determination

Students with disabilities should be instructed and provided opportunities to develop skills leading to self-determination as part of their social and academic experiences in school. Broadly, these skills include making choices, setting goals, and monitoring progress towards one's goals (Lee, Palmer, &

Wehmeyer, 2009). The Self-Determined Learning Model of Instruction (SDLMI) is one strategy for incorporating skills leading to self-determination in inclusive settings (Shogren, Palmer, Wehmeyer, Williams-Diehm, & Little, 2012) that has evidence of promoting participation in inclusive settings (Agran, Cavin, Wehmeyer, & Palmer, 2006).

Resource Allocation and Funding

School staff and administrators should identify and acquire needed resources so optimal teaching and learning can occur. Inclusive schools benefit from organized, planned resource allocation. In a case study of a highly effective inclusive elementary school, McLeskey, Waldron, and Redd (2014) noted all teachers sacrificed autonomy over their teaching schedules to permit supports and resources to be distributed across the school. For example, teachers were told when to teach reading to ensure that co-teachers, paraprofessionals, and other needed supports would be available. Similarly, related services providers should deliver services such as speech or occupational therapy in inclusive settings, thus enabling teachers and paraprofessionals to understand how to provide related services goals throughout the school day (Downing & Peckham-Hardin, 2007). Finally, effective inclusive schools should have personnel resources allocated meaningfully. In a study of 174 special education teachers and paraprofessionals, Giangreco, Suter, and Hurley (2013) found a persistent problem of high student caseloads for teachers coupled with a large number of paraprofessionals to supervise. Together, these factors contributed to limited teacher time for actual instruction. These authors argue that effective schools limit the number of paraprofessionals supervised while reducing teacher caseload, thus shifting teaching responsibilities from paraprofessionals to teachers (Giangreco et al., 2013).

Related to school funding and its relationship to inclusive schools, Sailor (2015) notes the impact of separate funding for special and general education in the United States. This practice enables special education to separate from general education and become "a separate self-contained system" (p. 96). With this in mind, Sailor advocates a new fiscal approach to special education in which braided funding is realized to enable unified education programs. Schools and districts can support this unification of special and general education by funding programs, curricula, activities, and personnel that benefit all students.

Inclusive Leadership

Leadership for inclusive practices from schools and school districts is an important factor in developing and implementing effective inclusive practices (Sailor & Roger, 2005). As articulated by Sailor and Roger, inclusive education is most successful when it is seen as a core value of the school for all students, not just those with disabilities, and not when it is viewed as a special education issue. Furthermore, a strong and supportive relationship between schools and their districts is necessary for sustainable school reform (McLaughlin & Talbert, 2003). At the school and district level, the allocation of supports, personnel, and leadership are all crucial to successful inclusive education. Specifically, schools and districts support inclusive practices by allocating sufficient time for scheduling and planning for transdisciplinary teaming. Collaborative teaching has gained support for implementing inclusive practices. However, teachers often have limited coplanning time, and infrequently have established roles and responsibilities related to lesson planning and delivery (Magiera & Zigmond, 2005). Thus, schools and districts support collaborative teaming by designating common planning time, providing in-service opportunities to learn about their roles and responsibilities in these teams, and provide problem solving support as teachers navigate these new roles (McLeskey, Waldron, & Redd, 2014).

Furthermore, the beliefs, actions, and preferences of schools and districts have a great impact on educational programming and services available in schools (Sindelar, Shearer, Yendol-Hoppey, & Liebert, 2006). Thus, school leaders with a dedication to inclusive education are critical for inclusive education to exist and persist. In their analysis of a successful inclusive elementary school, McLeskey, Waldron, Spooner and colleagues (2014) identified effective leadership practices. First, school leaders distributed decision making. Leaders set high expectations, but allowed teachers to reach these expectations using the strategies and materials that best suited them. Second, school leaders in effective schools used data to monitor progress and make timely decisions. Third, school leaders provided high-quality professional development focused on teacher-identified needs; this professional development was embedded and provided over time with a focus on teachers as part of a learning community. Finally, effective inclusive school leaders developed and shared a vision of meeting the needs of all students in inclusive settings. That is, inclusive education is not considered a special education issue, but an issue of setting high expectations for all students. Thus, inclusive schools value the contributions and membership of all students. Further, these schools presume all students are competent and therefore students with disabilities pursue the same learner outcomes as students without disabilities.

Practices that Have Evidence for Implementing Inclusive Education

Conceptually, inclusive education is similar to co-teaching in that it is an "organizational approach" (Cook, McDuffie-Landrum, Oshita, & Cook, 2011). Therefore, inclusive education is not an intervention per se, but is a way of organizing evidence-based practices (EBPs) within inclusive settings. Furthermore, the effectiveness of an organizational approach is highly determined by how the approach is implemented as well as the component parts and the skills by which practitioners implement them. While No Child Left Behind (2001) emphasizes the need to use instructional practices that are evidence-based, the identification of EBPs for students with intellectual disability is complicated by the variability of students with this classification, the low prevalence of the disability resulting in small sample sizes, and the continuum of special education contexts in which students are educated (Odom et al., 2005). Together, these factors make it challenging for practices to meet the standards of EBP. As a result, many inclusive practices that have scientific evidence simply do not have sufficient evidence to meet these requirements. However, the promising practices presented here are backed by scientific research, and many may eventually meet the standards of EBP.

There exists a range of instructional practices that have great promise for ensuring that students with intellectual disability learn important skills within general education settings. Table 17.1 provides an overview of practices identified in recent studies focusing on students with intellectual disability learning general education content or skills. Unfortunately, most of these intervention studies were not conducted in general education settings. Those that were conducted in inclusive settings are indicated in the table. Yet, as one reviews the key features of each practice, irrespective of setting, there is nothing to suggest that each intervention could not be implemented in general education settings. There is also a significant body of research on effective practices for teaching students with intellectual disability (see for example, Browder, Wood, Thompson, & Ribuffo, 2014); again, many of those practices can be applied in a variety of settings.

There are many effective instructional practices for improving inclusive education in general education classrooms that have been shown to have strong evidence even though they have not been researched specifically with students with intellectual disability (see for example, Harrower & Dunlap, 2001). Those practices are not listed in Table 17.1. However, it seems that most of the instructional practices that have strong evidence with other disability populations could be effective with students with intellectual disability, and more research is needed in this area.

Table 17.1 Inclusive practices for students with intellectual disability having research evidence

Instructional Practice	Key Features	Evidence
Collaboration and Co-teaching	Focus on coordinating curriculum changes. Both general and special education teachers knowledgeable about how to plan for diverse learner needs. Shared planning time.	Murawski, W. W., & Goodwin, V. A. (2014). Effective inclusive schools and the co-teaching conundrum. In J. McLeskey, N. L. Waldron, F. Spooner, & B. Algozzine (Eds.) *Handbook of Effective, Inclusive Schools: Research and Practice* (pp. 292). New York: Routledge. Solis, M., Vaughn, S., Swanson, E., & Mcculley, L. (2012). Collaborative models of instruction: The empirical foundations of inclusion and co-teaching. *Psychology in the Schools, 49*, 498–510.
Systematic and Intensive Instruction using Embedded Instruction	Applied Behavior Analysis practices, such as time delay, task analysis, reinforcement, and progress monitoring. Multiple distributed learning trials.	* Jameson, J. M., McDonnell, J., Johnson, J. W., Riesen, T., & Polychronis, S. (2007). A comparison of one-to-one embedded instruction in the general education classroom and one-to-one massed practice instruction in the special education classroom. *Education and Treatment of Children, 30*, 23–44. *Jimenez, B. A., Browder, D. M., Spooner, F., & Dibiase, W. (2012). Inclusive inquiry science using peer-mediated embedded instruction for students with moderate intellectual disability. *Exceptional Children, 78*, 301–317. * Johnson, J. W., & McDonnell, J. (2004). An exploratory study of the implementation of embedded instruction by general educators with students with developmental disabilities. *Education and Treatment of Children, 27*, 46–63. * Johnson, J. W., McDonnell, J., Holzwarth, V. N., & Hunter, K. (2004). The efficacy of embedded instruction for students with developmental disabilities enrolled in general education classes. *Journal of Positive Behavior Interventions, 6*, 214–227.
Instructional Grouping Involving Typical Peers and Use of Peers for Instructional Support	Peer use of system of least prompts. Peer use of constant time delay. Peers implement embedded Instruction program. Clear roles and training of peers. Two or more typical peers.	* Collins, B.C., Branson, T. A., Hall, M., & Rankin, S. W. (2001). Teaching secondary students with moderate disabilities in an inclusive academic classroom setting. *Journal of Developmental & Physical Disabilities, 13*, 41–59. Harrower, J. K., & Dunlap, G. (2001). Including children with autism in general education classrooms a review of effective strategies. *Behavior Modification, 25*, 762–784. *Jimenez, B. A., Browder, D. M., Spooner, F., & Dibiase, W. (2012). Inclusive inquiry science using peer-mediated embedded instruction for students with moderate intellectual disability. *Exceptional Children, 78*, 301–317. * McDonnell, J., Mathot-Buckner, C., Thorson, N., & Fister, S. (2001). Supporting the inclusion of students with moderate and severe disabilities in junior high school general education classes: The effects of classwide peer tutoring, multi-element curriculum, and accommodations. *Education & Treatment of Children, 24*, 141–160.

Instructional Practice	Key Features	Evidence
Providing Modifications and Supports for Literacy Instruction	Modified text passages. Time delay. Shared stories. Task analysis.	Browder, Ahlgrim-Delzell, Spooner, Mims and Baker (2009); Browder, D., Ahlgrim-Delzell, L., Spooner, F., Mims, P. J., & Baker, J. N. (2009). Using time delay to teach literacy to students with severe developmental disabilities. *Exceptional Children, 75*, 343–364.
		Browder, D. M., Hudson, M. E., & Wood, A. L. (2013). Teaching students with moderate intellectual disability who are emergent readers to comprehend passages of text. *Exceptionality, 21*, 191–206.
		Browder, D. M., Lee, A., & Mims, P. (2011). Using shared stories and individual response modes to promote comprehension and engagement in literacy for students with multiple, severe disabilities. *Education and Training in Autism and Developmental Disabilities, 46*, 339–351.
		Browder, D. M., Trela, K., & Jimenez, B. (2007). Training teachers to follow a task analysis to engage middle school students with moderate and severe developmental disabilities in grade-appropriate literature. *Focus on Autism and Other Developmental Disabilities, 22*, 206–219.
Providing Modifications and Supports for Science Instruction	Constant time delay. Graphic organizers. Systematic instruction.	*Jimenez, B. A., Browder, D. M., Spooner, F., & Dibiase, W. (2012). Inclusive inquiry science using peer-mediated embedded instruction for students with moderate intellectual disability. *Exceptional Children, 78*, 301–317.
		Knight, V. F., Spooner, F., Browder, D. M., Smith, B. R., & Wood, C. L. (2013). Using systematic instruction and graphic organizers to teach science concepts to students with autism spectrum disorders and intellectual disability. *Focus on Autism and Other Developmental Disabilities, 28*, 115–126.
Providing Modifications and Supports for Mathematics Instruction	Adapted word problems combined with picture symbols based on grade-level standards.	Browder, D. M., Trela, K., & Jimenez, B. (2007). Training teachers to follow a task analysis to engage middle school students with moderate and severe developmental disabilities in grade-appropriate literature. *Focus on Autism and Other Developmental Disabilities, 22*, 206–219.
	Graphic organizers and manipulatives. Task-analytic procedures.	Browder, D. M., Spooner, F., Ahlgrim-Delzell, L., Harris, A. A., & Wakeman, S. (2008). A meta-analysis on teaching mathematics to students with significant cognitive disabilities. *Exceptional Children, 74*, 407–432.

* Indicates that source was an intervention study that was conducted in general education setting.

Collaboration and Co-teaching

An important organizational element at the classroom level is use of collaboration and co-teaching (Magiera & Zigmond, 2005; Villa, Thousand, & Nevin, 2004). However, the evidence base for such practices has been mixed (Solis, Vaughn, Swanson, & Mcculley, 2012). Solis and colleagues noted the importance of examining how the co-teaching and collaboration structure is set up.

Co-teaching or collaborative teaching can take several forms, including: one teacher teaching with the other assisting; station teaching whereby teachers teach groups of students at the same time; and alternative teaching when teachers take turns teaching the whole class (Murawski & Swanson, 2001). Regardless of form, the ideal is that both general and special education teachers should share equal responsibility for lesson planning, lesson implementation, and assessment (Austin, 2001). Typically the general education teacher is viewed as the content expert, whereas the special education teacher is viewed as the expert in accommodations and differentiation (Austin, 2001). In their meta-analysis of co-teaching, Solis and colleagues (2012) found that fewer than 15% of the 146 studies on co-teaching systematically examined the influence of co-teaching. They concluded that the most promising interpretation of the evidence for co-teaching is that there might be small gains on student outcomes when c-teaching is implemented appropriately. Of interest is their conclusion that,

> Findings from these syntheses also suggest that when specialists "recommend" improved instructional practices to teachers (such as the model in which the general education teacher provides most of the instruction and the special education teacher provides support), instructional changes are unlikely to be realized in the classroom. However, when the specialists coordinate curriculum changes, significant changes are more likely to occur. . . . An example of this type of curriculum change is the use of alternative grouping formats, such as small groups, peer-pairing, and cooperative groups, as a means to accomplish academic and behavioral goals.
>
> *(p. 510)*

Based on Solis and colleague's analysis, it is important to note both special and general education teachers must be knowledgeable about how to plan for diverse learner needs. One way that this can be accomplished is through UDL and use of MTSS.

For students who require extensive supports to participate in inclusive classrooms, more substantial supports will be needed. The challenge for school teams is to develop strategies for incorporating these supports within typical classroom routines rather than pulling the student out for individualized sessions. Perhaps, there will be times where intensive remediation may be needed. However, most individualized supports are best provided within daily routines, or typical classroom routines.

Providing supports within daily routines will also require school teams to think about other types of supports and how to address those needs within typical classroom routines. For some students with intellectual disability, mobility and health supports are important considerations for the student to participate in instructional and classroom routines. Consideration of these support needs should be approached through an interdisciplinary/transdisciplinary team process involving physical therapists, occupational therapists, and educational team members. Such an approach requires ongoing collaboration amongst the various team members, as well as team members becoming comfortable with sharing roles, or what has been referred to as "role-release." An ecological analysis of the typical classroom routines will assist in providing team members with priority needs as well as ensuring that the health and physical supports maximize access to the classroom lessons and activities, and to identify which school team members can best be used during specific lessons and activities.

Systematic and Intensive Instruction Using Embedded Instruction

Throughout the history of special education interventions, researchers have identified the importance of systematic instruction as a method for delivering instruction in a way that would maximize the learning of students with intellectual disability. This type of approach is grounded in behavioral learning theory and is now widely accepted under the umbrella term of Applied Behavior Analysis (ABA). Interestingly, these instructional principles, when used to provide instruction to students with intellectual disability, were often applied in separate settings. However, it is becoming increasingly clear that ABA principles can be implemented in any type of setting, and researchers are finding that natural environmental teaching (NET), which involves teaching skills in the child's natural environment and focusing on the child's immediate interests, is either as effective, or more effective, than isolated teaching episodes using massed trials. This is important because, historically, use of one-to-one massed trial teaching has been a cornerstone of special education instructional delivery.

An instructional delivery approach that employs ABA principles within a NET approach is embedded instruction. Embedded instruction consists of delivering intensive and systematic instruction on priority tasks within the context of ongoing routines in the classroom (Johnson et al., 2004). In other words, rather than providing massed trial opportunities, learning trials are distributed throughout the day during natural learning opportunities (Browder, Hudson, & Wood, 2014). The model stresses key instructional practices that have a strong evidence base (i.e., time delay, task analysis, reinforcement, progress monitoring; see, Browder et al., 2009; Browder, Trela, & Jimenez, 2007; Lloyd, Forness, & Kavale, 1998; Shapiro, 2008). According to McDonnell, Johnson, and McQuivey (2008), critical features of embedded instruction are:

1. Learning outcomes for each student are clearly defined, including goals and criterion for judging the effectiveness of the intervention.
2. Instructional opportunities are designed to accommodate the presence or absence of naturally occurring opportunities for instruction during the activities and routines of the inclusive setting.
3. Instructional trials are distributed within or across the typical routines or activities in the general education classroom.
4. The number and approximate timing for the delivery of embedded instructional trials is planned.
5. Instruction is based on empirically validated instructional procedures.
6. Instructional decisions are directly linked to student performance data.

A number of studies by McDonnell, Jameson, and colleagues have shown that embedded instruction can be just as effective as one-to-one massed trial teaching procedures (Jameson, McDonnell, Johnson, Riesen, & Polychronis, 2007; Johnson & McDonnell, 2004; Johnson et al., 2004; McDonnell et al., 2006; Polychronis, McDonnell, Johnson, Riesen, & Jameson, 2004). In addition, concepts learned through embedded instruction procedures have greater potential for enabling instruction in general education settings, and when done well, can better facilitate generalization of skills. For example, Jameson and colleagues (2007) compared the effectiveness of one-to-one embedded instruction vs. one-to-one massed trials with four middle school students with intellectual disability who were taught general education content. Although one student reached criterion more rapidly in the embedded instruction, all students were successful in meeting criteria for their specific targeted skill. In another study, McDonnell and colleagues (2006) compared the effectiveness of embedded instruction in general education with small group instruction in special education classes. Four middle school students with intellectual disability were taught to verbally define words drawn from the general education lessons. The instructional delivery formats were equally effective in promoting vocabulary acquisition. Embedded instruction has been found to be feasible and effective at teaching a variety of skills without disrupting the general education classroom routine (Johnson et al., 2004). Furthermore, this research has shown that interventions can be implemented by paraprofessionals, educators, and nondisabled peers, making this intervention a feasible practice within typical school settings (Jameson et al., 2007; Johnson & McDonnell, 2004).

Instructional Grouping Involving Typical Peers & Use of Peers for Instructional Supports

Another important classroom practice that has gained wide acceptance is use of peers in supporting students with disabilities in inclusive classrooms. Peer supports and peer collaborative groupings involve utilizing one or more peers to provide academic and social support to classmates with a disability (Fennick & Royle, 2003). The successes of peer tutoring have been well documented in the literature (Collins, Branson, Hall, & Rankin, 2001; Harrower & Dunlap, 2001; Lieberman, Dunn, van der Mars, & McCubbin, 2000; Mastropieri, Scruggs, Spencer, & Fontana, 2003; McDonnell, Mathot-Buckner, Thorson, & Fister, 2001). Peers have successfully been taught to complete tasks such as adapting curriculum, providing instruction, implementing behavior plans, providing feedback, and promoting communication (Carter, Cushing, Clark, & Kennedy, 2005). Furthermore, peers can be taught to effectively do drills and practice from study guides, ask content questions and summarize information, and do oral readings of English novels and summarize these for their peer tutees (Mastropieri & Scruggs, 2001). In addition, peers have been successfully taught to implement accommodations, ranging from rewording, paraphrasing questions, breaking assignments into smaller tasks, facilitating partial participation in class activities, and modifying course materials (Carter et al., 2005). The use of peer supports in classrooms has been associated with higher levels of engagement for students both with and without disabilities, increases in social interactions, decreases in problem behavior, and improved academic performance (Mastropieri et al., 2003). Carter and colleagues (2005) further found that use of two peers was more effective than use of one peer to provide supports for their peers with disabilities.

Providing Modifications and Supports for Literacy, Science, and Math Instruction

The work of Browder and colleagues has shown that when students with intellectual disability are provided adapted materials and systematic teaching, they are able to learn general education content (Browder et al., 2009; Browder, Hudson, & Wood, 2013; Browder, Jimenez, & Trela, 2012; Browder, Lee, & Mims, 2011; Hudson, Browder, & Wood, 2013). The theme emerging from this body of work is that students with intellectual disability, when provided with instruction based on effective teaching practices and appropriately modified materials, are able to successfully learn academic content that was previously thought to be beyond the cognitive capacity of these students. In other words, as a result of inclusive practices, the content of education for students with intellectual disability is changing. Rather than focusing only on "functional" skills or "life skills" taught in separate environments, important functional skills are being incorporated into academic subjects.

Academic core content, such as literacy (Browder et al., 2009; Browder et al., 2013; Browder et al., 2011), mathematics (Browder et al., 2012; Browder et al., 2008), and science (Browder et al., 2012; Jimenez, Browder, Spooner, & Dibiase, 2012) for students with intellectual disability have been the focus of more recent inclusive practices research. Browder and colleagues' (2008) meta-analysis of mathematics instruction for students with significant intellectual disability led to the conclusion that teaching math using systematic instruction within typical settings had strong evidence. Similarly, these same researchers have conducted a number of studies focused on teaching core literacy skills based on general education content within general education settings that resulted in students with intellectual disability increasing their sight word reading, passage comprehension skills, vocabulary, and science concepts.

Future Directions

In many ways, we as a field have cause to celebrate that there are tools for creating meaningful and effective educational opportunities for students with intellectual disability in inclusive settings. As schools and classrooms implement evidence-based practices to create effective learning for students with intellectual disability, team members will be pushed to think about how they work with each other as well as how they will deliver services.

The research of the past 30 years has shown that inclusive practices can and should employ evidence-based practices. Yet, examination of current practices in schools and classrooms continues to reveal that such practices are the exception. Despite the current breadth of our knowledge, too many students with intellectual disability are being educated in segregated settings, with almost no access to the general education curriculum (Kleinert et al., 2015; Kurth, Morningstar, & Kozleski, 2014). Further, trends towards including more students with intellectual disability in general education settings are flat and stable, suggesting students with intellectual disability will remain unlikely to be educated in general education settings in the next decades, if not centuries, if present trends continue (Morningstar, Kurth, & Johnson, 2015).

Researchers have continued to demonstrate the importance of high expectations and the presumption of competence for students who were previously deemed unable to learn. We are beginning to see that when students with intellectual disability have failed to learn, this failure to learn is more likely due to our poor delivery of instruction and supports rather than any inherent inability in the student. This certainly opens many exciting possibilities as we continue to explore how our understanding of systematic teaching along with provision of appropriate modifications and supports within inclusive settings can create opportunities for students with intellectual disability to learn academic content.

Future researchers and policy makers have a reasonable foundation to build upon to make inclusive schooling a reality for students with intellectual disability. This has been a gradual effort, and as was noted in historical trends, has been long overdue. We are learning that without inclusive schooling opportunities, students with intellectual disability cannot exercise self-determination into adulthood—and society as a whole cannot move towards a strengths-based perspective that honors people regardless of disability status.

In order for the inclusive practices to benefit students, there must be a concerted effort to have school personnel use them. To do this, more research on how to incorporate evidence-based practices in general education subject areas is needed. Additionally, an important future direction for inclusive practices is to explore how school teams can be supported to effectively utilize implementation science processes (Cook & Odom, 2013; Fixsen, Blase, Metz, & Van Dyke, 2013; Fixsen, Blase, Naoom, & Wallace, 2009).

The Need to Engage School Teams Through Implementation Science and Scaling Up Efforts to Implement Inclusive Practices

Recent attention has focused on the need for school and district teams to engage in a systematic process to create more systemic and enduring change. Implementation science provides a framework for planning for implementation, bringing together school and district teams (see Active Implementation Hub, n.d.). The essential components center around the following five stages of implementation: (1) Exploration, (2) Installation, (3) Initial Implementation, (4) Full Implementation, and (5) Expansion and Scale-Up. The overall purpose is to guide the team towards identifying key practices to support implementation. When a team focuses on creating an inclusive school, it examines and identifies which practices will be the focus of efforts. Using what we know about instructional practices discussed in this chapter, the team would identify areas of need and practices to address these needs. Linking the area of need to a practice is essential for keeping a consistent path towards addressing any barriers and enabling the facilitators to move a school or district towards including more students with intellectual disability in the general education classroom and curriculum. To date, there are no studies using the implementation-science processes that focus on inclusive education for students with intellectual disability. Therefore, it will be important for research and implementation teams to share what they are learning so that other teams can learn from those efforts and a knowledge base can be created.

The Need for Additional Research on Implementing Effective Instruction in Inclusive Settings

While important research has documented the potential of students with intellectual disability to learn general education content (e.g., Browder et al., 2006), far too much of this research has occurred in separate special education settings. Indeed, few studies have taught students with intellectual disability core content in general education settings. Most of those have employed embedded instruction, as discussed previously, to teach vocabulary (e.g., Riesen, McDonnell, Johnson, Polychronis, & Jameson, 2003), sight words (e.g., Johnson & McDonnell, 2004), and academic facts (e.g., Collins, Evans, Creech-Galloway, Karl, & Miller, 2007) in inclusive settings. Emerging research has employed other methods, but remains limited in scope. For example, Wood and Allison (2014) have developed a task analysis that includes systematic instruction for teaching science concepts to students with severe disabilities in general education settings. Certainly, further investigations of instructional methods in general education settings, across age ranges and curricular content, are needed.

Conclusion

There is no denying that creating and providing inclusive educational environments for students with intellectual disability takes hard work by committed school, family, and community personnel with a unified mission. In this chapter, we have reviewed the historical context and the evolving views of the LRE for students with disabilities and then provided a review of the evidence base for inclusive educational strategies, especially for students with intellectual disability. We as a field no longer have to make 'forced educational choices' between effective practices and inclusive education for students with intellectual disability—these learners should, and can be, valued, welcome school community members with supports and services provided in their inclusive educational environments. There is a body of knowledge demonstrating that this is not only possible, but is absolutely necessary in order for students with intellectual disability to receive the quality of education they deserve.

References

Active Implementation Hub (n.d.). The National Implementation Research Network's Active Implementation Hub. Retrieved from http://implementation.fpg.unc.edu/

Agran, M., Cavin, M., Wehmeyer, M., & Palmer, S. (2006). Participation of students with moderate to severe disabilities in the general curriculum: The effects of the self-determined learning model of instruction. *Research & Practice for Persons with Severe Disabilities, 31,* 230–241.

Austin, V. L. (2001). Teachers' beliefs about co-teaching. *Remedial & Special Education: Special Curriculum Access, 22,* 245–255. doi: http://dx.doi.org/10.1177/074193250102200408

Ayres, K. M., Lowrey, K. A., Douglas, K. H., & Sievers, C. (2011). I can identify Saturn but I can't brush my teeth: What happens when the curricular focus for students with severe disabilities shifts. *Education & Training in Developmental Disabilities, 46,* 11–21.

Bellini, S., Peters, J., Benner, L., & Hopf, A. (2007). A meta-analysis of school-based social skills interventions for children with autism spectrum disorders. *Remedial and Special Education, 28,* 153–162.

Bouck, E. C., & Satsangi, R. (2015). Is there really a difference? Distinguishing mild intellectual disability from similar disability categories. *Education and Training in Autism and Developmental Disabilities, 50,* 186–198. doi: 10.1177/002221949602900601

Brock, M. E., & Carter, E. W. (2013). A systematic review of paraprofessional-delivered educational practices to improve outcomes for students with intellectual and developmental disabilities. *Research & Practice for Persons with Severe Disabilities, 38,* 211–221. doi: 10.1177/154079691303800401

Browder, D., Ahlgrim-Delzell, L., Spooner, F., Mims, P. J., & Baker, J. N. (2009). Using time delay to teach literacy to students with severe developmental disabilities. *Exceptional Children, 75,* 343–364.

Browder, D., Spooner, F., Ahlgrim-Delzell, L., Harris, A. A., & Wakeman, S. (2008). A meta-analysis on teaching mathematics to students with signifiant cognitive disabilities. *Exceptional Children, 74,* 407–432.

Browder, D., Wakeman, S., Spooner, F., Ahlgrim-Delzell, L., & Algozzine, B. (2006). Research in reading instruction for individuals with significant cognitive disabilities. *Exceptional Children, 72,* 392–408.

Browder, D. M., Hudson, M. E., & Wood, A. L. (2013). Teaching students with moderate intellectual disability who are emergent readers to comprehend passages of text. *Exceptionality, 21*, 191–206.

Browder, D. M., Hudson, M. E., & Wood, L. (2014). Using principles of high quality instruction in the general education classroom to provide access to the general education curriculum. In J. McLeskey, N. L. Waldron, F. Spooner, & B. Algozzine (Eds.), *Handbook of research and practice for effective inclusive schools* (pp. 339–351). New York: Routledge.

Browder, D. M., Jimenez, B. A., & Trela, K. (2012). Grade-aligned math instruction for secondary students with moderate intellectual disability. *Education and Training in Autism and Developmental Disabilities, 47*, 373–388.

Browder, D. M., Lee, A., & Mims, P. (2011). Using shared stories and individual response modes to promote comprehension and engagement in literacy for students with multiple, severe disabilities. *Education and Training in Autism and Developmental Disabilities, 46*, 339–351.

Browder, D. M., Spooner, F., Ahlgrim-Delzell, L., Harris, A. A., & Wakeman, S. (2008). A meta-analysis on teaching mathematics to students with significant cognitive disabilities. *Exceptional Children, 74*, 407–432.

Browder, D. M., Trela, K., & Jimenez, B. (2007). Training teachers to follow a task analysis to engage middle school students with moderate and severe developmental disabilities in grade-appropriate literature. *Focus on Autism and Other Developmental Disabilities, 22*, 206–219.

Browder, D. M., Wood, L., Thompson, J., & Ribuffo, C. (2014). Evidence-based practices for students with severe disabilities (Document No. IC-3). University of Florida, Collaboration for Effective Educator, Development, Accountability, and Reform Center website. Retrieved from http://ceedar.education.ufl.edu/tools/innovation-configurations/

Brown, L., Wilcox, B., Sontag, E., Vincent, B., Dodd, N., & Gruenewald, L. (1977). Toward the realization of the least restrictive environments for severely handicapped students. *JASH, 2*, 195–201. doi: 10.1177/154079697700200402

Burstein, N., Sears, S., Wilcoxen, A., Cabello, B., & Spagna, M. (2004). Moving toward inclusive practices. *Remedial & Special Education, 25*, 104–116.

Burton, T. A., & Hirshoren, A. (1979a). The education of severely and profoundly retarded children: Are we sacrificing the child to the concept? *Exceptional Children, 45*, 598–602.

Burton, T. A., & Hirshoren, A. (1979b). Some further thoughts and clarifications on the education of severely and profoundly retarded children. *Exceptional Children, 45*, 618–625.

Carrington, S., & Elkins, J. (2002). Bridging the gap between inclusive policy and inclusive culture in secondary schools. *Support for Learning, 17*, 51–57.

Carter, E., Cushing, L. S., Clark, N. M., & Kennedy, C. H. (2005). Effect of peer support interventions on students' access to the general curriculum and social interactions. *Research & Practice for Persons with Severe Disabilities, 30*, 15–25.

Carter, E. W., Cushing, L., & Kennedy, C. (2009). *Peer support strategies for improving all students' social lives and learning*. Baltimore, MD: Paul H. Brookes.

Cate, D., Diefendorf, M., McCullough, K., Peters, M. L., & Whaley, K. (Eds.). (2010). *Quality indicators of inclusive early childhood programs/practices: A compilation of selected resources*. Chapel Hill: The University of North Carolina, FGP Child Development Institute, National Early Childhood Technical Assistance Center.

Causton-Theoharis, J. N., Theoharis, G. T., Orsati, F., & Cosier, M. (2011). Does self-contained special education deliver on its promises? A critical inquiry into research and practice. *Journal of Special Education Leadership, 24*, 61–78.

Cole, C. L., Waldron, N. L., & Majd, M. (2004). Academic progress of students across inclusive and traditional settings. *Mental Retardation, 42*, 136–144.

Collins, B. C., Branson, T. A., Hall, M., & Rankin, S. W. (2001). Teaching secondary students with moderate disabilities in an inclusive academic classroom setting. *Journal of Developmental & Physical Disabilities, 13*, 41–59.

Collins, B. C., Evans, A., Creech-Galloway, C., Karl, J., & Miller, A. (2007). Comparison of the acquisition and maintenance of teaching functional and core content sight words in special and general education settings. *Focus on Autism & Other Developmental Disabilities, 22*, 220–233.

Cook, B. G. (2001). A comparison of teachers' attitudes toward their included students with mild and severe disabilities. *Journal of Special Education, 34*, 203–213.

Cook, B. G., McDuffie-Landrum, K. A., Oshita, L., & Cook, S. C. (2011). Co–teaching for students with disabilities: A critical analysis of the empirical literature. In J. M. Kauffman & D. P. Hallman (Eds.) *Handbook of special education* (pp. 147–160). New York: Routledge.

Cook, B. G., & Odom, S. L. (2013). Evidence-based practices and implementation science in special education. *Exceptional Children, 79*, 135–144.

Cosier, M., Causton-Theoharis, J., & Theoharis, G. (2011). Economic and demographic predictors of inclusive education. *Remedial & Special Education, 32*, 496–505. doi: 10.1177/0741932510362513

Courtade, G., Spooner, F., & Browder, D. (2007). Review of studies with students with significant cognitive disabilities which link to science standards. *Research & Practice for Persons with Severe Disabilities, 32,* 43–49.

Courtade, G., Spooner, F., Browder, D., & Jiminez, B. (2012). Seven reasons to promote standards-based instruction for students with severe disabilities: A reply to Ayres, Lowrey, Douglas, & Sievers (2011). *Education & Training in Developmental Disabilities, 47,* 3–13.

Dessemontet, R., & Bless, G. (2013). The impact of including children with intellectual disability in general education classrooms on the academic achievement of their low-, average-, and high-achieving peers. *Journal of Intellectual & Developmental Disability, 38,* 23–30.

Dessemontet, R. S., Bless, G., & Morin, D. (2012). Effects of inclusion on the academic achievement and adaptive behaviour of children with intellectual disabilities. *Journal of Intellectual Disability Research, 56,* 579–587.

Donnellan, A. M. (1984). The criterion of the least dangerous assumption. *Behavioral Disorders, 9,* 141–150.

Downing, J. E., & Eichinger, J. (2008). Educating students with diverse strengths and needs together: Rationale for inclusion. In J. E. Downing (Ed.), *Including students with severe and multiple disabilities in typical classrooms: Practical strategies for teachers.* Baltimore, MD: Paul H. Brookes.

Downing, J. E., & Peckham-Hardin, K. D. (2007). Inclusive education: What makes it a good education for students with moderate to severe disabilities? *Research and Practice for Persons with Severe Disabilities, 32,* 16–30.

Downing, J. E., & Peckham-Hardin, D. (2008). Inclusive education: What makes it a good education for students with moderate to severe disabiltiies? *Research & Practice for Persons with Severe Disabilities, 32,* 16–30.

Etscheidt, S. K. (2006). Progress monitoring: Legal issues and recommendations for IEP teams. *Teaching Exceptional Children, 38,* 56–60.

Farmer, J., Gast, D., Wolery, M., & Winterling, V. (1991). Small group instruction for students with severe handicaps: A study of observational learning. *Education and Training in Mental Retardation, 26,* 190–201.

Fennick, E., & Royle, J. (2003). Community inclusion for children and youth with developmental disabilities. *Focus on Autism & Other Developmental Disabilities, 18,* 20–27.

Ferguson, D. L. (1995). The real challenge of inclusion: Confessions of a "rabid inclusionist". *Phi Delta Kappan, 77,* 281–287.

Fisher, M., & Meyer, L. H. (2002). Development and social competence after two years for students enrolled in inclusive and self-contained educational programs. *Research & Practice for Persons with Severe Disabilities, 27,* 165–174. doi: http://dx.doi.org/10.2511/rpsd.27.3.165

Fixsen, D., Blase, K., Metz, A., & Van Dyke, M. (2013). Statewide implementation of evidence-based programs. *Exceptional Children, 79,* 213–230.

Fixsen, D. L., Blase, K. A., Naoom, S. F., & Wallace, F. (2009). Core implementation components. *Research on Social Work Practice, 19,* 531–540.

Florida Inclusion Network. (n.d.) Best practices for inclusive education (BPIE): School level assessment. Retrieved July 30, 2015, from http://www.floridainclusionnetwork.com/wp-content/uploads/2015/03/BPIE-School-Indicators-At-A-Glance-3-5-15.pdf

Foreman, P., Arthur-Kelly, M., Pascoe, S., & King, B. (2004). Evaluating the educational experiences of students with profound and multiple disabilities in inclusive and segregated classroom settings: An Australian perspective. *Research & Practice for Persons with Severe Disabilities, 29,* 183–193. doi: 10.2511/rpsd.29.3.183

Foster, M., & Pearson, E. (2012). Is inclusivity an indicator of quality of care for children with autism in special education? *Pediatrics, 130,* S179–S185.

Fuchs, D., & Fuchs, L. (1994). Inclusive schools movement and the radicalization of special education reform. *Exceptional Children, 60,* 294–309.

Fuchs, D., Fuchs, L., & Stecker, P. M. (2010). The "blurring" of special education in a new continuum of general education placements and services. *Exceptional Children, 76,* 301–323.

Giangreco, M. (1996). *Vermont interdependent services team approach: A guide to coordinating educational support services.* Baltimore, MD: Paul H. Brookes Publishing Co.

Giangreco, M., York, J., & Rainforth, B. (1989). Providing related services to learners with severe handicaps in educational settings: Pursuing the least restrictive option. *Pediatric Physical Therapy, 1,* 55–63.

Giangreco, M. F., & Broer, S. M. (2005). Questionable utilization of paraprofessionals in inclusive schools: Are we addressing symptoms or causes? *Focus on Autism & Other Developmental Disabilities, 20,* 10–26.

Giangreco, M. F., Suter, J. C., & Hurley, S. M. (2013). Revisiting personnel utilization in inclusion-oriented schools. *The Journal of Special Education, 47,* 121–132. doi: 10.1177/0022466911419015

Harrower, J. K., & Dunlap, G. (2001). Including children with autism in general education classrooms a review of effective strategies. *Behavior Modification, 25,* 762–784.

Heller, K. A., Holtzman, W. H., & Messick, S. (Eds.). (1982). *Placing children in special education: A strategy for equity.* Washington, DC: National Academy Press.

Horn, E., & Banerjee, R. (2009). Understanding curriculum modifications and embedded learning opportunities in the context of support all children's success. *Language, Speech, and Hearing Services in Schools, 40,* 406–415.

Hudson, M. E., Browder, D. M., & Wood, L. A. (2013). Review of experimental research on academic learning by students with moderate and severe intellectual disability in general education. *Research and Practice for Persons with Severe Disabilities, 38*, 17–29.

Individuals with Disabilities Education Improvement Act (IDEA), H.R. 1350, Pub. L. No. P.L. 108–446 (2004).

Jackson, L., Ryndak, D. L., & Wehmeyer, M. L. (2008–2009). The dynamic relationship between context, curriculum, and student learning: A case for inclusive education as a research-based practice. *Research & Practice for Persons with Severe Disabilities, 33–4*, 175–195.

Jameson, J. M., McDonnell, J., Johnson, J. W., Riesen, T., & Polychronis, S. (2007). A comparison of one-to-one embedded instruction in the general education classroom and one-to-one massed practice instruction in the special education classroom. *Education and Treatment of Children, 30*, 23–44.

Jimenez, B. A., Browder, D. M., Spooner, F., & Dibiase, W. (2012). Inclusive inquiry science using peer-mediated embedded instruction for students with moderate intellectual disability. *Exceptional Children, 78*, 301–317.

Johnson, J. W., & McDonnell, J. (2004). An exploratory study of the implementation of embedded instruction by general educators with students with developmental disabilities. *Education and Treatment of Children, 27*, 46–63.

Johnson, J. W., McDonnell, J., Holzwarth, V. N., & Hunter, K. (2004). The efficacy of embedded instruction for students with developmental disabilities enrolled in general education classes. *Journal of Positive Behavior Interventions, 6*, 214–227.

Jorgensen, C. M., McSheehan, M., Schuh, M. C., & Sonnenmeier, R. M. (2012a). *Essential best practices in inclusive schools*. Durhan, NH: National Center on Inclusive Education, Institute on Disability.

Jorgensen, C. M., McSheehan, M., Schuh, M. C., & Sonnenmeier, R. M. (2012b). Quality indicators of inclusive education. Retrieved July 30, 2015, from http://www.cherylmjorgensen.com/upload/QualityIndicatorsof InclusiveEducation040113.docx

Kalambouka, A., Farrell, P., & Dyson, A. (2007). The impact of placing pupils wiht special educational needs in mainstream schools on the achievement of their peers. *Educational Research, 49*, 365–382.

Kauffman, J. M., Bantz, J., & McCullough, J. (2002). Separate and better: A special public school class for students with emotional and behavioral disorders. *Exceptionality, 10*, 149–170. doi: 10.1207/S15327035EX1003_1

Kavale, K. A., & Forness, S. (2000). History, rhetoric and reality: Analysis of the inclusion debate. *Remedial & Special Education, 21*, 279–296.

Kleinert, H., Garrett, B., Towles, E., Garrett, M., Nowak-Drabik, K., Waddell, C., & Kearns, J. (2002). Alternate assessment scores and life outcomes for students with significant disabilities: Are they related? *Assessment for Effective Intervention, 28*, 19–30. doi: 0.1177/073724770202800103

Kleinert, H., Towles-Reeves, E., Quenemoen, R., Thurlow, M., Fluegge, L., Weseman, L., & Kerbel, A. (2015). Where students with the most significant cognitive disabilities are taught: Implications for general curriculum access. *Exceptional Children, 81*, 312–328. doi: 10.1177/0014402914563697

Kleinert, H. L., Miracle, S. A., & Sheppard-Jones, K. (2007). Including students with moderate and severe disabilities in extracurricular and community recreation activites: Steps to success. *Teaching Exceptional Children, 39*, 33–38.

Knight, V. F., Spooner, F., Browder, D. M., Smith, B. R., & Wood, C. L. (2013). Using systematic instruction and graphic organizers to teach science concepts to students with autism spectrum disorders and intellectual disability. *Focus on Autism and Other Developmental Disabilities, 28*, 115–126.

Kurth, J. A., Born, K., & Love, H. (2015). *Ecobehavioral characteristics of self-contained high school classrooms for students with severe cognitive disability*. Manuscript submitted for publication.

Kurth, J. A., Forber-Pratt, A., & Griswold, D. (2015). *Views of inclusive education from the perspectives of pre-service and mentor teachers*. Manuscript submitted for publication.

Kurth, J. A., & Mastergeorge, A. M. (2012). Impact of setting and instructional context for adolescents with autism. *Journal of Special Education, 46*, 36–48. doi: 10.1177/0022466910366480

Kurth, J. A., Morningstar, M. E., & Kozleski, E. (2014). The persistence of highly restrictive special education placements for students with low-incidence disabilities. *Research & Practice for Persons with Severe Disabilities, 39*, 227–239. doi: 10.1177/1540796914555580

Lauderdale-Littin, S., Howell, E., & Blacher, J. (2013). Educational placement for children with autism spectrum disorders in public and non-public school settings: The impact of social skills and behavior problems. *Education and Training in Autism and Developmental Disabilities, 48*, 469–478.

Lee, S. H., Palmer, S., & Wehmeyer, M. L. (2009). Goal setting and self-monitoring for students with disabilities: Practical tips and ideas for teachers. *Intervention in School & Clinic, 44*, 139–145.

Lieberman, L. J., Dunn, J. M., van der Mars, H., & McCubbin, J. (2000). Peer tutors' effects on activity levels of deaf students in inclusive elementary physical education. *Adapted Physical Activity Quarterly, 17*, 20–39.

Light, J. C., & McNaughton, D. (2014). Communicative competence for individuals who require augmentative and alternative communication: A new definition for a new ear of communication? *Augmentative and Alternative Communication, 30*, 1–18.

Lloyd, J. W., Forness, S. R., & Kavale, K. A. (1998). Some methods are more effective than others. *Intervention in School and Clinic, 33*, 195–200.

Luckner, J. L., & Bowen, S. K. (2010). Teachers' use and perceptions of progress monitoring. *American Annals of the Deaf, 155*, 397–406.

Magiera, K., & Zigmond, N. (2005). Co-teaching in middle school classrooms under routine conditions: Does the instructional experience differ for students with disabilities in co-taught and solo-taught classes? *Learning Disabilities Research & Practice, 20*, 79–85.

Martin, J. E., Van Dycke, J. L., Christensen, W. R., Greene, B. A., Gardner, J. E., & Lovett, D. L. (2006). Increasing student participation in IEP meetings: Establishing the self-directed IEP as an evidence-based practice. *Exceptional Children, 72*, 299–316.

Maryland Coalition for Inclusive Education. (n.d.) Quality indicators for inclusive building based practices. Retrieved July 30, 2015, from http://www.mcie.org/usermedia/application/8/quality_indicators_-_building-based_practices_2011.pdf

Mason, C. Y., McGahee-Kovac, M., Johnson, E., & Stillerman, S. (2002). Implementing student-led IEPs: Student participation and student and teacher reactions. *Career Development for Exceptional Individuals, 25*, 171–192.

Mastropieri, M. A., & Scruggs, T. E. (2001). Promoting inclusion in secondary classrooms. *Learning Disability Quarterly, 24*, 265–274.

Mastropieri, M. A., Scruggs, T. E., Spencer, V., & Fontana, J. (2003). Promoting success in high school world history: Peer tutoring versus guided notes. *Learning Disabilities Research & Practice, 18*, 52–65.

Mayton, M. R., Carter, S. L., Zhang, J., & Wheeler, J. J. (2014). Intrusiveness of behavioral treatments for children with autism and developmental disabilities: An initial investigation. *Education and Training in Autism and Developmental Disabilities, 49*, 92–101. doi: 10.1016/j.ridd.2013.10.023

McCart, A., Sailor, W., Bezdek, J., & Satter, A. (2014). A framework for inclusive educational delivery systems. *Inclusion, 2*, 252–264. doi: 10.1352/2326-6988-2.4.252

McDonnell, J., Johnson, J. W., & McQuivey, C. (2008). *Embedded instruction for students with developmental disabilities in general education classrooms.* Arlington, VA: Council for Exceptional Children.

McDonnell, J., Johnson, J. W., Polychronis, S. C., & Riesen, T. (2002). The effects of embedded instruction on students with moderate disabilities enrolled in general education classes. *Education & Training in Developmental Disabilities, 37*, 363–377.

McDonnell, J., Johnson, J. W., Polychronis, S. C., Riesen, T., Jameson, M., & Kercher, K. (2006). Comparison of one-to-one embedded instruction in general education classes with small group instruction in special education classes. *Education & Training in Developmental Disabilities, 41*, 125–138. doi: http://www.jstor.org/stable/23880175

McDonnell, J., Mathot-Buckner, C., Thorson, N., & Fister, S. (2001). Supporting the inclusion of students with moderate and severe disabilities in junior high school general education classes: The effects of classwide peer tutoring, multi-element curriculum, and accommodations. *Education & Treatment of Children, 24*, 141–160.

McLaughlin, M. J., & Talbert, J. (2003). Reforming districts: How districts support school reform. Retrieved June 28, 2015, from https://depts.washington.edu/ctpmail/PDFs/ReformingDistricts-09-2003.pdf

McLeskey, J., Waldron, N. L., & Redd, L. (2014). A case study of a highly effective, inclusive elementary school. *Journal of Special Education, 48*, 59–70.

McLeskey, J., Waldron, N. L., Spooner, F., & Algozzine, B. (2014). What are effective inclusive schools and why are they important? In J. McLeskey, N. L. Waldron, F. Spooner, & B. Algozzine (Eds.), *Handbook of effective inclusive schools* (pp. 3–16). New York: Routledge.

Miner, C. A., & Bates, P. E. (1997). The effect of person centered planning activities on the IEP/Transition planning process. *Education & Training in Mental Retardation & Developmental Disabilities, 32*, 105–112.

Mock, D. R., & Kauffman, J. M. (2002). Preparing teachers for full inclusion: Is it possible? *Teacher Educator, 37*, 202–215.

Morningstar, M. E., Kurth, J. A., & Johnson, P. J. (2015). *Examining the past decade of education settings for students with significant disabilities.* Manuscript submitted for publication.

Mulvibill, B. A., Cotton, J. N., & Gyaben, S. L. (2004). Best practices for inclusive child and adolescent out-of-school care: A review of the literature. *Family & Community Health, 27*, 52–64.

Murawski, W. W., & Goodwin, V. A. (2014). Effective inclusive schools and the co-teaching conundrum. In J. McLeskey, N. L. Waldron, F. Spooner, & B. Algozzine (Eds.) *Handbook of effective, inclusive schools: Research and practice* (p. 292). New York: Routledge.

Murawski, W. W., & Swanson, H. L. (2001). A meta-analysis of co-teaching research: What are the data? *Remedial & Special Education, 22*, 258–267.

No Child Left Behind Act of 2001, P.L. 107–110, 115 Stat. 1425 Stat. (2001).

Odom, S. L., Brantlinger, E., Gersten, R., Horner, R., Thompson, B., & Harris, K. R. (2005). Research in special education: Scientific methods and evidence-based practices. *Exceptional Children, 71*, 137–148.

Pivik, J., McComas, J., & LaFlamme, M. (2002). Barriers and facilitators to inclusive education. *Exceptional Children, 69*, 97–107.

Polychronis, S. C., McDonnell, J., Johnson, J. W., Riesen, T., & Jameson, M. (2004). A comparison of two trial distribution schedules in embedded instruction. *Focus on Autism & Other Developmental Disabilities, 19*, 140–151.

Rafferty, Y., Piscitelli, V., & Boettcher, C. (2003). The impact of inclusion on language development and social competence among preschoolers with disabilities. *Exceptional Children, 69*, 467–480.

Riesen, T., McDonnell, J., Johnson, J. W., Polychronis, S., & Jameson, M. (2003). A comparison of constant time delay and simultaneous prompting within embedded instruction in general education classes with students with moderate to severe disabilities. *Journal of Behavioral Education, 12*, 241–259.

Rose, D. H., & Meyer, A. (2000). Universal design for learning. *Journal of Special Education Technology, 15*, 67–70.

Ruijs, N. M., Van der Veen, I., & Peetsma, T. T. (2010). Inclusive education and students without special educational needs. *Educational Research, 52*, 351–390.

Ruppar, A. L., Dymond, S., & Gaffney, J. S. (2011). Individualized education program team decisions: A preliminary study of conversations, negotiations, and power. *Research & Practice for Persons with Severe Disabilities, 36*, 11–22.

Ryndak, D., Jackson, L., & Billingsley, F. (2000). Defining school inclusion for students with moderate to severe disabilities: What do experts say? *Exceptionality, 8*(2), 101–116.

Sailor, W. (2015). Advances in schoolwide inclusive school reform. *Remedial and Special Education, 36*, 94–99. doi:10.1177/0741932514555021

Sailor, W., & Roger, B. (2005). Rethinking inclusion: Schoolwide applications. *Phi Delta Kappan, 86*, 503–509.

Schalock, R. L. (2000). Three decades of quality of life. *Focus on Autism & Other Developmental Disabilities, 15*, 116–127.

Schnorr, R. (1990). "Peter? He comes and goes . . . ": First graders' perspectives on a part-time mainstream student. *JASH, 15*, 231–240.

Schwartz, I. (2000). Standing on the shoulders of giants: Looking ahead to facilitating memberships and relationships for children with disabilities. *Topics in Early Childhood Special Education, 20*, 123–128.

Shapiro, E. S. (2008). Best practices in setting progress monitoring goals for academic skill improvement. In A. Thomas & J. Grimes (Eds.), *Best practices in school psychology V* (pp. 141–158). Bethesda, MD: National Association of School Psychologists.

Shogren, K. A., Palmer, S. B., Wehmeyer, M. L., Williams-Diehm, K., & Little, T. D. (2012). Effect of intervention with the self-determined learning model of instruction on Access and goal attainment. *Remedial and Special Education, 33*, 320–330. doi: 10.1177/0741932511410072

Sindelar, P. T., Shearer, D. K., Yendol-Hoppey, D., & Liebert, T. W. (2006). The sustainability of inclusive school reform. *Exceptional Children, 72*, 317–331.

Solis, M., Vaughn, S., Swanson, E., & Mcculley, L. (2012). Collaborative models of instruction: The empirical foundations of inclusion and co-teaching. *Psychology in the Schools, 49*, 498–510.

Staub, D., Schwartz, I., Gallucci, C., & Peck, C. (1994). Four portraits of friendship at an inclusive school. *JASH, 19*, 314–325.

Taylor, S. (1988). Caught in the continuum: A critical analysis of the principle of the Least Restrictive Environment. *JASH, 13*, 41–53.

Thomson, C., Brown, D., Jones, L., Walker, J., Moore, D., Anderson, A., . . . Glynn, T. (2003). Resource teachers learning and behavior: Collaborative problem solving to support inclusion. *Journal of Positive Behavior Interventions, 5*, 101–111.

Turnbull, R. (1981). Least restrictive alternatives: Principles and practices. In J. W. Ellis, E. M. Boggs, P. O. Brookes, & D. P. Biklen (Eds.), Washington, DC: Amercian Association on Mental Deficiency.

Villa, R., Thousand, J. S., & Nevin, A. (2004). *A guide to co-teaching: Practical tips for facilitating student learning.* Thousand Oaks, CA: Corwin Press.

Wehmeyer, M. (2009). Autodeterminacion y la tercera generacion de la practices de inclusion [Self-determination and the third generation of inclusive practices]. *Revista de Educacion [Journal of Education], 349*, 45–67.

Wood, L., & Allison, C. (2014). Teaching science comprehension to students with severe disabilities. *DADD Online Journal, 1*, 24–36.

Zigmond, N. (2003). Where should students with disabilities receive special education services? Is one place better than another? *Journal of Special Education: Special Issue: What Is Special about Special Education?, 37*, 193–199. doi: doi.org/10.1177/00224669030370030901

18

Research-Based Practices for Fostering Trusting Partnerships with Families in Educating Students with Intellectual Disability

Kathleen Kyzar, Shana J. Haines,
Ann P. Turnbull, Jean Ann Summers

Families have long been considered the backbone of American society. Over a century ago, Progressive era reformer Jane Addams asserted, "America's future will be determined by the home and the school. The child becomes largely what it is taught, hence we must watch what we teach it, how we live before it" (Ryan, Cooper, & Bolick, 2016, p. 95). Today, US educational policy and research in general, and special education in particular, reflect the notion that family professional partnerships are essential in meeting the needs of all students. We base this chapter on the premise that when professionals establish trusting partnerships with families, the benefits to students, families, and professionals are greater than when families and professionals work in isolation.

Accordingly, the purpose of this chapter is to provide research-based family professional partnership strategies to enhance positive outcomes for students with intellectual disability and their families in pre-kindergarten through 12th grade school settings. We begin with a brief overview of the family-related aspects of the Individuals with Disabilities Education Act (IDEA). We then introduce a family-professional partnership framework, and finally, we describe how to use this framework and its associated principles to partner with families:

- during the special education eligibility process,
- during the development of individualized education programs (IEPs),
- in carrying out academic and behavioral supports, and
- during transition planning.

Overview of Family-Related Aspects of IDEA

Pre-IDEA Parent Roles

In the mid-1900s many children and youth with intellectual disability were still excluded from public schools. Parents provided instruction to their own children at home and were the organizers and volunteer teachers of special schools in communities, but outside of the public educational system (Boggs, 1985). Recognizing that their children could learn and were experiencing discrimination through their exclusion from school, parents of children with intellectual disability organized parent associations to share concerns about their child's right to an education (Turnbull, Turnbull, Erwin, Soodak, & Shogren, 2015). The National Association for Retarded Children (today known as The Arc), a product of this parental advocacy, was created in 1950 with a primary goal of furthering educational opportunities for children and youth with intellectual disability. Parents were at the educational helm, and their goal was to urge educators to partner with them in the delivery of educational services.

The Arc, other parent associations, and professional associations (e.g., the Council for Exceptional Children) brought right-to-education lawsuits in the early 1970s (*Pennsylvania Association for Retarded Citizens (PARC) v. Commonwealth of Pennsylvania, 1971, 1972*). The Pennsylvania lawsuit was a catalyst for 37 similar cases across the United States (Gilhool, 1997). These state initiatives provided a groundswell of parents and professionals working in partnership to lobby Congress to pass federal legislation asserting the right of all students with intellectual disability and other disabilities to a free and appropriate public education. Parents were prominent and forceful advocates in congressional hearings held throughout the country and to congressional committees (Turnbull, Shogren, & Turnbull, 2011). Clearly, parents' early demonstrations that their children could benefit from an education and their political organizing were potent influences in the successful passage of IDEA.

Parent Roles as Specified by IDEA

Given the influential role parents had in building national momentum for IDEA, it is not surprising that Congress revolutionized parental roles in education by requiring educators to partner with parents in making educational decisions for students. In fact, a comprehensive analysis of the Congressional Record indicated Congress operated under the fundamental premise that schools alone would not appropriately and fully implement IDEA (Turnbull, Turnbull, & Wheat, 1982). Thus, Congress viewed parents as accountability agents for schools in ensuring effective implementation.

In order to carry out the accountability agent role, Congress created requirements for parents to be shared decision makers and even monitors of professionals' decisions. For example, not only are parents to be included in their child's IEP meeting as full partners, but schools must also demonstrate that parents have agreed to the IEP, including all related services and placements. Further, IDEA provides mechanisms for procedural due process should the school and parents disagree on appropriate educational services, and for complete parental access to educational records for the student. In sum, IDEA reflects the belief of lawmakers that parents working in partnership with professionals are the lynchpin to assure that an individual child is receiving an "appropriate" education.

Unfortunately, this partnership vision for IDEA reflects more the ideal than the reality in special education services over the last 40 years, due in large part to a lack of understanding by both families and professionals about their roles and responsibilities. In terms of family information and training, this is not for lack of effort. The US Department of Education has established a national infrastructure of state Parent Training and Information Centers, supplemented by Community Parent Resource Centers in underserved communities, to provide information to parents about their rights and responsibilities under IDEA and other laws supporting people with disabilities (Turnbull, Turnbull, Erwin, Soodak, & Shogren, 2015). The website of the Center for Parent Information and Resources (http://www.parentcenterhub.org/) is the national technical assistance hub for the 73 Parent Training and Information Centers and 30 Community Parent Resource Centers. Although these centers have an impressive record of providing direct assistance (e.g., phone calls, emails, meetings) to 1.1 million parents and indirect assistance (e.g., website, newsletter) to approximately 25 million (National Parent Technical Assistance Center, 2013), many parents continue to report a lack of awareness and understanding about special education services in general and their rights under IDEA in particular (Mandic, Rudd, Hehir, & Acevedo-Garcis, 2012).

On the other side of the equation, teacher preparation programs are inadequate in preparing special education teachers to be partners. Nationwide, teachers report that communicating with families is their greatest challenge (MetLife, 2005; Miller & Losardo, 2002) and that their teacher preparation programs did not prepare them to work with families (Epstein & Sanders, 2006). A national study of early childhood special education teacher preparation programs found that only 57% included even one course on the topic of working with families (Chang, Early, & Winton, 2005). In short, it is critical to bridge this gap by providing a brief overview of family-professional partnerships and what they comprise before turning to research-based educational practices for partnering with families of students with intellectual disability.

Family-Professional Partnership: Conceptualization and Research

Development of the Family-Professional Partnership Framework

When we use the term *partnership*, we are referring to a "relationship in which families (not just parents) and professionals agree to build on each other's expertise and resources, as appropriate, for the purpose of making and implementing decisions that will directly benefit students and indirectly benefit other family members and professionals" (Turnbull et al., 2015, p. 161). Although we have cited that partnership was a fundamental premise in IDEA's original enactment (Turnbull, Turnbull, & Wheat, 1982), a clear, operational definition of partnership has been absent for most of IDEA's lifespan. An important initial step in developing that understanding was a qualitative study by Blue-Banning, Summers, Frankland, Nelson, and Beegle (2004). In this study, Blue-Banning et al. conducted a series of focus groups and individual interviews with 137 family members of children with disabilities and 53 education and human/social services professionals, asking them to talk about what a high-quality partnership meant to them. They found that these stakeholders defined partnership according to six major principles: communication, commitment, equality, skills, trust, and respect.

Summers et al. (2005) built on these findings to develop a reliable and valid partnership measure, the Family-Professional Partnership Scale (hereafter referred to as Partnership Scale), for practice and research use. These researchers began this task by developing survey items that represented the six major partnership principles identified in the Blue-Banning et al. study. They then asked a total of 496 families of children with disabilities to rate how important these items were. They used a statistical technique called *factor analysis*, which computed correlations between the item scores, to find out which items study participants rated similarly. This resulted in two factors: items related to how the professional treats the child, and those related to how the professional treats the family. This study provides an important insight for professionals: *Families think about the quality of their partnerships in terms of how the professional treats their child just as much, if not more, than the way the professional treats them.* In the end, the Summers et al. (2005) research boiled down the items from the Blue-Banning et al. qualitative study into 18 items that included nine items describing how well the family thinks the professional treats their child, and nine items describing how well the family thinks the professional treats them. Table 18.1 outlines the child- and family-focused items on the Summers et al. Partnership Scale.

Summers, Hoffman, Marquis, Turnbull, and Poston (2005) conducted a follow-up study examining families' ratings of the importance of and satisfaction with their partnerships with professionals utilizing a sample of 147 parents of children with disabilities ages birth to 12 years. Findings indicated that although importance ratings did not differ by child age (birth to 3 years, 3 to 5 years, and 6 to 12 years), satisfaction ratings did: Parents of older children rated their partnership less favorably than parents of younger children.

Studies have also utilized the Partnership Scale to examine the relationship of partnership to family outcomes. Zuna (2007) found that parents' satisfaction with partnership significantly predicted parent involvement and parent-teacher communication for families of kindergarten children with and

Table 18.1 Child- and family-focused partnership practices—Summers et al. (2005)

Child-Focused Partnership Practices	Family-Focused Partnership Practices
The service provider:	The service provider:
• Helps the family gain skills or information to get what their child needs	• Is available when the family needs him or her
• Has the skills to help their child succeed	• Is honest, even when he or she has bad news
• Provides services that meet the individual needs of their child	• Uses words that the family understands
• Speaks up for their child's best interests when working with other service providers	• Protects the family's privacy
• Lets the family know about the good things their child does	• Shows respect for the family's values and beliefs
• Treats their child with dignity	• Listens without judging the child or family
• Builds on their child's strengths	• Is a person the family can depend on and trust
• Values the family's opinion about their child's needs	• Pays attention to what the family has to say
• Keeps their child safe	• Is friendly

without disabilities. Burke and Hodapp (2014) examined the relationship between partnership and the stress of mothers of children with developmental disabilities. Findings indicated a significant inverse relationship between both the child- and family-focused subscales of the Partnership Scale and the outcome of maternal stress, suggesting that "when parents experienced stronger partnerships with the school, stress decreased" (p. 19).

Kyzar, Brady, Summers, Haines, and Turnbull (in press) found that partnership satisfaction predicted family quality of life (FQOL) for families of children birth to 21 with deaf-blindness, and that it also moderated the relationship between families' satisfaction with education/related services and FQOL. These findings indicate that when families are more satisfied with special education services, they are also more satisfied with FQOL; however, satisfaction with partnership impacts this relationship. Similar to Kyzar et al., Summers et al. (2007) found that partnership partially mediated the effect of families' perceptions of service adequacy and FQOL for families of young children with disabilities, suggesting that the "quality of relationships with professionals is also a critical component of effective service models" (p. 334). Summers et al. also found that families of young children with disabilities rated items on the child-focused partnership practices (e.g., helping parent gain skills/information to get what the child needs) lower than family-focused practices (e.g., provider is friendly). The importance of these two factors is also suggested in a study by Eskow, Chasson, Mitchell, and Summers (2015), which was a statewide survey of families of children with autism. Findings indicated that higher satisfaction with *child-focused* partnership items (but not the family-focused items) was significantly associated with families' perceptions about their child's improvement over the last 12 months, as well as higher FQOL. In sum, the research on partnership indicates (a) that partnership is associated with the outcomes of parent involvement, parent-teacher communication, FQOL, families' perceptions of their child's improvement, and maternal stress; and (b) that as children age, parents' satisfaction with partnership decreases.

Seven Principles of Partnership

In the previous section, we cited the Turnbull et al. (2015) definition of partnership, which built on research conducted over the last decade. In their work, Turnbull et al. have also expanded on Blue-Banning et al.'s findings in developing seven partnership principles professionals can implement in their work with families. We highlight these principles in Figure 18.1, which work together at the

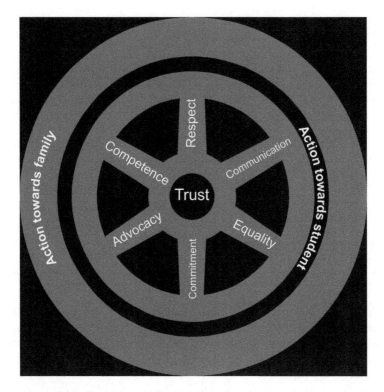

Figure 18.1   Framework of family-professional partnership

child and family level to create partnership. In this section, we draw from Turnbull et al. to define each of these seven partnership principles and then, in the remainder of the chapter, explain how these partnership principles can be applied to enhance positive outcomes for students and families.

The first principle, *communication*, involves paying attention to both the quality and quantity of communication. In communication with families, professionals should be friendly in their interactions, listen with empathy and without judgment, communicate using commonly understood terms (i.e., eliminate jargon and acronyms), be honest, and provide and coordinate information.

The second principle is *professional competence*. Parent participation and involvement in special education have been linked to parents' perceptions of professional competence and satisfaction with special education services (Bruder & Dunst, 2015; Laws & Millward, 2001; Zablotsky, Boswell, & Smith, 2012). Having professional competence involves providing an appropriate education through individualization, seeking professional development, and setting high expectations for students.

The third partnership principle is *advocacy*, which involves partnering with families to prevent problems, being mindful of making ethical decisions and actively pursuing advocacy opportunities, creating win-win solutions, forming alliances, and identifying and documenting problems.

The fourth principle is *respect*, which involves honoring cultural diversity by understanding families' cultures and their culturally based beliefs, affirming family and child strengths, and treating students and families with dignity.

Fifth, *commitment* involves being sensitive to families' emotional needs, being available and accessible through flexible scheduling, and going above and beyond through helping the family and student in a manner that extends the reach of their formal job description.

The sixth principle is *equality*, or "the condition in which families and professionals feel that each of them has roughly equal power to influence a student's education" (Turnbull et al., 2015, p. 174).

To achieve equality, professionals should share power, not exert "power over" (p. 175) families, foster empowerment through persistence in overcoming challenges, and provide options in finding solutions through being flexible and creative.

Trust, which is the seventh and final partnership principle, is the glue of the relationship. Turnbull et al. (2015) explain plainly to the educator: "You build trust when you practice each of these six partnership principles, for each leads to the seventh partnership principle, trust" (p. 184). Additionally, trust involves using sound judgment, maintaining confidentiality, being reliable, and trusting yourself.

Incorporating Trusting Family-Professional Partnerships into Educational Practices

Effective partnerships are not created in a vacuum; the best partnerships involve mobilizing the participants around a purpose that has meaning for everyone. Partnerships are about families and practitioners coming together to provide the best possible educational services for students with intellectual disability. In the following sections, we provide information on research-based partnership practices according to major aspects of special education service provision: assessment, IEP, behavioral support, academic support, self-determination, and transition. Within each section, we provide an overview of relevant family-related research and policies, review current challenges, present research-based practices, and connect the practices to the partnership framework presented in Figure 18.1.

Partnering With Families in Assessment for Special Education Eligibility

Importance of Partnerships Related to Assessment of Eligibility

A key principle of IDEA is nondiscriminatory evaluation. Although numerous court cases have highlighted the need for nondiscriminatory evaluation for special education eligibility, *Larry P. v. Riles* (1984), is the most prominent. In *Larry P.*, the court found that special education eligibility determination based on one assessment alone (in this case, an IQ test) is discriminatory, and the result of its use was the misdiagnosis of Black students as having a disability. Maydoxz and Maydoxz (2013) provide a comprehensive review of case law contributing to current special education policy on nondiscriminatory evaluation.

The history of discrimination in education has led to legally mandated procedural guidelines aimed at ensuring fair and timely evaluations for special education determination. These guidelines include providing written notice about the intent to evaluate a child to parents in their native language, obtaining consent prior to evaluating students, and conducting an evaluation within 60 calendar days from parental consent to the evaluation. Assessments must be selected and administered to minimize cultural and linguistic bias in order to fully show the student's academic, developmental, and functional competence.

Current Challenges

Despite these policies, discrimination within and as a result of the special education evaluation process persists (e.g., Maydoxz & Maydoxz, 2013). The disproportional representation of students from ethnic minority groups in special education is well documented (Harry & Klingner, 2014; Zhang, Katsiyannis, Ju, & Roberts, 2014). Problematically, Black students are 2.64 times more likely to receive special education services for intellectual disability than their chronological-age peers from all other racial/ethnic groups combined (Aud et al., 2013). Forming trusting partnerships with families during evaluation and early in the IEP process is one strategy professionals can use to enhance the nondiscriminatory intention of IDEA (Chen & Gregory, 2011). However, an inherent partnership barrier during the assessment for eligibility process relates to timing: The comprehensive evaluation is often the family's first experience with the special education system. During this time, the family is just beginning to learn about special education services and their role within them. Although IDEA mandates that schools send written notices to families and secure parental consent prior to conducting any evaluation, these procedures are often not sufficient in helping families understand their rights, the evaluation process, and/or potential outcomes of the process, even if they are written in the families' primary language (Mandic, Rudd, Hehir, & Acevedo-Garcia, 2012).

In a seminal study investigating special education assessment procedures in a large metropolitan school district, Klingner and Harry (2006) reported flaws in the assessment procedures, especially for students who spoke a language other than English at home, which resulted in discriminatory evaluation methods. They found that school staff saw multidisciplinary team meetings as the time to inform parents of premade assessment decisions instead of actively involving them in the evaluation and decision-making process. Further, specific mannerisms of school staff (e.g., ignoring parents' questions) resulted in parents' decreased participation in the remainder of the meeting, and negative views of a family increased the likelihood that a child would be placed in special education. Klingner and Harry observed that school staff in this district put little effort into discovering and building on family strengths and, in general, did not value families as members of the multidisciplinary evaluation team.

Research-Based Practices

Scant research validates effective practices aimed specifically at partnership during assessment for special education eligibility. However, three research-based family-professional partnership strategies show promise in addressing child and family outcomes within the context of the special education evaluation: providing information to families about eligibility, using a cultural liaison during the eligibility process, and encouraging family information sharing.

Parents need to be informed about the assessment process and their potential roles in it in order to be active members of the multidisciplinary evaluation team. Klein et al. (2011) conducted a descriptive study to investigate parents' perceptions of various types of information during diagnostic assessment. These parents wanted to have information about the assessment process available in multiple formats, including written, a flow chart of what to do and when, a parent-friendly reference guide for professional/diagnostic language that might be used during meetings, and a video tour of the process. This study also found that a strengths-based approach, which openly appreciates the child's and family's strengths and builds upon them to work towards goals, enabled parents to feel empowered and adopt a hopeful and positive approach to their child's disability. To implement this research-based practice, you can provide information to families in some of the multiple formats described by these researchers.

Research has also documented the benefit of information sharing that occurs between people who have similar linguistic and cultural backgrounds. Referred to as *cultural navigators* (Hardin, Mereoiu, Hung & Roach-Scott, 2009), *parent liaisons* (Hardin et al., 2009), or *school liaisons* (Howland, Anderson, Smiley, & Abbott, 2006), these liaisons serve as brokers for communication that occurs between families and schools in instances of a cultural or linguistic disconnect between the two parties. In a case study, Howland et al. found that the use of school liaisons (a) increased parents' beliefs about the importance of their active role in their children's education at school and at home and (b) increased parents' beliefs that their partnership with their children's teachers would help the children attain desired results. Therefore, utilizing cultural liaisons during the special education evaluation process to help communicate important information to families as well as understand families' unique functioning is a promising practice for improving child and family outcomes.

While providing information to families during the special education eligibility process is critical, professionals should expect to learn from families as well, to ensure that the evaluation is accurate and comprehensive. Establishing the importance of parents' sharing of family perspectives can help launch families as partners in their children's education (Turnbull et al., 2015). Professionals can employ strategies to facilitate information sharing from families such as building on the person-centered planning approach. Another promising practice that can facilitate parents' sharing information is the use of a Family Assessment Portfolio (FAP; Thompson, Meadan, Fansler, Alber, & Balogh, 2007). FAPs can consist of several components, including scrapbooks, web-based profiles, and movies, and they came about as a group of researchers realized the power of relatable, personal information about children under evaluation presented by families who brought informal items to meetings. Thompson et al. (2007) outlined steps to follow to make FAPs, but they suggest that the format of FAPs must be flexible enough to enable families to make them personal and relevant. Meadan et al. (2009) found that users were satisfied with using FAPs and that facilitators could systematically teach small groups of families how to make FAPs.

Relationship to Partnership Principles

In sum, research-based practices for partnering with families in the process of assessing students for special education eligibility provide guidance on providing information to families about eligibility, using a cultural liaison during the eligibility process, and encouraging family information sharing. In terms of our partnership framework (see Figure 18.1), *communication* is key to ensuring families understand the assessment process and the importance of their voice in depicting a comprehensive portrait of their child's strengths and needs. Providing information in multiple formats and using cultural liaisons are two research-based techniques for communicating the assessment process to families. These actions also demonstrate *commitment* to partnering with families. *Communication* is also necessary to implement strategies such as person-centered planning to ensure that families are encouraged to tell their family story. These strategies also demonstrate the partnership elements of *respect* and *equality*. Partnering with families during the assessment for eligibility process can help set the stage for trusting relationships as multidisciplinary teams work together to create students' IEPs.

Partnering With Families in Developing the IEP

Importance of Partnerships Related to the IEP

IDEA requires that students (ages 3 to 21) have an IEP. IDEA specifies requirements for the IEP document (content) and IEP meeting (process of development). The Congressional expectation is that the quality of appropriate education—individualization and benefit—is more likely to accrue when parents are shared educational decision makers. Furthermore, the US Supreme Court has ruled that the "cooperative process" occurring among IEP team participants, especially the parents, is the "core" of IDEA (*Schaffer v. Weast,* 2005). Therefore, key to the process of IEP development are the requirements that families must be invited to every meeting and that meetings should move forward without parents being present only when documentation exists that good faith efforts have been made to involve parents and they have declined the opportunity to attend. Good faith efforts involve scheduling meetings with parents in consideration of a broad range of factors including their job schedule, child-care needs, transportation availability, religious holy days, and other similar factors.

Current Challenges

Two longitudinal studies—the Special Education Elementary Longitudinal Study and the National Longitudinal Study-2—(Wagner, Newman, Cameto, Javitz, & Valdes, 2012) provide a national profile of parent attendance of and satisfaction with IEP conferences. These studies found that:

- Parents of students with intellectual disability were less likely to attend the IEP conference and experience satisfaction from it than parents of students from most other disability categories.

- Approximately 90% of parents reported attending the conference with about 70% of those attending perceiving their participation was the right amount and slightly over 25% reporting that they would like to have more involvement.
- Parents of students of color and parents of students with incomes below $25,000 were less likely to attend conferences and were less satisfied with their participation.

Besides attending IEP meetings, another key variable is the actual extent to which parents contribute to the discussion and decision making throughout the conference. Fish (2008) found that 50% of the parents indicated that they would like to be able to influence IEP decision making to a greater extent. Blackwell and Rossetti (2014) conducted a comprehensive review of literature on IEP development over a 16-year period. They indicated that, although the majority of parents attend conferences, they typically have a passive role, with the discussion being dominated by teachers and administrators. This study also reported that educators experience challenges in developing IEPs that (a) meet substantive requirements (i.e., performance levels, goals and objectives, instructional and related services supports) and (b) facilitate the participation of students in the general curriculum within general education classes. The authors speculate that these greater complexities to individualized planning present challenges to including families in substantive decision making. They concluded that: "the federal intention of parents and guardians being equal partners in collaborating with schools to develop IEPs is not being realized" (Blackwell & Rosetti, 2014, p. 11).

Research-Based Practices

Although the number of students with exceptionalities has varied over the years, an approximate annual figure is 6 million students. At the time of this writing, that means that there have been approximately 222 million conferences, with the vast majority having parents in attendance. Especially considering the hours invested in IEP conferences, it is regrettable that research on family-professional partnerships within this context has been so meager. The research that does exist highlights providing training to families about their involvement in the IEP process, having a parent advocate present during the IEP meeting, and IEP facilitation.

In a comprehensive search of the literature, Goldman and Burke (in press) focused on identifying multiple ways to provide training to parents to prepare them for their partnership role in IEP decision making. They identified six studies, but only one—conducted by Brinkerhoff and Vincent in 1986—had significant results. The authors provided an intervention to parents of preschoolers that consisted of (a) completing developmental assessments on their child (i.e., child's functioning at home, parent goals, and a description of the family's daily routine); and (b) attending a parent meeting with a school/community liaison in advance of the IEP conference to receive an overview of the IEP including the purpose, participants' roles, and a description of how the developmental assessment data they provided would be incorporated into the IEP. As compared to the control group of families who received only a handout describing the IEP conference, the families who received the intervention made significantly more contributions to the conference. The parent-completed assessment information prepared professionals to have more in-depth discussions with families about suggestions for helping their child at home. Interestingly, of the seven families in the intervention group, fathers attended two of the conferences, and these two fathers each contributed twice as much as any of the mothers. Even though this is one study involving a small number of families, three promising practices to consider include:

- Provide an orientation meeting in advance.
- Provide a structured way for mothers and fathers to provide input in advance on their child's functioning at home, parent goals, and daily routines.
- Encourage fathers to attend conferences through invitations and convenient scheduling.

Another research study, which was conducted in the early years after IDEA's passage and implementation, investigated the impact of having someone attend conferences at the elementary level in the role of a parent advocate (e.g., welcoming and introducing parents, directing questions to parents, clarifying jargon, indicating the value of parental contributions, summarizing at the end of the conference, highlighting next steps, and thanking parents for their attendance; Goldstein & Turnbull, 1982). Parents who had a parent advocate present made significantly more contributions at the conference as compared to the control group. In implementing this strategy, any member of the IEP team might be designated as the parent advocate. Professionals can invite parents to bring a friend or parent advocate from the community to the conference. The professional team might designate one of the team members to serve as a parent advocate for new parents; however, parents who know the professional team from past IEP experiences might prefer to select their own professional advocate.

The final strategy for consideration is IEP facilitation, which is based on research from the field of conflict resolution (Fisher, Ury, & Patton, 2011). It is a comprehensive approach to conducting IEP conferences that involves many strategies. In a nutshell, IEP facilitation involves having a committee leader, who is a neutral party both to families and the school staff, chair the IEP meeting for the primary purpose of insuring that the meeting is of high quality and that both parents and school staff have equal opportunity for influence and decision making. The seven key IEP facilitation components include:

- a neutral facilitator,
- an agenda linked to IDEA requirements and key educational decisions requiring attention,
- goals for the meeting from the perspectives of each participant shared with the group,
- sound ground rules for participation,
- an environmental set-up that promotes collaborative decision making,
- communication strategies to ensure an equal playing field for all participants, and
- the use of a "parking lot" to identify important issues to address later rather than going off on "tangents" during the meeting (Mueller, 2009).

Currently 30 states have policies and procedures on the use of IEP facilitation. We encourage you to follow the emerging research on IEP facilitation because our expectation is that the use of these strategies will be increasing in the future as a way to avoid more formal mediation and due process hearings, which are procedural safeguards addressed in IDEA. A key website for publications and training videos on IEP facilitation is the National Center for Dispute Resolution in Special Education (http://www.directionservice.org/cadre/index.cfm).

Relationship to Partnership Principles

The practices we recommend align with the partnership framework presented in Figure 18.1 in numerous ways. First, the goal of the IEP facilitation (Mueller, 2009) and parent advocacy strategies is to level the playing field for families, who, as we reported, do not perceive their participation in IEP conferences as equal to those of professionals. This ties directly to the partnership principle of *equality*. When a neutral party facilitates IEP meetings, families may have the opportunity to voice their perspectives with the same level of input as professionals. In this section, we also reported that parents of color and parents whose income is less than $25,000 report lower levels of satisfaction with IEP conferences and are less likely to attend them (Wagner et al., 2012). To address this, professionals should place more emphasis on understanding and viewing the diversity that exists among students and their families as an asset. This tone of *respect* is needed to promote a climate of inclusiveness for families who attend IEP meetings. Finally, the partnership principle of *communication* includes the action of providing and coordinating information with families in a clear manner. Chief among these communication skills is the ability to *listen* to parents by providing opportunities for them to feel comfortable speaking up. When an orientation meeting is provided in advance of the IEP, it is necessary to provide structured ways for parents to provide input in advance, have an advocate at the meeting to invite their participation, and ensure flexible and convenient scheduling. This leads to effective communication and demonstrated *commitment* on the part of professionals to students and their families.

Partnering With Families in Supporting Students' Positive Behavior

Importance of Partnerships Related to Behavior

IDEA requires the IEP team to consider positive behavior intervention and supports (PBIS) for any student whose behavior impedes his or her learning or the learning of others. Furthermore, IDEA underscores the effectiveness of whole-school PBIS approaches and directs Congress to provide grants for preservice and in-service PBIS training. PBIS is especially important for students with intellectual disability given that this group of students exhibit problem behavior at higher rates than children without intellectual disability (Dekker, Koot, van der Ende, & Verhulst, 2002). It is well documented that child/adolescent problem behavior is associated with increased family-related stress (Baker, Blacher, Crnic, & Edelbrock, 2002; Neece, Green, & Baker, 2012). Fox, Vaughn, Wyatte, and Dunlap (2002) qualitatively examined family perspectives on problem behavior and concluded: "we found it difficult to construct the prose that would adequately convey the emotional, physical, and structural impact of problem behavior on family life. Problem behavior relentlessly affected family relationships, physical circumstances, social networks, and daily activities" (Fox et al., 2002, p. 448). Therefore, efforts to involve families with joint home and school behavior programs have the potential to improve both student behavior and family well-being.

Current Challenges

Parents of students with behavior problems report being less satisfied with their child's school, teachers, and homework than the general population of parents (Duchnowski et al., 2012). On the whole, adults (teachers and parents) in the lives of students with intellectual disability and problem behavior may need increased levels of targeted support as compared to adults in the lives of students with and without intellectual disability who do not have problem behavior. There are many reasons for this higher level of support, including higher stress levels on the part of both teachers and parents that can impede the formation of trusting relationships (Baker et al., 2002; Singh & Billingsley, 1996). Further, there is an increased likelihood that teachers working with students with problem behavior have less teaching experience and lack the certification required to deal competently with problem behaviors (Billingsley, Fall, & Williams, 2006; Sutherland, Denny, & Gunter, 2005). In sum, both families of children with intellectual disability and behavior problems and the teachers who work with them may also be among those with the highest level of need when compared to all teachers of school-aged children.

Research-Based Practices

Research suggests a connection between partnership, problem behavior, and parent involvement. Kim, Sheridan, Kwon, and Koziol (2013) found that specific parent involvement factors—role construction, or parents' belief that it is their role to be involved in their child's education, and self-efficacy, or parents belief that they have the skills needed to be involved in their child's education—were related to (a) child problem behavior and (b) the parent-teacher relationship. The findings of this study indicate that parental involvement appears to be a key factor influencing student problem behavior and partnership. Therefore, professionals should support families in gaining the skills they need to address problem behavior at home within everyday routines. Lucyshyn et al. (2004) examined parent-child interactions for families of children with intellectual disability and problem behavior and concluded that, in order to address problem behavior, parents need to learn strategies from behavioral specialists. They explain that addressing problem behavior requires "some level of expertise" (p. 117). Therefore, it is important to realize that families can use some sort of structured intervention to manage challenging behavior, just as teachers do.

To this point, there is significant evidence that families are very capable of partnering with professionals on behavior interventions. Looking at one study in particular, Lucyshyn et al. (2007) examined the outcomes of a family-implemented PBIS plan in which parents implemented a specific behavior intervention in a case study design, to change one child's severe problem behavior across four family routines in home and community settings. The family's child had intellectual disability, severe problem behavior, and autism. Findings indicated that the child's problem behavior reduced to "zero or near zero levels" (p. 145) and participation in routines increased from zero to 75%. These impressive findings were maintained and even improved during the seven years of maintenance evaluations. In addition to the positive child outcomes, Lucyshyn et al. also observed improved parent outcomes as well. Prior to the intervention, the mother in this study was unable to seek paid employment due to the caregiving demands of her child with intellectual disability. However, after her daughter's improved behavior, the parents were able to enroll their child in a community respite program. This "newfound confidence and free time" (p. 145) was associated with decreased depression and an interest in finding work outside of the home for the mother.

The findings of Lucyshyn et al. (2007) are not unique. McLaughlin, Denney, Snyder, and Welsh (2012) conducted a literature review of 18 studies spanning 10 years on parent-implemented PBIS interventions for children with disabilities ages 3 to 8 years. Overwhelmingly, child behavior outcomes improved as a result of parent-implemented strategies. Most studies included interventions that had a family education program (e.g., demonstration of intervention, role play), featuring a collaborative approach whereby the family had input into the nature of the intervention, and were carried out in the home or other natural environment. Across studies, families implemented interventions with high levels of integrity. These findings indicate that partnering with families in implementing behavioral strategies at home may be an important element of a school-based PBIS program.

In addition to supporting parents in their involvement in their child's education and in teaching parents how to implement behavioral strategies in the home, there is evidence to suggest that paying particular attention to the emotional support that is provided to families and students with intellectual disability and problem behavior is also important. McCormick, Cappella, O'Connor, and McClowry (2013), for example, found teacher emotional support to students within the classroom to be an important mediator in the relationship of home-school communication and student problem behavior. Student-teacher relationship quality has been identified as a correlate to child problem behavior (Nurmi, 2012). Addressing student-directed emotional support may be particularly important for students with intellectual disability as they have been shown to have less favorable and less consistent relationships with their teachers as compared to students without intellectual disability (Blacher, Baker, & Eisenhower, 2009). In building relationships with students, professionals must value the family's opinion about their child's needs and consider how to build on students' strengths. Participating in person-centered planning can be a useful tool in establishing positive relationships with students who have intellectual disability and in providing emotional supports in the school setting given its focus on students' strengths from the student and family perspective.

Research indicates that emotional supports are also critical for the well-being of families. Fox et al. (2002) found that families of children with problem behavior described the emotional support they received from professionals or friends as most helpful in addressing their child and family needs. Participants did not place emphasis on practices that special educators typically see as their role—that is, "making [student] gains or achieving [student] outcomes" (p. 448). This research suggests that professionals should pay particular attention to their interactions and communication with families of children with intellectual disability and problem behavior: Be available when the family needs you, pay attention to what they have to say, and listen without judgment. Another strategy for providing emotional support to families is to connect them with other families of children with intellectual disability. Kutash, Duchnowski, Green, and Ferron (2013) found that a parent-to-parent intervention in which experienced parents offered emotional, informational, and instrumental support was associated with the target parents' increased engagement in their child's education and mental health services, increased perceived benefit of engagement, and increased beliefs that important people in their lives were involved in their child's education and mental health services. Parent-to-parent support has been documented elsewhere as an effective strategy for helping families deal positively with their child and family demands, view their lives more favorably, and make progress on important child/family goals (Singer et al., 1999). There are many parent-to-parent programs across the nation. You can find information about Parent to Parent USA by visiting this link: http://www.p2pusa.org/p2pusa/sitepages/p2p-home.aspx.

Relationship to Partnership Principles

Obviously, a child with intellectual disability who also experiences problem behavior presents challenges to all the adults in his or her life, both in the family and at school. Under these stressful conditions it is even more critical to maintain a high-quality partnership. A key feature is *communication*. In particular, it will be important to practice good *listening* skills to understand what the family is experiencing at home, strategies that seem to work for the parents, and additional needs they may have. Sometimes just listening when families are under stress is a major support in and of itself. Another feature that is important is demonstrating *respect* for the family, in particular avoiding judgments about the family that imply blame for the student's problem behaviors. Understanding the family culture and respecting that the family is doing the best they can within their own sphere of knowledge and experience may be difficult in some cases, but is essential in establishing a trusting relationship. Finally, working with students with intellectual disability and problem behaviors and their families requires a level of *commitment* on the part of professionals. Commitment is demonstrated by communicating that the student and the family are not "just a job" and indicating availability in crisis situations; these actions go a long way toward building *trust*.

Partnering With Families in Supporting Students' Academics

Importance of Partnerships Related to Academics

A key IDEA theme is that students with disabilities must make progress in the general curriculum. The general curriculum is based on academic standards (reading, math, science, etc.) states adopt in order to document and report on student academic proficiency. Students with disabilities lag far behind their typical peers in standards-based assessment scores related to general curriculum content. For example, three times as many students with disabilities are "below basic" in eighth grade math as compared to their peers without disabilities (65% vs. 21%) (US Department of Education, 2012).

Research has documented that parental involvement in academics is associated with positive outcomes for children (Hill & Tyson, 2009). Galindo and Sheldon (2012), for example, found that family involvement at school was associated with kindergarten students' math and reading achievement, and Sonnenschein and Galindo (2015) documented the favorable link between reading at home and math achievement. Duchnowski et al. (2012) found that students with emotional and behavioral disorders (EBD) performed better on a test of problem-solving skills if their parents were more involved in their education.

Current Challenges

It is well documented that students with culturally and linguistically diverse backgrounds are disproportionally represented in special education (US Department of Education, 2012). Therefore, educators must consider not only the impact of disability on parental involvement, but also families' cultural characteristics, which may conflict with the school's family involvement practices or policies. Parent involvement practices and discourses have been criticized for assuming that the parents' role is to serve as a resource for addressing schools' interests, and for imposing mainstream values of involvement on families (Lai & Vadeboncoeur, 2012). Trainor (2010) cited the inflexibility of the special education service provision and the systemic bias of schools toward privileged students who are "typical or able" (p. 261) as possible explanations for what is impeding parents' ability to connect with schools and establish effective involvement. The following research-based practices include specific recommendations aimed at promoting equality among parents of children with intellectual disability and professionals in supporting students' academics.

Research-Based Practices

Hill and Tyson (2009) conducted a meta-analysis of 50 studies examining the relationship between research-based strategies for parent involvement and academic achievement from 1985 to 2006. They defined parental involvement according to the following three typologies: home-based involvement, school-based involvement, and academic socialization. Academic socialization (e.g., communicating expectations for the value of education, teaching their child learning strategies) was the strongest predictor of student academic success. School-based involvement (e.g., attending school events, communicating with the teacher) was also a significant predictor. However, home-based involvement was more complex in that not all types of home involvement predicted academic achievement. Educationally enriching activities (e.g., making books and other educational materials available, taking children to museums and to the library) predicted academic achievement whereas help with homework did not. We should interpret this finding with caution, however, since homework help may be a proxy variable for other factors that are correlated negatively with academic achievement such as parents tending to work more on homework with students who were already struggling, or parental interference with their child's autonomy. Building on the research of Hill and Tyson and others, we report practices to promote parent involvement in the academic experiences of their child with intellectual disability in Table 18.2.

Relationship to Partnership Practices

Connecting to the partnership framework illustrated in Figure 18.1, involving families in their child's academics requires effective *communication*. Several studies (e.g., Anderson & Minke, 2007; Walker, Ice, Hoover-Dempsey, & Sandler, 2011) have underscored the influence of specific teacher invitations in parents' overall involvement at home and at school. In order to carry out these research-based partnership practices for academics, it is necessary to demonstrate *commitment* to the child and family. Although many state teacher standards include family involvement as an indicator, teachers may not be held accountable for encouraging family involvement; therefore, in doing so, teachers will go above and beyond an indicator of commitment. A second *commitment* indicator is flexible scheduling, which will be critical in achieving meetings with families that enable professionals to learn about a family's specific needs for involvement and brainstorm strategies to address those needs. Finally, the research on family involvement highlights the mismatch between the values held at the school about family involvement and family values about involvement. Therefore, it is critical that *respect* is demonstrated in partnerships with families by learning about their culturally based beliefs related to involvement, affirming their strengths, and treating families with dignity.

Table 18.2 Research-based partnership practices for supporting students' academics

Research-Based Practice	Practice Considerations
Support parents in providing enriching educational experiences for their child.	Send parents information about libraries or other community educational opportunities that align with the curriculum or unit students are learning at school. Provide tips on how families can incorporate educational experiences into their routine.
Support families in communicating with their child about school.	Develop tip sheets that include questions or conversation starters parents can ask to encourage their child to talk about what they are learning at school.
Support families in communicating with their child about his or her future.	During a conference, ask parents about their educational goals for their child. Problem-solve an action plan for accomplishing the goals, which may include utilizing the family's natural supports.
Encourage students to talk with their parents about what they are learning.	Fishman and Nickerson (2015) found that when students ask their parents for assistance, home-based involvement increases. Provide students with the necessary supports (modeling, direct instruction) to ensure that they have the skills to communicate with families about their school day.
Teach families how to use learning strategies at home.	Ask parents what strategies they have used at home that they have found effective. Since they know their child well, it is possible that you will pick up some effective strategies you might not otherwise have considered.
Send invitations to families about school- and classroom-related events and volunteer and/or leadership opportunities	Specific invitations from teachers have been shown to predict families' school-based involvement (Anderson & Minke, 2007). Encourage and support parents in taking on leadership roles at the school level. Under IDEA, parents are entitled to membership on the state advisory council for special education. Parent training and information centers and parent-to-parent organizations also provide excellent leadership opportunities.

Partnering With Families in Teaching Self-Determination

Importance of Partnerships Related to Self-Determination

IDEA stipulates four long-term results for students with disabilities: equality of opportunity, full participation, independent living, and economic self-sufficiency. Across the board, the National Organization on Disability (2010) reports that there are substantial gaps for adults with disabilities in meeting these goals. For example, only one-third of adults with disabilities report that they are very satisfied with their quality of life, as compared to two-thirds of adults without disabilities. It is especially noteworthy that higher levels of self-determination in adolescent students with disabilities has been linked with more positive employment and independent living outcomes (Shogren, Wehmeyer, Palmer, Rifenbark, & Little, 2015; Wehmeyer & Palmer, 2003), as well as more positive quality of life and life satisfaction (Lachapelle et al., 2005; Shogren, Lopez, Wehmeyer, Little, & Pressgrove, 2006).

As described elsewhere, promoting self-determination for students with intellectual disability has been identified as a critical component of inclusive educational practices, especially for secondary students, but increasingly also for younger students. Wehmeyer (2007) sees self-determination as related to volitional action, which means acting as the primary causal agent in one's life and making choices and decisions. Self-determination includes both beliefs (a student feels he or she has the right to and the ability for personal empowerment) and skills that enable the student to act autonomously, including self-regulation in goal setting and using problem-solving skills to attain desired outcomes (Rodriguez & Cavendish, 2013).

Evidence suggests that instruction in self-determination has both direct and indirect impacts on cognition, including problem solving (Shogren, Palmer, Wehmeyer, Williams-Diehm, & Little, 2012), self-regulation and engagement (Erwin, et al., 2015), and goal setting (Palmer & Wehmeyer, 2002). The importance of involving families in teaching self-determination has been recognized by investigators who focus on self-determination (Peralta & Arellano, 2010; Shogren & Turnbull, 2006). There is qualitative evidence that families influence the development of skills leading to self-determination in the home (Brotherson, Cook, Erwin, & Weigel, 2008) and that families actively engage in strategies to teach their children with disabilities how to make age-appropriate choices, encourage self-regulation, and help their children engage appropriately with their environment (Summers et al., 2014).

Current Challenges

Some studies document that families do not always encourage self-awareness and autonomy in children with disabilities (Zulueta & Peralta, 2008). Parents may place high value on the individual components of skills leading to self-determination (e.g., choice-making skills, goal-setting skills, problem-solving skills, self-advocacy and leadership skills, self-awareness and self-knowledge, and self-management and self-regulation skills), but may not have confidence that their son or daughter has the capacity to learn these skills, particularly as the severity of the disability increases (Carter & Lane, 2013). IDEA requires that students with disabilities must be invited to participate in their transition planning (National Center on Secondary Education and Transition, 2002); however, promoting students' effective involvement in the planning process remains challenging (Woods, Sylvester, & Martin, 2010). Evidence suggests that students who participate in goal setting and problem solving are more engaged in their learning (Reschly & Christenson, 2006). The key to promoting students' involvement in self-directing their transition planning is in convincing both parents and teachers of the value and efficacy of the effort to teach students these skills (Martin, Van Dycke, Christensen, Greene, Gardner, & Lovett, 2006).

Furthermore, self-determination is seen by some researchers as more of a reflection of Anglo-European values (Frankland et al., 2004; Zhang, Landmark, Grenwelge, & Montoya, 2010), and thus, that families from cultures with a greater emphasis on collective and family-centered decision making may not see the importance of self-determination for their son or daughter with a disability. However, in a review of literature about culture and self-determination, Shogren (2011) noted that self-determination has a common meaning across cultures, in that learning to problem-solve and make decisions—whether individually or as part of a collective—is universal.

Research-Based Practices

There is limited research suggesting that families can be successfully involved in teaching self-determination. Kim and Park (2012) used the Self-Determination Learning Model of Instruction (SDLMI; Shogren et al., 2012) with students in middle school language classes in South Korea. The approach involves providing training to families including support for goal setting, homework assistance, talking about school goals, and checking their child's homework assignments. Results showed a significant increase in students' academic engagement and goal attainment, as compared to a control group. In a study examining teaching skills related to precursors of self-determination for preschool children, Palmer et al. (2015) used a problem-solving rubric to help family and teacher dyads collaborate to select goals for preschoolers in self-regulation, choice making, or engagement, and determine specific strategies to teach and put in place at both home and school. Investigators found that when home and school goals for the child were focused on the same target outcome related to precursors to self-determination (i.e., both goals were focused on self-regulation, choice making, *or* engagement), children made significantly more gains in goal attainment as compared to those in which parents and teachers were pursuing different goals (Palmer et al., 2015). Rodger, O'Keefe, Cook, and Jones (2012) showed both parents and professionals benefited from collaborative goal setting, which resulted in positive outcomes for children and positive experiences for adults.

Relationship to Partnership Principles

These studies show both that families can be effectively involved in strategies to teach self-determination, and that their involvement results in more effective outcomes for students. In terms of our partnership framework (see Figure 18.1), it is clear that *communication* is a critical factor. Families need to understand the meaning of self-determination as well as be reassured about some common misconceptions. For example, self-determination does *not* mean that the adults in a student's life are turning over all decision-making power to him or her, but rather that the student will learn how to problem-solve and make appropriate choices in a developmentally appropriate context. This example also illustrates the importance of *respect,* in that educators need to validate families' fears about their child's safety and the need to protect them from potential exploitation and the consequences of poor decision making. It is important to talk about problem solving and the value of learning self-determination in helping to provide further protection to the young person by helping him or her to make good choices. Another aspect of *respectful* involvement is that families from different cultural backgrounds may need training to support self-determination to reflect problem solving and choice-making activities that are culturally relevant to their family. Finally, involving families in teaching skills leading to self-determination implies the principle of *equality*, in that fostering a coordinated strategy to enable the student to work on his or her goals both at home and school is likely to produce more effective results (Palmer et al., 2015).

Partnering With Families in Planning for the Transition to Adulthood

Importance of Partnerships Related to Transition to Adulthood

Navigating the world after secondary school requires many skills and coordination for everyone. For students with disabilities, IDEA requires advanced preparation for the transition from school to adulthood. Transition planning must begin by the time a child is 16 years old in order to enable students with disabilities to successfully thrive in the postsecondary community with appropriate services and supports. Although writing the plan for a student's transition to adulthood is the responsibility of the transition planning team, it is important to acknowledge the reality that the family and student are typically responsible for the student's well-being and service coordination once the student leaves school (Gross & Francis, 2015; Lindstrom, Doren, & Miesch, 2011; Shogren & Plotner, 2012). Teachers who prioritize family involvement during transition planning have higher family involvement and partnership rates (Hirano & Rowe, 2015; Landmark, Roberts, & Zhang, 2013). Research has shown that family involvement in the transition process is a predictor of postschool employment (Test, Mazzotti, et al., 2009). In addition, families' expectations for postsecondary school employment greatly affect employment outcomes for students with intellectual disability: When parents expected a student to have a paying job after high school, the student was five times more likely to do so (Carter, Austin, & Trainor, 2011). Simply stated, the role of high family expectations and family partnership in transition planning cannot be understated (Gross & Francis, 2015; King, Baldwin, Currie, & Evans, 2006; Landmark et al., 2010; Turnbull et al., 2015)

Current Challenges

The biggest challenges impeding family-professional partnerships during transition to adulthood for students with intellectual disability stem from low expectations. In addition to teachers having low expectations for partnership, teachers may also have lower expectations of their students' success in postsecondary education or employment, which may affect families' expectations and advocacy efforts (Cooney, 2002). Martinez, Conroy, and Cerreto (2012) found that, while families overall expressed positive beliefs about the future for their transition-aged youth with intellectual disability, approximately 25% of parents felt their children's teachers had much lower expectations. Furthermore, these researchers found that only 26% of parents were certain there was a transition plan in their child's IEP.

Similarly, in a survey study conducted with 108 families of transition-age students with intellectual disability, Griffin, McMillan, and Hodapp (2010) found that families were hopeful about pursuing postsecondary education programs, but they felt educators were less supportive of this option. Shogren and Plotner (2012) found that only 62% of families of transition-aged youth with intellectual disability in a national sample had received any information about postsecondary school services. Griffin et al.'s study revealed numerous barriers to students with intellectual disability transitioning to postsecondary education; 73% of respondents highlighted the lack of information and guidance readily available for families as the primary impediment to pursuing this option, and 36% of respondents reported not receiving any guidance about postsecondary education options from teachers. Thirteen percent of participants admitted that "written and online materials were difficult to understand" (p. 342).

Research-Based Practices

Despite these challenges, there are several research-based practices that can be implemented to increase family and professional expectations in the transition process and family knowledge of the numerous postsecondary options for their children with intellectual disability. First and foremost, in order to partner with families during this important part of their children's lives, high expectations are important and must be tailored to each student's strengths and dreams (Cooney, 2002). As discussed earlier, research shows that family involvement in the transition process correlates with higher postschool outcomes. Stated bluntly by Hirano and Rowe (2015): "The role of teachers in engaging parents cannot be underestimated. Parents respond with involvement to teachers who invite them to be involved" (p. 9).

Teaching families about transition planning and postschool options is an evidence-based practice (Test, Fowler, et al., 2009). Increasing family knowledge has been shown to increase families' expectations for postschool employment outcomes. Young, Morgan, Callow-Heusser, and Lindstrom (2014) conducted a study in which they compared two approaches to increase knowledge of transition resources: giving parents a brochure about local transition services or providing the brochure supplemented with one hour of small-group training. They randomly assigned parents to each of these conditions. One month after the informational session, 64% of the parents in the training session had contacted community service providers while no parents who had received only the brochure had contacted a community service provider. These results suggest that meeting with families to discuss information may enhance their ability to use the information they have received in a written or lectured format.

The Family Employment Awareness Training project (FEAT; Francis, Gross, Turnbull, & Parent-Johnson, 2013; Francis, Gross, Turnbull, & Turnbull, 2014; Gross & Francis, 2015; Gross, Francis, & Pijem, 2015) is a research-based program for increasing expectations for competitive employment and raising understanding of the myriad federal and state employment resources available. FEAT focuses on employment options, potential family roles in supporting employment for their children, how to access disability benefits in education and health care, the available resources to support employees and employers who hire people with intellectual disability, laws that protect people with intellectual disability from discrimination, and local and national funding opportunities.

In the first part of FEAT, called *Building the Dream of Employment*, participants imagine a vision and expectation for competitive employment for the family member with a disability. This part uses a person-centered planning approach (discussed previously in this chapter). The second part, *Identifying and Accessing Employment Resources*, focuses on improving participants' knowledge of state and federal resources that can support employment. FEAT includes a variety of small-group activities for individuals with intellectual disability and their families (both together as a family and separated into peer groups), opportunities to network with local experts (including people with intellectual disability and their families who have been successfully employed as well as local representatives of employment agencies). Families develop an action plan for employment as a part of FEAT, and local parent training and information centers or teachers follow up with families to support the plan's implementation.

Using person-centered planning to imagine postschool outcomes, for example, is one research-based component of transition planning that promotes family involvement in the process (Shepherd, Kervick, & Salembier, 2015). Connecting families with other local families who have recently gone through the transition planning process can bring together families who may feel isolated, foster their self-awareness and ability to situate their beliefs about their children's futures within the larger context of possibilities, and increase their role in active transition planning (Kingsnorth, Gall, Beayni, & Rigby, 2011). Developing an understanding of programs will enable families to be critical consumers of programs for their children across the lifespan (Hirano & Rowe, 2015).

Relationship to Partnership Principles

These studies show both that families should and can be integral participants in transition planning. Teachers and service providers must provide information about transition planning and postschool options in a variety of formats and have high expectations for students and families. In terms of our partnership framework (see Figure 18.1), *communication* is a critical factor in partnering with families during this time of complex options and tasks. It is important to remember and *respect* the fact that families will continue to be the primary support for most people with intellectual disability postschool. Showing *respect* for families and their sons and daughters during this transition from the coordinated school context to the more fragmented postschool context is paramount to partnership. *Advocating* for students and their families to receive the information they need demonstrates *commitment* and high expectations. Using person-centered planning and establishing students are critical partners in transition planning will help demonstrate competence and solidify trusting family professional partnerships.

Conclusion

As you conclude this chapter, we hope that you are convinced of the importance of developing and implementing trusting partnerships with families of students with intellectual disability (and, in fact, all students). You have learned about the powerful role of families in starting schools for their children with intellectual disability and in advocating for the passage and effective implementation of IDEA. Because it truly is "on families' shoulders we stand" in the field of special education, and research clearly documents the importance of and positive outcomes of trusting partnerships. It is of paramount importance to recognize the challenges and become competent in research-based practices related to the seven principles of partnership—communication, professional competence, advocacy, respect, commitment, equality, and trust—and to understand ways to apply these principles to the particular topics we have addressed, including assessment for special education eligibility, IEPs, behavior support, academic support, training to support self-determination, and transition planning. Don't stop there, however. The key is to apply the partnership principles to *every aspect of educational practice.*

References

Anderson, K. J., & Minke, K.M. (2007). Parent involvement in education: Toward an understanding of parents' decision making. *The Journal of Educational Research, 100*, 311–323.

Aud, S., Wilkinson-Flicker, S., Kristapovich, P., Rathbun, A., Wang, X., & Zhang, J. (2013). *The condition of education 2013* (NCES 2013-037). US Department of Education, National Center for Education Statistics. Washington, DC. Retrieved from http://nces.ed.gov/pubs2013/2013037.pdf

Baker, B.L., Blacher, J., Crnic, K.A., & Edelbrock, C. (2002). Behavior problems and parenting stress in families of three-year-old children with and without developmental delays. *American Journal on Mental Retardation, 107*, 433–444.

Billingsley, B.S., Fall, A.M., & Williams, T.O. (2006). Who is teaching students with emotional and behavioral disorders?: A profile and comparison to other special educators. *Behavior Disorders, 31*, 252–264.

Blacher, J., Baker, B.L., Eisenhower, A.S. (2009). Student-teacher relationship stability across early school years for children with intellectual disability or typical development. *American Journal on Intellectual and Developmental Disabilities, 114*, 322–339. doi: http://dx.doi.org/10.1352/1944-7558-114.5.322

Blackwell, W.H., & Rossetti, Z.S. (2014). The development of individualized education programs: Where have we been and where should we go now? *SAGE Open*, 1–15. doi: 10.1177/2158244014530411

Blue-Banning, M., Summers, J.A., Frankland, H.C., Nelson, L.L., & Beegle, G. (2004). Dimensions of family and professional partnerships: Constructive guidelines for collaboration. *Exceptional Children, 70*, 167–184.

Boggs, E.M. (1985). Who is putting whose head in the sand? (Or in the clouds, as the case may be). In H.R. Turnbull & A.P. Turnbull (Eds.), *Parents speak out: Then and now* (2nd ed., pp. 39–55). Englewood Cliffs, NJ: Merrill/Prentice Hall.

Brinkerhoff, J. L., & Vincent, L. J. (1986). Increasing parental decision-making at the individualized educational program meeting. *Journal of Early Intervention, 11*(1), 46–58.

Brotherson, M. J., Cook, C.C., Erwin, E. J., & Weigel, C. J. (2008). Understanding self-determination and families of young children with disabilities in home environments. *Journal of Early Intervention, 31*, 22–43.

Bruder, M.B., & Dunst, C.J. (2015). Parental judgments of early childhood intervention personnel practices: Applying a consumer science perspective. *Topics in Early Childhood Special Education, 34*, 200–210. doi: 10.1177/0271121414522527

Burke, M.M., & Hodapp, R.M. (2014). Relating stress of mothers of children with developmental disabilities to family-school partnerships. *Intellectual and Developmental Disabilities, 52*, 13–23. doi: 10.1352/1934-9556-52.1.13

Carter, E.W., Austin, D., & Trainor, A.A. (2011). Predictors of postschool employment outcomes for young adults with severe disabilities. *Journal of Disability Policy Studies, 23*, 50–63.

Carter, E.W., & Lane, K.L. (2013). Self-determination among transition age youth with autism or intellectual disability: Parent perspectives. *Research and Practice for Persons with Severe Disabilities, 38*, 129–138.

Chang, F., Early, D.M., & Winton, P. J. (2005). Early childhood teacher preparation in special education at 2- and 4-year institutions of higher education. *Journal of Early Intervention, 27*, 110–124.

Chen, W.B., & Gregory, A. (2011). Parental involvement in the prereferral process implications for schools. *Remedial and Special Education, 32*, 447–457.

Cooney, B.F. (2002). Exploring perspectives on transition of youth with disabilities: Voices of young adults, parents, and professionals. *Mental Retardation, 40*, 425–435.

Dekker, M.C., Koot, H.M., van der Ende, J., & Verhulst, F.C. (2002). Emotional and behavioral problems in children and adolescents with and without intellectual disability. *Journal of Child Psychology and Psychiatry, 43*, 1087–1098.

Duchnowski, A. J., Kutash, K., Green, A.L., Ferron, J.M., Wagner, M., & Vengrofski, B. (2012). Parent support services for families of children with emotional disturbances served in elementary school special education settings: Examination of data from the special education elementary longitudinal study. *Journal of Disability Policy Studies, 24*, 36–52. doi: 10.1177/1044207312460889

Epstein, J.L., & Sanders, M.G. (2006). Prospects for change: Preparing educators for school, family, and community partnerships. *Peabody Journal of Education, 81*, 81–120.

Erwin, E. J.; Maude, S.P., Palmer, S.B., Summers, J.A., Brotherson, M. J., Haines, S. J., . . . Peck, N.F. (2015). Fostering the foundations of self-determination in early childhood: A process for enhancing child outcomes across home and school. *Early Childhood Education Journal, 44*(325). doi 10.1007/s10643-015-0710-9

Eskow, K., Chasson, G., Mitchell, R., & Summers, J.A. (2015). *Association between parent-teacher partnership satisfaction and outcomes for children and families with autism.* Towson, MD: Towson University. Manuscript submitted for publication.

Fish, W.W. (2008). The IEP meeting: Perceptions of parents of students who receive special education services. *Preventing School Failure, 53*, 8–14.

Fisher, R., Ury, W.L., & Patton, B. (2011). *Getting to yes: Negotiating agreements without giving in.* London: Penguin.

Fishman, C.E., & Nickerson, A.B. (2015). Motivations for involvement: A preliminary investigation of parents of students with disabilities. *Journal of Child and Family Studies, 24*, 523–535. doi: 10.1007/s10826-013-9865-4

Fox, L., Vaughn, B. J., Wyatte, M.L., & Dunlap, G. (2002). "We can't expect other people to understand": Family perspectives on problem behavior. *Exceptional Children, 68*, 437–450.

Francis, G.L., Gross, J.M.S., Turnbull, H.R., & Parent-Johnson, W. (2013). Evaluating the effectiveness of the Family Employment Awareness Training in Kansas: A pilot study. *Research and Practice for Persons with Severe Disabilities, 38*, 1–14.

Francis, G.L., Gross, J.M.S., Turnbull, A.P., & Turnbull, H.R. (2014). Understanding the barriers to competitive employment. *Inclusion, 2*(1), 37–53.

Frankland, H.C., Turnbull, A.P., Wehmeyer, M.L., & Blackmountain, L. (2004). An exploration of the self-determination construct and disability as it relates to the Diné (Navajo) culture. *Education and Training in Developmental Disabilities, 39*, 191–205.

Galindo, C., & Sheldon, S.B. (2012). School and home connections and children's kindergarten achievement gains: The mediating role of family involvement. *Early Childhood Research Quarterly, 27*, 90–103. doi: 10.1016/j.ecresq.2011.05.004

Gilhool, T. (1997, Spring). The parent movement: Reflections and directions. *Coalition Quarterly, 14*, 1.

Goldman, S.E., & Burke, M.M. (in press). The effectiveness of interventions to increase parent involvement in special education: A systematic literature review and meta-analysis. *Exceptionality.*

Goldstein, S., & Turnbull, A.P. (1982). The use of two strategies to increase parent participation in IEP conferences. *Exceptional Children, 48*, 360–361.

Griffin, M.M., McMillan, E.D., & Hodapp, R.M. (2010). Family perspectives on post-secondary education for students with intellectual disabilities. *Education and Training in Autism and Developmental Disabilities, 45*, 339–346.

Gross, J. M. S., & Francis, G.L. (2015). Role of expectations and knowledge in transition to employment. In *Way Leads on to Way: Paths to Employment for People with Intellectual Disability* (pp 63–83). Washington, DC: American Association on Intellectual and Developmental Disabilities (AAIDD).

Gross, J.M.S., Francis, G.L., & Pijem, M. A. (2015). Family Employment Awareness Training (FEAT) in Kansas: Description of a family-focused and rationale supporting it. *Journal of Vocational Rehabilitation, 43*, 217–228.

Hardin, B.J., Mereoiu, M., Hung, H.F., & Roach-Scott, M. (2009). Investigating parent and professional perspectives concerning special education services for preschool Latino children. *Early Childhood Education Journal, 37*, 93–102.

Harry, B., & Klingner, J. (2014). *Why are so many minority students in special education?* New York: Teachers College Press.

Hill, N.E., & Tyson, D.F. (2009). Parental involvement in middle school: A meta-analytic assessment of the strategies that promote achievement. *Developmental Psychology, 45*, 740–763. doi: 10.1037/a0015362

Hirano, K.A., & Rowe, D.A. (2015). A conceptual model for parent involvement in secondary special education. *Journal of Disability Policy Studies*. Advance online publication. doi: 10.1177/1044207315583901

Howland, A., Anderson, J.A., Smiley, A.D., & Abbott, D.J. (2006). School liaisons: Bridging the gap between home and school. *School Community Journal, 16*, 47–68.

Kim, E.M., Sheridan, S.M., Kwon, K., & Koziol, N. (2013). Parent beliefs and children's social-behavioral functioning: The mediating role of parent-teacher relationships. *Journal of School Psychology, 51*, 175–185. doi: http://dx.doi.org/10.1016/j.jsp.2013.01.003

Kim, N.H., & Park, J. (2012). The effects of the family-involved SDLMI on academic engagement and goal attainment of middle school students with disabilities who exhibit problem behavior. *International Journal of Special Education, 27*, 117–127.

King, G.A., Baldwin, P.J., Currie, M., & Evans, J. (2006). The effectiveness of transition strategies for youth with disabilities. *Children's Health Care, 35*, 155–178.

Kingsnorth, S., Gall, C., Beayni, S., & Rigby, P. (2011). Parents as transition experts? Qualitative findings from a pilot parent-led peer support group. *Child: Care, Health, and Development, 37*, 833–840. doi: 10.1111/j.1365-2214.2011.01294.x

Klein, S., Wynn, K., Ray, L., Demeriez, L., LaBerge, P., Pei, J., & Pierre, C.S. (2011). Information sharing during diagnostic assessments: What is relevant for parents? *Physical & Occupational Therapy in Pediatrics, 31*, 120–132.

Klingner, J.K., & Harry, B. (2006). The special education referral and decision-making process for English language learners: Child study team meetings and placement conferences. *Teachers College Record, 108*, 2247–2281.

Kutash, K., Duchnowski, A.J., Green, A.L., & Ferron, J. (2013). Effectiveness of the parent connectors program: Results from a randomized controlled trial. *School Mental Health, 5*, 192–208. doi: 10.1007/s12310-013-9106-4

Kyzar, K.B., Brady, S., Summers, J.A., Haines, S.J., & Turnbull, A.P. (in press). Services and supports, partnership, and FQOL for families of children with deaf-blindness. *Exceptional Children.*

Lachapelle, Y., Wehmeyer, M.L., Halewyck, C., Courbois, Y., Keither, K.D., Schalock, R., . . . Walsh, P.N. (2005). The relationship between quality of life and self-determination: An international study. *Journal of Intellectual Disability Research, 49*, 740–744.

Lai, Y., & Vadeboncoeur, J.A. (2012). The discourse of parent involvement in special education: A critical analysis linking policy documents to the experiences of mothers. *Educational Policy, 27*, 867–897. doi: 10.1177/0895904812440501

Landmark, L.J., Ju, S., & Zhang, D. (2010). Substantiated best practices in transition: Fifteen plus years later. *Career Development for Exceptional Individuals, 33*, 165–176.

Landmark, L.J., Roberts, E.L., & Zhang, D. (2013). Educators' beliefs and practices about parent involvement in transition planning. *Career Development and Transition for Exceptional Individuals, 36*, 114–123.

Larry P. v. Riles, 343 F. Supp. 1306 (N.D. Cal. 1972), 502 F. 2d 963 (9th Cir. 1974), No. C-71-2270 RFP (N.D. Cal., October 16, 1979), 793 F. 2d 969 (9th Cir. 1984).

Laws, G., & Millward, L. (2001). Predicting parents' satisfaction with the education of their child with Down's syndrome. *Educational Research, 45*, 209–226. doi: 10.1080/00131880110051173

Lindstrom, L., Doren, B., & Miesch, J. (2011). Waging a living: Career development and long-term employment outcomes for young adults with disabilities. *Exceptional Children, 77*, 423–434.

Lucyshyn, J.M., Albin, R.W., Horner, R.H., Mann, J.C., Mann, J.A., & Wadsworth, G. (2007). Family implementation of positive behavior support for a child with autism: Longitudinal, single-case, experimental, and descriptive replication and extension. *Journal of Positive Behavior Interventions, 9*, 131–150.

Lucyshyn, J.M., Irvin, L.K., Blumberg, E.R., Laverty, R., Horner, R.H., & Sprague, J.R. (2004). Validating the construct of coercion in family routines: Expanding the unit of analysis in behavioral assessment with families of children with developmental disabilities. *Research & Practice for Persons with Severe Disabilities, 29*, 104–121.

Mandic, C.G., Rudd, R., Hehir, T., & Acevedo-Garcia, D. (2012). Readability of special education procedural safeguards. *Journal of Special Education, 45*, 195–203.

Martin, J.E., Van Dycke, J.L., Christensen, W.R., Greene, B.A., Gardner, J.E., & Lovett, D.L. (2006). Increasing student participation in their transition IEP meetings: Establishing the self-directed IEP as an evidenced-based practice. *Exceptional Children, 72*, 299–316.

Martinez, D.C., Conroy, J.W., & Cerreto, M.C. (2012). Parent involvement in the transition process of children with intellectual disabilities: The influence of inclusion on parent desires and expectations for postsecondary education. *Journal of Policy and Practice in Intellectual Disabilities, 9*, 279–288.

Maydoxz, A., & Maydoxz, D. (2013). Culturally and linguistically diverse students with disabilities: Case law review. *Multicultural Learning and Teaching, 8*, 65–80.

McCormick, M.P., Cappella, E., O'Connor, E.E., & McClowry, S.G. (2013). Parent involvement, emotional support, and behavior problems: An ecological approach. *The Elementary School Journal, 114*, 276–300.

McLaughlin, T.W., Denney, M.K., Snyder, P.A., & Welsh, J.L. (2012). Behavioral support interventions implemented by families of young children: Examination of contextual fit. *Journal of Positive Behavioral Interventions, 14*, 87–97. doi: 10.1177/1098300711411305

Meadan, H., Thompson, J.R., Hagiwara, M., Herold, J., Hoekstra, S., & Manser, S. (2009). Evaluating the acceptability and effectiveness of family assessment portfolios. *Education and Training in Developmental Disabilities, 44*, 421–430.

MetLife. (2005). *The MetLife survey of the American teacher.* Hartford, CT: Author.

Miller, P.S., & Losardo, A. (2002). Graduates' perceptions of strengths and needs in interdisciplinary teacher preparation for early childhood education: A state study. *Teacher Education and Special Education, 25*, 309–319.

Mueller, T.G. (2009). IEP facilitation: A promising approach to resolving conflicts between families and schools. *Teaching Exceptional Children, 41*(3), 60–67.

National Organization on Disability. (2010). *National Organization on Disability/Harris Survey of Americans with Disabilities.* Washington, DC: Author.

National Parent Technical Assistance Center. (2013). *Parent centers helping families: Outcome data 2012–2013.* Minneapolis, MN: Parent Technical Assistance Center Network.

Neece, C.L., Green, S.A., & Baker, B. (2012). Parenting stress and child behavior problems: A transactional relationship across time. *American Journal on Intellectual and Developmental Disabilities, 117*, 48–66. doi: 10.1352/1944-75558-117.1.48

Nurmi, J.E. (2012). Students' characteristics and teacher-child relationships in instruction: A meta-analysis. *Educational Research Review, 7*, 177–197.

Palmer, S.B., Summers, J.A., Fleming, K., Brotherson, M.J., Maude, S.P., Erwin, E.J., . . . Zheng, Y. (2015). *Foundations for self-determination in early childhood intervention: Fidelity, feasibility, and outcomes.* Manuscript under review.

Palmer, S.B., & Wehmeyer, M.L. (2002). *A teacher's guide to the self-determined learning model of instruction: Early elementary version.* Lawrence, KS: The Beach Center on Disability.

Pennsylvania Association for Retarded Citizens (PARC) v. Commonwealth of Pennsylvania. (1971, 1972).

Peralta, F., & Arellano, A. (2010). Family and disability: A theoretical perspective on the family centered approach for promoting self-determination. *Electronic Journal of Research in Educational Psychology, 8*, 1339–1362.

Reschly, A., & Christenson, S.L. (2006). Prediction of dropout among students with mild disabilities. *Remedial and Special Education, 27*, 276–292.

Rodger, S., O'Keefe, A., Cook, M., & Jones, J. (2012). Parents' and service providers' perceptions of the family goal setting tool: A pilot study. *Journal of Applied Research in Intellectual Disabilities, 25*, 360–371.

317

Rodriguez, R., & Cavendish, W. (2013). Ethnicity and gender as moderators of the relationship between perceived family environments and self-determination among students with disabilities. *Career Development and Transition for Exceptional Individuals, 36*, 152–162.

Ryan, K., Cooper, J.M., & Bolick, C.M. (2016). *Those who can, teach* (14th ed.). Boston, MA: Cengage Learning.

Schaffer v. Weast. (2005). 126 S. Ct. 528.

Shepherd, K.G., Kervick, C.T., & Salembier, G. (2015). Person-centered planning: Tools for promoting employment, self-direction, and independence among persons with intellectual disability. In *Paths to employment for people with intellectual disability* (pp. 299–320). Washington, DC: AAIDD.

Shogren, K.A. (2011). Culture and self-determination: A synthesis of the literature and directions for future research and practice. *Career Development for Exceptional Individuals, 34*, 115–127. doi: 10.1177/0885728811398271

Shogren, K.A., Lopez, S., Wehmeyer, M.L., Little, T.D., & Pressgrove, C.L. (2006). The role of positive psychology constructs in predicting life satisfaction in adolescents with and without cognitive disabilities: An exploratory study. *The Journal of Positive Psychology, 1*, 37–52.

Shogren, K.A., & Plotner, A.J. (2012). Transition planning for students with intellectual disability, autism, or other disabilities: Data from the National Longitudinal Transition Study-2. *Intellectual and Developmental Disabilities, 50*, 16–30. doi: 10.1352/1934-9556-50.1.16

Shogren, K.A., & Turnbull, A.P. (2006). Promoting self-determination in young children with disabilities: The critical role of families. *Infants & Young Children, 19*, 338–352.

Shogren, K.A., Palmer, S.B., Wehmeyer, M.L., Williams-Diehm, K., & Little, T. (2012). Effect of intervention with the self-determined learning model of instruction on access and goal attainment. *Remedial and Special Education, 33*, 320–330.

Shogren, K.A., Wehmeyer, M.L., Palmer, S.B., Rifenbark, G.G., & Little, T.D. (2015). Relationships between self-determination and postschool outcomes for youth with disabilities. *Journal of Special Education, 48*, 256–267.

Singer, G.H.S., Marquis, J., Powers, L.K., Blanchard, L., DiVenere, N., Santelli, B., . . . Sharp, M. (1999). A multi-site evaluation of Parent to Parent programs for parents of children with disabilities. *Journal of Early Intervention, 22*, 217–219.

Singh, K., & Billingsley, B.S. (1996). Intent to stay in teaching: Teachers of students with emotional disorders versus other special educators. *Remedial & Special Education, 17*, 37–47.

Sonnenschein, S., & Galindo, C. (2015). Race/ethnicity and early mathematics skills: Relations between home, classroom, and mathematics achievement. *The Journal of Educational Research, 108*, 261–277. doi: 10.1080/0022/671.2014.880394

Sutherland, K.S., Denny, R.K., & Gunter, P.L. (2005). Teachers of students with emotional and behavioral disorders reported professional development needs: Differences between fully licensed and emergency-licensed teachers. *Preventing School Failure: Alternative Education for Children and Youth, 49*, 41–46. doi: 10.3200/PSFL.49.2.41-46

Summers, J.A., Brotherson, M.J., Erwin, E.J., Maude, S.P., Palmer, S.B., Haines, S.J., . . . Zheng, Y.Z. (2014). Family reflections on the foundations of self-determination in early childhood. *Inclusion, 2*, 175–194. doi: 10.1352/2326-6988-2.03.175

Summers, J.A., Hoffman, L., Marquis, J., Turnbull, A., Poston, D. (2005). Relationship between parent satisfaction regarding partnerships with professionals and age of child. *Topics in Early Childhood Special Education, 25*, 48–58.

Summers, J.A., Hoffman, L., Marquis, J., Turnbull, A., Poston, D., & Nelson, L.L. (2005). Measuring the quality of family-professional partnerships in special education services. *Exceptional Children, 72*, 65–81.

Summers, J.A., Marquis, J., Mannan, H., Turnbull, A.P., Fleming, K., Poston, D.J., . . . Kupzyk, K. (2007). Relationship of perceived adequacy of services, family-professional partnerships, and family quality of life in early childhood service programmes. *International Journal of Disability, Development and Education, 54*, 319–338. doi: 10.1080/1034912071488848

Test, D.W., Fowler, C.H., Richter, S.M., White, J., Mazzotti, V.L., Walker, A.R., . . . Kortering, L. (2009). Evidence-based practices in secondary transition. *Career Development for Exceptional Individuals, 32*, 115–128.

Test, D.W., Mazzotti, V.L., Mustian, A.L., Fowler, C.H., Kortering, L., & Kohler, P. (2009). Evidence-based secondary transition predictors for improving post-school outcomes for students with disabilities. *Career Development for Exceptional Individuals, 32*, 160–181.

Thompson, S., Meadan, H., Fansler, K.W., Alber, S.B., & Balogh, P.A. (2007). Family assessment portfolios: A new way to jumpstart family/school collaboration. *Teaching Exceptional Children, 39*, 19–25.

Trainor, A.A. (2010). Reexamining the promise of parent participation in special education: An analysis of cultural and social capital. *Anthropology & Education Quarterly, 41*, 245–263. doi: 10.1111/j.1548-1492.2010.01086.x

Turnbull, A., Turnbull, R., Erwin, E.J., Soodak, L.C., & Shogren, K.A. (2015). *Families, professionals, and exceptionality: Positive outcomes through partnerships and trust* (7th ed.). Upper Saddle River, NJ: Pearson Education, Inc.

Turnbull, H.R., Shogren, K.A., & Turnbull, A.P. (2011). Evolution of the parent movement: Past, present, and future. In J.M. Kauffman & D.P. Hallahan (Eds.), *Handbook of special education* (pp. 639–653). New York: Routledge.

Turnbull, H.R., Turnbull, A.P., Wheat, M. (1982). Assumptions concerning parent involvement: A legislative history. *Exceptional Education Quarterly, 3*(2), 1–8.

US Department of Education. (2012). *31ˢᵗ annual report to Congress on the implementation of the Individuals with Disabilities Education Act, 2009.* Washington, DC: Author.

Wagner, M., Newman, L., Cameto, R., Javitz, H., & Valdes, K. (2012). A national picture of parent and youth participation in IEP and transition planning meetings. *Journal of Disability Policy Studies, 23*, 140–155.

Walker, J.M., Ice, C.L., Hoover-Dempsey, K.V., & Sandler, H.M. (2011). Latino parents' motivations for involvement in their children's schooling: An exploratory study. *The Elementary School Journal, 111*, 409–429.

Wehmeyer, M.L. (2007). *Promoting self-determination in students with developmental disabilities.* New York: Guildford.

Wehmeyer, M.L., & Palmer, S.B. (2003). Adult outcomes for students with cognitive disabilities three years after high school: The impact of self-determination. *Education and Training in Developmental Disabilities, 38*, 131–144.

Woods, L.L., Sylvester, L., & Martin, J.E. (2010). Student directed transition planning: Increasing student knowledge and self efficacy in the transition planning process. *Career Development and Transition for Exceptional Individuals, 33*, 106–114.

Young, J., Morgan, R.L., Callow-Heusser, C.A., & Lindstrom, L. (2014). The effects of parent training on knowledge of transition services for students with disabilities. *Career Development and Transition for Exceptional Individuals.* Advance online publication. doi: 2165143414549207

Zablotsky, B., Boswell, K., & Smith, C. (2012). An evaluation of school involvement and satisfaction of parents of children with autism spectrum disorders. *American Journal on Intellectual and Developmental Disabilities, 117*, 316–330. doi: 10.1352/1944-7558-117.4.316

Zhang, D., Katsiyannis, A., Ju, S., & Roberts, E. (2014). Minority representation in special education: 5-year trends. *Journal of Child and Family Studies, 23*, 118–127.

Zhang, D., Landmark, L., Grenwelge, C., & Montoya, L. (2010). Culturally diverse parents' perspectives on self-determination. *Education & Training in Autism and Developmental Disabilities, 45*(2), 175–186.

Zulueta, A., & Peralta, F. (2008). Parents' perceptions about the self-determined behavior of their children with intellectual disabilities. *Siglo Cero, 39*, 31–43.

Zuna, N.I. (2007). *Examination of family-professional partnerships, parent-teacher communication, and parent involvement in families of kindergarten children with and without disabilities* (Doctoral dissertation). Retrieved from ProQuest Dissertations & Theses Global. (3266511).

19

Teaching Reading and Literacy Skills to Students with Intellectual Disability

Susan R. Copeland, Elizabeth B. Keefe

Introduction

Being able to read is a critically important skill for children and adults. The United Nations Educational, Scientific, and Cultural Organization (UNESCO, 2004) underscored the importance of being able to read when it noted that acquiring literacy skills contributes to quality of life and full participation in society. Reading forms the foundation for learning other academic skills (e.g., acquiring social studies and science knowledge). Reading also opens up opportunities for full participation in social activities (e.g., corresponding with friends and family; Forts & Luckasson, 2011), employment (e.g. using literacy skills to complete work-related activities; Vaccarino, Culligan, Comrie, & Sligo, 2006), and civic activities (e.g., learning about issues that affect one's rights; Reichenberg & Lofgren, 2013). Having basic reading skills is also associated with improved health outcomes (Institute on Medicine [IOM], 2011).

Despite acknowledgement of the critical importance of learning to read, people with intellectual disability do not always acquire the skills needed to do so (Channell, Loveall, & Conners, 2013). Research over an extended period of time has clearly documented that children and adults with intellectual disability *can* learn to read (Browder, Wakeman, Spooner, Ahlgrim-Delzell, & Algozzine, 2006; Burgoyne et al., 2012; Channell et al., 2013). Yet, many people with intellectual disability do not read or do not read at a level that supports increased participation in daily activities. Koritas and Iacono (2011), in a survey of support providers, found that 67% rated reading difficulties as a significant problem for the adults with intellectual disability they supported.

The reasons for people with intellectual disability's lack of reading skills are varied. One issue that contributes to this problem is that many teachers and other professionals have low expectations of the potential of children with intellectual disability to acquire reading skills. These low expectations too often lead to limited or poor-quality instruction, resulting in very low levels of reading skill (Copeland & Keefe, 2007). For example, although researchers have documented that very young children with intellectual disability can learn foundational reading skills (e.g., acquire sight words and print knowledge), not all children in early intervention receive systematic instruction that builds these foundational skills (Goldstein, 2011). Similarly, although research findings show that students with intellectual disability do best if provided sustained high-quality reading instruction across all of their formal schooling, reading instruction may stop or be significantly limited in quantity and quality past the first few years of school (Burgoyne, Baxter, & Buckley, 2014). Related to this, teacher preparation programs frequently do not provide teacher candidates with information about research-based practices that could be incorporated into reading instruction for students with intellectual disability or give teacher candidates opportunities to practice applying these strategies during field-based experiences (Copeland, Keefe, Calhoon, Tanner, & Park, 2011; Moni & Jobling, 2014). Lack of understanding or knowledge of how to utilize assistive technology (AT) to create access to reading materials or as a means of facilitating instruction also contributes to poor-quality reading instruction for students with intellectual disability. A recent survey of more than 1,000 educators in a Midwestern state found that although respondents used technology daily in their own lives, most reported not using technology with their students with disabilities (including students with severe disabilities) daily or even weekly (Okolo & Diedrich, 2014).

The past 15 years have seen an increase in the number and type of studies investigating reading instruction for students with intellectual disability. This is likely due to several factors. In the United States, the No Child Left Behind Act (NCLB, 2001) and the reauthorization of the Individuals with Disabilities Education Act (IDEA) in 2004 required that schools focus on improving access to the general curriculum for all students and monitor their progress towards meeting grade-level academic standards. NCLB and IDEA also required teachers to implement evidence-based instruction with students with disabilities. These mandates created new interest in developing effective reading interventions for children with intellectual disability. Adding to this, the recent adoption of the Common Core State Standards (CCSS) by many states requires teachers to prepare students to meet more rigorous learning standards that require higher-level literacy skills. Teachers and schools will need to revisit the types of reading instruction they are providing to students with intellectual disability if students are to acquire such skills. Previous strategies, such as simply teaching sight words using stimulus response strategies, for example, will not be sufficient for students to meet more rigorous academic standards.

Another factor affecting reading instruction for students in K–12 schools is the increase in the number of youth with intellectual disability attending postsecondary education programs. The reauthorization of the Higher Education Opportunity Act (2008) created greater access to postsecondary programs for people with intellectual disability by providing ways to secure financial support and setting up guidelines for these programs. The result has been an increase in the number of students attending postsecondary programs. Grigal, Hart, and Weir (2014) pointed out that as more young adults with intellectual disability attend college or university programs, there will be a need to better prepare them during their K–12 education to participate academically in postsecondary program coursework. Seeing students go on to postsecondary education may also create positive changes in expectations of academic potential held by teachers, parents, and students themselves. This could in turn create changes in the quality of reading instruction provided.

Another factor that has positively influenced research on reading instruction is a growing awareness that people with intellectual disability, like their peers without disability, have the capability to be lifelong learners (Moni & Jobling, 2014). Much more is known about effective reading instruction for children and adolescents with intellectual disability, but researchers are now beginning to increase examinations of reading instruction for adults with intellectual disability (Copeland, McCord, & Kruger, 2016). The available research with adults shows that learning does not stop when people leave formal school programs. Adults with intellectual disability, like their peers, may have increased motivation and focus when pursuing learning opportunities of their own choosing and for their own purposes. Thus, literacy instruction should be available for adults who wish to expand their skills.

Each of these factors has influenced research on reading instruction for children, youth, and adults with intellectual disability. The increased number of studies conducted across the world in this area in the last 15 years has expanded our knowledge of effective reading instruction. It has also enlarged our understanding of what is literacy and how it may look in the lives of people with intellectual disability, and it is changing expectations of what is possible for people with intellectual disability.

Research-Based Practices

Prior to discussing ways to support reading and literacy skill development in people with intellectual disability, there are general issues related to learning that must be considered. The first relates to the need for support that many people with intellectual disability have in generalizing knowledge and skills across contexts (Fox, 1989). This is relevant to reading instruction because of the long history of teaching people with intellectual disability reading skills in a decontextualized manner (e.g., sight words) (Browder et al., 2006; Erickson, Hatch, & Clendon, 2010). Students may acquire isolated skills with this approach, but reading for meaning requires integration of multiple skills. Learning isolated skills is not likely to lead to reading for meaning outside of the intervention setting. More recent research supports comprehensive instruction (i.e., instruction that teaches all the components needed for effective reading) within meaningful contexts if students are to use these skills in ways that enhance their participation in school, community, or employment settings (Allor, Champlin, Gifford, & Mathes, 2010; Browder, Ahlgrim-Delzell, Flowers, & Baker, 2012). Practitioners should strive to use topics and materials that are familiar and of interest to students and to build on their current knowledge (e.g., using familiar spoken vocabulary when selecting words for decoding instruction) if they want students to transfer and use what they are learning to authentic tasks in their lives (Allor et al., 2010).

Another issue to consider is assessment. Accurately assessing the reading skills of people with intellectual disability is difficult. Each person with intellectual disability has a unique profile of cognitive abilities and support needs. Some people may experience speech delays or disorders that affect their ability to respond to standardized measures (Burgoyne et al., 2014; Ratz & Lenhard, 2013). Meaningful assessment data that can inform instruction and monitor progress often requires development of classroom based or informal measures that have been adjusted for a person's mode of communication. Practitioners should be familiar with both standardized and informal assessments that can be used to plan and monitor instruction (e.g., Nonverbal Literacy Assessment; Ahlgrim-Delzell, Browder, Flowers, & Baker, 2008–2009). Knowledge of and expertise with these tools is especially helpful when working with people who are emergent literacy learners and those who have communication support needs.

Finally, because of the wide range of language and cognitive skills across people with intellectual disability, there will be variation in outcomes of reading instruction. Many people will become conventional readers and writers when given sustained, intensive, and appropriate reading instruction. Others may not become conventional readers but will still benefit in numerous ways from having high-quality instruction. Much pleasure and useful information, for example, is learned in listening to someone else read aloud on a topic of interest or in using symbols or objects to communicate a message. Many people need sustained instruction to acquire reading skills. It is critically important that practitioners do not deny reading instruction to any person, and that they do not stop instruction if students do not make progress at a rapid rate. To do so is a denial of the person's rights to an individualized and appropriate education, and will have long-term negative consequences for the person's participation in schools, communities, and workplaces.

In the following sections we will examine research-based reading instruction practices for children and adults with intellectual disability. For ease of organization, this overview of research is structured using the core components of effective reading instruction. However, we acknowledge that effective instruction is comprehensive in nature and includes instruction in all components of reading, not merely in one or two skill areas (Allor, Mathes, Roberts, Cheatham, & Al Otaiba, 2014; Browder et al., 2012; Burgoyne et al., 2014).

Language and Communication

People with intellectual disability have wide-ranging language abilities, although most people with intellectual disability have at least some need for support related to language and communication (Snell et al., 2010). This is relevant when discussing reading and literacy instruction because oral language forms the foundation for learning to read (Scherba de Valenzuela & Tracey, 2007). Providing early language and communication intervention is essential in building vocabulary and ensuring that children have a way to express their thoughts, needs, and preferences. It is beyond the scope of this chapter to fully describe research-based practices in this area. However, findings from many years of language intervention studies support providing frequent, engaging, and meaningful communication opportunities, combined with a literacy-rich environment and high expectations to build a strong foundation on which later reading skills can expand (Downing, 2011). Teaching parents to support their child's language development is one practice with a strong research base (Kaiser & Roberts, 2013). This can take multiple forms such as parents providing frequent opportunities to participate in literacy activities (e.g., reading books together, drawing, writing; Ricci, 2011). Parents can also learn systematic language-intervention strategies to build their child's skills. Parent implemented strategies gives children more frequent opportunities to practice new language skills and facilitate their generalization to natural environments (Kaiser & Roberts, 2013).

Word Recognition

The majority of research investigating reading and people with intellectual disability has focused on word recognition (Browder et al., 2006; Ruppar, 2015). Word recognition is influenced by a number of underlying skills. Phonological processing (comprised of phonological memory and phonological awareness), orthographic processing (recognition of visual patterns), and rapid automatized naming are thought to be related to word recognition for both children with and without intellectual disability (Channell et al., 2013; Wise, Sevcik, Romski, & Morris, 2010). There is also an association between word recognition and vocabulary (Burgoyne et al., 2012). This latter finding underscores the need to build strong language skills as a foundation for developing literacy.

Sight Word Instruction

Readers use two means of identifying words: recognizing them automatically by sight (i.e., recognizing a word based on its visual properties) or applying decoding skills (i.e., applying phonics knowledge to sound out a word). Much of the older research on word recognition investigated only sight word interventions because researchers and practitioners presumed that people with lower cognitive abilities could not acquire and apply phonics knowledge (Browder et al., 2006; Wise et al., 2010). More recent research has shown this not to be the case. People with intellectual disability can acquire and utilize phonemic skills to recognize words (Conners, Rosenquist, Sligh, Atwell, & Kiser, 2006; Lemons, Mrachko, Kostewicz, & Paterra, 2012). Teaching students to recognize words by sight is useful, however. Certainly, as children increase their reading skills, they learn to recognize large numbers of words based on their orthographic patterns (i.e., recognize them automatically) and apply decoding skills only when they encounter novel words. Also, many common words in English have irregular spellings that make decoding difficult or impossible (e.g., was, sight, of) so acquiring a basic sight word vocabulary is useful for all children (Reutzel & Cooter, 2012). Additionally, researchers have found that learning sight words seems to facilitate acquisition of other reading skills in children with intellectual disability (Lemons & Fuchs, 2010).

DIRECT INSTRUCTION TO TEACH SIGHT WORDS

Researchers have identified several effective interventions to teach sight words to people with intellectual disability. Many of these approaches include techniques derived from applied behavior analysis. Browder, Ahlgrim-Delzell, Spooner, Mims, and Baker (2009) conducted a review of word-recognition intervention studies that included participants with intellectual disability. Applying Horner and colleagues' (2005) quality indicators for single-case research design to studies in this area, they concluded that time delay is an evidence-based intervention to teach word recognition. They defined time delay as beginning instruction by showing and saying the target word simultaneously (0-sec delay), having the student repeat the word, and on subsequent trials, inserting a brief delay between presenting the word and providing a prompt to the student. This processes allows the student to respond to the word (stimulus) during the delay. Response prompts, actions the interventionist takes to elicit a correct response, are used if a student does not respond within the delay or makes an error; differential reinforcement for responses is also typically provided. Other researchers (Ruwe, McLaughlin, Derby, & Johnson, 2011; Spector, 2011) identified related research-based sight word interventions that included massed trials using direct instruction (e.g., presenting flash cards to teach sets of words using time delay and response prompting), differential reinforcement of responses (e.g., providing positive reinforcement for correct word recognition and error correction for mistakes), and systematic prompting (e.g., using a system of least prompts).

IMPLICATIONS FOR SIGHT WORD INSTRUCTION

There is a strong evidence base supporting use of direct, systematic instruction to teach sight words to people with intellectual disability. It is critical for practitioners to remember, however, that sight word instruction should never be the only reading instruction provided to students with intellectual disability and that these words must not be taught in isolation. Acquiring a base of sight words is a useful part of learning to read, but without additional instruction, students will not likely achieve levels of literacy that increase their meaningful participation in their daily lives.

Practitioners should select words for sight word instruction with care to ensure that they are meaningful and useful to the student (Allor et al., 2010). Instruction should be paced appropriately for students and include many opportunities to actively engage instead of relying solely on massed trial instruction. Massed trials may be helpful if used briefly to review previously taught words and build fluency, but instruction must go beyond this. Reading comprehension is the ultimate goal of instruction, so practitioners implementing sight word instruction should teach word meaning simultaneously with word recognition. Instruction should include opportunities to read targeted words in connected text as soon as possible (Alberto, Waugh, & Fredrick, 2010; Allor et al., 2010). Students with intellectual disability need to learn target words in different types of contexts to have maximum benefit from instruction (e.g., reading target words in books, digital texts, handwritten letters). A concern for practitioners is that many schools increasingly use boxed curricula marketed to teach sight words to students with intellectual disability. Students may not achieve the levels of literacy of which they are capable if teachers do not regularly supplement these curricula with vocabulary, fluency, reading comprehension, and writing instruction to provide comprehensive reading instruction (Copeland & Cosbey, 2008–2009).

Decoding Instruction

A second means of recognizing words is applying knowledge of letter sounds to decode a word. As noted earlier, researchers and practitioners have not always recognized that people with intellectual disability can acquire and utilize phonemic skills. Although people with intellectual disability may have additional needs related to learning phonemic skills (van Tilborg, Segers, van Balkom, & Verhoeven, 2014), recent research supports providing phonemic instruction, in addition to sight word approaches, so that students have multiple word attack options. Having even basic decoding skill provides increased opportunities to recognize novel words rather than relying solely on memory for word recognition.

Phonological decoding is comprised of both phonemic awareness and phonological memory. Phonological memory (i.e., the ability to hold and manipulate sounds in working memory to decode words) in particular seems to be weaker in students with intellectual disability (Channell et al., 2013). However, researchers have concluded that interventions that teach phonemic awareness and phonics are useful for students with intellectual disability since we cannot predict who will or will not acquire these important skills based on a disability label or an IQ score (Allor et al., 2014).

EXPLICIT, SYSTEMATIC INSTRUCTION TO TEACH DECODING

Effective phonemic interventions for participants with intellectual disability should incorporate explicit, systematic instruction. In other words, instruction should begin with careful assessment of what students already know about letters, sounds, and decoding; provide sequenced activities to teach new skills that are based on the assessment information; and use motivating materials and engaging activities (Allor et al., 2010). Pacing appropriate for learners' current skill levels and using a structured format is also important. Cologon, Cupples, and Wyver (2011) conducted a study with young children with Down syndrome that illustrates these characteristics of effective instruction. These researchers taught phonological and word reading skills using a routine in which participants practiced reading words and matched them to pictures, blending onset/rimes, segmenting phonemes, and completing sentences by selecting the correct word. All participants demonstrated improved phonological awareness and word-reading skills after 10 weeks of intervention.

Most studies teaching decoding have used an adult-directed format in which the interventionist leads participants through a carefully sequenced set of learning activities. One promising exception to this approach is a study by Hansen, Wadsworth, Roberts, and Poole (2014). They taught three phonemic skills (syllable segmentation, identification of initial sounds in words, and phoneme segmentation) to kindergarten students with intellectual disability and/or autism spectrum disorders within the context of 15-minute naturally occurring play activities. Interventionists followed each child's interest in toys and other objects and used those naturally occurring opportunities to explicitly teach the target skills. All the children demonstrated increased skills after intervention.

It is essential to also describe the research base for phonics instruction for students with intellectual disability who do not speak. This population of students has been especially marginalized when it comes to effective reading instruction because of misconceptions and lack of knowledge on the part of teachers. Recent research has found that many students who do not speak or who use augmentative and alternative communication (AAC) devices can acquire reading skills, including learning to decode words. Heller and Coleman-Martin (2007), for example, have conducted several studies using the Nonverbal Reading Approach (NRA) in conjunction with a published phonics program to teach students with complex communication needs to decode words. This approach employs principles of direct instruction to teach students to use internal speech (subvocalization) to first segment the sounds in a word, blend them, and then say them quickly using internal speech. Students across all studies employing this approach made gains in the number of words they could decode. More recently, Ahlgrim-Delzell, Browder, and Wood (2014) used systematic instruction and an AAC device to teach beginning phonics skills (i.e., phoneme identifying, blending phonemes to form words, and reading words and matching the word to a picture) to students with intellectual disability who did not speak. All three students improved both phoneme identity and blending skills.

IMPLICATIONS FOR DECODING INSTRUCTION

Teaching decoding skills to people with intellectual disability has a smaller research base than sight word instruction, but results are promising. Effective instruction requires direct, systematic instruction that builds on students' current skill levels and introduces new skills in a planned, structured manner. It is also important to use engaging activities and materials to enhance motivation and generalization of skills across contexts. Instruction, as with other aspects of reading, should begin early (Burgoyne et al.,

2012) and should continue across grade levels (Allor et al., 2014). Researchers whose interventions have produced strong, durable outcomes emphasize the need for intensive, sustained intervention to achieve maximum growth.

Comprehensive Approaches to Teach Word Recognition

A promising trend in recent research has been investigations of comprehensive models to teach word recognition in which teaching sessions incorporate core components of instruction (Allor et al., 2014; Browder, Ahlgrim-Delzell, Courtade, Gibbs, & Flowers, 2008; Browder, Ahlgrim-Delzell, Flowers, & Baker, 2012). Browder and colleagues (2008) examined the impacts of a program called *Early Literacy Skills Builder* (ELSB) when implemented with elementary school students with intellectual disability with moderate or severe intellectual impairment. ELSB was developed by adapting instructional practices found to be effective with students without disabilities to be accessible to students with significant intellectual and communication challenges (e.g., offering nonverbal means of responding). Using a randomized control group design, 23 students were randomly assigned to either a group receiving ELSB instruction or a group receiving sight word/picture instruction using the *Edmark Reading Program* sight word curriculum. Scores on standardized assessment measures showed that students who received the comprehensive instructional program significantly outperformed their peers who received sight word–only instruction.

Allor et al. (2014) examined the effects of another comprehensive instructional program on the reading skills of elementary school students with intellectual disability across four years. The intervention employed evidence-based practices identified in research (e.g., direct instruction) and included strategies targeting concepts about print, word recognition (sight words and decoding), oral language, fluency, vocabulary, and comprehension. The decoding portion of the intervention taught participants to decode increasingly complex phonemic patterns across time and supplemented this direct instruction with motivating activities to provide additional practice opportunities (i.e., games and puzzles that included words with targeted patterns). Students also read target words in connected text during every lesson (e.g., using specially created books that used target decodable and sight words). Intervention occurred daily for 45–50 minutes in small groups led by highly trained interventionists. Participants in the intervention group showed significant progress on all reading measures except untimed word identification when compared to participants in the control group who received whatever reading instruction their school typically provided to children with intellectual disability.

In a related study, Allor, Gifford, Al Otaiba, Miller, and Cheatham (2013) used an intensive and comprehensive intervention with participants who had demonstrated limited progress in the larger study described earlier. The purpose was to increase participants' fluency and generalization of decoding skills. Specifically, these students struggled to move from letter-by-letter decoding to unitizing words (recognizing them automatically). These individual sessions took place daily for 45 minutes across 14 weeks. The researchers created storybooks that included the targeted words and skills, and they taught the skills just as they did in the larger study except that they used the story books as the primary instructional materials. All the students acquired new word-reading skills (moving from five to 20 words read at baseline to 50 to 70 at the end of the intervention). This study underscores the importance of incorporating students' interests into lessons and teaching word recognition skills within a meaningful context.

Vocabulary

Vocabulary is most simply defined as the knowledge of words and word meanings. Vocabulary instruction can thus be defined as teaching words and word meanings (NRTAC, 2010; Reutzel & Cooter, 2012). The National Reading Panel (NRP; 2000) noted that vocabulary instruction has historically been viewed as a subset of comprehension, but proposed that comprehension was one of the five critical components of reading instruction in its own right. Research indicates that vocabulary development is a critical area of instruction for all children and is related to all other areas of reading instruction, not just comprehension (Beck, McKeown, & Kucan, 2013; NRP, 2000; Reutzel & Cooter, 2012). Research also indicates that effective literacy instruction for students with intellectual disability must be comprehensive and include explicit vocabulary instruction (Allor et al., 2014; Browder et al., 2012).

This simple definition of "vocabulary" can be misleading when it comes to identifying research-based instructional practices. Often the term "vocabulary" is not explicitly defined in reading research in general and is used interchangeably with sight word instruction in the research relating to students with intellectual disability (Browder et al., 2006). As noted earlier, the majority of research in reading for students with intellectual disability has focused on word recognition, so it might be assumed that vocabulary has been sufficiently addressed in the research. This is untrue because vocabulary instruction incorporates much more than being able to recognize a word. A narrow focus on sight word instruction has led to a long history of teaching students with intellectual disability limited vocabulary skills in a decontextualized manner (Browder et al., 2006; Copeland & Keefe, 2007).

There are generally four types of vocabulary recognized in the literature: listening, oral, reading, and writing. Sight word recognition is an element of reading vocabulary. For students without disabilities these vocabularies are usually viewed as a hierarchy from listening as the largest vocabulary to writing as the smallest vocabulary. For students with intellectual disability this view of vocabulary is not necessarily accurate or useful (Keefe, 2007b). First, the concept of *oral* vocabulary must be broadened for students with intellectual disability to *expressive vocabulary* to include sign language, gestures, symbols, objects, and AAC (Keefe & Copeland, 2011; Kliewer, 2008a; Mims, Lee, Browder, Zakas, & Flynn, 2012; Scherba de Valenzuela & Tracey, 2007). Second, for students with intellectual disability, the size of their expressive vocabulary may be smaller than their reading and/or writing vocabulary due to, for example, physical or sensory needs. Instructional decisions in the area of reading for students with intellectual disability should not be made based on the size of a student's expressive vocabulary because this can result in low expectations and lack of access to comprehensive reading instruction (Copeland & Keefe, 2007).

Further complicating the evaluation of research-based practices in the area of vocabulary instruction is the challenge inherent in defining what it means to "know" a word. Beck et al. (2013) note, "It is not the case that one either knows or does not know a word. In fact, word knowledge is a rather complex concept" (p. 10). Beck et al. describe word knowledge as falling along a continuum from no knowledge of the word, a general sense of the word meaning, a narrow context-based knowledge of the word, to a rich decontextualized knowledge of the word. One example of the challenge facing researchers is how to assess the impact of instructional practices on vocabulary knowledge. A common dependent measure for students with intellectual disability is the Peabody Picture Vocabulary Test III (PPVT III), which measures receptive vocabulary by asking a student to point to a picture after the examiner presents the word orally. Allor et al. (2014) used Expressive Vocabulary Test (EVT) as a dependent measure for vocabulary. The EVT measures expressive vocabulary and word retrieval. Both of these tests address the lower end of the continuum of word knowledge so do not indicate a rich decontextualized understanding of the word.

Direct and Systematic Instruction to Teach Vocabulary

Similarly to the findings discussed for word recognition, the research does indicate research-based instructional methods for increasing listening, expressive, and reading vocabulary in students with intellectual disability. The use of direct and systematic instruction is recommended for teaching vocabulary. Interestingly, this parallels the recommendations that direct and explicit instruction in vocabulary constitute evidence-based practice for students without disabilities (NRP, 2000; NRTAC,

2010; Reutzel & Cooter, 2012). The form that such instruction takes will be more intensive for students with intellectual disability. Specifically, time delay, response prompting, differential reinforcement of responses, and systematic prompting have been used with students with intellectual disability to improve vocabulary in general (Allor et al., 2014; Browder et al., 2006; Browder et al., 2009; Browder, Hudson, & Wood, 2013) and in content areas such as science (Spooner, Knight, Browder, Jimenez, & DiBase, 2011), middle school language arts (Mims et al., 2012), and in general education settings (Hudson, Browder, & Wood, 2013).

Shared Stories

A review of the research on shared stories indicates moderate evidence that this is a research-based practice to increase literacy skills, including vocabulary, for students with extensive support needs (Hudson & Test, 2011). An overview of the six single-subject research studies included in the review identify the following instructional practices in common:

- Shared reading of a text
- Systematic instruction
- Task analysis
- System of least prompts
- Adapted books and use of AAC/AT

Shared stories have been shown to increase vocabulary in students with students without disabilities (NRTAC, 2010) and students with disabilities (Katims, 1991). Shared stories are a good example of a practice that embodies one of the most important recommendations for teaching vocabulary to all students, namely active engagement in vocabulary-rich environments where children have repeated exposure to words and word meanings (Beck et al., 2013; NRP, 2000; NRTAC, 2012; Reutzel & Cooter, 2012).

Comprehensive Reading Approaches to Teach Vocabulary

Comprehensive or multicomponent reading programs show promise for increasing vocabulary skills of students with intellectual disability (Allor et al., 2014; Browder et al., 2012; Mims et al., 2012). Comprehensive approaches combat the historical tendency to teach vocabulary through decontextualized sight word approaches. Multicomponent approaches use systematic instruction, including time delay and system of least prompts, to build vocabulary knowledge and go beyond word recognition to understanding and applying word knowledge in connected text.

As described previously with regard to word recognition, Allor et al. (2014) conducted a longitudinal study to examine the effectiveness of "comprehensive scientifically based reading instruction" (p. 289) that had been effective with struggling readers. Allor et al. (2010) describe the ways in which vocabulary instruction occurred in the *Early Interventions in Reading* intervention. First, the vocabulary instruction targeted words and concepts that held meaning for the students. Second, the meaning of words was taught through pictures, conversation, and connected text. Third, puzzles and games were developed for independent and supported practice. Allor et al. reported moderate to high effect sizes for the impact of the intervention measures of vocabulary for the treatment group.

Browder et al. (2012) compared a multicomponent literacy curriculum, the ELSB, described previously, with a sight word approach (*Edmark Reading Program*) across three years for students with severe developmental disabilities. The vocabulary objectives included reading vocabulary words, pointing to sight words to complete sentences to demonstrate comprehension, and pointing to pictures of spoken words using a variety of pictures for the same word. These encompass all levels of word knowledge by building word recognition, definition, and conceptual understanding. Methods used to teach the vocabulary objectives included flash card drills with constant time delay and system of least prompts. Browder et al. (2012) used the PPVT III as the dependent measure for receptive vocabulary. While the treatment group had significantly higher mean literacy scores over the control group, the smallest effect size was seen for receptive vocabulary in comparison to the conventions of reading and phonics skills subtests.

In a smaller-scale study, Mims et al. (2012) piloted the use of a multicomponent treatment package in middle school English language arts (ELA), self-contained classrooms serving 15 students with moderate to severe disabilities. The study used a one group pre-posttest nonrandomized design. The curriculum materials were organized around four themed units, targeting skills in the areas of vocabulary, comprehension, story elements, and writing. Vocabulary words were assigned based on student symbolic level and taught using flash cards, pictures, and time delay. Instruction occurred in groups and incidental learning was encouraged by having all students attend as their peers responded to the prompts. Students pointed to named words and were instructed to find words/pictures that correspond with definitions. The dependent measure was a pre- and posttest based on the scripted lessons and middle school ELA target skills. The vocabulary assessment included 5–15 words and definitions. The most significant gains were found in the area of vocabulary compared to comprehension and writing measures.

These three studies demonstrate that vocabulary can be improved through systematic direct instruction in a comprehensive or multicomponent program. This provides support for including vocabulary instruction as part of comprehensive reading instruction for all students with intellectual disability. However, it should be noted that all three studies reported improved growth across almost all areas of reading instruction. The reality is that the different areas of reading instruction are interrelated and no area should be taught in a decontextualized and isolated way. Vocabulary has been shown to be significantly related to word recognition, comprehension, and fluency for students without disabilities (NRP, 2000) so it should come as no surprise that the same would be true for students with intellectual disability.

Implications for Practice to Teach Vocabulary

As with other areas of reading instruction discussed in this chapter, it is clear that effective vocabulary instruction must be direct and systematic. Research demonstrates the positive effects of using time delay and system of least prompts in teaching recognition and definition of vocabulary words. Vocabulary instruction should be one element of a comprehensive reading program and taught concurrently with other areas of reading.

We know that students must have multiple opportunities to engage with listening, expressive, reading, and writing vocabularies in order to develop a rich decontextualized knowledge of words. Shared stories are one example of a promising practice teachers can implement in classrooms to improve vocabulary together with other reading skills. Teachers still need to plan instruction systematically using principles of universal design for learning (UDL), task analysis, and prompting systems to make text accessible to all students. Teachers need to become familiar with a range of literature that is age appropriate and matches the interests of their students. Fortunately there are many age-appropriate books that can be adapted (see the Tar Heel Reader website at http://tarheelreader.org) and engaging picture books or graphic novels (see illustrator David Wiesner's website at http://www.davidwiesner.com). Teachers need to consider multiple ways to go beyond shared stories to make their classrooms vocabulary-rich environments. Strategies such as "reading the room" and using environmental print may not have a specific research base for students with intellectual disability, but they build on the accepted practice of using ecological inventories to guide instructional planning (Brown et al., 1979; Downing, 2005). Direct and systematic instruction, together with incidental learning, can be used to teach vocabulary words selected from important people, objects in the classroom and school environment, and print that appears in signs, labels, and logs in the environment (Keefe, 2007b; Keefe, Copeland, & DiLuzio, 2010). These vocabulary words can then be used in sentences, other connected text, puzzles, and games. In this way teachers can build vocabulary knowledge by actively engaging students and building on their prior knowledge.

The NRP (2000) synthesis on research on vocabulary can provide guidance for teaching literacy to students with intellectual disability. The eight recommendations of NRP are as summarized as follows:

- Direct instruction of vocabulary words should be provided.
- Effective instruction incorporates repetition and multiple exposure.
- Vocabulary words need to be useful in multiple contexts.
- Vocabulary tasks should be restructured as necessary.
- Vocabulary instruction should require active engagement and go beyond definition.
- Computer technology can be useful.
- Vocabulary can be acquired through incidental learning.
- Dependence on a single method will not optimize learning.

Each of these recommendations can be applied to teaching vocabulary to students with intellectual disability.

Fluency

Rasinski (2009) notes "The multidimensional nature of reading fluency has led to it having different definitions" (p. 2). According to the NRP (2000) "Fluent readers can read text with speed, accuracy, and proper expression" (p. 3–1). Reutzel and Cooter (2012) expand this definition to include automaticity in word identification, grade level–appropriate reading rate; expressive or prosodic features such as volume, pitch, and stress; and correct text phasing. Allor and Chard (2011) propose a definition of fluency that reflects the complex reciprocal relationship between fluency and comprehension such that "Reading fluency refers to efficient, effective word recognition skills that permit the reader to construct the meaning of text. Fluency is manifested in accurate, rapid, expressive oral reading and is applied during, and makes possible, silent reading comprehension" (p. 1). Despite the multidimensional nature of fluency, most research in this area has focused on oral reading rate rather than prosody and text phrasing (Rasinski, 2003). Automaticity has typically been considered in the area of sight word recognition (research on word recognition for students with intellectual disability has been covered in an earlier section).

Fluency for students without disabilities is the area of reading that has received the least amount of attention from researchers (Allington, 2006; NRP, 2000). Similarly, fluency historically has been the most neglected area of reading instruction in schools (Allington, 1983) and in reading textbooks and curricula (Rasinski, 2003). However, increased research and instruction is being directed to reading fluency as a result of the emphasis placed on fluency by the NRP and the recognition of the critical importance of reading fluency to comprehension and overall reading competence (Allington, 2006; Rasinski, 2009). However, a quick perusal of one popular text in reading instruction (Reutzel & Cooter, 2012) reveals that reading fluency is still the area of reading with the shortest chapter.

Research into reading fluency for students with intellectual disability has also received limited attention from researchers (Browder et al., 2006). Although Browder et al. found more studies addressing fluency than phonemic awareness and phonics, most studies were conducted in the 1980s and focused primarily on error rate. Only one instructional practice—system of least prompts—was found to have research supporting its use to increase fluency for students with intellectual disability. Browder et al. conclude "For the most part, research on individuals with significant cognitive disabilities has occasionally measured fluency, but rarely taught this component of reading" (2006, p. 402). Ruppar (2015) reported the results of an observational study of the literacy experiences of eight middle and high school students with severe disabilities. Reading fluency instruction was not observed for any of these students. These findings suggest the situation has not greatly improved since Browder and colleagues' research review.

Repeated Reading to Teach Fluency

Two studies were found specifically addressing reading fluency for students with intellectual disability and other developmental disabilities since 2003. Hua, Therrien, Hendrickson, Woods-Groves, Ries, and Shaw (2012) used a multiple-baseline design to investigate the effectiveness of Reread-Adapt and Answer-Comprehend (RAAC) with three postsecondary learners with intellectual disability. Hua, Hendrickson et al. (2012) replicated this study with three postsecondary students with autism and intellectual disability. RAAC is a repeated reading intervention designed to improve both fluency and comprehension. Hua, Hendrickson et al. noted RAAC has previously been shown to be an effective instructional strategy for learners with reading and behavioral difficulties. The general RAAC procedure is to first have students read generic questions related to the text to be read prior to reading. Students then read and re-read text at their instructional level to a tutor who corrects decoding errors. Once the student reaches performance criteria such as correct words per minute (CWPM) the student moves to a more difficult passage. The student is also asked factual and inferential questions to monitor comprehension.

The RAAC procedure was slightly modified for students with intellectual disability and autism in the two previously mentioned studies (Hua, Hendrickson et al., 2012; Hua, Therrien et al., 2012). Before reading a passage, the participants were asked to read four generic questions related to components of narrative passages. The student then read the passage three consecutive times and the tutor timed each attempt. Following each reading, the tutor followed an error correction procedure until all the missed words were read correctly. The tutor also gave feedback on fluency, accuracy, and prosody using a feedback sheet. After reading the passage three times, the student was asked to answer the four generic comprehension questions plus eight passage-specific comprehension questions (four factual and four inferential). Outcomes were measured using CWPM for the third reading of each passage, the number of correct answers to the eight passage-specific questions, and the total number of decoding errors per passage. Participants were tested prior to and after the intervention on unpracticed passages using the Dynamic Indicators of Basic Early Literacy Skills (DIBELS) Oral Reading Fluency (ORF) subtest.

Hua, Therrien et al. (2012) found that RAAC improved fluency and comprehension of narrative passages in all three participants with intellectual disability. In addition, improvements in fluency transferred to unseen passages. Hua, Hendrickson et al. (2012) replicated this study with three young adults with autism and intellectual disability. The modified RAAC intervention again resulted in improved fluency and comprehension scores. All three students also generalized improved CWPM to unpracticed passages.

Repeated reading is considered an evidence-based practice for improving reading fluency for students without disabilities (NRP, 2000; Rasinski, 2009) and students with learning and behavioral difficulties (Hua, Hendrickson et al. 2012; Strickland, Boon, & Spencer, 2013). Hua, Therrien et al. (2012) and Hua, Hendrickson et al. (2012) results suggest that an intervention incorporating repeated reading to improve reading fluency and comprehension can also have a positive impact on young adults with intellectual disability and autism. These results taken together suggest that repeated readings could be a useful intervention to improve fluency for students with intellectual disability.

Comprehensive Programs to Teach Fluency

The multicomponent programs studied by Browder et al. (2012) and Mims et al. (2012) do not include intervention or results related to the component of reading fluency. Allor et al. (2014) compared a treatment group using a comprehensive reading program with a contrast group over four academic years. Allor et al. specifically targeted all components of reading integrated across lessons. Fluency is addressed through "repeated reading in unison to paired reading and independent timed reading" (p. 293). Fluency growth across the treatment and contrast group was measured using the DIBELS ORF subtest. Allor et al. report statistically significant differences in ORF for the treatment groups compared to the contrast group. They further reported that students with higher IQs *tend* to perform at a higher level in ORF but caution that the results were highly variable with some students with lower IQ scores outperforming some students with higher IQ scores in ORF.

Implications for Practice to Teach Fluency

There is a notable lack of research in the area of teaching reading fluency to students with intellectual disability. However, the research that is available indicates that students and young adults with intellectual disability can improve reading fluency using the system of least prompts (Browder et al., 2006), through targeted interventions such as RAAC (Hua, Hendrickson et al., 2012; Hua, Therrien et al., 2012), or as part of a comprehensive reading program (Allor et al., 2014). In short, there is no research-based justification for denying students with intellectual disability access to reading fluency instruction. Critical features for providing fluency instruction can be extrapolated from instructional practices accepted for use with students without disabilities, struggling readers, and students with other disabilities, including those described in the following sections.

HEARING TEXT READ FLUENTLY

The importance of fluent reading is generally accepted for all children (Allor & Chard, 2011). The development of fluency can occur in many ways. Shared stories/read alouds are recommended for all students (Fisher & Frey, 2008; Rasinski, 2009; Reutzel & Cooter, 2012) and have been shown to increase literacy skills of students with extensive support needs (Hudson & Test, 2011). Read alouds should be planned and prepared ahead of time (Keefe, 2007a), include interaction and active participation by students (Rasinski, 2003), and incorporate best practices for teaching students with intellectual disability (Hudson & Test, 2011). Other ways for students to hear fluent reading include technology-assisted reading (Rasinski, 2009; Reutzel & Cooter, 2012), paired reading (e.g., Allor et al. 2014; Rasinski, 2009), choral reading (Keefe, 2007a) and peer tutors (e.g., Kamps, Locke, Delquadri, & Hall, 1989).

REPEATED GUIDED ORAL READING

The NRP (2000) identified repeated reading and guided oral reading as evidence-based practices in the area of reading fluency. While the idea of repeated reading may sound simple, it involves careful planning and preparation. Requiring students to repeatedly read a passage without modeling and feedback is not only tedious but may result in students practicing dysfluent reading. Teachers must always make sure that the passage to be read is at the student's instructional level and motivating (Allor & Chard, 2011; Allor et al., 2014; Rasinski, 2009; Reutzel & Cooter, 2012). This can be challenging for students with intellectual disability and other disabilities because the reading passages also need to be age appropriate (Allor et al., 2010). Students need to receive corrective feedback about word reading errors (Allor & Chard, 2011; NRP, 2000). An example of how this might look can be found in Hua, Hendrickson et al. (2012) who describe a model-prompt-check procedure. Another consideration is whether to have students repeatedly read the passage until they reach a predetermined CWPM (Allington, 2006; Rasinski, 2009) or a set number of times (e.g., Hua, Hendrickson et al., 2012). Students may be motivated by participating in recording their progress (Allington, 2006; Allor et al., 2010). Repeated reading can be varied and modified as necessary. For example, repeated reading can be combined with paired reading (Rasinski, 2009).

PERFORMANCE READING

It can be challenging to motivate students to read the same text repeatedly and find ways to integrate repeated reading into literacy curricula (Rasinski, 2009). An authentic and engaging way to build repeated reading into classrooms is to find ways to incorporate performance reading into instruction. Some examples of performance reading are Readers Theatre, poetry readings, puppet shows, and plays (Keefe, 2007a; Rasinski, 2009; Reutzel & Cooter, 2012).

WIDE READING FOR PLEASURE

The NRP (2000) did not find that sustained silent reading in the classroom was a research-based strategy for increasing reading fluency. Allor and Chard (2011) note this finding but suggest that independent and silent reading should be included as a way to address fluency for students with disabilities, with the recommendation that silent reading should be monitored to ensure students are reading successfully—by asking comprehension questions, for example. Students with intellectual disability may need access to adapted books, AT or AAC, and/or careful selection of age-appropriate books with low decoding demands (e.g., high-interest low-vocabulary books from Oxford Readers or wordless/picture books) (Allor et al., 2010; Copeland & Keefe, 2007).

Reading Comprehension

Reading comprehension is the ultimate goal of reading instruction. Comprehension is an active process that requires the reader to understand the words an author uses, reflect on his or her own experience, and then use this information for a particular purpose. Perhaps most importantly, it is a crucial skill in acquiring new knowledge (e.g., understanding a science concept or being able to prepare a new food from a recipe). Text comprehension is a complex process made up of multiple components that must operate smoothly and concurrently. This process includes (a) the ability to fluently decode words; (b) adequate language comprehension (i.e., grammar, syntax, and pragmatic skills as well as ample vocabulary); (c) familiarity with varied text structures (narrative and expository); (d) and working memory, planning, organizing, and monitoring skills (i.e., executive function skills; Sesma, Mahone, Levine, Eason, & Cutting, 2009). The level of influence of each of these skill areas on comprehension changes as children develop their reading abilities (Ouellette & Beers, 2010). For example, decoding is more strongly linked to reading comprehension in early readers, and oral language abilities are more strongly linked to comprehension in more skilled readers.

Students with intellectual disability can struggle with reading comprehension. Although much remains to be understood about how people with intellectual disability comprehend text, research findings to date suggest that students with intellectual disability frequently have a need for support to build decoding skills and language comprehension (van Wingerden, Segers, van Balkom, & Verhoeven, 2014). Despite these challenges, researchers have successfully developed several interventions to build reading comprehension in students with intellectual disability.

Strategy Instruction and Reciprocal Teaching for Reading Comprehension

Strategy instruction and reciprocal teaching are two promising reading comprehension interventions. Strategies are cognitive processes that people use to help them understand what they read. There are multiple strategies that can be applied to understand a text, depending on the reading task and the learner's needs (e.g., strategies to find a main idea, to summarize key information). Reciprocal teaching is an approach that involves the student and teacher or peers taking turns reading portions of a text and using strategies such as prediction, generating questions, summarizing, and clarifying to deepen understanding. Reading comprehension is an active process. Both reciprocal teaching and strategy instruction actively engage students with the text so are helpful in facilitating comprehension.

Strategy instruction and reciprocal teaching have been shown to be effective in increasing reading comprehension of students without disabilities. Investigations of their use with students with intellectual disability have also resulted in positive outcomes. Van den Bos, Nakken, Nicolay, and van Houten (2007) taught adults with intellectual disability to use four reading strategies (summarizing, questioning, predicting, and clarifying) to improve comprehension of written texts. They compared two conditions to each other and to a control group. In the first condition they used direct instruction to teach the strategies in a one-to-one format. In the second condition they provided strategy instruction in small groups using elements of reciprocal teaching. Results showed that while both groups performed better than the control group, there were no significant differences in strategy performance between small group and individual formats. Participants in both groups acquired the strategies and demonstrated improved reading comprehension that was maintained across three months. Hua and colleagues also investigated the effects of strategy instruction (see earlier section on fluency). They conducted two studies in which they found that young adults with intellectual disability had increased reading comprehension and fluency skills and decreased reading errors after learning to utilize the RAAC strategy (Hua, Hendrickson et al., 2012; Hua, Therein et al., 2012). In another example, Morgan, Moni, and Jobling (2004) taught a young adult with intellectual disability to use prediction, generating questions, and retelling to improve his ability to comprehend simple stories.

Graphic Organizers for Reading Comprehension

Teaching students to use graphic organizers is another research-based comprehension strategy (Dexter & Hughes, 2011). Only a few researchers have examined their use in students with intellectual disability, but the results are promising. Ozman (2011) taught five adolescents with intellectual disability with mild cognitive impairment to use a compare/contrast graphic organizer to improve comprehension of expository texts. Browder et al. (2013) used time delay and a modified system of least prompts in combination with a graphic organizer to teach three middle school students with intellectual disability to improve comprehension of adapted grade-level texts. They used the graphic organizer and time delay to teach *wh* question definitions and examples to the participants. They then asked students to use their graphic organizers to help them answer comprehension questions after reading short chapters of the adapted texts. They utilized time delay and a modified system of least-intrusive prompts to teach answering comprehension questions during the instructional phase. All participants learned to define *wh* questions and improved their skill in answering these types of comprehension questions related to adapted stories (i.e., stories written in simple language, often accompanied by pictures or graphics). Moreover, generalization probes indicated that participants increased correct reading comprehension responses to novel texts after intervention.

Other researchers such as Allor et al. (2014) have included reading comprehension instruction as a central component of comprehensive reading instruction programs. The reading comprehension portion of the intervention in Allor et al.'s (2014) study included instruction in vocabulary and oral language as well as applying specific strategies to both narrative and expository texts. Participants in the intervention group demonstrated significantly higher reading comprehension scores postintervention than those in the control (i.e., business as usual) group.

Role of Listening Comprehension Strategies

Because people with intellectual disability have widely varying reading and language abilities, it is important to also examine the research base that has focused on teaching academic content via listening comprehension strategies. Many people with intellectual disability do not have sufficiently developed word recognition skills to read grade level–connected text yet could benefit from access to information in textbooks. Strategies that teach these learners to comprehend text read aloud are useful in building content knowledge. Listening to texts read aloud can also be a pleasurable leisure experience for people of any age.

Interventions to build listening comprehension generally include the same strategies used to teach reading comprehension: systematic, explicit instruction and some type of visual support (e.g., graphic organizers) to support comprehension. Browder and colleagues have conducted a number of studies examining strategies to improve comprehension of narrative and expository texts in students with intellectual disability (Browder, Trela, & Jimenez, 2007). These studies have demonstrated positive results, but most have taken place in self-contained classrooms and often used very simplified texts. More recently, Wood, Browder, and Flynn (in press) taught two special education teachers to implement an intervention to improve their fifth grade students with intellectual disability comprehension of a grade-level social studies text. Teachers read aloud a section of the social studies text, taught the students to use a graphic organizer to generate *wh* questions about the passage, and then read the passage aloud again. Students then answered the questions they had generated based on the read aloud of the text. Once students learned the strategy, they applied it in their general education social studies classroom in small cooperative learning groups. All students increased the number of questions they generated and improved their comprehension of the grade-level text in this setting. These findings are particularly exciting because they document that students with intellectual disability can acquire critical content knowledge alongside their peers, using the same grade-level texts as their peers and within the same classrooms.

Implications for Reading Comprehension Instruction

Reading comprehension remains an under-researched but essential area of reading instruction for students with intellectual disability (Browder et al., 2013). Several researchers have conducted promising studies suggesting that many of the research-based strategies used with students without identified disabilities or those with high-incidence disabilities are also effective with students with intellectual disability (e.g., strategy instruction and use of graphic organizers). The research base confirms that students with intellectual disability need systematic, direct instruction to learn these strategies. It is also evident that comprehension is best taught from the beginning of word recognition instruction and as a part of a comprehensive reading program. Instructional materials that are based on students' interests promote engagement and meaning making and facilitate comprehension. Finally, as noted by Allor's research team (2014), students with intellectual disability require sustained, intensive reading instruction to make meaningful progress. It is critical to continue quality, intensive instruction throughout the school years if students are to achieve at the levels of which they are capable.

Writing

Writing instruction is an important, but often neglected, part of a comprehensive reading program (Mason, 2013). This is unfortunate because reading and writing are reciprocal processes (Staples & Edmister, 2012). Students' literacy skills are enhanced when teachers provide instruction in both areas. Sturm (2012) emphasized the importance of teaching students writing skills, saying that writing "allows individuals to engage in authentic communication with themselves and others to express basic and abstract ideas" (p. 336). Among other things, acquiring writing skills builds academic knowledge (Troia, 2014), increases opportunities for social participation (Forts & Luckasson, 2011), supports and builds self-advocacy and skills leading to self-determination (Cannella-Malone, Konrad, & Pennington, 2015), and develops important employment skills (Pennington, Delano, & Scott, 2014).

Just as with reading instruction, education professionals' low expectations of people with intellectual disability have likely influenced the amount and type of writing instruction provided to them (Sturm, 2012). Recent research examining writing instruction in general has shown several practices to be effective. Researchers have investigated several of these practices specifically with children and young adults with intellectual disability and found them to be effective (Joseph & Konrad, 2009).

Multiple, Authentic Writing Opportunities

One important component of effective writing instruction substantiated in the literature is giving students multiple, authentic opportunities to write every day (Sturm, 2012; Troia, 2014). This seems simple but is not common practice, even in general education classrooms (Troia, 2014). Students with intellectual disability need repeated opportunities to engage in writing for multiple purposes to hone skills and to learn how to use writing in ways that are meaningful to them. For example, instead of asking students to copy lists of words or even paragraphs that an adult has written on the board, as is often done, students would be asked to write columns for weekly newsletters. For example, one high school student was asked to write a weekly column in a city recreational program newsletter that was disseminated across the city to multiple recreational sites (J. Tatz, personal communication, 2015). This young man, with appropriate support from peers and staff, regularly wrote short news stories for the paper. Because this was a highly socially valued activity, it offered a very motivating reason to learn and practice writing skills.

Explicit, systematic instruction combined with writing for authentic purposes is needed to support students' learning. Pennington et al. (2014) taught three young adults with intellectual disability who were seeking employment to write cover letters using explicit, systematic instruction. They presented models of correctly written letters and, using this instructional approach, taught participants to self-monitor and correct their own letters, and to graph their writing progress. All participants learned to include the six components of a cover letter, were able to generalize these skills to create a letter for a novel job posting, and all maintained at least five of the component skills up to four weeks post intervention.

Strategy Instruction and Process Writing

Strategy instruction (teaching students to follow carefully structured steps to conceptualize and create a piece of text) has been used successfully with students with high-incidence disabilities (e.g., Self-Regulated Strategy Development [SRSD]; Mason, 2013). One group of researchers has adapted this approach for use with students with intellectual disability with promising results. Konrad, Trela, and Test (2006) taught three high school students to write paragraphs using the GO 4 It NOW strategy, an adaptation of the SRSD instructional approach. Students improved their paragraph writing skills on the training topic (writing about their goals) and generalized their skills to other types of paragraphs.

Process-writing instruction is also a widely used writing instructional approach with a sound research base (Troia, 2014). This approach incorporates multiple components, including providing writing assignments for specific, meaningful purposes and teaching students to follow a specific set of steps to create a plan for what they will write (i.e., create a draft, review and edit the draft, and then rewrite the draft based on their review). It has not been as widely studied with students with intellectual disability. However, strategy instruction has successfully been combined with process-writing approaches to teach writing. Sturm (2012) created an intervention, Enriched Writer's Workshop, that incorporates both approaches. This intervention shows encouraging results with children and young adults with a range of cognitive abilities. The Workshop is comprised of teacher-led mini-lessons on a particular writing skill, numerous opportunities for students to self-select topics to write about, and individualized supports and adaptations to help students learn to organize and write about their ideas. Students also regularly share their writing with peers and teachers through the Author's Chair. This activity is highly motivating and provides opportunities for additional feedback.

Assistive Technology (AT) and Writing Instruction

Students with intellectual disability may have support needs that must be considered when learning to compose text (e.g., cognitive, motor, and sensory needs; Sturm, 2012). AT has an important role as a component of effective writing instruction for students with intellectual disability (Cannella-Malone et al., 2015). Surprisingly few studies, however, have examined the use of technology to teach writing to students with intellectual disability. Erickson et al. (2010) described using alternative keyboards, screen readers, and word prediction software to support students in learning to spell and to write words and texts. These authors emphasized the need to select technology based on the person's unique needs. Technology tools are just tools: They do not take the place of effective teacher instruction but allow access to the writing process. As technology continues to advance, it will be increasingly important for teachers to learn how to effectively use various types of technology to create access to writing for students and as an instructional method.

Implications for Writing Instruction

The scant research available on writing instruction for students with intellectual disability suggests that many of the practices found effective for teaching writing in general are effective with students with intellectual disability when combined with explicit, systematic instruction. Practitioners must begin instruction with high expectations for their students, combined with appropriate supports, including technological supports. Instruction is more effective when the teacher provides authentic reasons for students to write and allows them to select topics that are of high interest. Strategy instruction paired with process writing is a promising approach that can incorporate several promising intervention components. Teaching students how to plan before writing, write, share their writing to receive feedback, and then revise their draft based on that feedback seems effective, especially when paired with brief direct instruction on specific writing strategies. Use of visuals is also helpful in this process, both as an aid to determining topics and as a way to facilitate organization of ideas.

Conclusion

This is an exciting time to be involved in research and practice related to reading and literacy instruction for people with intellectual disability. The burgeoning research in this area is highlighting new ways of conceptualizing and delivering instruction. One question that research has emphatically answered is that children with intellectual disability benefit from reading instruction. It is time to move from arguing about whether people with intellectual disability should have access to reading instruction to focusing on how to deliver that instruction more effectively.

Although there is a great need for additional research to guide practice, we simply cannot wait to teach students until that future research is completed and disseminated. Reading and literacy skills are crucial for a person's well-being. Instead of waiting for a larger body of research to substantiate a complete set of evidence-based instructional practices, we must teach students *now* so that they do not miss out on the opportunities that having reading skills offer (e.g., enhanced employment choices). One way to approach instruction when there is not a substantial amount of research in a given area (e.g., writing instruction) is to examine what research with students without disabilities and those with high-incidence disabilities tells us. We can use and build on these practices while researchers continue to extend our knowledge base about specific instructional practices for students with intellectual disability (Browder et al., 2008).

This chapter's brief examination of what we know about research-based instructional practices highlights critical guidelines for educators and parents. First, effective reading education begins with holding high expectations and requires carefully structured, systematic, and sustained instruction. Next, language support and intervention forms the foundation for later literacy, so attention must be paid to this from the beginning of a child's life. Third, structured (but age appropriate) literacy instruction should begin in the preschool years and continue across formal schooling. People with intellectual disability are increasingly taking advantage of opportunities for postsecondary education—another important issue is that instruction should continue within these programs and into adulthood if an individual wishes to continue to expand his or her literacy skills.

Fourth, students with intellectual disability learn best when reading education includes concurrent instruction in all the core components of reading (Allor et al., 2014; Browder et al., 2008, 2012). We must prepare teachers to go beyond highly scripted intervention programs focused on only one reading component and instead provide instruction across skill areas using engaging materials and activities. One way to facilitate this is to move away from segregated instruction. Accumulating evidence shows that children with intellectual disability learn to read in a similar manner to their peers (Wise et al., 2010). They should be taught alongside their peers in order to tap into the natural supports, motivation, and incidental learning opportunities this arrangement provides. Thus, inclusive learning environments are important for literacy learning for all children. Students with intellectual disability need individualized and intensive instruction, but this can be successfully embedded within general education contexts (Hudson et al., 2013; Ryndak, Moore, Orlando, & Delano 2008–2009; Ryndak, Morrison, & Sommerstein, 1999). Research has demonstrated that children with intellectual disability acquire higher levels of reading skills when receiving instruction in general education classrooms, regardless of cognitive abilities (de Graaf & van Hove, 2015). What is needed now are changes to teacher education programs that ensure preservice teachers have the skills to provide quality instruction within these settings. Preservice teachers must have both coursework and fieldwork to apply research-based reading instructional practices for students with intellectual disability. This should include knowledge of UDL lesson design, use of technology, and a solid understanding of research-based literacy instructional practices.

Creation of high-quality reading education for students with intellectual disability is the responsibility of educators, policy makers, researchers, and families. Kliewer (2008b) challenged us to work toward the goal of "literate citizenship" for all individuals. As documented in this chapter, the field now has clear guidelines for how to achieve this end. There can no longer be any justification for denying comprehensive reading instruction to students with intellectual disability. What is called for now is to work together to make changes to teacher preparation and educational systems so that the accumulating body of knowledge is implemented consistently for all students.

References

Ahlgrim-Delzell, L., Browder, D., Flowers, C., & Baker, J. (2008–2009). *Nonverbal literacy assessment.* Charlotte, NC: University of North Carolina.

Ahlgrim-Delzell, L., Browder, D., & Wood, L. (2014). Effects of systematic instruction and an augmentative communication device on phonics skills acquisition for students with moderate intellectual disability who are nonverbal. *Education and Training in Autism and Developmental Disabilities, 49,* 517–532.

Alberto, P. A., Waugh, R. E., & Fredrick, L. D. (2010). Teaching the reading of connected text through sight-word instruction to students with moderate intellectual disabilities. *Research in Developmental Disabilities, 31,* 1467–1474.

Allington, R. L. (1983). Fluency: The neglected goal. *The Reading Teacher, 36,* 556–561.

Allington, R. L. (2006). *What really matters for struggling readers.* Boston: Person, Allyn, & Bacon.

Allor, J. H., Champlin, T. M., Gifford, D. B., & Mathes, P. G. (2010). Methods for increasing the intensity of reading instruction for students with intellectual disabilities. *Education and Training in Autism and Developmental Disabilities, 45,* 500–511.

Allor, J. H., & Chard, D. J. (2011). A comprehensive approach to improving reading fluency for students with disabilities. *Focus on Exceptional Children, 43,* 1–12.

Allor, J. H., Gifford, D. B., Al Otaiba, S., Miller, S. J., & Cheatham, J. P. (2013). Teaching students with intellectual disability to integrate reading skills: Effects of text and text-based lessons. *Remedial and Special Education, 34,* 346–356.

Allor, J. H., Mathes, P. G., Roberts, J. K., Cheatham, J. P., & Al Otaiba, S. (2014). Is scientifically based reading instruction effective for students with below-average IQs? *Exceptional Children, 80,* 287–306.

Beck, I. L., McKeown, M. G., & Kucan, L. (2013). *Bringing words to life.* New York: The Guilford Press.

Browder, D. M., Ahlgrim-Delzell, L., Courtade, G., Gibbs, S. L., & Flowers, C. (2008). Evaluation of the effectiveness of an early literacy program for students with significant developmental disabilities. *Exceptional Children, 75,* 33–52.

Browder, D. M., Ahlgrim-Delzell, L., Flowers, C., & Baker, J. (2012). An evaluation of a multicomponent early literacy program for students with severe developmental disabilities. *Remedial and Special Education, 33,* 237–246.

Browder, D. M., Ahlgrim-Delzell, L., Spooner, F., Mims, P. J., & Baker, J. N. (2009). Using time delay to teach literacy to students with severe developmental disabilities. *Exceptional Children, 75,* 343–364.

Browder, D. M., Hudson, M. E., & Wood, A. L. (2013). Teaching students with moderate intellectual disability who are emergent readers to comprehend passages of text. *Exceptionality, 21,* 191–206.

Browder, D. M., Trela, K., & Jimenez, B. (2007). Training teachers to follow a task analysis to engage middle school students with moderate and severe developmental disabilities in grade-appropriate literature. *Focus on Autism and Other Developmental Disabilities, 22,* 206–219.

Browder, D. M., Wakeman, S. Y., Spooner, F., Ahlgrim-Delzell, L., & Algozzine, B. (2006). Research on reading instruction for individuals with significant cognitive disabilities. *Exceptional Children, 72,* 392–408.

Brown, L., Branston, M. B., Hamre-Nietupski, S., Pumpian, I., Certo, N., & Gruenewald, L. (1979). A strategy for developing chronological and age-appropriate and functional curricular content for severely handicapped adolescents and young adults. *Journal of Special Education, 13,* 81–90.

Burgoyne, K., Baxter, B., & Buckley, S. (2014). Developing the reading skills of children with Down syndrome. In R. Faragher & B. Clarke (Eds.), *Educating learners with Down syndrome: Research, theory, and practice with children and adults* (pp. 195–220). New York: Routledge.

Burgoyne, K., Duff, F. J., Clarke, P. J., Buckley, S., Snowling, M. J., & Hulme, C. (2012). Efficacy of a reading and language intervention or children with Down syndrome: A randomized controlled trial. *Journal of Child Psychology and Psychiatry, 53,* 1044–1053.

Cannella-Malone, H. I., Konrad, M., & Pennington, R. C. (2015). ACCESS! Teaching writing skills to students with intellectual disability. *TEACHING Exceptional Children, 47,* 272–280.

Channell, M. M., Loveall, S. J., & Conners, F. A. (2013). Strengths and weaknesses in reading skills of youth with intellectual disabilities. *Research in Developmental Disabilities, 34,* 776–787.

Cologon, K., Cupples, L., & Wyver, S. (2011). Effects of targeted reading instruction on phonological awareness and phonic decoding children with Down syndrome. *American Journal of Intellectual and Developmental Disabilities, 11,* 111–129.

Conners, F. A., Rosenquist, C. J., Sligh, A. C., Atwell, J. A., & Kiser, T. (2006). Phonological reading skills acquisition by children with mental retardations. *Research in Developmental Disabilities, 27,* 121–137.

Copeland, S. R., & Cosbey, J. (2008–2009). Making progress in the general curriculum: Rethinking effective instructional practices. *Research and Practice for Persons with Severe Disabilities, 33,* 214–227.

Copeland, S. R., & Keefe, E. B. (2007). *Effective literacy instruction for students with moderate or severe disabilities.* Baltimore, MD: P. H. Brookes.

Copeland, S. R., Keefe, E. B., Calhoon, A. J., Tanner, W., & Park, S. (2011). Preparing teachers to provide literacy instruction to all students: Faculty experiences and perceptions. *Research and Practice for Persons with Severe Disabilities, 36,* 126–141.

Copeland, S. R., McCord, J. A., & Kruger, A. (2016). Literacy instruction for adults with extensive needs for supports: A review of the intervention literature. *Journal of Adolescent and Adult Literacy.* Advance online publication. doi: 10.1002/jaal.548

de Graaf, G., & van Hove, G. (2015). Learning to read in regular and special schools: A follow-up study of students with Down syndrome. *Life Span and Disability, 1,* 7–39.

Dexter, D. D., & Hughes, C. A. (2011). Graphic organizers and students with learning disabilities: A meta-analysis. *Learning Disabilities, 34,* 51–72.

Downing, J. E. (2005). *Teaching literacy to students with significant disabilities: Strategies for the K–12 inclusive classroom.* Thousand Oaks, CA: Corwin Press.

Downing, J. E. (2011). Teaching communication skills. In M. E. Snell & F. Brown (Eds.), *Instruction of students with severe disabilities* (7th ed., pp. 461–491). Boston: Pearson.

Erickson, K., Hatch, P., & Clendon, S. (2010). Literacy, assistive technology, and students with significant disabilities. *Focus on Exceptional Children, 42,* 1–16.

Fisher, D., & Frey, N. (2008). *Improving adolescent literacy.* Upper Saddle River, NJ: Pearson.

Forts, A. M., & Luckasson, R. (2011). Reading, writing, and friendship: Adult implications of effective literacy instruction for students with intellectual disability. *Research & Practice for Persons with Severe Disabilities, 36,* 121–125.

Fox, L. (1989). Stimulus generalization of skills and persons with profound mental handicaps. *Education and Training in Mental Retardation, 24*, 219–229.

Goldstein, H. (2011). Knowing what to teach provides a roadmap for early literacy intervention. *Journal of Early Intervention, 33*, 268–280.

Grigal, M., Hart, D., & Weir, C. (2014). Postsecondary education for students with intellectual disabilities. In M. Agran, F. Brown, C. Hughes, C. Quirk, & D. Ryndak (Eds.), *Equity and full participation for individuals with severe disabilities: A vision for the future* (pp. 275–298). Washington, DC: TASH.

Hansen, B. D., Wadsworth, J. P., Roberts, M. R., & Poole, T. N. (2014). Effects of naturalistic instruction on phonological awareness skills of children with intellectual and developmental disabilities. *Research in Developmental Disabilities, 35*, 2790–2801.

Heller, K. W., & Coleman-Martin, M. B. (2007). Strategies or promoting literacy for students who have physical disabilities. *Communication Disorders Quarterly, 28*, 69–72.

Higher Education Opportunity Act of 2008, PL 110–315, 122 Stat. 3078.

Horner, R. H., Carr, E. G., Halle, J., McGee, G., Odom, S., & Wolery, M. (2005). The use of single-subject research to identify evidence-based practice in special education. *Exceptional Children, 71*, 165–179.

Hua, Y., Hendrickson, J. M., Therrien, W. J., Woods-Groves, S., Rice, P. S., & Shaw, J. J. (2012). Effects of combined reading and question generation on reading fluency and comprehension of three young adults with autism and intellectual disability. *Focus on Autism and Other Developmental Disabilities, 27*, 135–146.

Hua, Y., Therrien, W. J., Hendrickson, J. M., Woods-Groves, S., Ries, P. S., & Shaw, J. W. (2012). Effects of combined repeated reading and question generation intervention on young adults with cognitive disabilities. *Education and Training in Autism and Developmental Disabilities, 47*, 72–83.

Hudson, M. E., Browder, D. M., & Wood, L. A. (2013). Review of experimental research on academic learning by students with moderate and severe intellectual disability in general education. *Research and Practice for Persons with Severe Disabilities, 38*, 17–29.

Hudson, M. E., & Test, D. W. (2011). Evaluating the evidence base of shared story reading to promote literacy for students with extensive support needs. *Research and Practice for Persons with Severe Disabilities, 36*, 34–45.

Individuals with Disabilities Education Improvement Act (IDEA) of 2004, PL 108–446, 20 US C. §§ 1400 *et seq.*

Institute on Medicine. (2011). *Innovations in health literacy research: Workshop summary*. Washington, DC: The National Academies Press.

Joseph, L. M., & Konrad, M. (2009). Teaching students with intellectual or developmental disabilities to write: A review of the literature. *Research in Developmental Disabilities, 30*, 1–19.

Kaiser, A. P., & Roberts, M. Y. (2013). Parent-implemented enhanced milieu teaching with preschool children who have intellectual disabilities. *Journal of Speech, Language, and Hearing Research, 56*, 295–309.

Kamps, D., Locke, P., Delquadri, J., & Hall, R. V. (1989). Increasing academic skills of students with autism using fifth grade peers as tutors. *Education & Treatment of Children, 12*, 38–51.

Katims, D. D. (1991). Emergent literacy in early childhood special education: Curriculum and instruction. *Topics in Early Childhood Special Education, 11*, 69–84.

Keefe, E. B. (2007a). Fluency. In S. R. Copeland & E. B. Keefe (Eds.), *Effective literacy instruction for students with moderate or severe disabilities* (pp. 63–77). Baltimore: Paul H. Brookes.

Keefe, E. B. (2007b). Vocabulary development. In *Effective literacy instruction for students with moderate or severe disabilities* (pp. 95–108). Baltimore: Paul H. Brookes.

Keefe, E. B., & Copeland, S. R. (2011). What is literacy? The power of a definition. *Research & Practice for Persons with Severe Disabilities, 36*, 92–99.

Keefe, E. B., Copeland, S. R., & DiLuzio, H. (2010). Creating print-rich literacy environments to support literacy instruction. In C. Carnahan & P. Williamson (Eds.), *Quality literacy instruction for students with autism spectrum disorders* (pp. 161–187). Shawnee Mission, KS: Autism Asperger Publishing Company.

Kliewer, C. (2008a). Joining the literacy flow: Fostering symbol and written language learning in young children with significant developmental disabilities through the four currents of literacy. *Research and Practice for Persons with Severe Disabilities, 33*, 103–121.

Kliewer, C. (2008b). *Seeing all kids as readers*. Baltimore, MD: P. H. Brookes.

Konrad, M., Trela, K., & Test, D. W. (2006). Using IEP goals and objectives to teach paragraph writing to high school students with physical and cognitive disabilities. *Education and Training in Developmental Disabilities, 41*, 111–124.

Koritas, S., & Iacono, T. (2011). Secondary conditions in people with developmental disability. *American Journal on Intellectual and Developmental Disabilities, 116*(1), 36–47.

Lemons, C. J., & Fuchs, D. (2010). Modeling response to reading intervention in children with Down syndrome: An examination of predictors of differential growth. *Reading Research Quarterly, 45*, 134–168.

Lemons, C. J., Mrachko, A. A., Kostewicz, D. E., & Paterra, M. F. (2012). Effectiveness of decoding and phonological interventions for children with Down syndrome. *Exceptional Children, 79*, 67–90.

Mason, L. H. (2013). Teaching students who struggle with learning to think before, while, and after reading: Effects of self-regulated strategy development instruction. *Reading and Writing Quarterly, 29,* 124–144.

Mims, P. J., Lee, A., Browder, D. M., Zakas, T., & Flynn. S. (2012). Effects of a treatment package to facilitate English/language arts learning for middle school students with moderate to severe disabilities. *Education and Training in Autism and Developmental Disabilities, 47,* 414–425.

Moni, K. B., & Jobling, A. (2014). Challenging literate invisibility: Continuing literacy education for young adults and adults with Down syndrome. In R. Faragher & B. Clarke (Eds.), *Educating learners with Down syndrome: Research, theory, and practice with children and adults* (pp. 221–237). New York: Routledge.

Morgan, M., Moni, K., & Jobling, A. (2004). What's it all about? Investigating reading comprehension strategies in young adults with Down syndrome. *Down Syndrome Research & Practice, 9*(2), 37–44.

National Reading Panel (NRP). (2000). *Teaching children to read: An evidence-based assessment of the scientific literature on reading and its implications for reading instruction.* Washington, DC: US Department of Health and Human Services (NIH Pub. No.00–4754).

National Reading Technical Assistance Panel. (2010). *A review of the current research on vocabulary instruction.* Retrieved from http://www2.ed.gov/programs/readingfirst/support/rmcfinal1.pdf

No Child Left Behind (NCLB) Act of 2001, Pub. L. No. 107–110 (2002).

Okolo, C. M., & Diedrich, J. (2014). Twenty-five years later: How is technology used in the education of students with disabilities? Results of a statewide study. *Journal of Special Education Technology, 29,* 1–20.

Ouellette, G., & Beers, A. (2010). A not-so-simple view of reading: How oral vocabulary and visual-word recognition complicate the story. *Reading & Writing, 23,* 189–208.

Ozman, R. G. (2011). Comparison of two different presentations of graphic organizers in recalling information in expository texts with intellectually disabled students. *Educational Sciences: Theory & Practice, 11,* 785–793.

Pennington, R., Delano, M., & Scott, R. (2014). Improving cover-letter writing skills of individuals with intellectual disabilities. *Journal of Applied Behavior Analysis, 47,* 204–208.

Rasinski, T. V. (2003). *The fluent reader.* New York: Scholastic.

Rasinski, T. V. (2009). *Essential readings on fluency.* Newark: International Reading Association.

Ratz, C., & Lenhard, W. (2013). Reading skills among students with intellectual disabilities. *Research in Developmental Disabilities, 34,* 1740–1748.

Reichenberg, M., & Lofgren, K. (2013). The social practice of reading and writing instruction in schools for intellectually disabled pupils. *Psychological and Pedagogical Survey, 14*(3–4), 43–60.

Reutzel, D. R., & Cooter, Jr., R. B. (2012). *Teaching children to read.* Boston: Pearson.

Ricci, L. (2011). Home literacy environments, interest in reading and emergent literacy skills of children with Down syndrome versus typical children. *Journal of Intellectual Disability Research, 55*(6), 596–609.

Ruppar, A. L. (2015). A preliminary study of the literacy experiences of adolescents with severe disabilities. *Remedial and Special Education, 36,* 235–245.

Ruwe, K., McLaughlin, T. F., Derby, K. M., & Johnson, J. (2011). The multiple effects of direct instruction flashcards on sight word acquisition, passage reading, and errors for three middle school students with intellectual disabilities. *Journal of Developmental and Physical Disabilities, 23,* 241–255.

Ryndak, D. L., Moore, M. A., Orlando, A. M., & Delano, M. (2008–2009). Access to general education: The mandate and role of context in research-based practices for students with extensive support needs. *Research and Practice for Persons with Severe Disabilities, 33–34,* 199–213.

Ryndak, D. L., Morrison, A., & Sommerstein, L. (1999). Literacy before and after inclusion in general education settings. *The Journal of the Association for Persons with Severe Handicaps, 24,* 5–22.

Scherba de Valenzuela, J., & Tracey, M. M. (2007). The role of language and communication. In S. R. Copeland & E. B. Keefe (Eds.), *Effective literacy instruction for students with moderate or severe disabilities* (pp. 23–40). Baltimore: Paul H. Brookes.

Sesma, H. W., Mahone, E. M., Levine, T., Eason, S. H., & Cutting, L. E. (2009). The contribution of executive skills to reading comprehension. *Child Neuropsychology, 15,* 232–246.

Snell, M. E., Brady, N., McLean, L., Ogletree, B. T., Siegel, E., Sylvester, L., . . . Sevick, R. (2010). Twenty years of communication intervention research with individuals who have severe intellectual and developmental disabilities. *American Journal on Intellectual and Developmental Disabilities, 115,* 364–380.

Spector, J. E. (2011). Sight word instruction for students with autism: An evaluation of the evidence base. *Journal of Autism and Developmental Disorders, 42,* 1411–1422.

Spooner, F., Knight, V., Browder, D., Jimenez, B., & DiBase, W. (2011). Evaluating evidence-based practice in teaching science content to students with severe developmental disabilities. *Research and Practice for Persons with Severe Disabilities, 36,* 62–75.

Staples, A., & Edmister, E. (2012). Evidence of two theoretical models observed in young children with disabilities who are beginning to learn to write. *Topics in Language Disorders, 32,* 319–334.

Strickland, W. D., Boon, R. T., & Spencer, V. G. (2013). The effects of repeated reading on the fluency and comprehensions skills of elementary-age students with learning disabilities, 2001–2011: A review of research and practice. *Learning Disabilities: A Contemporary Journal, 11*, 1–33.

Sturm, J. (2012). An enriched writers' workshop for beginning writers with developmental disabilities. *Topics in Language Disorders, 32*, 335–360.

Troia, G. (2014). *Evidence-based practices for writing instruction* (Document No. IC-5). Retrieved from http\\ceedar. education.ufl.edu/tools/innovation-configuration/

UNESCO. (2004). *The plurality of literacy and its implications for policies and programmes.* UNESCO Education Sector Position Paper.

Vaccarino, F., Culligan, N., Comrie, M., & Sligo, F. (2006). School to work transition: Incorporating workplace literacy in the curriculum for individuals with disabilities in New Zealand. *International Journal of Learning, 13*, 69–81.

van den Bos, K. P., Nakken, H., Nicolay, P. G., & van Houten, E. J. (2007). Adults with mild intellectual disabilities: Can their reading comprehension ability be improved? *Journal of Intellectual Disability Research, 51*, 835–849.

van Tilborg, A., Segers, E., van Balkom, H., & Verhoeven, L. (2014). Predictors of early literacy skills in children with intellectual disabilities: A clinical perspective. *Research in Developmental Disabilities, 35*, 1674–1685.

van Wingerden, E., Segers, E., van Balkom, H., & Verhoeven, L. (2014). Cognitive and linguistic predictors of reading comprehension in children with intellectual disabilities. *Research in Developmental Disabilities, 35*, 3139–3147.

Wise, J. C., Sevcik, R. A., Romski, M. A., & Morris, R. D. (2010). The relationship between phonological processing skills and word and non-word identification performance in children with mild intellectual disabilities. *Research in Developmental Disabilities, 31*, 1170–1175.

Wood, L., Browder, D. M., & Flynn, L. (in press). Teaching students with intellectual disability to use a self-questioning strategy to comprehend social studies text for an inclusive setting. *Research and Practice for Persons with Severe Disabilities*.

20

Teaching Mathematics and Science to Students with Intellectual Disability

Alicia F. Saunders, Diane M. Browder, Jenny R. Root

In the 21st century, positive experiences with mathematical and scientific learning can provide students with enhanced opportunities for independence and inclusion in an increasingly technological society. Through mathematical learning, students gain skills to manage the numerical problem solving required in many of life's activities. Through science students learn about the natural world and ways to engage in inquiry. Recent comprehensive reviews have indicated that the mathematics and science focus for students with intellectual disability has been extremely narrow. In mathematics, nearly all research for students with intellectual disability with moderate and severe intellectual impairment has focused on money and simple computation (Browder, Spooner, Ahlgrim-Delzell, Harris, & Wakeman, 2008). Limited research exists for students with intellectual disaiblity with mild intellectual impairment due to being aggregated with other high-incidence disabilities (e.g., learning disabilities and emotional/ behavioral disorders) or with students with intellectual disaiblity with moderate and severe intellectual impairment (Hord & Bouck, 2012). Studies on science included only a few basic concepts needed to learn daily living tasks (Spooner, Knight, Browder, Jimenez, & DiBiase, 2011). In the last decade, educators have focused on expanding access to general curriculum content to help students prepare for state assessments. These assessments, including the alternate assessments for students with more severe disabilities, are aligned with state standards in language arts, mathematics, and science. With this focus, new intervention strategies have emerged for teaching both content that aligns with a student's grade level and for teaching the foundational skills needed to enhance learning this content. This chapter provides an overview of these recent innovations for mathematics and science.

Mathematical Learning for Students with Intellectual Disability

The National Council of Teachers of Mathematics established six principles that are fundamental for high-quality mathematics education; the first being the equity principle, which calls for high expectations for *all* students. This principle articulates that *all* students must have opportunities and adequate support to learn mathematics "regardless of personal characteristics, backgrounds, or physical challenges" (NCTM, 2000, pg. 12), including learners with intellectual disability. In addition, technological advances have increased the need for students to have greater mathematical skills. Students with mathematical competence will have greater independent living outcomes and greater employment options. The Common Core State Standards Initiative (CCSSI, 2015) recognizes this need and has called for all students to be college and career ready. The illustration of what "college and career ready" may look like for students that fall under the intellectual disability umbrella may vary widely, but without a doubt, it maintains high expectations that students with intellectual disability can engage in mathematical learning with sound instruction. Because of these national movements and federal law, mathematics instruction has transformed and now emphasizes problem solving, conceptual understanding, and communication about mathematics (Montague & Jitendra, 2006).

Foundations for Mathematics Instruction

Students with intellectual disability have a number of support needs in learning mathematics due to characteristics of their disability, including working-memory deficits, attention deficits, language processing and comprehension deficits, weak early numeracy skills, and difficulty with self-regulation (Donlan, 2007). For this reason, students with intellectual disability will often need supports to make mathematics accessible. These may include individualized instruction, repeated opportunities for practice, reduction in requirements for the number of problems to complete, extended time, reading problems aloud, peer tutoring, cue cards of strategy steps, color coding, calculators, graphic organizers, mathematical manipulative materials, mnemonics, technology-assisted instruction, and contextualizing the instruction with real-world applications (Maccini & Gagnon, 2006). Browder et al.'s (2008) review also identified systematic instruction, such as task analysis and prompting with feedback, as evidence-based practices for teaching mathematics.

For students with intellectual disability to have full access to general-curriculum mathematics, they need the opportunity to learn the full range of content reflected in their state's standards. For students who take alternate assessments, the standards might be simplified and prioritized, but they will generally be the same content. For example, an elementary student with intellectual disability will be learning to find the perimeter of a rectangle the same as students who are nondisabled. What may differ is the student working towards alternate achievement may solve simpler problems involving smaller numbers and fewer steps. Some students with intellectual disability will be working towards grade-level achievement and may need explicit instruction to catch up on underdeveloped concepts. These students will take their state's mathematics assessment with or without an accommodation such as the use of a calculator or manipulatives. This chapter will describe research on meeting both types of learning challenges, but with an emphasis on alternate achievement in mathematics. What is key is that a ceiling not be placed on how much mathematics students will learn by denying them opportunity to be exposed to the content.

When students with intellectual disability receive this grade-aligned instruction, some will enter the content far below grade-level achievement expectations. For this reason, a twofold approach is needed to mathematics instructions. Figure 20.1 shows this twofold approach to math. Students not only need access to the grade-aligned content, but they also need the opportunity to continue to develop their foundational skills. For example, while finding perimeter, students also can be learning to recognize larger numbers or to use a standard measure, skills typically acquired at an earlier grade. Jimenez and Staples (2015) demonstrated this by teaching three students with intellectual disability with moderate intellectual impairment early numeracy skills using a scripted, systematic instruction curriculum, *Early Numeracy* (Jimenez, Browder, & Saunders, 2013) in the context of general education lessons. All three students showed a gain in proficiency of early numeracy skills, which also resulted in a gain in access to grade-aligned math content.

Early Numeracy Instruction

Just as phonics is the essence of reading, early numeracy skills are the essence of mathematics. Number sense can be defined as an individual's ability to comprehend numbers and operations and use these concepts and strategies to make mathematical judgments and apply them to more complex problem solving

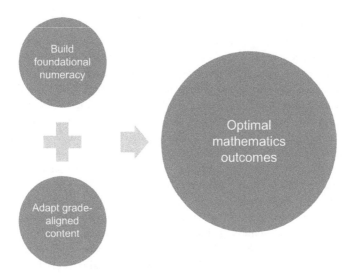

Figure 20.1 Using a twofold approach to mathematics instruction for students with intellectual disability

(McIntosh, Reys, & Reys, 1992). Numerous skills fall under the umbrella term of *early numeracy skills* including number identification, rote counting, representation of numbers and counting with one-to-one correspondence, number conservation, composing and decomposing numbers, magnitude of numbers, early measurement concepts, understanding the effects of operations, and patterning.

The development of number sense, including what numbers are and how they relate to one another, begins before the first year of life and grows extensively in the first five years of life (Sarama & Clements, 2009). Even children whose development is delayed demonstrate more advanced mathematical concepts in the early years than once thought possible (Baroody, 1998). Most children enter formal schooling in kindergarten with some early numeracy skills. The early numeracy skills a student possesses by first grade are a strong predictor of future quantitative understanding and mathematical achievement (Sarama & Clements, 2009). They also are a predictor of future reading ability. However, students with intellectual disability may not possess these skills because of a lack of exposure in the early years of their life due to their home environment, culture, or lack of formalized schooling (e.g., preschool or daycare with curriculum), or because of developmental deficits in memory and cognition (Sarama & Clements, 2009). For students who do not have these skills, the gap in mathematical achievement and accessing the general curriculum continues to widen with each grade level. This does not have to be the case. With sound, explicit instruction, students can develop these skills and bridge the gap (Gersten & Chard, 1999).

Mathematical researchers have proposed empirically based learning trajectories and progressions of early numeracy skills and number sense (Sarama & Clements, 2009). When educators understand the natural progressions, they can teach these skills in an explicit manner that is both developmentally appropriate and effective for learners. For example, a child naturally progresses from rote counting to counting small groups of objects (e.g., 1–4) with one-to-one correspondence to counting larger sets and representing the quantity with a number (e.g., counts 10 blocks and writes "10"). When following a learning progression developed for typically developing children, it is important to note that students with intellectual disability may have splinter skills in which they are more proficient in some early numeracy skill progressions than in others. Students also may work on multiple progressions at one time, especially because students with intellectual disability may grasp the concepts of one content area faster than another. For this reason, it is important not to limit students' future learning because of an early numeracy skill that is taking a long time to master. Often these skills can be reviewed while working on other mathematical content (e.g., reviewing numbers while working on measurement). The following section will describe interventions designed to teach early numeracy skills.

There are research-based curricula available for purchase to teach early numeracy skills following recommended learning trajectories. The degree of research on each of these curricula for students with intellectual disability may vary as most of the research has focused on typically developing children or children with mathematical difficulties. *Number Worlds* (Griffin, Clements, & Sarama, 2008) is a curriculum that has shown an increase in numeracy skills in students with mathematical difficulties and mathematics learning disabilities, but has not been directly studied with students with intellectual disability. *SRA Real Math Building Blocks PreK* (Clements & Sarama, 2007) is another example of a research-based curriculum that emerged from a National Science Foundation grant, which has shown positive outcomes in preschool children from low-income families, but has not been directly studied with students with intellectual disability. *SRA Connecting Math Concepts: Comprehensive Edition* (Engelmann, Engelmann, Carnine, & Kelly, 2012) is a Direct Instruction mathematics program that has shown positive effects in preschool-aged students with developmental delays.

There are also research-based approaches developed for students with more intensive support needs related to learning math. Tzanakaki, Hastings, Grindle, Hughes, and Hoare (2014) combined an adapted version of the *Math Recovery* curriculum (Wright, Stanger, Stafford, & Martland, 2006) with Discrete Trial Training (DTT) to teach emergent numeracy skills to 11 students with severe intellectual impairment using a group experimental design where the remaining 11 students received mathematics as usual. DTT was comprised of three steps: (a) delivery of instructional cue; (b) the child's response, which is paired with teacher response when first teaching; and (c) immediate, brief reinforcement. Once the child showed correct responding, the teacher's response was faded. The *Math Recovery* curriculum consists of five progressive stages: Emergent, Perceptual, Figurative, Counting-on and Counting-back, and Facile. The majority of participants in this study were at the "emergent" stage and targeted skills including rote counting to 20, identifying numerals 1 to 10, counting objects or visible items, subitizing spatial patterns to 6 (i.e., recognizing dot patterns, like dice configurations, with automaticity without counting), and finger counting. A few participants were at the Perceptual or Figurative stages and were working on counting to 100, counting backwards from 30 to 1, adding items of two groups when one group was screened, and ordering numbers from 30 to 100. The study used two distal measures to measure effects; students showed an average of 8.18 months of mathematical age growth, versus the control group that showed a 0.27 month growth. The experimental group also showed a moderate effect size on oral counting and a small effect on number identification.

Attainment's *Early Numeracy* (Jimenez et al., 2013) is a research-based curriculum for students with intellectual disability with moderate and severe intellectual impairment that has shown positive effects in early numeracy skill acquisition (Browder, Jimenez, Spooner et al., 2012; Jimenez & Kemmery, 2013; Jimenez & Staples, 2015). The *Early Numeracy* curriculum (Jimenez et al., 2013) is a treatment package composed of several evidence-based and research-based instructional practices for students with moderate and severe intellectual impairment, including story-based mathematical problems to provide a context for instruction, systematic instruction (time delay and least-intrusive prompting with error correction and feedback), graphic organizers, multiple exemplar training, and repeated opportunities for practice. The curriculum is comprised of four units with six lessons in each unit that cover nine early numeracy skills that build in difficulty over units. Each lesson within a unit covers the same skills, but changes context and numbers to build generalization with repeated opportunities for practice. Skills include rote counting, number identification, counting with one-to-one correspondence, making sets, adding sets, comparing quantities, measurement, and calendar skills. Browder, Jimenez, Spooner et al. (2012) examined the effects of the *Early Numeracy* curriculum (Jimenez et al., 2013) with systematic instruction and repeated practice on the acquisition of early numeracy skills in seven students with moderate intellectual impairment during a pilot study using three of the four units. Participants also were included in a general-education mathematics classroom with their chronological-age peers, and paraprofessionals were trained to embed instruction in naturally occurring opportunities during the lesson. All participants showed growth in early numeracy skills and were able to generalize to the general education setting. Some students generalized early numeracy skills across units, thus indicating they may not have needed skills broken down into that small of increments. For example, once students mastered making a set of three in Unit 1, some were able to make sets of five and ten in Units 2 and 3 without being taught. This has great implications for practice from the standpoint of teachers, who may be able to condense instruction and teach more concepts or prioritize accessing the general curriculum using the early numeracy skills. Jimenez and Kemmery (2013) replicated this study in a different geographical location using a multiple probe across three groups of students. All but one participant showed positive outcomes linked to instruction. Both studies show promise that *Early Numeracy* may have positive effects on early numeracy acquisition for students with moderate and severe intellectual impairment.

Although the skills taught in these curricula are not an exhaustive list of numeracy skills to target, they provide a basis for teaching these skills in a progressive manner based on learning trajectories with high-quality practices. Teachers can certainly choose to teach skills on their own if a purchasable curriculum is not an option. For example, Skibo, Mims, and Spooner (2011) taught three students with severe intellectual impairment to receptively identify numerals 1–5 using response cards and a system of least prompts. The experimenter's cards during instruction also had the quantity represented in picture form (e.g., three balloons). Students were asked to receptively identify a number. The participant was given 5 seconds before a prompt was given. The prompting hierarchy included a verbal prompt, model prompt, partial physical prompt, and physical prompt. This was a fairly quick strategy, which included both active responding and systematic instruction at little cost.

Because students with intellectual disability have difficulty generalizing skills learned in isolation, it is important to promote the development of these skills in the students' naturally occurring routines and environments. Embedding trials of these skills whenever possible and wherever possible will produce the greatest degree of learning and application. Early numeracy skills provide a strong foundation for all domains of mathematics, but students also must develop mathematical reasoning and problem solving in order to perform higher level mathematics.

Mathematical Problem Solving

Learning how to solve story problems is the basis for learning how to apply these skills to real-world problems in a child's everyday life (Van de Walle, 2004). In contrast, story problems pose difficulties for most students with intellectual disability because of their cognitive and memory support needs. To be successful problem solvers, students with intellectual disability must receive mathematics instruction that accommodates their developmental and cognitive characteristics using evidence-based practices. One evidence-based practice for teaching problem solving is schema-based instruction (SBI), which uses a conceptual teaching approach by combining reading comprehension strategies to teach students to identify the underlying problem structure before solving the problem (Fuchs et al., 2006; Jitendra & Hoff, 1996).

Schema-based instruction is thought to be effective because it lessens the cognitive demands placed on the student and teaches a highly structured format for solving the problem. SBI focuses on conceptual knowledge by enhancing comprehension to ensure students can effectively create representations of the problem situation, thus developing an understanding of the underlying problem structure. This step is imperative to successful problem solving because most errors in word problem solving are actually a result of students misunderstanding the problem situation, rather than computation errors (Jitendra, 2008). In SBI, students learn to understand the semantic structure of word problems through text analysis in order to identify quantitative relations between sets or actions between sets, and then learn to create a visual model of these relationships (Jitendra & Hoff, 1996). From this mathematical representation, or model, students can select the operation to solve. The procedural rules for solving problem types are directly related to the underlying concepts. For example, rather than just teaching students to add when the total is unknown (i.e., the procedural rule), SBI would teach a rule that relates the concept to the algorithmic procedure (e.g., two small parts are combined to create a whole, or "part-part-whole"; Jitendra, 2008).

Problem Type and Schematic Diagrams

There are three main types of arithmetic word problem situations (i.e., schemata) that have been identified: *group, change,* and *compare* (Marshall, 1995). In SBI, students are explicitly taught to identify the structural features of the problem (e.g., part-part-whole) in order to identify the problem schemata (e.g., group problem). Visual representations go far beyond simply a pictorial representation of the information in the word problem. These representations, called *schematic diagrams,* provide students with a way to visually organize and summarize the information from the word problem so that it is concrete and shows the relationship among numbers in the problem. Known values in the word problem are written into their corresponding parts of the selected schematic diagram, and the unknown values are either left blank or a question mark is placed in the diagram to indicate the unknown.

Group schema (Figure 20.2) involves two or more small groups combined to make a larger group, emphasizing the part-part-whole relationship. For example, *Sarah picked 8 squash from her garden. She also picked 7 carrots. How many vegetables did she pick?* Eight squash and seven carrots represent the "part" relationships and the unknown quantity (i.e., vegetables) represents the "whole."

Change schema (Figure 20.3) involves a dynamic process, where an initial quantity is either increased or decreased over time to result in a final quantity. An example of a *change increase* problem is shown in Figure 20.3, and would be presented as: *Marcus earned $2 for sweeping the kitchen. He earned $5 more for mowing the lawn. How much money did Marcus earn?* An example of a *change decrease* problem is shown next: *Marcus raked 5 piles of leaves. He bagged 2 piles of leaves. How many more piles of leaves does he have left to bag?* In both examples, Marcus starts with an initial set ($2 and 5 piles). The initial set was changed by adding more or taking away from the set ($5 and 2 piles), resulting in a final amount, which is unknown. The *change-subtraction* problem also illustrates one issue that can result in incorrect operation when using the key word strategy. Specifically, the question uses both key words "more" and "left," which usually denote addition and subtraction, respectively; however, the problem requires the student to subtract to solve.

The compare schema (Figure 20.4) involves comparing two differing sets that are related in some way, and requires finding the difference between the sets, regardless of whether the question is asking "How many more?" or "How many fewer?" For example: *Xavier has 24 DVDs in his collection. His*

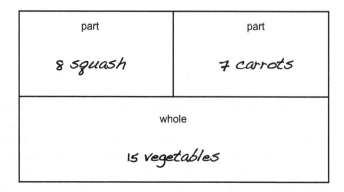

Figure 20.2 Sample *group* problem type schema

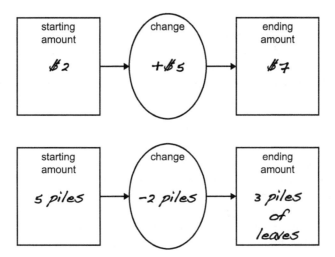

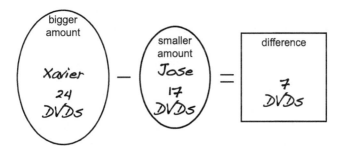

Figure 20.3 Sample *change-addition* and *change-subtraction* problem type schemas

Figure 20.4 Sample *compare* problem type schema

brother, *Jose, has 17 DVDs in his. How many more DVDs does Xavier have than Jose?* The two numbers being compared are the number of DVDs Xavier has (24) and Jose has (17), and the relation between these two sets is the difference of 7.

All of these examples displayed the unknown quantity in the final position of a number sentence. More complex problems may place the unknown in the initial or medial position, requiring some level of algebraic thinking to solve. Additionally, problems similar to those found in the general education classroom may include extraneous information in the word problem. Larger numbers and multistep problems also increase the difficulty level.

Key Components of SBI

SBI has four main components, including: (a) identifying the underlying problem structure, using visual representations known as schematic diagrams; (b) explicitly teaching problem solving through the use of a heuristic (called a *mnemonic* in other disciplines); (c) using explicit instruction to teach the four-step problem-solving heuristic (i.e., problem schema identification, representation, planning, and solution); and (d) metacognitive strategy knowledge instruction, which includes activities such as analyzing the problem, self-monitoring of strategy use, and checking the outcome for accuracy. Students can be taught to organize information using a schematic diagram and show their solution using a mathematical equation (Griffin & Jitendra, 2009). Explicit, teacher-delivered instruction is essential to SBI. Initially, teachers model problem solving by demonstrating how to analyze text in the word problem to find key information and represent it in schematic diagrams. Rules and procedures are explicitly explained. According to Jitendra (2008), in SBI, students are taught to identify the problem type first and fill in the corresponding schematic diagram, using story situations with all known values. This is known as *schema induction*. The purpose of doing so is to teach students to analyze the story situation structure rather than acting impulsively, selecting numbers, and computing (Jitendra, 2008).

Once students have shown mastery identifying the problem type, selecting the corresponding schematic diagram, and filling in the known and unknown values, they are taught to solve the problem. They also are taught to represent the schema in a number sentence. Students practice these skills repeatedly within each problem type, as well as with mixed problem types once they have learned all types. For metacognitive strategy knowledge, students are taught to use think-alouds to explain their reasoning (e.g., "Why is this a *change* problem?" It is a *change* problem because there was an initial set, a change set, and an ending set.). In addition, students are given a four-step strategy checklist with the heuristic to help transition from teacher-led instruction to student-led instruction. Jitendra, Griffin, Deatline-Buchman, and Sczesniak (2007) use a specific heuristic of *FOPS* (e.g., *F:* Find the problem type, *O:* Organize the information in the problem using the schematic diagram, *P:* Plan to solve the problem, and *S:* Solve the problem). Rockwell, Griffin, and Jones (2011) use a shortened version of Jitendra's heuristic, namely *RUNS* (e.g., *R:* Read the problem, *U:* Use a diagram, *N:* Number sentence, and *S:* State the answer), with a student with autism spectrum disorder (ASD) and mild intellectual impairment.

Numerous studies have shown that students with learning disabilities can be taught problem solving using SBI both at the elementary level and at the middle school level (Jitendra, DiPipi, & Perron-Jones, 2002; Jitendra, Hoff, & Beck, 1999; Xin, Jitendra, & Deatline-Buchman, 2005; Xin & Zhang, 2009). Some research has also shown that the use of schematic diagrams can be faded, so students gradually transfer their skills of using a schematic diagram to using mathematical equations to represent the structure of a word problem, known as schema-broadening instruction (Fuchs et al., 2008; Fuchs et al., 2009). Xin, Wiles, and Lin (2008) further built on SBI by using word-problem story grammar to enhance problem solving in elementary students with math difficulties. With modifications, these strategies may also be applicable for students with intellectual disability.

SBI for Students With Intellectual Disability

Rockwell et al. (2011) examined the effects of SBI to teach all three types of addition and subtraction word problems (i.e., compare, change, and group) to one female student with intellectual disability with mild intellectual impairment and ASD using a multiple probe across behaviors (problem type) design. Scripted lessons were used for each instructional session. First, students were taught the four-step RUNS heuristic. Next, each problem type was introduced one by one. The student was shown a story problem with all quantities known to facilitate schema induction. Direct instruction (i.e., teacher modeling, guided practice, independent practice, and continual feedback) was used to teach the salient features of word problems. Then the student was asked to sort the problems into categories as belonging or not belonging to the type being taught. Once the student was able to discriminate problem type, she was taught to solve the problems of that type where the final quantity was the unknown. During generalization, an instructional session was given on using algebraic reasoning to solve problems of any problem type with unknown quantities in the initial or medial position. The student was 100% correct for all three problem types. During generalization, she was 100% correct for all three sessions of each problem type with the exception of change, in which she made a computation error which resulted in her earning 3 out of 6 possible points for the session. At a six-week follow-up, the student was able to maintain the problem-solving skills at a high level.

Neef, Nelles, Iwata, and Page (2003) taught two students with intellectual disability with mild and moderate intellectual impairment to solve change problems by teaching precurrent behaviors. Four different training phases were conducted in which the students were taught to identify precurrent behaviors (i.e., component parts of the word problem) including the initial set, the change set, key words to identify the operation, and the resulting set. The unknown for each problem could be in any location (i.e., the initial set, the change set, or the resulting set). Within each training phase, supports and prompts were strategically faded. Results showed that teaching precurrent behaviors was successful in promoting accurate problem solving. There are several important aspects to note in this study that offer implications and needed adaptations in SBI for students with more severe intellectual impairment. First, traditional SBI was broken into much smaller steps by teaching precurrent behaviors across four training phases. Second, it took the students several sessions to learn to solve one problem type (i.e., 80 sessions for the student with moderate intellectual impairment and 51 sessions for the student with mild intellectual impairment). Third, a strategic prompt fading procedure was used in each phase to aid in the transfer from teacher-led instruction to student-led instruction. Finally, all problems were read aloud to the students.

Two additional studies have investigated the effects of a modified SBI approach with students with moderate intellectual impairment and ASD (Root, Browder, Saunders, & Lo, 2016; Saunders, 2014). Saunders (2014) investigated the effects of a modified SBI approach delivered through computer-based video instruction on the acquisition of mathematical problem-solving skills, as well as the ability to discriminate problem type and generalize to paper-and-pencil format. *Group* and *change* problem types were taught. In this modified SBI approach, the heuristic typically found in SBI was replaced with a task analysis of the steps to solve the problem supports with picture prompts and a read-aloud feature. Explicit instruction was combined with a system of least prompts, and virtual manipulatives were provided for solving problems. All three students demonstrated an increase in mathematical problem solving skills for the *group* and *change* problem types. These students also were able to increase their discriminations of problem type and generalize to the paper-and-pencil format. Root et al. (2016) also investigated the effects of a modified SBI approach on the acquisition of mathematical problem-solving skills for the *compare* problem type using both virtual and concrete manipulatives in three students with moderate intellectual impairment and ASD. Similar to Saunders (2014), the treatment package consisted of task-analytic instruction with picture supports, read-aloud feature, explicit instruction, and system of least prompts. All three students acquired the skill of solving *compare* word problems.

The studies by Neef et al. (2003), Root et al. (2016), and Saunders (2014) offer some direction for teaching word-problem solving through SBI with adaptions for students with intellectual disability who may need additional strategies and support. Problems will need to be simplified in reading level and extraneous information will need to be removed to accommodate the difficulty in reading comprehension. Read alouds offer necessary accommodation to support students who are emerging or nonreaders. Some precurrent skills will need to be taught to not overload cognitive demands. Manipulatives may be needed to represent the problem for students who lack fact recall. Task-analytic instruction with system of least prompts can be incorporated into explicit instruction typical of SBI. Existing research for students with intellectual disability has addressed addition and subtraction problem types only, so future research is needed to expand this to multiplication and division problem types.

Promoting Learning in Grade-Aligned Mathematics

As described earlier, it is important to provide students with intellectual disability the opportunity to learn the general-education mathematics curriculum so as not to place a ceiling on their learning outcomes. When given the opportunity to learn, students may reveal unexpected aptitude and interest in mathematics. For some this could lead to future careers or special interests that build on this learning. For all students, benefits can be achieved by increasing knowledge of numerical problem solving.

In teaching grade-aligned content, educators will want to refer closely to the mathematical standards targeted for the student's assigned grade level. Several states have adopted the Common Core State Standards in Mathematics (CCSSM). Because the majority of published research to date used the National Council of Teachers of Mathematics principles and standards (NCTM, 2000), these standards are used in the following section. Collaboration with general educators who know the mathematics content deeply is an essential starting point. Often the grade-level mathematics teachers can help to identify the most important standards addressed in the grade level.

Saunders, Bethune, Spooner, and Browder (2013) suggest a series of steps to teach grade-aligned mathematics standards to students with intellectual disability with moderate and severe intellectual impairment. The first is to select the standard and write specific objectives for the target student's learning. Many mathematics standards in both the NCTM standards and the CCSSM encompass many skills under one standard. For students with intellectual disability, it is important to prioritize the targeted skill. Rather than going an inch deep and a mile wide in content, prioritization allows students to reach mastery of several skills across standards and various domains. This takes careful planning but can be most beneficial for students to succeed at accessing the big idea of several standards. Next, a real-world application or activity is selected that incorporates the mathematical concept. This gives the instruction meaning for the student and promotes maintenance and generalization. The real-life activity is used to create the mathematical problems to solve. See Table 20.1 for an example of sample mathematics standards

Table 20.1 Sample mathematics standards from the CCSSM at three grade levels, the targeted objective, and the real-world application selected

CCSS	Objective	Real-world application
3.OA.A.3		
Use multiplication and division within 100 to solve word problems in situations involving equal groups, arrays, and measurement quantities, e.g., by using drawings and equations with a symbol for the unknown number to represent the problem.	Solve real-world multiplication and division word problems with the support of a graphic organizer and manipulatives.	Create problems related to an upcoming bowling field trip the students have planned. Student selects appropriate operation and uses supports to solve. For example, if 25 students go on the trip and the school rents 5 lanes, how many students will be in each lane?
7.NS.A.1.D		
Apply and extend previous understandings of addition and subtraction to add and subtract rational numbers; represent addition and subtraction on a horizontal or vertical number line diagram. (D) Apply properties of operations as strategies to add and subtract rational numbers.	Solve real-world problems with rational numbers (fractions) using the supports of fraction bars and a number line.	Create problems related to measurement. For example, the class walked ½ mile on Monday, ¾ mile on Tuesday, and ½ mile on Wednesday. How many miles total has the class walked?
HSA.REI.B.3		
Solve linear equations and inequalities in one variable, including equations with coefficients represented by letters.	Solve real-world linear equations with one variable that include coefficients and a calculator.	Solve equations related to earning money at various job sites. For example, if Sam earns $25 per lawn mowed and $10 per hour of additional yard work completed, how much will Sam have earned after x hours? ($y = 10x + 25$).

at three grade levels, (e.g., third grade, seventh grade, and high school), the targeted objective, and real-world application selected. The skill itself is taught using evidence-based practices, such as using a task analysis of the steps to solve the problem and systematic prompting with feedback. If needed, the teacher also plans instructional supports like technology, graphic organizers, or concrete manipulatives. Using these plans, the instructor implements the lesson-monitoring progress to make decisions about changing instruction if needed to promote progress. This monitoring should include checking for generalization across materials and contexts.

Numbers and Operations

Skills within the numbers and operations standard provide understanding of and proficiency with the number system. Many of the early numeracy skills previously addressed can be found within this standard. The central focus of this standard is to develop number sense, or a foundational understanding of numbers and their conceptual role within mathematics. Research has addressed this focus through teaching both basic math facts and calculation skills.

Automaticity in recalling basic math facts, such as $4 + 2 = 6$ and $2 \times 5 = 10$, will assist students in completing higher-level calculations and mathematics. For example, knowledge of addition math facts will facilitate procedural components of solving a word problem, reducing the overall cognitive load. Vaughn, Bos, and Schumm (2007) cite lack of knowledge of basic math facts as a common impediment to learning higher-level math for all students, including those with intellectual disability. Researchers have highlighted several strategies for teaching basic math facts and increasing automaticity for students with intellectual disability.

One method for teaching automaticity of math facts is simultaneous prompting with response cards. Rao and Mallow (2009) used this systematic instruction technique to teach multiplication facts to junior high students with intellectual disability. Multiplication facts were written on $3'' \times 5''$ index cards and divided into six sets of five facts. Daily probe sessions were conducted prior to instruction on all 30 multiplication facts. Following the probe, one training session was conducted on one set of five multiplication facts. The cards were presented one at a time with simultaneous controlling prompt (correct answer) from the instructor. After students heard the answer, they were expected to repeat it (e.g., "six times five equals thirty"). All participants were able to master each of the six sets of five facts.

A continuum of research-based strategies for teaching mathematical computation was identified by Mastropieri, Bakken, and Scruggs (1991). The strategies ranged from concrete (manipulative) to abstract (numeral). Manipulatives can supplement a student's current level of procedural knowledge and facilitate calculation. Although manipulatives can take many different forms (e.g., physical objects, virtual objects, or picture/symbol notations), their purpose is to give students an opportunity to interact with objects to learn target information (Carbonneau & Marley, 2012). Within the continuum, the easiest manipulatives to use would be physical objects that can be moved or arranged. Research has shown that both virtual and concrete manipulatives can be effective in teaching calculation, and that participants may prefer virtual learning materials (Root et al., 2016). Virtual manipulatives are those which are displayed and manipulated through technology. Virtual manipulatives can be accessed using free online resources such as the National Library of Virtual Manipulatives or created using technology such as SMART Board®.

The concrete-representational-abstract sequence and strategic instruction model (CRA-SIM) systematically moves instruction along the continuum suggested by Mastropieri et al. (1991). This strategy has been used to teach computation strategies by first using manipulatives, then moving to drawings and pictures once mastery with concrete objects is met, and finally progressing to a strategy that uses numbers only. The CRA-SIM strategy has been used effectively to teach addition, subtraction, and multiplication facts to students with intellectual disability.

Drawings are used as manipulatives in the dot-notation method, first evaluated by Kramer and Krug (1973) and incorporated into a mathematics curriculum by Bullock, Pierce, and McClelland (1989). The dot-notation method, (also known as "touch math" or "touch points") embeds stimulus prompts within numbers that students are instructed to touch as they count aloud. For example, numbers 1 through 5 have single dots, or "touch points," that students count (i.e., the number 3 has three dots). Numbers 6 through 10 have double touch points (i.e., the number 6 has three dots that are touched two times each). This may be an appropriate strategy for students who are able to count with one-to-one correspondence and are able to count on from a number when adding to it. The dot-notation method has been shown to be effective in teaching single-digit calculation (Cihak & Foust, 2008), and possibly to be more effective than the number line strategy (Fletcher, Boon, & Cihak, 2010).

The use of calculators for students with intellectual disability is supported by research and may be a way to compensate for limited recall of basic math facts. Yakubova and Bouck (2014) compared the effectiveness of graphing and scientific calculators in both calculation and story problems for students with mild intellectual impairment. Both formats were effective for all students, although the difference between the two varied. Findings included an increase in correct performance of subtraction computation and word problem-solving questions using both types of calculators and a decrease in the amount of time spent on answering questions. Therefore, calculators are one method for addressing numbers and operations procedural skills that decreases the cognitive load and allows for increased focus on conceptual understanding.

One overall caution in teaching numbers and operations, whatever approach is used, is to include real-life word problems. These may be introduced contextually by doing the activity related to the problem or simply by using a few props or pictures to make the word problem realistic. If students learn computation only, they know how to perform the operations, but not when or why, so have little functional use in everyday contexts.

Algebra

Algebra is closely linked with other domains of mathematics, especially geometry and data analysis, and serves as a way to unify them (NCTM, 2000). The foundations of algebraic reasoning are developed through early numeracy skills. As students build an algebraic foundation with number sense, they also must begin to apply reasoning skills. Structured mathematical experiences in earlier grades build the required foundation for algebraic thinking for later success in algebra (Dougherty, Bryant, Bryant, Darrough, & Pfannenstiel, 2015). For example, relational understanding of the equal sign and evaluation of equations in elementary grades leads to later skill of using properties of operations to generate equivalent expressions (e.g., $5 + 2 = 2 + 5$).

In a review of teaching mathematics to students with intellectual disability with moderate and severe intellectual impairment, Browder et al. (2008) identified systematic prompting with feedback and task-analytic instruction as evidence-based practices. Task-analytic instruction on how to "count up" using a number line is an effective strategy for teaching how to use an algebraic equation. In the first study to teach algebra to students with intellectual disability, Jimenez, Browder, and Courtade (2008) taught high school students with moderate intellectual impairment to solve an algebraic equation. The multicomponent intervention included concrete representation of solving a simple linear equation, task-analytic instruction on the steps to solve the equation in a total task format, multiple trials for learning, and systematic prompting with fading to promote errorless learning. Participants were taught to "count up" through a system of least prompts that included a verbal prompt and a physical prompt. A series of studies have successfully taught high school students with moderate intellectual impairment to "count up" to solve equations within story problems (Browder, Jimenez, & Trela, 2012; Browder, Trela et al., 2012). Word problems that are based on a student's future and current environments can provide a meaningful context for solving algebraic equations.

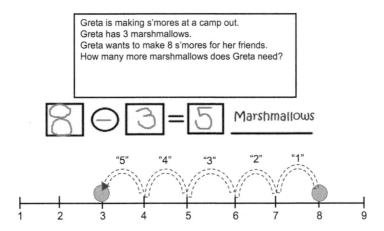

Figure 20.5 Graphic organizer to support algebraic problem solving

Graphic organizers may be useful tools for teaching students to solve algebraic equations. As shown in Figure 20.5, a graphic organizer combined with a real-world story problem can provide both context and support for solving grade-aligned word problems. The student would first read the problem aloud or use an adult or e-reader. Next, the student would identify the known components of the word problem (e.g., have 3 marshmallows, need 8) and the operation (subtraction). The graphic organizer provides a stimulus support for writing the equation (i.e., 8 − 3 =). The number line is a support for completing the procedural act of solving the problem. A student would be taught to start at the 8 and "jump back" three spaces to 5. Conversely, for an addition problem students would be taught to "jump forward." Finally, it is important the student label the answer (i.e., 5 *marshmallows*) to show conceptual understanding of the relationship between the quantity and item being counted.

Measurement

The measurement standard is very important because of its immediate practical implications. Throughout the measurement standard, students become familiar with standard (e.g., inches) and nonstandard (e.g., paper clips) units of measurement. Demonstration of an understanding of time is an important measurement skill. Skills in this area include being able to read digital and analog clocks, as well as understanding the passage of time. Systematic instruction incorporating prompting procedures, such as constant time delay or simultaneous prompting, can facilitate acquisition of these skills.

Mastery of vocabulary and concepts are essential to conceptual understanding of measurement skills. The most basic concept of "more" and "fewer" is necessary when comparing attributes of figures and using nonstandard measurements (e.g., paper clips to measure different-size pencils). Similarly, vocabulary words such as *cup, pint,* and *gallon* are essential to understanding volume and have application within real-world contexts. Students with intellectual disability will need to be explicitly taught vocabulary and concepts. Multiple exemplar training is one method that has been successful for students with intellectual disability. In multiple exemplar training, the instructor presents both examples and nonexamples (e.g., items that are thick and items that are thin). First, the instructor models with rapid succession, pointing to an example and stating the concept (e.g., "This is thick.") and then pointing to a nonexample and stating that it is not the concept (e.g., "This is not thick"). Massed trials are conducted with instructor models. After sufficient modeling, the instructor may test for either expressive or receptive understanding. To test expressive understanding an instructor may say "What is this?" and require the student to say "thick" or "not thick." To test receptive understanding, an instructor may say, "Touch thick" or "Touch not thick." A rule would be set for the number of errors a student can make before the instructor resumes modeling (i.e., two consecutive errors results in five additional modeling rounds). Only once mastery is met on the concept (thick) would the instructor introduce the opposite concept of thin. Multiple exemplar training has been used to teach measurement concepts such as few, old, long, and thick (Celik & Vuran, 2014) and same, different (Saunders, 2014) to students with intellectual disability.

Many purchasing skills fall within the measurement standard, such as the ability to assign coins and bills to a price, either using the exact amount (e.g., five one dollar bills, one dime, and one nickel for a price of $5.15) or a counting-up strategy such as the next-dollar method (e.g., six one dollar bills for a price of $5.15). Technology in the form of video models and software programs can assist teachers in providing instruction on purchasing-related skills. Embedded supports such as text to speech, visual supports, auditory enhancements, and video models can enhance instruction. For example, video models embedded within the intervention package allow the video to provide explicit instruction and visual demonstrations of the skill. The model can be provided by any model type (i.e., self, point of view, peer, or adult) and can be embedded within a program such as Microsoft PowerPoint® to provide a multimedia, interactive learning opportunity (Mechling, 2005). When the two evidence-based practices of video modeling and computer-assisted instruction are combined, they are referred to as computer-based video instruction (CBVI).

Grade-aligned purchasing skills have been taught through CBVI. Recently, Burton, Anderson, Prater, and Dyches (2013) used video self-models displayed on an Apple iPad® to teach middle school students with intellectual disability with moderate intellectual impairment and ASD to solve purchasing-related story problems. Student materials included five story problems with specific price tags, a cash register containing simulated money, and an iPad with a video of each step of the task with the directions to calculate a total cost and give change. CBVI has many benefits, including the ability for the task to be student-directed, promote independence, and reduce dependency on adults for prompts. In this study, each student controlled the video (rewinding) to rewatch the steps as necessary without teacher facilitation. All students were able to use the video self-modeling intervention to solve story problems and generalize skills to novel problems. CBVI was used to provide access to the story problem as well as to provide prompting to solve the problem. One limitation of this study was the repetition of story problems throughout the intervention. Students should be presented with multiple exemplars, using novel problems with novel prices throughout baseline and intervention, to build generalization and ensure acquisition of skills rather than simply memorizing the answer.

Geometry

The geometry standard focuses on the development of spatial relations and reasoning skills. Grade-aligned geometry skills involve the incorporation of several skills from different standards. For example, perimeter and area are important concepts within the geometry standard. Not only should students be able to demonstrate conceptual understanding of perimeter and area of a shape, such as by moving a finger along the outside of a rectangle for perimeter and rubbing the inside for area, but they should also be able to calculate perimeter and area when given the required information. Tiling is one concrete method for teaching calculation of perimeter and area. Given flat tiles, such as 1″ by 1″ algebra tiles, students can be taught to fill up the inside of the figure with tiles and count to find the area. They can be taught to align tiles with the edges of the figure and count to find the perimeter. Explicit instruction using the "model, lead, test" procedure is an effective method of teaching this skill. In the "model," the teacher would instruct students to watch as she or he puts tiles around the outside of a figure (e.g., rectangle) and counts to find the perimeter. The next round would be the "lead," where the teacher would encourage students find the perimeter together, either by assisting him or her in tiling a figure and counting to find the perimeter, or all students would tile their own figures in unison. Finally, in the "test" round the teacher would instruct students to try it on their own as they watch to determine the level of proficiency. If needed, the teacher may return to a "model" or "lead" round depending on errors made by the student. Explicit instruction using the "model, lead, test" method is effective in teaching many chained tasks within the geometry standard.

Another evidence-based practice for teaching mathematics to students with intellectual disability that works well with geometry skills is task-analytic instruction. In a series of studies, Browder, Jimenez, and Trela (2012), and Browder, Trela et al. (2012) evaluated the use of a task analysis and systematic instruction to teach high school students with intellectual disability to find points on a coordinate plane. The geometry standard addressed in the intervention was "identify and describe the intersection of figures on a plane, draw line segments and a coordinate plane to demonstrate spatial sense for familiar contexts." Story problems related to familiar contexts, such as a grocery store, were used. For example, students were provided a list of grocery items to buy and a map of the grocery store; then were asked to map out the most efficient route for purchasing the items. The task analysis consisted of the following steps: (a) identify the problem statement, (b) identify points on a map using facts from the story, (c) draw line segments formed from identified points, (d) identify the plane figure formed by line segments, (e) state the solution to the story problem, and (f) state the solution in the story context. It is important that students connect the answer or solution with the context of the story problem to facilitate generalization to real-world settings and ensure conceptual understanding.

Task-analytic instruction with systematic prompting is also an effective strategy to teach geometric formulas. High school students with intellectual disability have successfully learned to solve geometry problems using the Pythagorean theorem and simultaneous prompting through steps of a task analysis (Creech-Galloway, Collins, Knight, & Bausch, 2013). The 32 steps of the task analysis taught students how to find an unknown hypotenuse of a right triangle ("c") when given a calculator and the measurements for the other two sides of a right triangle ("a" and "b") using the Pythagorean theorem ($a^2 + b^2 = c^2$). To anchor grade-aligned instruction in a real-world context, students were shown videos of real-world instances of right triangles, such as a man on a ladder painting a house or patches on a quilt.

Data Analysis

The data analysis standard develops student's abilities to collect data, organize and display data, and ask or answer reasonable questions using the data. This standard can be addressed from early elementary through secondary grades and can easily be a means to address problem-solving skills. For example, in elementary grades, students should learn how to interpret data from multiple types of graphs. The data may be presented in a variety of formats, including pictures, shapes, or numbers. Students should be exposed to graphical data and instructed on how to display data in early grades so that skills can build and increase in difficulty, working towards real-world applications of data analysis. For example, a pictograph depicting pets within a family may show two cats, one dog, and three fish. Students could be asked to simply identify the number of a given animal ("How many cats does the family have?"), or to evaluate the data (e.g., "What animal does the family have the most of?"). A more difficult skill addressed in later grades would be a similar pictograph depicting pets in a pet store and may have four frogs, two birds, and five rabbits. However, a key at the bottom of the graph may state that each picture represents two animals. In this case, students would need to multiply each of the numbers by two, or be taught to "double count" before answering questions. Naturalistic opportunities for data analysis can be embedded in students' daily routines in a variety of ways, such as self-monitoring behavior, graphically displaying the month's weather, and reading a schedule.

Generalization to Real-World Applications of Mathematics

Although there is a heavy emphasis on teaching academics to students with intellectual disability, it is of utmost importance to try to deliver the content in meaningful, purposeful ways for the students. Mathematics instruction will have little value to this population if they are taught only *how* to solve the problem, without being taught *when* or *why* to apply these skills. Therefore, teachers should strive to teach applicable contexts with relevant applications to real-world situations and scenarios. This may include some functional skills, such as time management, budgeting, and banking, but it also can include skills students may need for potential jobs, practical applications to real-world situations the students may encounter in everyday life, or even independence or skills leading to self-determination.

Contextualized and Functional Mathematics

Although past mathematics education may have overemphasized a few functional applications of mathematics, these skills continue to be important. Real-life skills can be targeted through the use of either contextualized or functional mathematics approaches. The difference between the two is that contextualized instruction focuses on the development of a mathematical concept whereas functional mathematics focuses on completing an everyday task. Real-life activities are used to achieve both goals. Browder et al. (2008) provides many examples of how to teach use of money or everyday computation in a functional mathematics approach.

Contextualized mathematics focuses on the development of the mathematics concept. An example of how this format can be combined with the systematic and explicit instruction needed by many students with intellectual disability can be found in the MASSI (Math Activities with Scripted Systematic Instruction) lessons developed by the National Consortium and State Collaborative Project (https://wiki.ncscpartners.org). For example, in elementary data analysis, students may learn about posing questions, collecting data, and graphing while centering the activity on ways students in the class get to school. In high school, students may target writing equations that represent problems they may have to solve in a potential work site, such as a hardware store.

An illustration using the computation of tax can illustrate why a contextualized approach may be needed to develop a mathematics concept. In functional math, the student would be taken to the store or restaurant (or some simulation of it) and taught to compute the current tax amount. This might be done with the help of some support like the calculator on a cellphone. In contrast, contextualized math teaches the student the variations that can occur in pricing an item. For example, if given an original price of $20.00 and a sale amount of 20%, an individual needs to be able to find 20% of $20.00 ($4.00). Next, he or she needs to understand that *sale* indicates a reduction in cost, and therefore $4.00 should be subtracted from $20.00. Then, the sales tax would be applied to the reduced amount. Also, sales tax can change over time and across states or cities so it is not always the same percent.

Technology to Promote Generalization

The generalization of mathematical skills may be enhanced with the use of technology supports. With the advancement of technology innovation, mobile technology is now able to take technology-assisted instruction (TAI) into the community and use visual supports as a type of visual cue. Visual cues have been used to teach students with intellectual disability to independently complete chained purchasing tasks. Visual cues in TAI can guide participants through a task analysis for completing a chained behavior. For example, Alberto, Cihak, and Gama (2005) evaluated the use of static picture prompts and video modeling during simulated instruction to teach eight middle school students with moderate intellectual impairment to use a debit card to withdraw cash from an ATM and purchase two items. Both the static picture prompts and the video modeling were effective in teaching purchasing skills. In addition, Scott, Collins, Knight, and Kleinert (2013) taught adults with intellectual disability with moderate intellectual impairment to use an ATM using an Apple iPod®. A combination of instructional technology was used to create the intervention, including Microsoft® Photo Story 3 to create the video models and record auditory prompts, which were then uploaded to a podcast that individuals used to listen to and watch each step of the task analysis. The combination of video prompting and audio prompting presented on an iPod was effective in teaching the students to use an ATM to withdraw $20.00 in a community setting. Visual cues have been shown to be effective in teaching chained mathematics skills related to purchasing. Visual cues displayed using touch-based technology allow for individuals to control the pace and intensity of prompts. Research is warranted to evaluate the effectiveness of visual cues on increased independence within grade-aligned mathematics tasks.

Science Instruction

Science instruction provides students with intellectual disability the means to investigate and understand their natural world. This curricular area is also where many key concepts are acquired to help students know how to be safe in their world. In earth science, understanding can be gained about severe weather patterns and how to respond and the importance of recycling. Through chemistry, students learn about the dangers of mixing certain substances. Besides these safety concepts, students also can gain an appreciation and wonder for their world through learning about the universe, life cycles, and geographic landforms. Science also helps students learn to pose questions and gain information about their world.

Focus on Inquiry-Based Learning

Because our understanding of the world changes with new discoveries, students need to approach science with more than memorization of key terms and facts. Students need to develop skills in inquiry. Inquiry is the process of exploring, posing questions, forming hypotheses, researching answers, and conducting experiments to gain knowledge about a phenomena. Teaching students with intellectual disability to learn to explore and ask questions of their world can be an exciting process.

The Next Generation Science Standards currently provide a conceptual framework for science instruction that many states follow. These new science standards place a strong emphasis on all students gaining competence in scientific inquiry throughout their school career. The standards emphasize eight science and engineering practices that include: (1) asking questions, (2) developing and using models, (3) planning and carrying out investigations, (4) analyzing and interpreting data, (5) using mathematics and computational thinking, (6) construction explanations, (7) engaging in argument from evidence, and (8) obtaining, evaluating, and communicating information.

There have been several recent studies in which students with intellectual disability learned the process of inquiry, including those with moderate and severe intellectual impairment. In Smith, Spooner, Jimenez, and Browder (2013) students with multiple disabilities engaged in lessons that had guided inquiry on topics related to elementary science standards (e.g., phases of moon, life cycle, rocks vs. crystals). The teacher first read a "wonder" story to give the students a real-life situation that raised questions about the science concept and ended with a wonder statement (e.g., "I wonder why the moon changes shape."). Students were then allowed to explore materials that would be used for an experiment and make a prediction about the concept. Using vocabulary acquired to communicate about the science concept, the students completed a science lesson.

In Browder, Trela et al. (2012) middle and high school students with intellectual disability with moderate and severe intellectual impairment learned a variety of science concepts related to their grade level. The teachers who implemented the intervention followed a step-by-step task analysis to help the students learn a process for engaging in inquiry. The students analyzed materials, made predictions, compared materials before and after the experiment, and reported on their findings.

In Jimenez, Browder, Spooner, and DiBiase (2012), students with intellectual disability with moderate intellectual impairment engaged in the process of science inquiry in an inclusive general education classroom. In cooperative learning groups, the students used a KWHL chart to describe what they Know (K), Want to know (W), How to find out (H), and what they Learned (L) about the science phenomena to be explored. In Jimenez, Browder, and Courtade (2009), students with moderate intellectual impairment used a similar chart and were able to demonstrate knowledge of the concept explored with a novel set of materials.

Teachers may not have had the opportunity to learn how to adapt inquiry-based learning for students with intellectual disability. Courtade, Browder, Spooner, and DiBiase (2010) showed how teachers could learn to follow a step-by-step task analysis for inquiry. As the teachers' implementation of the steps improved, the students' performance of the inquiry responses all increased.

Teach Science Communication Skills

Although teaching students to investigate their natural world is key to science learning, students cannot engage in the other skills of inquiry such as posing hypotheses or communicating findings if they lack the skills to communicate about the concepts explored. Students often will need repeated instruction to learn the core vocabulary related to the concepts to be acquired. This can often be achieved by using constant time delay. In constant time delay, the instructor identifies the key term (e.g., points to the word *precipitation* in an array of words) and has the student repeat the response. At this first step, there is an immediate prompt for every response so students engage in few to no errors. Over trials, small intervals of time (e.g., 4 seconds) are used between showing the target stimulus (e.g., science term) and prompting the answer. This allows the student to anticipate the correct response. Time delay was used successfully by Johnson, McDonnell, Holzwarth, and Hunter (2004) to teach students with intellectual disability to identify the parts of an insect or plant cell in a general education context. In Jimenez et al. (2012) peers taught students with moderate intellectual impairment in a middle school science class to match a picture illustrating a science concept with a science term and definition (e.g., kinetic energy).

Although learning the science terms and definitions is an important starting point to be able to communicate about science discoveries, students may also need help to gain a deeper understanding of the concept. Two options are to use some explicit instruction strategies and to provide graphic organizers that depict the concept. Two studies with students with ASD offer possible guidance for how this might be applied for students with intellectual disability. In Knight, Smith, Spooner, and Browder (2012) the instructor used models of the concept (e.g., demonstrating the concept of change) and had students then illustrate the concept. Not all concepts can be demonstrated with manipulatives, but may require models or graphic organizers. Knight, Spooner, Browder, Smith, and Wood (2013) illustrated the stages of the water cycle by having students label the depiction with key words like *evaporation, condensation, convection,* and *precipitation.* Similarly, Courtade et al. (2010) included models such as a small globe to show land masses and graham crackers to depict plate tectonics of the Earth.

Personal Relevance

Jimenez and Carlone (2014) have described the importance of making science learning personally relevant for all students. This relevance can be promoted by helping students to generalize their science learning to everyday contexts. Even young students develop ideas about their world. Applying science learning involves encouraging them to use their newly acquired vocabulary to share these ideas with others and to apply inquiry skills when novel phenomena are encountered. For example, a student might be encouraged to use new vocabulary for the concept of "change" to notice variations in the school schedule or the school menu. A student who seems keenly interested in a coming snow storm might be asked to make a prediction, identify how to find out more about the potential for snow, and communicate what is learned. Communication with parents can include information about science lessons with encouragement to discuss and explore the same ideas at home. For example, a student might make a chart on the phases of the moon with his or her parents and communicate what is learned with the class. Some students might enjoy participating in a science fair or club to have additional learning experiences with peers. Through these types of generalization activities, science can become a tool for engaging with the natural world.

Summary

Twenty years ago it would have been difficult to identify practices focused on mathematical instruction for students with intellectual disability beyond "plug and chug" computation or counting money. Science was often minimally addressed and sometimes focused on having students memorize terms that had no meaning to them. What recent research has revealed is that students with intellectual disability can benefit from a much broader range of mathematics and science instruction. Mathematics can become much more applicable as students learn to apply their skills to problem scenarios using realistic word problems and real life activities. Although 20 years ago mathematics was embedded in real-life activities, the focus was often applying whatever skills the student had to get the activity achieved (e.g., make the purchase). With contextualized mathematics, the student can gain conceptual knowledge while working with engaging activities.

Similarly in science, the focus is on gaining the inquiry skills that can help students engage more fully with their natural world. Some students may gain their first real skills in posing questions through a science context. At its best, science will help them see more of their world, explore its wonder, and learn what they want and need to know. Practically it can help them learn safety skills. Overall, opening educational opportunities to students with intellectual disability to have the opportunity learn the full range of mathematics and science removes ceilings on achievement created by past low expectations. Students will be better prepared to understand the world in which they live.

References

Alberto, P. A., Cihak, D. F., & Gama, R. I. (2005). Use of static picture prompts versus video modeling during simulation instruction. *Research in Developmental Disabilities, 26*, 327–339.

Baroody, A. J. (1998). Mental-addition development of children classified as mentally handicapped. *Educational Studies in Mathematics, 19*, 369–388.

Browder, D. M., Jimenez, B. A., Spooner, F., Saunders, A., Hudson, M., & Bethune, K. (2012). Early numeracy instruction for students with moderate and severe developmental disabilities. *Research & Practice for Persons with Severe Disabilities, 37*, 308–320.

Browder, D. M., Jimenez, B. A., & Trela, K. (2012). Grade-aligned math instruction for secondary students with moderate intellectual disability. *Education and Training in Autism and Developmental Disabilities, 47*, 373–388.

Browder, D. M., Spooner, F., Ahlgrim-Delzell, L., Harris, A. A., & Wakeman, S. (2008). A meta-analysis on teaching mathematics to students with significant cognitive disabilities. *Exceptional Children, 74*, 407–432.

Browder, D. M., Trela, K., & Jimenez, B. (2007). Training teachers to follow a task analysis to engage middle school students with moderate and severe developmental disabilities in grade-appropriate literature. *Focus on Autism and Other Developmental Disabilities, 22*, 206–219.

Browder, D. M., Trela, K., Courtade, G. R., Jimenez, B. A., Knight, V., & Flowers, C. (2012). Teaching mathematics and science standards to students with moderate and severe developmental disabilities. *The Journal of Special Education, 46*, 26–35.

Bullock, J., Pierce, S., & McClelland, L. (1989). *TouchMath.* Colorado Springs, CO: Innovative Learning Concepts.

Burton, C. E., Anderson, D. H., Prater, M. A., & Dyches, T. T. (2013). Video self-modeling on an iPad to teach functional math skills to adolescents with autism and intellectual disability. *Focus on Autism and Other Developmental Disabilities, 28*, 67–77.

Carbonneau, K. J., & Marley, S. C. (2012). Activity-based learning strategies. In J. A. C. Hattie & E. M. Anderman (Eds.), *The international guide to student achievement* (pp. 282–284). New York: Routledge.

Celik, S., & Vuran, S. (2014). Comparison of direct instruction and simultaneous prompting procedure on teaching concepts to individuals with intellectual disability. *Education and Training in Autism and Developmental Disabilities, 49*, 127–144.

Cihak, D. F., & Foust, J. L. (2008). Comparing number lines and touch points to teach addition facts to students with autism. *Focus on Autism and Other Developmental Disabilities, 25*, 131–137.

Clements, D. H., & Sarama, J. (2007). *Real math building blocks.* Columbus, OH: SRA/McGraw-Hill.

Common Core State Standards Initiative (CCSSI). (2015). *Mathematics Standards.* Retrieved from http://www.corestandards.org/Math/

Courtade, G. R., Browder, D. M., Spooner, F., & DiBiase, W. (2010). Training teachers to use an inquiry-based task analysis to teach science to students with moderate and severe disabilities. *Education and Training in Autism and Developmental Disabilities, 55*, 378–399.

Creech-Galloway, C., Collins, B. C., Knight, V., & Bausch, M. (2013). Using a simultaneous prompting procedure with an iPad to teach the Pythagorean Theorem to adolescents with moderate intellectual disability. *Research & Practice for Persons with Severe Disabilities, 38*, 222–232.

Donlan, C. (2007). Mathematical development in children with specific language impairments. In D. B. Berch & M. M. M. Mazzocco (Eds.), *Why is math so hard for some children? The nature and origins of mathematical learning difficulties and disabilities* (pp. 151–172). Baltimore, MD: Brookes.

Dougherty, B., Bryant, D. P., Bryant, B., Darrough, R. L., & Pfannenstiel, K. H. (2015). Developing concepts and generalizations to build algebraic thinking: The reversibility, flexibility, and generalization approach. *Intervention in School and Clinic, 5*, 273–281.

Engelmann, S., Engelmann, O., Carnine, D., & Kelly, B. (2012). *Connecting math concepts: Comprehensive edition.* Columbus, OH: SRA/McGraw-Hill.

Fletcher, D., Boon, R. T., & Cihak, D. F. (2010). Effects of the TOUCHMATH program compared to a number line strategy to teach addition facts to middle school students with moderate intellectual disabilities. *Education and Training in Autism and Developmental Disabilities, 45*, 449–458.

Fuchs, L. S., Fuchs, D., Finelli, R., Courey, S. J., Hamlett, C. L., Sones, E. M., & Hope, S. K. (2006). Teaching third graders about real-life mathematical problem solving: A randomized controlled study. *The Elementary School Journal, 106*, 293–311.

Fuchs, L. S., Powell, S. R., Seethaler, P. M., Cirino, P. T., Fletcher, J. M., Fuchs, D., . . . Zumeta, R. O. (2009). Remediating number combination and word problem deficits among students with mathematical difficulties: A randomized control trial. *Journal of Educational Psychology, 101*, 561–576.

Fuchs, L. S., Seethaler, P. M., Powell, S. R., Fuchs, D., Hamlett, C. L., & Fletcher, J. M. (2008). Effects of preventative tutoring on the mathematical problem solving of third-grade students with math and reading difficulties. *Exceptional Children, 74*, 155–173.

Gersten, R., & Chard, D. (1999). Number sense rethinking arithmetic instruction for students with mathematical disabilities. *The Journal of Special Education, 33*, 18–28.

Griffin, C. C., & Jitendra, A. K. (2009). Word problem solving instruction in inclusive third grade mathematics classrooms. *Journal of Educational Research, 102*, 187–202.

Griffin, S., Clements, D. H., & Sarama, J. (2008). *SRA number worlds.* Richmond, VA: McGraw-Hill.

Hord, C., & Bouck, E. C. (2012). Review of academic mathematics instruction for students with mild intellectual disability. *Education and Training in Autism and Developmental Disabilities, 47*, 389–400.

Jimenez, B. A., Browder, D. M., & Courtade, G. R. (2008). Teaching an algebraic equation to high school students with moderate developmental disabilities. *Education and Training in Developmental Disabilities, 43*, 266–274.

Jimenez, B. A., Browder, D. M., & Courtade, G. R. (2009). An exploratory study of self-directed science concept learning by students with moderate intellectual disabilities. *Research and Practice for Persons with Severe Disabilities, 34*, 33–46.

Jimenez, B. A., Browder, D. M., & Saunders, A. (2013). *Early numeracy: A skill building math program for students with moderate and severe disabilities.* Verona, WI: Attainment Company.

Jimenez, B. A., Browder, D. M., Spooner, F., & Dibiase, W. (2012). Inclusive inquiry science using peer-mediated embedded instruction for students with moderate intellectual disability. *Exceptional Children, 78*, 301–317.

Jimenez, B. A., & Carlone, H. (2014). Chapter ten: Science as inquiry. In D. Browder & F. Spooner (Eds.), *More language arts, math, and science for students with severe disabilities* (pp. 195–214). Baltimore, MD: Brookes.

Jimenez, B. A., & Kemmery, M. (2013). Building the early numeracy skills of students with moderate intellectual disability. *Education and Training in Autism and Developmental Disabilities, 48*, 479–490.

Jimenez, B. A., & Staples, K. (2015). Access to the common core state standards in mathematics through early numeracy skill building for students with significant intellectual disability. *Education and Training in Autism and Developmental Disabilities, 50*, 17–30.

Jitendra, A. K. (2008). Using schema-based instruction to make appropriate sense of word problems. *Perspectives on Language and Literacy, 34*, 20–24.

Jitendra, A. K., DiPipi, C. M., & Perron-Jones, N. (2002). An exploratory study of word problem-solving instruction for middle school students with learning disabilities: An emphasis on conceptual and procedural understanding. *The Journal of Special Education, 36*, 23–38.

Jitendra, A. K., Griffin, G. C., Deatline-Buchman, A., & Sczesniak, E. (2007). Mathematical word problem solving in third-grade classrooms. *The Journal of Educational Research, 100*, 283–302.

Jitendra, A. K., & Hoff, K. (1996). The effects of schema-based instruction on the mathematical word-problem-solving performance of students with learning disabilities. *Journal of Learning Disabilities, 29*, 422–431.

Jitendra, A. K., Hoff, K., & Beck, M. (1999). Teaching middle school students with learning disabilities to solve multistep word problems using a schema-based approach. *Remedial and Special Education, 20*, 50–64.

Johnson, J. W., McDonnell, J., Holzwarth, V. N., & Hunter, K. (2004). The efficacy of embedded instruction for students with developmental disabilities enrolled in general education classes. *Journal of Positive Behavior Interventions, 6*(4), 214–227.

Knight, V. F., Smith, B. R., Spooner, F., & Browder, D. (2012). Using explicit instruction to teach science descriptors to students with autism spectrum disorder. *Journal of Autism and Developmental Disorders, 42*, 378–389.

Knight, V. F., Spooner, F., Browder, D., Smith, B., & Wood, C. (2013). Using systematic instruction and graphic organizers to teach science concepts to students with autism spectrum disorders and intellectual disability. *Focus on Autism and Other Developmental Disabilities, 28*, 115–126.

Kramer, T., & Krug, D. A. (1973). A rationale and procedure for teaching addition. *Education and Training of the Mentally Retarded, 8*(3), 140–150.

Maccini, P., & Gagnon, J. C. (2006). Mathematics instructional practices and assessment accommodations by secondary special and general educators. *Exceptional Children, 72*, 217–234.

Marshall, S. P. (Ed.). (1995). *Schemas in problem solving.* New York: Cambridge University Press.

Mastropieri, M. A., Bakken, J. P., & Scruggs, T. E. (1991). Mathematics instruction for individuals with mental retardation: A perspective and research synthesis. *Education and Training in Mental Retardation, 26*, 115–129.

McIntosh, A., Reys, B. J., & Reys, R. E. (1992). A proposed framework for examining basic number sense. *For the Learning of Mathematics, 12*, 2–8.

Mechling, L. (2005). The effect of instructor-created video programs to teach students with disabilities: A literature review. *Journal of Special Education Technology, 20*(2), 25.

Montague, M., & Jitendra, A. J. (2006). *Teaching mathematics to middle school students with learning disabilities.* New York: Guilford.

National Council of Teachers of Mathematics. (2000). *Principles and standards for school Mathematics.* Reston, VA: NCTM.

Neef, N. A., Nelles, D. E., Iwata, B. A., & Page, T. P. (2003). Analysis of precurrent skills in solving mathematics story problems. *Journal of Applied Behavior Analysis, 36*, 21–33.

Rao, S., & Mallow, L. (2009). Using simultaneous prompting procedure to promote recall of multiplication facts by middle school students with cognitive impairment. *Education and Training in Developmental Disabilities, 44*, 80–90.

Rockwell, S. B., Griffin, C. C., & Jones, H. A. (2011). Schema-based strategy instruction in mathematics and the word problem-solving performance of a student with autism. *Focus on Autism and Other Developmental Disabilities, 26*, 87–95. doi:10.1177/1088357611405039

Root, J. R., Browder, D. M., Saunders, A. F., & Lo, Y.-y. (2016). Schema-based instruction with concrete and virtual manipulatives to teach problem solving to students with autism. *Remedial and Special Education.* Advance online publication. doi: 10.1177/0741932516643592

Sarama, J., & Clements, D. H. (2009). *Early childhood mathematics education research: Learning trajectories for young children.* New York: Routledge.

Saunders, A. F. (2014). Effects of modified schema-based instruction delivered through computer-based video instruction on mathematical word problem solving of students with autism and moderate intellectual disability. (Unpublished doctoral dissertation). University of North Carolina: Charlotte.

Saunders, A. F., Bethune, K. S., Spooner, F., & Browder, D. (2013). Solving the common core equation teaching mathematics CCSS to students with moderate and severe disabilities. *Teaching Exceptional Children, 45*(3), 24–33.

Scott, R., Collins, B., Knight, V., & Kleinert, H. (2013). Teaching adults with moderate intellectual disability ATM use via the iPod. *Education and Training in Autism and Developmental Disability, 48*, 190–199.

Skibo, H., Mims, P., & Spooner, F. (2011). Teaching number identification to students with severe disabilities using response cards. *Education and Training in Autism and Developmental Disabilities, 46*, 124–133.

Smith, B. R., Spooner, F., Jimenez, B. A., & Browder, D. (2013). Using an early science curriculum to teach science vocabulary and concepts to students with severe developmental disabilities. *Education and Treatment of Children, 36*, 1–31.

Spooner, F., Knight, V., Browder, D. M., Jimenez, B., & DiBiase, W. (2011). Evaluating evidence-based practice in teaching science content to students with severe developmental disabilities. *Research and Practice in Severe Disabilities, 36*, 62–75.

Tzanakaki, P., Hastings, R. P., Grindle, C. F., Hughes, J. C., & Hoare, Z. (2014). An individualized numeracy curriculum for children with intellectual disabilities: A single blind pilot randomized controlled trial. *Journal of Developmental and Physical Disabilities, 26*, 615–632.

Van de Walle, J. A. (2004). *Elementary and middle school mathematics: Teaching developmentally* (5th ed.). Boston, MA: Allyn & Bacon.

Vaughn, S., Bos, C. S., & Schumm, J. S. (2007). *Teaching students who are exceptional, diverse, and at risk.* Upper Saddle River, NJ: Pearson.

Wright, R. J., Stanger, G., Stafford, A. K., & Martland, J. (2006). *Teaching number in the classroom with 4–8 year olds.* London: Paul Chapman Publishing.

Xin, Y. P., Jitendra, A. K., & Deatline-Buchman, A. (2005). Effects of mathematical word problem solving instruction on students with learning problems. *The Journal of Special Education, 39,* 181–192.

Xin, Y. P., Wiles, B., & Lin, Y.-Y. (2008). Teaching conceptual model-based word problem story grammar to enhance mathematics problem solving. *The Journal of Special Education, 42,* 163–178. doi:10.1177/0022466907312895

Xin, Y. P., & Zhang, D. (2009). Exploring a conceptual model-based approach to teaching situated word problems. *Journal of Educational Research, 102,* 427–442. doi:10.3200/JOER.102.6.427–442

Yakubova, G., & Bouck, E. C. (2014). Not all created equally: Exploring calculator use by students with mild intellectual disability. *Education and Training in Autism and Developmental Disabilities, 49,* 111.

Part IV
Education Across the Lifespan

21

Early Intervention and Early Childhood Education

Michaelene M. Ostrosky, Rosa Milagros Santos,
Hasan Y. Zaghlawan

In the United States, federal legislation has established specialized services for the nation's youngest children with disabilities, birth through 5 years old, and their families. Part B of Public Law (PL) 108–446, the Individuals with Disabilities Education Improvement Act of 2004 (IDEA), delineates programs and services for preschool-aged children with disabilities (3–5 years old). Part C of IDEA defines programs and services specific to infants and toddlers (birth–3 years old) with disabilities and their families, known as Early Intervention or EI.

With federal support, states established processes and procedures for families to access and receive specialized services through a local educational agency for Part B services and/or a state-based agency (e.g., Departments of Public Health, Human Services, Rehabilitation Services, and Economic Security) for Part C services. In many states, such as Alabama, Kentucky, Illinois, and Virginia, Part B and Part C programs are administered separately through different agencies. To ensure that children and families do not experience a gap in services when they transition from Part C to Part B programs, states are required to develop a plan that ensures a coordinated and seamless implementation of programs and services across both systems.

Within Part B, Section 619 specifies that children with disabilities, 3–5 years old, are eligible for a free appropriate public education (also known as FAPE) in the Least Restrictive Environment (or LRE). Thus, most states deliver special education services to eligible preschoolers within school systems, while EI or services for children birth to 3 years old can be delivered in a variety of natural environments in which infants and toddlers may be found if they do not have a disability. These natural environments may include but are not limited to the children's homes, inclusive child-care and community programs, clinics, and medical facilities. In 2012, 87% of infants and toddlers who were deemed eligible for EI services were served in their homes (US Department of Education Office of Special Education Programs, 2014). Regardless of the settings in which they are served, EI and Early Childhood Special Education (EI/ECSE) services for infants, toddlers, and preschoolers with disabilities typically focus on meeting their developmental needs in the cognitive/academic, physical, social, communication, and adaptive domains.

Characteristics of Young Children Served Under IDEA

Eligibility for Part B and Part C services is determined by criteria set within each state. Generally, young children are found eligible based on a variety of factors including a specified percent delay in one or more areas of development, medically based diagnoses that can impact a child's development such as Down syndrome or Spina Bifida, and risk factors that can impact the child's development such as prematurity. The World Health Organization (2012) currently estimates that approximately 24 million infants are born at low birth weight each year. These infants, along with infants with identified disabilities (e.g., Fragile X syndrome) will be most in need of specialized services to support optimal development throughout the early childhood years. In 2012, a total of 333,982 infants and toddlers received Part C EI services and 750,131 preschoolers qualified for ECSE services in the United States (US Department of Education, 2014).

In 2012, 48 states used the category of developmental delay to identify young children for special education services. IDEA allows the use of developmental delay only for children 3–9 years old; and 37% of children who received services under Part B were identified as having developmental delays. Speech and language impairment was the most prevalent disability category under which children qualified for Part B services (45% of children), while "other combined disabilities" (10%) and autism (8%) were the remaining disability categories for children 3–5 years old. The Part B data is mirrored in Part C data, where in 2007, the majority of infants and toddlers referred for Part C services were diagnosed as having speech or communication delays (41%), followed by prenatal/perinatal problems (19%), motor delays (17%), or an overall delay in development (12%) (Hebbeler et al., 2007).

Young Children With Intellectual Disability

Recent data suggest that people with intellectual disability comprise 1.5%–2.5% of the US population (Bethesda Institute, 2012). In 2012, approximately 8% of students between the ages of 6–21 received Part B services under the disability category of intellectual disability (36th Annual Report to Congress, 2014). According to the Centers for Disease Control (CDC, 2015), intellectual and developmental disabilities are often caused by maternal infections that are passed on to the fetus. Biological, genetic, and other chromosomal conditions such as Down syndrome, Fetal Alcohol Syndrome, and Fragile X are also common causes of intellectual disability that occur early in a child's development. Furthermore, recent advances in medical technology have resulted in infants surviving at earlier points in gestation (i.e., 24 weeks); prematurity and concomitant conditions associated with early birth such as low birth weight are linked to increased risks for intellectual and developmental delays.

Specific data on young children with intellectual disability, birth–5 years old, is difficult to determine. The current categories used to identify children for EI/ECSE services make it difficult to ascertain definitive numbers of infants, toddlers, and preschoolers with intellectual disability. However, given the existing prevalence data on older children with intellectual disability, it is likely that many of them have been, or are currently, served under Part C and Part B.

Research-Based and Recommended Practices in EI/ECSE Services

The purpose of this chapter is to highlight seven key characteristics in the education of society's youngest members, those under age 5, in an attempt to describe empirically based practices that distinguish EI/ECSE services from K–12 services for children and youth with disabilities, including those with intellectual disability. These seven characteristics are: (a) family practices, (b) teaming and collaboration, (c) routines-based interventions in natural environments, (d) assessment, (e) integrated developmental domains, (f) transitions, and (g) professional development. Given the frequent use of classifications including developmental delay in EI/ESCE as described previously, this chapter is structured around research-based and recommended practices that facilitate the development and learning of infants, toddlers, and preschoolers with developmental delays or disabilities. The leading professional organization in early childhood special education, the Division for Early Childhood of the Council for Exceptional Children (DEC), and the Office of Special Education Program (OSEP) of the US Department of Education, Technical Assistance Community of Practice (Part C Settings) provide a framework or guiding principles for birth–5 services; this framework is used to present information in this chapter. While the words "education" and "educating" are used throughout this chapter, these terms are intended to include services provided across settings (home, hospital, preschool, child care etc.), and they include an emphasis on caregiver–child interaction whereby "caregiver" might include adults such as parents, extended family members, preschool teachers, developmental therapists, paraprofessionals, child-care providers, pediatric speech-language pathologists, and many others. See Table 21.1 for a glossary of terms that are commonly used in the EI/ECSE field and are used throughout this chapter.

Family Practices

The role of the family as decision makers, intervention planners, and intervention implementers cannot be overstated in facilitating the learning and development of infants, toddlers, and preschoolers with disabilities. PL 99-457, passed in 1986 to establish the eligibility of infants and young children with disabilities for special education services and supports, first reflected the central role of families in the EI/ECSE process and the recognition of the effectiveness and cost benefits of intervening in the early years (Public Law 99-457, 1986). Families are truly the experts on their young children with disabilities, for they typically spend more time with their children than any professional at this age. It is during the early childhood years that many families have their concerns about their children's delayed or atypical development are confirmed, and therefore professionals serve the critical role of helping family members understand Part C and Part B of IDEA, the philosophy of EI/ECSE, and their parental rights under the law. The importance of strong parent-professional partnerships as well as positive parent-child relationships is the foundation for high-quality EI/ECSE as the goal is to strengthen child, parent, and family functioning. Additionally, given children's strengths and needs, the families' priorities and concerns are situated within their unique cultural, linguistic, and socioeconomic context and drive services provided to them and their children (Division for Early Childhood, 2014). DEC's *Position Statement on Responsiveness to Family Cultures, Values and Languages* (2010) stresses that "individuals who work with children must respect, value, and support the cultures, values, and languages of each home and promote the active participation of all families." (p. 1). During the early childhood years, families are encouraged to choose their preferred roles and level of engagement based on cultural and linguistic background, values and beliefs, resources, family structure, and priorities for their children (Trivette, Dunst, & Hamby, 2010).

The family is in the optimal position to support their young children's developmental needs and the acquisition of new skills, partly because of the amount of time that they spend with their children, but also because they have a vested interest in their child's well-being (Keilty, 2010). As parental competence and confidence are enhanced while a child with disabilities receives EI/ECSE services, parents hopefully recognize the positive impact they can have on their child and the family as a whole (Dunst & Trivette, 2009). Research has shown a relation between families that are functioning in a positive manner and children's growth and developmental progress (Keilty, 2010). Therefore, in EI/ECSE, professionals recognize and utilize the strengths of each family, empower families to make informed decisions based on their priorities and concerns, engage them in open and honest communication, and demonstrate flexibility and willingness to change services based on child and family needs (Bailey, Raspa, & Fox, 2012).

The families' role is crucial in the development, implementation, and evaluation of their children's services as delineated in the individualized plan required by IDEA. For children birth to 3 years old, legislation requires an Individualized Family Service Plan (IFSP) that addresses supports for both the child and family, and while in preschool–12th grade (3–21 years old) an Individualized Education Program (IEP) is used to develop a focused plan based on child strengths and needs. The IFSP planning process may be used further into the early childhood years after 3 years old if the state, family, and local service program agree to its use (IDEA, 1997, Part B). Within 45 days of an infant or toddler's referral to EI

Table 21.1 Glossary of key terminology

Individualized Family Service Plan (IFSP)	A written document used to guide the early intervention process for young children with disabilities and their families; designed to reflect individual concerns, priorities, and resources (The IRIS Center, 2015)
Neonatal Intensive Care Unit (NICU)	A nursery in a hospital that provides around-the-clock care to sick or premature babies (March of Dimes Foundation, 2015)
Early Intervention (EI)	Specialized services provided to very young children (birth–3) at risk for or showing signs of developmental delay. (The IRIS Center, 2015)
Early Childhood Special Education (ECSE)	The provision of customized services crafted to meet the individualized needs of young children with disabilities; generally used when referring to children with disabilities from birth to 5 years old (The IRIS Center, 2015)
The Division for Early Childhood (DEC)	One of 17 divisions of the Council for Exceptional Children, the largest professional organization dedicated to improving the educational success of individuals with disabilities and/or gifts and talents. DEC promotes policies and advances evidence-based practices that support families and enhance the development of young children who have or are at risk for developmental delays and disabilities (Division for Early Childhood, 2016).
Natural Environments	Settings in which children without disabilities spend time, including homes, child-care programs, family child-care homes, and community settings (Division for Early Childhood, 2015)
Routines-Based Intervention	When caregivers use daily routines (i.e., diapering, mealtime) as the context for the child's learning and they embed the child's goals in these naturally occurring daily routines (Jennings, Hanline, & Woods, 2012)
Transition	Any of a number of routine aspects of a person's learning or educational experience involving movement to new classes, grade levels, programs, or school systems (hospital to home, EI to preschool, etc.) (The IRIS Center, 2015)
Developmental Delays	Term used to encompass a variety of disabilities in infants and young children indicating that they are significantly delayed in one or more areas of development, including motor development, socialization, independent functioning, cognitive development, or communication (The IRIS Center, 2015)
Developmental Therapists and EI Service Providers	A person who is responsible for and paid to enhance the development of young children who have or are at risk for developmental delays/disabilities. This includes providing care, education, or therapy to the child, as well as support to the child's family (Division for Early Childhood, 2015).
PL 99–457	An amendment to the Education of the Handicapped Act in 1986, which extended free appropriate public education to include preschool children (3–5 years) and offered a national policy for infants and toddlers at risk for and with identified disabilities
IDEA Part B/619	A law that ensures services to children with disabilities throughout the nation. IDEA governs how states and public agencies provide early intervention, special education, and related services to more than 6.5 million eligible infants, toddlers, children, and youth with disabilities. Children and youth (ages 3–21) receive special education and related services under IDEA Part B. IDEA Part B Section 619 specifically refers to the laws and regulations for preschool grants and funding.
IDEA Part C	Infants and toddlers with disabilities (birth–3) and their families receive early intervention services under IDEA Part C.

services, an IFSP is developed. While IFSPs may differ across states, seven key components are included in the plan: (a) present levels of development; (b) family information including resources, priorities, and concerns; (c) measurable child and family outcomes; (d) EI services that will be provided; (e) the environment in which services will occur; (f) who will be responsible for paying for services; and (g) the plan for transitioning the child from EI to an appropriate educational-based setting upon his or her third birthday. However, the IFSP is not only designed to delineate the frequency and dose of intervention strategies, but also to serve as a vehicle for parents and professionals to partner and select meaningful outcomes and a framework for achieving them (Blasco, 2001). In other words, the "heart of the IFSP is the outcome statements, which define a planning team's shared vision for the child" (Rosenkoetter & Squires, 2004, p. 51).

In sum, families play a critical role in the development and learning of infants, toddlers, and preschoolers. DEC's (2014) recommended practices related to the family are listed in Table 21.2, and reflect three key principles (Trivette & Banerjee, 2015, pp. 66–67):

- Parents are the constant in the lives of young children with disabilities or at-risk for disabilities and thus are the primary unit of family-centered services;
- Promoting confidence and affirming the competency of the parents to support their child's development and learning is essential in every parent-professional interaction;
- The unique characteristics of the family, including but not limited to ethnicity, culture, family structure, and the family's goals, must be respected.

Thus, through ongoing conversation and collaboration, family members and EI/ECSE professionals can best support the individual needs of young children with disabilities, including those with intellectual disability.

Table 21.2 DEC recommended family practices

F1.	Practitioners build trusting and respectful partnerships with the family through interactions that are sensitive and responsive to cultural, linguistic, and socioeconomic diversity.
F2.	Practitioners provide the family with up-to-date, comprehensive and unbiased information in a way that the family can understand and use to make informed choices and decisions.
F3.	Practitioners are responsive to the family's concerns, priorities, and changing life circumstances.
F4.	Practitioners and the family work together to create outcomes or goals, develop individualized plans, and implement practices that address the family's priorities and concerns and the child's strengths and needs.
F5.	Practitioners support family functioning, promote family confidence and competence, and strengthen family-child relationships by acting in ways that recognize and build on family strengths and capacities.
F6.	Practitioners engage the family in opportunities that support and strengthen parenting knowledge and skills and parenting competence and confidence in ways that are flexible, individualized, and tailored to the family's preferences.
F7.	Practitioners work with the family to identify, access, and use formal and informal resources and supports to achieve family identified outcomes or goals.
F8.	Practitioners provide the family of a young child who has or is at risk for developmental delay/ disability, and who is a dual-language learner, with information about the benefits of learning in multiple languages for the child's growth and development.
F9.	Practitioners help families know and understand their rights.
F10.	Practitioners inform families about leadership and advocacy skill-building opportunities and encourage those who are interested to participate.

Source: Division for Early Childhood, 2014.

Teaming and Collaboration

EI/ECSE services are typically provided by professionals from a variety of disciplines such as medical doctors, speech-language pathologists, occupational therapists, social workers, physical therapists, teachers, and developmental specialists. The family is an essential member of the team, and at no time is their input more important than during the early childhood years. According to the DEC's (2014) recommended practices, the quality of the relationships and interactions among the adults on the team affects the success of the intervention programs. Additionally, one of the key EI principles regarding Part C practices highlights the importance of family-provider partnerships: "The primary role of the service provider in early intervention is to work with and support the family members and caregivers in a child's life" (p. 4). Such collaborations require EI providers to view their role as that of a "coach" or "mentor" instead of "expert" on child and family needs. When authentic collaboration occurs, the parent' role shifts from being seen as passive participants to agents of change for their child (James & Chard, 2010).

Professionals typically work with families to access support, mobilize resources, and identify their existing strengths, concerns, and priorities for meeting the developmental needs of the whole child (Fowler, Ostrosky, & Yates, 2014). As professionals and families collaborate, they share knowledge, expertise, and information, thereby building capacity and working together to solve problems. Unfortunately, early childhood services are provided in a fragmented fashion at times, with families having to seek services for every developmental and medical need that their child faces. It is important for collaboration to occur among the community-based systems that provide services for young children with disabilities, including medical, mental health, and educational services. Ideally, professionals and family members work together as a team to determine outcomes and create services to best meet the complex and varied needs of infants, toddlers, and preschoolers with disabilities, including those with intellectual disability. As the DEC's (2014) recommended practices state, "Team members assist each other to discover and access community-based services and other informal and formal resources to meet family-identified child and family needs" (p. 14). Research has shown that when systems collaborate to meet the unique needs of families, children demonstrate more positive outcomes in both educational and community-based settings (Adams et al., 2013). Finally, "through a strengths- and assets-based collaborative process, the competence and confidence of both families and professionals are enhanced" (Fowler et al., 2014, p. 621).

Routines Based Interventions in the Natural Environments

"Natural environments are defined as settings that are natural or normal for the child's age peers who have no disabilities and go beyond 'place' to include families' everyday routines and activities" (Fowler et al., 2014, p. 618). However, as Odom, Buysse, and Soukakou (2011) remind us, "placement in a least restrictive environment is not sufficient to meet the intent of inclusion, but rather, participation, social relationships and learning outcomes for all children are common goals" (p. 345). Ideally, EI/ECSE services are implemented in a child's natural environment. IDEA defines a natural environment as any setting that a child without a disability might routinely participate in or access, such as preschool or child care (36th Annual Report to Congress, 2014). This mandate has changed the attitude of many professionals within the EI and ECSE systems as well as related services professionals. Service provision is changing from a therapeutic approach, where skills are taught during decontextualized activities that cannot be replicated in the child's natural environment, to a more meaningful and functional approach, where learning opportunities occur in the natural routines and activities (Hanft & Pilkington, 2000). There is evidence that children learn best through naturalistic opportunities that involve their preferred materials and familiar people (Snyder et al., 2015). Using natural routines and activities as the contexts (i.e., diapering, mealtime) for learning experiences makes the entire family, and not only the child, the center of services. It encourages caregivers and service providers to work together to identify the family's needs as well as the children's needs, interests, and preferences. Therefore, the focal tenant of EI/ECSE becomes not *where* services are implemented but *how* they are implemented (Bruder, 2010). A multitude of learning opportunities exists in any natural environment, regardless of the location (Dunst, Bruder, Trivette, Raab, & Mclean, 2001). Within typical early childhood settings such as homes, schools, and the community, "every moment that adults and children interact provides an opportunity to build positive adult-child relationships that are the basis for developing more advanced skills" (Fowler et al., 2014, p. 621). For example, a preschooler with intellectual disability can learn numerous skills by helping a caregiver prepare a meal, whether that occurs at home, during a picnic in the park, or in a Head Start classroom. Each family function, community event, or classroom activity is a potential location that might offer a continuum of naturally occurring learning opportunities for a child (Dunst et al., 2001). These embedded learning opportunities, although they may happen in different locations in the presence of different people and materials, reinforce the same target skill (i.e., helping a caregiver during meal preparation). In the event that the child is able to generalize target skills to different locations, with other people, and using different materials, the natural environments in fact would be supporting skill development and providing the child with more opportunities to practice skills, leading to increased independence and engagement.

Once families become familiar with embedded learning strategies, they become more empowered and understand *when*, *where*, and *how* they can influence their children's development (Wade, Llewellyn, & Matthews, 2008). This can encourage them to generalize their skills to other contexts. Research has shown that these strategies are effective because they address the family's needs during typical routines. In addition, families are able to measure their children's progress in learning new skills, and they see the positive impact of their work with their children reflected in their quality of life.

This unique approach in providing EI/ECSE services in natural environments strengthens the collaboration between families and service providers. Currently, EI/ECSE professionals are more inclined to learn about and understand a family's ecology in order to support the family in identifying learning opportunities that are present during natural routines. Moreover, the families and EI/ECSE professionals can engage in conversations to identify adaptations, modifications, and assistive technology to increase a child's participation and engagement in the natural environment. For example, a child with intellectual disability might use an augmentative device during mealtime to ask for a preferred food item or to express his or her desire to be finished eating.

McWilliam (2000) stressed the importance of differentiating between service and intervention in the EI/ECSE system. On one hand, he refers to service as providing the family with three levels of support: information, emotional, and material support. On the other hand, intervention is what caregivers provide a child on a daily basis throughout the different routines and activities. Hence, although a child may be receiving one or more hours per week of direct services, it is up to the family to embed intervention strategies in routines the rest of the time. This will increase the child's participation in his or her natural environment, the child will have more opportunities to practice the target skills, and the child will become more engaged in family and community events. As IFSP and IEP outcomes are written to address functional skills, embedding strategies into daily routines where a child has multiple times to practice them has been found to support developmental outcomes (McWilliam, Casey, & Sims, 2009).

Assessment

According to DEC's (2014) recommended practices, "Assessment is the process of gathering information to make decisions. Assessment informs intervention and, as a result, is a critical component of services for young children who have or are at risk for developmental delays/disabilities and their families" (p. 5). Assessment in the early years is similar to assessment for older students served in special education. The purpose of assessments within EI/ECSE for children includes identifying children and youth who may qualify for services through Child Find and screening, determining children and families' eligibility for services, individualizing plans and interventions, monitoring child and family progress, and measuring child and family outcomes (Division for Early Childhood, 2014). However, key practices that distinguish assessments for young children served in early intervention and early childhood special education include: (a) conducting Child Find and screening for children with or at-risk for disabilities and developmental delays; (b) using multiple sources when conducting assessments; and (c) engaging parents and family members in the assessment process.

Conducting Child Find and Screening

IDEA (2004) requires states that receive federal support conduct a systematic process for identifying, locating, and screening all children with or at-risk for disabilities and developmental delays. Within Part C of IDEA, states are required to establish "a comprehensive Child Find system, consistent with Part B, including a system for making referrals to service providers that includes timelines and provides for participation by primary referral sources and that ensure rigorous standards for appropriately identifying infants and toddlers with disabilities for services under this part that will reduce the need for future services" (20 USC. 1435(a)(5)). Just as schools are required to conduct Child Find for students eligible for special education services, the lead agency for EI in each state must systematically conduct outreach to locate and identify families of infants and toddlers who may qualify for EI services under Part C. Furthermore, Child Find efforts continue as children transition out of Part C services when they reach the age of 3 years old. Thus, Child Find efforts for young children often focus on community-based programs (e.g., child-care programs, faith-based settings, crisis nurseries, etc.), public service programs (e.g., public health clinics, Women, Infants, and Children [WIC] offices, park services, etc.), and medical facilities (e.g., pediatricians' offices, rehabilitation clinics, etc.) where infants, toddlers, and preschoolers may be served.

However, every state is given the latitude to determine characteristics that might qualify young children for early intervention and early childhood special education services (Ringwalt, 2012). For Part C services, most children with intellectual disability will fall within predetermined factors for eligibility that include but are not limited to an identified developmental delay and/or a diagnosis such as Down syndrome or traumatic brain injury that impacts young children's overall development. Furthermore, states may differ in how they define *at-risk* status to determine eligibility for EI/ECSE services. For example, a young child may be identified as at-risk due to exposure to one or more environmental risk factors that may impact his or her development, such as poverty, abuse, and parental health (IDEA). Thus, young children and their families may qualify for EI services in one state and not necessarily qualify for such services in other states.

Using Multiple Sources to Conduct Assessments

According to DEC's (2014) recommended practices, the goals of assessment are to provide an ongoing process to determine strengths, needs, resources, concerns, and priorities for young children and their families. Child and family information gathered from assessments serve as the basis for developing individualized support plans, IFSPs and IEPs, that focus on facilitating the child's overall development within the context of responsive environments, primarily through their family and community networks (Workgroup on Principles and Practices in Natural Environments, 2008).

Assessment for young children, whether it is to determine eligibility or monitor progress towards learning goals, can involve both formal and informal ways to gather information on children, families, and their environment (US Department of Health and Human Services and US Department of Education, 2015). As such, DEC's (2014) recommended practices on assessment noted that the

Table 21.3 DEC recommended practices on assessment

A1.	Practitioners work with the family to identify family preferences for assessment processes.
A2.	Practitioners work as a team with the family and other professionals to gather assessment information.
A3.	Practitioners use assessment materials and strategies that are appropriate for the child's age and level of development and accommodate the child's sensory, physical, communication, cultural, linguistic, social, and emotional characteristics.
A4.	Practitioners conduct assessments that include all areas of development and behavior to learn about the child's strengths, needs, preferences, and interests.
A5.	Practitioners conduct assessments in the child's dominant language and in additional languages if the child is learning more than one language.
A6.	Practitioners use a variety of methods, including observation and interviews, to gather assessment information from multiple sources, including the child's family and other significant individuals in the child's life.
A7.	Practitioners obtain information about the child's skills in daily activities, routines, and environments such as home, center, and community.
A8.	Practitioners use clinical reasoning in addition to assessment results to identify the child's current levels of functioning and to determine the child's eligibility and plan for instruction.
A9.	Practitioners implement systematic ongoing assessment to identify learning targets, plan activities, and monitor the child's progress to revise instruction as needed.
A10.	Practitioners use assessment tools with sufficient sensitivity to detect child progress, especially for the child with significant support needs.
A11.	Practitioners report assessment results so that they are understandable and useful to families.

Source: DEC, 2014.

current evidence base suggests that, "Practitioners use a variety of methods, including observation and interviews, to gather assessment information from multiple sources, including the child's family and other significant individuals in the child's life" (p. 5). EI/ECSE professionals may utilize tools such as commercially available developmental checklists or tests. In addition, they may conduct structured or unstructured observations of children and families engaging in a variety of routine environments (i.e., "Practitioners obtain information about the child's skills in daily activities, routines, and environments such as home, center, and community" (Division for Early Childhood, 2014, p. 5). This and the other DEC recommended practices highlighted in Table 21.3 describe what has been learned through research regarding how assessments should be conducted during the early childhood years.

Engaging Families in Assessment

The role of family members during screening and assessment in EI/ECSE cannot be overlooked. The children's parents, extended family members, and significant caregivers are key to ensuring that professionals are able to gather high-quality and valid information about young children's strengths and needs. The recently released policy statement codeveloped by the US Department of Health and Human Services and US Department of Education (2015) specifically states, "Teachers and providers should also have ongoing conversations with families on their children's learning and development, regularly share information on developmental screening and child assessment, ask for their perspectives on their children's strengths and needs, and connect them to additional services and supports, as needed, such as family to family health resource centers or specialized service providers" (p.15).

This statement highlights three of the DEC's recommended practices on assessment (see A1, A2, and A11 in Table 21.3) regarding how EI/ECSE professionals should engage families during the assessment process, from beginning to end. Of note is the importance of understanding that at the same time families are important sources of information about their children, they also are recipients of the assessment results. As such, professionals must be intentional in ensuring that families can access information about the assessment process and results in a way that is respectful and supportive of a family's background and preferences.

Integrated Developmental Domains

Outcomes for young children with or at-risk for disabilities and developmental delays highlight the integrated way domain areas (e.g., physical and motor, cognitive, social and emotional, communication and language, adaptive) develop in the early years. Fogel (2009) emphasized that young children's skills do not develop in isolation. The development of each domain is integrally connected to the development of the other areas. For example, a toddler who persists through the process of stacking a block tower even as some of the blocks topple over (e.g., the blocks are not balanced) is demonstrating growth and development in the emotional, cognitive, perceptual, and motor domain areas. Hence, for young children with disabilities, while their areas of need may focus on one or two domains (i.e., a child with intellectual disability may exhibit delays in the cognitive and speech domains), other aspects of the child's development may be affected as well (e.g., social). Therefore while early childhood interventions may target one or more specific areas (e.g., enhancing speech and vocabulary), they should be designed and implemented with the child's other skills in mind as well (e.g., increasing social and communication and language development).

IDEA (2004) identifies three outcomes for young children served in Part C and Part B programs: (a) social relationships, which includes getting along with other children and relating well with adults; (b) use of knowledge and skills, which refers to thinking, reasoning, problem solving, and early literacy and math skills; and (c) taking action to meet needs, which includes feeding, dressing, self-care, and following rules related to health and safety. The focus of each of these outcomes highlights the way special education and early intervention services in the early childhood years are distinctively different from special education services for school-aged children and youth. Notably, each of these child outcomes is underscored by social-emotional development.

Over the years, there has been an emphasis on the importance of facilitating the social-emotional development of young children with and without disabilities (Conroy, Brown, & Olive, 2008). Inarguably, social-emotional development influences every domain of children's development. The three child outcomes delineated by IDEA highlight the extent to which social-emotional development is integrally connected to the ability of young children to develop social relationships, engage with cognitive-based and preacademic learning, and gain adaptive skills. To form healthy relationships means that children also need to have a way to communicate, self-regulate, and empathize with others (Diamond & Aspinwall, 2003). To learn preliteracy or early math skills, children also must to learn to persist, work in a group, pay attention, and follow directions (Hamre & Pianta, 2005). To meet their needs, children must communicate effectively, recognize and label their feelings and emotions, and manage disappointment (Webster-Stratton & Reid, 2003). Researchers have noted that healthy social-emotional development in the early years is directly linked to academic success and positive adult outcomes (Jones, Greenberg, & Crowley, 2015). Children with intellectual and other developmental disabilities may need support to develop and apply social-emotional skills (Guralnick, 2005; Smith & Matson, 2010).

Many children with intellectual and developmental disabilities experience delays in social-emotional development (American Psychiatric Association, 2013). Young children with disabilities may exhibit challenging behaviors as a result of delays in social-emotional and communication skills (Conroy et al., 2008). Challenging behaviors impact young children's ability to access and participate in inclusive settings such as in their home, school, and in the community. Gilliam (2005) found that young children who exhibit challenging behaviors are twice more likely to be expelled compared to all children in kindergarten–12th grade combined. Furthermore, children with disabilities who exhibit challenging behaviors have limited opportunities to form important social relationships with their peers and caregivers, which in turn further limits their opportunities to learn and acquire much-needed skills across domain areas within naturally occurring routines and activities (Hemmeter, Ostrosky, & Fox, 2006). In sum, outcomes for young children with intellectual and other developmental disabilities are based on the integrated relationship among all domain areas of development, with social-emotional skills serving as a common thread that connects all domain areas together.

Transitions

Across age groups, transition planning should ensure continuity of services, minimize disruptions, prepare children and their families for the next setting, and meet legal requirements (Pianta, Cox, & Snow, 2007). An important component of service delivery and coordination is the successful transition of children and their families from one service delivery model or program to another (Fowler, 2010; Rous, 2015; Rous & Hallam, 2006). In EI/ECSE, if one considers the range of transitions that young children with disabilities might experience within a very short period of time, those include but are not limited to: hospital (i.e., neonatal intensive care unit, or NICU) to home, the transition into a Part C program, movement from a birth–3 EI program (center or home based) to an inclusive preschool environment (school-based, community-based), and the transition from preschool to kindergarten and elementary school. In addition to staff and location changes, the diversity of settings and systems-level variables such as eligibility requirements, funding, class enrollment size (i.e., preschool to kindergarten), and unique policies and procedures can make transitions difficult for even the most well-informed families and the most flexible infants, toddlers, or preschoolers with disabilities.

The most potentially disruptive transition for many infants and toddlers with disabilities and their families is the move from early intervention or Part C services to services through Part B upon the child's third birthday. This transition process often begins between four to six months prior to a child's third birthday, thereby ensuring that the receiving agency (i.e., typically a public preschool program) has the most current reports with which to determine eligibility and develop an IEP. In 2012, 66% of children enrolled in EI services were eligible for Part B pre-K services (36th Annual Report to Congress, 2014).

The time period surrounding a child's transition can be overwhelming for families. Therefore, structures should be in place to support families during this time and ensure the smooth transfer of information and communication between each family and its new program, and between the sending and receiving programs (Fowler, 2010; Petrakos & Lehrer, 2011; Rous & Hallam, 2012). The Workgroup on Principles and Practices in Natural Environments (2008) lists the following as one of the seven key early intervention principles: "The early intervention process, from initial contacts through transition, must be dynamic and individualized to reflect the child's and family members' preferences, learning styles, and cultural beliefs" (p. 5). This principle includes an understanding that families are the ultimate decision makers in the amount and type of assistance needed, as well as how much support they receive. With regard to information sharing and support related to transitions, the DEC's recommended practices (2014) highlight the need for "practitioners in sending and receiving programs to exchange information before, during, and after transitions about practices most likely to support a child's successful adjustment and positive outcomes," (p.15) and the need for "practitioners to use a variety of planned and timely strategies with the child and family before, during, and after the transition to support the successful adjustment and positive outcomes for both the child and the family" (p. 15). Given the numerous transitions between programs or environments that are likely to occur during the early childhood years, it is imperative that professionals and family members work together in support of young children with disabilities.

Professional Development

Another feature that differentiates EI/ECSE services from special education services for school-aged children are the types, preparation, and training of professionals who work with young children and their families. Not surprisingly, EI/ECSE professionals tend to be mostly female (Hebbeler et al., 2007; Saluja, Early, & Clifford, 2002). For children receiving Part C services in particular, early intervention professionals may come from a broad range of professional backgrounds including medicine (e.g., developmental pediatricians and nurses); allied medical programs (e.g., speech language pathologists, audiologists, occupational therapists, and physical therapists); education (e.g., early childhood teachers, special education teachers, child-care providers, and developmental therapists); social work, psychology, and counseling (e.g., family therapists, mental health counselor); and other related fields (e.g., dietitians, hearing specialists, vision specialists, and orientation and mobility specialists) (Hebbeler et al., 2007).

For Part B services, Markowitz et al. (2006) reported that the majority of professionals are licensed teachers, in diverse areas including special education (36%), early childhood special education (31%), elementary/secondary education (31%), early childhood education (28%), and other licenses (>20%). Interestingly, speech and language therapy is the most common service provided to children enrolled in Part C and Part B programs. The range of professions working in Part C and Part B programs requires professionals to collaborate as members of interdisciplinary teams. The extent to which professionals are prepared to work collaboratively across disciplines remains a challenge for preservice personnel preparation and in-service professional development programs.

While the US Department of Education and professional organizations have endorsed a set of principles and practices when working with young children with disabilities and their families, systemic barriers prevent professionals from fully embracing and employing these principles and practices (Early Childhood Technical Assistance Center, 2014). For example, there are no national standards specifically for early intervention providers. Instead, specific disciplines determine standards of practice for their professionals to enable them to obtain and maintain their licensure—for example, the American Speech-Language-Hearing Association (ASHA), the American Physical Therapy Association (APTA), and the American Occupational Therapy Association (AOTA). This can be problematic given that preservice programs for these professions are likely to offer broad-based training on their topic area (e.g., motor development across the human lifespan for physical therapists). Weglarz-Ward and Santos (2015) found that while many preservice personnel preparation programs address the topic of young children within their training, the depth to which the content is covered to prepare professionals to address the unique needs of young children with disabilities is severely lacking.

Nonetheless, federal statutes provide some structure for states to begin to support professionals who work with young children with disabilities and their families. Each state determines the requirements for their licenses, certificates, or credentials for professionals working with children and families served in Part C and Part B programs. To support professionals to obtain and maintain their license, certificate, or credentials, states have created statewide professional development systems for their early childhood workforce. Furthermore, states also have identified standards and/or early learning guidelines not unlike standards that have been developed for school-aged children. Finally, some professional organizations provide guidance for their specific disciplines on evidence-based practices for young children with disabilities.

The 2015 joint policy statement by the US Departments of Health and Human Services and Education highlights the need to systematically work across disciplines: "An effective early childhood workforce is a key component of expanding access to inclusive high-quality early childhood programs. States should ensure that their professional development efforts are ongoing, coordinated and differentiated so that inclusion is meaningfully addressed, and that efforts are inclusive of paraprofessionals and aides, center-based and family child care providers, teachers, directors and principals, and other leaders" (US Department of Health and Human Services and US Department of Education, 2015, p. 11). Through continued research and high-quality professional development provided to those who work with and on behalf of young children with intellectual and other developmental disabilities, the early childhood field can continue to move forward in terms of achieving positive outcomes for infants, toddlers, preschoolers, and their families.

Challenges and Future Directions

As services focused on addressing the unique needs of infants, toddlers, and preschoolers with disabilities and their families will reach yet another significant milestone (2016 will mark the 30th year since the passage of PL 99–457 in 1986), challenges remain for the EI/ECSE field. Foremost is the fact that full funding and implementation of PL 99–457 is yet to be realized. While policies supporting early childhood services remain a staple in state and national politics, there is a markedly decreasing trend for supporting essential services for young children with disabilities and their families (Lazara, Danaher, & Goode, 2014). Advocacy on behalf of children and families and research-informed policy statements are key to ensuring that local, state, and national policies and legislations focus on the importance of addressing the individual developmental needs of children early in their development *and* within the context of responsive environments and caregivers.

Another challenge for the EI/ECSE field is the need to continue to build the knowledge base to support the development and learning of infants, toddlers, and preschoolers with developmental delays and disabilities. The most recent version of DEC's recommended practices (Division for Early Childhood, 2014) highlights strategies that have empirical evidence to promote positive change in young children and their families. However, much more work is needed to further define these strategies and to identify additional interventions that can address the unique needs of young children with disabilities and their families (Division for Early Childhood, 2014). Furthermore, it is equally important that EI/ECSE professionals and families have the capacity to implement these strategies and interventions with fidelity. Changes in our society such as those brought about by advancements in science and technology, and shifting migration patterns, will serve as a driving force for EI/ECSE field to continue to reflect upon its role in addressing the needs of young children with a variety of disabilities and their families representing a broad spectrum of experiences and backgrounds. Further research is required to better understand how to extend and enhance the overall mission and goals of EI/ ECSE to include and better serve the growing diversity of children with disabilities and families who are entering the system and ways to prepare and support professionals who work with them.

As such, there is a clear need for a more comprehensive, unified, and seamless approach to the preservice and in-service training of EI/ECSE professionals. While there is guidance in the field on what works for young children with disabilities and their families, the extent to which these practices and principles are implemented with fidelity is debatable. Not only is there a need to ensure that EI/ECSE professionals receive training specific to their discipline but also they must have the necessary skills to understand and support the unique needs of infants, toddlers, and preschoolers with disabilities. It is imperative that their preservice and in-service training is consistent with the current knowledge base. Furthermore, policies and procedures that govern the various disciplines within EI/ECSE should serve as a guide and not a hindrance to the development, implementation, and evaluation of the professional development of EI/ECSE professionals.

References

Adams, R. C., Tapia, C., Murphy, N. A., Norwood, K. W., Burke, R. T., Friedman, S. L., . . . Wiley, S. E. (2013). Early intervention, IDEA Part C services, and the medical home: Collaboration for best practice and best outcomes. *Pediatrics, 132*, e1073–e1088.

American Psychiatric Association. (2013). *Diagnostic and statistical manual of mental disorders* (5th Edition). Washington, DC: Author.

Bailey, D. B., Raspa, M., & Fox, L. C. (2012). What is the future of family outcomes and family centered services? *Topics in Early Childhood Special Education, 31*, 216–223.

Bethesda Institute. (2012). *How prevalent are intellectual and developmental disabilities in the United States?* Retrieved from http://bethesdainstitute.org/document.doc?id=413

Blasco, P. M. (2001). Curriculum and teaching strategies in early intervention. In P. M. Blasco (Ed.), *Early intervention strategies for infants, toddlers, and their families* (pp. 191–212). Boston: Allyn & Bacon.

Bruder, M. B. (2010). Early childhood intervention: A promise to children and families for their future. *Exceptional Children, 76*, 339–355.

Centers for Disease Control and Prevention. (2015, September 1). *Facts about intellectual disability.* Retrieved from http://www.cdc.gov/ncbddd/actearly/pdf/parents_pdfs/IntellectualDisability.pdf

Conroy, M. A., Brown, W. H., & Olive, M. L. (2008). Social competence interventions for young children with challenging behaviors. In W. H. Brown, S. L. Odom, & S. R. McConnell (Eds.), *Social competence of young children: Risk, disability, and intervention* (pp. 205–231). Baltimore, MD: Paul Brookes.

Diamond, L. M., & Aspinwall, L. G. (2003). Emotion regulation across the life span: An integrative perspective emphasizing self-regulation, positive affect, and dyadic processes. *Motivation and Emotion, 27*, 125–156.

Division for Early Childhood. (2010, September). *Responsiveness to all children, families, and professionals: Integrating cultural and linguistic diversity into policy and practice.* Retrieved from http://dec.membershipsoftware.org/files/Position%20Statement%20and%20Papers/Position%20Statement_Cultural%20and%20Linguistic%20Diversity.pdf

Division for Early Childhood. (2014). *DEC recommended practices in early intervention/early childhood special education 2014.* Retrieved from http://www.dec-sped.org/recommendedpractices

Division for Early Childhood. (2015). *DEC recommended practices in early intervention/early childhood special education glossary 2015.* Retrieved from http://www.dec-sped.org/recommendedpractices

Division for Early Childhood (2016, July 4). Retrieved from http://www.dec-sped.org/

Dunst, C. J., Bruder, M. B., Trivette, C. M., Raab, M., & McLean, M. (2001). Natural learning opportunities for infants, toddlers, and preschoolers. *Young Exceptional Children, 4*(3), 18–25.

Dunst, C. J., & Trivette, C. M. (2009). Capacity-building family systems intervention practices. *Journal of Family Social Work, 12*, 119–143.

Early Childhood Technical Assistance Center. (2014). *Training resources for early interventionists and service coordinators: Assuring qualified providers: Training required for certification or enrollment in the early intervention program.* Chapel Hill: The University of North Carolina, FPG Child Development Institute, Author.

Fogel, A. (2009). *Infancy: Infant, family and society* (5th Edition). Cornwall-on-Hudson, NY: Sloan Publishing.

Fowler, S. A. (2010). Early transition of children with special needs. In P. Peterson, E. Baker, & B. McGraw (Eds.), *International encyclopedia of education* (Vol. 2, pp. 613–620). Oxford, UK: Elsevier.

Fowler, S. A., Ostrosky, M. M., & Yates, T. J. (2014). Teaching and learning in the early years. In L. Florian (Ed.), *The SAGE handbook of special education* (2nd Edition, pp. 613–631). Thousand Oaks, CA: SAGE Publishers.

Gilliam, W. S. (2005). *Prekindergarteners left behind: Expulsion rates in state prekindergarten systems.* New York: Foundation for Child Development.

Guralnick, M. J. (2005). Early intervention for children with intellectual disabilities: Current knowledge and future prospects. *Journal of Applied Research in Intellectual Disabilities, 18*, 313–324.

Hamre, B. K., & Pianta, R. C. (2005). Can instructional and emotional support in the first-grade classroom make a difference for children at risk of school failure? *Child Development, 76*, 949–967.

Hanft, B. E., & Pilkington, K. O. (2000). Therapy in natural environments: The means or end goal for early intervention? *Infants & Young Children, 12*, 1–13.

Hebbeler, K., Spiker, D., Bailey, D., Scarborough, A., Mallik, S., Simeonsson, R., . . . Nelson, L. (2007). *Early intervention for infants and toddlers with disabilities and their families: Participants, services, and outcomes.* Menlo Park, CA: SRI International.

Hemmeter, M. L., Ostrosky, M., & Fox, L. (2006). Social and emotional foundations for early learning: A conceptual model for intervention. *School Psychology Review, 35*, 583–601.

Individuals with Disabilities Education Improvement Act of 2004, P.L. 108–446. (2004). Retrieved September 28, 2015 from https://www.congress.gov/bill/108th-congress/house-bill/1350

Individuals with Disability Education Act Amendments of 1997 [IDEA]. (1997). Retrieved from http://thomas.loc.gov/home/thomas.php

The IRIS Center. (2015). *Glossary.* Retrieved from http://iris.peabody.vanderbilt.edu/glossary/

James, C., & Chard, G. (2010). A qualitative study of parental experiences of participation and partnership in an early intervention service. *Infants & Young Children, 23*, 275–285.

Jennings, D., Hanline, M. F., & Woods, J. (2012). Using routines-based interventions in early childhood special education. *Dimensions for Early Childhood, 40*, 13–22.

Jones, D. E., Greenberg, M., & Crowley, M. (2015). Early social-emotional functioning and public health: The relationship between kindergarten social competence and future wellness. *American Journal of Public Health*, e1–e8. doi:10.2105/AJPH.2015.302630.

Keilty, B. (2010). *The early intervention guidebook for families and professionals: Partnering for success*. New York: Teachers College Press.

Lazara, A., Danaher, J., & Goode, S. (2014). *Part C infant and toddler program federal appropriations and national child count 1987–2013*. Chapel Hill: The University of North Carolina, FPG Child Development Institute, Early Childhood Technical Assistance Center.

March of Dimes Foundation. (2015). *In the NICU*. Retrieved from http://www.marchofdimes.org/baby/in-the-nicu.aspx

Markowitz, J., Carlson, E., Frey, W., Riley, J., Shimshak, A., Heinzen, H., . . . Klein, S. (2006). *Preschoolers' characteristics, services, and results: Wave 1 overview report from the Pre-Elementary Education Longitudinal Study (PEELS)*. Rockville, MD: Westat. Available at www.peels.org.

McWilliam, R. A. (2000). It's only natural. . . to have early intervention in the environments where it's needed. In S. Sandall & M. Ostrosky (Eds.), *Young exceptional children monograph series no. 2: Natural environments and inclusion* (pp. 17–26). Denver, CO: The Division for Early Childhood of the Council for Exceptional Children.

McWilliam, R. A., Casey, A. M., & Sims, J. (2009). The routines-based interview: A method for gathering information and assessing needs. *Infants & Young Children, 22*, 224–233.

Odom, S. L., Buysse, V., & Soukakou, E. (2011). Inclusion for young children with disabilities: A quarter century of research perspectives. *Journal of Early Intervention, 33*, 344–356.

Petrakos, H. H., & Lehrer, J. S. (2011). Parents' and teachers' perceptions of transition practices in kindergarten. *Exceptionality Education International, 21*(2), 62–73.

Pianta, R. C., Cox, M. J., & Snow, K. L. (2007). *School readiness and the transition to kindergarten in the era of accountability*. Baltimore: Brookes.

Public Law 99-457 (1986). Education of the Handicapped Act Amendments of, 100, 1145-1177. Retrieved July 4, 2016 from https://www.gpo.gov/fdsys/pkg/STATUTE-100/pdf/STATUTE-100-Pg1145.pdf

Ringwalt, S. (2012) Summary table of states' and territories' definitions of/criteria for IDEA PART C eligibility. Retrieved from http://ectacenter.org/~pdfs/topics/earlyid/partc_elig_table.pdf

Rosenkoetter, S. E., & Squires, S. (2004). Writing outcomes that make a difference for children and families. In E. M. Horn, C. Peterson, & L. Fox (Eds.), *Young exceptional children monograph series on linking curriculum to child and family outcomes* (pp. 51–60). Missoula, MT: DEC.

Rous, B. S. (2015). Using the recommended practices to support continuity and transitions. In *DEC recommended practices: Enhancing services for young children with disabilities and their families* (pp. 109–118). Missoula, MT: The Division of Early Childhood.

Rous, B. S., & Hallam, R. A. (2006). *Tools for transition in early childhood: A step-by-step guide for agencies, teachers, and families*. Baltimore: Brookes.

Rous, B. S., & Hallam, R. A. (2012). Transition services for young children with disabilities: Research and future directions. *Topics in Early Childhood Special Education, 31*, 232–240.

Saluja, G., Early, D. M., & Clifford, R. M. (2002). Demographic characteristics of early childhood teachers and structural elements of early care and education in the United States. *Early Childhood Research and Practice, 4*(1). Retrieved from http://ecrp.uiuc.edu/v4n1/saluja.html

Smith, K. R., & Matson, J. L. (2010). Social skills: Differences among adults with intellectual disabilities, co-morbid autism spectrum disorders and epilepsy. *Research in Developmental Disabilities, 31*, 1366–1372.

Snyder, P. A., Rakap, S., Hemmeter, M. L., McLaughlin, T. W., Sandall, S., & McLean, M. E. (2015). Naturalistic instructional approaches in early learning a systematic review. *Journal of Early Intervention, 37*, 69–97. doi:10.1177/1053815115595461

Trivette, C. M. & Banerjee, R. (2015). Using the recommended practices to build parent competence and confidence. In *DEC recommended practices: Enhancing services for young children with disabilities and their families* (pp. 66–75). Missoula, MT: The Division of Early Childhood.

Trivette, C. M., Dunst, C. J., & Hamby, D. W. (2010). Influences of family system intervention practices on parent-child interactions and child development. *Topics in Early Childhood Special Education, 30*, 3–19.

US Department of Education, Office of Special Education and Rehabilitative Services, Office of Special Education Programs. (2014). *34th annual report to Congress on the implementation of the Individuals with Disabilities Education Act, 2012*. Washington, DC: Author.

US Department of Education. (2014). *36th annual report to Congress on the implementation of the Individuals with Disabilities Education Act*. Washington DC: Author.

US Department of Health and Human Services and US Department of Education. (2015, September 14). *Policy statement on inclusion of children with disabilities in early childhood programs*. Washington, DC: Author.

Wade, C., Llewellyn, G., & Matthews, J. (2008). Review of parent training interventions for parents with intellectual disability. *Journal of Applied Research in Intellectual Disabilities, 21,* 351–366.

Webster-Stratton, C., & Reid, M. J. (2003). Treating conduct problems and strengthening social and emotional competence in young children: The Dina Dinosaur treatment program. *Journal of Emotional and Behavioral Disorders, 11,* 130–143.

Weglarz-Ward, J., & Santos, R. M. (2015). *The inclusion of early intervention content in personnel preparation programs across disciplines.* Unpublished manuscript. Champaign, IL: University of Illinois at Urbana-Champaign.

Workgroup on Principles and Practices in Natural Environments, OSEP TA Community of Practice: Part C Settings. (2008, March). *Seven key principles: Looks like/doesn't look like.* Retrieved from http://www.ectacenter.org/~pdfs/topics/families/Principles_LooksLike_DoesntLookLike3_11_08.pdf

World Health Organization. (2012). *Newborns: Reducing mortality.* Retrieved from http://www.who.unt/mediacentre/factsheets/fs333/en/index.html

22

High-Quality Educational Programs for Students with Intellectual Disability in Elementary School

Kendra L. Williams-Diehm, Susan B. Palmer

Introduction

Students with intellectual disability in elementary school can be served within the general education curriculum. According to Browder and Spooner (2014): "[it] is now clearly possible to teach more advanced academic content to students with significant cognitive disabilities as educators translate longstanding evidence-based practices into use with core curriculum" (p. 5). As discussed throughout this text, a philosophical shift has occurred in education pertaining to the educational experience of students with intellectual disability. Emphasis on learning strong academic skills in core subjects is growing, and students with intellectual disability are expected to make the same or similar academic growth as compared to their peer groups (Browder & Spooner, 2006).

Teachers should have high expectations for all student outcomes, even though it can be difficult for students with intellectual disability to achieve at the same rate as all other students. Teachers focusing on academics should find encouragement from their teacher peers, administrators, and families, rather than skepticism. Students benefit by being included with their peers, and academic skills increase when compared to groups educated in segregated classrooms (Fisher & Meyer, 2002, Foreman, Arthur-Kelly, Pascoe, & King, 2004). Research has also demonstrated associated positive outcomes including empathy and acceptance (Copeland et al., 2004) while ensuring that negative effects are not found within academic skills (Jameson, McDonnell, Polychronic, & Riesen, 2008).

For students with intellectual disability with more extensive support needs to attain their full potential, educators teaching these students from an early age must possess the knowledge and skills to facilitate positive outcomes. The inability to ensure highly qualified and trained teachers will result in a negative impact on student learning and achievement (Downing & MacFarland, 2010). In fact, because many current teachers lack knowledge on how to effectively teach reading and other core content, students are not excelling to their full potential (Foorman & Torgesen, 2001).

Educators and families should be aware of barriers that may impact quality education for students with intellectual disability that could include low expectations for learning, teachers who do not have adequate training, and limited family involvement (Downing & MacFarland, 2010). In addition, education systems should avoid instructional models that fail to recognize inclusion leading to access to the general curriculum as being possible or best practice. These systemic models perpetuate the "fallacy of perceived incompetence" (Downing & MacFarland, 2010) in which expectations are low, children with intellectual disability are not provided with high-quality curriculum, instruction is in segregated settings, and little or no direct instruction occurs.

An ongoing challenge for teachers, administrators, and families is to be able to support an increasing number of students with more extensive support needs to be educated in the general education curriculum along with all other students in the same general education settings. We must work on functional skills and academics in a coordinated, rather than separate effort. Social inclusion is not enough to support academic progress. Issues discussed at the National Goals Conference in 2015 identified the need for more research:

> To ensure that policies, practices, and administrative supports produce scalable, universally designed, inclusive, and culturally and linguistically competent educational systems that are responsive to the needs of all students, research is essential to enable school systems to improve their practices, policies, and activities, and to facilitate the learning and academic achievement of all students in inclusive environments.
>
> *(Thoma & Palmer, 2015, p. 2)*

This chapter on the education of students with intellectual disability during the elementary years is based on the premise that students with intellectual disability belong in the same instructional space as other students and should receive instruction with the same aim as their peers, to access the general education curriculum using research-based practices; there is no reason for students with intellectual disability to be in separate spaces for much of their instructional day. Pursuing evidence-based practices promotes a new way to integrate and coordinate instruction for all students, including students with intellectual disability, to receive access to the general curriculum and advance cognitive process within academic and social learning.

Evidence-Based Practices

Evidence-based practices have come to the forefront in special education. Such practices meet specific criteria concerning research design, quality, quantity, and statistical effect size and are one way to address the research-to-practice gap of special instruction (Cook & Cook, 2015). However, when one searches the What Works Clearinghouse (http://ies.ed.gov/ncee/wwc/), few if any practices for students with intellectual disability are evident. This site compiles reports from research designs using large-scale randomized control trials and is considered to reflect the highest level of evidence. We can look at related practices for fulfilling instruction in the general education curriculum for students without disabilities but must be cautious in implementing individualized instruction to promote overall learning.

Several levels of recommendation for effective instructional practice exist. Teachers should question best or recommended practices as to why and who/which group is supporting the statements. For example, some recommended practices suggested in a publication from the Center for International Rehabilitation Research Information Exchange include "learning with peers without disabilities, systematic instruction that takes into account their chronological age, culture, interests and needs, strong family involvement, collaborative teamwork for a unified approach, and positive behavior support that keeps the focus on desired behavior" (Downing & MacFarland, 2010, p. 11). Although these listed practices are generally accepted in education, teachers could seek additional information on each of these to ensure that a research base exists and obtain information about employing these practices, if they are not already doing so.

Further, if a practice is research-based, how many students or groups using a similar research design show positive student outcomes? Correlational research may show increased student outcomes for a particular practice, but causation cannot be assumed (Cook & Campbell, 1979). Teachers should look to outcomes from research designs such as group experimental, group quasi-experimental, and single-subject designs to consider evidence-based practices (Gersten et al., 2005; Gersten et al., 2005; Horner et al., 2005). Educators can review studies that test alternative co-occurring reasons for a change in student outcomes (Cook & Cook, 2015).

Once promising practices are confirmed, teachers must also decide whether evidence-based and research-based practices are effective for students in a particular setting, if these practices are difficult to use, and whether or not instructional results help effective decision making for evaluation or next instructional steps (Cook & Cook, 2015). No matter the level of evidence, teachers must also work to integrate their understanding of student needs based on practical wisdom and common sense into decision making for effective instruction.

Organizing Instruction

Although this chapter will provide specific guidance and practices for instruction organized by various content areas, there are instructional strategies that are universally beneficial to providing instruction for students with intellectual disability. Although this list is extensive, we focus on some of the newer practices. Some of these practices are system-driven, depending on decisions made by administrators or coordinators (e.g., co-teaching or school-wide positive behavior support). Others are practices or strategies—such as planning via Universal Design for Learning (UDL), and other instructional supports such as time delay—that teachers can employ within their classrooms in order to provide quality instruction for all students, including students with intellectual disability.

System-Driven Practices

Co-teaching

A general and special educator will most likely be co-teaching partners delivering differentiated instruction to students with disabilities in an inclusive elementary classroom (Thousand, Villa, & Nevin, 2007). One teacher may take the lead on a particular instructional objective, while the other is secondary, or a shared parallel model of teaching can be used where students are assigned to groups led by one teacher or the other within a classroom. Co-teaching requires careful planning and evaluation, and a great deal of consultation, especially at the start of the process.

School-Wide Positive Behavior Support

The concept of School-Wide Positive Behavioral Interventions and Supports (SWPBIS) has emerged as an effective practice for addressing student needs and improving outcomes (Freeman et al., 2016). SWPBIS is part of a multitiered system that helps with student success (Lewis & Sugai, 1999; see Chapter 13 for fuller discussion). The multi-tiered system generally involves three levels of success: Tier 1, the primary level, involves all school staff and students (Sugai & Horner, 2006). Tier 2, secondary level, is targeted to small groups and typically occurs in the general education setting. Tier 3, tertiary level, is reserved for students needing individualized instruction and supports (Freeman et al., 2016). SWPBIS "restructures the educational system by creating a culture in which there is shared responsibility and collaboration between general education and special education for the purpose of ensuring that the educational needs of every student are met" (Colorado Department of Special Education, 2014, p. 1). Greenwood (2009) reminds us that children with Individualized Education Programs (IEPs) are not limited to participation in Tier 3 and that SWPBIS is applicable to all children in a class within a school. SWPBIS has shown positive results in the academic achievement of all students (Freeman et al., 2016).

Classroom or Teacher-Driven Strategies

Universal Design for Learning (UDL)

As discussed in detail in Chapter 14, UDL is a method of planning for curriculum delivery that provides a more efficient way to promote access for all children to address a range of user abilities and needs within the general education curriculum by incorporating flexible goals, methods, and materials that accommodate learner differences from the start. UDL encompasses three primary principles: (a) multiple means of representation to give learners a variety of ways to access information and content, (b) multiple means of engagement to gain and maintain learners' interest, and (c) multiple means of expression to provide learners with a variety of ways for demonstrating what they know (CAST, 2011).

On a basic level, UDL provides a framework for educators to design engaging learning opportunities that incorporate a variety of ways to access the curriculum content, offer multiple methods to recruit children's active attention and sustained engagement, and include a range of formats for children to respond and demonstrate what they know and have learned. The principles of UDL are essential for ensuring not only access to, but also meaningful participation across daily routines and activities for all children, particularly those with disabilities or who are at risk for developing disabilities. Using UDL in planning instruction in the elementary grades enhances instructional activities and often reduces the amount of accommodations and supports needed by most students in a class. However, the implementation of UDL does not take the place of instructional individualization to meet individual child needs.

Time Delay and Task-Analytic Instruction

Spooner, Knight, Browder, and Smith (2012) reviewed literature published between 2003 and 2010 on teaching students with extensive support needs literacy, mathematics, and science. Using time delay and task-analytic instruction met the criteria for evidence-based practices. Time delay involves fading prompts over time and as needed, with either an immediate prompt as children are learning the skills or an extended time delay of prompts as learning occurs (Neitzel & Wolery, 2009). First, teachers watch a student to identify a target behavior that can be documented and measured by observable means. Then a teacher identifies a target stimulus, selects the cuing response, and identifies reinforcers and the time needed before cuing begins. Teachers use task analysis to break skills into smaller teachable steps, helping students to master smaller parts of a skill and become increasingly independent learners over time.

Embedded Instruction

The practices of systematic and explicit instruction have extensive literature to validate their effectiveness (Downing, 2008; Snell & Brown, 2006). Systematic instruction refers to a carefully designed and planned sequence of instruction that includes targeting learning outcomes. Systematic instruction incorporates ensuring students have the prior knowledge to successfully gain the targeted skills and then through a series of modeling, guided practice, and independent practice, students acquire skill sets. Explicit instruction is often delivered through direct teaching strategies. Lessons are always a teacher-directed process that is usually delivered in small, face-to-face instructional groups (Carnine, Silbert, Kame'enui, & Tarver, 2004). Carefully derived lessons break skills into small, deliberately sequenced, highly scripted lessons with constant and immediate feedback. Although little detail is provided on systematic and explicit teaching, these strategies have been found successful with students with intellectual disability (Downing, 2008), and incorporating these strategies into teaching content areas or typical routines will yield positive results (Engelmann, Haddox, Hanner, & Osborn, 2002; Flores & Ganz, 2009).

Partnerships and Collaboration

The following practices are ones that involve teachers interacting in strategic ways with other adults to impact instruction for students in their classrooms, including students with intellectual disability. These activities often involve role release and perspective taking on the part of a lead teacher but are well worth the time and energy to enhance educational practice.

FAMILY-PROFESSIONAL PARTNERSHIPS

"In partnership, educators, families, and community members work together to share information, guide students, solve problems, and celebrate successes," (Epstein, 2010, p. 4). This approach supports learning, communication, activities, decisions, and other connections between school and other entities such as home and the community, according to Epstein. Teachers who understand their students and the contexts in which they live, work, and play can extend educational supports in meaningful ways and help students see school and home being connected within learning situations. Although the Individuals with Disabilities Education Act (IDEA) mandates family participation in the IEP process, it also helps teachers to maintain and extend linkages with families, especially for students with intellectual disability who may present with limited communication or less ability to interact without prompting or generalizing learning across contexts. Peacock and Collett (2010) suggested that parents not only play an important role in the lives of their children, but also are part of effective and efficient partnerships carrying out intervention programs and plans for their children's academic and social outcomes.

COLLABORATION AMONG TEAM MEMBERS

Partners collaborate, communicate, share opinions and resources, and participate in any other number of activities to build relationships and enhance educational opportunities for students with intellectual disability. People who are either assigned to work with a student with intellectual disability, as an IEP team member (administrator, general education teacher, special educator, speech-language therapist, occupational therapist, physical therapist, or other related service providers, to name just a few), or family or community providers should engage in collaborative practices to benefit the academic and social outcomes of elementary students with intellectual disability. According to Jackson, Ryndak, and Billingsley (2000), collaboration between team members can help establish a common set of practices around inclusive services, define roles for team members, and create a shared focus by teachers and related service providers on educational outcomes that support education.

Positive Behavior Support—Classroom Level

Even if a system does not embrace SWPBIS, a teacher can still use the principles within a classroom to emphasize respect for each and every class member by identifying situations and learning opportunities that focus on what students can and should do, as opposed to negative impacts. First, a teacher should post simple, consistent classroom rules and refer to these when needed to guide behavior and engagement in learning, using both words and icons for understanding and interest. Teachers can observe ongoing activities over time to determine if some students may need more direction in order to follow classroom routines. In the case of challenging behaviors, there is a series of actions that a teacher can use, including identifying and describing the behavior, sharing information about the need across other adults in the classroom and beyond, determining the function of the behavior (avoidance, misunderstanding directions, other reasons), planning an intervention to reduce challenging behavior, teaching replacement behaviors, and monitoring the plan over time to determine progress (Palmer, Butera, Classen, & Kang, 2016).

Self-Determined Learning

As discussed in Chapter 16, promoting self-determination has beneficial impacts for students (Deci & Ryan, 1985; Palmer & Wehmeyer, 2003; Wehmeyer & Shogren, 2008; Wehmeyer et al., 2007). According to Wehmeyer and Shogren (2013), individuals who are self-determined have knowledge of their own interests, strengths, and needs and carry out their own desires. Persons who are self-determined will "make or cause things to happen in their own lives" (Wehmeyer & Shogren, 2008, p. 95). Promoting self-determined learning is, as such, important during early years.

English Language Arts and Literacy

The Common Core State Standards (CCSS) collectively group not only language arts with literacy, but also address literacy within history/social studies, science, and technical subjects (see http://www. corestandards.org/assets/Appendix_A.pdf). It is important to focus on grade-level standards for students of all ages with intellectual disability, with appropriate accommodations and individualization provided, if necessary.

Literacy is defined as reading, writing, and communicating. The literacy experience includes the concept of reading, writing, and interacting with books and other printed material, but this experience for children with disabilities often differs from that of their peers. This holds true for students with intellectual disability (Simmons & Kame'enui, 1998). It is also possible that children with intellectual disability may not be encouraged or provided the accommodations to explore literacy materials in homes and schools. Students with this disability are less likely to be read to and to engage in other literacy activities (Koppenhaver & Yoder, 1993). Other studies mirror this trend to deemphasize reading (Katims, 2000; Kliewer, Bilken, & Kasa-Hendrickson, 2006).

Reading

Reading is linked with outcomes not only in the K–12 setting but into postsecondary education as well (Nguyen, 2010); no one would argue the importance of literacy and reading. Children who are unable to reach specific reading benchmarks by first grade are already at a higher rate of potential negative school outcomes (Borman & Dowling, 2010). Learning to read is one of the most fundamental academic strategies. The ability to read also has lifelong consequences, as adult illiteracy is associated with unemployment and lower wages (Kutner et al., 2007). Francis (1996) determined that 75% of struggling readers in third grade still struggled in ninth grade, demonstrating the need for targeted intervention.

Traditional reading intervention for students with intellectual disability has focused on functional reading (Brown, Nietupski, & Hamre-Nietupski, 1976) or sight word recognition only (Downing, 2005; Ryndak & Alper, 2003). As discussed in detail in Chapter 19, we must strive to teach reading skills to maximize reading potential. Students with intellectual disability are often compared to students with learning disabilities, but it has been shown that students with intellectual disability make smaller gains and the ability to transfer information is difficult (Caffrey & Fuchs, 2007). However, it has been demonstrated that in a longitudinal randomized-control trial investigating reading instruction, students with intellectual disability show significant progress as contrasted to comparison groups when provided evidence-based reading instruction over an extended period of time (Allor, Mathes, Roberts, Cheatham, & Otaiba, 2014). The five principles of (a) phonological/phonemic awareness, (b) word study and phonics, (c) vocabulary, (d) fluency, and (e) comprehension should be the primary focus of targeted reading intervention (National Reading Panel, 2000).

Phonological/Phonemic Awareness

Phonological awareness is a collection of skills related to the ability to recognize and identify the sound structure in spoken words that are created in speech (Carnine et al., 2004). Children who have mastered the subskill of phonemic awareness, that letters have different associated sounds, by first grade experience more success in reading than their peers who have not mastered this skill (Smith, Simmons, & Kame'enui, 1998). Letter-sound correspondence and identifying first sounds in words are two target skills in this category. Students with intellectual disability will most likely need systematic instruction in phonemic awareness across time. Browder et al. (2009) suggested consistently pairing phonemes with corresponding pictures to promote this awareness skill.

Word Study and Phonics

Letter recognition is critical in reading (Durrell, 1958). The ability to connect spoken words and words in print is imperative. Decoding words while reading is correlated with reading success (Mraz, Padak, & Rasinski, 2008). For students with intellectual disability, word study becomes important in the understanding of book orientation, making connections between text and picture, and text prediction. These skills will assist in beginning to read. Students with intellectual disability have been successful in obtaining mastery on letter sounds, written-letter sounds, and then word reading (Bradford, Shippen, Alberto, Houchins, & Flors, 2006). Researchers also found significant gains in phonemic decoding and letter-word recognition for students with intellectual disability but that gains were not seen until 15–20 weeks into the intervention (Allor, Mathes, Jones, Chanokun, & Cheatham, 2010), speaking to the need for long-term targeted intervention and the possibility that this population will take longer to master objectives.

Vocabulary

Both receptive and expressive language are critically important for vocabulary development. Students must have appropriate vocabulary to understand what is being read (Beck, McKowan, & Kucan, 2002). Browder, Wakeman, Spooner, Ahlgrim-Delzell, and Algozzine (2006) found success in providing systematic procedures for teaching vocabulary. However, for students to truly develop vocabulary, students must engage with the text as opposed to recognizing sight words only. Developing vocabulary results in significantly higher overall literacy scores (Browder, Ahlgrim-Delzell, Flowers, & Baker, 2012).

Fluency

LaBerge and Samuels (1974) first defined fluency as reading words without effort. Fluency involves a connection between decoding and comprehension and can be a problem with students with developmental disabilities due to cognitive abilities and communication concerns. Fluent readers are able to focus more on comprehension of text as opposed to decoding (Institute for the Development of Educational Achievement, 2004). Similar to previous topics, careful consideration must be applied to this population. Fluency rates are typically based on a words-per-minute ratio. This may need to be reconsidered for students who are nonverbal or have speech impairments (Browder et al., 2009). Lemons, Mrachko, Kostewicz, and Paterra (2012) determined that although students with Down syndrome showed an increase in phonics and high-frequency words, this skill was not generalized to oral reading fluency. This topic is in need of additional research.

Comprehension

One must be able to process and interpret reading into meaning (Snow, 2002). Effective readers engage in text through asking questions, monitoring comprehension, and knowing when to go back and reread. Browder et al. (2006) found that comprehension is mostly addressed through word recognition and functional activity, not through literacy-based teaching. It is suggested that comprehension can be developed over time through systematic questioning by the teacher (Browder et al., 2009). However, we do know that when students obtain targeted reading instruction that includes phonemic awareness, phonics, vocabulary, and comprehension, students with severe disabilities consistently perform better than their control-group counterparts (Browder, Gibbs, Ahlgrim-Delzell, Courtade, & Lee, 2007).

For individuals to become successful readers, teachers can employ instruction in the five areas of reading simultaneously. Systematic instruction in any area of reading can show overall reading improvement for all students (O'Connor, Cappella, McCormick, & McClowry, 2014). Although these components are easily incorporated into any curriculum and instructional methods, finding a method to teach them for students with intellectual disability is not easy. Through a meta-analysis of teaching reading to students with severe developmental disabilities, the vast majority of studies ($n = 117$) addressed vocabulary only, with a small number ($n = 23$) addressing comprehension. Teaching phonics has rarely been studied, but shows promise (Barbetta, Heward, & Bradley, 1993). Research supports the idea that instruction should include direct teaching of certain skills and creating opportunities for students to actively engage with tests (National Reading Panel, 2000). Effective reading instruction should be responsive to differentiated student needs across a classroom (Denton & Hocker, 2006), including balance between grouping students so that not all students are of the same ability (Chorzempa & Graham, 2006), which is not always practiced.

Read Aloud/Shared Reading

Reading aloud to students has been a strong component of early childhood education for years, because it gives students access to literature and other appropriate reading materials prior to being able to decode words and read stories. Students can appreciate and develop enjoyment from listening to others read (Burgess, Hecht, & Lonigan, 2002). The recommendation of daily reading to young children is longstanding (Morrow & Gambrell, 2002). Vecca et al. (2006) determined that young children who are exposed to reading daily through oral reading score higher on assessments of vocabulary and comprehension.

Browder et al. (2009) proposes that read-alouds be structured to consider the student's age and grade as opposed to reading level and ability so that students with disabilities have access to similar age-appropriate materials as their peers are using. This may require accommodations such as enlarged print, carefully constructed book summaries and technological adaptations including screen readers. Early childhood and elementary-age students should begin to learn the skills of prediction from pictures and book orientation. Upper-elementary students with intellectual disability can continue to learn more about print awareness through chapter sequence while also still being held responsible for comprehension. However, regardless of the skills being learned, students with developmental disabilities can work on self-regulated learning skills by setting a reading goal and increasing involvement in the process (Browder et al., 2009).

Seven strategies were reported by Fisher, Flood, Lapp, and Frey (2004) for teachers or parents to maximize learning and instruction during read-aloud activities: (a) select books of interest, (b) practice sections ahead of time, (c) establish the purpose of the passage, (d) model oral reading, (e) read with appropriate expression and inflection, (f) pause to check for understanding and engage in a meaningful questioning process, and (g) give enough time for children to make connections to the passage.

Teachers are always encouraged to think outside of the box and to come up with creative and accessible formats for literacy instruction, including audiobooks and utilizing peers in the process. Using UDL, reading can be made much more accessible (Hitchcock, Meyer, Rose, & Jackson, 2005).

Adjustments for Reading

Although it is important to increase reading independence for students with intellectual disability, there may continue to be a reliance on additional assistance when reading (Browder et al., 2009; Goldstein, 2011). Teachers must be creative to overcome boundaries for access and engagement of students with intellectual disability to literacy. Teachers can provide physical access to books and other literature, and time during the day for reading and interaction with books. To ensure students have physical access to literature, a teacher can place books strategically in the classroom and facilitate how some students may physically handle books. At the elementary level, taking books apart and laminating pages may be beneficial. In addition, lots of titles are becoming available in a board-book format, and can be used as long as the titles are age-appropriate. Utilizing popsicle sticks or another grip to assist with turning pages is one suggestion. Above all, students need to be given opportunities to enjoy interaction with printed materials.

Access to books for students with cognitive disabilities could mean that teachers help students to understand parts of the story or book, but not necessarily the entire selection (Browder et al., 2009). Teachers can limit new vocabulary or simplify text. Many age-appropriate elementary books already encompass strategies such as repeated lines, colorful pictures to illustrate the print, and rhyming words to help predict text. Carefully choosing books with such features will benefit all students in the classroom. It is important to use teacher, peer, or technology-supported adaptations so that struggling readers are encouraged to become more interested and successful in reading (Browder et al., 2009).

Computer and technological advances provide a wealth of opportunity for students. Prerecorded audiobooks also allow for greater independence as students can learn to navigate accessing literature on their own. Many public libraries are expanding digital library and audiobook sections; school libraries can do the same. Software programs and online resources also provide technology-related access through websites and other print-to-speech apps that are designed to convert text into speech, to assist in decoding print. Key supports for learning are a large number of apps for hand-held devices such as tablets and smartphones. Teachers can critically evaluate the educational value of apps for specific students beyond the technical aspects of platform and download ease. There are websites that critically review educational apps (IEar.org, learninhand.com), but teachers must consider the specific needs of their students, the general curriculum content, standards for the area of study, level of complexity that the app presents, and a host of other concerns. Walker (2010) suggested a rubric to evaluate apps for the Apple iPad looking at curriculum connection, authenticity of learning environment, feedback differentiation, feasibility of use, and student motivation. App feedback should be specific, support student learning, and motive students to learn, while using flexible settings to meet individual student needs.

Past studies demonstrate that the amount of time children spend reading not only predicts understanding but also academic achievement (Guthrie, Wigfield, Metsala, & Cox, 1999) but that motivation in reading starts declining in elementary schools as students start aging (Guthrie & Davis, 2003). This motivation is greatly tied to self-determination as defined by intrinsic motivation (Noels, Pelletier, Clement, & Vallerand, 2000; Ryan & Deci, 2000). In one of the first attempts to directly connect reading achievement with principles of self-determination, Deci and Ryan (2000) viewed intrinsic motivation as a predecessor of fully autonomous self-determination. It has also been found that increasing motivation in reading can assist with academic achievement (Taboada, Tonks, Wigfield, & Guthrie, 2009). Leary (1999) took this one step further in hypothesizing that motivation and self-esteem are beginning steps in facilitating goal achievement. He even went on to make the connection that students who achieve goals related to academics increase motivation and self-esteem.

Multiple studies have connected reading achievement, student self-competence, and belief of success (Chapman, Tunmer, & Prochnow, 2000; Mata, 2011). Belief in self-competence is highly linked to self-efficacy and other aspects of self-determination. In simple terms, if a child believes they can accomplish a task, they are already more apt to perform at a higher level (Bandura, 1994; Guthrie & Knowles, 2001). This all relates back to intrinsic motivation and positive psychology, which is heavily linked to self-determination (Wehmeyer, Shogren, Little, & Lopez, in press). It has been shown that there is a positive association between self-concept and reading level (phonemic awareness and vocabulary) demonstrated through attitude and perceived competences of early elementary students who were labeled at risk of reading failure (Fives et al., 2014). The notion of using personal goal setting to enhance reading levels has been demonstrated to improve reading outcomes in curriculum-based measures (Jenkins & Terjeson, 2011) and based upon student ability and interest (Cabral-Marquez, 2015).

In general, Browder and Spooner (2011) suggested focusing reading instruction on themes of everyday life and texts that support more independent reading. However, these authors are quick to point out that because targeted reading instruction is in its infancy for students with severe disabilities, "we must remain optimistic that students will acquire additional reading skills through systematic teaching procedures" (p. 130).

Writing

Writing is an important component of expressive communication, literacy, and learning. It is a part of the curriculum for all students, including students with intellectual disability, at the elementary grades (Graham, Gillespie, & McKeown, 2013). Once again, teachers in elementary grades can promote writing development via planning and structure using UDL, targeting grade-level standards, using accommodations, and employing individualized supports for particular students within selected, meaningful applications. Early grade standards involve the act of writing, representing text, and understanding the purpose of writing. Standards in grades three to five include writing to persuade, inform, and narrate as well as using writing to recall, organize, analyze, interpret, and build content knowledge and enhance reading skills across domains (Graham et al., 2013).

Collaboration among team members from different disciplines can support the development or comprehension of writing skills in academic activities. For example, a student's IEP team might contain a variety of professionals, including occupational and speech therapists, who can focus on physical or communicative aspects of writing skills. Teachers can both model and encourage written expression via a number of avenues. Written/expressive communication can use symbols, icons, pictures, tactile, and artistic expression. Teachers or peers can take dictation or otherwise elicit information that can be represented in print or visual modalities. Learning to write is a generative process, but there is no specific road map to develop writing skills. Some see writing as more cognitive while others focus on the motivational nature of writing according to Graham et al. (2013).

Communication

Communication is one of the most critical skills for students with intellectual disability because of the effect this skill has on learning content and quality of life (Browder, Spooner, & Mims, 2011). Communication takes place in three major components of form, context, and function. The form of speech can be achieved through the spoken word, or augmentative or alternative systems. Form also includes the intentional and symbolic components of communication (Sigafoos, Arthur-Kelly, & Butterfield, 2006). Context includes the actual words, vocabulary, and topics of discussion (Browder, Spooner, & Mims, 2011) as well as the people with whom the communication is taking place (Siegel-Causey & Bashinski, 1997). Finally, function refers to the purpose such as social, obtaining information, or making requests

(Arthur-Kelly, Foreman, Bennett, & Pascoe, 2008). In order to help students with intellectual disability obtain and utilize communication skills, all three areas must be addressed.

Unfortunately, students with intellectual disability often rely on alternative forms of communication at the symbolic level such as shortened words, phrases, and pictures, and nonsymbolic eye movement, vocalizations, and gestures. These nonverbal communication attempts rely heavily on someone who can understand and attach meaning to the communication (Foreman, Arthur-Kelly, Bennett, Neilands, & Colyvas, 2014). However, evidence-based practices are emerging that show advancement in the use of both alternative and augmentative communication systems (Arthur-Kelly et al., 2008). These emerging practices include strategies like picture-exchange communication systems (Frost & Bondy, 2002), voice output devices (Dicarlo & Meher, 2000), and naturalistic communication techniques—which simply refer to providing and encouraging communication learning and efforts through the naturally occurring events within the day. Time delays (Hancock & Kaiser, 2002) and mand training (Webber & Scheuerman, 2009) in conjunction with naturalistic communication opportunities have shown success.

Literacy Instruction

Browder et al. (2009) provided a conceptual framework for establishing literacy instruction for students with intellectual and other disabilities focused on promoting opportunities for accessing literature and learning the needed access skills. Literacy will potentially appear different for students with intellectual disability due to cognitive and/or physical limitations of individual students. Since it is recommended that children now be held to higher standards, Browder and colleagues (2009) encourage special education teachers to deliver targeted reading instruction to students with intellectual and developmental disabilities (Browder et al., 2009).

Rather than focus on the traditional but functional literacy of reading community signs, ordering from menus, or memorizing simple sight words (Browder & Xin, 1998), literacy for all students must promote individual literacy skills to satisfy personal interest and enjoyment. Unfortunately, educators continue to focus on teaching sight words as the predominant way to develop reading skills for children with intellectual disability (Katims, 2000) despite the fact that this strategy does not necessarily promote actual reading skills (Browder et al., 2006). Teachers must provide access to and adapt reading materials, since simply increasing intensity and instructional time for students with intellectual disability is not likely to be successful.

Social Studies

"Social studies is an important subject that influences citizenship, teaches about key events and figures, and integrates literacy skills" (Ciullo, 2015, p. 108). A shift has occurred in social studies instruction from that of memorizing historical dates and pointing out places of interest on a map to the emphasis on helping individuals become meaningful and respected citizens (National Council for Social Studies, 2002). Providing access to the curriculum in social studies has been neglected in favor of a greater emphasis on literacy and mathematics (Zakas, Browder, & Spooner, 2009).

The National Council for the Social Studies (NCSS, 2002) identified five disciplinary standards including (a) history, (b) geography, (c) civics and government, (d) economics, and (e) psychology. History and geography are the standards typically addressed in social studies instruction involving the understanding of timelines and past events, and the spatial locations in which these events occurred. The concepts of civics and government are directly related to being a responsible citizen living within a democratic country, while economics brings concepts of supply and demand and services into reality. Psychology, the final discipline standard in social study instruction, is the study of human behavior and how it affects the other four standards (NCSS, 2002). Teachers can use the following themes to address the five standards for social studies instruction: (a) culture; (b) time, continuity, and change; (c) people, places, and environments; (d) individual development and identity; (e) individuals, groups, and institutions; (f) power, authority, and governance; (g) production, distribution, and consumption; (h) science, technology, and society; (i) global connection; and (j) civic ideas and practices (NCSS, 2002).

Unfortunately, there is little or no research regarding teaching social studies content areas to students with intellectual disability (Browder, Spooner, & Zakas, 2011). Until substantial research can be conducted and published, special educators must adapt concepts and practices from other academic areas and apply these to the social studies domain. Thus, strategies to use in teaching elementary students with learning disabilities may be helpful, with some adaptations, when needed. Ciullo (2015) suggests that teachers review their specific state's social studies standards and determine topics while also looking over English language arts standards that could be jointly addressed through literacy within social studies content. In addition, teachers can look for alternate sources of information to address standards beyond text books, including websites, apps, and simple to complex videos that are prescreened to ensure application and feasibility for the particular classroom. *Get the Gist* (Klinger & Vaughan, 1999) is a strategy used in reading comprehension that students can use for learning essential details within social studies. Teachers work with students to help them identify the most important *who* or *what* in a portion of text or within a story that is read to them. Next, teachers guide students to identify two to three details about the *who* or *what* previously identified. Then, the student is supported to put this information into a main idea sentence to determine comprehension and continuity.

Students with intellectual disability in elementary school need access to high-quality social studies content. Teachers must carefully articulate goals objectives, and purposes of lessons by identifying the central content and main ideas of each lesson and adapting curriculum content. It is recommended to use strategies such as systematic instruction, known vocabulary strategies, and graphic organization to assist in teaching content (Browder et al., 2011).

Science

The current National Science Education Standards were published in 1996 by the National Research Council (NRC, 1996). There is limited research that focuses on teaching science to students with intellectual disability (Courtade, Jimenez, Trella, & Browder, 2008; also see Chapter 20). The NRC standards identify six scientific content areas: (a) unifying concepts and processes, (b) inquiry, (c) physical, (d) life, (e) earth, space, and the environment, (f) technology, (g) history and nature of science, and (h) personal and social perspectives (NRC, 1996). Now, science concepts have long been incorporated into teaching daily living skills (Courtade et al., 2008), but Spooner, Stem, and Test (1989) documented targeted instruction in these living skills. The reasons for providing systematic and targeted instruction in the sciences to students with intellectual disability include (a) providing access to the full scope of educational subjects, (b) ensuring adequate yearly gains are made under federal law, (c) exposing students to the world, and (d) helping students figure out answers to questions to explore (Spooner, Knight, Browder, Jimenez, & DiBiase, 2011).

Jimenez, Spooner, Browder, DiBiase, and Knight (2008) provided a full conceptual model using the six content areas identified by the NRC (1996). Interesting, the NRC (1996) specifically notes that students will experience various levels of understanding and interest in the domains (NRC, 1996)—potentially laying ground work for the importance of introducing and exposing students to the breadth of content to ensure, expose, and pique potential interest. The scope, sequence, and progression of objectives are provided by the NRC (1996). Browder et. al. (2012) and, later, Smith, Spooner, Jimenez, and Browder (2013) showed that students with severe disabilities can be successful in the science curriculum. These findings support previous information that students with intellectual disability benefit from graphic organization and carefully designed questions and scaffolding within science content (Scruggs & Mastropieri, 1995). The remainder of this section will provide instructional strategies for ensuring access to high-quality science instruction.

Providing inquiry skills is perhaps one of the central concepts in science. The National Science Education Standards state that inquiry is the critical component of a science curriculum. The ability to fully understand inquiry is linked to overall achievement (Shymansky, Kyle, & Alport, 1983). Students with cognitive disabilities are capable of following inquiry-based science exploration and interacting with the vocabulary related to such lessons (Jimenez, Browder, & Courtade, 2009). Courtade, Browder, Spooner, and DiBiase (2010) later demonstrated that students with severe disabilities can successfully engage in the scientific process through a carefully designed task analysis. This process truly becomes a life-long skill of learning how to discover answers (Spooner, Browder, & Jimenez, 2011). The process of inquiry includes (a) asking a scientific question, (b) giving a response from what is known, (c) organizing evidence, (d) making connections to scientific knowledge, and (e) communicating results. Every step of this process can be modified to provide access to scientific inquiry and the ability to participate in such inquiry. Teachers can benefit from learning how to provide instruction and assistance to students as they learn to modify the inquiry process (Courtade et al., 2010).

Vocabulary related to science can be specific and challenging to all students, but teachers must bypass text comprehension and use strategies discussed in literacy to learn new word meanings in general vocabulary building (Hudson, Browder, & Jimenez, 2014). To make the vocabulary meaningful, teachers need to ensure instruction builds the background knowledge and provides hand-on experience (Courtade et al., 2008). Another science vocabulary accommodation is to have students focus on the broad concepts or "big ideas" only and then determine ability to generalize this learning into new settings. The teaching technique called *multiple exemplars,* which involves providing the students with multiple examples so that generalization is achieved (Cooper, Heron, & Heward, 2007), has been shown to be successful with this population (Gena, Krantz, McClannahan, & Poulson, 1996; Taylor, Collins, Schuster, & Kleinert, 2002).

Recently, science, technology, engineering, and math (STEM) has been associated with instruction at all levels, from preschool to secondary grades. The acronym has even been extended to STEAM, including the arts, or artistic expression related to art, drama, and music (http://steamedu.com/). Students with intellectual disability are often included and instructed in the same artistic expression classes as students without disabilities, but when these subjects are integrated and recombined, STEAM provides an organizer for meaningful instruction for all students in integrating academics and the arts. Students may have similar or different abilities within the arts that do not depend on intellectual ability. Hammel (2004) suggests using open communication to support highly motivated students in music, since there is a wide variation in music aptitude and achievement that transcends disability category. By modifying the instructional program, knowing how to modify the physical environment, encourage social interaction, and adapt materials for individual differences, elementary teachers supporting the arts and music can provide effective instruction to all students.

Mathematics

As with English language arts and literacy, teachers must also provide instruction in mathematics to students with intellectual disability. Historically, instruction for this population focused on the functional skills of money and time measurement (Ryndak & Alper, 2003; Snell & Brown, 2006)—but now it is believed that students with intellectual disability can absorb more difficult skills than first imagined (Jimenez, Browder, & Courtade, 2008). Browder, Spooner, and Trela (2011) mention that although instruction may have focused on functional skills, we need to prepare students for the community with skills beyond understanding and counting money. In a meta-analysis examining more than 70 studies in math for students with severe disabilities, almost all instruction was in numbers and operations ($n = 37$) or money management ($n = 36$) (Browder, Spooner, Spooner, Ahlgrim-Delzell,

Wakeman, & Harris, 2008). Rather than limiting students with intellectual disability to a small amount of information, teachers should set priorities to broaden instruction to all areas of math to which peers are exposed (Browder et al., 2011). Teachers should develop instructional strategies to address each of the broad areas of mathematics listed in the next sections.

Broad Areas of Mathematics

The National Council of Teachers in Mathematics (NCTM) identified five broad areas of math that underline all curriculum outcomes: (a) numbers and operations, (b) measurement, (c) data analysis, (d) geometry, and (e) algebra. Students in the elementary grades can benefit from instruction in each and every one of these areas.

Number and Operations

The concepts of number and operations are the foundation of all mathematics and a primary focus of elementary schools (NCTM, 2000). Concepts under this domain include the basics of 1:1 correspondence through fractions and decimals in upper elementary grades. Students with severe disabilities typically need instruction in these fundamental concepts beyond elementary school. Teachers have historically focused on continuous practice of basic computational skills without allowing students to progress in concepts. An underlying belief permeated the field that students must first master prerequisite skills prior to moving onto advanced concepts (Woodward & Montague, 2002). However, to expose students to the breadth of math concepts, teachers must learn to move to higher-order concepts while continuing to develop number and operations. Many strategies exist to aid teachers with developing these concepts in early grades. The use of manipulation, mnemonics, and songs can be beneficial. Typically, in the beginning, teachers pair visuals with the abstract representation of numerals to help advance such concepts.

Measurement

Measurement involves the concepts that objects have attributes and there is a common language in mathematics to describe them. Elementary terms such as *big* and *small* fall in this category. Students in early grades may separate or categorize objects by simple attributes while in upper elementary grades concepts of area, volume, and weight are explored (NCTM, 2000). Many measurement concepts such as money and time management are included in the broad category of functional math. The majority of research related to teaching math involves these skills (Browder & Grasso, 1999). Multiple strategies including *Next-Dollar* (Ayres, Langone, Bon, & Norman, 2006; Colyer & Collins, 1996) and determining dollar equivalence (Stoddard, Brown, Hurlbert, Manoli, & McIlvane, 1989) have been researched and found effective for students with intellectual disability. More current studies with students with intellectual disability (Ayres et al., 2006) are stressing the importance of community settings and utilizing technology. Similarly, an evidence base exists for teaching time management with popular strategies such as schedule following (Browder, Cooper, & Lim, 1998) and using the clock to signify important times (Thurlow & Turnure, 1977).

Data Analysis

Generally speaking, data analysis allows students to organize information in a meaningful way to communicate findings through charts and graphs (NCTM, 2000). Leinhardt, Zaslavsky, and Stein (1990) stressed that children with disabilities should be able to interpret graphs and charts. Thus, there is more emphasis on visually presented information. Starting at early grades may allow this skill (the ability to interpret graphical information) to develop. Teachers can then, through prompting, scaffolding, and targeting questions, help students to interact with the information. Because no research on this skill exists, it is difficult to know the possibilities of educational outcomes. However, given that students with intellectual disability have been successful with other targeted skills (Browder, Jimenez, & Trela, 2012; Wei, Lenz, & Blackorby, 2012), it is certainly a promising area to explore.

Geometry

Geometry includes simple recognition of shapes, but it also involves additional concepts. Researchers in mathematics (Browder et al., 2011) suggest shape recognition creates a foundation but instruction should focus on additional skills. The concepts embedded in the geometry domain include an entire framework for learning to work in various planes and spatial-geometric concepts is critical. Sarama, Clements, Swaminathan, McMillen, and Gonzalez Gomez (2003) associate this reasoning with the ability to read maps and understand place in space. Early elementary objectives include exposure to directional terms used in spatial orientation while upper elementary instruction develops the Cartesian plane and precise location on grids and maps (NCTM, 2000). Browder et al. (2011) suggested the use of Investigations Geo-Logo software (TERC, 2006), which has been used repeatedly in elementary classrooms to assist young children in understanding the relationships within coordinate planes.

Algebra

Algebra instruction encourages students to see patterns, relations, and functions through numbers (NCTM, 2000). Students will build on early patterns, through numbers and colors, into complex numerical patterns required to predict future outcomes. Algebra may be considered a topic that is unobtainable or inappropriate to students with intellectual disability in elementary schools. However, Jimenez et al. (2008) were able to utilize a nine-step task analysis for students to learn a functional task in algebra. Their findings suggest that students with intellectual disability are capable of completing complex tasks with the correct supports. Skills to target in elementary school to promote critical thinking in secondary grades include reading or having access to story problems that are based on real life. This involves the comprehension of what is being asked and the ability to determine needed and unneeded information. Another skill targeted in elementary school is determining what operation is needed (addition, subtraction, multiplication, and division) to solve each problem (Browder et al., 2011).

Instructional Methods within Mathematics

Browder et al. (2008) recommend the use of systematic instruction coupled with task-analytic instruction and prompting as an instructional strategy to promote math skills. Task analysis has long been identified as a positive instructional strategy for teaching functional skills (Browder, Snell, & Wildonger, 1988; Haring Kennedy, Adams, & Pitts-Conway, 1987). There is emerging research that shows students with intellectual disability who are receiving targeted instruction in mathematics make gains in curriculum-based assessment (Browder et al., 2010). Promising emerging practices include systematic prompting, task analysis, and connecting learning to real-life situations (Browder et al., 2008). However, teachers must accept that mathematics skills do not have to be taught in a sequential order: Students can progress to broader skills without mastering each and every initial skill thought to be necessary. It is unrealistic or inappropriate to expect students with limited cognitive ability and other limitations to master every sequential skill. However, providing accommodations such as a calculator or other technological accommodations can help students to move forward. Using graphic organizers is another option for providing accommodations and support (Garjaria, Jitendra, Sood, & Sacks, 2007).

Even though we are discussing elementary grades, the overarching goal in all instruction, whether for students receiving special education services or not, is to increase independence and improve future postsecondary outcomes. This is imperative for students with intellectual disability. Therefore, Browder et al. (2011) argued that the most critical mathematical skills should enable students to solve real-world problems. Although research in this field is preliminary, findings suggest that most math difficulties relate to "poor computation skills, difficulties with long-term and working memory, poor conceptual understanding, poor strategy selection for problem solving, and impaired self-monitoring" (Wei, Lenz, & Blackorby, 2012, p. 154). Students with intellectual and developmental disabilities are at higher risk of facing these challenges. However, with systematic instruction (Browder et al., 2008) students with these disabilities can be successful in learning advanced math skills.

Social-Emotional and Other Learning

Elementary teachers must also implement social-emotional instruction, which is integrated into all areas of the CCSS. For example, a search of the CCSS in literacy or mathematics results in words such as *discussing, collaborating, questioning,* and *describing.* These words implicitly embed social-emotional learning into the decidedly academic CCSS, and teachers must be prepared to integrate social awareness and ability into classroom practices. A number of other concepts related to social awareness and relationship management call for students to be good listeners, use perspective taking, and be able to predict behavior of others.

Self-regulation in both academic and social activities is another aspect related to social-emotional support that elementary teachers must address. Achievement goals are driven by motivation, according to Zimmerman (2000). Mithaug (2013) describes self-determined learning as having three factors: (a) self-interest (to drive self-regulating behaviors), (b) self-regulation (or thoughts and actions), and (c) persistent adjustment (continuous regulation of thoughts and actions to achieve learning). In other words, you become a self-determined learner by being interested in what you are learning, regulating yourself within the task, and constantly discovering what works or doesn't for specific learning activities or being persistent in finding a way to learn. Mithaug also suggests having a plan of action to achieve. One method that uses all of these elements, including a plan of action, is the Self-Determined Learning Model of Instruction (SDLMI; Wehmeyer et al., 2000). This model consists of three phases for a student to accomplish (Set a Goal, What's Your Plan?, Evaluate Your Plan or Goal) with the teacher scaffolding Teacher Objectives and Learning Support strategies.

With student input as the process unfolds, a plan is set up, and self-evaluation takes place, thus infusing motivation into the learning process for young learners of strategies and principles of self-determination. Cognitive engagement is a direct outcome of both motivation and self-determination (Walker, Greene, & Mansell, 2006). Payton et al. (2008) reviewed studies that promoted social-emotional competence and decision making and found a positive impact on academic outcomes, including on school grades and standardized achievement test scores. Miller and Brickman (2004) stated that students will put forth effort only in an activity or towards a goal they perceive as important. In addition, understanding goal mastery related to self-determined learning leads to better social adjustment (Levy & Williams, 2004).

Summary

Effective and evidence-based instruction at the elementary school level encourages children with intellectual disability in accessing the general curriculum via grade-level standards, in this instance represented by the CCSS. Inclusive education means education for all in a common environment that supports learning. Using UDL as a planning mechanism encourages all students to engage in activities via less-individualized instruction. However, many students may still need additional accommodations, alterations, and scaffolding to access curricular content. Use of evidence-based practices ensures that all students receive effective instructional practices in the areas of literacy (reading, writing, and communication) beyond reading instruction in the cognitive areas of social studies and science. In addition, teaching all areas of mathematics to all students provides access to this essential part of learning, no matter what teachers often perceive about every student's abilities. High expectations drive instruction and learning, both for teachers and families. Directed and embedded instruction in social-emotional learning also supports all students. Self-determined learning is one strategy that students of all ages can use to become more motivated to learn while targeting needed areas of emphasis, which are self- and teacher-identified.

Research shows that in the past we have underestimated the ability and interest of students with intellectual disability to engage in learning at all levels. Starting in the preschool and then elementary grades is one way to ensure that students with intellectual disability are included in classrooms with their general education peers, gain access to the same general curriculum that peers without disabilities experience, have more robust postschool outcomes, are better prepared for a career, and better informed for life. Teachers at the elementary level should embrace high expectations and self-determined learning. They should also bring positive attitudinal expectations and methodologies to school each day to support excellent instruction within inclusive settings for students with intellectual disability.

References

Allor, J. H., Mathes, P. G., Jones, F. G., Chanokun, T. M., & Cheatham, J. P. (2010). Individualized research-based reading instruction for students with intellectual disabilities: Success stories. *Teaching Exceptional Children, 42*, 6–12.

Allor, J. H., Mathes, P. G., Roberts, J. K., Cheatham, J. P., & Otaiba, S. A. (2014). Is scientifically based reading instruction effective for students with below-average IQs? *Exceptional Children, 80*, 287–306.

Arthur-Kelly, M., Foreman, P., Bennett, D., & Pascoe, S. (2008). Interaction, inclusion and students with profound and multiple disabilities: Toward an agenda for research and practice. *Journal of Research in Special Education Needs, 9*, 161–166.

Ayres, K. M., Langone, J., Bon, R. T., & Norman, A. (2006). Computer-based instruction for purchasing skills. *Education and Training in Developmental Disabilities, 41*, 253–263.

Bandura, A. (1994). *Self-efficacy: The exercise of control.* New York: Academic Press.

Barbetta, P. M., Heward, W. L., & Bradley, D. M. C. (1993). Relative effects of whole-word and phonetic—prompt error correction on the acquisition and maintenance of sight words by students with developmental disabilities. *Journal of Applied Behavior Analysis, 26*, 99–110.

Beck, J., McKowan, M., & Kucan, L. (2002). *Robust vocabulary instruction.* New York: Guilford.

Borman, G., & Dowling, M. (2010). Schools and inequality: A multilevel analysis of Coleman's equality of educational opportunity data. *The Teachers College Record, 112*, 1–2.

Bradford, S., Shippen, M. E., Alberto, P., Houchins, D., & Flors, M. (2006). Using systematic instruction to teach decoding skills to middle school students with moderate intellectual disabilities. *Education and Training in Developmental Disabilities, 41*, 333–343.

Browder, D. M., Ahlgrim-Delzell, L., Flowers, C., & Baker, J. N. (2012). An evaluation of multicomponent early literacy program for students with severe developmental disabilities. *Remedial and Special Education, 33*, 237–246.

Browder, D. M., Cooper, K., & Lim, L. (1998). Teaching adults with severe disabilities to express their choice of settings for leisure activities. *Education and Training in Mental Retardation and Developmental Disabilities, 33*, 226–236.

Browder, D. M., Gibbs, S. L., Ahlgrim-Delzell, L., Courtade, G., & Lee, A. (2007). *Early literacy skills builder.* Verona, WI: Attainment.

Browder, D. M., Gibbs, S. L., Ahlgrim-Delzell, L., Courtade, G., Mraz, M., & Flowers, C. (2009). Literacy for students with severed developmental disabilities: What should we teach and what should we hope to achieve? *Remedial and Special Education, 30*, 269–282.

Browder, D. M. & Grasso, E. (1999). Teaching money skills to individuals with mental retardation: A research review with practical applications. *Remedial and Special Education, 20*, 297–308.

Browder, D. M., Jimenez, B., & Trela, K. (2012). Grade-aligned math instruction for secondary students with moderate intellectual disabilities. *Education and Training in Autism and Developmental Disabilities, 47*, 373–388.

Browder, D. M., Snell, M. E., & Wildonger, B. (1988). Simulation and community-based instruction of vending machines with time delay. *Education and Training in Mental Retardation, 23*, 175–185.

Browder, D. M., & Spooner, F. (2006). *Teaching language arts, math, and science to students with significant cognitive disabilities*. Baltimore: Brooks.

Browder, D. M., & Spooner, F. (2011). *Teaching students with moderate and severe disabilities*. New York: Guilford Press.

Browder, D. M., & Spooner, F. (2014). *More language arts, math, and science*. Baltimore, MD: Paul H. Brookes.

Browder, D. M., Spooner, F., Ahlgrim-Delzell, L., Wakeman, S. Y., & Harris, A. (2008). A meta-analysis on teaching mathematics to students with significant cognitive disabilities. *Exceptional Children, 74*, 407–432.

Browder, D. M., Spooner, F., & Mims, P. (2011). Communication skills. In D. M. Browder, & F. Spooner (Eds.), *Teaching students with moderate and severe disabilities* (pp. 262–282). New York: Guilford Press.

Browder, D. M., Spooner, F., & Trela, K. (2011). Mathematics. In D. M. Browder & F. Spooner (Eds.), *Teaching students with moderate and severe disabilities* (pp. 168–200). New York: Guilford Press.

Browder, D. M., Spooner, F., & Zakas, T. L. (2011). Social student. In D. M. Browder & F. Spooner (Eds.), *Teaching students with moderate and severe disabilities* (pp. 222–240). New York: Guilford Press.

Browder, D. M., Trela, K., Courtade, G. R., Jimenez, B. A. Knight, V., & Flowers, C. (2010). Teaching mathematics and science standards to students with moderate and severed developmental disabilities. *The Journal of Special Education, 46*, 26–35. doi:10.1177/0022466910369942

Browder, D. M., Wakeman, S. Y., Spooner, F., Ahlgrim-Delzell, L., & Algozzine, B. (2006). Research on reading instruction for individuals with significant cognitive disabilities. *Exceptional Children, 72*, 392–408.

Browder, D. M., & Xin, Y. P. (1998). A meta-analysis and review of sight word research and its implications for teaching functional reading to individuals with moderate and severe disabilities. *The Journal of Special Education, 32*, 130–153.

Brown, L., Neitupski, J., & Hamre-Neitupski, S. (1976). The criterion of ultimate functioning. In M. A. Thomas (Ed.), *Hey, don't forget about me* (pp. 2–15). Reston, VA: Council for Exceptional Children.

Burgess, S., Hecht, S., & Lonigan, C. (2002). Relations of the home literacy environments (HLE) to the development of reading-related abilities: A one-year longitudinal study. *Reading Research Quarterly, 37*, 408–426.

Cabral-Marquez, C. (2015). Motivating readers: Helping students set and attain personal reading goals. *Reading Teacher, 68*, 464–472.

Caffrey, E., & Fuchs, D. (2007). Difference in performance between students with learning disabilities and mild mental retardation: Implications for categorical instruction. *Learning Disabilities Research and Practice, 22*, 119–128.

Carnine, D. W., Silbert, J., Kame'enui, E. J., Tarver, S. G. (2004). *Direct instruction reading* (4th ed.). Upper Saddle River, NJ: Pearson Prentice Hall.

CAST. (2011). Universal design for learning guidelines version 2.0. Retrieved from http://www.udlcenter.org/aboutudl/udlguildeines/downloads

Chapman, J. W., Tunmer, W. E., & Prochnow, J. E. (2000). Early reading-related skills and performance, reading self-concept, and the development of academic self-concept: A longitudinal study. *Journal of Educational Psychology, 92*, 703–708.

Chorzempa, B. F., & Graham, S. (2006). Primary-grade teachers' use of within-class ability grouping in reading. *Journal of Educational Psychology, 98*, 529–541.

Ciullo, S. (2015). Improving access to elementary school social studies instruction: Strategies to support students with learning disabilities. *Teaching Exceptional Children, 48*, 102–109.

Colorado Department of Special Education. (2014, January). Special education within a multi-tiered system of supports. Retrieved from http://www.cde.state.co.us/sites/default/files/SPEDandMTSS_2_5_14.pdf

Colyer, S. P. & Collins, B. C. (1996). Using national cues within prompt levels to teach the next dollar strategy to students with disabilities. *Journal of Special Education, 30*, 305–318.

Cook, B. G., & Cook, S. C. (2015). Unraveling evidence-based practices in special education. *The Journal of Special Education, 47*, 71–82. doi:10.1177/0022466911420877

Cook, T. D., & Campbell, D. T. (1979). *Quasi-experimentation: Design and analysis issues for field settings*. Boston: Houghton Mifflin.

Copeland, S. R., Hughes C., Carter, E. W., Guth, C., Pressley, J. A., Williams, C. R, & Fowler, S. E. (2004). Increasing access to general education: Perspectives of participants in a high school peer support program. *Remedial and Special Education, 25*, 342–352.

Cooper, J. O., Heron, T. E., & Heward, W. L. (2007). *Applied behavior analysis* (2nd ed.). Upper Saddle River, NJ: Pearson Prentice Hall.

Courtade, G., Browder, D. M., Spooner, F., & DiBiase, W. (2010). Training teachers to use an inquiry-based task analysis to teach science to students with moderate ad severe disabilities. *Education and Training in Developmental Disabilities, 45*, 378–399.

Courtade, G. Jimenez, B., Trella, K., & Browder, D. M. (2008). *Teaching to standards: Science: A inquiry-based approach for middle and high school students with moderate and severe disabilities.* Verona, WI: Attainment.

Deci, E. L., & Ryan, R. M. (1985) *Intrinsic motivation and self-determination in human behavior.* New York: Plenum.

Deci, E. L., & Ryan, R. M. (2000). The "what" and "why" of goal pursuits: Human needs and the self-determination of behavior. *Psychological Inquiry, 11*(4), 227–268. doi:10.1207/s15327965pli1104_01

Denton, C. A., & Hocker, J. L. (2006). *Responsive reading instruction: Flexible intervention for struggling readers in the early grades.* Longmont, CO: Sopris West.

Dicarlo, C. F., & Meher, B. (2000). Using voice output devises to increase initiations of young children with disabilities. *Journal of Early Intervention, 23*, 191–199.

Downing, J. E. (2005). *Teaching communication skills to students with severe disabilities* (2nd ed.). Baltimore: Brookes.

Downing, J. E. (2008). *Including students with severe and multiple disabilities in typical classrooms: Practical strategies for teachers* (3rd ed.). Baltimore, MD: Brookes.

Downing, J. E. & MacFarland, S. (2010). Education and individuals with severe disabilities: Promising practices. In *International encyclopedia of rehabilitation* (pp. 1–11). Buffalo, NY: Center for International Rehabilitation Research Information and Exchange.

Durrell, D. D. (1958). Success in first-grade reading. *Journal of Education, 148*, 1–8.

Engelmann, S., Haddox, P., Hanner, S., & Osborn, J., (2002). *Corrective reading thinking basics: Comprehension level A.* Columbus, OH: SRA/McGraw-Hill.

Epstein, J. L. (2010). *School, family, and community partnerships: Preparing educators and improving schools.* New York: Westview Press.

Fisher, D., Flood, J., Lapp, D., & Frey, N. (2004). Interactive read-alouds: Is there a common set of implementation practices? *Reaching Teacher, 58*, 8–17.

Fisher, M, Meyer, L. H. (2002). Development and social competence after two years for students enrolled in inclusive and self-contained educational programs. *Research and Practice for Persons with Severe Disabilities, 27*, 165–174.

Fives, A., Russell, D., Kearns, N., Lyons, R., Eaton, P., Canavan J.,. . . O'Brien, A. (2014). The association between academic self-beliefs and reading achievement among children at risk of reading failure. *Journal of Research in Reading, 37*, 215–232.

Flores, M. M., & Ganz, J. (2009). Effects of direction instruction on the reading comprehension of students with autism and developmental disabilities. *Education and Training in Developmental Disabilities, 44*, 39–53.

Foorman, B. R., & Torgesen, J. (2001). Critical elements of classroom and small-group instruction promote reading success in all children. *Learning Disabilities Research & Practice, 16*, 203–212.

Foreman, P., Arthur-Kelly, M., Bennett, D., Neilands, J., & Colyvas, K. (2014). Observed changes in the alertness and communicative involvement of students with multiple and severe disability following in-class mentor modeling for staff in segregated and general education classrooms. *Journal of Intellectual Disability Research, 58*, 704–720.

Foreman, P., Arthur-Kelly, M., Pascoe, S., King, B. S. (2004). Evaluating the educational experiences of children with profound and multiple disabilities in inclusive and segregated classroom setting: An Australian perspective. *Research and Practice for Persons with Severe Disabilities, 29*, 183–193.

Francis, D. J. (1996). Development of lag versus deficit models of reading disability: A longitudinal, individual growth curse analysis. *Journal of Educational Psychology, 88*, 3–17.

Freeman, J., Simonsen, B., McCoach, B., Sugai, G., Lombardi, A., & Horner, R., (2016). Relationship between school-wide positive behavior interventions and supports and academic, attendance, and behavior outcomes in high schools. *Journal of Positive Behavior Interventions, 18*, 41–51.

Frost, L., & Bondy, A. (2002). *The pictures exchange communication system training manual.* Newark, DE: Pyramid Educational.

Garjaria, M., Jitendra, A. K., Sood, S., & Sacks, G. (2007). Improving comprehension of expository text in students with LD: A research synthesis. *Journal of Learning Disabilities, 40*, 210–225.

Gena, A., Krantz, P. J., McClannahan, L. E., & Poulson, C. L. (1996). Training and generalization of affective behavior displayed by youth with autism. *Journal of Applied Behavior Analysis, 29*, 291–304.

Gersten, R., Fuchs, L. S., Compton, D., Coyne, M., Greenwood, C., & Innocenti, M. S. (2005). Quality indicators for group experimental and quasi-experimental research in special education. *Exceptional Children, 71*, 149–164.

Goldstein, H. (2011). Knowing what to teach provides a roadmap for early literacy intervention. *Journal of Early Intervention, 33*, 268–280.

Graham, S., Gillespie, A., & McKeown, D. (2013). Writing: Importance, development, and instruction. *Reading and Writing, 26,* 1–15.

Greenwood, C. (2009). *Introduction roadmap to pre-K RTI: Applying response to intervention in preschool settings.* New York: National Center for Learning Disabilities.

Guthrie, J. T., & Davis, M. (2003). Motivating struggling readers in middle school through an engagement model of classroom practice. *Reading & Writing Quarterly, 19,* 59–85. doi:10.1080/10573560308203

Guthrie, J. T., & Knowles, K. (2001). Promoting reading motivation. In L. Verhoven & C. Snow (Eds.), *Literacy and motivation: Reading engagement in individuals and groups* (pp. 159–176). Mahwah, NJ: Lawrence Erlbaum.

Guthrie, J. T., Wigfield, A., Metsala, J. L., & Cox, K. E. (1999). Motivational and cognitive predictors of text comprehension and reading amount. *Scientific Studies of Reading, 3,* 231–256. doi:10.1207/s1532799xssr0303_3

Hammel, A. M. (2004). Inclusion strategies that work. *Music Educator's Journal, 90,* 33–37.

Hancock, T. B., & Kaiser, A. P. (2002). The effects of trainer-implemented enhanced milieu teaching on the social communication of children with autism. *Topics in Early Childhood Special Education, 22,* 39–54.

Haring, T. G., Kennedy, C. H., Adams, M. J., & Pitts-Conway, V. (1987). Teaching generalization of purchasing skills across community settings to autistic youth using videotape modeling. *Journal of Applied Behavior Analysis, 20,* 89–96.

Hitchcock, C. G., Meyer, A., Rose, D., & Jackson, R. (2005). Equal access, participation, and progress in the general education curriculum. In D. Rose, A. Meyer, & C. Hitchcock (Eds.), *The universally designed classroom: Accessible curriculum and digital technologies* (pp. 37–68). Cambridge, MA: Harvard Education Press.

Horner, R. H., Carr, E. G., Halle, J., McGee, G., Odom, S., & Wolery, M. (2005). The use of single-subject research to identify evidence-based practice in special education. *Exceptional Children, 71,* 165–179.

Hudson, M. E., Browder, D. M., & Jimenez, B. (2014). Effects of a peer-delivered system of least prompts intervention and adapted science read-alouds on listening comprehension for participants with moderate intellectual disabilities. *Education and Training in Autism and Developmental Disabilities, 49,* 60–77.

Institute for the Development of Educational Achievement. (2004). *Big ideas in reading.* Retrieved from http://reading.uoregon.edu/

Jackson, L., Ryndak, D. L., & Billingsley, F. (2000). Useful practices in inclusive education: A preliminary view of what experts in moderate to severe disabilities are saying. *The Journal of the Association for Person with Severe Handicaps, 25,* 129–141.

Jameson, J. M., McDonnell, J., Polychronic, S., & Riesen, T. (2008). Embedded, constant time delay instruction by peers without disabilities in general education classrooms. *Intellectual and Developmental Disabilities, 46,* 346–363.

Jenkins, J., & Terjeson, K. J. (2011). Monitoring reading growth: Goal setting, measurement frequency, and methods of evaluation. *Learning Disabilities Research & Practice, 26,* 28–35.

Jimenez, B. A., Browder, D. M., & Courtade, G. R. (2008). Teaching an algebraic equation to high school students with moderate developmental disabilities. *Education and Training in Developmental Disabilities, 43,* 266–274.

Jimenez, B. A., Browder, D. M., & Courtade, G. R. (2009). An exploratory study of self-directed science concepts learning by students with moderate intellectual disabilities. *Research and Practice for Persons with Severe Disabilities, 34,* 33–46.

Jimenez, B. A., Spooner, F., Browder, D. M., DiBiase, W., & Knight, V. (2008). A conceptual model for science for students with significant cognitive disabilities. [Brochure]. Retrieved from education.uncc.edu/access on December 21, 2015

Katims, D. S. (2000). Literacy instruction for people with mental retardation: Historical highlights and contemporary analysis. *Education and Training in Mental Retardation & Developmental Disabilities, 35,* 3–15.

Kliewer, C., Biklen, D., & Kasa-Hendrickson, C. (2006). Who may be literate? Disability and resistance to the cultural denial of competence. *American Education Research Journal, 12,* 163–192.

Klinger, J. K., & Vaughan, S. (1999). Promoting reading comprehension, content learning, and English acquisition through collaborative strategic reading. *Reading Teacher, 52,* 738–747.

Koppenhaver, D. A. & Yoder, D. E. (1993). Classroom literacy instruction for children with severe speech and physical impairments: What is and what might be. *Topics in Language Disorders, 13,* 1–15.

Kutner, M., Greenberg, E., Jin, Y., Boyle, B., Hsu, Y., & Dunleavy, E. (2007). *Literacy in everyday life: Results from the 2003 National Assessment of Adult Literacy (NCES 2007–480).* Washington, DC: National Center for Education Statistics, Institute of Education Sciences, US Department of Education.

LaBerge, D., & Samuels, S. (1974). Toward a theory of automatic information processing in reading. *Cognitive Psychology, 6,* 293–323.

Leary, M. R. (1999) Making sense of self-esteem. *JSTOR, American Psychological Society,* 32–35.

Leinhardt, G., Zaslavsky, O., & Stein, M. K. (1990). Functions, graphs, and graphing: Tasks, learning, and teaching. *Review of Educational Research, 60,* 1–64.

Lemons, C. J., Mrachko, A. A., Kostewicz, D. E., & Paterra, M. F. (2012). Effectiveness of decoding and phonological awareness intervention for children with Down Syndrome. *Exceptional Children, 79,* 67–90.

Levy, P. E. & Williams, J. (2004). The social context of performance appraisal: A review and framework for the future. *Journal of Management, 30*, 881–905.

Lewis, T. J., & Sugai, G. (1999). Effectives behavior support: A systems approach to proactive school wide management. *Focus on Exceptional Children, 31*, 1–24.

Mata, L. (2011). Motivation for reading and writing in kindergarten children. *Reading Psychology, 32*, 272–299.

Miller, R. B. & Brickman, S. J. (2004). A model of future-oriented motivation and self-regulation. *Education Psychology Review, 16*(1), 9–35.

Mithaug, D. E. (2013). Self-determined learning. In M. L. Wehmeyer (Ed.), *The Oxford handbook of positive psychology and disability* (pp. 137–153). New York: Oxford University Press.

Morrow, L. M. & Gambrell, L. B. (2002) Literature-based instruction in the early years. In S. B. Neuman & D. K. Dickinson (Eds.), *Handbook of early literacy research* (pp. 348–360). New York: Guilford.

Mraz, M., Padak, N. D., & Rasinski, T. V. (2008). *Evidence-based instruction in reading: A professional development guide to fluency instruction.* Boston: Allyn & Bacon.

National Council for Social Studies. (2002). *National standards for social students teachers.* Washington, DC: Author. Retrieved from www.socialstudies.org

National Council of the Teachers of Mathematics (NCTM). (2000). *Principles and standards for school mathematics.* Reston, VA: Author.

National Reading Panel. (2000). *Teaching children to read: An evidence-based assessment of the scientific research literature on reading and its implications for reading instruction.* Rockville, MD: NICHD.

National Research Council. (1996). *National science education standards.* Washington, DC: National Academy Press.

Neitzel, J., & Wolery, M. (2009). *Steps for implementation: Time delay.* Chapel Hill, NC: The National Professional Development Center on Autism Spectrum Disorders, Frank Porter Graham Child Development Institute, The University of North Carolina. http://csesa.fpg.unc.edu/sites/csesa.fpg.unc.edu/files/ebpbriefs/Time Delay_Steps_0.pdf

Nguyen, N. (2010). Early post-school outcomes of indigenous youth: The role of literacy and numeracy: Longitudinal surveys of Australian youth (Vol. Briefing Paper 22). Adelaide, South Australia NCVER.

Noels, K. A., Pelletier, L. G., Clement, R., & Vallerand, R. J. (2000). Why are you learning a second language? Motivational orientations and self-determination theory. *Language Learning, 50*, 57–85. doi:10.1111/0023–8333.00111

O'Connor, E. E., Cappella, E., McCormick, M. P., & McClowry, S. G. (2014). An examination of the efficacy of INSIGHTS in enhancing academic and behavioral development of children in early grades. *Journal of Educational Psychology.* Advance online publication. http://dx.doe.org/10.1037/a0036615

Palmer, S. B., Butera, G. D., Classen, A., & Kang. J. (2016). Addressing challenging behaviors. In E. M. Horn, S. B. Palmer, G. D. Butera, & J. Lieber (Eds.), *Six steps to inclusive preschool curriculum* (pp. 161–182). Baltimore, MD: Paul H. Brookes.

Palmer, S. B., & Wehmeyer, M. L. (2003). Promoting self-determination in early elementary school: Teaching self-regulated problem-solving and goal-setting skills. *Remedial and Special Education, 24*, 115–126.

Payton, J., Weissberg, R. P., Durlak, J. A., Dyminicki, A. B., Taylor, R. D., Schellinger, K. B., & Pachan, M. (2008). The positive impact of social and emotional learning for kindergarten to eighth-grade students. Retrieved from http://files.eric.ed.gov/fulltext/ED505370.pdf

Peacock, G. G., & Collett, B. R. (2010). *Collaborative home/school interventions: Evidence-based solutions for emotional, behavioral, and academic problems.* New York: Guildford.

Ryan, R. M., & Deci, E. L. (2000). Self-determination theory and the facilitation of intrinsic motivation, social development, and well-being. *American Psychologist, 55*, 68–78. doi:10.1037/0003–066X.55.1.68

Ryndak, D. L., & Alper, S. (2003). *Curriculum and instruction for students with significant disabilities in inclusive settings* (2nd ed.). Boston: Allyn & Bacon.

Sarama, J., Clements, D. H., Swaminathan, S., McMillen, S., & Gonzalez Gomez, R. M. (2003). Development of mathematical concepts of two-dimensional space in grid-environments: An exploratory story. *Cognition and Instruction, 21*, 285–324.

Scruggs, T. E., & Mastropieri, M. A. (1995). Science and students with mental retardation: An analysis of curriculum features and learner characteristics. *Science Education, 79*, 251–271.

Shymansky, J. A., Kyle, W. C., & Alport, J. M. (1983). The effects of new science curriculum on student performance. *Journal of Research in Science Teaching, 20*, 387–404.

Siegel-Causey, E., & Bashinski, S. M. (1997). Enhancing initial communication and responsiveness of learners with multiple-disabilities: A tri-focus framework for partners. *Focus on Autism and Other Developmental Disabilities, 12*, 105–120.

Sigafoos, J., Arthur-Kelly, M., & Butterfield, N. (2006). *Enhancing everyday communication for children with disabilities.* Baltimore, MD: Brookes.

Simmons, D. C., & Kame'enui, E. J. (1998). *What reading research tells us about children with diverse learning needs: Bases and basics*. Mahwah, NJ: Lawrence, Erlbaum.

Smith, B. R., Spooner, F., Jimenez, B., & Browder, D. M. (2013). Using early science curriculum to teach science vocabulary concepts to students with severe developmental disabilities. *Education & Treatment of Children, 36*, 1–31.

Smith, S. B., Simmons, D. C., & Kame'enui, E. J. (1998). Phonological awareness: Instructional and curricular basics and implications. In D. C. Simmons & E. J. Kame'enui (Eds.), *What reading research tells us about children with diverse learning needs: Bases and basics* (pp. 129–140). Mahwah, NJ: Lawrence Erlbaum.

Snell, M. E., & Brown, F. (2006). *Instruction of students with severe disabilities* (6th ed.). Upper Saddle River, NJ: Pearson.

Snow, C. (2002). *Reading for understanding: Toward a research and development program in reading comprehension*. Santa Monica, CA: Rand.

Spooner, F., Browder, D. M., Jimenez, B. (2011). Science. In D. M. Browder & F. Spooner (Eds.), *Teaching students with moderate and severe disabilities* (pp. 201–221). New York: Guilford Press.

Spooner, F., Knight, V. F., Browder, D. M., Jimenez, B., & DiBiase, W. (2011). Evaluating evidence-based practices in teaching science content to students with severe developmental disabilities. *Research and Practice for Persons with Severe Disabilities, 36*, 62–75.

Spooner, F., Knight, V. F., Browder, D. M., & Smith, B. R. (2012). Evidence-based practices for teaching academic skills to students with severe developmental disabilities. *Remedial and Special Education, 33*, 374–387.

Spooner, F., Stem, B., & Test, D. (1989). Teaching first-aid skills to adolescents who are moderately mentally handicapped. *Education and Training of the Mentally Retarded, 19*, 114–124.

Stoddard, L. T., Brown, J., Hurlbert, B., Manoli, C., & McIlvane, W. J. (1989). Teaching money skills through stimulus class formation, exclusion, and component matching methods: Three case studies. *Research in Developmental Disabilities, 10*, 413–439.

Sugai, G., & Horner, R. H. (2006). A promising approach for expanding and sustaining school-wide positive behavior support. *School Psychology Review, 35*, 245–259.

Taboada, A., Tonks, S. M., Wigfield, A., & Guthrie, J. T. (2009). Effects of motivational and cognitive variables on reading comprehension. *Reading and Writing, 22*, 85–106. doi:10.1007/s11145–008–9133-y

Taylor, P., Collins, B. C., Schuster, W. J., & Kleinert, H. (2002). Teaching laundry skills to high school students with disabilities: Generalization of targeted skills and non-targeted information. *Education and Training in Mental Retardation and Developmental Disabilities, 37*, 172–183.

TERC, The Investigations Curriculum. (2006). *Geo-logo* (1st ed.) [Computer Software]. Glenview, IL: Pearson Scott Foresman.

Thoma, C., & Palmer, S. B. (2015, December). Issue brief: Education of students with IDD. http://aaidd.org/docs/default-source/National-Goals/education-of-students-with-idd.pdf?sfvrsn=0

Thousand, J. S., Villa, R. A., & Nevin, A. (2007). *Differentiating instruction: Collaborative planning and teaching for universally designed learning*. Thousand Oaks, CA: Corwin Press.

Thurlow, M. L., & Turnure, J. E. (1977). Children's knowledge of time and money: Effective instruction for the mentally retarded. *Education and Training of the Mentally Retarded, 12*, 203–212.

Vecca, J., Vacca, R., Grove, M., Burkey, L., Lenhart, L., & Mckeon, C. (2006). Reading and learning to read (6th ed.). Boston: Allyn & Bacon.

Walker, C., Greene, B., & Mansell, R. (2006). Identification with academics, intrinsic/extrinsic motivation, and self-efficacy as predictors of cognitive engagement. *Learning and Individual Differences, 16*, 1–12.

Walker, H. (2010). Evaluating the effectiveness of apps for mobile devices. *Journal of Special Education Technology, 26*, 59–63.

Webber, J., & Scheuerman, B. (2009). Using naturalistic teaching strategies to build communication skills in students with severe disabilities. In W. L. Heward (Ed.), *Exceptional children: An introduction to special education* (9th ed., pp. 476–477). Upper Saddle River, NJ: Pearson.

Wehmeyer, M. L., Agran, M., Hughes, C., Martin, J. E., Mithaug, D. E., & Palmer, S. B. (2007). *Promoting self-determination in students with developmental disabilities*. New York: Guilford Press.

Wehmeyer, M. L., Palmer, S. B., Agran, M., Mithaug, D. E., & Martin, J. (2000). Teaching students to become causal agents in their lives: The self-determined learning model of instruction. *Exceptional Children, 66*, 439–453.

Wehmeyer, M. L., & Shogren, K. A. (2008). The self-determination of adolescents with intellectual disability. In S. Lopez (Ed.), *Positive psychology perspective series volume III: Growing in the face of diversity* (pp. 89–108). Westport, CT: Greenwood Publishing Group.

Wehmeyer, M. L., & Shogren, K. A. (2013). Self-determination: Getting students involved in leadership. In P. Wehman (Ed.), *Life beyond the classroom: Transition strategies for young people with disabilities* (pp. 41–68). Baltimore, MD: Paul H. Brookes.

Wehmeyer, M. L., Shogren, K. A., Little, T. D., & Lopez, S. (in press). *Handbook on the development of self-determination.* New York: Springer.

Wei, X., Lenz, K. B., & Blackorby, J. (2012). Math growth trajectories of students with disabilities: Disability category, gender, racial, and socioeconomic status differences from ages 7 to 17. *Remedial and Special Education, 34*(3), 154–165. doi:10.1177/0741932512448253

Woodward, J., & Montague, M. (2002) Meeting the challenge of mathematics reform for students with LD. *The Journal of Special Education, 36*, 89–101.

Zakas, T., Browder, D., & Spooner (2009). Effects of using a task analysis to train peers without disabilities to share adapted grade level books with middle school aged students with severe developmental disabilities. Manuscript submitted for publication.

Zimmerman, B. J. (2000). Attaining self-regulation: A social cognitive perspective. In M. Boekaerts, P. R. Pintrich, & M. Zeidner (eds.), *Handbook of self-regulation: Theory, research and applications* (pp. 13–39). San Diego, CA: Academic Press.

23

High-Quality Educational Programs for Students with Intellectual Disability in Middle and Junior High School

Colleen A. Thoma, Kim W. Fisher, Sarah A. Hall,
LaRon A. Scott, Irina Cain, Andrew Wojcik, Brittany Sterret

Introduction

Early adolescence is a time of considerable change in physical, social, cognitive, and moral development for all young people, including students with intellectual disability. Most sources that describe this time period, generally between the ages of 11 through 14, indicate that it is a time of rapid physical development coupled with confusion, excitement, new social situations, and increased reasoning abilities—all of which make this time a thrilling and sometimes challenging time for students, parents, and teachers alike (Repetto, 2012). This chapter will investigate the qualities of educational programs designed for early adolescents with intellectual disability that address these development challenges and that meet the educational goals for students in this age range. We begin with a brief overview of developmental issues that are important for all students.

Middle School Versus Junior High School Model

Although they are often thought to be synonymous, the junior high and middle school models offer two different approaches to create a bridge for students between elementary and high school (Repetto, 2012). Junior high school was created at the beginning of the twentieth century in an effort to encourage young adolescents to stay in school. It typically includes the seventh and eighth grades, exposing students to an environment very similar to high school (Cuban, 1992; Repetto, 2012). Powell (2005) described the junior high model as subject-centered and focused on the students' cognitive development. Classes are academic in nature, and teachers are organized based on the subjects they teach (Powell, 2005). Critics of the junior high school model suggest that it does not address the developmental needs of the young adolescents it serves (Repetto, 2012).

In response to these criticisms, the middle school model was created to provide a curriculum responsive to young adolescents' unique needs and interests (Repetto, 2012). This student-oriented model typically expands its reach to the sixth, seventh, and eighth grades (Powell, 2005; Repetto, 2012). It seeks to promote both cognitive and affective development (Powell, 2005). Much like the junior high model, students move through different classes throughout the day; however, in middle school, teachers and students work in interdisciplinary teams that support learning and provide a sense of community. Academic classes are prerequisite courses used to develop critical skills needed for students to be successful in high school (Repetto, 2012). In addition to the core curriculum, students are provided with exploratory and nonacademic courses, along with mentoring opportunities, in a more flexible schedule (Powell, 2005). These elements of the middle school model work together in an effort to provide a solid learning and social foundation in a time of transition.

Development of Early Adolescents

According to Caskey and Anfara (2014): "[i]n early adolescence, the young adolescent body undergoes more developmental change than at any other time except from birth to two years old" (Physical Development Characteristics section, para. 1). In the middle school years, students experience numerous biological and cognitive changes (Caskey & Anfara, 2014). Between the ages of 10 and 15 years, individuals' bodies grow in height and weight, physically mature, and transition towards becoming sexual beings with the emergence of puberty (Caskey & Anfara, 2014; Repetto, 2012). Although this age span is marked by significant growth and change, it occurs unevenly and causes numerous difficulties for young adolescents. Uneven development leads to clumsiness and physical injuries, while changing hormone levels result in mood swings and irritability (Repetto, 2012). Young adolescents are susceptible to poor health habits, improper nutrition, and high-risk behaviors, including drug and alcohol use and sexual activity (Caskey & Anfara, 2014). Parents and educators must provide support during this time to help young adolescents understand these changes are normal and will eventually settle (Caskey & Anfara, 2014; Repetto, 2012). Caskey and Anfara (2014) suggested: "[s]chools can support physical development by offering responsive educational opportunities for young adolescents" (Physical Development Characteristics section, para. 5). These opportunities can include curriculum embedded into health and other appropriate courses that instruct students on how to make good decisions regarding their bodies (Caskey & Anfara, 2014).

Cognitive Development in Early Adolescence

Cognitively, young adolescents experience a wide range of intellectual development. Students at this age build from their concrete knowledge and begin to think abstractly; become more efficient with completing tasks; and begin to use higher order thinking skills, including making inferences, testing hypotheses, explaining connections among topics, and thinking reflectively (Caskey & Anfara, 2014). During this time, young adolescents also begin to understand themselves as students by developing academic and vocational preferences (Repetto, 2012). Students at this age prefer authentic learning experiences that allow for real-life connections and peer interactions (Caskey & Anfara, 2014). It is not uncommon for young adolescents to develop perceptions about themselves as students that will carry through the duration of their secondary education. In response to this critical cognitive period, it is imperative that parents and teachers encourage students' development of independent learning, a positive self-image in relation to education, and skills leading to self-determination (Repetto, 2012).

Social Development in Early Adolescence

When students with intellectual disability move into middle school, the social environment and expectations for social behavior change (Sitlington, Neubert, & Clark, 2010). As peer conformity grows, students struggle with self-esteem and self-perception. This may be even more complicated with the convergence of multiple identities, such as race and disability (Banks, 2014). Like their peers, students with intellectual disability are interested in belonging to social groups and developing romantic relationships. Many students with intellectual disability have difficulty with social relationships, are less accepted by peers, and have few friends outside of school (Friend, 2011). The challenges they have in developing friendships may be the result of immature behaviors and interests, inappropriate ways of dealing with social situations, and difficulty interpreting subtle social cues.

Increasing the social inclusion of students with intellectual disability, including meaningful involvement in activities and reciprocal relationships, is essential for enhancing the quality of life of students with intellectual disability (Hall, 2009). Since adolescents with intellectual disability tend to spend less time with friends outside of school (Tipton, Christensen, & Blacher, 2013), teachers and parents may help identify activities and events that reflect the students' interests and provide instruction, practice, and support to spend time with peers. Teachers may provide direct instruction in communication, social skills, problem solving, and leisure activities. To facilitate friendships and other meaningful relationships, teachers should promote social acceptance and provide social supports in a variety of settings (Hughes & Carter, 2000). When students with intellectual disability have more-developed social skills and few behavior problems, they tend to have higher levels of friendship quality (Tipton et al., 2013).

Physical Development and Health Care Needs in Early Adolescence

Early adolescents face significant changes in their bodies during this time of their development, and middle school students with intellectual disability are no exception. People with intellectual disability are at higher risk for a number of health challenges and are less likely to receive preventative health care compared to people without disabilities (Horner-Johnson, Dobbertin, Lee, Andresen, & the Expert Panel on Disability and Health Disparities, 2014). Adults with intellectual disability also have greater risks of acquiring Alzheimer's disease, obesity, heart disease, and cancer (Krahn, Hammond, & Turner, 2006; Sohler, Lubetkin, Levy, Soghomonian, & Rimmerman, 2009). In addition, children with intellectual disability are more likely to have at least one chronic health condition requiring ongoing care that could have been prevented or remedied through healthy decisions about activities and lifestyle (McQueen, Spence, Garner, Pereira, & Winsor, 1987; van Schrojenstein Lantman-deValk et al., 1997; Waldman, Perlman, & Swerdloff, 2001). Despite this, researchers have found that a low percentage of children with intellectual disability participate in health-promoting activities, such as taking their own temperature, exercising regularly, choosing or preparing healthy meals, or using a seat belt (Bechtel & Schreck, 2003; Steele, 1986), and they access health care providers less often than typically developing children (Horwitz, Kerker, Owens, & Zigler, 2001; Krauss, Gulley, Sciegaj, & Wells, 2003). Further of concern are challenges that children and adults with intellectual disability face in terms of access to adequate medical and dental care, and insurance to cover costs (i.e., Horner-Johnson et al., 2014).

Academic Instruction of Students with Intellectual Disability in Middle/Junior High Schools

Changes in US educational policy for students with intellectual disability have evolved since the late 1990s when, in conjunction with school reform efforts driven by the No Child Left Behind Act (NCLB, 2002), the Individuals with Disabilities Education Act (IDEA) required that all students receiving special education be involved with and progress in the general education curriculum. Prior to this, students with intellectual disability enrolled in public schools were typically taught functional-life-skills curricula (Browder et al., 2003). Since IDEA and NCLB, students with intellectual disability are expected to have access to, learn, and be assessed on general education curriculum content that is aligned with their grade level (Karvonen, 2013). For students with intellectual disability in middle and junior high school, access to the general education curriculum means the right to academic content and supports in reading, mathematics, science, social studies, and other general education opportunities they were once denied.

Promoting Access to the General Education Curriculum

Promoting access to the general education curriculum for students with intellectual disability in middle school has its challenges. For example, Karvonen (2013) identified three challenges to providing meaningful access: (a) limited existing research on strategies to teach core academic content, (b) difficulty in addressing both general education curriculum content and functional academic/Individualized Education Program (IEP) priorities for students, and (c) general and special education teacher–perceived efficacy about their preparation to teach academic content to students with intellectual disability. To address these challenges, resources and supports are being generated to support teachers' efforts in providing access to the general education curriculum for students with disabilities (Kleinert & Kearns, 2010).

The access mandates in IDEA have forced schools to reexamine student participation in the general education curriculum; it is important for practitioners to recognize the reasons students should be included in academic curricula (Browder, 2015; Courtade, Spooner, Browder, & Jimenez, 2012). As a result of changes in national education policy, students have acquired the legal right to access challenging academic standards (Courtade et al., 2012; Wehmeyer, 2006), which, it is presumed, will raise expectations and improve outcomes. The academic work completed by students with intellectual disability is important to postsecondary outcomes, including students accessing the growing number of postsecondary education programs available for students with intellectual disability (see Chapter 26; Courtade et al., 2012; Thoma, 2013; Thoma, Lakin, Carlson, Domzal, & Boyd, 2011). Finally, students with intellectual disability can learn functional skills while simultaneously learning academic skills (Ayers, Lowrey, Douglas, & Sievers, 2012).

Evidence-Informed Teaching Strategies to Promote Access to the General Education Curriculum

In its simplest form, embedded instruction is the provision of educational services in the general education classroom, alongside peers without disabilities learning the same academic content. Students attend class with peers, and as the special education teacher identifies barriers to access, the teacher adapts materials or the presentation of the materials (Jimenez & Kamei, 2015). Embedding students in the general education environment means that as much as possible the student engages with the general education teacher, the general education peers, and the general education curriculum. Embedded supports utilize a wide variety of teaching techniques and methods, including Universal Design for Learning (UDL), natural, peer, and individualized supports.

Universal Design for Learning

Students with and without disabilities can become overwhelmed in the general education environment. Confusing directions, novel activities, and academic rigor challenge all students. The UDL model attempts to provide students (with or without disabilities) with redundant support systems (Meyer, Rose, & Gordon, 2014). For students with intellectual disability, teachers can build lessons and activities to include the students with the greatest needs (Spooner, Baker, Harris, Ahlgrim-Delzell, & Browder, 2007). The UDL approach encourages teachers to plan for a diverse group of students with a range of support needs. Teachers design the classroom and activities allowing students to (a) access multiple representations of concepts, (b) engage with the material in multiple ways and, (c) demonstrate mastery of skills or concepts with multiple means of expression (Meyer, Rose, & Gordon, 2014).

For example, a teacher might choose to use a UDL approach to teach a lesson to help students to identify the colonists' grievances during the American Revolution. To help students access the material in multiple ways, stations might be set up to let students (a) read a paragraph or two from the *Declaration of Independence,* (b) watch movie clips of people reading the document, or (c) listen to a text-to-speech reading of the document. To assist students to engage in the material in multiple ways, they might be asked to highlight the document, participate in a jigsaw activity focused on the document, or prioritize grievances. To help students express their knowledge, they might choose to act out, draw, or write about a grievance. With UDL, students have the opportunity to choose their path of performance. The students would choose their preferred way to access, engage, and perform (see Chapter 14 for an extensive discussion of UDL).

Peer Supports

Using peers in instructional support roles is also an evidence-informed practice. The utilization of peers can help avoid stigma associated with typical instructional support (e.g., paraeducators). For example, teachers can utilize cooperative learning strategies to support students with intellectual disability. The cooperative learning process formally divides students into groups. Each group member has an assigned task, and the group works together to complete a common task (Slavin, 1980). Cooperative learning has a long history of effectiveness for supporting students with disabilities in inclusive settings (Madden & Slavin, 1983). Peers can also deliver intensive instruction using prompting strategies. Jimenez and Kamei (2015) pointed out that peers can deliver intensive systematic instructional programs to students. For example, peers without disabilities could be trained to deliver a constant time delay prompt with accuracy and fidelity (Jameson, McDonnell, Polychronis, & Riesen, 2008).

Structured Teaching

Structured teaching can be blended into the general education classroom and can be implemented by peers, paraprofessionals, teachers, or parents. Structured teaching uses concrete objects, task analysis, and prompting strategies to deliver instruction to students (Browder et al., 2003). Prompting strategies provide the student with supportive feedback before he or she has a chance to make an error during a practice assignments. Cohen, Heller, Alberto, and Fredrick (2008) demonstrated the effectiveness of a constant time delay–prompting strategy to teach reading. Specifically, they described providing an instructional prompt to encourage students to blend letters into sounds after a five-second delay.

Inquiry-Based Teaching

Inquiry-based teaching supports students in investigating and reporting on phenomena. Primarily used in literature, science, and social science classes, the process encourages students to ask questions and to seek answers. Students are encouraged to be curious. Courtade, Browder, Spooner, and DiBiase (2010) demonstrated that teachers could develop a list of steps necessary for students to investigate the world. For example, a student could be taught to (a) look for something different, (b) ask a question, and (c) seek answers.

Other Approaches

Another approach encourages students to engage with concrete objects, then semi-concrete objects, then abstract representations of the objects. Hord and Xin (2014) demonstrated the effectiveness of this strategy to teach middle school students methods for calculating surface area and volume for shapes. First students worked with concrete three-dimensional shapes, then they worked with semi-concrete representative drawings, and finally they worked with dimensions.

Other alternative approaches utilize technology. Most people recognize that calculators can aid students with basic calculations, but the graphing calculators found in most middle and high schools can help students simplify fractions, graph functions, and create formula charts. As a tool, graphing calculators can help students access more conceptual parts of the curriculum (Yakubova & Bouck, 2014).

Universal Design for Transition (UDT) is a framework designed to help educators in middle and high school link academic and functional/transition goals and content (Thoma, Bartholomew, & Scott, 2009). The UDT framework establishes a model for stakeholders that support meaningful access to the general education curriculum for students with disabilities, including students with intellectual disability, in junior and middle school, without sacrificing functional/transition priorities (Best, Scott, & Thoma, 2015). The UDT framework builds on principles of UDL (i.e., multiple representation, multiple engagement, multiple expression) and adds four additional principles to the UDL framework: (a) multiple life domains, (b) multiple means of assessment, (c) student self-determination, and (d) multiple resources/perspectives. For students with intellectual disability in middle and junior high school, the UDT framework can offer a model for a quality educational program that can offer access to both the general curriculum and functional academic/IEP priorities (Best et al., 2015; Thoma et al., 2009).

Social Instruction of Students with Intellectual Disability in Middle/Junior High Schools

In both late childhood and adolescence, peers play a significant role in a child's cognitive and social development in that peer relationships or peer social networks can help mitigate the difficulties children experience (Hartup, 1979; Ladd, 1989; Parker & Gottman, 1989; Parker, Rubin, Erath, Wojslawowicz, & Buskirk, 2006). In their discussion on the impact of adolescent peer relationships, Bukowski and Hoza (1989) stated that peers (a) are critical for fundamental skill development, (b) "contribute to a child's sense of social support and security" (p. 17), and (c) help develop a child's self-concept.

Peer Interaction

As children transition to adolescence, the way in which adolescents interact changes. In turn, the ways in which adolescents seek and offer social support (i.e., exchange resources), the ways in which friendships are made, and the design and function of social relations change (Parker & Gottman, 1989). "Structural changes in social networks begin to occur as children are increasingly exposed to children of various ascribed statuses (e.g., race, sex, and ethnicity) and children encounter variability in peer personalities that were heretofore unimagined" (Parker & Gottman, 1989, p. 112). Of particular importance during this transition period are the adolescent's understanding of (a) social status and its importance, (b) the influence of histories and confirmation bias in forming opinions (resulting in selection effect), (c) how information is transferred between peers and groups, and (d) how group behavior influences individual behavior (Bukowski, Velasquez, & Brendgen, 2008; Price & Dodge, 1989). The adolescent's desire for friendship groups (i.e., social networks) is often so great that they work hard to maintain social status and avoid peers that may thwart their status or limit access to desirable friendship groups, referred to as "selection effect" (Carter, Sisco, Brown, Brickham, & Al-Khabbaz, 2008; Kandel, 1978; Parker & Gottman, 1989). They begin to readily recognize similarities and differences amongst their peers, establish themselves within social groups, and develop networks with adolescents who are similar to them. This is what Lazarsfeld and Merton (1954) referred to as "homophily," or as Cairns, Cairns, Neckerman, Gest, and Gariepy (1988) coined, "cliques."

More specifically, adolescents begin to view their status as determined by their peers and become keenly aware of how their behavior or the behaviors of others can disrupt or topple their social status and social group membership (Prinstein & Dodge, 2008). For adolescents, peers become a critical part of their social network, so much so that adolescents will interact with and navigate many different peers groups of peers obtain or maintain a particular social status within a formed social network (Ladd, 1989). In fact, peers play such a significant role in the cognitive and social development of children (Erath, Flanagan, Bierman, & Tu, 2010; Hartup, 1979; Parker et al., 2006) that their effects are nearly impossible to replicate (Ladd, 1989). Given this, understanding how social networks are formed and the multiple ecologies experienced by adolescents with intellectual disability in middle and junior high schools is necessary to understand the multifaceted nature of interventions and supports for social interaction and social networks.

Social Networks

While social networks and social capital in adults can be diverse, a child's or adolescent's social networks and social capital involve peers with whom they interact regularly. Individual and peer characteristics and beliefs play a significant role in the social inclusion of individuals with intellectual disability (Siperstein, Parker, Norins-Bardon, & Widaman, 2007). Peer relationships can help mitigate the difficulties children and adolescents experience (Parker & Gottman, 1989; Parker et al., 2006) and influence an adolescent's sense of personal identity (Bukowski & Hoza, 1989; Damon & Phelps, 1989). While not all children utilize social networks and social capital with the same effectiveness, children and adolescents with intellectual disability, in particular, may not experience these benefits when their social interaction, communication, and social skill–related support needs are not addressed. Despite the positive effects interaction interventions have produced, students with disabilities continue to have few interactions with their peers beyond specifically scheduled opportunities (e.g., Carter, Hughes, Guth, & Copeland, 2005; Chung, Carter, & Sisco, 2012). They also continue to be isolated from either peer social networks or peripheral social network members (Chamberlain, Kasari, & Rotheram-Fuller, 2007; Farmer, Hall, Leung, Estell, & Brooks, 2011; Pearl, et al., 1998). In fact, there is data to suggest that children and adolescents with disabilities, for whom forming and maintaining peer relationships is difficult, are at significant risk for isolation, loneliness, and antisocial behavior (Pearl et al., 1998; Price & Dodge, 1989; Williamson, McLeskey, Hoppey, & Rentz, 2006).

Because of this, accessing and entering social networks may become difficult for students with limited access to opportunities for social network membership. Students who experience smaller networks or difficulties obtaining network membership may attempt to enter desired networks through assimilated behavior. For instance, adolescents with lower status often emulate adolescents with high status (Prinstein & Cillessen, 2003). The highly connected peer can choose to invite the isolated student into the network or not. Students wanting to fit in will begin to assimilate or socialize in ways similar to these peers. Awareness of differences, then, becomes an influencing factor for the creation of an adolescent's social networks. However, it is not clear that social capital works for adolescents in this way, particularly for adolescents with disabilities who have different support needs, have limited exposure to different peers and activities, and can experience limited adolescent peer relationships.

Adolescents With Disabilities, Peer Relationships, and Social Capital

Typically developing children and adolescents often develop positive peer relationships and social connections through natural opportunities and supports (e.g., extracurricular clubs, after-school activities, neighborhood activities). However, adolescents with intellectual disability can experience isolation from peer relationships (Wagner, Newman, & Cameto, 2004) and fewer opportunities to access social activities that build peer relationships (e.g., Bult, Verschuren, Jongmans, Lindeman, & Ketelaar, 2011; Shields, King, Corbett, & Imms, 2014; Simeonsson, Carlson, Huntington, McMillen, & Brent, 2001). Adolescents with intellectual disability who may look or behave differently (e.g., communicate and socialize in different ways) are at even greater risk for social isolation and bullying and victimization because the natural supports provided by peers may not be available.

Bullying and Victimization

Middle schools can be a jarring experience for adolescents as they leave the highly structured elementary school process and move to the frequently changing environments of the middle schooler's daily schedule (Eccles & Midgley, 1989). However, middle schools can create diverse school-wide opportunities for social interaction, and individual classroom teachers can provide social interaction opportunities embedded within instruction. Middle and junior high schools, specifically, are places where social and emotional learning can be emphasized, where community cohesion can be encouraged and fostered, and where social opportunities both within and after the school day can occur on a regular basis. In this sense, schools should be hubs for social networks and social activity to occur. However, with increased numbers of students, larger campuses, and frequent changing of classes, direct adult supervision of peer interactions declines and adolescents without the protective structure of peer friendships and support are at greater risk of bullying and victimization (Erath, Flanagan, & Bierman, 2008). Since adolescents with intellectual disability continue to experience limited access to social networks (e.g., Pearl et al., 1998; Kef & Deković, 2004) and participate in social activities at a much lower rate than same-age peers (King et al., 2009; Larson & Verma, 1999; Simeonsson etal., 2001), they experience fewer opportunities to develop those supportive social networks that can provide protective features in times of stress or need, or during instances of bullying and harassment.

Defining Bullying

Bullying occurs within a relationship and is reinforced by a series of antecedents and consequences that continue the cycle (Rodkin, Espelage, & Hanish, 2015). The cycle of bullying has four distinct features: It is a series of (a) intentional, (b) repeated acts that reveal a (c) power imbalance between the bully and the victim and bystander, (d) leaving the victim negatively affected while the perpetrator is unphased (Espelage & Swearer, 2003). While the reasons may be related to social status and the developmental nature of adolescent development, students in segregated environments who look different, act different, or interact differently experience substantially more incidences of bullying (Rose, Espelage, Monda-Amaya, Shogren, & Aragon, 2013). However, Rose et al.'s (2013) review of the research also indicated that students with and without disabilities in inclusive environments experience similar levels of bullying. These findings indicate the protective nature that inclusive education policies can have for students with disabilities. However, other research has indicated that this benefit does not extend to adolescents with intellectual disability (Whitney, Smith, & Thompson, 1994) or with physical or hearing impairments (Reiter & Lapidot-Lefler, 2007), who can experience higher levels of victimization than their peers despite being in inclusive environments. Unfortunately, there is a paucity of literature on factors specific to adolescents with intellectual disability and on ways to reduce victimization rates for adolescents with intellectual disability. Researchers have suggested that high incidence rates may be related to developmental factors in peer relationships and social status or the support needs some adolescents with intellectual disability require to build social networks.

Despite this, researchers have identified key components of bullying prevention programs that may provide some promise for adolescents with intellectual disability, although future research is needed. School-wide evidence-based bullying prevention programs that promote prosocial behaviors, create a school climate where bullying is not tolerated, ensure that punishments are enforced against perpetrators, and train students to be intervening bystanders can address bullying incidences (Polanin, Espelage, & Pigott, 2012). Specifically, focusing on both the bullying perpetrator, and also training and supporting bystanders to intervene in bullying activities and develop empathy towards the victim, appear to be key components of bullying prevention plans. Finally, teachers can create classrooms where bullying is defined, is not tolerated, and consequences are provided while embedding social and communication skills instruction for adolescents with intellectual disability and their peers to develop social interaction opportunities and a positive school environment (Rose et al., 2013).

Social Capital

Social capital of students with intellectual disability results from the people they know who provide both direct and indirect access to resources (Trainor, Morningstar, Murray, & Kim, 2013). Their social networks may include family members, teachers, coaches, peers, church members, and other members of the community. It is critical for students with intellectual disability to know people from different parts of the community to increase their opportunities for community involvement and employment (Trainor et al., 2013). To enhance social capital, teachers can promote social interactions, teach skills leading to self-determination, and promote the strengths of students with intellectual disability (Hughes & Carter, 2000).

Both social and cultural capital may bring about significant increases in the area of self-determination (Banks, 2014). Meaningful inclusion and instruction in both general and vocational curricula provide access to cultural capital from the general education materials and social networks in the community. Teachers should identify sociocultural barriers and supports to improve the social capital of students with intellectual disability. The development of self-awareness is needed to increase self-esteem and reframe negative messages about disability and culture identity (Banks, 2014).

The development of friendships is important to expanding social networks. Friendships can be fostered through supporting inclusive practices, encouraging peer-mediated support interventions, and addressing attitudinal and support barriers (Carter, Asmus, & Moss, 2013; Friend, 2011). To increase shared activities with peers, opportunity barriers need to be addressed. Teachers should also address barriers created by teachers and paraprofessionals that interfere with the interactions between students (Carter et al., 2013). Peer-mediated strategies that allow students to develop relationships are important because peers can provide both academic and social support to students with significant intellectual disability (Kleinert, Jones, Sheppard-Jones, Harp, & Harrison, 2012). For example, as communication partners, peers can make a positive impact on the communication skills of students who use augmentative and alternative communication (AAC) devices (Wolowiec Fisher & Shogren, 2012).

Peer Networks and Social interaction

Positive peer relationships for typically developing children often develop through natural supports (e.g., extracurricular clubs, after-school activities; neighborhood activities). For students with intellectual disability, who may have communication and social interaction support needs, natural supports may not provide enough support for successful peer relationships to develop. Students with more extensive support needs often need environmental supports to develop the communication skills that are critical for developing social networks. More specifically, adolescents with intellectual disability and their communication partners may benefit from specified communication and social skills training (see Carter & Hughes, 2005; McConnell, 2002; Wong et al., 2014) and AAC supports (see Chung, Carter, & Sisco, 2012; Snell, Chen, & Hoover, 2006) to develop peer relationships and create and obtain social networks.

Social Interaction Interventions

Carter and Hughes (2005) outlined social interaction interventions as being skill based and supports based. Skill-based interventions address specific communication skills taught to the target student or to a peer. Supports-based interventions address the person-environment gap where intervention supports address the gap between the environmental demands and the individual's support needs. Some researchers have focused on narrowly defined interventions that exclusively remediate specific deficits in areas such as requesting (Hamilton & Snell, 1993), initiating (Haring & Lovinger, 1989; Hughes, et al., 2000), turn taking (Hunt, Alwell, & Goetz, 1991; Weiner, 2005; Kamps, Leonard, Vernon, Dugan, & Delquadri, 1992), asking questions (Carter & Maxwell, 1998; Koegel, Camarata, Koegel, Ben-Tall, & Smith, 1998), or commenting (Hunt et al., 1991; Goldstein, Kaczmarek, Pennington, & Shafer, 1992). While these studies helped to develop evidence-based technologies for teaching social interaction to individuals with intellectual disability, much of the work concentrated on the skill deficits of the individual.

As the field has moved to a social-ecological framework (as discussed in earlier chapters), social interaction research has begun to reflect this transition. Interventions have addressed specific skills and supports (e.g., peer skill needs, environmental arrangements) necessary for effective social interactions to occur (for a review, see Carter & Hughes, 2005). For instance, Carter, Sisco, Brown, Brickham, and Al-Khabbaz (2008) explored the frequency and content of social interactions of adolescents with intellectual disability in academic and elective classes. Their work suggests small-group instruction increases the rate of social interaction over large-group or other instructional formats for this population. Interestingly, the content of interactions that were social in nature were higher when general or special education teachers were not present than when they were. This indicates that teachers may be cognizant of their proximity in facilitating social interactions and networks.

AAC Interventions

Students with intellectual disability can have difficulty communicating using conventional methods (Downing, 2005). Without effective and efficient communication means or supports, students with severe disabilities can experience isolation from their peers. One such support used by many students with severe disabilities is AAC. In an effort to capitalize on the influence that peers exert on each other, some researchers have utilized peers as interventionists or communication partners when teaching children with disabilities to use AAC systems (Buzolich, King, & Baroody, 1991; Buzolich & Lunger, 1995; Hunt et al., 1991; Ratcliff & Cress, 1999; Shukla, Kennedy, & Cushing, 1999). With the support of peer-mediated strategies (Goldstein et al., 1992), children with disabilities were able to learn new communicative functions, such as initiating, turn taking, and commenting, utilizing their AAC systems. Researchers have also implemented social skills training to promote peer interaction (for review, see Brown, Odom, & Conroy, 2001; Carter & Hughes, 2005). Some of these studies have used small social networks to improve social interactions of children with disabilities (Garrison-Harrell, Kamps, & Kravits, 1997; Haring & Breen, 1992).

Despite the need for ecologically based interventions that consider multiple ecologies, the majority of research on building relationships for children with disabilities has focused on micro-system level interventions (Carter & Hughes, 2005) and used single measurements to assess change. For instance, researchers have intervened with children with disabilities to remediate communication and social deficits but only rarely involved peers as communication partners or as trainers (Fisher & Shogren, 2012). A small subset of researchers has created interventions for individuals with significant communication needs (those who use AAC) focused on changing the environment to promote peer relationships. Specifically, these researchers structured activities to support social interaction through play groups (Schleien, Mustonen, & Rynders, 1995), peer networks (Garrison-Harrell et al., 1997), or cooperative learning groups (Cushing, Kennedy, Shukla, Davis, & Meyer, 1997; Hunt et al., 1991). This focus suggests the potential utility of multifaceted interventions (e.g., inclusive environments, skills training) that utilize multiple measures (e.g., skill assessment, peer ratings) to assess changes in social interaction and, with that, the social network membership of individuals with disabilities.

Transition Instruction

Secondary transition planning and instruction prepares students for adulthood in the areas of education, employment, and independent living. IDEA 2004 requires transition plans based on student strengths, preferences, interests, and needs (Flexer, Baer, Luft, & Simmons, 2013). Though IDEA mandates that secondary transition begin at age 16, best practice recommends that it begin earlier, in middle school, to fully engage students and parents in the process (Hetherington et al., 2010; Martinez, Conroy, & Cerreto, 2012; Mazzotti et al., 2009). Middle school students with disabilities also need support in navigating the transition to high school and the physical, social, and cognitive changes that occur during these years (Repetto, 2012). Those students who struggle with these transitions are less likely to meet their goals for the future (Jerald, 2006; National Longitudinal Transition Study-2, 2005) and may be at risk of dropping out or otherwise distancing themselves from school. This section will focus on strategies that middle school educators can use to engage students and build a foundation that can be used to support a successful transition to adult life (more information about transition planning and education can be found in Chapter 10).

Transition Assessment

Transition assessment is a process of gathering information to inform transition planning that begins in middle school and continues throughout high school (Mazzotti et al., 2009; Thoma & Tamura, 2013). Transition assessments include a combination of formal and informal assessments such as student and family interviews, observations in the community, vocational evaluations, and curriculum-based assessments in order to understand the student's strengths, support needs, interests, and preferences (Walker, Kortering, & Fowler, 2007). The assessments should be selected based on the main concerns of the IEP team and assist in determining the student's strengths, interests, preferences, and priorities related to adulthood (Kellems & Morningstar, 2009).

While transition assessment in the high school years focuses on helping students set specific goals for life after high school and steps to help them achieve those goals, the focus for middle school students is one of exploration (Thoma & Tamura, 2013). Middle school students with disabilities need opportunities to learn about their communities, about career options, and about their strengths, needs, preferences, and interests. Repetto (2012) suggests that middle school students with disabilities engage in career exploration activities to help them gain a broader understanding of the types of postschool outcomes that could be possible. Without this broader perspective, student goals tend to focus only on those careers with which they are familiar (either those of their parents or those highly visible careers such as entertainers, sports stars, or doctors) and that often do not match their strengths and needs (Repetto, 2012; Thoma & Tamura, 2013).

Career exploration for this group of students can include activities such as Internet searches, job shadowing, visits to vocational and technical schools, attending career fairs, interviewing adults about their careers, and/or having guest speakers talk with them about adult life and careers (Flexer et al., 2013; Repetto, 2012). In middle school, students may begin with interest inventories, employability surveys, and career development questionnaires to help them identify broad career areas to explore further. When students have difficulty expressing their strengths and experiences, situational assessments in different work settings may be effective (Kellems & Morningstar, 2009). Teachers may invite speakers and performers to class, simulate jobs in the classroom, and bring students to job fairs. Video modeling may be used to demonstrate work skills for students who are interested in specific careers (Kellems & Morningstar, 2009). Students may begin researching jobs and volunteer opportunities and explore careers of interest through job shadowing. Service-oriented projects in the community have also been effective in practicing employability skills and exploring careers (Sitlington et al., 2010). To find the right fit, students may research and practice a variety of jobs to find a balance between their needs and the supports in the environment (Henninger & Taylor, 2014).

Transition Services

Transition services for middle school students with intellectual disability should identify a course of study, accommodations, and supports (Flexer et al., 2013). A direct link should be made between the student's postsecondary goals and the course of study beginning in middle school and continuing through high school (Shogren & Plotner, 2012). Additional services may include community experiences, instruction in daily living, and related services (Mazzotti et al., 2009). Students with intellectual disability would also benefit from involvement in clubs, organizations, and leadership positions. These experiences can inform transition plans, promote self-determination, enhance a sense of belonging, and encourage friendship development (McGuire & McDonnell, 2008).

Self-Determination

Chapter 16 provides a comprehensive look at issues pertaining to self-determination and self-advocacy. Much of the focus on self-determination and self-advocacy for students with disabilities centers on the high school years (Wehmeyer, Abery, Mithaug, & Stancliffe, 2003; Wehmeyer et al., 2007), and the majority of the research on self-determination addresses the connection between higher levels of self-determination and improved postschool outcomes (i.e., Martorell, Gutierrez-Recacha, Pereda, & Ayuso-Mateos, 2008; Nota, Ferrari, Soresi, & Wehmeyer, 2007; Shogren, Lopez, Wehmeyer, Little, & Pressgrove, 2006; Thoma & Getzel, 2005; Wehmeyer & Palmer, 2003). In this section, we will examine only those issues that are pertinent to middle school.

Middle school is a time when students with and without disabilities learn many of the skills they will need to be successful in high school and are provided opportunities to be increasingly autonomous. As such, these years provide an excellent time to teach skills leading to self-determination and provide opportunities for students to practice behaviors that support problem solving, goal setting, and self-regulation (Wehmeyer, Agran, & Hughes, 1998) to positively impact a student's academic productivity (Konrad et al., 2008; Lachapelle et al., 2005).

Students not only need to have the attitudes, skills, and knowledge to be self-determined, but they also need to have the opportunity to make choices on their own. Students may have limited opportunities for self-determination if they are from low-income backgrounds, speak a different language, or are from a culture that does not value individual choice and self-expression (Leake & Black, 2005). This highlights the importance of intentionally creating opportunities to practice these skills in school, home, and community settings (Shogren, 2013). Embedding self-determination into existing practices, such as school-wide approaches and UDL, will increase opportunities for students to engage in goal setting, choice making, problem solving, and self-advocacy throughout the day (Bohanon, Castillo, & Afton, 2015). This will make the academic content relevant and have lasting effects on school and postsecondary outcomes for students with intellectual disability (Rowe, Mazzotti, & Sinclair, 2015). Learning generic strategies for self-management, such as using checklists, may assist students in applying them in further settings (Hughes & Carter, 2000).

There are multiple strategies for teachers to embed self-determination into instruction. The use of the Self-Determined Learning Model of Instruction (Agran, Blanchard, & Wehmeyer, 2000) introduces students to the use of a problem-solving strategy that they can use to identify academic, social, and/or transition-related goals (Agran, Cavin, Wehmeyer & Palmer, 2008) and the steps they can take to achieve their goals. Teachers support students through three phases as they (a) set attainable goals, (b) develop a plan to reach their goals, and (c) monitor their progress. Students increase their self-awareness by examining their skills, identifying supports, monitoring progress, and making adjustments when needed. They may practice self-advocacy and problem-solving skills with peers by sharing their goals and providing positive feedback (Rowe et al., 2015). Teachers may help students identify self-management strategies by matching their strengths and needs with their preferences and interests. Visual prompts, such as picture schedules and picture lists, can be used to practice self-management, prioritizing, and choice making (Hughes & Carter, 2000).

Addressing Physical and Health Care Needs

The general education of students in middle school includes a focus on health and physical education that is designed to address their need to learn to establish and maintain healthy lifestyles. In general, middle schools address these health and physical development needs in a number of inter-connected ways: courses in health and physical education; extracurricular activities designed to provide opportunities for youth to engage with others; health-care services and screenings, including mental health services; and a safe and healthy school environment (Kann, et al., 2013). This section will describe some of these practices that have been demonstrated to be effective for middle school students with intellectual disability: health education, physical education, and ensuring a safe and healthy school environment.

Health Education

The main objective of health education in middle schools is the establishment of healthy lifestyles to prevent future diseases and/or at-risk behaviors. Health education includes teaching strategies and learning experiences that provide students with opportunities to acquire the knowledge, attitudes, and skills necessary for making health-promoting decisions, achieving health literacy, adopting health-enhancing behaviors, and promoting the health of others (Kann et al., 2013). Nationally, health education curriculum includes instruction on human immunodeficiency virus (HIV) prevention, human sexuality, nutrition and dietary behavior, other sexually transmitted disease (STD) prevention, physical activity and fitness, pregnancy prevention, violence prevention, emotional and mental health, infectious disease prevention, suicide prevention, tobacco use prevention, and illegal drug use prevention (Kann, Telljohann, Hunt, Hunt, & Haller, 2013).

For students with intellectual disability, learning to establish and maintain a healthy lifestyle requires that goals be expanded to address some of the unique challenges faced by this group of students. For example, students with intellectual disability can struggle with reading and, in particular, reading at the level that many health-care resources use to disseminate information about common diseases and preventative care. The teaching materials used in health education classes must be made accessible for this group of students; Turnbull, Wilkie, McKenzie, and Powell (2005) found that converting materials so they are available in electronic formats and can include video to accompany step-by-step written instructions was effective in teaching health curriculum to students with intellectual disability.

Another study found that providing health-care education to both students with intellectual disability and their parents or other caregivers, either simultaneously or in parallel, also results in an increase in establishing and/or maintaining healthy habits such as following recommendations for oral health care (Fickert & Ross, 2012; Glassman & Miller, 2006) or preventative health care and screenings (Felce et al., 2008). This type of educational training included information about the importance of the behavior, the role in maintaining health, and contact information for community services that provide related health care or screening services.

Physical Education and Physical Activity

A large number of research studies have demonstrated the relationship between regular exercise and improved health, mood, and cognitive ability (i.e., Office of the Surgeon General, 2002; Ouellette-Kuntz, 2005), but for individuals with intellectual disability, the results have not been quite as clear.

There have been a few studies that have demonstrated that exercise does have positive benefits for adolescents with intellectual disability, particularly on improving mood (Vogt, Schneider, Abeln, Anneken, & Studer, 2012) and a quality of life (Blick, Saad, Coreczney, Roman, & Sorensen, 2015).

Students with intellectual disability, however, face some challenges when it comes to participation in physical education classes. Often they are not interested in physical activities, preferring activities that are more sedentary (Pitetti, Beets, & Combs, 2009). Students with intellectual disability may also struggle physically with participating in the activities, either as a result of coordination issues that are associated with physical growth at this age or because of physical challenges associated with their disability (Frey & Chow, 2006). In addition, many of the studies designed to determine the impact on fitness levels for youth with intellectual disability who participated in physical education classes and activities did not demonstrate that they made significant improvements in body mass index (BMI), weight loss in general, or in aerobic conditioning (Davis, Zhang, & Hodson, 2011; Frey & Chow, 2006; Halle, Gabler-Halle, & Chung, 1999).

One study did find that daily participation in a daily, thirty-minute program that consisted of activities designed to focus on cardiovascular endurance, flexibility, and muscular strength and endurance activities did result in an increase in fitness levels and a slight decrease in BMI (Davis et al., 2011). Greater decreases in BMI levels were attained from an exercise program that included assisted cycling, a stationary bike with a motor that encourages the exerciser to pedal at a pace greater than what they would do without the assistance (Ringenbach, Albert, Chen, & Alberts, 2014). Lastly, another study found that participation in a regular exercise program resulted in a decrease in anxiety levels of individuals with intellectual disability as measured by a common self-rating anxiety scale (Carraro & Gobbi, 2012). Although more research is needed to determine the best approaches to providing physical education and activities, it remains important that students with intellectual disability participate in physical education classes during the middle school years.

Safe and Healthy School Environment

There is a growing body of literature that examines instances of bullying behavior or peer victimization in middle schools, finding that students with disabilities are more likely to be victims than peers without disabilities (Blake, Lund, Zhou, Kwok, & Benz, 2012). This has implications for school administrators charged with maintaining a safe and healthy school environment as youth who are chronically involved in peer victimization have a range of adjustment difficulties, including social problems, low academic achievement, and mental health disorders (Biggs et al., 2010; Burk et al., 2011; Hanish & Guerra, 2004; Menesini, Modena, & Tani, 2009). Students with disabilities, including students with intellectual disability, were more likely to be socially marginalized, which was associated with "stable peer victimization involvement" (Chen, Hamm, Farmer, Lambert, & Mehtaji, 2015, p. 321). A safe and healthy school environment that decreases social marginalization consists of teachers who are trained to "merge the management of academic engagement, the positive management of students' behavior, and the management of the social ecology" (Chen et al., 2015, p. 321). Practices such as implementing school-wide positive behavior supports that describe clear expectations for student, faculty, and staff behavior (Kartub, Taylor-Greene, March, & Horner, 2000; Lewis Powers, Kelk, & Newcomber, 2002; Safran & Oswald, 2003; Simonsen, Sugai, & Negron, 2008) and involving students with and without disabilities in setting school and/or classroom rules and consequences can be particularly effective in middle school, providing an opportunity for students to improve social capital and status.

Collaboration

Inclusion requires that members of an interdisciplinary team work cooperatively to ensure that students with disabilities are not only fully integrated in the general education classroom, but also benefit from individually tailored instruction and classroom accommodations. Ideally, this team includes both school personnel (e.g., special and general education teachers, related services personnel, instructional assistants, and administrators), and the students' caregivers. The team is involved in all stages, from planning and delivering instruction to assessing the progress of students. Planning begins when the whole interdisciplinary team meets to make decisions about goals and the course of action for delivering instruction; we will delve deeper into the team approach to the IEP meeting later in this chapter. Subsequently, service professionals collaborate to implement the instructional plan, to teach, and to assess progress. This collaboration will be our focus for this section.

One aspect of inclusion is the tailoring of support to meet varying student needs. A recurring theme in terms of the amount of support provided is "only as much as necessary," with the understanding that the needs of each student are monitored and the support is regarded as dynamic over time (Murawski, 2009; Villa, Thousand, Nevin, & Liston, 2005). Some students merely need to be monitored, while others learn more effectively in a one-on-one or small group setting. Regardless of the intensity of supports, all models require professional collaboration between the general education teachers and other service providers. Importantly, students in a classroom differ not only in their ability levels, but also on other essential characteristics that must be accounted for during instruction planning. Characteristics such as gender, race or ethnicity, socioeconomic status, and culture of students and team members can have a significant impact on the successful inclusion of all students (Waitoller & Artilles, 2013).

There are a variety of factors leading to successful collaboration. One is the acknowledgement that both general and special education teachers are credentialed, are able to perform unique functions, and have complementary skill sets. In cases when instructional assistants are placed in a classroom to support inclusion, it is important that they function as co-teachers and are regarded as such, rather than just offering support for one or a few students with disabilities (Villa et al., 2005).

Another essential element that can make a difference in successful inclusion is professional buy in. When decisions to integrate classrooms are purely administrative, with no support for the inclusive vision from staff, any reorganization effort is bound to fail (Fox & Ysseldyke, 1997). Buy-in is not only a matter of being willing to modify instruction, but also the belief that all students are able to learn middle school grade-level curriculum (Santoli, Sachs, Romey, & McClurg, 2008).

It is also worth considering that change, especially at the middle school level where instruction is delivered by a multitude of educators, takes time (Fox & Ysseldyke, 1997). In addition to changing mindsets, there must be a learning process by which teachers are trained not only to work collaboratively, but also have time to implement their knowledge and develop a comfortable style of collaboration (Murawski, 2009).

Co-teaching

In terms of instructional delivery, a specific model that has received attention and support from research in the past decade is co-teaching shared instruction by special and general educators in a general education setting (Friend, Cook, Hurley-Chamberlain, & Shamberger, 2010). There have been numerous studies identifying benefits of co-teaching, both for students (with and without disabilities) and their teachers (e.g., Murawski, 2009; Lipsky & Gartner, 1996). Co-teaching is embodied in different models. In addition to the traditional models described by Friend and Cook (1992), in middle schools the same class of students can benefit from co-teaching in one or all academic areas, depending on their needs, with different special educators collaborating in teams centered around subject areas (Friend et al., 2010). Co-teaching models require achieving a fine balance between the time spent with the general education teacher and more individualized services from the special education teacher. One of the most frequently cited impediments to achieving this balance is lack of administrative support (Scruggs, Mastropieri, & McDuffie, 2007), which can take many forms. For instance, administrators should allow for common planning time among general and special education teachers, and time for general education teachers to participate in IEP meetings for their students with disabilities (Santoli et al., 2008).

Villa et al. (2005) called for reorganization at the middle school level to promote a more collaborative environment. In addition to advising a restructure of the educational environment, the authors emphasized the need for a collective, school-wide inclusion mindset, beginning with collaborative teaching teams, and ending with administrative support for inclusion practices.

Beginning in middle school, the instructional model for professional collaboration is different from elementary education due to changes in school organization. General educators become specialized in a specific subject and possibly grade level, which means their academic understanding becomes more focused. Middle school special educators are also content specialists, although not in academic content, but in differentiating instruction according to varying student needs. While elementary school teachers generally team up according to grade level, in middle schools such an arrangement is less frequent, with teachers grouping by subject, unless they teach in larger schools where several faculty members are teaching the same subject for a grade level. The difference between the traditional team teaching in middle school and co-teaching is that educators have different skills and the teacher/student ratio is reduced (Friend et al., 2010)

At the upper-elementary level and beyond, general education teachers who would be responsible for making the inclusion process successful face a unique challenge: They are held accountable for their students' test scores. This can lead to disincentivizing voluntary inclusion of students with disabilities who are perceived as less capable of performing well on standardized tests (Mackey, 2014).

Parent Involvement

We have known for some time that parental involvement in education is associated with better student outcomes (e.g., Fan & Chen, 2001), and collaborating with parents is, in some respects, similar to collaborating with other professionals. Parents bring expertise about their child (Cook, Shepherd, Cook, & Cook, 2012), just as teachers supply expertise in content knowledge or differentiation strategies. Although they might not hold the same understanding of evidence-based practices or instruction delivery, parents are an important part of the team by extending instruction into nonschool hours and providing insight into their children's interests and personalities. By becoming members of the decision-making team, parents can learn what practices are available and contribute to the selection of the best ones for their children (Cook et al., 2012).

Designing Interdisciplinary IEPs

Federal legislation has attempted to expand educational opportunities for students with disabilities by providing access to the general curriculum, assessing progress toward meeting standards, and providing individualized supports (Altman et al., 2010). As a result, it is even more essential that a focus is placed on designing interdisciplinary IEPs that will offer access to the general education curriculum and support functional curricula for students with intellectual disability. Standards-based IEPs and student-directed IEPs have both emerged as interdisciplinary models of practice to support the design of IEPs that consider academic learning and student involvement in the IEP process.

Standards-Based IEPs

Standards-based IEPs can be defined by their principal target to align state content standards in developing goals and objectives for the IEP (National Association of State Department of Special Educators, 2007). It has been customary to have the IEP emphasize functional skills development and focus less on academic skills (Ahearn, 2010). With a standards-based approach, student achievement and access to the general curriculum is facilitated by aligning grade-level standards with annual IEP goals and objectives (Ahearn, 2010)—but as it turns out, having a standards-based approach does not mean ignoring the functional and developmental needs of students with disabilities. Browder, Spooner, and Jimenez (2011) underlined the fact that standards-based IEPs can have both goals aligned with state standards and functional and developmental goals for students with intellectual disability. This point about the standards-based IEP becomes incredibly significant for students with intellectual disability across the lifespan, but it is particularly important during the developmental stages of middle and junior high school.

As with developing a traditional IEP, the standards-based approach depends on required members of the traditional IEP team (i.e., parents, general education teachers, special education teachers, test evaluators, administrators, related services staff specialist, student; IDEA, 2004) to be active and contributing members of the development process. In addition to being active and contributing members, according to the National Association of State Directors of Special Education (NASDE, 2007), team members must also be acquainted with the general education curriculum. This also includes being familiar with the state academic standards and the assessments associated with the academic standards. The NASDE and Office of State Superintendent of Education (OSSE), Division of Specialized Education underlined the major steps in the creation of a standards-based IEP: (a) team members consider the student's grade-level content (for this purpose the IEP team would consider the middle and junior high school content in which the student with intellectual disability is enrolled); (b) review student data to examine gaps between current performance and grade-level content; (c) develop the present-level and academic performance narrative; (d) develop measurable annual goals that are specifically aligned with the grade-level academic content; (e) access, review, and disseminate students' progress towards annual goals; (f) identify and incorporate necessary accommodations and modifications that will support students' access and advancement towards grade-level content; and (g) determine which assessments will be used to assess the student's progress (NASDE, 2007; OSSE, 2013). Once more, it is important to emphasize that standards-based IEPs can have both academic and functional goals (Courtade et al., 2012) so the major steps for the creation of a standards-based IEP prescribed by the NASDE can include the development of functional goals for students with intellectual disability.

Student-Directed IEPs

Best practice supports the active involvement of students with disabilities in the development of their IEPs (Agran & Hughes, 2008; Barnard-Brak & Lecgtenberger, 2010; Mason, McGahee-Kovac, & Johnson, 2004). Student-directed IEPs involve the practice of teaching students with disabilities how to become meaningful and active participants in their IEP meetings and provide a way for students to practice and apply skills leading to self-determination in settings that have relevance and meaning (Agran & Hughes, 2008). For students with intellectual disability in middle and junior high schools, the student-directed process can prove to be vital as they navigate rights to education, independent living, personal needs, and making transition choices that are often critical decisions during this time period.

Konrad and Test (2004) found four different paths by which students may become involved in the IEP process: (a) drafting the IEP document, (b) planning and developing the IEP document, (c) implementing the components of the IEP document, and (d) meeting again to make additions or revisions to the IEP document. Several models support meaningful student participation in the IEP, including the Self-Directed IEP (Martin, Marshall, Maxson, & Jerman, 1996), the *NEXT S.T.E.P. Curriculum* (2nd Ed.) (Halpern, Herr, Doren, & Wolf, 2000), and *Whose Future Is It Anyway?* (Wehmeyer et al., 2004).

Students with disabilities who are involved in transition planning are required to be invited to their IEP meetings (IDEA, 2004), but active involvement in the educational planning process requires more than being present at the meetings. Thoma, Rogan, and Baker (2001) found that little was done to prepare students for IEP meetings or to help adults learn to facilitate student participation in these meetings. The student-directed IEP processes listed earlier can be effective in preparing middle school students to be active participants in the educational planning process, to enhance their skills leading to self-determination, and to increase their knowledge of transition (Wehmeyer & Lawrence, 1995). Research studies about the use of lessons that are part of *Whose Future Is It Anyway?* curriculum (Wehmeyer et al., 2004) demonstrate that they were effective in increasing skills leading to self-determination of students with disabilities, and the greatest increases occurred for those in the middle school years (Wehmeyer, Palmer, Lee, Williams-Diehm, & Shogren, 2011). In addition, the use of a computer-assisted screen reader (Rocket Reader) to deliver instruction of the *Whose Future Is It Anyway?* curriculum (Wehmeyer et al., 2004) resulted in enhanced self-determination, self-efficacy, and outcome expectancy for educational planning for middle school–aged students with disabilities (Lee et al., 2011). A student-directed IEP approach with appropriate supports and accommodations during the middle school years can not only improve student skills leading to self-determination, but can also prepare students to be causal agents in the transition planning process during their high school years.

Conclusions

This chapter provided an introduction to the educational needs of early adolescents between the ages of 11 and 14 with intellectual disability. Students in this age group with disabilities are in an important developmental period between the elementary and high school years. While middle school and junior high school models differ in approach, they each strive to address the academic, social, health, and early transition needs of this group of students as they set the foundation for the transition planning and services that typically begin in high school.

Educators who work with this population of students need a variety of strategies to help students become independent learners, develop skills leading to self-determination, learn to make choices to create a healthy lifestyle, and explore the world at large. These skills and experiences provide a rich educational experience while providing sufficient experiences for students to use to make decisions about their strengths, needs, preferences, and interests that will ultimately guide their plans for adult life.

References

Agran, M., Blanchard, C., & Wehmeyer, M. L. (2000). Promoting transition goals and self-determination through student self-directed learning: The Self-Determined Learning Model of Instruction. *Education & Training in Mental Retardation & Developmental Disabilities, 35*, 351–364.

Agran, M., Cavin, M., Wehmeyer, M. L., & Palmer, S. (2008). Promoting student active classroom participation skills through instruction to promote self-regulated learning and self-determination. *Research and Practice for Persons with Severe Disabilities, 31*, 230–241.

Agran, M., & Hughes, C. (2008). Students' opinions regarding their individualized education program involvement. *Career Development for Exceptional Children, 31*(2), 69–76.

Ahearn, E. (2010). *Standards-based IEP implementation update* (US Department of Education No. H326F050001). Retrieved from http://www.projectforum.org

Altman, J. R., Lazarus, S. S., Quenemoen, R. F., Kearns, J., Quenemoen, M., & Thurlow, M. L. (2010). *2009 survey of states: Accomplishments and new issues at the end of a decade of change*. Minneapolis, MN: University of Minnesota, National Center on Educational Outcomes.

Ayres, K. M., Lowrey, K. A., Douglas, K. H., & Sievers, C. (2012). The question still remains: What happens when the curricular focus for students with severe disabilities shifts? A reply to Courtade, Spooner, Browder, and Jimenez (2012). *Education and Training in Autism and Developmental Disabilities, 47,* 14–22.

Banks, J. (2014). Barriers and supports to postsecondary transition: Case studies of African American students with disabilities. *Remedial and Special Education, 35*(1), 28–39.

Barnard-Brak, L., & Lecgtenberger, D. (2010). Student IEP participation and academic achievement across time. *Remedial and Special Education, 31*(5), 343–349.

Bechtel, J. J., & Schreck, K. A. (2003). Balancing choice with health considerations in residential environments. *Mental Retardation, 41*, 465–467.

Best, K., Scott, L. A., & Thoma, C. A. (2015). Starting with the end in mind: Inclusive education designed to prepare students for adult life. In E. Brown, R. G. Craven, & G. McLean (Eds.), *International advances in education: Global initiatives for equity and social justice: Vol. 9, inclusive education for students with intellectual disabilities* (pp. 45–72). Charlotte, NC: Information Age Press.

Biggs, B. K., Vernberg, E., Little, T. D., Dill, E. J., Fonagy, P., & Twemlow, S. W. (2010). Peer victimization trajectories and their association with children's affect in late elementary school. *International Journal of Behavioral Development, 34*, 136–146. doi:10.1177/0165025409348560

Blake, J., Lund, E. M., Zhou, Q., Kwok, O., & Benz, M. (2012). National prevalence rates of bully victimization among students with disabilities in the United States. *School Psychology Quarterly, 27*, 210–222. doi:10.1037/spq0000008

Blick, R. N., Saad, A. E., Coreczney, A. J., Roman, K., & Sorensen, C. H. (2015). Effects of declared levels of physical activity on quality of life of individuals with intellectual disabilities. *Research in Developmental Disabilities, 37*, 223–229.

Bohanon, H., Castillo, J., & Afton, M. (2015). Embedding self-determination and futures planning within a school wide framework. *Intervention in School and Clinic, 50*(4), 203–209.

Browder, D. M. (2015). What should we teach to students with moderate and severe developmental disabilities. In B. Bateman, J. W. Lloyd, & M. Tankersley (Eds.), *Enduring issues in special education: Personal perspectives* (pp. 52–72). New York: Routledge.

Browder, D. M., Spooner, F., Ahlgrim-Dezell, L., Flowers, C., Algozzine, R., & Karvonen, M. (2003). A content analysis of the curricular philosophies reflected in states' alternate assessment performance indicators. *Research & Practice for Persons with Severe Disabilities, 28*, 165–181.

Browder, D. M., Spooner, F., & Jimenez, B. (2011). Standards-based IEPs. In D. M. Browder & F. Spooner (Eds.), *Teaching students with moderate and severe disabilities* (pp. 42–91). New York: Guilford.

Brown, W. H., Odom, S. L., Conroy, M. A. (2001). An intervention hierarchy for promoting young children's peer interactions. *Topics in Early Childhood Special Education, 21*, 162–175.

Bukowski, W. M., & Hoza, B. (1989). Popularity and friendship: Issues in theory, measurement, and outcome. In T. J. Berndt & G. W. Ladd (Eds.), *Peer relationships in child development* (pp. 15–45). New York, NY: John Wiley & Sons.

Bukowski, W. M., Velasquez, A. M., & Brendgen, M. (2008). Variations in patterns of peer influence: Considerations of self and other. In M. J. Prinstein & K. A. Dodge (Eds.), *Understanding peer influence in child and adolescent development* (pp. 125–140). New York, NY: The Guilford Press.

Bult, M. K., Verschuren, O., Jongmans, M. J., Lindeman, E., & Ketelaar, M. (2011). What influences participation in leisure activities of children and youth with physical disabilities? A systematic review. *Research in Developmental Disabilities, 32*(5), 1521–9. doi:10.1016/j.ridd.2011.01.045

Burk, L. R., Armstrong, J. M., Park, J. H., Zahn-Waxler, C., Klein, M. H., & Essex, M. J. (2011). Stability of early identified aggressive victim status in elementary school and associations with later mental health problems and functional impairments. *Journal of Abnormal Child Psychology, 39*, 225–238. doi:10.1007/s10802-010-9454-6

Buzolich, M., King, J., & Baroody, S. (1991). Acquisition of the commenting function among system users. *Augmentative and Alternative Communication, 7*, 88–99. doi:10.1080/07434619112331275753

Buzolich. M. J., & Lunger, J. (1995). Empowering system users in peer training. *Augmentative and Alternative Communication, 11*, 37–48. doi:10.1080/07434619512331277129

Cairns, R. B., Cairns, B. D., Neckerman, H. J., Gest, S. D., & Gariepy, J. L. (1988). Social networks and aggressive behavior: Peer support or peer rejection? *Developmental Psychology, 24*, 815–823.

Carraro, A., & Gobbi, E. (2012). Effects of an exercise programme on anxiety in adults with intellectual disabilities. *Research in Developmental Disabilities, 33*, 1221–1226.

Carter, E. W., Asmus, J., & Moss, C. K. (2013). Fostering friendships: Supporting relationships among youth with and without developmental disabilities. *Prevention Researcher, 20*(2), 14–17.

Carter, E. W., & Hughes, C. (2005). Increasing social interaction among adolescents with intellectual disabilities and their general education peers: Effective interventions. *Research and Practice for Persons with Severe Disabilities (RPSD), 30*(4), 179–193. doi:10.2511/rpsd.30.4.179

Carter, E. W., Hughes, C., Guth, C. B., & Copeland, S. R. (2005). Factors influencing social interaction among high school students with intellectual disabilities and their general education peers. *American Journal on Mental Retardation, 110*, 366–377. doi:10.1352/0895–8017

Carter, E. W., Sisco, L. G., Brown, L., Brickham, D., & Al-Khabbaz, Z. A. (2008). Peer interactions and academic engagement of youth with developmental disabilities in inclusive middle and high school classrooms. *American Journal on Mental Retardation, 26*, 479–494. doi:10.1352/2008.113:479–494

Carter, M., & Maxwell, K. (1998). Promoting interaction with children using augmentative communication through a peer-directed intervention. *International Journal of Disability, Development, and Education, 45*, 75–96. doi:10.1080/1034912980450106

Caskey, M., & Anfara, V. A. (2014). *Developmental characteristics of young adolescents*. Retrieved from http://www.amle.org/BrowsebyTopic/WhatsNew/WNDet.aspx?ArtMID=888&ArticleID=455

Chamberlain, B., Kasari, C., & Rotheram-Fuller, E. (2007). Involvement or isolation? The social networks of children with autism in regular classrooms. *Journal of Autism and Developmental Disorders, 37*(2), 230–242. doi:10.1007/s10803–006–0164–4

Chen, C. C., Hamm, J. V., Farmer, T. V., Lambert, K., Mehtaji, M. (2015). Exceptionality and peer victimization involvement in late childhood. *Remedial and Special Education, 36*, 312–324.

Chung, Y. C., Carter, E. W., & Sisco, L. G. (2012). Social interactions of students with disabilities who use augmentative and alternative communication in inclusive classrooms. *American Journal on Intellectual and Developmental Disabilities, 117*(5), 349–367. doi:10.1352/1944–7558–117.5.349

Cohen, E. T., Heller, K. W., Alberto, P., & Fredrick, L. D. (2008). Using a three-step decoding strategy with constant time delay to teach word reading to students with mild and moderate mental retardation. *Focus on Autism and Other Developmental Disabilities, 23*(2), 67–78.

Cook, B. G., Shepherd, K. G., Cook, S. C., & Cook, L. (2012). Facilitating the effective implementation of evidence-based practices through teacher-parent collaboration. *Teaching Exceptional Children, 44*(3), 22–30.

Courtade, G., Browder, D., Spooner, F., & DiBiase, W. (2010). Training teachers to use an inquiry-based task analysis to teach science to students with moderate and severe disabilities. *Education and Training in Developmental Disabilities, 45*, 378–399.

Courtade, G., Spooner, F., Browder, D. M. & Jimenez, B. (2012). Seven reasons to promote standards-based instruction for students with severe disabilities: A reply to Ayres, Lowrey, Douglas, and Sievers. *Education and Training in Autism and Developmental Disabilities, 47*(1), 3–13.

Cuban, L. (1992). What happens to reforms that last? The case of the junior high school. *American Educational Research Journal, 29*(2), 227–251.

Cushing, L. S., Kennedy, C. H., Shukla, S., Davis, J., & Meyer, K. A. (1997). Disentangling the effects of curricular revision and social grouping within cooperative learning arrangements. *Focus on Autism and Other Developmental Disabilities, 12*(4), 231–240. doi:10.1177/108835769701200405

Damon, W., & Phelps, E. (1989). Strategic uses of peer learning in children's education: Peer relationships in child development. In T. J. Berndt & G. W. Ladd (Eds.), *Peer relationships in child development* (pp. 135–157). Oxford, England: John Wiley & Sons.

Davis, K., Zhang, G., & Hodson, P. (2011). Promoting health-related fitness for elementary students with intellectual disabilities through a specifically designed activity program. *Journal of Policy and Practice in Intellectual Disabilities, 8*(2), 77–84.

Downing, J. (2005). Inclusive education for high school students with severe intellectual disabilities: Supporting communication. *Augmentative & Alternative Communication, 21*, 132–148.

Eccles, J. S., & Midgley, C. (1989). Stage-environment fit: Developmentally appropriate classrooms for young adolescents. *Research on Motivation in Education, 3*, 139–186.

Erath, S. A., Flanagan, K. S., & Bierman, K. L. (2008). Early adolescent school adjustment: Associations with friendship and peer victimization. *Social Development, 17*(4), 853–870.

Erath, S. A., Flanagan, K. S., Bierman, K. L., & Tu, K. M. (2010). Friendships moderate psychosocial maladjustment in socially anxious early adolescents. *Journal of Applied Developmental Psychology, 31*(1), 15–26. doi:10.1007/s10802–007–9099–2

Espelage, D. L., & Swearer, S. M. (2003). Research on school bullying and victimization: What have we learned and where do we go from here? *School Psychology Review, 32*(3), 365–383.

Fan, X., & Chen, M. (2001). Parental involvement and students' academic achievement: A meta-analysis. *Educational Psychology Review, 13*(1), 1–22.

Farmer, T. W., Hall, C. M., Leung, M.-C., Estell, D. B., & Brooks, D. (2011). Social prominence and the heterogeneity of rejected status in late elementary school. *School Psychology Quarterly, 26*(4), 260–274. doi:10.1037/a0025624

Felce, D., Baxter, H., Lowe, K., Dunstan, F., Houston, H., Jones, G., Felce, J., & Kerr, M. (2008). The impact of repeated health checks on adults with intellectual disabilities. *Journal of Applied Research in Intellectual Disabilities, 21*, 585–594.

Fickert, N. A., & Ross, D. (2012). Effectiveness of a caregiver education program on providing oral care to individuals with intellectual and developmental disabilities. *Intellectual and Developmental Disabilities, 50*, 219–232.

Fisher, K. W., & Shogren, K. A. (2012). Integrating augmentative and alternative communication and peer support for students with disabilities: A social-ecological perspective. *Journal of Special Education Technology, 27*, 23–39.

Flexer, R. W., Baer, R. M., Luft, P., & Simmons, T. J. (2013). *Transition planning for secondary students with disabilities* (4th ed.). Upper Saddle River, NJ: Pearson Education.

Fox, N. E., & Ysseldyke, J. E. (1997). Implementing inclusion at the middle school level: Lessons from a negative example. *Exceptional Children, 64*(1), 81–98.

Frey, G. C., & Chow, B. (2006). Relationship between BMI, physical fitness, and motor skills in youth with mild intellectual disabilities. *International Journal of Obesity, 30*, 861–867.

Friend, M. (2011). *Special education: Contemporary perspectives for school professionals.* Upper Saddle River, NJ: Pearson Education Inc.

Friend, M., & Cook, L. (1992). *Interactions: Collaboration skills for school professionals.* White Plains, NY: Longman Publishing Group.

Friend, M., Cook, L., Hurley-Chamberlain, D., & Shamberger, C. (2010). Co-teaching: An illustration of the complexity of collaboration in special education. *Journal of Educational and Psychological Consultation, 20*(1), 9–27.

Garrison-Harrell, L., Kamps, D., & Kravits, T. (1997). The effects of peer networks on social-communicative behaviors for students with autism. *Focus on Autism and Other Developmental Disabilities, 12*(4), 241–235. doi:10.1177/108835769701200406

Glassman, P., & Miller, C. E. (2006). Effect of preventive dentistry training program for caregivers in community facilities on caregiver and client behavior and client oral hygiene. *New York State Dental Journal, 72*(2), 38–46.

Goldstein, H., Kaczmarek, L., Pennington, R., & Shafer, K. (1992). Peer-mediated intervention: Attending to, commenting on, and acknowledging the behavior of preschoolers with autism. *Journal of Applied Behavior Analysis, 25*, 289–305.

Hall, S. A. (2009). The social inclusion of people with disabilities: A qualitative meta-analysis. *Journal of Ethnographic and Qualitative Research, 3*, 162–173.

Halle, J. W., Gabler-Halle, D., & Chung, Y. B. (1999). Effects of a peer-mediated aerobic conditioning program on fitness levels of youth with mental retardation: two systematic replications. *Mental retardation, 37*(6), 435–448.

Halpern, A. S., Herr, C. M., Doren, B., & Wolf, N. K. (2000) *NEXT S.T.E.P.: Student transition and educational planning* (2nd ed.). Austin, TX: ProEd.

Hamilton, B., & Snell, M. E. (1993). Using the milieu approach to increase spontaneous communication book use across environments by an adolescent with autism. *Augmentative and Alternative Communication, 9*, 259–272.

Hanish, L. D., & Guerra, N. G. (2004). Aggressive victims, passive victims, and bullies: Developmental continuity or developmental change? *Merrill-Palmer Quarterly: Journal of Developmental Psychology, 50*, 17–38. doi:10.1353/mpq.2004.0003

Haring, T. G., & Breen, C. G. (1992). A peer-mediated social network intervention to enhance the social integration of persons with moderate and severe disabilities. *Journal of Applied Behavior Analysis, 25*(2), 319–333. doi:10.1901/jaba.1992.25–319

Haring, T. G., & Lovinger, L. (1989). Promoting social interaction through teaching generalized play initiation responses to preschool children with autism. *Journal of the Association for Persons with Severe Handicaps, 14*(1), 58–67.

Hartup, W. W. (1979). The social worlds of childhood. *American Psychologist, 34*, 944–950.

Henninger, N. A., & Taylor, J. L. (2014). Family perspectives on a successful transition to adulthood for individuals with disabilities. *Intellectual and Developmental Disabilities, 52*(2), 98–111.

Hetherington, S. A., Durant-Jones, L., Johnson, K., Nolan, K., Smith, E., Taylor-Brown, S., & Tuttle, J. (2010). The lived experiences of adolescents with disabilities and their parents in transition planning. *Focus on Autism and Other Developmental Disabilities, 25*(3), 163–172.

Hord, C., & Xin, Y. P. (2014). Teaching area and volume to students with mild intellectual disability. *The Journal of Special Education.* doi:10.1177/0022466914527826

Horner-Johnson, W., Dobbertin, K., Lee, J. C., Andresen, E. M., & the Expert Panel on Disability and Health Disparities. (2014). Disparities in health care access and receipt of preventative services by disability type: Analysis of the medical expenditure panel survey. *Health Research and Educational Trust, 49*, 1980–1999. doi:10.1111/1475–6773.12195

Horwitz, S. M., Kerker, B. D., Owens, P. L., & Zigler, E. (2001). *The health status and needs of individuals with mental retardation.* Washington, DC: Special Olympics.

Hughes, C., & Carter, E. W. (2000). *The transition handbook: Strategies high school teachers use that work!* Baltimore, MD: Paul H. Brookes.

Hughes, C., Rung, L. L., Wehmeyer, M. L., Agran, M., Copeland, S. R., & Hwang, B. (2000). Self-prompted communication book use to increase social interaction among high school students. *The Journal of the Association for Persons with Severe Handicaps, 25*, 153–166.

Hunt, P., Alwell, M., & Goetz, L. (1991). Interacting with peers through conversation turn taking with a communication book adaptation. *Augmentative and Alternative Communication, 7*, 117–126. doi:10.1080/07434619112331275783

Individuals with Disabilities Education Act, 20 USC. § 1400 (2004).

Jameson, J. M., McDonnell, J., Polychronis, S., & Riesen, T. (2008). Embedded, constant time delay instruction by peers without disabilities in general education classrooms. *Intellectual and Developmental Disabilities, 46*(5), 346–363.

Jerald, C. (2006). *Identifying potential dropouts: Key lessons for building on early warning system.* Achieve, Inc. Retrieved from http://www.achieve.org/measuresthatmatter

Jimenez, B. A., & Kamei, A. (2015). Embedded instruction: An evaluation of evidence to inform inclusive practice. *Inclusion, 3*(3), 132–144. doi:10.1352/2326–6988–3.3.132

Kamps, D. M., Leonard, B. R., Vernon, S., Dugan, E. P., & Delquadri, J. C. (1992). Teaching social skills to students with autism to increase peer interactions in an integrated first-grade classroom. *Journal of Applied Behavior Analysis, 2*(2), 281–288.

Kandel, D. B. (1978). Similarity in real-life adolescent friendship pairs. *Journal of personality and social psychology, 36*(3), 306.

Kann, L., Telljohann, S., Hunt, H., Hunt, P., & Haller, E. (2013). Health education. In Centers for Disease Control and Prevention (Ed.), *Results from the school health policies and practices study 2012* (pp. 21–32). Available at: http://www.cdc.gov/healthyyouth/data/shpps/pdf/shpps-results_2012.pdf#page=27

Karvonen, M. (2013). Factors associated with access to the general curriculum for students with intellectual disability. *Current Issues in Education, 16*(3), 1–20.

Kartub, D. T., Taylor-Greene, S., March, R. E., & Horner, R. H. (2000). Reducing hallway noise a systems approach. *Journal of Positive Behavior Interventions, 2*(3), 179–182.

Kef, S., & Deković, M. (2004). The role of parental and peer support in adolescents' well-being: a comparison of adolescents with and without a visual impairment. *Journal of Adolescence, 27*(4), 453–466. doi:10.1016/j.adolescence.2003.12.005

Kellems, R., & Morningstar, M. E. (Ed.). (2009). *Tips for transition.* Division of Career Development and Transition and the Transition Coalition. Retrieved from http://transitioncoalition.org/tc-materials-display/?cat_ID=331

King, G., McDougall, J., Dewit, D., Petrenchik, T., Hurley, P., & Law, M. (2009). Predictors of change over time in the activity participation of children and youth with physical disabilities. *Children's Health Care, 38*(4), 321–351. doi:10.1080/02739610903237352

Kleinert, H. L., Jones, M. M., Sheppard-Jones, K., Harp, B., Harrison, E. M. (2012). Students with intellectual disabilities going to college? Absolutely! *TEACHING Exceptional Children, 44*(5), 26–35.

Kleinert, H. L., & Kearns, J. F. (Eds.). (2010). *Alternate assessment for students with significant cognitive disabilities: An educator's guide.* Baltimore, MD: Paul H. Brookes.

Koegel, R. L., Camarata, S., Koegel, L. K., Ben-Tall, A., & Smith, A. E. (1998). Increasing speech intelligibility in children with autism. *Journal of Autism and Developmental Disorders, 28*(3), 241–251. doi:10.1023/A:1026073522897

Konrad, M., & Test, D. W. (2004). Teaching middle-school students with disabilities to use an IEP template. *Career Development for Exceptional Individuals, 27*, 101–124.

Konrad, M., Walker, A. R., Fowler, C. H., Test, D. W., & Wood, W. M. (2008). A model for aligning self-determination and general curriculum standards. *TEACHING Exceptional Children, 40*(3), 53–64.

Krahn, G. L., Hammond, L., & Turner, A. (2006). A cascade of disparities: Health and health care access for people with intellectual disabilities. *Mental Retardation and Developmental Disabilities Research Reviews, 12*, 70–82.

Krauss, M. W., Gulley, S., Sciegaj, M., & Wells, N. (2003). Access to specialty medical care for children with mental retardation, autism, and other special health care needs. *Mental Retardation, 41*, 329–339.

Lachapelle, Y., Wehmeyer, M. L., Haelewyck, M.-C., Courbois, Y., Keith, K. D., Schalock, R., Verdugo, M. A., & Walsh, P. N. (2005). The relationship between quality of life and self-determination: An international study. *Journal of Intellectual Disability Research, 49*(10), 740–744.

Ladd, G. W. (1989). Toward a further understanding of peer relationships and their contributions to children development. In T. J. Berndt, & G. W. Ladd (Eds.), *Peer Relationships in Child Development* (pp. 1–11). New York, NY, USA: John Wiley & Sons, Inc.

Larson, R. W. & Verma, S. (1999). How children and adolescents spend time across the world: Work, play, and developmental opportunities. *Psychological Bulletin, 125*(6), 701–736. doi:10.1037/0033–2909.125.6.701

Lazarsfeld, P. F. & Merton, R. K. (1954). Friendship as social process: A substantive and methodological analysis. In P. L. Kendall (Ed.). *The varied sociology of Paul F. Lazarsfeld* (pp. 18–66). New York, NY: Columbia University Press.

Leake, D., & Black, R. (2005). *Essential tools: Cultural and linguistic diversity: Implications for transition personnel.* Minneapolis, MN: University of Minnesota, Institute on Community Integration, National Center on Secondary Education and Transition.

Lee, Y., Wehmeyer, M. L., Palmer, S. B., Williams-Diehm, K., Davies, D. K., & Stock, S. E. (2011). The effect of student-directed transition planning with a computer-based reading support program on the self-determination of students with disabilities. *The Journal of Special Education, 42*(2), 104–117.

Lewis, T. J., Powers, L. J., Kelk, M. J., & Newcomer, L. L. (2002). Reducing problem behaviors on the playground: An investigation of the application of schoolwide positive behavior supports. *Psychology in the Schools. 39*(2), 181–190.

Lipsky, D. K., & Gartner, A. (1996). Inclusion, school restructuring, and the remaking of American society. *Harvard Educational Review, 66*(4), 762–797.

Mackey, M. (2014). Inclusive education in the United States: Middle school general education teachers' approaches to inclusion. *International Journal of Instruction, 7*(2), 5–21.

Madden, N. A., & Slavin, R. E. (1983). Effects of cooperative learning on the social acceptance of mainstreamed academically handicapped students. *The Journal of Special Education, 17*(2), 171–182.

Martin, J. E., Marshall, L. H., Maxson, L. M., & Jerman, P. L. (1996). *The self-directed IEP.* Longmont, CO: Sopris West.

Martinez, D. C., Conroy, J. W., & Cerreto, M. C. (2012). Parent involvement in the transition process of children with intellectual disabilities: The influence of inclusion on parent desires and expectations for postsecondary education. *Journal of Policy and Practice in Intellectual Disabilities, 9*(4), 279–288.

Martorell, A., Gutierrez-Recacha, P., Pereda, A., & Ayuso-Mateos, J. L. (2008). Identification of personal factors that determine work outcome for adults with intellectual disability. *Journal of Intellectual Disability Research, 52*(12), 1091–1101.

Mason, C. Y., McGahee-Kovac, M., & Johnson, L. (2004). How to help students lead their IEP meetings. *Teaching Exceptional Children, 36*(3), 18–24.

Mazzotti, V. L., Rowe, D. A., Kelley, K. R., Test, D. W., Fowler, C. H., Kohler, P. D. . . . Kortering, L. J. (2009). Linking transition assessment and postsecondary goals: Key elements in the secondary transition planning process. *TEACHING Exceptional Children, 42*(2), 44–51.

McConnell, S. R. (2002). Interventions to facilitate social interaction for young children with autism: Review of available research and recommendations for educational intervention and future research. *Journal of Autism and Developmental Disorders, 32*, 351–372.

McGuire, J., & McDonnell, J. (2008). Relationships between recreation and levels of self-determination for adolescents and young adults with disabilities. *Career Development for Exceptional Individuals, 31*, 154–163.

McQueen, P. C., Spence, M. W., Garner, J. B., Pereira, L. H., & Winsor, E. J. T. (1987). Prevalence of major mental retardation and associated disabilities in the Canadian Maritime Provinces. *American Journal of Mental Deficiency, 91*, 460–466.

Menesini, E., Modena, M., & Tani, F. (2009). Bullying and victimization in adolescence: Concurrent and stable roles and psychological health symptoms. *Journal of Genetic Psychology, 170*, 115–133. doi:10.3200/GNTP.170.2.115–134

Meyer, A., Rose, D. H., & Gordon, D. (2014). *Universal design for learning: Theory and practice.* Wakefield, MA: CAST.

Murawski, W. W. (2009). *Collaborative teaching in secondary schools: Making the co-teaching marriage work!* Thousand Oaks: Corwin Press.

National Association of State Department of Special Educators (NASDE). (2007, June). *A seven-step process to creating standards-based IEPs.* Retrieved from http://www.nasdse.org/Portals/0/SevenStepProcesstoCreatingStandards-basedIEPs.pdf

National Longitudinal Transition Study-2. (2005). *Facts from NLTS2: High school completion by youth with disabilities.* Menlo Park, CA: SRI International. Retrieved from http://www.lts2.org/fact_sheets

No Child Left Behind Act of 2001, Pub. L. No. 107–110, 115 Stat. 1425 (2002).

Nota, L., Ferrari, L., Soresi, S., & Wehmeyer, M. L. (2007). Self-determination, social abilities, and the quality of life of people with intellectual disabilities. *Journal of Intellectual Disability Research, 51*, 850–865.

Office of the State Superintendent of Education (OSSE). (2013). *Standards-based IEP guide: A resource for local education agencies.* Washington, DC: Division of Specialized Education.

Office of the Surgeon General. (2002). *Closing the gap: A national blueprint to improve the health of people with mental retardation.* Rockville, MD: US Department of Health and Human Services.

Ouellette-Kuntz, H. (2005). Understanding health disparities and inequalities faced by individuals with intellectual disabilities. *Journal of Applied Research in Intellectual Disabilities, 18*, 113–121.

Parker, J. G., & Gottman, J. M. (1989). Social and emotional development in a relational context: Friendship interaction from early childhood to adolescence. In T. J. Berndt & G. W. Ladd (Eds.), *Peer relationships in child development* (pp. 95–131). New York, NY: John Wiley & Sons.

Parker, J. G., Rubin, K. H., Erath, S. A., Wojslawowicz, J. C., & Buskirk, A. A. (2006). Peer relationships, child development, and adjustment: A developmental psychopathology perspective. In D. Cicchetti & D. J. Cohen (Eds.), *Developmental psychopathology: Vol. 1: Theory and methods* (2nd ed., pp. 96–161). New York: Wiley.

Pearl, R., Farmer, T. W., Acker, R. Van, Rodkin, P. C., Bost, K. K., Coe, M., & Henley, W. (1998). The social integration of students with mild disabilities in general education classrooms: Peer group membership and peer-assessed social behavior. *The Elementary School Journal, 99*(2), 167. doi:10.1086/461921

Pitetti, K. H., Beets, M. W., & Combs, C. (2009). Physical activity levels of children with intellectual disabilities during school. *Medicine and Science in Sports and Exercise, 41*, 1580–1586.

Polanin, J. R., Espelage, D. L., & Pigott, T. D. (2012). A meta-analysis of school-based bullying prevention programs' effects on bystander intervention behavior. *School Psychology Review, 41*, 47–65.

Powell, S. (2005). *Introduction to middle school.* New York: Pearson Allyn Bacon Prentice Hall.

Price, J. M., & Dodge, K. A. (1989). Peers' contributions to children's social maladjustment. In T. J. Berndt & G. M. Ladd (Eds.), *Peer relationships in child development* (pp. 341–370). New York, NY: John Wiley & Sons.

Prinstein, M. J., & Cillessen, A. H. N. (2003). Forms and functions of adolescent peer aggression associated with high levels of peer status. *Merrill-Palmer Quarterly, 49*, 310–342. doi:10.1353/mpq.2003.0015

Prinstein, M. J., & Dodge, K. A. (2008). Current issues in peer influence research. In M. J. Prinstein & K. A. Dodge (Eds.), *Understanding peer influences in children and adolescents* (pp. 3–13). New York, NY: The Guillford Press.

Ratcliff, A. E., & Cress, C. J. (1999). Guidelines for enhancing reciprocal peer communication with adolescents who use augmentative/alternative communication. *Communication Disorders Quarterly, 20*, 25–35. doi:10.1177/152574019902000204

Reiter, S., & Lapidot-Lefler, N. (2007). Disabilities : Differences in social adjustment and social skills. *Intellectual and Developmental Disabilities, 45*(3), 174–181.

Repetto, J. B. (2012). Middle school transition education planning and services. In M. L. Wehmeyer & K. W. Webb (Eds.), *Handbook of adolescent transition education for youth with disabilities* (pp. 267–270). New York: Taylor and Francis.

Ringenbach, S. D. R., Albert, A. R., Chen, C. C., & Alberts, J. R. (2014). Acute bouts of assisted cycling improves cognitive and upper extremity movement functions in adolescents with Down syndrome. *Intellectual and Developmental Disabilities, 52*, 124–135.

Rodkin, P. C., Espelage, D. L., & Hanish, L. D. (2015). A relational framework for understanding bullying. *American Psychologist, 70*(4), 311–321.

Rose, C. A., Espelage, D. L., Monda-Amaya, L. E., Shogren, K. A., & Aragon, S. R. (2013). Bullying and middle school students with and without specific learning disabilities: An examination of social-ecological predictors. *Journal of Learning Disabilities,* doi:10.1177/0022219413496279

Rowe, D. A., Mazzotti, V. L., & Sinclair, J. (2015). Strategies for teaching self-determination skills in conjunction with the common core. *Intervention in School and Clinic, 50*(3), 131–141.

Safran, S. P., & Oswald, K. (2003). Positive behavior supports: Can schools reshape disciplinary practices? *Exceptional Children, 69*, 361–373.

Santoli, S. P., Sachs, J., Romey, E. A., & McClurg, S. (2008). A successful formula for middle school inclusion: Collaboration, time, and administrative support. *RMLE Online: Research in Middle Level Education, 32*(2), 1–13.

Schleien, S. J., Mustonen, T., & Rynders, J. E. (1995). Participation of children with autism and nondisabled peers in a cooperatively structured community art program. *Journal of Autism and Developmental Disorders, 25*, 297–413.

Scruggs, T. E., Mastropieri, M. A., & McDuffie, K. A. (2007). Co-teaching in inclusive classrooms: A metasynthesis of qualitative research. *Exceptional Children, 73*(4), 392–416.

Shields, N., King, M., Corbett, M., & Imms, C. (2014). Is participation among children with intellectual disabilities in outside school activities similar to their typically developing peers? A systematic review. *Developmental Neurorehabilitation, 17*(1), 64–71. doi:10.3109/17518423.2013.836256

Shogren, K. A. (2013). A social–ecological analysis of the self-determination literature. *Intellectual and Developmental Disabilities, 51*(6), 496–511.

Shogren, K. A., Lopez, S. J., Wehmeyer, M. L., Little, T. D., & Pressgrove, C. L. (2006). The role of positive psychology constructs in predicting life satisfaction in adolescents with and without cognitive disabilities: An exploratory study. *The Journal of Positive Psychology, 1*, 37–52.

Shogren, K. A., & Plotner, A. J. (2012). Transition planning for students with intellectual disability, autism, or other disabilities: Data from the National Longitudinal Transition Study-2. *Intellectual and Developmental Disabilities, 50*(1), 16–30.

Shukla, S., Kennedy, C., & Cushing, L. (1999). Intermediate school students with severe disabilities: Supporting their social participation in general education classrooms. *Journal of Positive Behavior Interventions, 1*, 130–140. doi:10.1177/109830079900100301

Simeonsson, R. J., Carlson, D., Huntington, G. S., McMillen, J. S., & Brent, J. L. (2001). Students with disabilities: A national survey of participation in school activities. *Disability and Rehabilitation, 23*, 49–63. doi:10.1080/096382801750058134

Simonsen, B., Sugai, G., & Negron, M. (2008). Schoolwise positive behavior supports: Primary systems and practices. *Teaching Exceptional Children, 40*(6), 32–40.

Siperstein, G. N., Parker, R. C., Norins-Bardon, J., & Widaman, K. F. (2007). A national study of youth attitudes toward the inclusion of students with intellectual disabilities. *Exceptional Children, 73*(4), 435–455. Retrieved from http://cec.metapress.com/content/f834815370373485/

Sitlington, P. L., Neubert, D. A., & Clark, G. M. (2010). *Transition education and services for students with disabilities* (5th ed.). Upper Saddle River, NJ: Merrill.

Slavin, R. E. (1980). Cooperative learning. *Review of Educational Research, 50*(2), 315–342.

Snell, M. E., Chen, L., & Hoover, K. (2006). Teaching augmentative and alternative communication to students with severe disabilities: A review of intervention research 1997–2003. *Research and Practice for Persons with Severe Disabilities, 31*, 203–214.

Sohler, N., Lubetkin, E., Levy, J., Soghomonian, C., & Rimmerman, A. (2009). Factors associated with obesity and coronary heart disease in people with intellectual disabilities. *Social Work in Health Care, 48*, 76–89.

Spooner, F., Baker, J. N., Harris, A. A., Ahlgrim-Delzell, L., & Browder, D. M. (2007). Effects of training in universal design for learning on lesson plan development. *Remedial and Special Education, 28*(2), 108–116.

Steele, S. (1986). Assessment of functional wellness behaviors in adolescents who are mentally retarded. *Issues in Comprehensive Pediatric Nursing, 9*, 331–340.

Thoma, C. A. (2013). Postsecondary education for students with intellectual disability: Complex layers. *Journal of Postsecondary Education and Disability, 26*, 285–302.

Thoma, C. A., Bartholomew, C. C., & Scott, L. A. (2009) *Universal design for transition: A roadmap for planning and instruction.* Baltimore: Paul H. Brookes.

Thoma, C. A., & Getzel, E. E. (2005). "Self-determination is what it's all about": What post-secondary students with disabilities tell us are important considerations for success. *Education and Training in Developmental Disabilities, 40*, 217–233.

Thoma, C. A., Lakin, K. C., Carlson, D., Domzal, C., & Boyd, K. S. (2011). Post-secondary education for students with intellectual disabilities: A review of the literature. *Journal on Post-Secondary Education for Disabilities, 24*(3), 175–191.

Thoma, C. A., Rogan, P., & Baker, S. R. (2001). Student involvement in transition planning: Unheard voices. *Education and Training in Mental Retardation and Developmental Disabilities, 36*, 16–29.

Thoma, C. A., & Tamura, R. (2013). *Demystifying transition assessment.* Baltimore: Paul H. Brookes.

Tipton, L. A., Christensen, L., & Blacher, J. (2013). Friendship quality in adolescents with and without an intellectual disability. *Journal of Applied Research in Intellectual Disabilities, 26*, 522–532.

Trainor, A. A., Morningstar, M., Murray, A., & Kim, H. (2013). Social capital during the postsecondary transition for young adults with high incidence disabilities. *Prevention Researcher, 20*(2), 7–10.

Turnbull, C., Wilkie, F., McKenzie, K., & Powell, H. (2005). Health promotion: How to spread the word. *Learning Disability Practice, 8*(7), 16–19.

van Schrojenstein Lantman-de Valk, H. M. J., van den Akker, M., Maaskant, M. A., Havman, M. J., Urlings, H. F. J., Kessels, A. G. H., ... Crebolder, H. F. J. M. (1997). Prevalence and incidence of health problems in people with intellectual disability. *Journal of Intellectual Disability Research, 41*, 42–51.

Villa, R. A., Thousand, J. S., Nevin, A., & Liston, A. (2005). Successful inclusive practices in middle and secondary schools. *American Secondary Education, 33*(3) 33–50.

Vogt, T., Schneider, S., Abeln, V., Anneken, V., & Studer, H. K. (2012). Exercise, mood and cognitive performance in intellectual disability–A neurophysiological approach. *Behavioral Brain Research, 226*, 473–480.

Wagner, M., Newman, L., & Cameto, R. (2004). *Changes over time in the secondary school experiences of students with disabilities: A report of findings from the National Longitudinal Transition Study (NLTS) and the National Longitudinal Transition Study-2 (NLTS2).* Menlo Park, CA: SRI International.

Waitoller, F. R., & Artiles, A. J. (2013). A decade of professional development research for inclusive education: A critical review and notes for a research program. *Review of Educational Research, 83*(3), 319–356.

Waldman, H. B., Perlman, S. P., & Swerdloff, M. (2001). Children with mental retardation/developmental disabilities: Do physicians ever consider needed dental care? *Mental Retardation, 39*, 53–56.

Walker, A. R., Kortering, L. J., & Fowler, C. H. (2007). *Age-appropriate transition assessment guide.* National Secondary Transition Technical Assistance Center. Retrieved from http://education.nh.gov/instruction/special_ed/documents/age_app_trans_assess.pdf

Wehmeyer, M. L. (2006). Beyond access: Ensuring progress in the general education curriculum. *Research & Practice for Persons with Severe Disabilities, 31*(4), 322–326.

Wehmeyer, M. L., Abery, B., Mithaug, D. E., & Stancliffe, R. J. (2003). *Theory in self-determination: Foundations for educational practice.* Springfield, IL: Charles C. Thomas Publisher, LTD.

Wehmeyer, M. L., Agran, M., & Hughes, C. (1998). *Teaching self-determination to students with disabilities: Basic skills for successful transition.* Baltimore: Paul H. Brookes.

Wehmeyer, M. L., Agran, M., Hughes, C., Martin, J., Mithaug, D. E., & Palmer, S. (2007). *Promoting self-determination in students with intellectual and developmental disabilities.* New York: Guilford Press.

Wehmeyer, M. L., & Lawrence, M. (1995). Whose future is it anyway? Promoting student involvement in transition planning. *Career Development for Exceptional Individuals, 18*, 69–83.

Wehmeyer, M., Lawrence, M., Kelchner, K., Palmer, S., Garner, N., & Soukup, J. (2004). *Whose future is it anyway? A student-directed transition planning process* (2nd ed.). Lawrence, KS: Beach Center on Disability.

Wehmeyer, M. L., & Palmer, S. B. (2003). Adult outcomes for students with cognitive disabilities three years after high school: The impact of self-determination. *Education and Training in Developmental Disabilities, 38*, 131–144.

Wehmeyer, M. L., Palmer, S., Lee, Y., Williams-Diehm, K., & Shogren, K. (2011). A randomized-trial evaluation of the effect of *Whose future is it, anyway?* On self-determination. *Career Development and Transition for Exceptional Individuals, 34*, 45–56.

Weiner, J. S. (2005). Peer-mediated conversational repair in students with moderate and severe disabilities. *Research and Practice for Persons with Severe Disabilities, 30*, 26–37.

Whitney, I., Smith, P. K., & Thompson, D. (1994). Bullying and children with special educational needs. In P. K. Smith & S. Sharp (Eds.). *School bullying: Insights and perspectives* (pp. 213–240). London: Routledge.

Williamson, P., McLeskey, J., Hoppey, D., & Rentz, T. (2006). Educating students with mental retardation in general education classrooms. *Exceptional Children, 72*(3), 347–361.

Wolowiec Fisher, K., & Shogren, K. A. (2012). Integrating augmentative and alternative communication and peer support for students with disabilities: A social-ecological perspective. *Journal of Special Education Technology, 27*(2), 23–39.

Wong, C., Odom, S. L., Hume, K., Cox, A. W., Fettig, A., Kucharczyk, S., . . . Schultz, T. R. (2014). *Evidence-based practices for children, youth, and young adults with autism spectrum disorder.* Chapel Hill. Retrieved from http:// autismpdc.fpg.unc.edu/sites/autismpdc.fpg.unc.edu/files/2014-EBP-Report.pdf

Yakubova, G., & Bouck, E. C. (2014). Not all created equally: Exploring calculator use by students with mild intellectual disability. *Education and Training in Autism and Developmental Disabilities, 49*(1), 111.

24

High-Quality Educational Programs for Students with Intellectual Disability in High School

Mary E. Morningstar, Jennifer Kurth,
Michael L. Wehmeyer, Karrie A. Shogren

The transition to adulthood is typically marked by the high school graduation ceremony, a ritual that takes place for hundreds of thousands of youth across the country each spring. Students exit high school and enter postsecondary educational settings, go straight to work, or perhaps take some time off before they decide what direction their life will take. Youth with intellectual disability, however, far too often do not have similar adult life trajectories, and continue to experience negative post–high school outcomes (Sanford et al., 2011). Too often, young adults with intellectual disability transition to segregated work and residential settings without opportunities to engage in inclusive community settings. Innovative supports for a quality adult life are still mostly unobtainable (Braddock et al., 2013), despite existing and emerging models of positive and inclusive transitions (Certó & Luecking, 2006).

Why are high schools not adequately preparing youth with intellectual disability for successful transition to adulthood? As would be expected, a myriad of school factors may influence effective implementation of research-based transition practices that lead to valued postschool outcomes. Federal legislation requires that all students receiving special education services be involved with and progress in the general education curriculum as well as receive instruction to address their unique learning needs (Carter & Kennedy, 2006). However, transition-related instruction and content has not typically been included in the general education curriculum, despite its importance for all students. Too often, only core content instruction (math, science, literacy) has been emphasized within secondary core academic classes. Core content areas are, of course, important for all learners, but not at the exclusion of transition-related instruction and instructional supports for other unique student learning needs (Ryndak, Jackson, & White, 2013). Further, teachers may not sufficiently emphasize students' personal capacities through appropriate supports and modifications within the general education context (Turnbull, Turnbull, Wehmeyer, & Shogren, 2013). In addition, practitioners may not possess the pedagogical skills of emergent research-based interventions in literacy, math, and science that support secondary content (Browder, Spooner, Ahlgrim-Delzell, Harris, & Wakeman, 2008).

A factor influencing secondary schools is a result of educational reform driven by the almost nation-wide adoption of the Common Core State Standards (CCSS, National Governors Association, 2010) and college and career readiness (CCR) initiatives (US DOE, 2010). Along with academic standards, the CCSS maintain a long view to ensure that students are college and career ready (Council of Chief State School Officers, 2010). Unfortunately, most students with intellectual disability graduate from K–12 systems without the skills necessary to be college and career ready (Kearns, Towles-Reeves,

Kleinert, O'Regan Klienert, & Kliene-Kracht, 2011). Limited opportunities to fully participate in secondary school curricula and environments often result in young adults with intellectual disability achieving outcomes substantially lower than those of their peers without disabilities (Carter et al., 2012; Newman, Wagner, Cameto, Knokey, & Shaver, 2010). While evidence points to inclusion in general education as a predictor contributing to postschool success (Test et al., 2009), students with intellectual disability are least likely to spend significant time in general education classrooms and, when they are included in the general education classroom, rarely receive the modifications and accommodations that would ensure their success in the general education curriculum (Lee, Wehmeyer, Soukup, & Palmer, 2010; Soukup, Wehmeyer, Bashinski, & Bovaird, 2007). Thus, there is a pressing need for secondary programs for students with intellectual disability to reflect rigorous, high-quality instruction that clearly promotes CCR and the transition to inclusive postschool outcomes.

Promoting inclusive educational opportunities that adequately prepare youth with intellectual disability to be college and career ready, and to transition to meaningful postschool opportunities and outcomes, has brought major alterations to how schools implement secondary education for students with intellectual disability. New roles (e.g., teaching core content, using universal design for learning (UDL), promoting self-determined learning, collaborating to facilitate inclusion) and skills (e.g., co-teaching, adapting core curriculum, supporting peer supports; see Villa, Thousand, Nevin, & Liston, 2005) are needed to ensure successful transitions to colleges and careers (Morningstar, Lombardi, Fowler, & Test, 2015). Although research and legislation support the changing nature of secondary education for students with intellectual disability, states and districts often lag in offering research-based services and supports that ensure success.

The purpose of this chapter is to review critical features of effective secondary education for students with intellectual disability, with a focus on practices that promote CCR and the transition to inclusive adult lives. We begin by defining the Individuals with Disabilities Education Act (IDEA) transition requirements, using this to provide a framework for describing key features of research-based inclusive secondary education. We then describe requirements related to access to the general education curriculum, and strategies for promoting access to core content and transition programming in inclusive environments. Finally, we describe other research-based practices that are critical in supporting inclusive secondary education focused on CCR and the transition to inclusive, supported postschool outcomes.

IDEA Definition and Requirements for Transition

In the United States, transition planning and services were first mandated under the reauthorization to the 1990 IDEA (20 USC. §1400), with subsequent amendments in 1997 and 2004. More recently, other countries have acknowledged the importance of transition through laws and regulatory policies that mirror the US mandates and principles of IDEA. Understanding the compliance requirements of the transition Individualized Education Program (IEP) is important, but it is even more important to support students to achieve positive adult outcomes by using research-based strategies for student-focused transition planning. Equally relevant is that educators implement effective interventions and practices for preparing youth for adulthood. Assisting students and their families to connect with services both within and outside of the school system is a cornerstone of transition.

From early research on postschool outcomes (Blackorby & Wagner, 1996), it was evident that the first generation of students with disabilities who had received special education services were not experiencing successful outcomes in adulthood. This was especially true for students with the most significant support needs and intellectual disability (Will, 1984). Thirty years since the first federal transition initiatives were articulated, research reveals students with disabilities have been making steady progress toward achieving more positive adult outcomes (Sanford et al., 2011). Unfortunately, substantially fewer positive outcomes exist for students with intellectual disability when compared to their peers with and without disabilities, and inclusive adult outcomes are even less likely to be obtained (Carter et al., 2012; Newman et al., 2010). The urgency to improve both planning and transition services for this group of students is undeniable and can be felt by advocates, families, researchers, and practitioners.

The 2004 reauthorization of IDEA mandated that transition planning must begin by the time the student turns 16 years old. In some states, the requirement for starting transition planning begins even younger, with many beginning the process by age 14. Of course, for students with intellectual disability and their families, transition planning should begin as early as possible, to allow substantial time to create the supports and opportunities leading to inclusive adult outcomes. If the secondary school IEP is a road map for facilitating a future adult life, then sufficient time and energy must be given to quality transition planning and the provision of effective transition services.

IDEA mandates that when the purpose of an IEP team meeting is to consider a student's postsecondary goals, then the student must be invited to attend the meeting as a team member. Because the IEP is based upon a student's needs, strengths, preferences, and interests, it makes sense for the student to be present and actively engaged during transition meetings. This requires schools to implement research-based student-directed planning approaches (Martin et al., 2006; Wehmeyer, Palmer, Lee, Williams-Diehm, & Shogren, 2011). The law also makes it clear that parents are to be active members of IEP teams. Therefore, informing and supporting families to fully engage during transition planning is essential.

Transition planning entails reviewing students' postsecondary goals, educational services, and transition activities with the focus on supporting the interests, preferences, and strengths of the student. IEP teams must develop and specify measurable postsecondary goals (MPGs) in the areas of employment, education and/or training, and, where appropriate, independent living. Once a transition plan is developed, schools must also provide the educational and transition services required to facilitate the movement toward the employment, education and/or training, and independent living goals. Transition services are used to help the student achieve his or her desired postsecondary goals. When identifying transition services for students with intellectual disability, the educational team should be able to answer yes to the following three questions:

1. Do the transition services focus on improving the student's academic and functional achievement?
2. Do the transition services facilitate the student's movement from school to postsecondary settings?
3. Are the transition services listed appropriate for helping the student to meet his or her postsecondary goal(s)?

Transition services are much broader than annual IEP educational goals and services, and are included in transition plans to ensure that schools provide relevant experiences leading to improved postsecondary outcomes. In addition, parents, students, and other outside agencies can be listed as partners in providing transition services. Of course, involving families in transition planning requires more than just having them at the IEP meeting (Kim & Morningstar, 2005). Such research-based practices as communicating with families, providing family friendly information, offering parent training, hosting parent support groups, and meeting with families in the community are all identified as strategies that improve transition planning (Turnbull, Zuna, Turnbull, Poston, & Summers, 2007).

The transition IEP is only the first step: How schools implement effective services to increase relevant skills and the opportunities provided to students throughout their secondary school years are substantial contributors to success. For students with intellectual disability, this means participating in real-life and inclusive experiences such as work-based learning, and accessing the general education curriculum and context. It also means focusing on building systems of support that carry over into adulthood.

Broadening the Focus of Transition to Supported Adulthood

In discussing their son's transition from school to adult life, Diane and Phil Ferguson described a perspective of adulthood combining theories of chronological development with societal perceptions of adulthood: autonomy, membership, and change (Ferguson & Ferguson, 2006). This framework expands traditional notions of adulthood by emphasizing the "dual sense of independence and belonging as the most basic benefits of social support programs" (Ferguson & Ferguson, 2006, p. 626). Components of supported adulthood require high-quality educational programs to: (a) promote inclusion in the natural context, (b) blend informal and formal supports within natural settings, (c) ensure services meet the unique preferences of the individual and his or her family, and (d) maintain a school and community-focused point of view. School experiences should align with the skills, experiences, and supports needed to support the transition from school to a supported adult life (Buntinx & Schalock, 2010). Early on, Halpern (1993) introduced a quality adult life framework that encompasses three domains: (a) physical and material well-being, (b) performance of adult roles (e.g., employment/career, relationships/social networks, education, citizenship, and (c) personal fulfillment. Using an individualized supports approach to bring together practices such as person-centered planning, school inclusion, and personal growth and empowerment (Schalock et al., 2010) ensure that critical elements of supported adult life are considered and addressed.

The transition to supported adulthood for students with intellectual disability requires educators to develop new ways to plan and prepare for quality adult outcomes. Unfortunately, educational and adult service delivery systems often operate in ways that deny the full participation of adulthood for students, and that perpetuate "unfinished transitions by encouraging dependency, social isolation and personal chronicity" (Ferguson & Ferguson, 2006, p. 625). While strategies leading to inclusive supported adulthood have been developed and taken root in many school settings, gaps in replicating systems of support still exist.

Developing inclusive educational and adult life goals means holding high expectations for students with intellectual disability and recognizing that the general education curriculum provides key learning opportunities to promote CCR and a transition to inclusive postschool outcomes. The IEP team will also need to provide examples and role models to share with families if transition planning is to focus on supported transition to inclusive adult life engagement. In the following sections, we review the access to the general education curriculum mandates and the implications of these mandates for inclusive secondary education for students with intellectual disability.

IDEA and Access to the General Education Curriculum

Since the inclusion of IDEA mandates requiring "access" to the general education curriculum, there has been a growing need for evidence-based practices to promote involvement with and progress in general education for students with intellectual disability. Broadly speaking, continued improvements toward greater access to general education have been found (McLeskey, Landers, Williamson, & Hoppey, 2012). However, the extent to which this holds true for students with significant disabilities (i.e., intellectual disability, autism, multiple disabilities, deaf-blindness) is not clear. Recent research has indicated that students with intellectual disability and autism are less likely to be included in general education classes (Brock & Schaefer, 2015; Morningstar, Kurth, & Johnson, 2016). Researchers point to limited systemic change in schools, resulting in the little progress toward inclusion (Ryndak et al., 2013) for students with intellectual disability in the full range of general education contexts and curricula. The most salient characteristic of promoting access to the general education curriculum is that the focal point has shifted primarily from *where* a student receives his or her educational program, to *what* and *how* the student is taught (Wehmeyer, 2014). Today, the least dangerous assumption for teaching students with intellectual

disability is to consider their presence in the general education classroom with the emphasis on the quality of learning taking place.

Unfortunately, placement decisions on the basis of a disability label rest on assumptions that certain students cannot learn in or benefit from participation in a "regular" classroom; in a large part, we have seen a retrenchment toward segregated services for these students (Jackson, Ryndak, & Wehmeyer, 2010; Kurth, Morningstar, & Kozelski, 2014). Such assumptions exist despite the fact that research has consistently documented that students with intellectual disability can learn *academic* (Browder et al., 2008; Dessemontet, Bless, & Morin, 2012; Kurth & Mastergeorge, 2012), *communication* (Foreman, Arthur-Kelly, Pascoe, & King, 2004), and *social* (Boutot & Bryant, 2005; Carter, Moss, Hoffman, Chung, & Sisco, 2011; Fisher & Meyer, 2002) skills, in addition to skills leading to *self-determination* (Shogren, Palmer, Wehmeyer, Williams-Diehm, & Little, 2012; Wehmeyer et al., 2012). It has been shown that simply being placed in a general education setting can increase learning expectations of all students (Kurth & Mastergeorge, 2012).

The research-based technologies that have emerged over several decades related to engaging secondary students with intellectual disability in school and classroom-wide learning serve as a basis for high-quality educational programs leading to CCR. How teams plan for inclusive experiences and opportunities should incorporate fundamental principles of: aligning transition goals, holding high expectations for students, and promoting access to and progress in the general education curriculum.

Supporting Access to Inclusive Secondary General Education

Inclusive education presents unique challenges in secondary schools. The complexity of content and pace of instruction, as well as consequences of high-stakes testing (Mastropieri & Scruggs, 2001; Munk & Bursuck, 2001) pose particular challenges for those supporting the inclusion of students with intellectual disability in secondary schools. Further, special education teachers at the secondary level must teach academic content across grade levels (Wasburn-Moses, 2005), which can pose a challenge for teachers with limited pedagogical background. Moreover, special education teachers in secondary settings must plan for and prepare students with intellectual disability for the transition to adulthood (Conderman & Katsiyannis, 2002). Because special education programs for students with intellectual disability often focused on age-appropriate and functional skills (e.g., daily living, employment, using transportation), an emphasis on "functional life skills" may be viewed as competing with access to and inclusion in core content (Ayres, Lowrey, Douglas, & Sievers, 2011). In fact, most secondary students with intellectual disability receive the majority of special education services in functional classes with an emphasis on "life skills" (Bouck, 2012), effectively limiting their opportunities to learn both core content as well as critical communication, social, and problem-solving skills alongside their peers without disabilities.

Despite these challenges, a number of effective practices have been identified to promote inclusive secondary schools. Effective inclusive secondary schools engage in collaboration, regular communication, ongoing professional development, and authentic assessment to meet academic and transition-related needs (Deppeler, Loreman, & Sharma, 2005; Villa et al., 2005). Further, many effective programs have implemented evidence-based peer tutoring and mentoring to support student engagement and learning (e.g., Carter, Cushing, Clark, & Kennedy, 2005; Collins, Branson, Hall, & Rankin, 2001).

Additional critical principles and practices have emerged to meet the challenge of promoting learning for all students. Applying principles of UDL in secondary classrooms promotes flexibility in representing and presenting content as well as how students demonstrate learning. Classrooms with high levels of UDL are less likely to need accommodations, adaptations, and modifications for students with disabilities because they can access and engage in learning in ways that best meet their needs and styles (Morningstar, Shogren, Lee, & Born, 2015). In conjunction with classroom-wide transformations, effective secondary classrooms provide individualized supports for students with intellectual disability. Implementing evidence-based and individualized supports such as peer and social supports (Carter et al., 2011) are further components of effective inclusive secondary programs. Collaborative supports and arrangements for modifying curricular and instructional elements to ensure full access to all educational settings is another element in promoting full access to general education.

Aligning CCR and CCSS to Secondary Education of Students with Intellectual Disability

Recently, advocates have called for the field of secondary transition to become more involved in high school reform efforts (Morningstar, Knollman, Semon, & Kleinhammer-Tramill, 2012), directing attention to concepts of transition-focused education to prepare all students for success after high school (Kohler & Field, 2003). In addition to education reform driven by CCSS and CCR, reform movements such as Response to Intervention (RTI; National Center for Response to Intervention, 2011) and Positive Behavior Supports (PBIS; Flannery & Sugai, 2009) are examples of multitiered systems of supports (MTSS). MTSS is defined as "a whole-school, data-driven, prevention-based framework for improving learning outcomes for all students through a layered continuum of evidence-based practices and systems" (Sugai, 2012, p. 1). While originally developed for elementary schools, given the traction MTSS has gained within secondary schools, it is critical that teachers, including teachers of students with intellectual disability, understand and can effectively work within existing MTSS systems.

At the secondary level, however, MTSS must incorporate an adolescent and transition-focused frame of reference to bridge the unique contextual factors found in secondary schools and with adolescent learners (Morningstar et al., 2012). Such a model expands learning beyond core academic skills to support all students with performing nonacademic skills such as critical thinking, self-monitoring, self-determination, self-motivation, and engagement (Conley, 2010; Farrington et al., 2012; Kearns et al., 2011; Savitz-Romer, 2013; Shogren, 2012).

Research on Instructional Strategies to Promote Positive Outcomes for Secondary Students with Intellectual Disability

In previous sections we highlighted the IDEA requirements related to transition and access to the general education curriculum, discussing implications and strategies for using these mandates to promote inclusive secondary education focused on CCR. In the following sections we provide an overview of evidence-based transition planning practices, research and interventions to promote self-determination, access to communication supports, strategies for supporting community membership, and preparing youth for the transition to supported living and community participation.

Evidence-Based Transition Planning

The most current innovations in transition are the results of an increase in the research and implementation of evidence-based practices (Test, Fowler et al., 2009). By examining published literature, research studies, and model transition programs, Kohler (1996) created the *Taxonomy for Transition Programming Framework,* which comprises five domains: student-focused planning, student development, interagency collaboration, family involvement, and program structure. The *Taxonomy* is conceptually organized as a diverse set of practices for delivering transition-focused education and services (Kohler & Field, 2003). Subsequently, researchers have launched rigorous research studies to identify a body of evidence that supports the range of transition practices.

As part of the *What Works in Transition Research Synthesis,* Cobb and Alwell (2007) examined studies that met the definition of *transition planning/coordinating interventions* to identify approaches that successfully "facilitate the child's movement from school to post-school activities" (p. 11). Only a limited number of rigorous research studies were found to include student-focused planning; however, sufficient evidence was found that providing student-centered transition planning holds great promise for leading to positive postsecondary outcomes. The most effective methods of transition planning include involving students during transition IEP meetings and supporting them to be highly engaged during the planning process by ensuring that they have a valued place on the team. In addition, several of the qualitative studies supported the notion that adding transition to an already full IEP meeting is not sufficient: Transition planning requires enough time and space to be implemented well. Finally, Cobb and Alwell (2007) found that focusing specifically on person-centered planning approaches leads to more positive experiences for all involved in transition planning.

More recently, Test, Fowler and colleagues (2009) completed a systematic review of transition research. They identified specific practices with moderate to high evidence of success, including: (a) teaching students to be actively involved in transition IEP meetings (Test et al., 2004), (b) utilizing evidence-based self-advocacy strategies and skills (Van Reusen & Bos, 1994), (c) teaching students strategies for the Self-Directed IEP (SDIEP; Martin et al., 2006), and (d) promoting skills leading to self-determination that are more likely to lead to improved postsecondary outcomes in employment and independent living (Shogren, Wehmeyer, Palmer, Rifenbark, & Little, 2015; Wehmeyer & Palmer, 2003). Research- and evidence-based transition planning strategies include person-centered planning processes and processes to promote student involvement in education and transition planning, as discussed in the next two sections.

Implementing Person-Centered Transition Planning

When students and families are placed at the center of planning and a strengths-based approach is used, the resulting transition plans will be more individualized, comprehensive, and collaborative (Keyes & Owens-Johnson, 2003). Person-centered planning (discussed further in Chapter 11) is a strategy one can embed within transition planning that focuses on students' strengths and empowers families, thereby establishing collaborative relationships (Michaels & Ferrara, 2005). By illuminating the students' preferences, connecting them to formal and informal supports in the community, and involving family and community members, one can provide students with inclusive experiences (Kincaid & Fox, 2002; Rasheed, Fore, & Miller, 2006).

Using person-centered approaches specifically to plan for the transition to adulthood has been discussed for some time (Stineman, Morningstar, Bishop, & Turnbull, 1993). One approach embeds person-centered planning into transition by adapting *Making Action Plans* (MAP, O'Brien & Forest, 1989). The adaptation, *Making Dreams Happen* (Furney, 1993), begins by having a team respond to five questions: What is the student's history? What are his/her dreams? What are the fears for the future? Who is the student? and What are his/her current and future supports needed to achieve the dreams? Team members can include family members, peers, friends/neighbors, as well as teachers and other support staff. The team spends about an hour developing the student and family's vision for the future, as well as generating strategies for how to realize the student's dreams. As is typically found in a MAP meeting, the responses to the five questions are illustrated and displayed on large sheets of paper.

The team is then guided to complete specific transition planning for the IEP. Because this approach does not adhere to traditional planning methods and uses colorful graphics to record the planning, it easily accommodates students with a range of communication and intellectual supports, and it is much more appealing and accessible to students and other team members. The information generated from the MAP meeting often "sparks new ideas and creative ways to overcome barriers that have previously stood in the way of reaching a student's dreams for the future" (Furney, 1993, p. 6). The following four steps must be completed to develop a person-centered transition plan.

1. Hold a **MAP meeting** and summarize information from the MAP into charts.
2. Organize results of the MAP meeting into the following **Quadrants** to consider possible post-secondary goals: employment, community participation, education, and community living.
3. During the **IEP meeting**:
   a. Include results from the MAP meeting in the **transition assessments** section of the IEP;
   b. develop **measurable postsecondary goals** for the IEP based upon the dreams for the future generated during the MAP meeting and organized in the Quadrants;
   c. consider which **annual IEP goals** are to be developed and implemented to facilitate progress toward the measurable postsecondary goals;
   d. identify specific **transition services** needed (instruction, community experiences, etc.);
   e. include **interagency linkages and services** from outside agencies who are or may be involved in providing services.
4. **Implement the IEP**, track student progress toward goals and services provided, and reconvene the IEP team if needed.

The end result of the first meeting, notes from the MAP meeting, can then be used as a basis for developing the transition plan. The final step is to develop measurable postsecondary goals and annual IEP goals, and to identify specific transition services for the student—all of which are included in the IEP.

Implementing person-centered planning takes more time than the traditional IEP meeting, so keep in mind that it is most appropriate before a major change takes place, or when progress toward achieving a goal has been halted or stalled as a way to breathe life back into the process and get it moving again. If there have been recent changes in a student's life or if there is great uncertainty about future outcomes and services, a person-centered process can support the transition planning efforts.

Evidence-Based Practices to Promote Student Involvement

There are a number of instructional programs and packages to promote student involvement in educational and transition planning that are discussed in greater detail in Chapter 11. What is important to know is that research has consistently demonstrated that students across disability categories can be successfully involved in transition planning, and a number of programs, including those mentioned subsequently, are effective in increasing student involvement (Test et al., 2004). Several student-directed processes for promoting student involvement have been developed. *Whose Future Is It Anyway?* (WFA, Wehmeyer, Lawrence et al., 2004) is a student-directed process to support students with intellectual disability to learn skills that enable them to meaningfully participate in transition-planning meetings during their high school years (though can be used at the middle school level). The WFA process consists of 36 sessions introducing students to the concept of transition and transition planning and enabling students to self-direct instruction related to (a) self- and disability-awareness; (b) making decisions about transition-related outcomes; (c) identifying and securing community resources to support transition services; (d) writing and evaluating transition goals and objectives; (e) communicating effectively in small groups; and (f) developing skills to become an effective team member, leader, or self-advocate. Wehmeyer and colleagues (2011) conducted a randomized-trial, placebo-control group design to study the impact of intervention with the WFA process on skills leading to self-determination and transition knowledge, finding that instruction using the WFA process resulted in significant, positive differences in self-determination when compared with a placebo-control group. Similarly, Lee and colleagues (2011) conducted a randomized-trial study of the impact of the WFA process both with and without the use of technology, and determined significant gains in skills leading to self-determination and transition knowledge as a function of instruction with WFA.

The *ChoiceMaker Self-Determination Transition Curriculum* (Martin & Marshall, 1995) consists of three sections: (a) Choosing Goals, (b) Expressing Goals, and (c) Taking Action. One component of the

ChoiceMaker curriculum, the SDIEP, teaches students 11 steps for leading their own planning meeting. Martin and colleagues (2006) conducted a randomized-trial control group study of the SDIEP and determined that students who received instruction using the SDIEP increased their active participation and showed more leadership behaviors during IEP meetings. Seong, Wehmeyer, Palmer, and Little (2015) conducted a randomized-trial, placebo-control group study of the SDIEP, finding that instruction using the process resulted in enhanced knowledge relating to self-determination and transition.

Promoting Self-Determination

As further described in Chapter 16, promoting self-determination has become best practice in supporting students with intellectual disability to achieve more positive school and postschool outcomes, particularly as they pertain to secondary education and transition services. Early research confirmed that people with intellectual disability were less self-determined than many of their peers and that, in part, was a function of limited choice opportunities available in congregate living and work settings prevalent at the time (Wehmeyer & Bolding, 1999, 2001; Wehmeyer & Metzler, 1995). Research also confirmed that there were significant, positive correlations with self-determination status and more positive adult outcomes, including outcomes related to employment and community inclusion (Wehmeyer & Palmer, 2003; Wehmeyer & Schwartz, 1997), more positive quality of life (Lachapelle et al., 2005; Wehmeyer & Schwartz, 1998), and lifestyle satisfaction (Shogren, Lopez, Wehmeyer, Little, & Pressgrove, 2006).

The establishment of the importance of self-determination to people with intellectual disability, and the findings that people with intellectual disability were less self-determined than their peers, led to the development of interventions to promote self-determination, increase choice-making opportunities, and promote active involvement in educational and life-planning activities. These interventions are discussed in greater detail in Chapter 16, but several recent intervention studies contribute both to the establishment of an evidence base for practices to promote self-determination and knowledge about the importance of doing so, and warrant consideration at this point in the chapter.

Wehmeyer, Shogren, Palmer, Williams-Diehm, Little, & Boulton (2012) conducted a randomized-trial, control group study of the effect of multiple interventions to promote self-determination (i.e., goal setting, problem solving, self-advocacy skills) on the self-determination of high school students with intellectual disability or learning disabilities. Students in the treatment group received instruction using a variety of instructional methods to promote self-determination and student involvement in educational planning meetings over three years, while students in the control group received a placebo intervention. The self-determination of each student was measured using two norm-referenced measures across three measurement intervals (baseline, after two years of intervention, after three years of intervention). Using latent growth curve analysis, Wehmeyer and colleagues (2012) found that students with disabilities who participated in interventions to promote self-determination over a three-year period showed significantly more positive patterns of growth in their scores related to self-determination than did students not exposed to interventions to promote self-determination.

In a follow-up study of the treatment and control group students from Wehmeyer and colleagues (2012), Shogren, Wehmeyer, Palmer, Rifenbark, and Little (2015) investigated employment, community access, financial independence, and independent living outcomes one and two years after leaving school. Results indicated that self-determination status at the end of high school resulted in significantly more positive employment and community access outcomes. Students who were self-determined were significantly higher in all of these areas. These two studies study provided causal evidence that promoting self-determination results in enhanced self-determination, and that enhanced self-determination results in more positive adult outcomes, including employment and community inclusion.

A recent randomized-trial study by Powers and colleagues (2012) also provided causal evidence of the effect of promoting self-determination on postschool community inclusion. Powers and colleagues implemented the *TAKE CHARGE* intervention with youth in foster care who were receiving special education services, including students with intellectual disability. The *TAKE CHARGE* process involves in-situ coaching of youth to promote self-directed goal setting, mentoring, and parental support. Powers and colleagues conducted a randomized trial study of *TAKE CHARGE*. The intervention yielded moderate to large effect sizes at postintervention and at one year follow-up in student self-determination, a measure of quality of life, and youth utilization of transition services. Further, youth in the intervention group completed high school, obtained employment, and were living in the community at higher rates than were students in the control group. This body of work suggests the importance of teaching skills leading to self-determination and creating opportunities for students to use these skills in secondary education.

Access to Communication Supports

In addition to promoting active involvement in transition planning and student self-determination, it is important to focus on promoting effective support for communication for students with intellectual disability. Students who are able to access methods of communication can improve their quality of life by obtaining basic needs, engaging in desired activities, seeking information, and developing social closeness with others (Lund & Light, 2007). The communication supports that students with intellectual disability need will vary, but should focus on aligning support needs with goals related to inclusive postschool outcomes and engaging in meaningful communication related to learning the general education curriculum and in relation to meeting CCR standards.

For students with more extensive and pervasive communication support needs, their ability to make things happen in their world (i.e., become more self-determined) is highly dependent on one's ability to interpret meaning from unconventional methods (Brown, Gothelf, Guess & Lehr, 1998). This requires that educators be able to identify and interpret the functions of their students' unique, idiosyncratic, inconsistent, and unconventional communication styles, and respond accordingly. In order to facilitate self-determination, students must be offered many different opportunities to express their learning and their choices about postschool outcomes using a variety of means (e.g., written, verbal, body language, eye gaze, augmentative and alternative communication [AAC] devices). Unfortunately, many students with intellectual disability have limited opportunities to participate in inclusive settings, meaning they have limited opportunities to learn to communicate with or to make choices known to competent peers (McNaughton et al., 2008). Even when students with communication difficulties have access to AAC, there are barriers to expressing self-determination (McNaughton, Rackensperger, Wehmeyer, & Wright, 2010). Light and Gulens (2000) noted that acting in a self-determined manner is often more difficult for people using AAC, as they face challenges when sharing personal opinions, preferences, and interests. However, providing access to inclusive environments is necessary to enable these skills to develop and to prepare secondary youth for the transition to career and college environments.

To support students with complex communication needs, educational programs should use targeted and direct instruction to teach transition-focused communication skills (Cobb & Alwell, 2007). Other students with intellectual disability may not express their preferences though conventional means and, thus, may require alternative means to assess their personal preferences. Hughes, Pitkin, and Lorden (1998) identified several strategies for identifying student preferences, including:

- Pay attention to a student's behavior as he or she responds to situations in which choices are presented or occur naturally to determine preferences and choices.
- Use assistive technology, including switches, AAC, and computers to increase students' ability to indicate preferences.

- Consider the wide range of verbal, gestural, and other presymbolic communication behaviors as a means to determine preference.
- Gather information from those who know the student best, particularly the family, who will have considerable knowledge regarding preferences and interests.

Supported Membership and Friendships

In addition to providing communication supports, focusing on the role of social networks and friendships in inclusive general education and postschool environments is important. Families, educators, and many service providers now consider the importance of offering individual supports for sustained community inclusion. Not surprisingly, social isolation is often a top concern of families with young adults with intellectual disability in that they recognize the importance of having friends and a social network outside of the family (Kraemer & Blacher, 2001; Targett & Wehman, 2013). Ferguson and Ferguson (2006) describe the importance of supported membership for their son, Ian, in this way:

> The more hands that are there to catch him when he falls the better. We firmly believe that the more deeply embedded Ian is in the life of his neighborhood, workplace, and the city in general, the more people there will be who will notice if he is not there and who will work to keep him there as a member of his community.
>
> *(p. 615)*

A critical goal for adolescents with intellectual disability is to develop social connections in their communities to enrich their lives, and research has suggested the importance of social networks to community inclusion and career development opportunities. Unfortunately, people with intellectual disability rarely have the opportunities to develop social relationships outside of traditional approaches that involve only others with disabilities. Rather than being a mere presence at school, at home, and in the community, students with intellectual disability should experience a sense of community belonging (Hunt, Soto, Maier, & Doering, 2003).

Developing a community inclusive approach requires identifying both *individual* (e.g., personal friends) and *organized* social opportunities for students (e.g., participation in clubs and activities, including academic and career clubs). Building relationships involves more than teaching social skills; it requires educators to facilitate and support students in getting to know and be known by many different people in school and the community. Expanding the student's social network and maximizing a variety of relationships is the goal.

An effective strategy to increase student membership in school is to build intentional communities, or circles of friends (Forest & Pearpoint, 1992). Circles of friends began as a strategy to support inclusion for elementary students with intellectual disability, and are less commonly found in secondary schools. Secondary schools that use the circles approach often do so in conjunction with extracurricular clubs and sports teams as a better way to meet the structure and climate of the secondary school setting.

Another method to build community connections is to introduce students to a new setting that meets a strong preference or interest (e.g., high school poetry club), connect them to supportive members of the group, and continue to support them in building and sustaining new relationships (Walker, 2007). Taking advantage of volunteer and service opportunities can connect students with a broader community group, both within high school and in the community. It is important to remember to provide students with opportunities to make contributions, which helps to create a sense of belonging and builds opportunities to learn, which in turn generates respect from others (Miller, Hinterlong, & Green, 2010).

To successfully build inclusive communities for your students, it is often helpful to develop social support networks. An essential element of creating support networks is to encourage social relationships with peers without disabilities while the students are in school (Jorgensen, McSheehan, & Sonnenmeier, 2007). In other words, we must all make the shift from viewing students with intellectual disability as merely participating in activities in school and the community to one in which they are actively contributing to community groups and associations. Teachers and other team members can provide students with intellectual disability with opportunities to meet people with whom they can develop lasting and meaningful friendships. Providing opportunities to volunteer, to provide assistance to others, and to make contributions to their community at large are all essential and effective approaches. Friendships do not happen overnight, but rather require opportunities and support. The method of providing transition services should not hinder this vital part of the human experience.

In summary, planning for the transition to community-supported living for young adults with intellectual disability involves more than finding an agency that provides residential services. An inherent principle of supported living is promoting full community inclusion through individualized supports and services. Despite examples of remarkable outcomes, there remain limited opportunities for people with intellectual disability to live on their own with the supports they want and need. We should no longer be promoting a continuum mindset, but instead focusing on supported living and supported adulthood and the funding structures to support this model. The educational team must prepare students and families to develop a vision of supported living and to inform them of the new and innovative resources, funding structures, and policies that exemplify these values.

Preparing for the Transition to Supported Living and Community Participation

To enable supported living and community participation, we have to move from the traditional model in which the person with disabilities and his or her family either accept existing services (e.g., living in a group home) or they are not served by the community services agency. In some cases, group home providers have not provided services for people with significant medical and cognitive disabilities because they require too intensive a level of support and care (Morningstar et al., 2001). Ironically, it is families—who have been rejected from traditional service systems—who often create comprehensive and inclusive lifestyles for their adult children with intellectual disability (Turnbull & Turnbull, 2000).

Supported living means living in a home chosen by the individual with disabilities, shared with roommates determined by the individual, and in a home or apartment not owned or operated by an agency (Klein, Wilson, & Nelson, 2000). This model requires agencies and services to operate from a set of values predicated on the belief that people with intellectual disability should control the front door. These values include:

- Supporting and listening to what individuals with intellectual disability are "telling" us by ensuring they have access to a means of communication.
- Ensuring each individual's control over personal supports by developing a plan for self-directed care and services as well as involving informal supports from within his or her personal network.
- Supporting and facilitating friendships by ensuring students are a part of their community and engaging in activities that are of interest to them and others.
- Offering flexible services and supports so that students and families can determine which are best for them, rather than accepting an "all or nothing" approach.
- Ensuring that assistive technology is available across all areas of adult life, including communication, employment, living, and participating in the community.
- Valuing the role and contributions of students with intellectual disability for engaging in their community as fully participating citizens.

(Klein & Strully, 2000)

Educators must focus on teaching skills to prepare students for participating in home and community, leveraging opportunities related to the increased emphasis on access to the general education curriculum and CCR. While concerns have been raised that increased access to general education may dilute a focus on functional skills instruction (Ayres, Lowery, Douglas, & Sievers, 2011; Bouck, 2009), it is now apparent that curriculum decisions are not an either/or proposition. Students can participate in inclusive academic curricula while learning and practicing community-referenced skills that enable inclusive postschool outcomes (Wehmeyer, Field, Doren, Jones, & Mason, 2004). Unfortunately, teachers often perceive that inclusion in general education classes limits opportunities to learn life skills (Ruppar & Gaffney, 2011), even though functional life skills and access to general education can be mutually beneficial (McDonnell, Hunt, Jackson, & Ryndak, 2013). Research is clear: Critical skills needed for successful adult lives—communication, self-determination, teamwork, and problem solving—all are best learned in inclusive settings rather than in separate, special education functional/life skills classrooms. In fact, the movement within education to focus on CCR skills supports the movement toward inclusive education for students with intellectual disability.

Educators can support students with intellectual disability to gain the skills needed to prepare for living and participating in the community in several ways. Bambara, Koger, and Bartholomew (2011) describe several steps: (a) person-centered planning is used to create a vision for the student, (b) teachers partner with students and families to coordinate instruction, (c) student self-determination is considered as a critical domain of instruction, (d) school personnel examine the range of settings in which to teach home and community skills (e.g., general educational environments, school, home and community), and (e) transition planning targets home and community skills that should be considered.

Looking Toward the Future: Expanding Inclusive Educational Experiences; Equipping Youth for Successful Adulthood

In this chapter, we reviewed the IDEA transition and access to the general education curriculum mandates, highlighting how both of these requirements enable effective and inclusive secondary education focused on promoting CCR and transition to inclusive, supported postschool outcomes. We also reviewed research on key elements of secondary education programs related to teaching academic content in inclusive classrooms, providing high-quality transition planning, student involvement in the IEP and transition planning process, self-determination, communication, and social networks. Each of these elements is critical to enabling valued postschool outcomes in the community in ways that are preferred by young adults with disabilities and their families. Central to all of these efforts is the need for high expectations to guide the creation of educational programming for students with intellectual disability in inclusive secondary schools.

As we have highlighted, it is no longer a question of if students with intellectual disability can transition to inclusive postsecondary experiences; it is how the supports needed to enable these transitions to occur can be put in place. And, how can secondary education programming enable these outcomes and supports? Research is unequivocal that students with intellectual disability can access and progress in core academic content areas while also addressing transition-related goals, particularly when the focus is on promoting career and college readiness and when high-quality supports are in place. The range of transition outcomes is also expanding with the rapid emergence of postsecondary education options for students with intellectual disability, supported living models, and integrated work opportunities and supports. The quality of secondary education programs significantly impacts the degree to which students with intellectual disability are prepared to transition to such opportunities, and planning with these outcomes in mind and creating challenging, inclusive opportunities to access secondary education content and experiences that promote CCR in inclusive school environments has the potential to continue to enhance the outcomes of adults with intellectual disability.

References

Ayres, K. M., Lowrey, K. A., Douglas, K. H., & Sievers, C. (2011). I can identify Saturn but I can't brush my teeth: What happens when the curricular focus for students with severe disabilities shifts. *Education and Training in Autism and Developmental Disabilities, 46*, 11–21.

Bambara, L., Koger, F., & Bartholomew, A. (2011). Building skills for home and community. In M. E. Snell & F. Brown (Eds.), *Instruction of students with severe disabilities* (7th ed., pp. 529–568). Boston, MA: Pearson.

Blackorby, J., & Wagner, M. (1996). Longitudinal post-school outcomes of youth with disabilities: Findings from the National Longitudinal Transition Study. *Exceptional Children, 62*, 399–413.

Bouck, E. C. (2009). No child left behind, the individuals with Disabilities Education Act and functional curricula: A conflict of interest? *Education and Training in Developmental Disabilities, 44*(1), 3.

Bouck, E. C. (2012). Secondary students with moderate/severe intellectual disability: Considerations of curriculum and post-school outcomes from the National Longitudinal Transition Study-2. *Journal of Intellectual Disability Research, 56*, 1175–1186. doi: 10.1111/j.1365–2788.2011.01517.x

Boutot, E. A., & Bryant, D. P. (2005). Social integration of students with autism in inclusive settings. *Education and Training in Developmental Disabilities, 40*(1), 14–23.

Braddock, D., Hemp, R., Rizzolo, M. C., Tanis, E. S., Haffer, L., Lulinski-Norris, A., & Wu, J. (2013). *The state of the states in developmental disabilities* (8th ed.). Washington, DC: American Association on Intellectual and Developmental Disabilities.

Brock, M. E., & Schaefer, J. M. (2015). Location matters: Geographic location and educational placement of students with developmental disabilities. *Research and Practice for Persons with Severe Disabilities*. Advance online publication. doi: 10.1177/1540796915591988

Browder, D. M., Spooner, F., Ahlgrim-Delzell, L., Harris, A. A., & Wakeman, S. (2008). A meta-analysis on teaching mathematics to students with significant cognitive disabilities. *Exceptional Children, 74*, 407–432.

Brown, F., Gothelf, C. R., Guess, D., & Lehr, D. H. (1998). Self-determination for individuals with the most severe disabilities: Moving beyond chimera 1. *Research and Practice for Persons with Severe Disabilities, 23*(1), 17–26.

Buntinx, W. H., & Schalock, R. L. (2010). Models of disability, quality of life, and individualized supports: Implications for professional practice in intellectual disability. *Journal of Policy and Practice in Intellectual Disabilities, 7*(4), 283–294.

Carter, E. W., Austin, D., & Trainor, A. A. (2012). Predictors of post-school employment outcomes for young adults with severe disabilities. *Journal of Disability Policy Studies, 23*, 50–63.

Carter, E. W., Cushing, L. S., Clark, N. M., & Kennedy, C. H. (2005). Effect of peer support interventions on students' access to the general curriculum and social interactions. *Research & Practice for Persons with Severe Disabilities, 30*, 15–25.

Carter, E. W., & Kennedy, C. H. (2006). Promoting access to the general curriculum using peer support strategies. *Research and Practice for Persons with Severe Disabilities, 31*, 284–292.

Carter, E. W., Moss, C. K., Hoffman, A., Chung, Y. C., & Sisco, L. (2011). Efficacy and social validity of peer support arrangements for adolescents with disabilities. *Exceptional Children, 78*(1), 107–125.

Certo, N., & Luecking, R. (2006). Service integration and school to work transition: Customized employment as an outcome for youth with significant disabilities. *Journal of Applied Rehabilitation Counseling, 37*(4), 29.

Cobb, B., & Alwell, M. (2007). What works transition research synthesis project. Retrieved from http://www.ncset.org/publications/viewdesc.asp?id=714

Collins, B. C., Branson, T. A., Hall, M., & Rankin, S. W. (2001). Teaching secondary students with moderate disabilities in an inclusive academic classroom setting. *Journal of Developmental & Physical Disabilities, 13*, 41–59.

Conderman, G., & Katsiyannis, A. (2002). Instructional issues and practices in secondary special education. *Remedial and Special Education, 23*, 169–179. doi: http://dx.doi.org/10.1177/07419325020230030501

Conley, D. T. (2010). *College and career ready: Helping all students succeed beyond high school*. San Francisco, CA: Jossey-Bass.

Council of Chief State School Officers (CCSS). (2010). College and career ready standards. Retrieved from http://www.ccsso.org/

Deppeler, J., Loreman, T., & Sharma, U. (2005). Improving inclusive practices in secondary schools: Moving from specialist support to supporting learning communities. *Australasian Journal of Special Education, 29*, 117–127.

Dessemontet, R. S., Bless, G., & Morin, D. (2012). Effects of inclusion on the academic achievement and adaptive behaviour of children with intellectual disabilities. *Journal of Intellectual Disability Research, 56*, 579–587.

Farrington, C. A., Roderick, M., Allensworth, E., Nagaoka, J., Keyes, T. S., Johnson, D. W., & Beechum, N. O. (2012). *Teaching adolescents to become learners. The role of noncognitive factors in shaping school performance: A critical literature review*. Chicago: University of Chicago Consortium on Chicago School Research.

Ferguson, D. L., & Ferguson, P. M. (2006). The promise of adulthood. In M. E. Snell & F. Brown (Eds.), *Instruction of students with severe disabilities* (6th ed., pp. 614–637). Boston: Pearson.

Fisher, M., & Meyer, L. H. (2002). Development and social competence after two years for students enrolled in inclusive and self-contained educational programs. *Research and Practice for Persons with Severe Disabilities, 27*, 165–174.

Flannery, K. B., & Sugai, G. (2009). SWPBS implementation in high schools: Current practice and future directions. University of Oregon. Retrieved from http://www.pbis.org/school/high_school_pbis.aspx

Foreman, P., Arthur-Kelly, M., Pascoe, S., & King, B. S. (2004). Evaluating the educational experiences of students with profound and multiple disabilities in inclusive and segregated classroom settings: An Australian perspective. *Research and Practice for Persons with Severe Disabilities, 29*(3), 183–193.

Forest, M., & Pearpoint, J. C. (1992). Putting all kids on the MAP. *Educational Leadership, 50*, 26–31.

Furney, K. S. (1993). Making dreams happen: How to facilitate the MAPS process. *Burlington, VT: Vermont Transition Systems Change Project, University of Vermont.*

Halpern, A. S. (1993). Quality of life as a conceptual framework for evaluating transition outcomes. *Exceptional Children, 59*(6), 486–498.

Hughes, C., Pitkin, S. E., & Lorden, S. W. (1998). Assessing preferences and choices of persons with severe and profound mental retardation. *Education and Training in Mental Retardation and Developmental Disabilities, 33*, 299–316.

Hunt, P., Soto, G., Maier, J., & Doering, K. (2003). Collaborative teaming to support students at risk and students with severe disabilities in general education classrooms. *Exceptional Children, 69*(3), 315–332.

Individuals with Disabilities Education Act (IDEA), 20 USC. §1400 (1990).

Jackson, L., Ryndak, D., & Wehmeyer, M. (2010). The dynamic relationship between context, curriculum, and student learning: A case for inclusive education as a research-based practice. *Research and Practice in Severe Disabilities, 33–34*(1), 175–195.

Jorgensen, C. M., McSheehan, M., & Sonnenmeier, R. M. (2007). Presumed competence reflected in the educational programs of students with IDD before and after the beyond access professional development intervention. *Journal of Intellectual and Developmental Disability, 32*, 248–262.

Kearns, J. F., Towles-Reeves, E., Kleinert, H. L., O'Regan Kleinert, J., & Kleine-Kracht Thomas, M. (2011). Characteristics of and implications for students participating in alternate assessments based on alternate academic achievement standards. *Journal of Special Education, 45*, 3–14.

Keyes, M. W., & Owens-Johnson, L. (2003). Developing person-centered IEPs. *Intervention in School and Clinic, 38*, 145–152.

Kim, K.-H., & Morningstar, M. E. (2005). Transition planning involving culturally and linguistically diverse families. *Career Development for Exceptional Individuals, 28*, 92–103.

Kincaid, D., & Fox, L. (2002). Person-centered planning and positive behavior support. In S. Holburn & V. M. Vietze (Eds.), *Person-centered planning: Research, practice, and future directions* (pp. 29–49). Baltimore, MD: Paul H. Brookes Publishing Co.

Klein, J., & Strully, J. L. (2000). From unit D to the community: A dream to fulfilled. In M. L. Wehmeyer & J. R. Patton (Eds.), *Mental retardation in the 21st century* (pp. 165–178). Austin, TX: Pro-Ed.

Klein, J., Wilson, B., & Nelson, D. (2000). Postcards on the refrigerator: Changing the power dynamic in housing and assistance. In J. Nisbet & D. Hagner (Eds.), *Part of the community: Strategies for including everyone* (pp. 117–202). Baltimore, MD: Paul H. Brookes Publishing Company.

Kohler, P. D. (1996). *Taxonomy for transition programming: Linking research and practice.* Champaign-Urbana, IL: Transition Research Institute, University of Illinois.

Kohler, P. D., & Field, S. (2003). Transition-focused education foundation for the future. *The Journal of Special Education, 37*, 174–183.

Kraemer, B. R., & Blacher, J. (2001). Transition for young adults with severe mental retardation: School preparation, parent expectations, and family involvement. *American Journal on Mental Retardation, 106*, 173–188.

Kurth, J., & Mastergeorge, A. M. (2012). Impact of setting and instructional context for adolescents with autism. Journal of Special Education, 46, 36–48.

Kurth, J., Morningstar E., & Kozelski, E. B. (2014). *The tyranny of low expectations: The persistence of highly restrictive special education placements.* Manuscript submitted for publication.

Lachapelle, Y., Wehmeyer, M. L., Haelewyck, M. C., Courbois, Y., Keith, K. D., Schalock, R., Verdugo, M. A., & Walsh, P. N. (2005). The relationship between quality of life and self-determination: An international study. *Journal of Intellectual Disability Research, 49*, 740–744.

Lee, S. H., Wehmeyer, M. L., Soukup, J. H., & Palmer, S. B. (2010). Impact of curriculum modifications on access to the general education curriculum for students with disabilities. *Exceptional Children, 76*, 213–233.

Lee, Y., Wehmeyer, M., Palmer, S., Williams-Diehm, K., Davies, D., & Stock, S. (2011). The effect of student-directed transition planning using a computer-based reading support program on the self-determination of students with disabilities. *Journal of Special Education, 45*, 104–117.

Light, J. C., & Gulens, M. (2000). Rebuilding communicative competence and self-determination. In D. Beukelman, K. M. Yorkston, & J. Reichle (Eds.), *Augmentative and alternative communication for adults with acquired neurologic disorders* (pp. 137–179). Baltimore: Paul H. Brookes.

Lund, S. K., & Light, J. (2007). Long-term outcomes for individuals who use augmentative and alternative communication: Part III-Contributing factors. *Augmentative and Alternative Communication, 23*(4), 323–335.

Martin, J. E., & Marshall, L. H. (1995). Choice maker: A comprehensive self-determination transition program. *Intervention in School and Clinic, 30*, 147–156.

Martin, J. E., Van Dycke, J. L., Christensen, W. R., Greene, B. A., Gardner, J. E., & Lovett, D. L. (2006). Increasing student participation in IEP meetings: Establishing the self-directed IEP as an evidenced-based practice. *Exceptional Children, 72*, 299–316.

Mastropieri, M. A., & Scruggs, T. E. (2001). Promoting inclusion in secondary classrooms. *Learning Disability Quarterly, 24*, 265–274.

McDonnell, J., Hunt, P., Jackson, L., & Ryndak, D. (2013). Educational standards for students with significant intellectual disabilities: A response to Lou Brown. *TASH Connections, 38*(4), 30–33. Washington, DC: TASH.

McLeskey, J., Landers, E., Williamson, P., & Hoppey, D. (2012). Are we moving toward educating students with disabilities in less restrictive settings? *Journal of Special Education, 46*, 131–140.

McNaughton, D., Rackensperger, T., Benedeck-Wood, E., Krezman, C., Williams, M., & Light, J. (2008). "A child needs to be given a chance to succeed": Parents of individuals who use AAC describe the benefits and challenges of learning AAC technologies. *Augmentative and Alternative Communication, 24*, 43–55.

McNaughton, D., Rackensperger, T., Wehmeyer, M. L., & Wright, S. (2010). Self-determination and young adults who use alternative and augmentative communication. In J. Light & D. McNaughton (Eds.), *Transition services for youth who use alternative and augmentative communication* (pp. 17–32). Baltimore: Paul H. Brookes.

Michaels, C. A., & Ferrara, D. L. (2005). Promoting post-school success for all: The role of collaboration in person-centered transition planning. *Journal of Educational and Psychological Consultation, 16*, 287–313.

Miller, C. R., Hinterlong, J., & Green, A. D. (2010). Perspectives on inclusive service-learning from a state-wide model program. *School Social Work, 34*, 71–89.

Morningstar, M. E., Knollman, G., Semon, S., & Kleinhammer-Tramill, J. (2012). Accountability for what matters: Using post-school outcomes to build school and community renewal. In I. L. C. Burrello, W. Sailor, & J. Kleinhammer-Tramill (Eds.), *Unifying educational systems: Leadership and policy perspectives* (pp. 158–167). New York: Routledge.

Morningstar, M. E., Kurth, J. A., & Johnson, P. (2016). *Examining the past decade of education placements for students with significant disabilities.* Manuscript submitted for publication.

Morningstar, M. E., Lombardi, A., Fowler, C. H., & Test, D. W. (2015). A preliminary college and career readiness model for secondary students with disabilities. *Career Development and Transition for Exceptional Individuals.* doi:10.1177/2165143415589926

Morningstar, M. E., Shogren, K. A., Lee, H., & Born, K. (2015). Preliminary lessons about supporting participation and learning in inclusive classrooms. *Research and Practice for Persons with Severe Disabilities, 40*, 192–210.

Morningstar, M.E., Turnbull, H.R., Lattin, D.L., Umbarger, G., Reichard, A., & Moberly, R. (2001). Students supported by medical technology making the transition from school to adult life. *Journal of Developmental and Physical Disabilities, 13*(3), 229–259.

Munk, D. D., & Bursuck, W. D. (2001). What report card grades should and do communicate: Perceptions of parents of secondary students with and without disabilities. *Remedial and Special Education, 22*, 280–287.

National Center for Response to Intervention. (2011). The complex ecology of response to intervention. Retrieved from http://www.rti4success.org/pdf/complexEcology.pdf

National Governors Association Center for Best Practices, & Council of Chief State School Officers. (2010). *Common core state standards.* Washington, DC: National Governors Association Center for Best Practices, Council of Chief State School Officers.

Newman, L., Wagner, M., Cameto, R., Knokey, A.-M., and Shaver, D. (2010). *Comparisons across time of the outcomes of youth with disabilities up to 4 years after high school. A report of findings from the National Longitudinal Transition Study (NLTS) and the National Longitudinal Transition Study-2 (NLTS2) (NCSER 2010-3008).* Menlo Park, CA: SRI International.

O'Brien, J., & Forest, M. (1989). *Action for inclusion: How to improve schools by welcoming children with special needs into regular classrooms.* Toronto, Ontario, Canada: Inclusion Press.

Powers, L. W., Geenan, S., Powers, J., Pommier-Satya, S., Turner, A., Dalton, L. D., . . . Swank, P. (2012). My life: Effects of a longitudinal, randomized study of self-determination enhancement on the transition outcomes of youth in foster care and special education. *Children and Youth Services Review, 34*, 2179–2187.

Rasheed, S. A., Fore III, C., & Miller, S. (2006). Person-centered planning: Practices, promises, and provisos. *Journal for Vocational Special Needs Education, 28*, 47–59.

Ruppar, A. L., & Gaffney, J. S. (2011). Individualized education program team decisions: A preliminary study of conversations, negotiations, and power. *Research and Practice for Persons with Severe Disabilities, 36*, 11–22.

Ryndak, D., Jackson, L. B., & White, J. M. (2013). Involvement and progress in the general curriculum for students with extensive support needs: K–12 inclusive-education research and implications for the future. *Inclusion, 1*, 28–49. doi:10.1352/2326–6988–1.1.028

Sanford, C., Newman, L., Wagner, M., Cameto, R., Knokey, A.-M., & Shaver, D. (2011). The post-high school outcomes of young adults with disabilities up to 6 years after high school: Key findings from the national longitudinal transition study-2 (NLTS2). NCSER 2011–3004. *National Center for Special Education Research.* www.nlts2.org/reports/

Savitz-Romer, M. (2013). College readiness and life skills: Moving beyond academics. *Education Week Webinar.* Retrieved on January 31, 2013 from: www.edweek.org/go/webinars

Schalock, R. L., Borthwick-Duffy, S. A., Bradley, V. J., Buntinx, W. H., Coulter, D. L., Craig, E. M., . . . Yeager, M. H. (2010). *Intellectual disability: Definition, classification, and systems of supports* (Vol. 26). Washington, DC: American Association on Intellectual and Developmental Disabilities.

Seong, Y., Wehmeyer, M. L., Palmer, S. B., & Little, T. D. (2015). Effects of the self-directed individualized education program on self-determination and transition of adolescents with disabilities. *Career Development and Transition for Exceptional Individuals, 38*, 132–141.

Shogren, K. A., Lopez, S. J., Wehmeyer, M. L., Little, T. D., & Pressgrove, C. L. (2006). The role of positive psychology constructs in predicting life satisfaction in adolescents with and without cognitive disabilities: An exploratory study. *Journal of Positive Psychology, 1*, 37–52.

Shogren, K. A, Palmer, S., Wehmeyer, M. L., Williams-Diehm, K., & Little, T. (2012). Effect of intervention with the *Self-Determined Learning Model of Instruction* on access and goal attainment. *Remedial and Special Education, 33*, 320–330.

Shogren, K. A., Wehmeyer, M. L., Palmer, S. B., Rifenbark, G. G., & Little, T. D. (2015). Relationships between self-determination and post-school outcomes for youth with disabilities. *Journal of Special Education, 53*, 30–41. doi:10.1177/0022466913489733

Soukup, J. H., Wehmeyer, M. L., Bashinski, S. M., & Bovaird, J. (2007). Classroom variables and access to the general education curriculum of students with intellectual and developmental disabilities. *Exceptional Children, 74*, 101–120.

Stineman, R., Morningstar, M. E., Bishop, B., & Rutherford Turnbull, H. (1993). Role of families in transition planning for young adults with disabilities toward a method of person-centered planning. *Journal of Vocational Rehabilitation, 3*, 52–61.

Sugai, G. (2012, July). Multi-tiered systems of support: Features and considerations. Retrieved October 15, 2014 from www.pbis.org/presentations. Center on Positive Behavioral Interventions and Supports.

Targett, P., & Wehman, P. (2013). Families and young people with disabilities: Listening to their voices. In P. Wehman (Ed.), *Life beyond the classroom: Transition strategies for people with disabilities* (pp. 69–92). Baltimore, MD: Paul H. Brookes Publishing Company.

Test, D. W., Fowler, C. H., Richter, S. M., White, J., Mazzotti, V., Walker, A. R., Kortering, L. & Kholer, P. (2009). Evidence-based practices in secondary transition. *Career Development for Exceptional Individuals, 32*, 115–128. doi:10.1177/0885728809336859

Test, D. W., Mason, C., Hughes, C., Konrad, M., Neale, M., & Wood, W. (2004). Student involvement in individualized education program meetings. *Exceptional Children, 70*, 391–412.

Test, D. W., Mazzotti, V. L., Mustian, A. L., Fowler, C. H., Kortering, L., & Kohler, P. (2009). Evidence-based secondary transition predictors for improving post-school outcomes for students with disabilities. *Career Development for Exceptional Individuals, 32*, 160 181. doi:10.1177/0885728809346960

Turnbull, A. P., & Turnbull, R. (2000). Self-determination for individuals with significant cognitive disabilities and their families. *Research and Practice for Persons with Severe Disabilities, 26*, 56–62.

Turnbull, A. P., Turnbull, R., Wehmeyer, M. L., & Shogren, K. (2013). *Exceptional lives: Special education in today's schools* (7th ed.). Columbus, OH: Merrill.

Turnbull, A. P., Zuna, N., Turnbull, H. R., Poston, D., & Summers, J. A. (2007). Families as partners in educational decision-making: Current implementation and future directions. In S. L. Odom, R. H. Horner, Snell, M., & J. Blacher (Eds.), *Handbook on developmental disabilities* (pp. 570–590). New York: Guilford Press.

US Department of Education. (2010). Blueprint for reform. Retrieved from http://www2.ed.gov/policy/elsec/leg/blueprint/index.html

Van Reusen, A. K., & Bos, C. S. (1994). Facilitating student participation in individualized education programs through motivation strategy instruction. *Exceptional Children, 60*, 466–475.

Villa, R., Thousand, J. S., Nevin, A., & Liston, A. (2005). Successful inclusive practices in middle and secondary schools. *American Secondary Education, 33*, 33–50.

Walker, P. M. (2007). Promoting meaningful leisure and social connections: More than just work. In P. M. Walker & P. M. Rogan (Eds.), *Make the day matter!: Promoting typical lifestyles for adults with significant disabilities.* Baltimore, MD: Paul H Brookes Publishing Company.

Wasburn-Moses, L. (2005). Roles and responsibilities of secondary special education teachers in an age of reform. *Remedial and Special Education, 26*(3), 151–158.

Wehmeyer, M. L. (2014). Disability in the 21st century: Seeking a future of equity and full participation. In M. Agran, F. Brown, C. Hughes, C. Quirk, & D. Ryndak (Eds.), *Equity and full participation for individuals with severe disabilities: A vision for the future* (pp. 3–23). Baltimore, MD: Brookes Publishing.

Wehmeyer, M. L., & Bolding, N. (1999). Self-determination across living and working environments: A matched-samples study of adults with mental retardation. *Mental Retardation, 37*, 353–363.

Wehmeyer, M. L., & Bolding, N. (2001). Enhanced self-determination of adults with mental retardation as an outcome of moving to community-based work or living environments. *Journal of Intellectual Disability Research, 45*, 371–383.

Wehmeyer, M. L., Field, S., Doren, B., Jones, B., & Mason, C. (2004). Self-determination and student involvement in standards-based reform. *Exceptional Children, 70*(4), 413–425.

Wehmeyer, M. L., Lawrence, M., Kelchner, K., Palmer, S., Garner, N., & Soukup, J. (2004). *Whose future is it anyway? A student-directed transition planning process* (2nd ed.). Lawrence, KS: Beach Center on Disability.

Wehmeyer, M. L., & Metzler, C. (1995). How self-determined are people with mental retardation? The national consumer survey. *Mental Retardation, 33*, 111–119.

Wehmeyer, M. L., & Palmer, S. B. (2003). Adult outcomes for students with cognitive disabilities three-years after high school: The impact of self-determination. *Education and Training in Developmental Disabilities, 38*(2), 131–144.

Wehmeyer, M. L., Palmer, S. B., Lee, Y., Williams-Diehm, K., & Shogren, K. A. (2011). A randomized-trial evaluation of the effect of whose future is it anyway? On self-determination. *Career Development for Exceptional Individuals, 34*, 45–56.

Wehmeyer, M. L. & Schwartz, M. (1997). Self-determination and positive adult outcomes: A follow-up study of youth with mental retardation or learning disabilities. *Exceptional Children, 63*, 245–255.

Wehmeyer, M. L. & Schwartz, M. (1998). The relationship between self-determination, quality of life, and life satisfaction for adults with mental retardation. *Education and Training in Mental Retardation and Developmental Disabilities, 33*, 3–12.

Wehmeyer, M. L., Shogren, K. A, Palmer, S., Williams-Diehm, K., Little, T., & Boulton, A. (2012). The impact of the self-determined learning model of instruction on student self-determination. *Exceptional Children, 78*, 135–153.

Will, M. (1984). Bridges from school to working life. *Interchange, 20*(5), 2–6.

25

Transition to Employment

Paul Wehman, Lauren Avellone, Valerie Brooke,
Pam Hinterlong, Katherine Inge, Stephanie Lau,
Jennifer McDonough, Grant Revell, Carol Schall

Introduction

The purpose of this chapter will be to highlight and discuss the importance of employment for people with intellectual and developmental disabilities. Research increasingly shows that employment for youth with intellectual and developmental disabilities while in school correlates with employment after graduation (Carter, Austin, & Trainor, 2011, 2012; Siperstein, Heyman, & Stokes, 2014; Wehman, Sima, et al., 2015). In this chapter, while the focus is predominantly on youth and adults with intellectual disability, we know many persons with other developmental disabilities are struggling with similar issues and also may have intellectual impairments. We will therefore draw on this literature as we present an initial introduction on employment issues and then discuss different pathways to employment that teachers can encourage.

Unemployment

In 2014, The Bureau of Labor Statistics (2015) reported that the percentage of people with disabilities in the labor force was 17.1%, well below the employment–population ratio of 64.6% for people without a disability. Data collected from 2011 and 2012 by Siperstein, Parker, and Drascher (2013) found that only 34% of the sample of adults with intellectual disability were employed, compared to an estimated employment rate of 76% for people without disabilities (Erickson, Lee, & von Schrader, 2012). Siperstein et al. (2013) also found that only 44% of adults with intellectual disability were either employed or looking for work, in contrast with 83% of adults without disabilities in the same time period (Erickson et al., 2012). Findings from the American Community Survey (ACS) show that respondents with disabilities reported a 33.4% employment rate across all disability categories; however, people with ambulatory disabilities reported a 24.3% employment rate. Regarding specific types of physical disabilities, low employment rates were found for people with spinal cord injury (SCI; Boschen, Tonack, & Gargaro, 2003; Lidal, Huynh, & Biering-Sørensen, 2007), amputation (Burger & Marincek, 2007), cerebral palsy (Liptak, 2008; Michelsen, Uldall, Kejs, & Madsen, 2005), and others.

Schur, Kruse, Blasi, and Blanck (2009) analyzed approximately 30,000 employee surveys from 14 companies that had employees with disabilities. They found that compared to employees without disabilities, employees with disabilities were more likely to be in production jobs and less likely to be in professional, sales, and management and supervisory jobs; were more likely to be paid hourly and work fewer hours per week on average; had less job security; were more closely supervised; and had lower levels of participation in job decisions. Other reports also show that many individuals who return to work following a disability have done so in positions with fewer demands, lower work hours, and lower salaries (Boschen et al., 2003; Burger & Marincek, 2007).

Access to Health Care and Other Public Benefits

Brault (2012) reported that more than half of the adults aged 15 to 64 with severe disabilities received some form of public assistance (59%). Approximately 32.9% of adults with severe disabilities received Social Security benefits, compared to 8.8% with nonsevere disabilities and 2.6% without a disability. Brault also reported that people with severe disabilities were more likely to receive Medicare coverage than those with no disability (22.7% compared to 0.7%) and more likely to receive Medicaid (34.6% compared with 7.8%). All of these findings highlight the loss of potential benefits from people with intellectual and developmental disabilities being in the workforce and the absence of improvements in their employment outcomes despite public policies and resources expended to improve these outcomes.

As noted earlier, the primary target population we discuss in this chapter is comprised of people with intellectual and developmental disabilities whose disabilities substantially limit economic self-sufficiency as evidenced by unemployment or underemployment. This chapter emphasizes those people with intellectual and developmental disabilities with significant or secondary disabilities who have traditionally been unemployed or, when provided with day services, receive those services in facility-based programs such as sheltered workshops and other nonpaid segregated settings.

Competitive Employment and People With Intellectual and Developmental Disabilities

A body of evidence accumulated over the past three decades has consistently found that people with intellectual and developmental disabilities can be successfully employed in competitive, integrated positions and substantially increase earnings in comparison to segregated work or day support programs (Cimera, 2011; Wehman & Brooke, 2013; Wehman, Lau, et al., 2012; Wehman, Schall, et al., 2014). Moreover, the evidence indicates that the majority of people with disabilities and their families prefer competitive employment to segregated employment or day services (Siperstein et al., 2014).

Unfortunately, the use of non–community integrated day/work programs continues to grow noticeably faster than participation in competitive employment programming. For example, the number of people with intellectual and developmental disabilities in nonintegrated day programs grew by 96,300 from FY 2000 to FY 2011. In comparison, the growth in competitive employment outcomes during that same period was only 13,000 individuals. Many states and intellectual and developmental disabilities agencies are making substantial efforts to systematically transform their day and work programs by promoting community-integrated competitive employment as a first choice (Centers for Medicare and Medicaid Services, 2013). Despite these efforts, there is minimal growth in competitive employment outcomes for people with intellectual and developmental disabilities. For example, Braddock et al. (2013) reported that nationally in FY 2011, state intellectual and developmental disabilities agencies served approximately 455,600 people in day, work, and sheltered employment programs that did not involve competitive employment. In comparison, approximately 116,000 people with intellectual and developmental disabilities were in supported competitive employment, an approximate 4:1 ratio of nonintegrated day/programs to competitive work for people served by intellectual and developmental disabilities agencies.

Barriers to Competitive Employment for People With Intellectual and Developmental Disabilities

There are numerous reasons for the discouraging employment outcomes, ranging from individual characteristics and Social Security disincentives to system-level and family challenges. However, we believe that the critical underlying barrier is a lack of quality research documenting the efficacy of different pathways to employment. An overriding challenge to greater participation in the work-force by people with intellectual and developmental disabilities is the continued lack of high-quality research that documents the efficacy of the different pathways to employment. There are multiple ways people without disabilities procure jobs and find their way into competitive employment, includ-ing internship experiences, postsecondary education (PSE), and real work experiences. Usually people are self-determined and advocate for the type of work they want when they are young, then naturally flow into the nation's workforce. Why are people with intellectual and developmental disabilities so dramatically shut out of the labor force? When one carefully studies people with intellectual and developmental disabilities, as Siperstein and colleagues (2014) did in a recent Gallup Poll, it becomes clear that there are limited clinically proven employment interventions that are replicable and have efficacy. The US Department of Justice is making settlements in different states to extricate people with intellectual and developmental disabilities from sheltered workshops (United States Department of Justice, 2014, 2015), yet there are no clear, clinically proven guidelines as to how to enable and support people to enter the workforce.

While there is significant interest for people with intellectual and developmental disabilities to be engaged in customized employment programs with US Department of Labor initiatives, there are no controlled studies on efficacy and long-term follow-up data (Riesen, Morgan, & Griffin, in press; Wehman, in press). As was mentioned in Chapter 16, there is causal evidence linking enhanced self-determination for youth with disabilities, including youth with intellectual and developmental disabil-ities, to more positive employment outcomes. Although recent studies of the National Longitudinal Transition Study-2 (NLTS2) database strongly suggest that youth with intellectual and developmental disabilities who have a job while in school are more likely to have employment upon graduation (Carter et al., 2011, 2012; Wehman, Sima, et al., 2015), there is no proof of concept that actually shows this is an evidence-based practice. In addition, despite the fact that people with intellectual and devel-opmental disabilities clearly indicate they would prefer not to be in a sheltered workshop (Migliore, Mank, Grossi, & Rogan, 2007), little research exists that specifically drills down to find out how people with intellectual and developmental disabilities want to access employment—that is, what pathway is best for them. In short, there is a great deal to learn here and the lack of knowledge becomes a huge barrier for improving these egregious employment outcomes. Research needs to be devoted to specific interventions that are effective, similar to the work of Bond and Drake (2014) using the Individual Placement and Support (IPS) process to support people with severe mental illness in gaining competi-tive employment or the Project SEARCH model with youth with Autism Spectrum Disorder (ASD) by Wehman et al. (Wehman, Schall et al., 2014; Wehman, Schall et al., 2015).

As evidenced in the literature, Community Rehabilitation Provider (CRP) facility staff can be a major barrier to improving access to competitive employment (e.g., Brooks-Lane, Hutcheson, & Revell, 2005). Some of the opposition to change is based on personal factors, such as uncertainty of employment status and career implications, perceived scheduling inconveniences and the loss of the routine schedule typical with segregated employment, increase in responsibilities and accountability associated with placement and training in an employment setting, and an overall sense of feeling threatened (Brooks-Lane et al., 2005). Families are key stakeholders who can help remove barriers by motivating and advocating for change in services for people with disabilities.

Pathways to Employment

This chapter presents an overview of different pathways for supporting people with intellectual and developmental disabilities to enter competitive employment. These include (a) vocational rehabili-tation collaboration, (b) internships, (c) PSE programs, (d) supported employment, (e) customized employment, and (f) business partnerships. A description of each pathway is provided, along with a brief summary of pertinent research and a discussion of how the pathway is applied to promote desirable employment outcomes. The presentation of multiple pathways highlights the existing variety of available practices to support people with intellectual and developmental disabilities obtain paid work and, therefore, it is important for educators to consider the unique needs of the person when selecting one, or a combination, of approaches. Pathways described in this chapter are presented with an emphasis on the importance of continued efforts to develop and research effective interventions to significantly improve employment outcomes for people with intellectual and developmental disabilities.

Vocational Rehabilitation Collaboration

Vocational Rehabilitation Services

Vocational Rehabilitation (VR) is a cooperative program between state and federal governments designed to assist people with disabilities in obtaining meaningful work. VR agencies exist in all 50 states, the District of Columbia, and US territories. The Rehabilitation Act of 1973, amended most recently in 2014 by Title IV of the Workforce Innovations and Opportunities Act (Public Law 113–128), provides states with federal grants to operate comprehensive programs of VR services for people with disabilities. Throughout the transition years, VR should be the core service coordination resource used for youth with intellectual disability. VR agencies provide an array of supports and services that include, but are not limited to:

- assessment for determining eligibility for VR services;
- vocational counseling, guidance, and referral services;
- vocational and other training, including on-the-job training;
- personal assistance services, including training in managing and directing a personal assistant;
- rehabilitation technology services; and
- job placement and supported employment services.

Before any VR services can be accessed, an application must be completed. This application is reviewed and approved (or denied) by a VR counselor. Qualification for VR services is based on eligibility criteria including (a) the presence of a disability that impairs employment and (b) the expectation that VR services will result in the achievement of an employment outcome. Once eligibility for VR is determined, an Individualized Plan for Employment (IPE) is developed by the VR counselor. The IPE functions as a road map for a youth with intellectual disability as he or she transitions from high school to employment. It identifies both the employment goal chosen by the youth with a disability and the services needed to achieve that goal. The IPE should be developed with close cooperation from the youth with a disability, his or her family, and the transition team. Case management through VR continues until the case is officially closed by the VR agency. Ideally, case closure occurs after an individual is employed a minimum of 90 days in a job deemed consistent with the employment objective established in the IPE. Alternatively, case closure can also occur if the individual is not making progress towards achieving the target employment outcome.

VR agencies are well-positioned to function as coordination hubs for employment-oriented community services for eligible youth with intellectual disability as they transition from secondary-level programs. In addition to providing case management and service coordination, a key strength of VR agencies is their ability to reach out into the community to obtain individualized services for a youth with a disability because they often have extensive connections with other community agencies and employers. For example, a VR agency may arrange with other community providers to acquire services, such as rehabilitation technology or supported employment. Additionally, VR counselors also have access to case service funds that can be used to purchase services from authorized vendors. If the service supports the employment goal established in the IPE and the individual is financially eligible for VR services, VR funds can be used to purchase postsecondary education and training, supported employment, transportation, tools and uniforms, and a variety of other services. VR counselors are typically familiar with other funding sources that can be used to complement VR funding.

VR counselors can also serve as information resources about community services for transition teams during the earlier planning stages in the transition process. This information and referral resource is of value to younger students in the 14–16 age range. Students with intellectual disability are candidates for potential development of an IPE as a component of a formal transition plan. A disabling condition related to intellectual disability could also potentially meet the requirements for VR eligibility. As a youth with intellectual disability becomes involved in the transition process in his or her secondary education program, the VR counselor can be actively engaged with that individual so an IPE can be put in place as the student prepares to exit the school program. The IPE should be finished early enough in the transition process to ensure that needed school-to-work VR services are in place at the time the secondary-level education program is completed.

The community link between VR and any specific person seeking services is critically important. Although VR agencies work under federally mandated guidelines, there are variations from state to state regarding how VR eligibility guidelines are interpreted and applied. These variations have a substantial impact on the extent to which VR services are available in a specific state and community for youth with intellectual disability. Each state has a Client Assistance Program (CAP) that is set up to provide information, protection, and advocacy services for people with disabilities. Youth with intellectual disability and their families who have questions or concerns about a VR agency should consider utilizing the CAP in their state for information and assistance regarding the VR program. The Job Accommodation Network (2015) provides the following resources:

- A national directory of state VR agencies (http://askjan.org/cgi-win/TypeQuery.exe?902).
- A national directory of the associated CAP (http://askjan.org/cgi-win/TypeQuery.exe?039).

Research on VR Services

In the past, students with significant disabilities, including intellectual disability, have often left their secondary programs without exposure to employment opportunities. Recent research has found that having held a paid, community-based job while in school was strongly correlated with postschool employment success (Carter et al., 2012). Another study examined the effect of supported employment intervention on the employment outcomes of transition-age youth with intellectual and developmental disabilities served by the public VR system using a case-control study design. The sample studied included 23,298 youth with intellectual and developmental disabilities between the ages of 16 and 25 at time of application for VR services. Receipt of supported employment was found to increase employment rates across all sample group studies (Wehman, Chan, Ditchman, & Kang, 2014). Another research study examined data from the NLTS2 to determine variables associated with post–high school competitive employment. The strongest predictors of competitive employment were high school employment experiences and parental expectations of post–high school employment (Wehman, Sima et al., 2015).

VR Services as a Pathway to Employment

The Workforce Innovations and Opportunities Act of 2014 (WIOA, Public Law 113–128) created a number of revisions to pathways used by VR agencies to obtain employment for youth with intellectual disability. As noted in the preceding research on VR Services summary, actual work experience during secondary education is a primary predictor of successful employment outcomes for transitioning youth with a disability. WIOA builds on that research by placing emphasis on "pre-employment transition services." For example, 15% of state Title I VR Funds must be used for "pre-employment transition services" for in-school youth. These services include:

- job exploration counseling;
- work-based learning experiences;
- counseling on postsecondary opportunities;
- workplace readiness training; and
- training on self-advocacy.

Additional specified activities for VR area offices, based on availability of funds, include:

- attending Individualized Education Program (IEP) meetings;
- working with schools to ensure provisions of preemployment transition services;
- when invited, attending person-centered planning meetings; and
- working with Workforce Boards, One Stops, and employers to develop employment opportunities.

VR agencies are also required by WIOA to create partnerships with other agencies as follows:

- A Formal Cooperative Agreement must be established between VR, state Medicaid, and the intellectual and developmental disabilities agency on delivery of VR services, including delivery of extended services.
- A total of 50% of funds received by VR under the Supported Employment State Grants will be used to support youth with the most significant disabilities (up to age 24).
- Youth with the most significant disabilities may receive extended services (ongoing support to maintain an individual in supported employment) for up to four years.

Collaborative relationships between VR and Youth Workforce Programs were also changed by WIOA. Changes to Youth Workforce Services under WIOA include:

- Eligibility for out-of-school youth services changed from 16 to 21 years of age to 16 to 24.
- In-School Youth Services age remains at 14 to 21, except students with disabilities who can be served prior to age 14.
- Amount of youth funds spent on out-of-school youth increased from 30% to 75%.
- Virtually all youth with disabilities are now eligible.

Along with local education agencies and Workforce Investment resources, Community Rehabilitation Providers (CRPs) are primary pathway partners of VR agencies in providing employment services for youth in transition. CRPs, which can be not-for-profit or for-profit private agencies, assist people with disabilities in obtaining and maintaining competitive employment. Specific services offered by providers will vary. Many CRPs offer career counseling, assessments, job placement, and supported employment services designed to assist people with disabilities live and work in the community. Since many CRPs obtain much of their funding through contractual arrangements, access to their services can require a funding authorization from an agency such as VR.

CRPs can provide a variety of employment-related services, such as assistance with exploring potential job and career options, job preparation, job development, job placement, and jobsite training services. These services might include practicing job-interview skills, classes to build job-seeking skills, resume preparation, guided job searches, or negotiations with employers. As an example, imagine an employer has a job with multiple duties. Some of these duties match well to the abilities of the applicant with a disability; other features of the job responsibilities are a poor match for the applicant. The employment consultant, with the permission of the applicant, might work with the employer to negotiate a customized job carved out of the original job description that is a good match for the individual with a disability (Brooks-Lane et al., 2005). Once the job match is completed, the employment consultant can assist with training at the jobsite, help the worker with a disability adjust to job demands, and provide ongoing support as needed to help maintain the job or potentially assist with job change.

VR agencies are important resources for transitioning youth with intellectual disability. Collaborating with VR agencies enables access to beneficial services for eligible youth that both guide and support the transition process. Further, the inclusion of VR counselors in early transition planning can enable valuable opportunities for youth with intellectual disability to gain employment experiences prior to leaving their secondary education environment, which is recognized as a successful predictor of employment outcomes (Wehman, Sima, et al., 2015). Such experiences, which include internships or job-focused PSE training, are discussed in more detail next.

Internships

Description of Internships

The old saying, "it's easier to get a job when you have a job" is true. Indeed, there are logical reasons why this is the case. For example, it is easier to explain why an individual might want a *new* job than to sell them as an "unproven worker." Having a job also increases an individuals' access to the network of employment opportunities available while demonstrating a track record of success at work. Also, work breeds self-confidence and self-awareness regarding personal strengths and potential value to new employers. When marketing people with intellectual and developmental disabilities have the potential to contribute to the workforce, it helps to be confident in previous work success and knowledgeable about what a worker has to offer an employer. Thus, people with intellectual and developmental disabilities who have not worked or do not currently work miss the advantages that previous work experience may offer in the search for new jobs. Additionally, people with intellectual and developmental disabilities who have worked in a sheltered environment may also be disadvantaged when seeking community-based employment due to the stigma and lack of independence associated with sheltered employment.

One way to mitigate this disadvantage is to develop and offer internships to people with intellectual and developmental disabilities. An internship is a *time-limited work experience* where an individual learns *job skills in a real work environment*. Internships are common in most professions, where individuals work in their chosen career under the guidance of an experienced professional and receive supervision as would any other worker. Doctors, lawyers, teachers, psychologists, certified electricians, and athletic trainers are a few of the many professions that require internships prior to certification or licensure. It is also a concept that is becoming popular among new graduates regardless of their future career aspirations. In fact, internships often lead to first jobs for young graduates. After years of success among people without disabilities, the internship model is finally becoming a viable way for people with intellectual and developmental disabilities to get work experience, gain skills, and network among businesses as a pathway to their own careers.

Research Related to Internships for People with Intellectual and Developmental Disabilities

There has long been an expectation that students with intellectual and developmental disabilities would participate in community-based employment training (CBET) as a part of their high school curriculum (Kohler, 1996; Kohler & Field, 2003; National Collaborative on Workforce and Disability/

Youth [NCWD/Y], 2006; Wehman, 2013). While on one hand this expectation has improved access to work experiences for high school youth, it is likely that brief experiences resulting in two to three times a week with one to two hours each time of community-based employment training are not intensive enough to allow young people with intellectual and developmental disabilities to identify their strengths, interests, and preferences. Internships, on the other hand, typically involve a significant portion of a student's weekly educational time. Indeed, internships provide the intensity and experience necessary to allow youth with intellectual and developmental disabilities to learn the job skills and social behaviors that result in successful employment (Wehman, Schall, et al., 2014). Instead of being present a few times weekly to learn a few job skills, a young person in an internship earns real work experience (Schall et al., 2015).

There is a growing body of research indicating that participation in community-based internships, as a part of CBET, result in up to a five times greater chance of acquiring community-based employment after high school graduation (Carter et al., 2011, 2012; Holwerda, van der Klink, de Boer, Groothoff, & Brouwer, 2013; NCWD/Y, 2006; Schall et al., 2015; Simonsen & Neubert, 2013; United Cerebral Palsy, 2015). More recently, there have been two studies that demonstrated the power of internships for transition-aged youth with ASD. Wehman et al. (2014) subjected a modified Project SEARCH transition program for students with ASD (Project SEARCH Plus ASD Supports, or PS-ASD) to a randomized clinical trial. During this study, youth who participated in the intensive internship program gained employment after high school at a significantly higher rate than a control group who participated in high school. In a follow-up study, Schall et al. (2015) found that individuals who participated in PS-ASD required fewer hours of intervention to find a job than individuals in supported employment only. Additionally, individuals in PS-ASD had better job retention and earned a higher wage despite having lower educational attainment than individuals who received only supported employment services. This indicates that internships might provide advantages to the individual with intellectual and developmental disabilities beyond simply learning job skills.

Legal Requirements for Internships

While interns may or may not be paid, the US Department of Labor, Wage and Hour Division has developed six criteria for ensuring that unpaid interns are not taken advantage of by potential employers (US Department of Labor, Wage and Hour Division, April 2010). Those six criteria are:

1. The internship, even though it includes actual operation of the facilities of the employer, is similar to training that would be given in an educational environment.
2. The internship experience is for the benefit of the intern.
3. The intern does not displace regular employees, but works under close supervision of existing staff.
4. The employer that provides the training derives no immediate advantage from the activities of the intern, and on occasion its operations may actually be impeded.
5. The intern is not necessarily entitled to a job at the conclusion of the internship.
6. The employer and the intern understand that the intern is not entitled to wages for the time spent in the internship.

(US Department of Labor, Wage and Hour Division, April 2010, p. 1)

All of this indicates that internships must be time-limited training experiences. In addition, participating in an internship is vastly different from volunteering. Nonprofit businesses may have volunteers who work for charitable reasons, without pay; however, they often work without supervision on tasks that would otherwise go undone. Volunteers also do not seek employment or expect to be granted training in exchange for their time at the business. Likewise, businesses view volunteers and interns differently. Businesses rarely think of volunteers as potential employees, while they often look to qualified interns to fill open paid positions within their ranks. These differences are critical when thinking about internships as gateways to employment for people with intellectual and developmental disabilities.

Characteristics of Internships for People With Intellectual and Developmental Disabilities

When considering internships for people with intellectual and developmental disabilities, there are two important principles to enact. The first principle is that an intern should never complete tasks in an internship that are not tasks that would be part of a paid position. If a volunteer typically completes a given task, then that task is not a good match for an internship. Internships should be training interns to do jobs that they can one day be paid to complete. The goal is to train a person in work tasks that can be transferred to paid employment either in that business or another business in the community.

The second principle is focusing on the strengths and abilities of the potential intern. For people with intellectual and developmental disabilities, an employment specialist or job coach will be working with them on their internship to support them to learn their internship tasks. Getting to know the potential intern with intellectual and developmental disabilities is imperative prior to selecting an internship site. The employment specialist must understand the intern's likes and dislikes, interests, motivations, career aspirations, learning style, and abilities (both mental and physical) in order to match the individual to the best internship experience.

Once the employment specialist has a better understanding of the student with intellectual and developmental disabilities, he or she will need to identify the internship site as well as the supervisor and/or mentor. At this point in the process, the employment specialist will need to get to know local businesses and their needs. When meeting with businesses, the employment specialist will need to find out what their typical hiring needs are and where they see high turnover. Working with businesses to look at position descriptions is helpful. Taking a close look at what tasks are performed in each department and determining the specific skills that must be mastered to meet the qualifications for employment in a given position will help the employment specialist plan for an internship that is beneficial to the potential intern (Daston, Riehle, & Rutkowski, 2012). It is important to remember that the intern does not need all of the identified skills to enter the internship, but rather the ability to learn the skills so that he or she is better prepared for employment as a result of the internship.

An internship allows a student with intellectual and developmental disabilities to be totally immersed in a workplace where high expectations are the norm. It allows an intern to work on not only mastering work skills but also mastering social skills where strict business norms exist (Daston et al., 2012). Interns are given the opportunity to practice appropriate worksite interactions daily, including with coworkers, supervisors, and, many times, guests or visitors to the business. The practice an intern receives from these interactions allows for mastery of a key social skill that will benefit him or her when employment occurs. Finally, internships give people with disabilities a work history and references to add to their resume of educational experiences. The combination of these factors position people with intellectual and developmental disabilities to present competitive applications for post–high school employment.

Postsecondary Education and Employment

Advanced education and training are well-known means for successfully obtaining gainful employment. Not only is it common for high school students to pursue advanced education at colleges and technical schools to enhance job prospects, but those who do so tend to earn more over their lifetime (Carnevale, Rose, & Cheah, 2011; Marcotte, Bailey, Borkoski, & Kienzl, 2005). Recent advances in legislation have made PSEopportunities more accessible for students with intellectual and developmental disabilities than ever before. Chapter 26 addresses PSE for students with intellectual disability, generally, so we will deal only with issues pertaining to employment in this chapter.

Overview of Postsecondary Research and Employment Outcomes

PSE opportunities for students with intellectual disability have grown immensely in recent years. As a result, investigative efforts have focused more on describing programs rather than evaluating program effectiveness. Notably, wide variation in implementation has made it difficult to conduct a systematic comparison of programs (Grigal, Hart, & Weir, 2013). However, results of available research are promising and a process for more closely examining outcomes for students in PSE programs continues to be more rigorously defined (Lynch & Getzel, 2013).

Employment Coursework

PSE programs were designed to enable greater career development opportunities for youth with intellectual and developmental disabilities, with the ultimate goal of competitive employment (Grigal et al., 2015). Estimates of the extent to which PSE programs are employment focused range from 45% to 100% (McEathron, Beuhring, Maynard, & Mavis, 2013). Regardless of type, most programs contain vocational training in the form of academic coursework, which usually includes a career exploration component. Coursework is designed to not only offer training in terms of job skills, but also vocationally related social skills. Additionally, students are typically required to participate in either a paid or unpaid vocational internship to gain valuable work experience (McEathron et al., 2013).

Employment Outcomes

Positive gains in employment and independent living have been reported for students with intellectual disability following postsecondary training. For example, Zaft, Hart, and Zimbrich (2004) reported that students with intellectual disability who participated in a PSE program were more likely to obtain competitive employment and need fewer job supports than a matched sample of students who did not participate in a PSE program. Migliore, Butterworth, and Hart (2009) found that 3.4% of 16 to 26 year olds with intellectual disability who received VR services in 2007 pursued some form of PSE training and 1.5% ultimately completed their pursued training, ranging in credentials from nondegree to graduate degree. Further, researchers found that people with intellectual disability who received PSE training had a 48% employment rate compared to 32% for those who did not receive PSE training. Additionally, people with intellectual disability who completed PSE training earned more, approximately $316 per week, compared to $195 per week for those who did not receive PSE training (Migliore et al., 2009). Ross, Marcell, Williams, and Carlson (2013) found that 64% of graduates with intellectual and developmental disabilities of a PSE program reported income at or above minimum wage. A total of 88% of graduates managed their own living expenses and 94% lived independently, as defined as alone or with a partner, in a rented or purchased residence. Grigal et al. (2015) reported that, upon exit, 57% of students from model demonstration PSE programs for students with intellectual and developmental disabilities were either actively participating in an unpaid experience and working toward career development or were already in a paid employment position at the time they exited the program.

Supported Employment

Description of Supported Employment

Students with intellectual and developmental disabilities do not have to accept unemployment or underemployment after graduation. However, the expectations of teachers and family members, as well as students themselves, need to reflect the value that community-integrated employment is their first choice. Instead of accepting placement in segregated facility-based programs or employment in low-paying stereotypical jobs, transition teams need to be familiar with other options that can assist students in achieving their goals. One of these options is supported employment.

Supported employment was first mentioned in the Developmental Disabilities Act (Public Law 98–527) in 1984. In 1986, funding was provided through the Rehabilitation Act Amendments (Public Law 99–506). This legislation established supported employment as a service that can be funded by VR state agencies. Since that time, the definition of supported employment has remained fairly consistent in federal legislation most recently reauthorized as part of the Workforce Innovation and Opportunity Act of 2014 (Public Law 113–128). The definition now includes customized employment and reads as follows:

> (38) SUPPORTED EMPLOYMENT.—The term "supported employment" means competitive integrated employment, including customized employment, or employment in an integrated work setting in which individuals are working on a short-term basis toward competitive integrated employment, that is individualized and customized consistent with the strengths, abilities, interests, and informed choice of the individuals involved, for individuals with the most significant disabilities—
>
> (A)(i) for whom competitive integrated employment has not historically occurred; or
>
> (ii) for whom competitive integrated employment has been interrupted or intermittent as a result of a significant disability; and
>
> (B) who, because of the nature and severity of their disability, need intensive supported employment services and extended services after the transition described in paragraph (13)(C), in order to perform the work involved.

Supported employment is based on the value that all people, regardless of disability, can be competitively employed if provided an individualized set of supports that match their interests, strengths, and abilities. There are a number of quality indicators of supported employment that school personnel must be familiar with in order to facilitate successful postschool employment outcomes for students with intellectual and developmental disabilities (Wehman, Inge, Revell, & Brooke, 2007; Wehman, Revell, & Brooke, 2003). These include, but are not limited to, the following:

- The number of people with disabilities to employees without disabilities employed by the business is naturally proportioned.
- The individual with disabilities is paid by the business where the work is taking place, and not a service provider.
- The individual with disabilities performs real work tasks to an established standard that a person without disabilities in the same setting would be paid to complete.
- There are opportunities to interact with and develop relationships with coworkers who are not paid to be with the individual who has a disability.
- The individual with disabilities earns wages that are commensurate with the wages earned by people without disabilities who are doing similar work, which is at least the statutory minimum wage.
- The individual with disabilities has opportunities for advancement consistent with those available to coworkers without disabilities.

Fulfilling these indictors is possible due to the unique features of supported employment. Specifically, a job identified based on the individual's interests and abilities, and on-the-job training is provided by a service provider—referred to as an "employment specialist" or "job coach"—to assist in skill acquisition. These services are gradually faded until the employment specialist is no longer on the job with the individual. Ongoing supports are provided a minimum of twice monthly to ensure that person can continue to meet the expectations of the business.

Research on Supported Employment

Supported employment has assisted thousands of people with significant disabilities in achieving integrated employment outcomes (Wehman et al., 2007). However, people with intellectual and developmental disabilities continue to be left out of the nation's labor force. The Institute for Community Inclusion (ICI, 2015) reported that in 2012–2013 only 10% of working-age adults supported by state intellectual and developmental disabilities agencies worked in individual competitive or supported jobs. Supported employment emerged as a service in the 1980s and 1990s as a strategy to assist individuals who traditionally had been unemployed or underemployed (Wehman, 1981). During this time period, supported employment was described extensively in the literature to include concepts such as situational and functional assessments, working with the business community, consumer choice and control, natural supports, workplace supports, and other best practices (Brooke, Inge, Armstrong, & Wehman, 1997; Callahan, 1992; DiLeo, Luecking, & Hathaway, 1995; Fabian, Luecking, & Tilson, 1994; Moon, Inge, Wehman, Brooke, & Barcus, 1990). More recently, Wehman et al. (2007) provided a guide to employment for people with disabilities, including supported employment, to facilitate competitive employment outcomes.

Wehman et al. (2014) evaluated the effect of supported employment on VR outcomes of transition-age youth with intellectual and developmental disabilities. Findings suggested that supported employment is an effective support for facilitating employment outcomes of young adults with disabilities. Although extensive information is available on both how to implement supported employment and its positive impact, students with intellectual and developmental disabilities continue to leave school and do not achieve competitive employment outcomes.

Supported Employment as Pathway to Employment

There are a number of features unique to supported employment. Perhaps the most critical is the role of the employment specialist or job coach who assists the individual with intellectual and developmental disabilities in realizing his or her employment goals. Typically, employment specialists are hired by CRPs to provide these services. Also, VR agencies can purchase supported employment services for their clients from CRPs, which in turn implement the supports that are described in this section. Therefore, it is critical for schools to work closely with VR agencies, including having VR counselors actively involved in IEP development and transition planning, to ensure that supported employment services, when needed by a transitioning student, are included in that individual's VR plan for employment (the IPE). In addition, schools need to be familiar with the values of the CRPs in their communities to ensure that they practice the quality indicators described earlier in this chapter. This information needs to be shared with transition teams in an effort to promote integrated employment outcomes for students with intellectual and developmental disabilities.

Critical to the entire employment process is assisting the individual in identifying an employment goal, which has been referred to as "discovery," an "individual profile," and/or a "vocational profile." This step focuses on getting to know the individual's strengths and interests in order to match the person to a competitive job. This may include interviewing the individual and his or her family and friends, getting to know the person by participating with him or her in activities of the person's choosing, and conducting situational assessments in community businesses. Situational assessments allow the individual to briefly experience job types that he or she has expressed an interest in doing. The goal of community assessments is to identify the person's skills rather than assessing what the person cannot do in an employment setting. For students with intellectual and developmental disabilities, information from internships or community-based work experiences can also be used to determine his or her interests and strengths for an integrated job in a community business.

This vocational profile is used by the employment specialist to assist the person in finding employment during the job development and placement components of supported employment. The individual's employment specialist meets with employers that potentially have jobs reflecting the individual's interests and abilities. If necessary and requested by the individual, the employment specialist can accompany the person to the job interview to assist in presenting his or her skills to the employer. Potential jobs can be identified by networking with friends and family members as well as other members of the person's community.

At this point, the person with intellectual and developmental disabilities may not possess all of the skills required for the job that is selected. However, he or she has the ability to learn the skills once training is provided in the actual work setting. In other words, supported employment assumes a best match between the individual and the job once on-site work supports and training are provided. These workplace supports and training are provided until the person performs job duties independently to the employer's satisfaction. The employment specialist is also responsible for working with the employer to provide supports and supervision to the individual. These business or coworker supports are sometimes referred to as "natural supports" and require the employment specialist to transfer supervision to a supervisor or coworker to help ensure long-term success.

Once the worker with a disability is stable and independently performing his or her job, the ongoing-supports phase of supported employment begins. These supports are provided throughout the course of employment and have also been referred to as "follow-along services." The level and intensity of the supports vary depending on the individual's needs. Federal regulations for supported employment state that a minimum of twice-monthly follow-along services should be provided to the individual either at or away from the job site. This unique feature of supported employment makes it possible for people with intensive support needs, such as those with intellectual and developmental disabilities, to be placed into integrated employment settings. Follow-along supports can include additional skills training, work-related social skills training, transportation, or other support needs that the individual has related to job retention.

Some communities may also have CRPs that offer group-supported employment placements to include mobile work crews and enclaves. The people with intellectual and developmental disabilities in these group options are provided supervision from agency staff that is never faded. An enclave includes a group of employees who have disabilities that work together on a job site clustered in the same work station or area. Mobile work crews are defined as groups of employees with disabilities who typically move to different/multiple work sites. Contrary to best practices, typically, people with intellectual and developmental disabilities who are placed into enclaves or mobile work crews are not employees of the business. They receive their wages through the human service organization, and often make less than minimum wage. A major concern with the group option of supported employment is that it stands in direct conflict with the best practices presented earlier in this chapter to include job choice. The other primary concern related to group-supported employment placements is the limited employment choice regarding the work performed. Jobs are typically based on the local labor market economy and not selected based on the workers' preferences and interests. This type of placement is not recommended and should be carefully analyzed prior to selecting an employment outcome for students with intellectual and developmental disabilities. Customized employment and self-employment should be considered to meet the individual's intensive support needs as opposed to placing a student into a group placement.

Customized Employment

The Customized Employment Approach

Customized employment is a successful approach to finding meaningful community employment for people with significant disabilities. The US Department of Labor, Office of Disability and Employment Policy (ODEP) first defined "customized employment" in the Federal Register as follows:

> Customized employment means individualizing the employment relationship between employees and employers in ways that meet the needs of both. It is based on an individualized determination

of the strengths, needs, and interests of the person with a disability, and is also designed to meet the specific needs of the employer. It may include employment developed through job carving, self-employment or entrepreneurial initiatives, or other job development or restructuring strategies that result in job responsibilities being customized and individually negotiated to fit the needs of individuals with a disability. Customized employment assumes the provision of reasonable accommodations and supports necessary for the individual to perform the functions of a job that is individually negotiated and developed.

(Federal Register, June 26, 2002, Vol 67, No. 123 pp. 43154–43149)

The ODEP (2005) described a set of indicators that must be present in order to consider a placement customized employment. These include (a) personalized job description and/or employee expectations that did not exist prior to the negotiation process; (b) tangible contribution made by the employee to the employer's enterprise; (c) the individual is hired and paid directly by the employer; (d) customized employment can be utilized either prior to, or after, employment as a strategy to modify job duties and/or other employer expectations for an individual with complex needs; (e) opportunity for personal representation by a job developer, as appropriate, to assist the job seeker in negotiating with employers; (f) array of strategies can be implemented to allow for job duties to be tailored to satisfy both job seeker and employer needs; (g) use of personal budgets, individual training accounts, and other forms of individualized funding that provide choice and control to the person and promote self-determination; and (h) the employer, the workforce system, and/or funders of services should offer all accommodations and supports needed by the job seeker for success.

In 2014, the WIOA amended the Rehabilitation Act to improve employment outcomes for people with disabilities. WIOA defines customized employment as "competitive integrated employment, for an individual with a significant disability, that is based on an individualized determination of the strengths, needs, and interests of the individual with a significant disability, and is designed to meet the specific abilities of the individual with a significant disability and the business needs of the employer," and "carried out through flexible strategies" (p. 1634).

Benefits of Customized Employment

Customized employment is beneficial for students transitioning from school to work. The Individualized Career Planning model designed by Condon and Callahan (2008) for youth with developmental disabilities and/or physical disabilities provides a method to translate the information gathered during discovery into vocational profiles that aid in transition planning and customized employment outcomes. The model allows the user to capture the strengths, interests, contributions, and support needs of a student, and then use that information to negotiate a customized job in the community. The transition service delivery model described by Certo and Luecking (2006) provides customized employment strategies that benefit transition-aged youth with significant disabilities, specifically identifying and negotiating customized work tasks to create more employment opportunities. Rogers, Lavin, Tran, Gantenbein, and Sharp (2008) demonstrated that customized employment expands opportunities for young adults with significant disabilities when jobs are developed or created around their interests and abilities.

Research indicates that customized employment not only benefits people with disabilities, but is also well received by employers, which is essential given that it is intended to meet both employee and employer needs. Employer-reported gains as a result of customized employment practices include an increase in the attainment of sale goals, achievement of production objectives, and an increased ability for businesses to keep up with inventory (Luecking, Cuzzo, & Buchanan, 2006). Furthermore, surveyed employers indicated support for the customized employment approach by agreeing they would recommend its use to other employers (Luecking et al., 2006).

Customized Employment Process

As mentioned, customized employment is based on the match between the unique strengths, needs, and interests of the job candidate and the identified needs of the employer. Customized employment starts with *discovery*, which is a process for getting to know the person and the unique skills and talents he or she can bring to a community business. Information is gathered through a series of interviews, activities, and observations about the person's abilities, types of environments and activities in which the individual is at his or her best, effective supports, and present level of performance in actual life activities. Information is gathered from anyone who knows the person best, including family members, friends, teachers, and neighbors. The discovery process happens in both home and community settings, where the individual can be observed in both familiar and unfamiliar activities (Condon & Callahan, 2008).

The next step is *customized job development*, which focuses on negotiating a job with a business that matches the job seeker's needs, strengths, and interests, and leads to an employment proposal. The negotiation process addresses areas such as job duties, terms of employment, services and supports necessary to carry out the job duties, and expectations adapted to the needs of the job seeker (ODEP, 2005). Negotiating positions using employment proposals to meet the unique interests and abilities of job seekers is recommended (Inge, 2001). The outcome from the negotiation process with employers is that the employee with a disability has a personalized job description that did not exist previously and the employer has a qualified worker with a disability to perform valued job duties within the workplace. After a job has been negotiated, *individualized jobsite supports* are provided as needed. A personal representative or employment specialist may assist in providing on-the-job training and facilitating supports in the workplace. Jobsite supports for people with physical disabilities may also include personal assistance services, natural supports, and other accommodations including assistive technology.

Customized employment provides an opportunity for employment to be an outcome for all students. In customized employment, students are not required to prove readiness for work. Instead, through discovery, the transition team identifies characteristics of environments, supports, and tasks that enable the student to be successful. Work experiences are individualized as necessary to enable all students to participate fully. Ideally, by the time students exit school they will have gained valuable work skills through placement in a job well-matched to their strengths, interests, and abilities.

Customized employment allows us to consider work in a different light, understanding that it is unique for each student. Some people may choose to have jobs that are negotiated for them, or they may decide to develop their own business rather than pursue wage employment. Competitive employment skills such as learning to complete applications, create resumes, and prepare for interviews would be augmented with training around skills more typically required in customized employment such as requesting and negotiating accommodations on the job, development of task lists, and creation of visual resumes outlining skills, contributions, tasks, and experiences, as well as making a proposal to an employer. Customized employment gives us an individualized way to assist students in accessing employment.

Business Partnerships

Description of Business Partnership

Much of the current research on employers focuses on attitudes, opinions, and perceptions surrounding hiring people with disabilities. Employers often say they have positive attitudes about hiring people with disabilities; however, there is a significant gap between their willingness to hire and actual hiring and retention practices (Chan, Strauser, Gervey, & Lee, 2010). A survey conducted by the Kessler Foundation found that 36% of respondents with disabilities reported that employers assume they can't do the job (Kessler Foundation, 2015). Clearly, unemployment of people with disabilities cannot be addressed by changing employer attitudes alone (Fraser et al., 2010). Research on business practices and employment for people with disabilities has been plentiful and heavily studied over the past 15 years (Domzal, Houtenville, & Sharma, 2008; Employment and Disability Institute, 2012). Unfortunately, little change has occurred regarding business practices and subsequent labor force participation of people with disabilities (Chan et al., 2010; Rudstam, Hittleman, Pi, & Gower, 2013; Schur, Kruse, & Blanck, 2005). This underscores the need for creating business partnerships as a meaningful pathway to employment by addressing the business case for hiring persons with disabilities. Specifically, a partnership can educate businesses on the economic benefits of a diverse workforce that includes people with disabilities, assist with the recruitment and retention of people with disabilities by creating a talent pipeline, and influence workplace operations to increase accessibility for job candidates with disabilities.

Business partnerships seek to reverse the typical supply-side approach to securing employment. In a supply side approach, used by many CRPs providing supported employment services, job preferences are matched against available jobs. On-site job coaching or accommodations are used to address any discrepancy between the job seeker's abilities and job requirements (Unger, Wehman, & Green, 2011). Though supply-side approaches have been effective in addressing workforce barriers like application completion and interviewing, the role of the business and its workforce development needs have often been overlooked (Luecking, 2008; Luecking et al., 2006). In contrast, building a business partnership uses a demand-side placement model to create mutually beneficial partnerships between CRPs and employers by demonstrating the value of people with disabilities (Luecking et al., 2006; Unger et al., 2011). Emphasis is switched from fulfilling open positions to meeting business workforce and operations demands. Demand-side placement can be defined as working with businesses to identify employment opportunities, required skill sets, and qualified workers to fulfill in-demand positions (Chan et al., 2010).

This method can also be considered a dual-customer approach where both employer and job seeker are regarded as customers of VR. When the employer is treated as a customer, the business is no longer just an entity by which to gain job placements, but a customer whose specific needs are matched with qualified candidates. In essence, CRP professionals market to businesses much as supplemental staffing agencies do.

Why Business Partnerships Matter

Business partnerships can do much to mitigate misconceptions that continue to hinder the inclusion of people with disabilities in the workforce. There is still a resounding lack of knowledge on the part of businesses about the capability and value of hiring people with disabilities. Unfortunately, resistance to hiring is influenced by previous charitable appeals to "hire the handicapped" from the mid-20th century and employers have continued to hold prejudicial views of employees with disabilities (Luecking, 2008). These attitudinal barriers and stereotypical beliefs about what people can and cannot do has made employment of large numbers of people with disabilities extremely difficult. The truth is that the full range of abilities of people with disabilities is extremely diverse.

However, research demonstrates that attitudes towards employees with disabilities are changing. A survey of employers conducted by Unger, Kregel, Wehman, and Brooke (2002) found that employees with disabilities were rated on par or better than employees without disabilities in the areas of punctuality, attendance, work quality, task consistency, and overall proficiency. Furthermore, The Universal Access Program at Universal Studios reported a retention rate of 62.5% for employees with disabilities compared to 30% for nondisabled employees in 1998, and the average length of employment for employees through the transition program, Project SEARCH, was five years (as cited in Unger et al., 2011). Business partnerships can play an important role in the transmission of such information between CPRs and businesses by creating a working relationship and rectifying misconceptions before they hamper recruiting.

Furthermore, a growing body of evidence identifies exposure as the main factor that shapes employer perspectives. In short, employers who have had prior contact with people with disabilities tend to hold more favorable attitudes towards employees with disabilities than those who have not had previous exposure (Bartolotta, Skaff, & Klayman, 2014; Luecking, 2008). In fact, the disability of a productive employee, in the eyes of the employer, can become obscured or entirely eliminated. When it is perceived that people with disabilities offer something of value to businesses, employers are more likely to develop augmentative recruitment procedures and hire workers without the requisite skills (Luecking, 2008). Businesses interested in hiring people with disabilities require the expertise and support of VR professionals who are familiar with both disability support practices and are capable of developing and managing business relationships to reduce prejudices and provide education.

Employers consistently report they are unaware of the availability of job seekers with disabilities, or that when they are aware of resources there is confusion over the fragmentation of service groups (Bartolotta et al, 2014; Luecking, 2008). These reports indicate a failure in disability employment marketing efforts. Creation of a partnership can aid in supporting businesses through the recruitment and hiring of employees with disabilities, and reducing time and money spent on recruitment by presenting businesses with qualified candidates.

An analysis of employer survey responses clearly indicates that hiring decisions are based on demand-side factors. Businesses desire evidence of beneficial outcomes, information on agency services, increased recruitment pool, and third-party assistance to identify accommodations and job customization (Simonsen, Fabian, Buchanan, & Luecking, 2011). As in all cases, businesses need a reason to hire; it is important to explain the time, money, or efficiency benefits to hiring people with disabilities. A demand-side business partnership focuses not on charity but on the bottom line. In order to do so, a relationship built on trust and credibility must exist between CRP professionals and businesses.

Creation of Business Partnerships

Once a trusted relationship has been established, CRP professionals are in an excellent position to dispel common myths about people with disabilities. However, to create a relationship, CRP staff must be in the position to interact with businesses. Employer focus groups have voiced a desire to see CRP staff active in the business arena such as trade groups, business leader networks, and chambers of commerce (Luecking, 2008). By participating in these forums, CRP personnel are primed to both establish relationships with local businesses and to also clarify the mission and role of disability employment service providers. Participation can be as simple as requests to be a guest or to give presentations on employment services. Involvement in these environments also provides insight into the general workforce development needs of different businesses and may reduce the perception many employers hold of CRP personnel as being naïve about business practices.

When building a partnership, attention should be paid to demand-side concerns. Rather than convincing businesses to charitably offer positions to people with disabilities, emphasis should be placed on identifying and then meeting specific employers' needs. Requesting informational interviews is one means of learning more about a business or industry and potential workforce needs that may be filled by current or future job seekers with disabilities. Getting to know the specific desires of an employer may reveal hidden job opportunities where specific tasks can be reassigned in order to increase operations efficiency or production. Customizing a support position that allows highly trained employees to focus on skill-specific tasks is an example of reassigning work to create an employment demand in the hidden market. The more CRP professionals learn about a specific employer the more likely they are to increase job placement demand by demonstrating ways in which the employer can save money, increase production, or increase efficiency.

Once businesses in a partnership have recognized the value of hiring people with disabilities to fulfill workforce needs, CRPs are in a position to identify qualified candidates with disabilities. Fully understanding business needs prevents CRP staff from presenting nonviable candidates, which would reduce their credibility. Additionally, business partnerships may allay the growing trend for passive recruitment methods like online applications that reduce personal interactions and opportunities for disability disclosure.

When a person with a disability is hired, employers universally report the importance of maintaining credibility by providing necessary on-site support and maintaining a relationship (Simonsen et al., 2011). In a business partnership, the relationship does not end after placement of a job seeker; instead it is the role of the CRP staff to continue to provide customer service and ongoing consultation to the business. Consultation may take the form of additional education on disability awareness, adjustments to work supports to address or increase efficiency or production, or additional recruitment of qualified candidates.

Building business partnerships does not usurp the position of the job seeker as a customer of VR services. Focusing on a business's bottom line to create a demand for candidates with disabilities negates the charitable argument for hiring persons with disabilities and instead changes the argument to one of competency and ability. Candidates are no longer judged on their "job readiness" and are instead evaluated on the unique skills they possess that fulfill specific market needs.

Conclusion

The documented discrepancy in employment outcomes for people with intellectual and developmental disabilities compared to people without disabilities highlights the need for educators, who serve a key role in employment preparation and planning, to be aware of available avenues to decrease this gap. Along with educators, improvements in employment outcomes will require collaborative efforts on the part of many involved parties—including students with intellectual and developmental disabilities, families, researchers, service providers, and businesses—to ensure that available supports are being accessed, especially during pivotal transition-age years. It is important to stress that the subject of poor outcomes is comprehensive and extends far beyond the issue of objectionably low employment rates. Equally unacceptable is the fact that people with intellectual and developmental disabilities tend to work fewer hours, make less money, enjoy fewer employer-offered benefits, and have less control over their employment options (Schur et al., 2009). Unfortunately, these poor employment outcomes continue to be observed despite research indicating the contrary; people with intellectual and developmental disabilities can be successful in competitive employment positions (Cimera, 2011; Wehman & Brooke, 2013; Wehman, Lau, et al., 2012; Wehman, Schall, et al., 2014). To clarify, our initiative for improved employment outcomes refers to the attainment of a paid position, making competitive wages, in an integrated environment. Furthermore, such a position should encompass meaningful work, be considered an asset to the employer, and be matched to the person's interests as closely as possible.

Educators are in a unique position to assist students with intellectual and developmental disabilities obtain meaningful employment. All efforts should be made to provide students employment opportunities prior to exiting the secondary education environment (Schall et al., 2015). As described in this chapter, there are multiple pathways available to meet the needs of all students. VR agencies act as valuable resources and coordination hubs to help transitioning youth obtain available funding and support to be successful in paid work positions. Educators can enable students to learn about the benefits of contacting their local VR agency to apply for services. Educators can also encourage students to utilize other pathways to employment discussed in this chapter, such as taking advantage of available job-based internships or vocational training opportunities via PSE programs and learning about vocational services such as supported and customized employment. Educators play a critical role in supporting students with intellectual and developmental disabilities develop appropriate work skills, plan for transition to employment positions, and network for needed supports.

References

Bartolotta, R., Skaff, L., & Klayman, D. (2014). *Employer engagement strategy: Workforce inclusion*. Gaithersburg, MD: Social Dynamics, LLC.

Bond, G. R., & Drake, R. E. (2014). Making the case for IPS supported employment. *Administration and Policy in Mental Health and Mental Health Services Research, 41*(1), 69–73.

Boschen, K. A., Tonack, M., & Gargaro, J. (2003). Long-term adjustment and community reintegration following spinal cord injury. *International Journal of Rehabilitation Research, 26*(3), 157–164.

Braddock, D., Hemp, R., Rizzolo, M. C., Tanis, E. S., Haffer, L., Lulinski, A., & Wu, J. (2013). *State of the states in developmental disabilities 2013: The great recession and its aftermath*. Boulder, CO: Department of Psychiatry and Coleman Institute, University of Colorado and Department of Disability and Human Development, University of Illinois at Chicago.

Brault, M. W. (2012). *Americans with disabilities: 2010* (Current Population Reports No. P70–131). Washington, DC: US Census Bureau.

Brooke, V., Inge, K., Armstrong, A., & Wehman, P. (1997). *Supported employment handbook: A customer driven approach for persons with significant disabilities*. Richmond: Virginia Commonwealth University Rehabilitation Research and Training Center on Workplace Supports and Job Retention.

Brooks-Lane, N., Hutcheson, S., & Revell, G. (2005). Supporting consumer directed employment outcomes. *Journal of Vocational Rehabilitation, 23*(2), 123–134.

Burger, H., & Marincek, C. (2007). Return to work after lower limb amputation. *Disability and Rehabilitation, 29*(17), 1323–1329.

Callahan, M. (1992). Job site training and natural supports. In J. Nisbet (Ed.), *Natural supports in school, at work, and in the community for people with disabilities* (pp. 257–276). Baltimore: Paul H. Brookes Publishing Co.

Carnevale, A. P., Rose, S. J., & Cheah, B. (2011). *The college payoff: Education, occupations, lifetime earnings*. Retrieved from https://repository.library.georgetown.edu/handle/10822/559300

Carter, E. W., Austin, D., & Trainor, A. A. (2011). Factors associated with the early work experiences of adolescents with severe disabilities. *Intellectual and Developmental Disabilities, 49*(4), 233–247.

Carter, E. W., Austin, D., & Trainor, A. A. (2012). Predictors of post school employment outcomes for young adults with severe disabilities. *Journal of Disability Policy Studies, 23*(1), 50–63.

Centers for Medicare and Medicaid Services. (2013, May 20). *Guidance to states using 1115 demonstrations or 1915(b) waivers for managed long-term services and supports programs*. Retrieved from http://www.medicaid.gov/Medicaid-CHIP-Program-Information/By-Topics/Delivery-Systems/Downloads/1115-and-1915b-MLTSS-guidance.pdf

Certo, N. J., & Luecking, R. G. (2006). Service integration and school to work transition: Customized employment as an outcome for youth with significant disabilities. *Journal of Applied Rehabilitation Counseling, 37*(4), 29–35.

Chan, F., Strauser, D., Gervey, R., & Lee, E. J. (2010). Introduction to demand-side factors related to employment of people with disabilities. *Journal of Occupational Rehabilitation, 20*(4), 407–411.

Cimera, R. E. (2011). Does being in sheltered workshops improve the employment outcomes of supported employees with intellectual disabilities? *Journal of Vocational Rehabilitation, 35*(1), 21–27.

Condon, E., & Callahan, M. (2008). Individualized career planning for students with significant support needs utilizing the discovery and vocation profile process, cross-agency collaborative funding and social security work incentives. *Journal of Vocational Rehabilitation, 28*(2), 85–96.

Daston, M., Riehle, J. E., & Rutkowski, S. (2012). *High school transition that works: Lessons learned from Project SEARCH*. Baltimore: Paul H. Brookes Publishing.

DiLeo, D., Luecking, R., & Hathaway, S. (1995). *Natural supports in action: Strategies to facilitate employer supports of workers with disabilities*. St. Augustine, FL: Training Resource Network, Inc.

Domzal, C., Houtenville, A., & Sharma, R. (2008). *Survey of employer perspectives on the employment of people with disabilities: Technical report* (Prepared under contract to the Office of Disability and Employment Policy, US Department of Labor). McLean, VA: CESSI.

Erickson, W., Lee, C., & von Schrader, S. (2012). *2011 disability status report: United States*. Ithaca, NY: Cornell University, Employment and Disability Institute.

Fabian, E., Luecking, R., & Tilson, G. (1994). *A working relationship: The job development specialist's guide to successful partnerships with business*. Baltimore: Paul H. Brookes.

Fraser, R. T., Johnson, K., Hebert, J., Ajzen, I., Copeland, J., Brown, P., & Chan, F. (2010). Understanding employers' hiring intentions in relation to qualified workers with disabilities: Preliminary findings. *Journal of Occupational Rehabilitation, 20*(4), 420–426.

Grigal, M., Hart, D., Smith, F. A., Domin, D., Sulewski, J., & Weir, C. (2015). *Think College National Coordinating Center: Annual report on the transition and postsecondary programs for students with intellectual disabilities (2013–2014)*. Boston, MA: University of Massachusetts Boston, Institute for Community Inclusion.

Grigal, M., Hart, D., & Weir, C. (2013). Postsecondary education for people with intellectual disability: Current issues and critical challenges. *Inclusion, 1*(1), 50–63.

Holwerda, A., van der Klink, J. J., de Boer, M. R., Groothoff, J. W., & Brouwer, S. (2013). Predictors of sustainable work participation in young adults with developmental disorders. *Research in Developmental Disabilities, 34*(9), 2753–2763.

Inge, K. (2001). Supported employment for individuals with physical disabilities. In P. Wehman (Ed.), *Supported employment in business: Expanding the capacity of workers with disabilities* (pp. 153–180). St. Augustine, FL: Training Resource Network.

Institute for Community Inclusion (ICI). (2015). *Bringing employment first to scale.* Retrieved from http://thinkwork. org/img/issue1_F2.pdf

Job Accommodation Network. (2015). State vocational rehabilitation agencies. Retrieved from http://askjan.org/

Kessler Foundation. (2015). *The Kessler Foundation 2015 National Employment and Disability Survey: Report of main findings.* West Orange, NJ: Author. Retrieved from http://kesslerfoundation.org/sites/default/files/filepicker/5/KFSurvey15_Resultssecured. pdf

Kohler, P. (1996). *Taxonomy for transition programming: Linking research and practice.* Champaign: Illinois University, Transition Research Institute.

Kohler, P., & Field, S. (2003). Transition-focused education: Foundation for the future. *Journal of Special Education, 37*(3), 174–183.

Lidal, I. B., Huynh, T. K., & Biering-Sørensen, F. (2007). Return to work following spinal cord injury: A review. *Disability and Rehabilitation, 29*(17), 1341–1375.

Liptak, G. S. (2008). Health and well-being of adults with cerebral palsy. *Current Opinion in Neurology, 21*(2), 136–142.

Luecking, R. G. (2008). Emerging employer views of people with disabilities and the future of job development. *Journal of Vocational Rehabilitation, 29*(1), 3–13.

Luecking, R. G., Cuzzo, L., & Buchanan, L. (2006). Demand-side workforce needs and the potential for job customization. *Journal of Applied Rehabilitation Counseling, 37*(4), 5–13.

Lynch, K. B., & Getzel, E. E. (2013). Assessing impact of inclusive postsecondary education using Think College Standards. *Journal of Postsecondary Education and Disability, 26*, 385–393.

Marcotte, D. E., Bailey, T., Borkoski, C., & Kienzl, G. S. (2005). The returns of a community college education: Evidence from a national education longitudinal survey. *Educational Evaluation and Policy Analysis, 27*(2), 157–175.

McEathron, M. A., Beuhring, T., Maynard, A., & Mavis, A. (2013). Understanding the diversity: A taxonomy for postsecondary education programs and services for students with intellectual and developmental disabilities. *Journal of Postsecondary Education and Disability, 26*(4), 303–320.

Michelsen, S. I., Uldall, P., Kejs, A. M., & Madsen, M. (2005). Education and employment prospects in cerebral palsy. *Developmental Medicine & Child Neurology, 47*(8), 511–517.

Migliore, A., Butterworth, J., & Hart, D. (2009). Postsecondary education and employment outcomes for youth with intellectual disabilities. *Think College! Fast Facts, 1*, 1.

Migliore, A., Mank, D., Grossi, T., & Rogan, P. (2007). Integrated employment or sheltered workshops: Preferences of adults with intellectual disabilities, their families, and staff. *Journal of Vocational Rehabilitation, 26*(1), 5–19.

Moon, M. S., Inge, K. J., Wehman, P. W., Brooke, V., & Barcus, M. J. (1990). *Helping persons with severe mental retardation get and keep employment: Supported employment issues and strategies.* Baltimore: Paul H. Brookes Publishing Co.

National Collaborative on Workforce and Disability for Youth (NCWD/Y). (2006). *Guideposts for success.* Washington, DC: Institute on Educational Leadership.

Office of Disability Employment Policy (ODEP). (2005, June). *Customized employment—Practical solutions for employment success.* Washington, DC: US Department of Labor, ODEP and the National Center on Workforce and Disability/Adult.

Riesen, T., Morgan, R. L., & Griffin, C. (in press). Customized employment: A review of the literature. *Journal of Vocational Rehabilitation, 43*(3), 183–193.

Rogers, C., Lavin, D., Tran, T., Gantenbein, T., & Sharpe, M. (2008). Customized employment: Changing what it means to be qualified in the workforce for transition-aged youth and young adults. *Journal of Vocational Rehabilitation, 28*(3), 191–207.

Ross, J., Marcell, J., Williams, P., & Carlson, D. (2013). Postsecondary education employment and independent living outcomes of persons with autism and intellectual disability. *Journal of Postsecondary Education and Disability, 26*(4), 337–351.

Rudstam, H., Hittleman, M., Pi, S., & Gower, W. S. (2013). Bridging the knowing-doing gap: Researching a new approach to disability and employment programming. *Journal of Vocational Rehabilitation, 39*(1), 43–60.

Schall, C. M., Wehman, P., Brooke, V., Graham, C., McDonough, J., Brooke, A., . . . Allen, J. (2015). Employment interventions for individuals with ASD: The relative efficacy of supported employment with or without prior Project SEARCH training. *Journal of Autism and Developmental Disorders.* doi: 10.1007/s10803-015-2426-5

Schur, L., Kruse, D., & Blanck, P. (2005). Corporate culture and the employment of individuals with disabilities. *Behavioral Sciences and the Law, 23*(1), 3–20.

Schur, L., Kruse, D., Blasi, J., & Blanck, P. (2009). Is disability disabling in all workplaces? Disability, workplace disparities, and corporate culture. *Industrial Relations, 48*(3), 381–410.

Simonsen, M., Fabian, E. S., Buchanan, L., & Luecking, R. G. (2011). *Strategies used by employment service providers in the job development process: Are they consistent with what employer want?* Technical Report. Retrieved from http://heldrich.rutgers.edu/publications/publication-types/research-report

Simonsen, M. L., & Neubert, D. A. (2013). Transitioning youth with intellectual and other developmental disabilities: Predicting community employment outcomes. *Career Development and Transition for Exceptional Individuals, 36*(3), 188–198.

Siperstein, G. N., Heyman, M., & Stokes, J. E. (2014). Pathways to employment: A national survey of adults with intellectual disabilities. *Journal of Vocational Rehabilitation, 41*(3), 165–178.

Siperstein, G. N., Parker, R. C., & Drascher, M. (2013). National snapshot of adults with intellectual disabilities in the labor force. *Journal of Vocational Rehabilitation, 39*(3), 157–165.

Unger, D., Kregel, J., Wehman, P., & Brooke, V. (2002). *Employers' views of workplace supports: Virginia Commonwealth University charter business roundtable's national study of employers' experiences with works with disabilities.* Richmond, VA: Virginia Commonwealth University, Rehabilitation Research and Training Center (VCU-RRTC).

Unger, D., Wehman, P., & Green, H. (2011). An investigation of the efficacy of business and rehabilitation partnerships for promoting employment of persons with significant disabilities. *Journal of Applied Rehabilitation Counseling, 41*(1), 25–33.

United Cerebral Palsy. (2015). *The case for inclusion, 2015.* Washington, DC: Author.

United States Department of Justice. (2014). *Department of Justice reaches landmark Americans with Disabilities Act Settlement Agreement with Rhode Island.* Retrieved from https://www.justice.gov/opa/pr/department-justice-reaches-landmark-americans-disabilities-act-settlement-agreement-rhode

United States Department of Justice. (2015). *Justice Department reaches proposed ADA settlement agreement on Oregon's developmental disabilities system.* Retrieved from https://www.justice.gov/opa/pr/justice-department-reaches-proposed-ada-settlement-agreement-oregons-developmental

The US Bureau of Labor Statistics. (2015). *Persons with a disability: Labor force characteristics—2014.* Retrieved from http://www.bls.gov/news.release/pdf/disabl.pdf

US Department of Labor, Wage and Hour Division. (2010, April). *Fact sheet #71: Internship programs under the Fair Labor Standards Act.* Retrieved July 17, 2015, from http://www.dol.gov/whd/regs/compliance/whdfs71.htm

Wehman, P. (in press). Editorial. *Journal of Vocational Rehabilitation, 43*(3).

Wehman, P. (1981). *Competitive employment: New horizons for severely disabled individuals.* Baltimore: Paul H. Brookes Publishing Co.

Wehman, P. (2013). *Life beyond the classroom: Transition strategies for young people with disabilities* (5th ed.). Baltimore, MD: Paul H. Brookes.

Wehman, P., & Brooke, V. (2013). Securing meaningful work in the community. In P. Wehman (Ed.), *Life beyond the classroom: Transition strategies for young people with disabilities* (5th ed., pp. 326–329). Baltimore, MD: Brookes Publishing.

Wehman, P., Chan, F., Ditchman, N., & Kang, H. (2014). Effects of supported employment on vocational rehabilitation outcomes of transition-age youth with intellectual and developmental disabilities: A case control study. *Intellectual and Developmental Disabilities, 52*(4), 296–310.

Wehman, P., Inge, K. J., Revell, W. G., & Brooke, V. A. (2007). *Real work for real pay: Inclusive employment for people with disabilities.* Baltimore: Paul H. Brookes Publishing Co.

Wehman, P., Lau, S., Molinelli, A., Brooke, V., Thompson, K., Moore, C., & West, M. (2012). Supported employment for young adults with autism spectrum disorder: Preliminary data. *Research and Practice for Persons with Severe Disabilities, 37*(3), 1–10.

Wehman, P., Revell, G., & Brooke, V. (2003). Competitive employment: Has it become the first choice yet. *Journal of Disability Policy Studies, 14*(3), 163–173.

Wehman, P., Schall, C. M., McDonough, J., Graham, C., Brooke, V., Riehle, J. E., . . . Allen, J. (2015). *Effects of an employer based intervention on employment outcomes for youth with autism.* Manuscript submitted for publication.

Wehman, P. H., Schall, C. M., McDonough, J., Kregel, J., Brooke, V., Molinelli, A., . . . Thiss, W. (2014). Competitive employment for youth with autism spectrum disorders: Early results from a randomized clinical trial. *Journal of Autism and Developmental Disorders, 44*(3), 487–500.

Wehman, P., Sima, A. P, Ketchum, J., West, M. D., Chan, F., & Luecking, R. (2015). Predictors of successful transition from school to employment for youth with disabilities. *Journal of Occupational Rehabilitation, 25*(2), 323–334.

Workforce Innovation and Opportunity Act of 2014, Pub.L. 113–128, STAT, 1634.

Zaft, C., Hart, D., & Zimbrich, K. (2004). College career connections: A study of youth with intellectual disabilities and the impact of postsecondary education. *Education and Training in Developmental Disabilities, 39*(1), 45–53.

26

Postsecondary Education for Students with Intellectual Disability

Meg Grigal, Maria Paiewonsky, Debra Hart

If there is one thing most Americans have been able to agree on over the years, it is that getting an education, particularly a college education, is a key to human betterment and prosperity.

(Cassidy, 2015)

Higher education has been linked to improved employment, lifetime income, job satisfaction, and civic engagement for people regardless of age, race, or gender (Baum, Ma, & Payea, 2013). While enrollment in higher education continues to rise (NCES, 2015), the number of students with disability enrolled in postsecondary education has been difficult to confirm with accuracy (Leake, 2015). However, almost all public two-year and four-year institutions report enrolling students with disabilities (Raue & Lewis, 2011).

Although higher education was once considered an unrealistic goal for youth with intellectual disability, current thinking has expanded to see it not only as possible, but an increasingly viable option. While small numbers of programs serving students with intellectual disability existed since the 1970s (Neubert, Moon, Grigal, & Redd, 2001), the Higher Education Opportunities Act (HEOA), along with advocacy and research efforts, has increased the availability of higher education options in the United States (Hart & Grigal, 2010). As this field grows, so too does our knowledge about the potential of higher education in improving the quality of life, financial security, level of independence, and social value of people with intellectual disability in the United States.

This chapter will describe the recent growth in supply and demand for higher education options for people with intellectual disability and share the recent findings from a federally funded model demonstration program. Given the crucial role that transition services play in determining a student's postschool outcomes, the chapter will also describe how local education agencies partner with institutes of higher education (IHEs) to assist transitioning students with intellectual disability to access higher education via dual or concurrent enrollment experiences. A dual enrollment state initiative will be described along with current activities to demonstrate efficacy of the model. The roles and responsibilities of college, school, and family partners in dual enrollment transition services will be highlighted and implications for personnel preparation will be offered.

Overview of Current Postsecondary Education Options in the United States

IHEs are increasingly opening their doors to students with intellectual disability (Folk, Yamamoto, & Stodden, 2012; Grigal, Hart, & Weir, 2013; Kardos, 2011; Katovich, 2010; Mock & Love, 2012; Papay & Bambara, 2011). A 2010 National Center for Education Statistics survey of Title IV two-year and four-year IHEs found that 41% of reporting institutions indicated that they enrolled students with "cognitive difficulties or intellectual disability" (Raue & Lewis, 2011). As shown in Figure 26.1, the number of available options has expanded more than 900% in the past 11 years (Grigal, Hart, & Weir, 2013) and continues to grow.

According to a national database of higher education programs, there are now approximately 251 programs at IHEs in the United States that serve students with intellectual disability (Think College, 2016). Some of these programs focus on independent living–skill development and employment, and to a lesser extent on academics and social skill development (Grigal et al., 2012; Papay & Bambara, 2011). These programs exist in both two- and four-year IHEs and serve both transitioning youth (ages 18–21) and adult students with intellectual disability. Some of these programs are highly integrated with their IHE and others are substantially separate (Grigal et al., 2015). The programmatic structures and policies, the degree to which these align with the host IHE's infrastructure, and the levels of access to integrated learning and working experiences vary significantly (Grigal, Hart, & Weir, 2013).

Impact of the Higher Education Opportunities Act

Demand for postsecondary options in the United States has increased, as has federal and state investment. A number of states have developed legislation, created funding, and launched statewide and regional consortia to further program development efforts in higher education for students with intellectual disability (Grigal et al., 2015). In 2008 the HEOA reauthorized the Higher Education Act (HEA) of 1965 and provided unprecedented guidance related to students with intellectual disability and access to higher education and financial aid (Smith Lee, 2009). Unlike previous reauthorizations of the HEA, the HEOA included specific provisions regarding students with intellectual disability and outlined components that should be present in postsecondary education programs that serve them (see Figure 26.2). The HEOA indicated that a prevailing tenet of these postsecondary education programs should be inclusive academic access and that these experiences should result in gainful employment (Grigal et al., 2014).

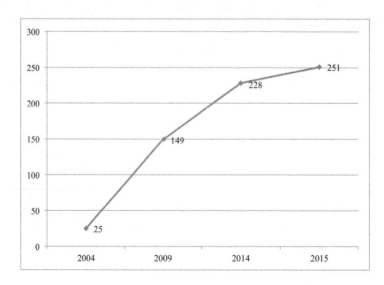

Figure 26.1 Growth in postsecondary education programs for students with intellectual disability

Higher Education Opportunities Act of 2008

Higher Education Act of 1965- Section 760(2)(A) of the Higher Education Act of 1965 (20 U.S.C. 1140(2)(A)) (updated October 2010 due to Rosa's Law)

A student—
(A) With a cognitive impairment, characterized by significant limitations in—
    (i) intellectual and cognitive functioning; and
    (ii) adaptive behavior as expressed in conceptual, social, and practical adaptive skills; and
(B) Who is currently, or was formerly, eligible for a free appropriate public education under the Individuals with Disabilities Education Act.

Definition Of Comprehensive Transition And Postsecondary Program For Students With Intellectual Disabilities (Final Regulations Federal Register/Vol. 74, No. 208/Thursday, October 29, 2009)

A Comprehensive transition and postsecondary program means a degree, certificate, nondegree, or noncertificate program that—
(1) Is offered by a participating institution;
(2) Is delivered to students physically attending the institution;
(3) Is designed to support students with intellectual disabilities who are seeking to continue academic, career and technical, and independent living instruction at an institution of higher education in order to prepare for gainful employment;
(4) Includes an advising and curriculum structure;
(5) Requires students with intellectual disabilities to have at least one-half of their participation in the program, as determined by the institution, focus on academic components through one or more of the following activities:
    (i) Taking credit-bearing courses with students without disabilities.
    (ii) Auditing or otherwise participating in courses with students without disabilities for which the student does not receive regular academic credit.
    (iii) Taking non-credit-bearing, nondegree courses with students without disabilities.
    (iv) Participating in internships or work-based training in settings with individuals without disabilities; and
(6) Provides students with intellectual disabilities opportunities to participate in coursework and other activities with students without disabilities.

Figure 26.2 HEOA definitions for students with intellectual disability and comprehensive transition programs

The HEOA also created a new Title IV or federal student aid access point for college students with intellectual disability called Comprehensive Transition Programs (CTPs). CTPs support students with intellectual disability who are seeking to continue academic, career and technical, and independent living instruction at an IHE and require that at least half of the program consist of coursework and other activities with students without disabilities (20 USC. 1091, 1140). IHEs that have approved CTPs can provide eligible students with intellectual disability access to certain forms of federal student aid. The HEOA also waived some previous requirements to qualify for federal student aid for students with intellectual disability attending CTPs, including the need to have a high school diploma or general equivalency diploma and the intent to matriculate and earn a standard degree or certificate. Students with intellectual disability who document their financial need and are out of high school are eligible to receive federal Pell Grants, federal Supplemental Educational Opportunity Grants, and federal work-study funds but are not eligible to receive student loans.

Despite the recent growth, the currently available 251 postsecondary education options represent only 3% of the more than 7,000 Title IV IHEs available to other students without or with different disabilities. Given this disparity, it is perhaps not surprising that until recently little aggregate data was available regarding the activities or outcomes of students with intellectual disability who accessed higher education. However, a federally funded program has led to significant growth in available data on postsecondary education access of students with intellectual disability.

Model Demonstration Projects for Students With Intellectual Disability

In 2010, as a result of some of the new provisions in the HEOA, the Department of Education's Office of Postsecondary Education (OPE), funded a new federal program aimed at creating, expanding, or enhancing high-quality, inclusive higher education experiences to support positive outcomes for people with intellectual disability. Five-year grants were awarded to 27 IHEs in 23 states to implement model demonstration projects called Transition Postsecondary Programs for Students with Intellectual Disability (TPSIDs; see Figure 26.3). In addition, a national center was established to provide technical assistance to these IHEs, evaluate the TPSID projects, and build a knowledge base around program components. This National Coordinating Center for Transition Postsecondary Programs for Students with Intellectual Disability (NCC) was administered by Think College at the Institute for Community Inclusion at the University of Massachusetts Boston. The NCC collected data from each of the 27 grantees and their respective satellite campuses between 2010 and 2015. These data, highlighted briefly in this chapter, provide the most comprehensive reflection of current and emerging practices supporting students with ID in higher education.

TRANSITION AND POSTSECONDARY PROGRAMS FOR STUDENTS WITH INTELLECTUAL DISABILITIES (TPSID) GRANTEES

Figure 26.3 Institutions of higher-education TPSID grantees by state, funded October 1, 2010–September 30, 2015

Reprinted with permission from Institute for Community Inclusion, University of Massachusetts Boston.

TPSID Demographics

After five years of funding, 15 TPSID programs operated on single college campuses and 12 operated as consortia, with various satellite college campuses. Fifteen of these sites were located at two-year IHEs, and 35 sites were located at four-year IHEs. As of September 2015 (the end of the funding period), 16 TPSID sites had been approved as CTPs and were able to offer eligible students with intellectual disability access to certain forms of Title IV student aid. Between 2010 and 2015, 2,246 students (primarily with intellectual disability and autism) were served by the 52 IHEs hosting a TPSID program. More than 90% of students were between the ages of 18 and 25, and 92% of enrolled students had intellectual disability and/or autism. In the final year of the projects, (2014–2015), 57% of students were male and 43% female. The majority of students were white (73%), 17% were black or African American, and 10% were Hispanic or Latino. Just under a quarter of students (24%) were dually enrolled (i.e., receiving special education transition services from a public school system while attending the TPSID program; see Grigal, Hart, Smith, Domin, Sulewski, & Weir, 2015).

Academic Access

Students attending TPSID programs were required to have an academic component to their college program. A majority of course enrollments (52%) were in academically specialized courses (i.e., courses designed for and delivered to only students with intellectual disability in the TPSID). The remaining 48% were in academically inclusive courses (i.e., typical college courses attended by students with intellectual disability and other college students). Some students audited courses; others took courses for academic credit. (See Figure 26.4 for a sample list of courses taken by students in TPSID programs.) The percentage of enrollments in inclusive courses was higher at two-year IHEs than at four-year IHEs. The most common accommodations were academic supports, such as note takers and readers. Students also received enrollment accommodations, such as modified course loads, substitutes for required courses, and priority registration, as well as academic accommodations, such as access to professors' notes, advance access to materials, and alternative test formats. A majority of students attending TPSIDs (79%) were seeking a credential. Peer mentors were used to provide academic supports to students in 86% of TPSID programs.

That a slim majority of the course enrollments for students with intellectual disability enrolled in the TPSIDs were in specialized courses, designed for and attended by students with disabilities only

---

- Crime in America
- Art Appreciation
- Music Appreciation
- Food & Society
- Introduction to Business
- The Theatre Experience
- World Civilization to 1600
- Intro to Sociology
- Environmental Science

- Spanish I
- Introduction to Social Work
- Intro to Graphic Design
- Sports Management II
- Foundations of College Writing II
- African American Music
- Intro to Computers
- Music In Your Life
- Formatting/Word Processing

Figure 26.4 Sample of college courses taken by students in TPSID programs

Reprinted with permission from Institute for Community Inclusion, University of Massachusetts Boston.

From: Grigal, M., Hart, D., Smith, F. A., Domin, D., Sulewski, J., & Weir, C. (2015). *Think College National Coordinating Center: Annual report on the transition and postsecondary programs for students with intellectual disabilities (2013–2014)*. Boston, MA: University of Massachusetts Boston, Institute for Community Inclusion.

(Grigal et al., 2015), was an area of concern noted by the NCC as it runs counter to the guidance offered by the authorizing language in the HEAO. It also creates the potential for other IHEs to replicate the segregated practices that are being implemented by these "model" projects. Segregated coursework reinforces the idea that individuals with intellectual disability have predetermined learning needs based upon their disability label. Often these specialized classes are focused on same "life skills" activities that have comprised the student's high school experiences and prohibit interactions with college peers. Equally often, these courses are designed and taught by program staff and are not formally approved as part of the college or university offerings. In contrast, inclusive courses provide the opportunity for students with intellectual disability to engage with college faculty and peers without disability in approved coursework and take advantage of a fuller range of college courses that align with their career goals and aspirations. Inclusive college courses also present opportunities for college students, faculty, and staff to better understand the educational goals of students with intellectual disability.

Career Development and Employment

A primary goal of the TPSID programs was to facilitate career development and the supports necessary for students to become employed. The TPSID programs offered internships, provided job coaches, and connected with adult service providers to address career development and employment. Rate of paid employment for students with intellectual disability enrolled in TPSIDs program rose each year, starting at 16% in 2011 and ending at 40% in 2015. Some students held the same job for multiple years and others held more than one paid job. Forty-eight percent of students employed had never held a paid job prior to entering the TPSID program. The length of student attendance impacted rates of employment: the longer students attended, the more likely they were to be employed. Challenges to engaging in paid employment included lack of preparation and career assessment prior to students entering their college program, as well as a lack of staff knowledge and training about state-of-the-art customized and integrated employment practices (Grigal et al., 2013).

Campus Membership and Housing

All of the TPSID programs reported facilitating or supporting student participation in campus social activities, including attending events on campus, going out with friends, and attending or participating in sporting events. Some students participated independently; others received support from staff or peer mentors. Approximately 50% of TPSID projects were located at commuter IHEs that did not provide housing for any students. Of the 25 TPSIDs located at IHEs that offered housing, 16 campuses provided students in the TPSID access to that housing, and nine campuses did not. Most of the TPSID students who engaged in housing lived in residence halls or off-campus apartments where most residents were other students attending the college. Nearly two thirds of those living off campus (but not with their families) lived independently, with another 20% in supervised living settings. Students who lived in TPSID or IHE housing generally had higher levels of participation in social activities.

Future Program Development

In October 2015 the OPE funded another cohort of 25 TPSID projects (see Figure 26.5). This next group of programs will help expand the number of available postsecondary options for students with intellectual disability in the United States and extend our knowledge base on effective practice and the impact and challenges of inclusive course access. It will also provide much-needed longitudinal data regarding the long-term employment and independent living outcomes of students who attend these programs. The TPSID programs, both old and new, represent only a small portion of available programs in the United States for students with intellectual disability. There are many programs that have been established without

TPSID Grantees 2015–2020

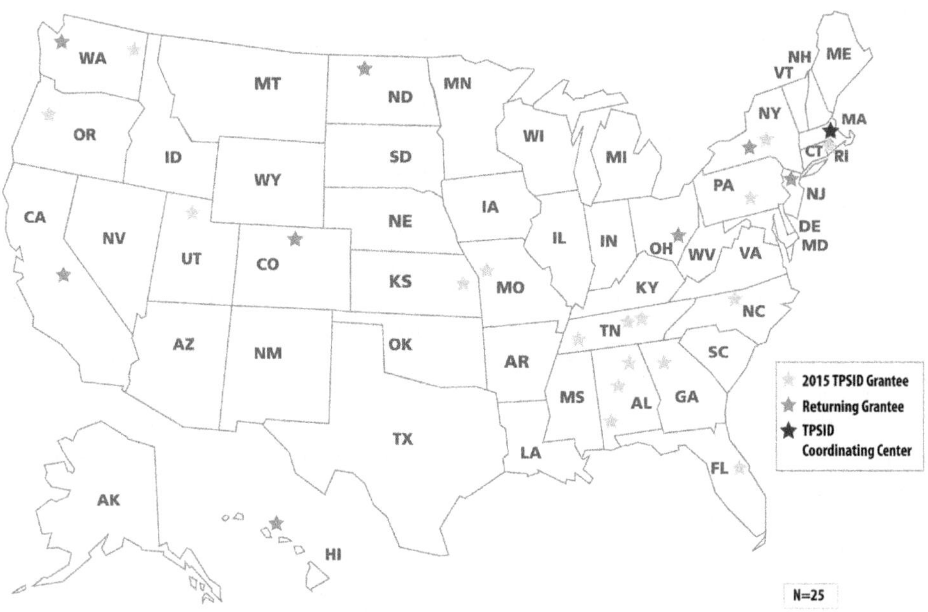

Figure 26.5 Institutions of higher education TPSID grantees by state, funded October 1, 2015–September 30, 2020

Reprinted with permission from Institute for Community Inclusion, University of Massachusetts Boston.

the assistance of federal grant funds; some have been developed with state funding, others with support from foundations or private donations (Katovich, 2010; Kleinert, Jones, Sheppard-Jones, Harp, & Harrison, 2012).

Another common method establishing postsecondary access for students with intellectual disability is via transition programs that are created through a partnership between an IHE and a local education agency (LEA). The next section of this chapter will describe the development of dual or concurrent enrollment transition programs for students with intellectual disability and roles and responsibilities of college partners, school partners, and families in these types of programs.

Dual Enrollment Transition Programs

Dual enrollment is a popular practice that permits high school students to be enrolled in high school and college simultaneously (Barnett & Stamm, 2010; Marken, Gray, & Lewis, 2013). Typically, dual enrollment experiences are offered to high school students in advanced placement courses, allowing them to seek high school and college credit simultaneously. A modified version of this practice has demonstrated promise for students with intellectual disability by providing them the opportunity to receive community-based transition services on a college campus with same-age peers instead of remaining in high school (Grigal, Dwyre, Emmett, & Emmett, 2012; Hart, Zimbrich, & Parker, 2005; Kleinert et al., 2012). Dual enrollment programs (also known as "concurrent enrollment programs") provide opportunities for transition-aged youth with intellectual disability between the ages of 18 and 22 access to college courses, internships, and employment, as well as other campus activities during their final two to three years of secondary education. Thirty percent of the postsecondary education programs available throughout the United States serve dually enrolled students (Think College, 2016) and approximately 24% of the students being served in the TPSIDs were dually enrolled.

Most dual enrollment programs are operated and funded by school districts, though some have been established initially via federal or state grants (Papay & Bambara, 2011). Similar to the TPSIDs, dual enrollment programs vary in the amount of access students with intellectual disability have to typical college classes. In some programs, students have greater access, but in others there is minimal to no access to typical college courses. In a national survey of dual enrollment programs, Papay and Bambara (2011) found that only about 25% of all students in postsecondary education programs were participating in college classes and that course access was dependent on the type of program model, the location of the program, and the level of academic ability of the student.

The focal areas of dual enrollment programs are similar to IHE programs serving adult learners with intellectual disability, including academic access, career development and integrated paid employment, independent living, and campus membership (Hart et al., 2005; Kleinert et al., 2012). College campuses can serve as a nexus for the transition experience, providing opportunities for personal growth and self-determination, access to adult learning and working environments, and new and expanded social networks (Grigal & Deschamps, 2012; Grigal & Dwyre, 2009). However, dual enrollment transition programs also must address issues related to the Individuals with Disabilities Education Act (IDEA) such as addressing Individualized Education Program (IEP) transition goals in a college setting; collaborating with secondary special education systems; dual funding structures; and schedule, staffing, and transportation issues (Grigal, Hart, & Paiewonsky, 2010).

Existing dual enrollment programs vary significantly in their practices, including in their commitment to offering access to college courses or support for paid internships or employment (Grigal et al., 2012; Papay & Bambara, 2011). There is little legislative guidance or oversight of the dual enrollment transition programs in the United States and few studies that have addressed the efficacy or outcomes of these practices. Current research on dual enrollment programs is primarily descriptive in nature and reflects that programs do not implement services in accordance with current HEOA provisions. A stronger evidence base is needed to expand implementation of high-quality dual enrollment practices more consistently for students with intellectual disability.

Creating an Evidence Base for Dual Enrollment Transition Services: The Think College Transition Project

The Institute for Community Inclusion at the University of Massachusetts Boston secured funding from the US Department of Education's Investing in Innovation Fund (i3) to conduct a four-year study to develop, implement, and evaluate an evidence-based inclusive dual enrollment transition model called the Think College Transition (TCT) Model. This project seeks to advance knowledge and practice in the fields of higher and special education by developing a transition model that that is fully inclusive, reflecting both current federal guidance and evidence-based transition practices. The TCT Model builds upon knowledge of effective and evidence-based practices from the field of special education, college and career readiness (CCR), dual and concurrent enrollment, career and technical education, supported employment, and school counseling, and it reflects guidance from the HEOA regarding students with intellectual disability.

To ensure the model reflected current knowledge of disability and higher education, researchers reviewed the Standards, Quality Indicators, and Benchmarks for Inclusive Higher Education (Grigal et al., 2012), the only existing standards for guiding the development or evaluation of inclusive higher education for students with intellectual disability. This framework is comprised of eight standards, of which four have been depicted as the cornerstone of inclusive high education: academic access, career development, campus membership and self-determination. The other four standards—integration with college systems and practices, coordination and collaboration, sustainability, and ongoing evaluation—provide the infrastructure for the cornerstone practices. These standards have been used nationally by IHEs and dual enrollment partnerships to create, expand, or enhance high-quality, inclusive postsecondary education to support positive outcomes for individuals with intellectual disability.

To reflect current guidance from the CCR field, Conley's (2011) four major components of college readiness were incorporated into the standards of academic access and career development. These components include: (1) key cognitive strategies, (2) academic knowledge and skills, (3) academic behaviors, and (4) contextual skills and awareness. Each of these components take into account the academic preparation, study skills, problem-solving skills, and college navigation skills that students—including students with intellectual disability—need to learn in order to be better prepared for postsecondary education (Kearns et al., 2012).

To ensure the model reflected knowledge from the field of dual and concurrent enrollment, researchers identified several standards, including the following: (1) course access and registration protocols are typical of any other college student, (2) concurrent paid work experiences are used to augment students' career awareness, and (3) course instructors meet the IHE's professional requirements (National Alliance of Concurrent Enrollment Partnerships, 2012).

From the field of career and technical education, components were included that emphasized that dually enrolled students begin with introductory courses at the secondary level that teach broad foundational knowledge and skills across careers and then progress to more occupationally specific courses at the postsecondary level (Perkins Collaborative Resource Network, 2015). The Association of People Supporting Employment First (APSE) provided a framework for Supported Employment Competencies, specifically standards focused on individualized work plans, building partnerships with businesses, and interagency collaboration for integrated employment opportunities (APSE, 2010). Finally, the American School Counselor Association emphasized the expectation that guidance staff provide all students with early planning, goal setting, and meaningful course and extra-curricular activities as a result of career assessment results (ASCA, 2016). Together these evidence-based practices provided the framework for the initial draft of the TCT Model.

Once developed, these initial components were reviewed via a Delphi study, conducted with transition and postsecondary education national content experts to assist in refining the essential TCT Model components. The Delphi method is a "group facilitation technique that seeks to obtain consensus on the opinions of 'experts' through a series of structured questionnaires (commonly referred to as rounds)" (Hasson, Keeney, & McKenna, 2000, p. 1009). It is used to achieve consensus among experts where little or no previous research exists and to address questions that are not easily quantifiable. The method allows for both quantitative and qualitative input. The results include the following eight components of the TCT Model:

1. **Community-based transition services:** Students learn necessary transition skills in naturally occurring environments in their community with supports as needed. School districts partner with IHEs, adult service agencies, and service providers so that students with intellectual disability or autism receive individualized transition services across all community-based environments including participation inclusive college courses, college- or community-based internships, service learning opportunities, competitive integrated employment, and the wide range of community organizations, businesses, and generic resources (Brooke, Revell, & Green, 2013; Fowler et al., 2014; NTACT, 2015). Adult service agencies (e.g., vocational rehabilitation, developmental disability services) participate to ensure the student has a seamless transition and the needed long-term supports to be successful (Simonsen, Stuart, Luecking, & Certo, 2013).

2. **Self-determination and self-advocacy:** Students first participate in a person-centered planning process to identify career and overall life goals (e.g., PATH, Whole Life Planning, Five Bold Steps). Students also learn to make choices, solve problems, set goals, evaluate options, take initiative to reach one's goals, and accept consequences for one's actions (Hagner, May, Kurtz, &

Cloutier, 2014; NTACT, 2015; Shogren et al., 2013). Students are provided with needed supports by education coaches, peer mentors, and/or other natural supports to learn and apply these skills in the actual environment in which they will be used, thereby increasing the likelihood that students will learn and use these skills.

3. **Family engagement and partnerships:** Services are designed to be focused on family involvement and therefore sensitive to the student's ethnic and cultural background and outreach strategies are used to ensure ongoing family participation (Greene, 2011; NTACT 2015). Family engagement is critical to postschool success (Dwyre, Grigal, & Fialka, 2010; Morningstar et al., 2012) and may include participation in program meetings and campus orientation events, along with materials that explain issues such as the difference between high school and college, the need for having high expectations for their child, the need for competitive integrated employment before exiting high school, and Social Security Administration work incentives. Parent and/or other family members are involved and supportive of all aspects of the students' participation in college, the community, and competitive integrated employment (Doren, Gau, & Lindstrom, 2012; NTACT, 2015).

4. **Advising, course of study, and enrollment:** Students and their college advisors use their postschool career goals from their person-centered plan to guide development of a course of study that will assist them in achieving their career goal and other personal areas of interest. Students take courses for audit or credit with needed supports (e.g., peer mentors and/or education coaches, accommodations, and technology).

5. **Student supports:** Students are provided with a range of services that are associated with an individualized supported education model and that lead to competitive integrated employment and other quality of life outcomes. These supports include but are not limited to: typical accommodations and technology available to any student with a disability, peer mentors, and education and job coaches. Funding is braided, demonstrating a shared responsibility among the students' LEA, the IHE, and adult services (e.g., vocational rehabilitation and developmental disability services) (Hart, Zimbrich, & Ghiloni, 2001).

6. **Integrated paid employment:** Students are supported, as needed, in integrated employment experiences such as discovery activities, job shadowing, work-based learning, paid/unpaid internships, service learning, and apprenticeships, all leading to competitive integrated employment prior to exiting high school (Luecking & Luecking, 2015; Simonsen et al., 2013). Students earn minimum wage or higher and their wages are paid by their employer.

7. **Staff development:** Staff receive training on evidence-based transition practices (Rowe et al., 2015), universal design for learning in higher education (Behring & Hart, 2008), college and career services (Conley, 2011; Fowler et al., 2014), competitive integrated employment (Simonsen et al., 2013), and interagency collaboration (Luecking & Luecking, 2015).

8. **Evaluation:** High school and/or college staff conducts accountability and evaluation of transition services and outcomes on a regular basis, including data from key stakeholders, such as students with and without disabilities, parents, faculty, disability services, district transition coordinators, and employers (Grigal et al., 2012; Test, Aspel, & Everson, 2006). Exit and follow up data are compiled and reviewed by interagency teams.

Building upon existing dual enrollment programs created in western Massachusetts via the Inclusive Concurrent Enrollment Initiative (see Figure 26.6), the TCT Model will be implemented with 60 students with intellectual disability over three years. Institute for Community Inclusion researchers, in conjunction with colleagues from the Education Development Center, will conduct a quasi-experimental evaluation to determine the impact of the TCT Model on students' levels of self-determination, job-seeking skills, career readiness, college self-efficacy, and competitive integrated employment outcomes. This study will provide some of the first evidence of the impact that inclusive dual enrollment transition practices has on students. It will also chronicle the practices and policies necessary to replicate this model in other states.

The Massachusetts Inclusive Concurrent Enrollment Initiative is the oldest, most comprehensive and inclusive state supported dual enrollment model nationwide. Since 2007, Massachusetts has had a statewide college-based inclusive transition initiative (ICEI) for students with intellectual disability, ages 18–22 who are still receiving special education services from their school district. Thus far, this initiative has been funded by a line item in the state budget that has ranged from 2 million dollars to $400,000 depending on state appropriations annually (Massachusetts Joint Committee on Higher Education, 2014). These funds have been used as seed money to establish partnerships between institutes of higher education (IHEs) and school districts in the surrounding geographic vicinity. Each partnership varies depending on the culture of the host IHE, subject focal areas that each IHE may specialize in (e.g., automotive, nursing, teacher preparation, theatre, liberal arts, technology), and how the initiative aligns student services and supports within the existing IHE infrastructure (e.g., registration, orientation, advising, credentialing, access to inclusive courses, disability services, actual placement of the initiative itself). Each funding cycle is for five years and partnerships have to reapply annually. On average, the ICEI supports between 100 to 125 students annually. The program is administered by the Massachusetts Executive Office of Education, which provides training and technical assistance, evaluation, and general oversight activities for each partnership.

The purpose of the ICEI is to provide students with intellectual disability the same opportunities that their peers without disabilities have as they prepare for and enter adult life. The emphasis is to ensure that students with intellectual disability meet with successful post-school outcomes by having a successful career and in becoming valued members of their home communities. To this end, students with intellectual disability are engaged in all campus activities including an inclusive course of study related to their career goals and other personal areas of interest, participating in campus-wide social and academic events, learning to use public transportation to and from campus, obtaining paid and unpaid internships and ultimately competitive integrated employment rather than staying in a high school or segregated community-based transition program only for students with disability.

The ICEI partnerships are typically formalized with a Memorandum of Understanding delineating the roles and responsibilities for each participating partner (e.g., LEA, IHE and adult service agencies such as Vocational Rehabilitation and/or state developmental disabilities agency). The needed core functions that personnel conduct include the following four key areas (MEOE, 2014):

1. **IHE Coordination** (IHEC) oversees all aspects of student services and supports and establishes communication mechanisms with the participating high schools and adult service agencies along with being the internal liaison for the IHE. The IHEC is responsible for convening partnership meetings to guide the operations of the initiative and to ensure a seamless transition to adult life for the student. The IHEC also works closely with Disability Services Office (DSO) personnel and Career Services and students with intellectual disability to ensure that student services are coordinated and that students learn how to self-advocate. The IHEC also arranges for and often provides professional development for coaches, peer mentors, college personnel and faculty.

2. **High School Liaison (HSL)** (sometimes a Transition Specialist) works directly with students in learning how to conducts person centered planning, coordinate their schedules, assist students in learning how to make transportation arrangements and how to navigate public or para-transportation. The HSL also communicates with families on what the difference between college and high school will be, the need to have high expectations for their son/daughter, the importance of competitive integrated employment before exiting high school, and Social Security Work Incentives. The HSL collaborates closely with the IHEC and adult service agencies to ensure that the student receives needed transition related services.

3. **Educational Coach and/or Peer Mentors** provide direct or indirect services to students via assistance with course assignments, tutoring, connecting with DSO personnel, homework help and overall wrap-around supports as need by the student. They may also involve classroom support, support with extracurricular and with navigating campus-wide social activities, and support with internships and integrated competitive employment.

Figure 26.6 Example of a statewide dual enrollment program: The Massachusetts Inclusive Concurrent Enrollment Initiative

4. **Career Specialist (CS)** or the HSL or IHE collaborates with adult employment service provider organizations to conduct career and job development activities for students. Career specialists work with students to review person-centered plans to ensure that their courses and campus activities are aligned with their career goals; collaborates with campus and community career & employment resources; collaborates with school and community providers to develop competitive integrated employment that aligns with student employment goals; and develops work-based learning plans with students and their work supervisor.

Dual enrollment initiatives nationwide have considerable variability in their design and staffing but overall have the need for these transition evidenced-based key practices if the initiative is going to be successful with supporting students with intellectual disability to achieve successful post-school outcomes such as competitive integrated employment, independent living, and overall life satisfaction. However, the field needs more comprehensive evaluation of dual enrollment initiatives for students with intellectual disability.

Figure 26.6 (Continued)

Establishing Effective Dual Enrollment Partnerships

Creating dual enrollment transition opportunities for students with intellectual disability requires thoughtful and organized collaboration among partnering colleges, schools, and families (Dwyre et al., 2010; Hart & Grigal, 2010; Griffin, McMillan, & Hodapp, 2010). Each partner has important, discrete tasks that, when combined, lead to college experiences for students that are meaningful and contribute toward their postsecondary goals (Folk et al., 2012; Hart & Grigal, 2010; Paiewonsky, Boyle, Hanson, et al., 2013; Paiewonsky & Ostergard, 2010). Understanding these tasks, and communicating their status regularly, is critical for partners who are focused on building a seamless transition to college and career. The following section describes the roles and responsibilities of each partner in a dual enrollment transition program for students with intellectual disability.

Roles and Responsibilities of College Partners

College partners in dual enrollment and other inclusive postsecondary education initiatives serve as the primary spokespeople for inclusive access to college (Leach, Helms, Foster, et al., 2013; Paiewonsky, Boyle, Hanson, et al., 2013). As the liaison between the student, family, and secondary school, college partners collaborate internally with various departments and personnel at the college or university and collaborate externally with school system administrations and teachers, as well as with adult agencies and families. College partners take responsibility for establishing memorandums of agreements (MOAs) that include cost sharing, orient partners to available college resources and schedules, and provide opportunities for professional development; they also collaborate on mutual outreach efforts to the college, schools, and community to promote dual enrollment or inclusive post–high school college opportunities.

Establishing Memorandums of Agreement

When colleges and schools offer dual enrollment experiences to students, partners often establish an MOA that outlines the responsibilities of each member partner (Grigal, Neubert, & Moon, 2005). College partners frequently initiate these agreements, which may include information about how many students the partnership can support each semester, how students will be supported, who will supervise educational coaches and mentors, what training will be provided, and what direct and indirect resources will be available to the students (Conroy, Hanson, Butler, & Paiewonsky, 2013).

Communicating with College Administration and Staff

Although there are a growing number of colleges that have developed inclusive postsecondary education initiatives to support students with intellectual disability, the idea of enrolling college students with intellectual disability in typical college classes can still seem unusual to many college staff and faculty. Kleinert et al. (2012) asserted that: "One of the greatest barriers to creating inclusive campus communities are the attitudes and preconceived notions about the limited ability of students with intellectual disability to meaningfully contribute to the collegiate environment" (p. 27). To respond to these attitudinal barriers, college partners must engage with their university colleagues to communicate the purpose of inclusive dual enrollment initiatives. College faculty and other staff can explain how both traditional and nontraditional college students benefit from this dual enrollment experience and highlight how the college community is enhanced by participating in inclusive college initiatives (Paiewonsky, Boyle, Hanson, et al., 2013). Sharing clear information about the goals and expectations of these experiences and how they can lead to better outcomes for students with intellectual disability can help broaden opportunities and advance college faculty and staff understanding of inclusive postsecondary education.

Orienting Students and Families and School Partners to College Expectations and Resources

College partners often provide students, families, and school partners with an overview of the differences between high school and college that will prepare them for the student's transition to a dual enrollment experience. Given that this opportunity is often the first experience the student has after at least 12 years in K–12 school settings, college partners know they need to take the time to orient their partners to the expectations of college. These include new expectations such as students advocating for themselves with disability services and with faculty, taking responsibility for following the course syllabus, learning to use accommodations rather than modifications, and seeking out academic tutoring independently rather that waiting for it to be offered.

College partners also may orient their school partners to college resources, either through the regularly scheduled partnership meetings or on a case-by-case basis as they mutually work to support students on campus. These resources are often new to school partners, and they are important to understand as they assist students to access and rely more on college resources rather than K–12 LEA resources. Examples of resources that college partners introduce students and school partners to include the campus academic support and learning center, the adaptive computer lab and related assistive technology, career services, student clubs and sports activities, and the campus calendar of events.

Addressing Systemic Barriers and Training Needs

College partners work with many departments to facilitate students' full access to college services and courses. Existing systems and protocol may not be set up to facilitate access for students with intellectual disability who may have a nontraditional course of study. Departments that college partners typically communicate and collaborate with include disability services, student affairs, and the bursar's office. Each of these departments play a role in course registration, accessing needed accommodations and supports, and engaging in campus activities.

Another role for college partners may be to arrange for needed professional development for their colleagues on universal design for learning and supported education, and an orientation to assistive technology. They may also assist LEA transition staff to access training on student preparation and self-determination for college, the role of educational coaches or mentors, and health and safety for first-year college students.

Meeting with College Faculty

College partners work behind the scenes discussing critical aspects of the dual enrollment program with faculty, including addressing course and performance expectations. They may help faculty understand the role of peer and professional support personnel such as education coaches and peer mentors. College partners may also work to increase the number of courses that are open and accessible to students with intellectual disability by arranging for faculty trainings that highlight universal design for learning methods and strategies.

Coordinating Partnership Meetings and Conducting Outreach

Dual enrollment partnerships between colleges and high schools are most productive when the partners meet regularly. Partnership meetings allow for information sharing about resources and supports for the students as well as the opportunity to discuss and resolve potential problems related to course access, transportation, and deadlines for academic advising and registration. Outreach efforts allow for sharing of information and resources regarding the dual enrollment program to the campus community as well as neighboring school districts and may include attending department and faculty meetings, sharing information at local transition fairs, speaking with interagency transition teams, and engaging with college administrators to highlight positive outcomes and systemic collaboration benefits.

Roles and Responsibilities of School Partners

Dual enrollment initiatives often involve a variety of school partners (Grigal et al., 2012; Kleinert et al., 2012; Plotner & Marshall, 2015)—including special education directors, transition specialists, special education teachers, and job/educational coaches—with unique roles in establishing, maintaining, and optimizing students' college-based transition experience.

Special education directors may take the lead role in addressing traditional school policies that may need to be adjusted to support students' participation in college and work activities that take place off school grounds or dealing with the need for flexible work hours for support staff. Transition specialists may take the lead role in coordinating transition services at both the individual student level (orienting and preparing students and families) and at the department or school level (organizing and collaborating with teachers and administrators). A primary responsibility is making colleagues and administrators aware of evidence-based transition practices (Test, Fowler, Kohler, & Kortering, 2010). Transition specialists and special educators often collaborate to orient students and families to the expected outcomes of the dual enrollment experience, including expectations for course access, campus or community employment, transportation, attendance, and costs (if applicable). Other staff may include job coaches or employment specialists and educational coaches, who are responsible for providing direct support to students with intellectual disability in the college and community.

Supporting Secondary Staff

Special education administrators and transition specialists must also address staff awareness of inclusive postsecondary education options and the skills required to succeed in college. Some of the preparatory skills students with intellectual disability must have include:

- Knowing how to advocate for needed supports or accommodations in learning and working environments;
- Articulating their postsecondary goals;
- Choosing courses the meet their personal or career goals;

- Knowing what their disability is and being able to describe how the disability impacts their learning and what accommodations they need; and
- Learning to travel to and navigate the college campus as independently as possible.

School personnel may also need to focus on students' personal development and evolving maturity, and to promote students' social and emotional well-being as well as their safety skills. One critical skill that may be overlooked in secondary school, but is critical in college, is the use of mobile technology. High school transition staff may need to learn how to incorporate a cell phone or smart phone, tablets, and apps into their students' skills development.

Supporting Families

Families are often not aware of supported education and inclusive postsecondary education (Benito, 2012; Doren et al., 2012; Griffin, McMillan, & Hodapp, 2010), so another role for school partners is to introduce these concepts to families. Part of this conversation includes sharing how college expectations differ from K–12 expectations, and the increased level of responsibility that children need to take to advocate for their own needs. School partners can use site visits, videos, and other students' stories to help parents grasp how college can be a good match for their child's transition from high school to adult life. Youth and families who have a low socioeconomic status and are from culturally and linguistically diverse backgrounds may require additional strategies as part of the college conversation. To address these needs, Green (2011) suggested that educators:

- Obtain knowledge of a family's culture and how to frame planning that is inclusive of a family's beliefs;
- Respect family perspectives related to their family member with intellectual disability;
- Provide families and students with accessible information and their rights under the law (and have material translated into the family's language when needed); and
- Take the time to establish a trusting relationship with families and demonstrate sensitivity to their schedules (e.g., schedule meetings when they are not working).

One primary family concern is student safety. School partners can include IEP goals such as learning to use public transportation, campus navigation, and respond to emergencies on the student's transition plan. School partners also need to communicate with families about their expectations regarding students' academic responsibilities, accessing campus events in the evenings or on weekends, and getting the student to and from jobs if work hours do not correspond with school hours.

Logistical Planning

Some existing school policies may need to be adjusted to support dual enrollment initiatives. Policies around student attendance, staff supervision and schedules, addressing free and reduced lunch for eligible students, and flexible schedules for support staff all must be addressed when creating dual enrollment initiatives. In some cases, school partners will need to collaborate with human resources staff and teacher unions to redesign support staff positions as roles and responsibilities in dual enrollment programs differ from the typical classroom-based paraprofessionals' work.

Roles and Responsibilities of Families

Families play a critical role in their loved one's participation in dual enrollment transition programs as they may be the first or the only adults who encourage them to pursue the goal of going to college (Benito, 2012; Griffin et al., 2010). Parent expectations have a significant impact on a student's path to postsecondary education and these expectations may be influenced by their son's or daughter's academic abilities.

Griffin et al. (2010) found that parents of students with lower reading levels were less likely to think that postsecondary education would help their son or daughter make the transition to adulthood, were less often encouraged by school staff to pursue postsecondary education, and were less likely to enroll their son or daughter in postsecondary education. These low expectations are also reflected in transition goals for students with intellectual disability (Grigal, Hart, & Migliore, 2011; Migliore & Domin, 2011; Papay & Bambara, 2011), which rarely include preparing for any level of postsecondary education.

Papay and Bambara (2011) found that parental expectations for employment and postsecondary education were some of the strongest predictors of successful postschool outcomes for youth with intellectual disability. Youth whose parents expected they would be employed were 28 times more likely to have enrolled in postsecondary education after leaving high school than youth whose parents did not expect employment (Papay & Bambara, 2011). The same study found that youth whose parents expected they would attend postsecondary education were three times more likely to have enrolled in postsecondary education than youth whose parents did not have that expectation. Family involvement was also significantly linked to students attending college after high school. Thus, it is crucial for families to be engaged in the college conversation. Their formal role may begin as part of the planning process, possibly during an IEP meeting or in a person-centered planning meeting where their son or daughter is invited to discuss their postsecondary plans. Parents may also be helpful in identifying potential networks for pursuing jobs (Luecking & Tilson, 2009). Parents can assist their son or daughter to practice articulating his or her learning style and offer examples of successful accommodations as the student prepares to request accommodations from the college's disability services staff.

Another important issue that families should address is that of transportation. Dual enrollment programs may use school system transportation or public transportation, or require families to assist their son or daughter to get to and from the campus and/or a job. Discussing expectations with families as they begin this experience can minimize some conflicts that may arise later if the expectations are not clearly outlined. A number of dual enrollment programs have implemented contracts with families that outline the parent responsibilities, the student responsibilities, and the program staff's responsibilities to ensure that all parties are familiar with their roles (Paiewonsky & Ostergard, 2010).

One crucial aspect of family participation in dual enrollment transition programs is the amount of privacy that student college records are afforded. Parents have full access to their child's educational records when their child is enrolled in K–12 education, under IDEA. However, once a student attends college, the parents' access to student records is protected under the Family Education Rights and Privacy Act. This law ensures that students, including students with intellectual disability, have sole rights to their education records and communications at college unless they say otherwise—meaning that they must consent to their parents having access to their college records. Given this shift in authority and responsibility, it is important that parents are provided with sufficient information and background about these policies as their child enters the dual enrollment experience (Hirano & Rowe, 2015; Larson, Goldberg, McDonald et al., 2011; Martinez, Conroy, & Cerreto, 2012).

Impact of Postsecondary Education for Students With Intellectual Disability on Transition Personnel Preparation

The preparation of transition personnel is recognized as a critical factor that leads to improved postschool outcomes for students with intellectual disability (Morgan et al., 2013; Morningstar & Benitez, 2013). To sufficiently prepare secondary special education and transition staff to support students with intellectual disability to access postsecondary education opportunities, personnel preparation programs need to address inclusive and evidence-based practices well beyond what is offered in typical preservice training. Given that personnel preparation programs may provide as few as one course on transition competencies (Anderson, Kleinhammer-Tramill, Morningstar et al., 2003), secondary special educators and other transition personnel may have only basic knowledge regarding the development of IEP goals that incorporate transition goals. Secondary special education teachers are less likely to have field-based expertise in transition assessment, interagency collaboration, transition-focused instruction, and instructional planning (Benitez, Morningstar & Frey, 2009; Morningstar & Kleinhammer-Trammel, 2005; Plotner, Mazzotti, Rose, & Carlson-Britting, 2016) and are most likely not aware of inclusive postsecondary education opportunities (Griffin et al., 2009; Martinez et al., 2012). It is critical that training programs for special educators, transition specialists, and special education administrators are aligned with up-to-date policies and practices that reflect current research, policy, and practice around inclusive postsecondary education.

Federal legislation and policies related to higher education, employment, and disability are constantly evolving. Students with intellectual disability must depend on the professionals in their schools to have current knowledge that extends beyond IDEA and includes understanding of the practical implications of the HEOA, Section 504 of the Rehabilitation Act, the Workforce Innovation and Opportunities Act (2014), Employment First, and Common Core and College Career Readiness. Transition and special education professionals who support secondary students with intellectual disability must be expected to demonstrate a range of state-of-the-art transition practices that support inclusive postsecondary education (e.g., person-centered planning, transition assessment, self-advocacy and self determination, career development, college and workplace accommodations, supported education, universal design for learning in higher education, interagency collaboration, teaming, resource mapping), and an in-depth knowledge of complex adult services systems (e.g., higher education, disability services, vocational rehabilitation, Social Security income, Medicaid, financial aid, developmental disability services, workforce development, benefits specialists, and community rehabilitation providers).

These are practices that go beyond writing IEPs or offering a handful of traditional vocational "readiness" activities (Benitez et al., 2009). Educators also need to understand the unique challenges that students with intellectual disability from culturally and linguistically diverse backgrounds face in attempting to pursue satisfactory postsecondary outcomes, including postsecondary education (Greene, 2014; Morningstar & Nix, 2011; Nix & Goff, 2013; Povenmire-Kirk, Lindstrom, & Bullis, 2010).

Needed Enhancements to Personnel Preparation Programs

To enhance personnel preparation programs for secondary special education staff, including special education administrators, teachers, and transition specialists, undergraduate and graduate education programs must include developing core competencies that are aligned with evidence-based practices that prepare students for inclusive postsecondary education and integrated paid employment. Courses should include both an overview of the theory and research that support evidence-based practices as well as multiple applied learning opportunities for scholars to learn how to integrate practices into their work (Papay & Bambara, 2014). Diverse and varied field-based experiences build upon the knowledge and skills acquired in the coursework, and provide the practical experience necessary to learn how these practices are implemented in authentic settings. A comprehensive training program should include skills and knowledge to prepare graduates to competently demonstrate:

- Facilitating person-centered career planning that includes postsecondary education (Hagner et al., 2014; Morningstar, Frey, Noonan, et al., 2010; O'Brien, 2014);
- Integrating CCR competencies into students' courses of study (Conley, 2011; Fowler et al., 2014);
- Coordinating inclusive education opportunities through the IEP process (Fowler et al., 2014; Test & Cease-Cook, 2012);
- Collaborating with families to prepare for their loved one's transition to postschool activities (Cobb & Alwell, 2009; Doren et al., 2012; Dwyre et al., 2010);
- Coordinating transition assessments that reflect students' postschool visions and inform IEP teams of appropriate planning for students preparing for postsecondary education (Rowe, Mazzotti, Hirano, & Alverson, 2015; Thoma, Bartholomew, & Scott, 2009);

- Assisting students to move from modifications they are entitled to under IDEA to accommodations they can request in higher-education settings (Newman & Madaus, 2015; Shaw, Madaus, & Dukes, 2010);
- Instructing students in self-determination, self-advocacy, and disability disclosure (Martin & Williams-Diehm, 2013; Shogren et al., 2013);
- Coaching students to access, and in some cases direct, a variety of supports and services at college (Eisenman & Mancini, 2010; Paiewonsky, Mecca, Daniels et al., 2010);
- Partnering with college, state disability agencies, and workforce development staff to develop inclusive college and career opportunities (Noonan, 2014; Reisen, Morgan, Schultz, & Kupferman, 2014);
- Developing early paid and unpaid work experiences for students (Carter, Austin, & Trainor, 2011; Lindstrom et al., 2014; Luecking & Luecking, 2015); and
- Creating a seamless transition pathway for students with intellectual disability to move from high school to college and work (Luecking & Luecking, 2015; Simonsen et al., 2013).

Comprehensive training on evidence-based transition practices, with an emphasis on an increased awareness of transition and postsecondary education state and national policies and implementation, will prepare transition staff to assume responsibility for effectively providing transition services and assisting their schools and districts to participate in state-of-the-art transition-related initiatives. Training also has the potential to prepare a growing cadre of transition professionals to successfully implement important disability-related and college- and career-related laws and initiatives. Their efforts and participation will, in turn, lead to positive secondary and postsecondary outcomes for students with intellectual disability.

Conclusion

The education of young people with intellectual disability needs to begin with the expectation that they will achieve the best possible outcome. And for many students, the best possible outcome can and should be accessing inclusive postsecondary education experiences that lead to employment. While the postsecondary education opportunities for students with intellectual disability in the United States have expanded significantly, there is still a great need for more colleges and universities to enroll students with intellectual disability. There is also a need to cultivate greater understanding and expertise related to how to plan, implement, and evaluate postsecondary education experiences both for transitioning youth and adults with intellectual disability.

Each of the preceding chapters has highlighted a variety of evidence-based practices that have a role in creating these college pathways. Person-centered planning, self-determination, integrated paid employment—all are part and parcel of creating the pathway to and through higher education. In some ways it might be better if the chapter on postsecondary education was the first and not the last chapter in every special education book. The ultimate outcome of a successful K–12 education for students with intellectual disability depends greatly on the expectations of the professionals and families who interact with that student. They create the vision for the student's future, and then systematically build the skills and experiences that to lead to that future. If the vision is to include postsecondary education, we must ensure that all special education and transition personnel are armed adequately with knowledge that supports the premise that students with intellectual disability are worthy and capable of lifelong learning.

References

American School Counselor Association (ASCA) (2016). *National model a framework for school counseling programs: Executive summary*. Retrieved from https://www.schoolcounselor.org/school-counselors-members/asca-national-model

Anderson, D., Kleinhammer-Tramill, P. J., Morningstar, M. E., Lehmann, J., Bassett, D., Kohler, P., et al. (2003). What's happening in personnel preparation in transition? A national survey. *Career Development for Exceptional Individuals, 26*(2), 145–160.

Association for Persons in Supported Employment (APSE), (2010). *APSE Position Papers, APSE Supported Employment Competencies.* Retrieved from http://apse.org/policy-advocacy/position-papers/

Barnett, E., & Stamm, L. (2010). *Dual enrollment: A strategy for educational advancement of all students.* Washington, DC: Blackboard Institute.

Baum, S., Ma, J., & Payea, K. (2013). *Education pays: The benefits of higher education for individuals and society.* New York: College Board.

Behring, K., & Hart, D. (2008). Universal course design: A model of professional development. In S. Bergstahler (Ed.), *Universal design of higher education: From principles to practice* (pp. 109–125). Cambridge, MA: Harvard Education Press.

Benitez, D. T., Morningstar, M. E., & Frey, B. B. (2009). A multistate survey of special education teachers' perceptions of their transition competencies. *Career Development for Exceptional Individuals, 32*(1), 6–16.

Benito, N. (2012). *Perspectives on life after high school for youth with intellectual and developmental disabilities: Findings of a statewide survey of families.* Think College Insight Brief, Issue No. 13. Boston, MA: University of Massachusetts Boston, Institute for Community Inclusion.

Brooke, V., Revell, W. G., & Green, H. (2013). Transition planning and community resources: Bringing it all together. In P. Wehman (Ed.), *Life beyond the classroom* (pp. 143–171). Baltimore: Paul H. Brookes Publishing Co.

Carter, E. W., Austin, D., & Trainor, A. A. (2011). Factors associated with the early work experiences of adolescents with severe disabilities. *Intellectual and Developmental Disabilities, 49*, 233–247.

Cassidy, J. (2015). *College Calculus: What's the real value of higher education?* Retrieved from http://www.newyorker.com/magazine/2015/09/07/college-calculus

Cobb, R. B., & Alwell, M. (2009). Transition planning/coordinating interventions for youth with disabilities: A systematic review. *Career Development for Exceptional Individuals, 32*(2), 70–81.

Conley, D. T. (2011). *Redefining college readiness* (vol. 5). Eugene, OR: Education Policy Improvement Center.

Conroy, M., Hanson, T., Butler, J., & Paiewonsky, M. (2013). *Massachusetts Inclusive Concurrent Enrollment: Shifting from state funds to IDEA funds.* Think College. Boston, MA: University of Massachusetts Boston, Institute for Community Inclusion.

Doren, B., Gau, J. M., & Lindstrom, L. (2012). The relationship between parent expectations and post school outcomes of adolescents with disabilities. *Exceptional Children, 79*, 7–23.

Dwyre, A., Grigal, M., & Fialka, J. (2010). Student and family perspectives. In M. Grigal & D. Hart (Eds.), *Think college: Postsecondary education options for students with intellectual disabilities* (pp. 189–227). Baltimore, MD: Paul H. Brookes Publishing Co.

Eisenman, L. T., & Mancini, D. K. (2010). College perspectives and issues. In M. Grigal & D. Hart (Eds.), *Think college: Postsecondary education options for students with intellectual disabilities* (pp. 176–179). Baltimore: Paul H. Brookes Publishing Co.

Folk, E. D., Yamamoto, K. K., & Stodden, R. A. (2012). Implementing inclusion and collaborative teaming in a model program of postsecondary education for young adults with intellectual disabilities. *Journal of Policy and Practice in Intellectual Disabilities, 9*, 257–269.

Fowler, C. H., Test, D. W., Cease-Cook, J., Toms, O., Bartholomew, A., & Scroggins, L. S. (2014). Policy implications on high school reform on college and career readiness of youth with disabilities. *Journal of Disability Policy Studies, 25*(1), 19–29.

Greene, G. (2011). *Transition planning for culturally and linguistically diverse youth.* The Brookes Transition to Adulthood Series. Baltimore, MD: Brookes Publishing Company.

Greene, G. (2014). Transition of culturally and linguistically diverse youth with disabilities: Challenges and opportunities. *Journal of Vocational Rehabilitation, 40*, 239–245.

Griffin, M. M., McMillan, E. D., & Hodapp, R. M. (2010). Family perspectives on postsecondary education for students with intellectual disabilities. *Education and Training in Autism and Developmental Disabilities, 45*(3), 339–346.

Grigal, M., & Deschamps, A. (2012). Transition education for adolescents with intellectual disability. In M. L. Wehmeyer & K. W. Webb (Eds.), *Handbook of adolescent transition education for youth with disabilities* (pp. 398–416). New York: Routledge.

Grigal, M. & Dwyre, A. (2009). *Employment activities and outcomes of college-based transition programs for students with intellectual disabilities [Insight Brief No. 3].* Boston: Institute for Community Inclusion, University of Massachusetts-Boston.

Grigal, M., Dwyre, A., Emmett, J., & Emmett, R. (2012). A program evaluation tool for dual enrollment transition programs. *Teaching Exceptional Children, 44*, 36–45.

Grigal, M., Neubert, D. & Moon, S. (2005). *Transition services for students with significant disabilities in college and community settings: Strategies for planning, implementation and evaluation.* Austin, TX: PRO-ED.

Grigal, M., Hart, D., & Paiewonsky, M. (2010). Postsecondary education: The next frontier for individuals with intellectual disabilities. In M. Grigal & D. Hart (Eds.), *Think College: Postsecondary education options for students with intellectual disabilities* (pp. 1–28). Baltimore, MD: Paul H. Brookes Publishing Co.

Grigal, M., Hart, D. & Migliore, A, (2011). Comparing the transition planning, postsecondary education and employment outcomes of students with intellectual and other disabilities. *Career Development for Exceptional Individuals, 34*(1), 4–17.

Grigal, M., Hart, D., Smith, F. A., Domin, D., Sulewski, J., & Weir, C. (2014).*Think College National Coordinating Center: Annual report on the transition and postsecondary programs for students with intellectual disabilities (2012– 2013)—Executive Summary.* Boston: University of Massachusetts Boston, Institute for Community Inclusion.

Grigal, M., Hart, D., Smith, F. A., Domin, D., Sulewski, J., & Weir, C. (2015). *Think College National Coordinating Center: Annual report on the transition and postsecondary programs for students with intellectual disabilities (2013– 2014).* Boston: University of Massachusetts Boston, Institute for Community Inclusion.

Grigal, M., Hart, D. & Weir, C. (2012). A survey of postsecondary education programs for students with intellectual disabilities in the United States. *Journal of Policy and Practice in Intellectual Disabilities, 9*(4), 223–233.

Grigal, M., Hart, D., & Weir, C. (2013). Postsecondary education for people with intellectual disability: Current issues and critical challenges. *Inclusion, 1*, 50–63.

Hagner, D., May, J., Kurtz, A., & Cloutier, H. (2014). Person-centered planning for transition-aged youth with Autism Spectrum Disorders. *Journal of Rehabilitation, 80*(1), 4–10.

Hart, D. & Grigal, M. (2010). *THINK College: Postsecondary education options for students with intellectual disabilities.* Baltimore, MD: Brookes Publishing.

Hart, D., Zimbrich, K., & Ghiloni, C. (2001). Interagency partnerships and funding: Individual supports for youth with significant disabilities as they move into postsecondary education and employment options. *Journal of Vocational Rehabilitation, 16*, 145–154.

Hart, D., Zimbrich, K., & Parker, D. R. (2005). Dual enrollment as a postsecondary education option for students with intellectual disabilities. In E. E. Getzel & P. Wehman (Eds.), *Going to college* (pp. 253–267). Baltimore, MD: Paul H. Brookes.

Hasson, F., Keeney, S., & McKenna, H. (2000). Research guidelines for the Delphi survey technique. *Journal of Advanced Nursing, 32*, 1008–1015.

Higher Education Act of 1965, PL 89–320, 20 USC. § 1001 et seq.

Higher Education Opportunity Act of 2008, PL 110–315, § 122 Stat. 3078. Retrieved from https://nces.ed.gov/fastfacts/display.asp?id=60

Hirano, K. A., & Rowe, D. A. (2015). A conceptual model for parent involvement in secondary special education. *Journal of Disability Policy Studies, 27*, 43–53.

Individuals with Disabilities Education Improvement Act (IDEA) of 2004, PL 108–446, 20 USC. §§1400 et seq.

Kardos, M.R. (2011). *Postsecondary education options for individuals with intellectual disability.* Ph.D. dissertation. Retrieved from Digital Commons at the University of Connecticut.

Katovich, D. M. (2010). *The power to spring up: Postsecondary education opportunities for students with significant disabilities.* Bethesda, MD: Woodbine House.

Kearns, J., Kleinert, H., Harrison, B., Sheppard-Jones, K. & Hall, M. (2012). *What does "college and career ready" mean for students with significant cognitive disabilities?* Unpublished manuscript. Lexington: University of Kentucky.

Kleinert, H. L., Jones, M. M., Sheppard-Jones, K., Harp, B., & Harrison, E. M. (2012). Students with intellectual disabilities going to college? Absolutely! *Teaching Exceptional Children, 44*, 26–35.

Larson, S. A., Goldberg, P., McDonald, S., Leuchovius, D., Richardson, V., & Lakin, K. C. (2011). *2010 fast family support survey: National results.* Minneapolis: PACER Center, University of Minnesota, Research and Training Center on Community Living, Institute on Community Integration (UCEDD).

Leach, D., Helms, L., Foster, M., Martin-Delaney, A., & Everington, C. (2013). *A dual enrollment postsecondary education program for students with intellectual disabilities: Winthrop transition to college.* Think College Insight Brief, Issue No. 19. Boston, MA: University of Massachusetts Boston, Institute for Community Inclusion.

Leake, D. (2015). Problematic data on how many students in postsecondary education have a disability. *Journal of Postsecondary Education and Disability, 28*, 73–87.

Lindstrom, L., Hirano, K., McCarthy, C., & Alverson, C. (2014). Just having a job: Case studies of low wage workers with intellectual and developmental disabilities. *Career Development and Transition for Exceptional Individuals, 37*(1), 40–49. Special Issue on Disability and Poverty.

Luecking, D. R., & Luecking, R. G. (2015). Translating research into a seamless transition model. *Career Development for Exceptional Individuals, 38*(1), 4–13.

Luecking, R., & Tilson, G. P. (2009). Job development in a tough economy: Mission impossible? *The Advance (APSE), 1*(2).

Marken, S., Gray, L., & Lewis, L. (2013). *Dual enrollment programs and courses for high school students at postsecondary institutions: 2010–11* (NCES 2013–002). US Department of Education. Washington, DC: National Center for Education Statistics.

Martin, J. E., & Williams-Diehm, K. (2013). Student engagement and leadership of the transition planning process. *Career Development and Transition for Exceptional Individuals, 36*(1), 43–50.

Martinez, D. C., Conroy, J. W., & Cerreto, M. C. (2012). Parent involvement in the transition process of children with intellectual disabilities: The influence of inclusion on parent desires and expectations for postsecondary education. *Journal of Policy and Practice in Intellectual Disabilities, 9*(4), 279–288.

Migliore, A., & Domin, D. (2011). *Setting higher employment expectations for youth with intellectual disabilities.* Boston: University of Massachusetts, Institute for Community Inclusion.

Mock, M. & Love, K. (2012). One state's initiative to increase access to higher education for people with intellectual disabilities. *Journal of Policy and Practice in Intellectual Disabilities, 9*(4), 289–297.

Morgan, R. L., Callow-Heusser, C. A., Horrocks, E., Hoffman, A. K., & Kupferman, S. (2013). Identifying transition teacher competencies through literature review and surveys of national experts and practitioners. *Career Development and Transition for Exceptional Individuals, 37*, 149–160. Published online 1 April 2013.

Morningstar, M. E., & Benitez, D. (2013). Teacher training matters: The results of a multistate survey of secondary special educators regarding transition from school to adulthood. *Teacher Education and Special Education, 36*(1), 51–64.

Morningstar, M., Erickson, A.G., Lattin, D.L., & Lee, H. (2012). *Quality indicators of exemplary transition program. Needs Assessment Instrument.* Lawrence, KS: University of Kansas.

Morningstar, M. E., Frey, B. B., Noonan, P. M., Ng, J., Clavenna-Deane, B., Graves, P., . . . Williams-Diehm, K. (2010). A preliminary investigation of the relationship of transition preparation and self-determination for students with disabilities in postsecondary educational settings. *Career Development for Exceptional Individuals, 33*(2), 80–94.

Morningstar, M. & Kleinhammer-Tramill, J. (2005). *Professional development for transition personnel: Current issues and strategies for success.* Information Brief. Minneapolis, MN: National Center on Secondary Education and Transition at the University of Minnesota.

Morningstar, M. E., & Nix, T. (2011). *Culturally responsive transition planning: Transforming transition coursework.* Presentation at NSTTAC Summit.

National Alliance of Concurrent Enrollment Partnerships. (2012). *National Concurrent Enrollment Partnership Standards.* Retrieved from http://nacep.org/docs/standards/NACEP-Standards-2011.pdf

National Technical Assistance Center on Transition (NTACT). (2015). *Effective practices and predictors matrix.* Retrieved from http://transitionta.org/effectivepractices

Neubert, D. A., Moon, M. S., Grigal, M., & Redd, V. (2001). Postsecondary educational practices for individuals with mental retardation and other significant disabilities: A review of the literature. *Journal of Vocational Rehabilitation, 16*, 155–168.

Newman, L. A., & Madaus, J. W. (2015). Reported accommodations and supports provided to secondary and postsecondary students with disabilities: National perspective. *Career Development and Transition for Exceptional Individuals, 38*(3), 173–181.

Nix, T., & Goff, C. (2013). *Collaborative transition planning from culturally, linguistically, and economically diverse backgrounds.* Retrieved from http://secondaryconnections.org/training/summits/2013-kssc-summit/handouts

Noonan, P. (2014). *Transition teaming: 26 strategies for interagency collaboration.* Arlington, VI: Council for Exceptional Children.

O'Brien, J. (2014). Person-centered-planning and the quest for systems change. In M. Agran, F. Brown, C. Hughes, C. Quirk & D. L. Ryndak (Eds.), *Equity and full participation for individuals with severe disabilities* (pp. 57–74). Baltimore, MD: Brookes Publishing.

Paiewonsky, M., Boyle, M., Hanson, T., Price, P., MacDonald, P., & Schwartz, S. (2013). *Establishing inclusive postsecondary education opportunities: Tips for effective communication.* Think College Insight Brief, Issue No. 20. Boston, MA: University of Massachusetts Boston, Institute for Community Inclusion.

Paiewonsky, M., Mecca, K., Daniels, T., Katz, C., Nash, J., Hanson, T., & Gragoudas, S. (2010). *Students and educational coaches: Developing a support plan for college.* Think College Insight Brief, Issue No. 4. Boston, MA: University of Massachusetts Boston, Institute for Community Inclusion.

Paiewonsky, M., & Ostergard, J. R. (2010). Local school systems perspectives. In M. Grigal & D. Hart (Eds.), *Think College: Postsecondary education options for students with intellectual disabilities.* Baltimore: Paul H. Brooks Publishing.

Papay, C., & Bambara, L. (2011). Postsecondary education for transition-age students with intellectual and other developmental disabilities: A national survey. *Education and Training in Autism and Developmental Disabilities, 46*, 78–93.

Papay, C., & Bambara, L. (2014). Best practices in transition to adult life for youth with intellectual disabilities. *Career Development and Transition for Exceptional Individuals, 37*(3), 136–148.

Perkins Collaborative Resource Network. (2015). *Office of career, technical, and adult education programs of study design framework.* Retrieved from http://cte.ed.gov/initiatives/octaes-programs-of-study-design-framework

Plotner, A. J. & Marshall, L. (2015). Postsecondary education programs for students with an intellectual disability: Facilitators and barriers to implementation. *Intellectual and Developmental Disabilities, 53*(1), 58–69.

Plotner, A., Mazzotti, V., Rose, C., & Carlson-Britting, K. (2016). Factors associated with enhanced knowledge and use of secondary transition evidence-based practices. *Teacher Education and Special Education, 39*(1) 1–19.

Povenmire-Kirk, T. C., Lindstrom, L., & Bullis, M. (2010). De Escuela a la Vida Adulta/From school to adult life: Transition needs for Latino youth with disabilities. *Career Development for Exceptional Individuals, 33*, 41–51.

Raue, K., & Lewis, L. (2011). *Students with disabilities at degree-granting postsecondary institutions.* Washington, DC: US Government Printing Office.

Reisen, T., Morgan, R., Schultz, J., & Kupferman, S. (2014). School-to-work barriers as identified by special educators, vocational rehabilitation counselors, and community rehabilitation professionals. *Journal of Rehabilitation, 80*(1), 33–44.

Rowe, D. A., Alverson, C. Y., Unruh, D. K., Fowler, C. H., Kellems, R., & Test, D. W. (2015). A Delphi study to operationalize evidence-based predictors in secondary transition. *Career Development and Transition for Exceptional Individuals, 38*(2), 113–126.

Rowe, D. A., Mazzotti, V., Hirano, K., & Alverson, C. (2015). Assessing transition skills in the 21st century. *Teaching Exceptional Children, 47*(6), 301–309.

Shaw, S. F., Madaus, J. W., & Dukes, L. L. (2010). Preparing students with disabilities for college success: A practical guide for transition planning. Baltimore, MD: Brookes Publishing.

Shogren, K. A., Wehmeyer, M. L., Palmer, S. B., Rifenbark, G., & Little, T. (2013). Relationships between self-determination and postschool outcomes for youth with disabilities. *Journal of Special Education, 48*(4), 256–267.

Smith Lee, S. (2009). *Overview of the Federal Higher Education Opportunities Act Reauthorization. [Think College! Policy Issue Brief No. 1].* Boston: Institute for Community Inclusion at the University of Massachusetts-Boston.

Simonsen, M., Stuart, C., Luecking, R., & Certo, N (2013). Collaboration among school and post-school agencies for seamless transition. In K. Storey & D. Hunter, *The road ahead: Transition to adult life for persons with disabilities* (pp. 137–154) Washington, DC: IOS Press.

Test, D. W., Aspel, N. P., & Everson, J. M. (2006). *Transition methods for youth with disabilities.* Columbus, OH: Merrill Prentice Hall.

Test, D. W., & Cease-Cook, J. (2012). Evidence-based secondary transition practices for rehabilitation counselors. *Journal of Rehabilitation, 78*(2), 30–38.

Test, D. W., Fowler, C., Kohler, P., & Kortering, L. (2010). *Evidence-based practices and predictors in secondary transition: What we know and what we still need to know.* National Secondary Transition Training Technical Center, IDEAS that Work. Retrieved from http://www.nsttac.org/sites/default/files/assets/pdf/pdf/ebps/Execsummary PPs.pdf

Think College Database, 2016. Retrieved at http://www.thinkcollege.net/component/programsdatabase/?view=programsdatabase&Itemid=339

Thoma, C. A., Bartholomew, C. C., & Scott, L. A. (2009). *Universal design for transition: A roadmap for planning and discussion.* Baltimore, MD: Brookes Publishing Co.

Workforce Innovation and Opportunities Act 2014, US Department of Labor. Retrieved from http://www.doleta.gov/wioa/

About the Editors

Michael L. Wehmeyer, Ph.D. is the Ross and Mariana Beach Distinguished Professor of Special Education, and Director and Senior Scientist, Beach Center on Disability at the University of Kansas. He is the author or coauthor of more than 350 peer-reviewed journal articles or book chapters and has authored, coauthored, edited, or coedited 35 books on disability and education–related issues, including issues pertaining to self-determination, positive psychology and disability, transition to adulthood, the education and inclusion of students with severe disabilities, and technology use by people with cognitive disabilities. Dr. Wehmeyer is a past president of the board of directors for and a Fellow of the American Association on Intellectual and Developmental Disabilities (AAIDD); a past president of the Council for Exceptional Children's (CEC) Division on Career Development and Transition (DCDT); a Fellow of the American Psychological Association (APA), Intellectual and Developmental Disabilities Division (Div. 33); and Vice President for the Americas and a Fellow of the International Association for the Scientific Study of Intellectual and Developmental Disabilities (IASSIDD). Dr. Wehmeyer has been recognized for his research and service with awards from numerous associations and organizations, including, recently, the American Psychological Association Distinguished Contributions to the Advancement of Disability Issues in Psychology Award, the AAIDD Research Award for contributions that have contributed significantly to the body of scientific knowledge in the field of intellectual and developmental disabilities, the Distinguished Researcher Award for lifetime contributions to research in intellectual disability by The Arc of the United States, and the Burton Blatt Humanitarian Award from the CEC Division on Autism and Developmental Disabilities, and the CEC Special Education Research Award recipient for 2016. Dr. Wehmeyer holds undergraduate and master's degrees in Special Education from the University of Tulsa and a master's degree in Experimental Psychology from the University of Sussex in Brighton, England, where he was a Rotary International Fellow from 1987 to 1988. He earned his doctoral degree in Human Development and Communication Sciences from the University of Texas at Dallas, where he received a 2014 Distinguished Alumni Award.

Karrie A. Shogren, Ph.D. is Professor of Special Education, Senior Scientist, and Director of the Kansas University Center on Developmental Disabilities, and Associate Director of the Beach Center on Disability, all at the University of Kansas. Dr. Shogren's research focuses on self-determination and systems of support for people with disabilities as well as applications of positive psychology and strengths-based approaches to people with intellectual and developmental disabilities. Her current work focuses on developing and researching the efficacy and effectiveness of assessment and intervention approaches for students with and without disabilities to promote self-determination, with a particular focus on the role of these approaches in the transition to adult life and engagement in meaningful adult roles and responsibilities. Dr. Shogren has published more than 100 articles in peer-reviewed journals, is the author or coauthor of 10 books, and is one of the coauthors of *Intellectual Disability: Definition, Classification, and Systems of Support,* the 11th edition of the American Association on Intellectual and Developmental Disabilities' seminal definition of intellectual disability (formerly "mental retardation") as well as the Supports Intensity Scale-Children and Adult versions. Dr. Shogren has received grant funding from several sources, including the Institute of Education Sciences (IES) and National Institute on Disability, Independent Living, and Rehabilitation Research (NIDILRR). Dr. Shogren is co-editor of *Inclusion* and *Remedial and Special Education,* and associate editor for *Intellectual and Developmental Disabilities* and *Research and Practice for Persons with Severe Disabilities.* She has received the CEC's Division for Research and the AAIDD Early Career Research Award. Dr. Shogren completed undergraduate and master's degrees in psychology at Ohio State University and the University of Dayton, respectively, and her doctoral degree at the University of Kansas.

About the Contributors

Lauren Avellone, Ph.D., BCBA is a research associate at the Rehabilitation Research and Training Center at Virginia Commonwealth University. She is also a Board Certified Behavior Analyst and has spent the majority of her clinical and professional career completing research and providing behavioral analytic services to youth and young adults with autism and intellectual disability. Dr. Avellone has extensive experience teaching in alternative school settings and coordinating research in a college program for students with intellectual disability. Her research interests include intervention and assessment methods related to employment and postsecondary education outcomes for young adults with developmental disabilities.

Jody Bartz, Ph.D. is Assistant Professor of Practice in the Department of Educational Specialties and Co–Principal Investigator for Project STRIDE (Strengthening Rural, Inclusive, Diverse, early Educators) at Northern Arizona University. Her research agenda includes studying the impact of educational, community, medical, and familial collaboration on outcomes for young children with intellectual and developmental disabilities, in addition to special health care needs. Dr. Bartz is an AzTASH Board member and is the faculty advisor for TASH@NAU—the only formal student chapter of TASH in the country.

Elizabeth E. Biggs, M.A. is a doctoral candidate in the Department of Special Education at Vanderbilt University. Her research interests focus on promoting social communication and language development for students with severe disabilities, particularly students with complex communication needs. Her present work addresses social and communication interventions, augmentative and alternative communication, paraprofessional and peer supports, and inclusive education.

Valerie Brooke, M.Ed has been a faculty member at Virginia Commonwealth University (VCU) and working in the field of employment for people with significant disabilities for more than 30 years. Ms. Brooke is the Director of Training for the VCU Autism Center for Excellence and Director of Employment Services at VCU-Research Rehabilitation and Training Center. She serves as the Principal Investigator/Project Director for several personnel training grants promoting employment for people with disabilities. In January 2015 Ms. Brooke was appointed to the Advisory Committee on Increasing Competitive Integrated Employment for Individuals with Disabilities (ACICIEID) by the US Secretary of Labor, as a provision of the Workforce Innovation and Opportunity Act (WIOA). Ms. Brooke has served on the editorial board for the *Journal of Vocational Rehabilitation* since 2000 and is interested in all issues and concerns that impact the employment rate and advancement of people with disabilities.

Diane M. Browder, Ph.D. is the Lake and Edward P. Snyder Distinguished Professor of Special Education at the University of North Carolina at Charlotte. Dr. Browder has more than two decades of research and writing on assessment and instruction for students with severe developmental disabilities.

She works closely with the Charlotte Mecklenburg School System in developing new interventions for students with autism spectrum disorders and intellectual disability. She recently completed IES federally funded research in Charlotte on early reading for students who are nonverbal and helped design a literacy approach for high school students with autism spectrum disorders. She is currently working with a team to develop a technology-based mathematical problem-solving intervention for students with intellectual disability. Dr. Browder's research has been recognized through multiple awards. She received the 2009 Distinguished Researcher Award in Special Education from the American Education Research Association and was the 2009 First Citizens Bank Scholar at the University of North Carolina at Charlotte. In 2011 Dr. Browder was recognized by the state of North Carolina with the O. Max Gardner Award for research that has made a contribution to humanity.

Irina Cain, M.Ed. is a doctoral student in Special Education at Virginia Commonwealth University. Her research interests include supporting students' transition to adulthood, evidence-based practices, and postsecondary outcomes, with an emphasis on residential choice, disability policy, and secondary data analysis. She has previously taught students with various disabilities in grades 2–15 and currently serves as the student representative for the AAIDD Education Division.

Erik W. Carter, Ph.D. is Professor of Special Education at Vanderbilt University and a Vanderbilt Kennedy Center investigator. His research and teaching have focused on evidence-based strategies for supporting inclusion and valued roles in school, work, and community settings for adolescents and young adults with intellectual disability, autism spectrum disorders, and multiple disabilities. He has published and presented widely in these areas in an effort to equip practitioners and policy makers with clear guidance on the most effective approaches for enhancing the relationships and outcomes of students with severe disabilities.

Susan R. Copeland, Ph.D., BCBA-D is a Regents' Lecturer and Professor of Special Education in the Department of Special Education at the University of New Mexico. Her research interests include developing strategies that allow individuals with disabilities to provide their own supports, direct their own lives, and enhance their active participation in their families, schools, and communities. This includes research on literacy instruction for individuals with intellectual disability and other severe disabilities, self-determination of individuals with developmental disabilities, and examining use of self-management strategies with children and adults with developmental disabilities. She is an associate editor for *Remedial and Special Education* and *Research and Practice for Persons with Severe Disabilities*. Dr. Copeland is an AAIDD Fellow.

Luann Ley Davis, Ph.D. is a graduate research assistant for an IES grant, The Solutions Project, which focuses on developing a mathematics word problem–solving curriculum for students with severe disabilities at the University of North Carolina at Charlotte. Her research focuses on providing students with intellectual and developmental disabilities access to the general curriculum through systematic instruction, technology, and positive behavior supports. She is a former classroom teacher of 14 years serving students from PK through Transition. Dr. Ley Davis has served on the Council for Exceptional Children's Canadian/US Committee at the national level and on the state executive board for both the Colorado and North Carolina Council for Exceptional Children as the CAN Coordinator for more than six years.

Stephanie N. DeSpain, Ed.D. is an Instructional Assistant Professor in the Department of Special Education at Illinois State University. Her research interests include the areas of support needs assessment and planning for students and adults with intellectual disability and related developmental disabilities, quality of life, and family support throughout the lifespan. Prior to joining Illinois State, she worked in a variety of professional roles in the public schools serving children at the preschool, elementary, and secondary levels.

Glen Dunlap, Ph.D. is a Research Professor at the University of Nevada, Reno. He has been involved with people affected by autism spectrum disorders and other developmental and intellectual disabilities for approximately 45 years in many capacities. His work is currently focused on families, family support, early intervention, and prevention of serious challenging behaviors.

Kim W. Fisher, Ph.D. is an Assistant Professor of Special Education in the Mary Lou Fulton Teachers College at Arizona State University, where she prepares special educators and conducts research. Her research focuses on augmentative and alternative communication, social networks, social capital, and information communication technology use of adolescents with intellectual disability who have complex communication needs. She has a particular interest in how access to social capital can improve long-term outcomes on independent living and employment for this population and how information communication technology can mediate this relationship. Prior to entering higher education, Dr. Fisher was a special education teacher and an assistive technology consultant for students with intellectual disability and complex communication needs.

Ashley Greenwald, Ph.D., BCBA-D is a faculty member in the College of Education at the University of Nevada, Reno and is the Project Director of the Nevada Positive Behavioral Interventions and Supports Technical Assistance Center, housed within the Nevada Center for Excellence in Disabilities. Dr. Greenwald manages more than $1.5 million per year in grant-funded projects, both at the federal and state level. She is a Board Certified Behavior Analyst with years of experience working with children and adults with intellectual disability and challenging behavior. Dr. Greenwald's areas of research include the assessment and treatment of challenging behaviors and behavioral medicine.

Meg Grigal, Ph.D. is a Senior Research Fellow at the Institute for Community Inclusion at University Massachusetts Boston and the Codirector of Think College, a national organization focused on research, policy, and practice in inclusive higher education and on people with intellectual disability. At Think College, she serves as a Principal Investigator on a variety of research grants, including the Investing in Innovation (i3)–funded TCT Model project, the Office of Postsecondary Education–funded National Coordinating Center for the Transition Programs for Students with Intellectual Disabilities (TPSID) Model Demonstration Programs and the Office of Special Education Program–funded Future Quest Island Stepping Up to Technology project. Dr. Grigal's work has led to expansion of higher-education options for students with intellectual disability throughout the United States and internationally. Dr. Grigal serves on the editorial board of the CEC Division on Career Development and Transition journal *Career Development and Transition for Exceptional Individuals*, the *Journal of Vocational Rehabilitation*, and the AAIDD journal *Inclusion*.

Shana J. Haines, Ph.D. is Assistant Professor of Special Education at the University of Vermont. Her research primarily focuses on the family-professional partnership and on refugee families whose children have disabilities.

Sarah A. Hall, Ph.D. is Associate Professor of Inclusive Services and Exceptional Learners at Ashland University. Her research focuses on the social inclusion of people with intellectual and developmental disabilities as well as on siblings of people with disabilities. She is the chair of Ohio SIBS (Special Initiatives by Brothers and Sisters) and co-coordinator of Sibs Looking Forward: Transition Retreat for students with developmental disabilities and their siblings. She participated in the social inclusion strand of the 2015 National Goals in Research, Practice, and Policy working meeting. Dr. Hall is an associate editor of *American Secondary Education* and on the editorial boards of the AAIDD journals *Inclusion* and *Intellectual and Developmental Disabilities*. She is a cochair of the AAIDD Student and Early Career Professional Special Interest Group.

Debra Hart, M.S. is the Director of Education and Transition for the Institute for Community Inclusion at the University of Massachusetts Boston. She has more than 30 years of experience working with students with intellectual disability, their families, and professionals to support youth in becoming valued members of their community via participation in inclusive K–12 education, inclusive higher education, and competitive integrated employment. Her research has focused on transition-related work in K–12 and adult-service agencies both in Massachusetts and nationwide. She has published considerably in the area of higher education for students with intellectual disability, especially with her work on the national Think College Coordinating Center.

Pam Hinterlong, M.S. is a research associate at Virginia Commonwealth University (VCU). She has extensive experience in policy development and program evaluation related to customized employment and supports for individuals with significant disabilities. Her specific interests are in customized employment and the transition from sheltered programs to community-based employment services. She currently serves on the Virginia Employment First Advisory Group. Prior to joining VCU, Ms. Hinterlong worked at the Florida Division of Vocational Rehabilitation (DVR) as the Supported Employment Program Administrator. She established policies and guidelines for supported employment services, mental health, self-employment, and other DVR program initiatives. She served on the Florida Developmental Disabilities Council, Florida Association of People Supporting Employment First (APSE) Board, START UP Florida advisory committee, and the Governor's Blue Ribbon Task Force for Developmental Disabilities.

Debra Holzberg, M.S. Ed. is a doctoral student at the University of North Carolina at Charlotte. Her research focuses on self-advocacy and academic skills as they relate to the transition of students with disabilities to postsecondary education. Additional interests and research include the disproportionate representation of culturally and linguistically diverse students in special education. Ms. Holzberg is the President of the North Carolina Division for Learning Disabilities, serves on the membership committee of the Division for Learning Disabilities, and is the student representative to the College of Education Graduate Curriculum Committee.

Carolyn Hughes, Ph.D. is Project Director of the Supports Intensity Scale-Children project and Visiting Professor at Queens College of the City University of New York (CUNY). Dr. Hughes has published numerous books, chapters, and articles addressing social interaction and self-directed learning skills among high school students with disabilities and their general education peers, and improving outcomes for youth from high-poverty backgrounds via mentoring programs. She is a coauthor of the Supports Intensity Scale-Children and -Adult versions. In 2012, she received the Education Award from AAIDD and was designated a Fellow of AAIDD in 2013.

Katherine Inge, Ph.D., O.T.R. has worked at Virginia Commonwealth University (VCU) since 1982 on federally funded projects through research and training efforts, including early demonstrations on employment for individuals with disabilities. Currently, she is Director of the VCU–Rehabilitation Resource and Training Center (RRTC) on Employment of People with Physical Disabilities. She is also Director for Instructional Technology and is responsible for developing and managing online continuing education courses for rehabilitation professionals. Dr. Inge is the coauthor of four books, including three on employment for people with significant disabilities and one on assistive technology. She is the editor and coeditor of numerous RRTC publications, including research monographs and newsletters. Most recently, she has edited a series of fact sheets on customizing employment and self-employment for individuals with significant disabilities.

Donald Jackson, Ph.D. is Senior Project Advisor and Coprincipal Investigator in the Nevada Positive Behavior Interventions and Support Technical Assistance Center, and Community Training and Technical Assistance Coordinator for the Nevada Center for Excellence in Disabilities, University of Nevada Reno. He was previously Lead Psychologist for Nevada's Aging and Disabilities Services Division and maintained a private practice focusing on persons with disabilities and behavioral health concerns. His contributions to the field of disabilities and behavioral challenges include instructional books, chapters, and journal publications, and numerous training workshops and professional presentations. His research focuses on positive behavior support policy and program design related to the implementation of services for organizations and for individuals of all ages.

Mindy Johnson, Ed.M. is an Instructional Designer, Social Media & Communications Strategist at CAST, an educational research and development organization focused on Universal Design for Learning (UDL). She is a former high school special education teacher who facilitated the inclusion of students with disabilities in general education courses of study, including those with developmental disabilities. Currently she participates in the formative development and research of technology-based universally designed learning environments and provides knowledge and expertise in social media, website development, online collaborative tools, and game design in education. Mindy is also a volunteer board member for the International Society for Technology in Education's (ISTE) Inclusive Learning Network.

Meagan Karvonen, Ph.D. is the Director of the Dynamic Learning Maps (DLM) Alternate Assessment Consortium and also Associate Director of the Center for Educational Testing and Evaluation at the University of Kansas. Dr. Karvonen has nearly 20 years of experience in research and assessment for students with intellectual disability, beginning with research on self-determination for children and youth with disabilities. For more than 15 years she has worked in the field of alternate assessments, assisting states with research and development on their assessments before joining the DLM project. Her interests lie especially in validity research and teachers' use of alternate assessments to improve student outcomes. Dr. Karvonen is a reviewer for *Exceptional Children* and the *Journal of Special Education*.

Elizabeth B. Keefe, Ph.D. is a Professor in the Department of Special Education at the University of New Mexico (UNM). She is committed to working with schools, school districts, community agencies, self-advocates, and families to implement effective inclusive practices for students with complex needs for support. Dr. Keefe prepares undergraduate and graduate students at UNM to teach and be leaders in inclusive classroom and school environments. Her research interests center on inclusive practices, literacy instruction, collaboration, and how system change occurs and is sustained in schools. Dr. Keefe has published numerous articles and books on effective inclusive practices and literacy instruction for individuals with complex needs for support.

Neal Kingston, Ph.D. is a Professor in the Educational Psychology Department at the University of Kansas and serves as Director of the Achievement and Assessment Institute. Dr. Kingston's research focuses broadly on improving large-scale assessments so they better support student learning, especially through the use of instructionally embedded, instructionally relevant assessments based on fine-grained learning maps. Dr. Kingston started his career as a high school science teacher and worked as Waterfront Director at summer camps for children with cognitive disabilities. Dr. Kingston received his doctorate in Educational Measurement and Research Design from Teachers College, Columbia University. He has authored more than 190 publications and presentations on assessment topics. While at the University of Kansas he was the founding director of the Dynamic Learning Maps Alternate Assessment, a consortium of 17 states working together to create an alternate assessment that supports the learning of children with significant cognitive disabilities as well as meets the requirements of state accountability systems. Before coming to the university in 2006, Dr. Kingston was a researcher and then executive at several educational testing companies and Associate Commissioner for Curriculum and Assessment at the Kentucky Department of Education during the early years of the Kentucky Educational Reform Act.

Jennifer Kurth, Ph.D. is an Assistant Professor of Special Education and the Principal Investigator for the Kansas Institute of Positive Behavior Supports at the University of Kansas. Her research focuses on inclusive education for students with intellectual and developmental disabilities, including methods of implementing instruction, educational decision making, and teacher preparation for inclusive practices. Dr. Kurth is a board member of TASH and is managing editor of the AAIDD journal *Inclusion*.

Kathleen Kyzar, Ph.D. is an Assistant Professor of Early Childhood Education in the College of Education at Texas Christian University (TCU) and a member of the associate faculty of the Alice Neeley Special Education Research and Service (ANSERS) Institute at the TCU College of Education. Her research focuses primarily on family-professional partnership in early childhood settings and family quality of life for families of young children with low-incidence disabilities.

Kathleen Lynne Lane, Ph.D. is a Professor in the Department of Special Education at the University of Kansas. Dr. Lane's research interests focus on school-based interventions with students at risk for emotional and behavioral disorders (EBD), with an emphasis on systematic screenings to detect students with behavioral challenges at the earliest possible juncture. She has designed, implemented, and evaluated comprehensive, integrated, three-tiered (CI3T) models of prevention in elementary, middle, and high school settings to (a) prevent the development of learning and behavior challenges and (b) respond to existing instances. Dr. Lane serves as the primary investigator of state-funded and federally funded projects. She is the coeditor of *Remedial and Special Education* and *Journal of Positive Behavior Intervention*. Dr. Lane has coauthored seven books and published more than 150 refereed journal articles and 30 book chapters.

Stephanie Lau, M.A.T. is a research associate at the Virginia Commonwealth University (VCU) Rehabilitation Research and Training Center. Her research and clinical experience lies in vocational rehabilitation for individuals with significant disabilities, with an emphasis on physical disabilities and customized employment. Ms. Lau is a member of the Virginia chapter of Association of People Supporting Employment First (APSE) board and serves as its public policy liaison. Ms. Lau is working on her doctorate in Public Policy and Administration at VCU.

Suk-Hyang Lee, Ph.D. is an Associate Professor of Special Education at Ewha Womans University in South Korea. Her research focuses on issues pertaining to self-determination and inclusive education, with a particular focus on evidence-based practices to promote transition outcomes, as well as access to the general education curriculum of students with intellectual and developmental disabilities. She has conducted several research projects on inclusive education and self-determination of students with intellectual disability that were supported by the National Research Foundation of Korea Grant funded by the Korean Government. Dr. Lee is a past Editor-in-Chief of *Journal of the Korean Association for Persons with Autism* and a member of the board of directors of the *Korean Association on Intellectual Disabilities*.

Susan Marks, J.D., Ph.D., BCBA-D is a Professor of Special Education at Northern Arizona University, where she teaches in the Special Education teacher preparation program and coordinates the graduate certificate in Autism. Dr. Marks teaches courses on positive behavioral supports and inclusive education, focusing primarily on the needs of students with developmental disabilities. She is also an attorney who focuses her practice on special education and disability-related issues. She is a board member of Arizona TASH, a state chapter of TASH International, and Vice President of The Arc of Arizona. Her primary interests are in supporting the self-determination of individuals with disabilities and in supporting their greater access to inclusive communities.

James E. Martin, Ph.D. is the Zarrow Family Professor and Endowed Chair at the University of Oklahoma, Department of Educational Psychology, and is Director of the University's Zarrow Center for Learning Enrichment. His professional interests focus upon identifying, assessing, and teaching secondary-aged youth and adults with disabilities generalizable self-determination and other skills that when learned will increase the likelihood of desired educational and employment outcomes. Dr. Martin has authored several books, numerous chapters for edited books, journal articles, several curriculum lesson packages, and instructional assessments. Most recently he and colleagues coauthored the online Transition Assessment and Goal Generator and wrote supporting materials. Federal, state, and private sources, including the Institute for Education Science's National Center for Special Education Research, provided Dr. Martin with approximately $15 million to conduct his research, demonstration, and writing activities. He has conducted presentations and professional development workshops across the United States, Canada, and in Europe. CEC's Division on Career Development and Transition honored Dr. Martin with the Oliver P. Kolstoe Award for his efforts to improve the quality and access to career and transition services for people with disabilities, and most recently his students nominated him for the University of Oklahoma graduate student mentoring award. He is currently the President of CEC's Division on Career Development and Transition.

Amber E. McConnell, Ph.D. is a research associate at the University of Oklahoma Zarrow Center for Learning Enrichment. Her research focuses on transition education, employability skills, skills leading to self-determination, and nonacademic skills that impact postschool outcomes for students with disabilities. She was the project coordinator for the Transition Assessment and Goal Generator (TAGG) and has presented transition education information for students with intellectual disability at numerous conferences including Division on Autism and Developmental Disabilities (DADD) and CEC webinars describing the transition process for students with significant cognitive disabilities.

Jennifer McDonough, M.S., C.R.C. is the Director of National Autism Research and the Virginia Project SEARCH Statewide Coordinator at Virginia Commonwealth University's Rehabilitation Research and Training Center. Ms. McDonough also serves as the Associate Director of Training for the Center and is a faculty member at VCU. Her research and experience focuses on the employment of individuals with significant disabilities, including intellectual disability and autism spectrum disorders. Ms. McDonough has more than 18 years of experience in the employment field and specializes not only in the areas listed but also in business development and relationships, jobsite training and supports for individuals with disabilities, and organizational collaboration.

Margaret H. Mehling, M.A. is a doctoral candidate in the Intellectual and Developmental Disabilities (IDD) Psychology program at Ohio State University. She received her undergraduate and master's degrees in Psychology from Ohio State University. Her research interests include evaluating social skills interventions for individuals with developmental disabilities, the neurological basis of social cognition in autism spectrum disorder, statistical modeling of social outcomes for individuals with developmental disabilities, and treatment process and outcome of psychiatric hospitalization for children and adults with autism and other developmental disabilities. She is the coauthor of five published peer-reviewed journal articles and book chapters, and she has presented research at numerous conferences and speaking engagements. She is the recipient of numerous awards including the Ohio State University Presidential Fellowship, the Ohio State University Graduate Associate Teaching Award (GATA), and the American Association on Intellectual and Developmental Disabilities Student Award.

Mary E. Morningstar, Ph.D. is Associate Professor in the Department of Special Education at the University of Kansas and Director of the Transition Coalition, which designs online and hybrid professional development for secondary special educators and transition practitioners. Her research includes evaluating the impact of teacher quality and professional development on transition practices and student outcomes, working with culturally diverse families during transition planning, and interagency collaboration for improved outcomes. She is a member of the AAIDD Education Committee and a coauthor of the 2016 AAIDD *National Goals for Research, Policy and Practice for Educating Students with Intellectual Disability.* She served three years as the Chair of the TASH Inclusive Education National Agenda Committee promoting research and advocacy for students with significant intellectual disability.

Loui Lord Nelson, Ph.D. is an educational consultant whose work focuses on UDL. A former special education teacher, she is the author of *Design & Deliver: Planning and Teaching using Universal Design for Learning,* which has received international attention. Currently, she works as the UDL Specialist with SWIFT, a national K–8 technical assistance center focused on improving behavioral and academic outcomes for all students, including those with developmental disabilities. She also supports schools, districts, states, and international partners as they work toward the full implementation of UDL. She is a fellow and former board member of the American Association on Intellectual and Developmental Disabilities.

Michaelene M. Ostrosky, Ph.D. is Head of the Department of Special Education at the University of Illinois. Her research focuses on social-emotional competence and challenging behavior of children with disabilities, including strategies for promoting acceptance. As a former teacher of adults with significant disabilities and young children who are deaf and blind, she is passionate about translating research to practice. Dr. Ostrosky has authored more than 100 publications, including numerous articles and monographs focusing on strategies to support the development and learning of children under age 6.

Maria Paiewonsky, Ed.D. is Director and Co–Principal Investigator of the Massachusetts Transition Leadership Specialist Initiative, a personnel preparation program that prepares master's level and graduate certificate level Transition Specialists at the University of Massachusetts Boston. Dr. Paiewonsky also directs the Think College Transition project, which is supported by an Investing in Innovation grant, developing and validating the first evidence-based inclusive college dual enrollment transition model for students with intellectual disability. Dr. Paiewonsky serves on the Massachusetts Department of Elementary and Secondary Education's Transition Specialist Endorsement Panel. She codeveloped criteria and a scoring rubric to review applications of teachers and Vocational Rehabilitation counselors seeking to be grandfathered into the endorsement. In the last 15 years, Dr. Paiewonsky has developed and delivered numerous professional development trainings and courses related to transition planning and postsecondary education and employment for people with intellectual disability. She has also produced many training and technical assistance modules and publications for professionals, families, and students related to preparing for transition to adult life. Dr. Paiewonsky has coordinated training for numerous state and federally funded initiatives that promote transition to inclusive secondary and postsecondary education and create collaborative partnerships with high-need school districts statewide. Her research interests are inclusive research with transition-aged students with intellectual and other disabilities and inclusive dual enrollment with college and school partners as well as participatory action research.

Susan B. Palmer, Ph.D. is Research Professor at the Beach Center on Disability and Associate Director for Applied and Translational Research for the Kansas University Center on Developmental Disabilities at the University of Kansas. She is also a Courtesy Professor in the Department of Special Education at the University. Her research focuses on self-determination, with a particular focus on the development of foundational skills for later self-determination during early childhood. Dr. Palmer is President and a Fellow of the AAIDD, and past president of the AAIDD's Education Division. She is also on the editorial board of the AAIDD journal *Inclusion*.

Carol Quirk, Ed.D. is the Executive Director of the Maryland Coalition for Inclusive Education (MCIE) and Executive Team member of the SWIFT Center, a national school reform center funded by the US Department of Education. Dr. Quirk has extensive experience in planning school-wide systems to address the learning needs of all students, developing positive behavior supports, promoting collaboration among educators, and providing high-quality professional development for general and special educators. She developed the MCIE Inclusive Schools Transformation Process that has been implemented in more than 50 schools in Maryland, demonstrating increased academic outcomes and participation in general education for students with disabilities. Dr. Quirk is one of the coeditors of *Equity & Full Participation for Individuals with Severe Disabilities* (2014). She served as President of the Board of Directors of TASH, and currently serves on the board of the Autistic Self-Advocacy Network. She was named to President Obama's Committee for People with Intellectual Disabilities in 2011 and was recognized as the 2012 Distinguished Alumna by the Johns Hopkins University.

Grant Revell, M.S., M.Ed. serves as a research associate in the areas of policy analysis related to state-level and national implementation of supported employment and customized employment. He served as Project Director for the National Supported Employment Consortium, a four-year national study funded by the Rehabilitation Services Administration of the US Department of Education to research best practices in supported employment services to persons with significant disabilities and to disseminate information on these best practices through technical assistance and training. He has extensive experience in program evaluation related to use of Outcome Based Funding of employment services. He currently serves on the Supported Employment Leadership Steering Committee for the Employment First initiative in Virginia. He has served as a member of the process evaluation team under contract with the Social Security Administration for the Ticket to Work. He most recently served as Project Director for the Great Expectations Employment Initiative, a cooperative program with the University of Kansas and the Kansas State Department of Vocational Rehabilitation that is focused on improving employment outcomes for individuals with significant disabilities.

Colleen Robertson, M.A. Ed., NBCT is a doctoral student at the University of North Carolina at Charlotte. Her research focuses on access to the general curriculum and applied behavior analysis specifically for students with moderate to severe intellectual disability. She has 10 years of teaching experience in the public schools of Virginia, Colorado, and North Carolina working with elementary school students with low-incidence intellectual disability. Additionally, she was the Curriculum and Disabilities Specialist for a birth-to-5 Early Head Start program for two years and presented at several national conferences.

Jenny R. Root, Ph.D., BCBA is the Snyder Fellow at the University of North Carolina at Charlotte. Her research focuses on providing students with intellectual and developmental disabilities access to the general curriculum through systematic instruction, technology, and positive behavior supports. She currently works for the Solutions Project, an IES grant focused on developing a mathematics word problem–solving curriculum for students with severe disabilities. Dr. Root is a board member for the Council for Exceptional Children's Division on Autism and Developmental Disabilities and is a recipient of the Alice Hayden Emerging Leader Award from TASH.

Rosa Milagros Santos, Ph.D. is a Professor in the Department of Special Education at the University of Illinois. Her research focuses on young children with disabilities and their families within the context of early intervention and early childhood special education services. She is interested in developing the field's understanding of the ecologic influence of families and culture on parents and professionals in facilitating young children's development and learning. Through her research activities she wants to make a positive impact on the lives of children with disabilities and their families by enhancing the practices of professionals who work directly with these children and families. She has authored more than 50 peer-reviewed articles, monographs, and book chapters. She serves on multiple review boards and most recently was the editor of the *Young Exceptional Children* journal and currently an associate editor for the *Journal of Early Intervention*.

Alicia F. Saunders, Ph.D. is the Project Coordinator and research associate for the Solutions project, which is supported by an IES grant, developing a mathematical word problem–solving curriculum for students with severe disabilities at the University of North Carolina at Charlotte. Her research focuses on access to the general curriculum for students with severe disabilities and autism spectrum disorder, specifically in the content areas of mathematics and science. She is one of the coauthors of *Early Numeracy*, a mathematics curriculum for students with severe disabilities.

Carol Schall, Ph.D. is the Codirector of the Virginia Commonwealth University Autism Center for Excellence, the Director of the Virginia Autism Resource Center, and the Principal Investigator in the development of the Community Based Functional Skills Assessment for Transition Aged Youth with Autism Spectrum Disorders, a grant funded by Autism Speaks. She has more than 30 years of experience supporting adolescents and adults with autism spectrum disorders. Dr. Schall has provided positive behavior support consultation and instructional technical assistance for the Project SEARCH Plus ASD Supports program for the past eight years at Virginia Commonwealth University and has consulted nationally and internationally on issues related to adolescents and young adults with autism spectrum disorders.

Robert L. Schalock, Ph.D. is Professor Emeritus at Hastings College (Nebraska), where he chaired the Psychology Department and directed the Cognitive Behavior Lab from 1967 to 2000. He currently has adjunct research appointments at the University of Kansas (Beach Center), University of Salamanca (Spain), Gent University (Belgium), and University of Chongqing (mainland China). Dr. Schalock has been involved in the field of intellectual disability for the last 40 years. Since 1972, his work has focused on the development and evaluation of community-based programs for people with disabilities and the key roles that the concept of quality of life and the supports paradigm play in planning and delivering individualized supports within a service delivery system. Dr. Schalock has published widely in the areas of personal and program outcomes, the supports paradigm, adaptive behavior, clinical judgment, quality of life, and the transformation of disabilities organizations. He has been actively involved in the AAIDD since 1972. He has served as the association's president (1997–1998) and is currently a member of the following AAIDD committees: Terminology and Classification, Supports Intensity Scale, and Diagnostic Adaptive Behavior Scale. Dr. Schalock is a frequent speaker at national and international conferences and has assisted a number of jurisdictions in their efforts to develop community-based programs for persons with intellectual and closely related developmental disabilities within the context of the supports paradigm, the quality of life construct, and outcomes-based evaluation.

LaRon A. Scott, Ed.D. is Assistant Professor of Special Education & Disability Policy and Director of the Special Education–General Education programs at Virginia Commonwealth University. His research focuses on universal design for transition, student-directed IEPs, and high-incidence special education personnel preparation and professional training. He served as an expert on teacher education issues at the National Goals Conference on Intellectual and Developmental Disabilities' Education strand. He helped to coauthor a book chapter in a book describing the goals of the education strand, published by AAIDD, and contributed to an article for the special edition of the *Inclusion* journal of the AAIDD organization on the National Goals work.

Karrie A. Shogren, Ph.D. is Professor of Special Education; Director and Senior Scientist, Kansas University Center on Developmental Disabilities, University of Kansas; and Associate Director of the Beach Center on Disability. Her research focuses on self-determination and systems of support for students with disabilities, and she has a specific interest in the multiple, nested contextual factors that impact student outcomes. She is one of the coauthors of *Intellectual Disability: Definition, Classification, and Systems of Support*, the 11th edition of the AAIDD's seminal definition of intellectual disability as well as the Supports Intensity Scale-Children and -Adult versions. Dr. Shogren is a Fellow of the American Association on Intellectual and Developmental Disabilities and is founding coeditor of the AAIDD journal *Inclusion*, as well as an associate editor for *Intellectual and Developmental Disabilities* and *Research and Practice for Persons with Severe Disabilities*. She is also coeditor of the journal *Remedial and Special Education*.

J. David Smith, Ph.D. is Professor Emeritus at the University of North Carolina at Greensboro. He is also a visiting professor at Virginia Commonwealth University. Dr. Smith's professional experience includes work as a public school teacher and counselor. In addition to his professorial appointments he has served as a department chair, dean, and provost during his career at several universities. Dr. Smith has given numerous invited presentations to national and international audiences and regularly contributes to the professional literature of special education and the human services. He is the author of 12 books. One of the integrating themes of Dr. Smith's research and writing has been a concern for the rights and dignity of people with disabilities. He has devoted much of his scholarship to the study of the history of eugenics and its impact on social and educational policy.

Fred Spooner, Ph.D. is a Professor in the Department of Special Education, and Child Development and Principal Investigator on a Personnel Preparation Project involving distance delivery technologies at the University of North Carolina at Charlotte, and Co–Principal Investigator on a US Department of Education, IES, Project to teach students with moderate/severe intellectual disability to solve mathematical problems. Prior work with IES has involved serving as a Co–Principal Investigator with Diane Browder on a project for determining evidence-based practices in the area of intellectual disability, and Co–Principal Investigator on a project focusing on high-quality mathematics and science instruction for students who participate in alternate assessments judged against alternate achievement standards (the 1%). Dr. Spooner has held numerous editorial posts, including coeditor of *TEACHING Exceptional Children* and coeditor of *Teacher Education and Special Education*, and currently he is the Co–Editor-in Chief for *The Journal of Special Education*, and Associate Editor for *Research and Practice for Persons with Severe Disabilities*. He is a member of the American Association on Intellectual and Developmental Disabilities, the Council for Exceptional Children's Division on Autism and Developmental Disabilities, the Association for Behavior Analysis International, and TASH. His research interests include instructional procedures for students with severe disabilities, alternate assessment, and validating evidence-based practices.

Brittany Sterret, M.Ed. is pursuing her doctorate in Special Education and Disability Policy at Virginia Commonwealth University. She received her undergraduate degree in Political Science with a concentration in Legal Studies from Virginia Tech and earned her master's in Special Education from Virginia Commonwealth University. She was a middle school special educator in the Richmond, Virginia, area before enrolling in her doctoral program as one of three scholars in the National Center for Leadership in Intensive Interventions consortium (led by Vanderbilt University). Her research interests include developing protocols for intensifying interventions for students at the middle school level with significant academic and behavioral challenges.

Jean Ann Summers, Ph.D. is a Research Professor at the Schiefelbusch Institute for Life Span Studies, Associate Director for Family Studies at the Beach Center on Disabilities, and Research Director at the Rehabilitation Research and Training Center on Independent Living at the University of Kansas. Her research focuses on development of interventions to provide supports and foster partnerships with families who have a member with a disability, and on developing interventions for adults with disabilities to support effective participation in the community.

Marc J. Tassé, Ph.D. is a Professor in the Departments of Psychology and Psychiatry and the Director of the Ohio State University Nisonger Center, a University Center for Excellence in Developmental Disabilities. Dr. Tassé is a coauthor of the 10th and 11th editions of the AAIDD's 2002 and 2010 terminology and classification manuals and associated users' guides. He has also coauthored several published standardized assessment instruments, including the assessment of adaptive behavior, assessment of problem behavior, and measurement of support needs. He is the senior author of the *Diagnostic Adaptive Behavior Scale*, to be published by AAIDD in 2016. Dr. Tassé is a fellow of the AAIDD, the American Psychological Association, Division on Intellectual and Developmental Disabilities, and the International Association for the Scientific Study of Intellectual and Developmental Disabilities. He also consults and testifies in capital cases involving the determination of intellectual disability. Dr. Tassé is a past president of AAIDD.

David W. Test, Ph.D. currently serves as a Co–Project Director of the National Technical Assistance Center on Transition, the North Carolina Indicator 14 Post-School Outcomes Project, the IES CIRCLES project, and the UNC Charlotte Ph.D. Program in Special Education Leadership Grant. Finally, he serves as a co-editor of *Career Development and Transition for Exceptional Individuals*. His research interests focus on preparing all students with disabilities to be successful in college or careers as they enter adulthood.

Colleen A. Thoma, Ph.D. is a Professor of Special Education and Disability Policy and Chair of the Department of Counseling and Special Education at Virginia Commonwealth University. Her research focuses on transition education for youth with disabilities with a particular focus on supporting student self-determination in the process, preparing special educators to facilitate student self-determination, and disability policy that improves transition outcomes. Dr. Thoma served as the leader of the Education strand of the 2015 National Goals in Research, Policy, and Practice for Individuals with Intellectual and Developmental Disabilities Conference. She is an AAIDD Fellow and President of the AAIDD's Education Division. Dr. Thoma is also a past president of the Division on Career Development and Transition and serves on the editorial board of a number of journals in the field, including the AAIDD journal *Inclusion*.

James R. Thompson, Ph.D. is Professor of Special Education and Associate Director and Senior Scientist, Kansas University Center on Developmental Disabilities, University of Kansas. His research focuses on support needs assessment and planning with children and adults with intellectual disability and related developmental disabilities. He is the lead author of the Supports Intensity Scale—Children and -Adult versions and is a coauthor of *Intellectual Disability: Definition, Classification, and Systems of Support,* the 11th edition of the AAIDD's definition and classification manual. Dr. Thompson is a Fellow and past president of the AAIDD. He has previously served on the board of the CEC's Division of Autism and Developmental Disabilities. He is editor of *Intellectual and Developmental Disabilities.*

Ann P. Turnbull, Ed.D. has been a professor, researcher, and advocate for individuals with disabilities, their families, and service providers for four decades. She is a Distinguished Professor Emerita at the University of Kansas, which has the number-one ranked doctoral program in special education. She has authored 32 books and more than 275 articles and chapters. In 1999, Ann and her husband, Rud, were selected by the National Historic Preservation Trust on Developmental Disabilities as two of 36 individuals who have "changed the course of history for individuals with intellectual and developmental disabilities in the 20th century." Her greatest learning has come from her son, Jay Turnbull (1967–2009), whom she has always called her "best professor" about the needs of individuals with significant disabilities over the lifespan.

Shawnee Wakeman, Ph.D. is a Clinical Associate Professor in the Department of Special Education and Child Development at the University of North Carolina at Charlotte. Her research interests include access to the general curriculum and how it is enacted for students with significant cognitive disabilities, alternate assessment, and alignment of the educational system for students with significant cognitive disabilities. Dr. Wakeman is one of the coauthors of the Links for Academic Learning Alignment model, which was developed to examine the alignment of academic content standards, professional development activities, and items within an alternate assessment system based on alternate achievement standards.

Virginia L. Walker, Ph.D. is a Board Certified Behavior Analyst and an Assistant Professor of Special Education at Illinois State University. Her research has focused on implementation of evidence-based practices within inclusive school settings, behavioral interventions, and communication-based interventions for learners with intellectual and related developmental disabilities. She has taught numerous university-level courses to prepare special education teachers to work with learners with high support needs. She also has extensive experience in providing consultation to school personnel in the area of support needs assessment and planning for learners with intellectual disability and related development disability. She is an active member of the AAIDD and the AAIDD Student and Early Career Professionals special interest group. She is on the editorial board of the TASH journal Research and Practice for Persons with Severe Disabilities and co-founder of the TASH Early Career Researcher Network.

Paul Wehman, Ph.D. is a Virginia Commonwealth University (VCU) Professor of Physical Medicine and Rehabilitation and Chairman of Rehabilitation Research with a joint appointment in the Departments of Special Education and Disability Policy and Rehabilitation Counseling. He pioneered the development of supported employment at VCU in the early 1980s. He has been heavily involved in the use of supported employment with people who have severe disabilities including people with severe intellectual disability, brain injury, spinal cord injury, or autism spectrum disorder, as well as transition from school to work for youth with disabilities. Dr. Wehman serves as Director of the VCU Rehabilitation Research and Training Center on Employment and Director of the VCU Autism Center for Excellence. He has researched, written, instructed, and presented extensively on issues related to transition from school to adulthood and special education as it relates to young adulthood. He is founding editor-in-chief of the *Journal of Vocational Rehabilitation.*

Michael L. Wehmeyer, Ph.D. is the Ross and Mariana Beach Distinguished Professor of Special Education and Director and Senior Scientist, Beach Center on Disability, University of Kansas. His research focuses on issues pertaining to self-determination, strengths-based, and supports-focused approaches to disability, defining and conceptualizing intellectual disability, and applied cognitive technologies. He is one of the coauthors of *Intellectual Disability: Definition, Classification, and Systems of Support,* the 11th edition of the AAIDD's seminal definition of intellectual disability as well as the Supports Intensity Scale-Child and -Adult versions. Dr. Wehmeyer is a past president and Fellow of the AAIDD; Vice President for the Americas and a Fellow of the International Association for the Scientific Study of Intellectual and Developmental Disabilities; publications chair and a board member for the CEC's Division on Autism and Developmental Disabilities; and a Fellow of the American Psychological Association, Intellectual and Developmental Disabilities Division. He is founding coeditor of the AAIDD journal *Inclusion.*

Kendra L. Williams-Diehm, Ph.D. is Associate Professor in Special Education in the Jeannine Rainbolt College of Education at the University of Oklahoma. She currently holds the Brian E. and Sandra L. O'Brien Presidential Professorship. Her research focuses on self-determination and postsecondary outcomes, with a particular focus on goal setting and goal acquisition, and how this looks for individuals with intellectual and developmental disabilities. She has recently begun working with elementary-aged students on how self-determination can be fostered at this age. She is an active member of the CEC's Division on Career Development and Transition, where she serves as Secretary. Prior to earning her doctoral degree, Dr. Williams-Diehm was a classroom teacher for students with developmental disabilities and autism spectrum disorder.

Andrew Wojcik, M.Ed. is a doctoral candidate at Virginia Commonwealth University (VCU). He is currently researching inclusion for students with intellectual disability in secondary schools. At the University, Mr. Wojcik works as an adjunct professor to support graduate students working to become general or special education teachers. Mr. Wojcik works as a special education teacher for the Albemarle County Public Schools. With 20 years of teaching experience, Mr. Wojcik has worked with a diverse group of students; currently, he is piloting the Building Accessible Supports with Evidence (BASE) program for students with autism spectrum disorder. The program supports high school students in the general education environment and curriculum using evidence-based practices.

Hasan Y. Zaghlawan, Ph.D. is an Assistant Professor and Coordinator of the Bachelor program in Special Education: Early Childhood in the School of Special Education at the University of Northern Colorado. His area of research focuses on promoting social and communicative skills for young children with disabilities, developing parent- and teacher-implemented interventions to increase children's engagement in naturalistic environments, and supporting culturally and linguistically diverse families in preventing and managing children's challenging behaviors. Dr. Zaghlawan serves on several editorial boards and as a guest reviewer for international and national journals in early childhood special education. He has published several articles and regularly presents at local, state, and national conferences.

Index

Page numbers in *italic* refer to figures, tables, and boxes.